The Business of
Tourism Management

Visit the *Business of Tourism Management* Companion
Website at **www.pearsoned.co.uk/beechchadwick**
to find valuable **student** learning material including:

- A Blog with links to tourism news, information and
  further resources

The Business of Tourism Management

Edited by

John Beech
Coventry Business School

and

Simon Chadwick
Birkbeck College, University of London

FT Prentice Hall
FINANCIAL TIMES

An imprint of **Pearson Education**
Harlow, England • London • New York • Boston • San Francisco • Toronto • Sydney • Singapore • Hong Kong
Tokyo • Seoul • Taipei • New Delhi • Cape Town • Madrid • Mexico City • Amsterdam • Munich • Paris • Milan

Pearson Education Limited

Edinburgh Gate

Harlow

Essex CM20 2JE

England

and Associated Companies throughout the world

Visit us on the World Wide Web at:

www.pearsoned.co.uk

_____

First published 2006

ISBN: 978-0-273-68801-3

British Library Cataloguing-in-Publication Data
A catalogue record for this book is available from the British Library

Library of Congress Cataloging-in-Publication Data
The business of tourism management / editied by John Beech and Simon Chadwick.
      p. cm.
    Includes bibliographical references and index.
    ISBN 0-273-68801-4 (alk. paper)
      1. Tourism--Management. I. Beech, John G., 1947-II. Chadwick, Simon, 1964-

  G155.A1B887 2005
  910'.68--dc22

                                                                2005051343

10 9 8 7 6 5 4 3 2
10 09 08

Typeset in 10/12.5pt Sabon by 30
Printed and bound in Malaysia   (CTP - VVP)

The publisher's policy is to use paper manufactured from sustainable forests.

Brief contents

Contents

Part 1

The context of tourism   1

Part 2

Business functions applied to tourism   59

Part 3

Management issues specific to tourism businesses   263

Supporting resources

Visit **www.pearsoned.co.uk/beechchadwick** to find valuable online resources

For students
• A blog with links to tourism news, information and further resources

For instrutors
• Complete, downloadable Instructor's Manual
• PowerPoint slides that can be downloaded and used as OHTs

For more information please contact your local Pearson Education sales representative or visit **www.pearsoned.co.uk/beechchadwick**

One**Key**
OneKey is
all you need
Convenience. Simplicity. Success.

Figures

Tables

Case studies

About the authors

Helen Atkinson

Helen is Principal Lecturer in Management Accounting in the School of Service Management at the University of Brighton. As a qualified management accountant, she is also a member of the British Association of Hospitality Accountants (BAHA) and teaches Accounting and Finance and Business Strategy. Her current research interests include Performance Management, Strategic Control and Implementation.

Marcjanna M. Augustyn

Marcjanna is the Senior Lecturer, Scarborough Management Centre, The Business School, at the University of Hull. Her research interests include tourism strategy, quality management, and tourism policy. She is a member of the International Association of Scientific Experts in Tourism (AIEST) and the Tourism Society. She is the Book Reviews Editor for *Tourism Analysis: An Interdisciplinary Journal*.

Ian Baxter

Ian is Associate Director of the Caledonian Heritage Futures Network and a Lecturer in Heritage and Tourism at Glasgow Caledonian University. His major research interest lies in the development of public policy for managing the historic environment, and the development of heritage auditing by national conservation agencies. He also undertakes work on heritage site management, and as a member of the ICOMOS-UK Cultural Tourism Committee is involved in work establishing the impact of World Heritage Status on areas and communities. He is a member of the UK-HERG (Historic Environment Research Group).

John Beech (co-editor)

John is the Head of the Department of Strategy and Management at Coventry Business School. He designed and teaches on both the BA (Tourism Management) and the half degree in Tourism, and has published widely on a range of tourism subjects, most recently on the image of Goa as a destination and on sports tourism as reconciliation. He is a committee member of ATLAS Europe. John has co-edited with Simon Chadwick *The Business of Sport Management*, also published by Financial Times Prentice Hall.

Karen Bill

Karen is Principal Lecturer at University College Worcester, where her main role is Development and Innovation within the School of Sport and Exercise Science. She has completed the Post graduate Diploma in Legal Studies (CPE) and has published in the *Legal Executive Journal*, written the chapter on sports law in *The Business of Sport Management* and presented at the International Association of Sports Law congress.

Dimitrios Buhalis

Dimitrios is Course Leader MSc in Tourism Marketing and Leader of eTourism Research at the School of Management, University of Surrey. He is also Adjunct

Professor at the MBA in Hospitality Management at IMHI (Cornell University-ESSEC) in Paris. Dimitrios has been an active researcher in the areas of ICTs and Tourism, was the University of Surrey based Principal Investigator for a number of projects and serves as Vice Chairman of the International Federation of Information Technology and Tourism (IFITT). He has written books on eTourism, Tourism Strategic Issues and Distribution Channels of Tourism and the future of tourism.

Simon Chadwick (co-editor)

Simon works at Birkbeck College, the University of London, where he is Programme Director for the MSc in Sport Management and the Business of Football. He is Editor of the *International Journal of Sports Marketng and Sponsorship* and also founder and leader of the Academy of Marketing's Sport Marketing Special Interest Group. Simon has researched and published extensively in the area of sport (including work on service quality in sport tourism) and is co-editor, along with John Beech, of *The Business of Sport Management* and *The Marketing of Sport* (both published by Financial Times Prentice Hall).

Beulah Cope

Beulah is Senior Lecturer in Bristol Business School, where she teaches Tourism Marketing and Operations. Her current research interests include business-travel buying behaviour and travel services distribution. She is a Chief Examiner for the Management Certificate of the Guild of Travel Management Companies (formerly the GBTA), a member of the City and Guilds National Advisory Committee for Travel, Tourism and Related Services and a visiting lecturer in tourism at the University of Perpignan and the Ecole Supérieure de Commerce in Rennes.

Carlos Costa

Carlos is an Associate Professor of the Department of Economics, Management and Industrial Engineering at the University of Aveiro, Portugal. He is course leader of the MSc programme on Management and Development of Tourism Destinations, and Director of the PhD Tourism Programme of the University of Aveiro. His research interests include tourism planning and development, tourism policy and education. He works as a consultant for several national and international tourism institutions.

Marcella Daye

Marcella is Lecturer in Tourism and Year Tutor for Tourism Management at Coventry University, where she lectures on Tourism in Developing Nations, Sport Tourism and International Tourism. Prior to her current position, Marcella worked for nine years in public relations and marketing at the Jamaica Tourist Board. Her main research interests are destination image, consumer behaviour in tourism and the relationship between tourism and the media.

Peter D. Dewhurst

Peter is Associate Dean within the University of Wolverhampton's School of Sport, Performing Arts and Leisure, where he teaches on the MA Tourism Management degree. Peter coordinates the delivery of management training to tourism businesses and his research and consultancy interests include the strategic and operational management of visitor attractions.

Helen Dewhurst

Helen is a Senior Lecturer within the University of Wolverhampton's School of Sport, Performing Arts and Leisure, where she is Course Leader for the BA Tourism Management degree. Helen's research and consultancy interests focus on small firms, public policy, sustainable tourism and training.

Tim Gale

Tim is Senior Lecturer in Tourism Geography at the University of the West of England, where he teaches on both undergraduate and postgraduate degrees in tourism, environmental management and sustainable development. His research interests include changing spatial patterns of tourism at the coast and their causes, and social science perspectives on tourism research.

George Goodall

George is Senior Lecturer in Tourism Management at Coventry Business School, where he teaches tourism, transport planning and heritage. His research and consultancy interests include the town and country planning system and its impacts on his teaching areas. He is a Chartered Town Planner.

Claire Haven-Tang

Claire is a Post-Doctoral Research Fellow in the Welsh School of Hospitality, Tourism and Leisure Management at the University of Wales Institute, Cardiff. Her current research interests are human resource issues in the tourism and hospitality industry. She has worked on a number of pedagogic research studies for the Learning and Teaching Support Network for Hospitality, Leisure, Sport and Tourism and her current research projects include exploring best practice in business, conference and event tourism and matching training provision to business need for the tourism industry in Wales.

Andrew Holden

Andrew is a Reader in Environment and Tourism at the University of Luton. He has undertaken tourism research and consultancy work related to development and environment projects in various countries, including Nepal, Indonesia, Russia, Turkey and Cyprus. He is the author of the *Environment and Tourism* published by Routledge.

Claire Humphreys

Claire is Senior Lecturer in Tourism at the University of Westminster. Her current research interests include destination development and niche tourism markets. She is involved in the management of an independent travel agent, operating in the UK.

John Jenkins

John is Associate Professor of Leisure and Tourism Studies at the Centre of Full Employment and Equity, the University of Newcastle, Australia. John is reviews editor for *Current Issues in Tourism*, and Managing Editor of *Annals of Leisure Research*. His main research areas include tourism policy and planning, outdoor recreation management and environmental politics.

Eleri Jones

Eleri is Head of the Welsh School of Hospitality, Tourism and Leisure Management at the University of Wales Institute, Cardiff. Her current research interests include tourism development in Wales and developing countries focusing in particular on the heterodoxy of the tourism SME. She project manages an extensive portfolio of European Union-funded human resource development projects for the tourism industry in Wales and collaborative links with higher education institutions in a number of developing countries.

David Litteljohn

David is Professor and Head of Tourism, Travel and Hospitality, Caledonian Business School, Glasgow Caledonian University. He has been publishing in hospitality and tourism management for over 15 years. His work spans strategic and economic aspects of the industry, with an orientation to internationalisation and corporate strategy. He also nurtures an interest in policy as it affects the hotel industry and the dynamics of the Scottish hotel and tourism industry.

Peter Mason

Peter is Professor of Tourism Management and Head of the Tourism, Leisure and HRM Department, University of Luton. He worked previously at the University of Plymouth and Massey University, New Zealand. His research interests include tourism impacts, planning and management. He is an elected member of the executive of the Association of Tourism in Higher Education.

John Old

John is Principal Lecturer at Coventry Business School, where he teaches economics and organisational management. His research and consultancy interests include sports and tourism organisations, organisational economics and the management of small businesses.

Lynn Parkinson

Lynn is a self-employed freelance training consultant and academic, working with commercial clients and UK business schools. She previously worked at the front end of tour management and in a research role in tourism in Scotland. Her academic research interests have focused on implementing relationship marketing within organisations.

Alice Pepper

Alice was admitted as a solicitor in 1992 and also worked as a senior lecturer at University of Wales Institute Cardiff from 1993 until 2004. During this time she was responsible for writing, developing and teaching courses in tourism, leisure and hospitality law. She has experience of teaching at universities and higher education colleges abroad including regular short courses at the Polytechnic of Helsinki for many years. Over the last ten years she has also acted as a legal consultant, specialising in the fields of tourism law, leisure law and health and safety.

Sherif Roubi

Sherif is a Lecturer in Accommodation Capacity Management and Real Estate at the Caledonian Business School, Glasgow Caledonian University. He undertook several consultancy projects and lectured on tourism real estate during the course of his career in North America, Europe and the Middle East. He has published and reviewed several articles for tourism and real estate journals. He is a member of several professional associations including the British Association of Hospitality Accountants, Urban Land Institute Europe, and the International Management Development Association. His research centres on tourism real estate valuation, investment and finance.

Resham Sandhu

Resham is a Senior Lecturer at Coventry Business School teaching Tourism, Sport and Leisure students. He is a member of ILAM, a member of their West Midlands Region Executive Committee and Regional Education and Training Officer.

John Tribe

John is Professor of Tourism at the University of Surrey, UK. He has authored books on strategy, economics and environmental management in tourism and his research concentrates on sustainability, epistemology and education in tourism. He is Chair of the ATHE (Association for Tourism in Higher Education) and edits the *Journal of Hospitality, Leisure Sport and Tourism Education* for the Higher Education Academy Subject Network.

Mike Weed

Mike is with the Institute of Sport and Leisure Policy in the School of Sport and Exercise Sciences at Loughborough University. He is interested in all aspects of the relationship between sport and tourism, but particularly in the behaviours and motivations of active sports tourists and travelling sports spectators. He is co-author (with Chris Bull, Canterbury Christ Church University College) of *Sports Tourism: Participants, Policy and Providers* (Elsevier).

The tourism industry offers an enormous choice of jobs for those who are suitably qualified. The World Travel and Tourism Council in their *Blueprint for New Tourism* (2003) described travel and tourism as 'one of the world's largest industries, responsible for 200 million jobs and over 10% of global GDP'. But what are your chances of getting a top job?

In the summer of 2003 one of the editors attended a meeting to discuss the possibilities of a major training scheme for employees in the travel and trade industry. Those present were mainly senior members of the Personnel or Human Resources Department of major players in the UK industry. They represented travel agents, tour operators, airlines and professional associations. Over lunch conversation turned to graduate recruitment. One of the industry practitioners who was responsible for graduate recruitment for one of the UK's largest travel companies offered the unsolicited comment that he would far rather recruit a graduate with a Business Studies degree than one with a Tourism Studies degree.

When pressed, he said that the skills he looked for in graduates were those of marketing, finance and human resource management, not those of sustainable tourism or sociology. He agreed that a graduate with a Tourism Management degree offered the business skills of a Business Studies graduate plus an understanding of tourism and the tourism industry. This conversation was the inspiration for this book.

As we shall see in Chapter 1, tourism programmes and tourism textbooks typically derive from a 'mother discipline' (see Figure 1.1). *The Business of Tourism Management* is firmly embedded in the management discipline. The two co-editors work in Business Schools and each has a Masters and a Doctorate in the management discipline. The team they have picked to contribute to this book are tourism experts who have years of experience teaching tourism in a business context. The chapters they have been asked to contribute provide an introduction to key aspects of tourism management for both undergraduate and postgraduate students. The book will also serve as a useful resource for staff involved in teaching on tourism-related modules and programmes, and for practitioners working as managers of tourism businesses.

The book consists of 24 chapters which are split into three parts: context, business functions and management issues in tourism. The rationale for this structure is a reflection of the underlying aim outlined above. The first part – context – explains how tourism management exists within both the worlds of both business and tourism. It shows how tourism as business has evolved, how the tourism and travel industry is structured and how tourism businesses operate within the political context of 'the State'. It is essential when approaching the subject to be familiar with this context; otherwise the more advanced areas of study are not realistically accessible.

Once an understanding of the context of tourism management has been achieved, the student can begin to assimilate the basics of business management theory, the subject of Part 2. This part comprises chapters whose titles would not be unfamiliar to the general business studies student. The content of each chapter is, however, presented with particular reference to tourism businesses. It thus concentrates on functions of business which are generic but which are presented from a tourism business perspective.

While it is generally accepted that any business needs to be customer-focused, a number of sectors have faced the difficulty of equating its 'customers' with the generic view of 'customers'. Examples are the health sector, the education sector and even the transport sector, where 'patients', 'students' and 'passengers' are more complex notions than simply 'customers'. In the tourism business sector, many organisations face difficulties with matching the notions of 'customers' and 'tourists'. As a result, a number of management issues have to be addressed that are unique to tourism businesses. These issues are covered in the 13 chapters of Part 3 of the book, which concludes with a consideration of the future prospects for tourism businesses.

Each of the chapters in this book contains the following:

- a statement of learning outcomes;
- a chapter overview;
- subject content appropriate to one of the sections mentioned above;
- case studies, including one extended case;
- a conclusion;
- guided reading;
- recommended websites;
- key words;
- a bibliography.

At the time of writing, all recommended websites were live. However, it may be the case that sites become inaccessible. In the event of this happening, readers are asked to contact the publisher with details of any problems.

Support materials

Materials for further study, including relevant annotated weblinks, are available at **www.pearsoned.co.uk/beechchadwick**

The BOTM Blog is a website designed to support this book with tourism management news stories and other internet resources. It is regularly updated by the editors at **businessoftourismmanagement.blogspot.com**

Acknowledgements

The editors would like to thank each of the chapter authors for their hard work and commitment in getting the book written. Special thanks are extended to those chapter authors who worked under especially tight time constraints.

Thanks are also due to the various organisations that have allowed us to use case material relating to their work in the tourism industry.

Respect is due to the patient staff at Financial Times Prentice Hall. After years of trying to get us to write *The Business of Sport Management*, they found two willing collaborators with this companion volume, not least because of the support they had given us with that book. Jacqueline Senior, Nicola Chilvers and Ben Greshon deserve a special mention, not only for all their help but also for putting up with our increasingly predictable BOTM jokes.

Both the editors reserve a special mention for Sue Beech and her excellent proof-reading work.

Special thanks are due to Natasha Brammer for her work in choosing and developing the longer case studies at the end of the book, and also preparing Cases 1.2 and 1.3.

John dedicates his work on the book to Sue, who has again tolerated a considerable amount of displacement activity. He still promises to return to the serious business of painting the house.

Simon dedicates his work on the book to Barbara and Tomasz.

Publisher's acknowledgements

We are grateful to the following for permission to reproduce copyright material:
Figure 1.1 adapted from 'Towards a framework for tourism education', in *Annals of Tourism Research*, Elsevier (Jafari, J. and Ritchie, J.R.B. 1981); Figure in Case 5.2 from Tourism Training Forum for Wales and Wales Tourist Board; Figure 5.5 adapted from 'A Theory of Human Motivation', in *Psychological Review*, American Psychological Association (Maslow, A. 1943); Case study 6.1 reproduced with permission of the Eden Project; Table 6.1 from *Services Marketing: People, Technology, Strategy*, Pearson Education, Inc. (Lovelock, C. 2001); Figure 6.2 from *Managing Services Marketing*, South-Western, a division of Thomson Learning (Bateson, J. and Hoffman, K. 1999); Figure 6.3 from www.ianallan.com/travel/index.htm, Ian Allan Travel Ltd; Figure 6.5 from *Principles of Services Marketing*, Open University Press/McGraw-Hill Publishing Company (Palmer, A. 2001); Tables in Cases 7.1 and 7.2 from *Go Ahead Group plc Annual Report 2003*, Go Ahead Group plc; Tables in Case 7.3 from *Ryanair Annual Report and Financial Accounts 2003*, Ryanair plc; Figure 7.5 from *Managerial Accounting in the Hospitality Industry*, Nelson Thornes (Harris, P. and Hazzard, P. 1992); Figure 7.6 from *Business Development; A Guide to Small Business Strategy*, Elsevier (Butler, D. 2001); Table 9.1 from 'From theory to practice: using new science concepts to create learning organizations' in *The Learning Organization*, Emerald Group Publishing Ltd (Shelton, C. and Darling, J. 2003); Table 9.2 from www.arrowhead.com/site/files/ breaker/2004springbuad4556southwestairlines.doc, Arrowhead University (Breaker, M. 2004); Figures 9.2 and 9.3 from *Competitive Advantage: Creating and Sustaining Superior Performance*, Free Press, a division of Simon & Schuster Adult Publishing Group (Porter, M.E. 1985, 1998); Table 10.1 from *Operations Management. An Active Learning Approach*, Blackwell Publishing Ltd (Bicheno, J. and Elliott, B.B. 1997); Figure 10.1 from *Operations Management*, Palgrave Macmillan (Hill, T. 2005); Figure 10.2 from *Operations Management*, Pearson Education Ltd (Slack, N., Chambers, S. and Johnston, R. 2004); Figure 10.3 from 'Yield Management Practices' in

Yield Management, Thomson Learning (EMEA) Ltd (Ingold, A., McMahon-Beattie, U. *et al.* 2000); Table 11.4 from 'The role of computerised reservation systems in the hospitality industry', in *Tourism Management*, Elsevier (Go, F. 1992); Table 13.1 from *Sightseeing in the UK 2000*, English Tourism Council (ETC 2001); Figure 13.1 from 'The nature and purpose of visitor attractions', in *Managing Visitor Attractions*, Elsevier (Leask, A. 2003); Table 14.1 based on *Mega-Events and Modernity*, Thomson Publishing/Routledge/Taylor & Francis (Roche, M. 2000); Figure 14.1 adapted from 'Integrating sport and tourism: a review of regional policies in England', in *Progress in Tourism and Hospitality Research*, John Wiley and Sons Ltd (Weed, M.E. and Bull, C.J. 1997); Tables 18.2, 19.1 and 24.2 Crown copyright material is reproduced with the permission of the Controller of HMSO and the Queen's Printer for Scotland; Table 18.3 from *Quality Standard for Hotels, Classification Scheme Manual*, English Tourism Council (ETC 2004); Table 18.5 from *Price Elasticity of Lodging Demand*, Pricewaterhouse Coopers (Hanson, B. 2000); Table 21.1 from *Yearbook of Statistics (1997–2001)*, World Tourism Organization (WTO 2003); Table 21.2 from *Eurostat Yearbooks 2002 and 2003*, Office for Official Publications of the European Communities (OPOCE 2002, 2003); Table 21.3 from *Eurostat Yearbook 2002*, Office for Official Publications of the European Communities (OPOCE 2002); Tables 22.1 and 22.2 from *Tourism and Poverty Alleviation*, World Tourism Organization (WTO 2002); Figure 22.1 from *Jamaica Observer*, Jamaica Observer Ltd (8.8.1996); Tables 24.4 and 24.5 from respectively www.greenglobe21.com/Benchmarking and *Green Globe 21 Essentials*, Green Globe Asia Pacific Pty Ltd (Green Globe 2004). Green Globe uses a series of Earthcheck indicators to benchmark aspects of performance. Earthcheck is a proprietary system of indicators used to measure environmental and social impacts; Table 24.7 from *Tourism, Technology and Competitive Strategies*, CABI Publishing (Poon, A. 1993).

Brilliant Weekends for an extract from their website www.brilliantweekends.co.uk (Case 6.4); Multilingual Matters for an extract from 'The World Wide Fund for Nature Arctic Tourism Project' by Mason, Johnston and Twynham published in *The Journal of Sustainable Tourism* 8 (4) (Case 16.2); Roger Bray for 'Agents suffer a squeeze from airlines', *The Financial Times Limited*, 21 January 2004, © Roger Bray (Case 20.7); Elsevier for an extract from 'The Great Barrier Reef' by Simmons and Harris in *Sustainable Tourism: An Australian Perspective* by Harris and Leiper (Case 22.2); Tourism Intelligence International for an extract from 'Succesful Tourism Destinations – Lessons from Leaders' by Boon; and Third World Network for extracts from *New Frontiers* available at www.twnside.org.sg/tour.htm (Case 22.1).

We are grateful to the Financial Times Limited for permission to reprint the following material:
Case 20.4 Inside track: Toeing the line versus do-it-yourself, © *Financial Times*, 28 May 2002; Case A Iranians rue loss of lucrative foreign tourist business, © *Financial Times*, 11 September 2004; Case B Germany's Tui reaches calmer waters, © *Financial Times*, 8 September 2004; Case C Mountain kingdom brave Maoist rebel blockade, © *Financial Times*, 28 August 2004; Case D Raising the bar high in order to perform well, © *Financial Times*, 6 August 2004; Case E 'Smoking ban' could benefit economy by £2.3bn, © *Financial Times*, 29 July 2004; Case F Dalmatia woos the 'in-crowd', © *Financial Times*, 13 July 2004; Case G Liechtenstein buys a new look, © *Financial Times*, 26 August 2004; Case H Priority is preserving unspoilt coast, © *Financial Times*, 11 July 2004; Case I Away from theme park Havana, © *Financial Times*, 16 August 2003; Case J The non-partisan middleman, © *Financial Times*, 27 October 2004; Case K Leader on the route to success, © *Financial Times*, 1 September 2004; Case L Vision of booming spiritual village, © *Financial Times*, 23 November 2004; Case M Image starts to wear a bit thin, from FT Investing Spain Supplement, © *Financial Times*, 26 October 2004; Case N The holiday package undone, © *Financial Times*, 21 May 2003.

In some instances we have been unable to trace the owners of copyright material, and we would appreciate any information that would enable us to do so.

ABTA	Association of British Travel Agents
ADR	Alternative dispute resolution
AITO	Association of Independent Tour Operators
ASEAN	Association of Southeast Asian Nations
CAA	UK's Civil Aviation Authority
CBA	Cost–benefit analysis
CEC	Commission of the European Communities
CRS	Computer reservations system
CIP	Critical incidental point
DDA	Disability Discrimination Act
DETR	UK's Department of the Environment, Transport and the Regions
DfES	UK's Department for Education and Skills
ECPAT	End Child Prostitution in Asian Tourism Organisation
ECTAA	The European Travel Agents' and Tour Operators' Associations
EMS	Environmental management system
ETC	English Tourism Council
EU	European Union
GATS	General Agreement on Trade and Services
GDS	Global distribution system
GDP	Gross domestic product
GNP	Gross national product
HDI	Human Development Index
ICAO	International Civil Aviation Organization
ICCROM	International Centre for the Study of the Preservation and Restoration of Cultural Property
ICOMOS	International Council on Monuments and Sites
ICT	Information and communication technologies
IUCN	International Union for Conservation of Nature and Natural Resources
IUOTO	International Union of Official Travel Organisations
LDC	Less Developed Countries
MMC	UK Monopolies and Mergers Commission
MNE	Multinational enterprise
OECD	Organization for Economic Co-operation and Development
OFT	Office of Fair Trading
SMEs	Small- and medium-sized enterprises
TNC	Transnational company/corporation
TPC	Tourism Policy Council
TSA	Tourism satellite account
UNDP	United Nations Development Programme
UNESCO	United Nations Educational, Scientific and Cultural Organization
USP	Unique selling proposition or point
VAT	Value added tax
VFR	Visiting friends and relatives
VSO	Voluntary Service Overseas
WTTC	World Travel & Tourism Council
WTO	World Tourism Organization[1]
WWF	World Wide Fund for Nature[2]

---

[1] Confusingly, WTO is *also* the abbreviation for the World Trade Organization, another United Nations agency.
[2] Formerly the World Wildlife Fund. Its Secretariat is known as WWF International. (Following a legal dispute, in 2002 the World Wrestling Federation Entertainment, which had used 'WWF' in its logo, rebranded as World Wrestling Entertainment.)

Useful websites

Academic associations

ALTIS: **www.altis.ac.uk**
ATHE: **www.athe.org.uk/**
ATLAS: **www.atlas-euro.org/**
ISTTE: **www.istte.org/index.html**
Tourism Society: **www.tourismsociety.org/**

Academic journals

Alastair M. Morrison's list of tourism journals: **omni.cc.purdue.edu/~alltson/journals_1.htm**

Government bodies

EU Tourism website: **http://europa.eu.int/comm/enterprise/services/tourism/index_en.htm**
OTTI: **http://www.tinet.ita.doc.gov/**
Star UK (statistics on tourism and research): **www.staruk.org.uk/**
Tourism Offices Worldwide Directory: **www.towd.com/**
World Tourism Organization e-Library: **miranda.wtoelibrary.org**
World Tourism Organization: **www.world-tourism.org/**

Others

John Beech's Travel and Tourism Management Information Gateway: **www.stile.coventry.ac.uk/cbs/staff/beech/tourism/index.htm**
René Waksberg's Tourism Research Links: **www.waksberg.com/**
Tourism Concern: **www.tourismconcern.org.uk/resources/resource-books.html**
Links to these websites and all other chapter-specific websites are available at: **www.pearsoned.co.uk/beechchadwick**
The BOTM Blog is a website with tourism management news stories and other internet resources. It is regularly updated by the editors at: **businessoftourismmanagement.blogspot.com**

Part 1
The context of tourism

- This section sets the context for the book. Given the main focus of the book – that of tourism businesses, whether in the public, private or voluntary sectors – the part begins by setting out how tourism emerged as a set of businesses with particular characteristics. The part outlines the core structure which can be ascribed to the tourism industry and its various subsectors, and acknowledges that tourism businesses must operate within a national state framework.

- The purpose of the part is to examine how and why the tourism industry and tourism businesses have evolved in the particular way they have, and in doing so an agenda within which the rest of book is written is established.

- The part contains chapters on the evolution of tourism as business, the structure of the tourism industry and the role of the state in tourism.

- In the part there is a variety of case studies and these include studies on Scarborough, a classic UK resort, the impact which information technology has had on the tourism industry and the role of the Italian state in the development of tourism.

Chapter 1

Introduction – the unique evolution of tourism as 'business'

John Beech and Simon Chadwick
Coventry Business School; Birkbeck College, University of London

Learning outcomes

On completion of this chapter the reader should be able to:

- outline the development of tourism, and mass tourism in particular;
- explain the significance of tourism in an economic context;
- identify the key factors which need to be present for mass tourism to emerge;
- identify the scope of the business of tourism and of tourism businesses, and the main tourism flows;
- identify the main business factors which are relevant to the management of tourism organisations;
- identify the main contents of this book.

Overview

This chapter provides both an overview and an introduction to the business of tourism management. It begins by establishing the historical context of today's mass tourism and explains how mass tourism emerged from an earlier era of tourism, one in which tourism was a pastime of the rich. As the development of tourism is tracked, key types of tourism are identified, as are the major tourism flows of the last century. The development of UK mass tourism is presented as an exemplar, and parallel developments in other parts of the world are discussed.

Next the main business dimensions of tourism are established and various applications of management theory which are specific to the study of tourism are outlined. This framework of management theory is used to establish the framework of the rest of the book.

Early travel

Early man was nomadic and by definition his lifestyle involved travel. Generally his wandering was confined to a clearly identifiable area, typically that in which he could hunt for the animals which formed a major part of his diet. Such a nomadic lifestyle could not be termed *tourism* in any modern sense of the word, as *tourism* presupposes a process of travel away from some form of home and a return to that home – until societies were based around a 'home', tourism could not be said to exist.

While early man was therefore no tourist, he showed great propensity to travel. His travelling might involve journeys of thousands of miles. The Celts, often characterised as a race which inhabited the north-west fringes of Europe, can be shown to have inhabited Halstadt in Austria and originated in central Asia. Such an enormous journey by an entire people again cannot be characterised as *tourism* since it does not involve a return to home. It does, however, involve a major change of home, the characteristic which identifies it as *migration* rather than *tourism*.

Early man did not simply either wander nomadically round a particular area or migrate in search of pastures new. Professor Trevor Sofield of the University of Tasmania has argued on the Trinet discussion forum for tourism academics that:

> Australian Aboriginals engaged in 'special annual events tourism' when the nomadic bands came together every year for a range of ceremonial activities and festivities as long ago as 30,000 years or more.
>
> Berndt and Berndt, 1964

Sofield makes this argument in the context of a plea for recognition of the fact that travel was not a great European invention. He points out that the Emperors of China appointed Ministers of Travel some 2000 years before the Roman Empire saw large-scale travel taking place systematically across much of Europe, the Near East and North Africa. He also points out that religious tourism – the pilgrimage to a holy place or shrine – was not an invention of the Rome-based Christian religion, but was, in fact, common practice in the Indian subcontinent, China, Nepal, Thailand, Iran, Vietnam and Myanmar well before the birth of Christ.

Some basic concepts

The notion of pilgrimage as *tourism* may appear strange at first sight. At this point it is worth looking at two definitions of tourism. One of the earliest official definitions is that made by the League of Nations in 1937:

> people travelling abroad for periods of over 24 hours.

This definition would not be acceptable today as it excludes all forms of domestic tourism, i.e. tourists visiting destinations in their own country. Such a definition excludes the massive flow of tourists from the northern USA, cities like Chicago for example, to Florida.

The most widely accepted modern definition of tourism is that given by the World Tourism Organization (WTO), the agency of the United Nations tasked with developing and promoting tourism:

> the activities of persons travelling to and staying in places outside their usual environment for not more than one consecutive year for leisure, business or other purposes.

By this definition pilgrimage clearly qualifies as tourism since it involves the temporary displacement of the pilgrim, or religious tourist, and his or her return to home. The reason that 'pilgrim' as 'tourist' strikes us as odd is that the purpose of a pilgrimage is not the purpose of travel that is normally associated with tourism – a holiday, a journey made for leisure purposes. The WTO definition contains, in fact, no restricting reference to the purpose of the journey – it includes 'or other purposes' – leaving us with a very wide definition. Most academics use the WTO definition, so studying tourism involves studying a much larger subject than the study of holiday-makers and holidays. Indeed, this element of tourism, the one which the lay person would readily identify as an essential part of tourism, is all too often neglected by tourism academics, with some notable exceptions. Lois Turner and John Ash wrote of 'the pleasure periphery' (1975) when describing the emergence of the Mediterranean as a major destination for the sun-seeking northern European tourist,[1] and Krippendorf (1987) and Urry (1990) have made major contributions to the study of the tourist *per se*. Krippendorf and Urry wrote from anthropological or sociological perspectives, and this raises an important question – from the perspective of which discipline should we study tourism?

Jafar Jafari, a seminal figure in the study of tourism, has suggested that the study of tourism can be made from the academic perspectives given in Figure 1.1.

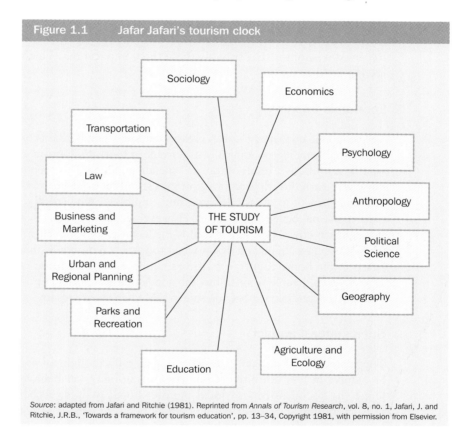

Figure 1.1   Jafar Jafari's tourism clock

Source: adapted from Jafari and Ritchie (1981). Reprinted from *Annals of Tourism Research*, vol. 8, no. 1, Jafari, J. and Ritchie, J.R.B., 'Towards a framework for tourism education', pp. 13–34, Copyright 1981, with permission from Elsevier.

These different academic perspectives have resulted in tourism being studied in different faculties or schools within universities, and in consequence it is unusual to find 'Tourism' courses on offer. Most frequent offerings are 'Tourism Studies', 'Tourism Management' and 'Tourism Geography'. This book is written from the management perspective, and is designed as a core textbook for either a tourism management degree or a tourism management module in a tourism studies or tourism geography degree programme.

There is an old joke: 'Tourism is good; it's tourists that are bad'. This raises two important points. First, tourism is a process that can be studied in its own right, whereas tourists are the actors who participate in that process. They could act alone, but in the

---

1 Authors of early studies of European and American tourists were often quite disparaging about their subjects, describing them, for example, as *The Golden Hordes* (Turner and Ash, 1975), and *The Offensive Tourist* (Pritchett, 1964).

modern world their actions are generally shaped to some extent by the tourism products that tourism producers offer. The core products which are offered typically include transport to and from a tourist destination, accommodation at that destination, and activities such as visits to tourist attractions within the destination. The offering of these tourism products is the nature of the tourism businesses which this book explores.

This distinction between tourists and producers of tourism products – both stakeholders in tourism – is important in understanding how tourism might be considered 'good' yet tourists might be considered as bad. The notions of 'good' and 'bad' in this context refer to the impacts which tourism and tourists have on the destinations visited. The three main impacts which have been studied are:

- economic;
- sociocultural;
- environmental.

Received wisdom is that broadly these three impacts may be characterised under the following headings.

Economic impact

The economic impact of tourism is expected to be 'good', that is, positive. In other words, the destination benefits economically as a result of tourism. Tourism creates jobs for local people who then profit as a result of tourists' spending money. This spending has a multiplier effect – those who earn directly from tourism jobs spend their earnings locally so there is a secondary economic benefit to other businesses and employees, who spend their earnings creating a tertiary economic benefit, and so on. However, economic impact can be reduced significantly through two effects: leakage, which is the leaking of profits back to the country from which the visitors have come and arises when tourists stay in hotels that are owned by companies based in the home country of visitors, and the demonstration effect, which is the process whereby local people want to buy the goods that have been imported to support the tourists' wants, e.g. Scandinavian beer on sale in a Mediterranean resort.

Sociocultural impact

The sociocultural impact of tourists is generally thought of as 'bad'. Tourists, who tend to behave in less inhibited ways when on holiday, set behaviour patterns which challenge the social norms of local people. Local people, especially those who work in tourism businesses and/or young people, begin to behave in ways that run against traditional cultural norms, and, if the exposure to tourists' behaviour is sufficiently sustained, the traditional way of life in a destination is irrevocably changed, in a way that traditional residents consider undesirable.

Environmental impact

The environmental impact of tourists is generally 'bad'. The continued presence of large numbers of tourists results in the degradation of the natural environment, through direct impact on the physical environment, through inappropriate use of land and water resources and through putting excessive pressure on the built environment, especially in the case of historical and cultural buildings.

When these three impacts are netted off, it can be seen whether the tourism process is sustainable at a particular destination. To return to Jafar Jafari's overview of how the study of tourism can be made from different perspectives, it will come as little surprise that economists have tended to concentrate on studying the economic sustainability of tourism whereas sociologists, anthropologists and geographers have tended to focus more on the sociocultural and environmental impacts of tourists. Although this book emphasises the managerial dimension of tourism businesses, it does not focus solely on economic impacts, positive or otherwise, at the expense of sociocultural and environmental impacts. It is to the emergence of the first businesses which might be considered as tourism businesses we now turn.

Early tourism businesses

The first businesses which we might view from a modern perspective as being tourism businesses emerge in two strands in medieval times. Historically the first of these that arose in Europe were associated with a cultural and educational phenomenon – The Grand Tour. This differed from our view of what might be considered conventional tourism in that the motivation was educational rather than for pleasure purposes. The sons of rich families were sent to broaden their education by visiting major centres of European culture and learning such as Paris, Vienna and Florence. It was common to employ a guide to accompany the travelling student, this guide acting as mentor, personal tutor and tourist guide. In this last capacity we can recognise a function which still offers employment to large numbers of people today. However, the 'Grand Tourists' came from a tiny elite of medieval society and often undertook Grand Tours lasting up to three or four years, a form of tourism which is effectively extinct today.

The second strand does, however, show some characteristics through which we might see it as a form of tourism recognisable as such today. As a wealthy middle class began to develop, with time and money available to travel, in many European countries spas began to emerge as 'tourist destinations', with visitors coming to spend two or three weeks to take the waters. While some undoubtedly came to seek medical treatments as cures for various ills, a large number started to come to these spas not only for some generally preventative medical treatment but also because of the lifestyle and status which started to emerge at the more successful spas. This form of tourism is still easily recognisable in spas in Belgium (the very name 'spa' comes from the town of Spa in Belgium), Germany, Austria and Switzerland, although in the United Kingdom (UK) it is perhaps difficult to imagine places such as Tunbridge Wells, Leamington Spa or Droitwich as health resorts which employed a master of ceremonies to arrange social activities which would give each of them a competitive edge. Today most inland spas in the UK show their origins mainly in the form of trying to develop heritage tourism – the best example of this is at the appropriately named spa of Bath, where the taking of waters re-emerged after years of inactivity following the withdrawal of the Romans in the early fifth century.

As the inland mineral-water spas started to decline, so a new form of 'spa' began to emerge – the coastal resort. Again, there was an emphasis on the health-giving aspect of visiting such a spa, with the added attraction of recreational activity in the form of swimming in the sea, but the social and recreational dimension of making such a visit remained to the fore.

It is with the growth of what are now considered traditional seaside resorts that we can clearly see the beginnings of today's mass tourism. While the inland spas had catered for a wealthy middle-class tourist, it is to the seaside resorts that working-class tourists first went in large numbers.

Case 1.1	Scarborough – a case of transformation

Scarborough is unique among UK spas in that not only does it have an early history as a spring-based mineral-water spa, but it survived the decline of such spas by transforming itself into a seaside spa – its possession of both spring water and sea water made it unique.

Granville's *Spas of England*, first published in 1841, describes Scarborough as 'the Queen of English sea-bathing places' and, while noting the facilities for sea-bathing, refers in detail to the two medicinal water springs which had been exploited since the seventeenth century. Facilities for visitors wishing to 'take the waters' from these springs had evolved in a similar way to those at the major inland spas such as Bath and Tunbridge – Assembly Rooms for social events, a Pump Room, a theatre, all presided over by a resident Master of Ceremonies. By the beginning of the nineteenth century, however, sea-bathing and drinking sea water had come to the fore, and bathing machines had spread along the beach.

Scarborough was thus well established as a destination by the time the railway arrived in the form of a branch line from York, then as now a major railway junction, in 1845; it was one of the first seaside resorts to be served by train. This proved to be a major influence on the scale of tourism development at Scarborough; its population grew from roughly ten thousand people in 1851 to more than thirty thousand by 1891. As the town grew, it developed all the major facilities and infrastructure that characterised British seaside resorts of the Victorian and Edwardian heyday:

- horse-drawn buses and a tramway system;
- cliff railways – four cable-hauled systems were built at Scarborough over the years to connect the town with the beach below;
- 'grand hotels' – many still operate, such as the Grand, the Royal and the Crown, although the marketing tag today tends very much to be 'restored to its former glory';
- an elegant crescent for those who wanted to take up residence in Scarborough on a grand scale;
- an esplanade to allow holiday-makers to stroll along the sea front;
- a pavilion – the first was designed by Sir Joseph Paxton, designer of London's Crystal Palace, but this burned down in 1876, to be replaced by the present Spa Pavilion;
- a pier – opened in 1869, Scarborough's pier was destroyed by a storm in 1905 and never rebuilt;
- a tower – opened shortly after Blackpool's, in 1897, but rather shorter and destined to survive only ten years;

and in more recent times:

- a miniature railway;
- a theme park – Kinderland;
- a mass of machine arcades, restaurants, nightclubs and souvenir shops;
- theatres – the Stephen Joseph Theatre and the Futurist Theatre.

As the twentieth century progressed, there was a gradual shift from an image of grandeur to one of sheer scale. The railway continued for many years to be a major element in the success of Scarborough as a destination. Picking up Granville's theme, the railway company which served Scarborough promoted it as 'Queen of Northern Watering Places'. A direct service from London was introduced under the brand 'The Scarborough Flyer'. To cater for such large numbers, Scarborough station boasted the longest station seat in Britain!

The availability of cheap package holidays in the Mediterranean during the last third of the century saw an inevitable fall in numbers of visitors. Scarborough was forced to reposition itself and redesign the tourism products it offered. This saw a growing market in weekend breaks, a growth in conference tourism – the Spa Complex, with its Grand Hall offering a capacity of 2000, was well positioned to make this switch – and an emphasis on heritage. Even the railways responded to this, establishing a heritage steam-train service from York.

In 2002 Scarborough won the English Tourism Council's Gold Award for Most Improved Resort, perhaps an indication both of how much it previously declined as well as of how much it had achieved in restoring its earlier status as a destination.

Sources: Various

For such mass tourism to emerge, four conditions had to be met:

Sufficient leisure time

The fulfilling of this condition came about in two phases. With the rise of industrial cities and a move from agricultural work to factory work, the traditional day of rest on a

Sunday became a true day of rest, with factories closed and workers not having to tend crops and animals on a seven-day-a-week basis. This meant that one day a week could be available for rest or recreation – excursionism, the less-than-twenty-four-hour variant of tourism, became a possibility. In many countries there was a legal imperative to give people guaranteed leisure time. In the UK an 1871 Act established Bank Holidays and within two decades many cities and towns had established formal half-day closing, and the 1901 Factory Act gave six days' holiday a year to women and young people.

Sufficient earnings to be able to spend money on holidays

This arose in a broader social and particularly economic context. In the late Victorian and Edwardian eras there was a growth in a movement for extending recreational activity in the fresh air, and this resulted in the provision of 'holiday camps' where such activity could be undertaken at affordable prices. Most such activity was, however, on a non-commercial basis. The increasing wealth of nations began to reflect itself in the increasing economic wealth of their citizens. Again there was often a legal imperative, for example the 1938 Holidays with Pay Act in the UK.

Cheap and easy means of transport

This manifested itself first in excursionism through the possibility of cheap transport by boat – Londoners were able to travel cheaply to the new resorts of Margate and Ramsgate in North Kent, for example, which began to grow from the 1820s. The next significant development came with the opening of railways. The first 'inter-city' route in the UK was opened between Liverpool and Manchester in 1830. Within the next twenty years most of today's rail network had been built. Although Thomas Cook is often credited with running the world's first railway excursion, the railway excursion was, in fact, an invention of the then private railway companies themselves. The significance of Thomas Cook's first organised excursion was that he was the first to establish a commercial tourism product based on the transport infrastructure which already existed. For over a century the railway not only provided the transport infrastructure for most tourism but it was also responsible for the growth of resorts such as Bournemouth and the Cornish Riviera.

After the Second World War, expectations of international holidays were raised, and the emergence of jet transport, notably in the form of the Boeing 707, opened up the possibility of cheap flights of reasonable duration from Northern Europe to the Mediterranean and from the industrial heartland of the North East of the United States to Florida, for example.

Commercial organisations producing and marketing tourism products

Although Thomas Cook and his son John Mason Cook were pioneers in developing guided tours (they were the first tour operators as we recognise them today), they catered not for the mass tourist but for the natural successors to the Grand Tourists. In the UK, the Regent Street Polytechnic was a pioneer tour operator and travel agent, organising overseas tours as early as 1889, and its Polytechnic Touring Association eventually becoming the 'Poly' of Lunn Poly, now part of the international TUI Group.

In the 1930s the 'holiday camp', an all-inclusive operation with all entertainment provided as well as board and lodging, became the major feature of mass tourism in the UK. The entrepreneurs who spearheaded this movement were once household names – Billy Butlin and Fred Pontin, for example.

The major emergence of large national tour operators and travel agents began immediately after the Second World War. The first major player in Europe was Club Mediterranée, with its Belgian founder, Gerard Blitz, operating his first holiday village in Majorca in 1950. Its early holiday villages were based on very simple accommodation, with a back-to-nature feel, but under the direction of Gilbert Trigano the company has grown to become a global player, with a variety of tourism products including ski holidays and cruises (Vichas, 1994).

Case 1.2   The Bay of Naples – a case of changing tourists

Widely thought of as the most beautiful coastline in Italy, the famous Bay of Naples lies on the west coast and is home to some of Italy's most popular tourist destinations. The small town of Sorrento is located on the southern arm of the bay, and is rapidly becoming as popular as its more renowned neighbours.

The most well-known of these is the city of Naples, which has catered for domestic tourists for centuries, and which, with its now diminishing reputation for crime and violence, is enjoying a successful and growing international tourism industry. The city itself, as well as the entire region, is steeped in history, culture and stunning architecture, and boasts friendly people, great cuisine and a warm climate, making it a popular destination for holiday-makers.

To the right of the city, the bay is overlooked by one of the most famous volcanoes in the world, Mount Vesuvius, the last active volcano on mainland Europe. Her most recent eruption was in 1944, but the most famous explosion was in AD 79, when the nearby Roman city of Pompeii was covered and destroyed by lava and ash. Located midway between Naples and Sorrento, Pompeii has been largely uncovered and restored and is now one of the most famous historical sights of Italy.

Leaving the bay behind and heading south along the beautiful Amalfi coast, the town of Salerno and the ancient Greek ruins of Paestum have fascinated the more adventurous traveller for centuries. At one point, Salerno was a most significant city, more so than Naples, and still houses a busy port and a spectacular Norman cathedral. A former Greek Colony, Paestum is made up of numerous magnificent and well-preserved temples and can tell the story of its history as far back as 600 BC.

In addition to these mainland attractions, the Bay of Naples is also home to three rocky island retreats: Procida, Ischia and Capri, the latter being the world-renowned holiday destination of many rich and famous people. A trip to these islands is well worth it, as 'the voyage across an aquamarine sea to experience their breathtaking loveliness is in itself a dream' (Leech and Shales, 2003). Once attached to the Sorrentine peninsula, Capri is the more developed and commercial of the islands, however, no less enchanting for it. The more allocentric tourists may enjoy the walks and wildlife of the less-visited Procida.

Standing between these contrasts of old and new is the town of Sorrento. Sorrento combines historical elements with modern aspects of tourism. As with the rest of Italy, the Bay of Naples is home to impressive museums, theatres, opera houses and cathedrals. Although on a smaller scale, Sorrento encapsulates all of these, and its stylish elegance has been attracting visitors for over 2500 years (Leech and Shales, 2003). The striking buildings are now surrounded with modern comfortable hotels and first-class restaurants, creating an all-encompassing holiday experience as well as being an ideal starting point and base for visiting all the surrounding areas. Tourism is now the most important industry in the region. The people of the area realised this potential a long time ago, and this has resulted in an adequate transport infrastructure in Sorrento. The islands, bay and coastline beyond are all joined by reliable air, road, rail and sea links, enabling tourists to move easily within the region.

As well as being the location of arguably the first holiday homes, this cluster of resorts has long been a destination of the rich and famous. In the nineteenth century Felix Mendelssohn, the composer, and Oscar Wilde, the playwright, spent holidays on Capri. Enrico Caruso returned from his spectacular worldwide success to stay in Sorrento, and W.H. Auden, the poet, became a resident of Ischia. Gracie Fields, the singer, and Noel Coward, the dramatist, composer and actor, were regular visitors to Capri. More recently, Tom Cruise, John Belushi and Duran Duran have holidayed on Capri. The area thus remains a destination for the rich and famous. Capri, with a population of 12,000, currently has four 5-star hotels. Today's visitor, however, is more typically a tourist making an excursion from a resort on the mainland such as Naples or Sorrento. At the height of the season the island currently receives 10,000 visitors a day, and these numbers greatly exceed the number of hotel residents.

Source: Various

Tourism as an evolutionary process

We have already seen the rise and fall of a group of destinations – the British inland spas – and it is all too apparent that their successors – the British seaside resorts – are now often in a state of serious decline. Butler (1980) developed a model of the evolutionary cycle of a destination (see Figure 1.2), a model which has been widely adapted as a marketing model to describe the lifecycle of virtually all products.

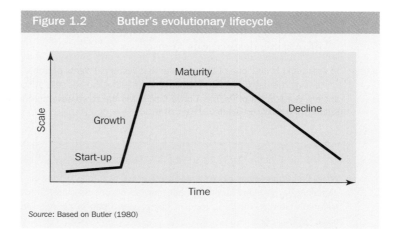

Figure 1.2   Butler's evolutionary lifecycle

Source: Based on Butler (1980)

Other theorists such as Thurot (1973) and Plog (1974) sought to explain what drives such an evolutionary lifecycle. Such models are dynamic – they emphasise the changing nature of the tourists who visit a particular destination, and especially a notion of 'succession'. In other words, there is a pattern in the change of the type of tourists who visit a particular destination, with one type of tourist moving on to new destinations to be succeeded by a different type of tourist. They differ in what they argue is the driver of this change process, as set out in Table 1.1.

Table 1.1   Evolutionary theories of destination development

Theorist	Driver	Resort discovered by:	Succeeded by:	Need for response by destination
Thurot (1973)	Class succession	The rich	Upper middle class; middle class; mass tourism	Changing types of hotels
Plog (1974)	Personality type	The allocentric tourists (the adventurous, outgoing, self-confident independent traveller)	Midcentric tourist (part- allocentric; part psychocentric; they constitute the *majority* of tourists); then psychocentric tourists (the timid tourist who prefers 'abroad' to be like 'home')	Changing types of attractions

Source: Based on information derived from WTO (www.wto.org)

Evolutionary theories have an obvious attraction – in many case they seem to work well, explaining how tourism to, for example, Torremolinos has changed in the last 50 years (see BBC, 1996). But difficulties with this kind of approach have emerged:

- They only make sense with respect to the destination from the perspective of the tourism-generating country – in the case of Torremolinos, or the Spanish Costas by extension, with respect to visitors from the UK and other Northern European countries. Do they really explain the growth in Spanish domestic tourism?
- The logical extension of these theories is that all destinations would ultimately be full of working-class psychocentric tourists only.
- Ultimately where do the rich allocentric tourists end up? They're going to run out of possible destinations to discover.

Some of these problems can be countered by recognising that any particular resort is not restricted to one lifecycle – they can reinvent themselves and attract a further round of visitation by upper-class allocentrics.

Case 1.3   Atlantic City – a case of reinvention

While first impressions would suggest Atlantic City is little more than a poor man's Vegas, this now chintzy gambling haven hides a complex and original history. Its current reputation began in the latter half of the twentieth century. However, tourism has played a part in Atlantic City's history for much longer, since the early 1800s in fact.

Absecon Island, home to Atlantic City, was also home to a prominent pioneering family, the Leeds. The Leeds set Atlantic City on a tourism lifecycle that is quite unlike that of most other tourism destinations. The first ever industry on Absecon Island was tourism, which began with a boarding house opened by Jeremiah Leeds' second wife. The original idea was to turn the island into a seaside health resort, but the isolated location and the lack of transport links were to be a problem. To solve this, in 1852 the Camden–Atlantic City railroad was born, and it was to set Atlantic City on a path of rapid change and development. Over the next three decades, following the initial influx of tourists by train, Atlantic City developed various alternative routes for its potential visitors to use: a busy seaport, a road from the mainland and an additional railway line.

With the rapid increase in the number of guests, the need for accommodation also grew. A vast number of then luxurious hotels were opened to cater for the influx of tourists, as were amusement parks to entertain them. In 1870, Atlantic City's most famous landmark was built – the Boardwalk. The first in the world, it began a trend and the boardwalk has become a symbol of seaside holiday resorts worldwide. At six miles long, the Boardwalk is still today at the very centre of Atlantic City's tourism industry.

The late 1800s and early 1900s were a great time for Atlantic City; industry, population and tourist numbers were growing. Its variety of amenities and amusements meant that it had something to interest everyone, and for a long while Atlantic City was the place to be. Like many other destinations, however, it suffered from seasonality, and while the summer months were buzzing, it struggled out of season. One solution to this came in 1921, with the first annual Miss America pageant. Along with the Boardwalk, the pageant has become synonymous with Atlantic City, and has brought followers from all over the world.

However, this was all to change. Before long, plenty of other destinations had taken their lead from Atlantic City's early success, and the once popular seaside resort looked dated in comparison. Combined with the increase in air travel after the Second World War, Atlantic City was soon losing out to more modern and glamorous international competitors.

By 1960, Atlantic City was definitely not 'the place to be'. Something was needed to restore the city's former glory. That something was thought to be gambling. In 1976, Atlantic City was given a second chance, with the passing of the Casino Gambling Referendum. Suddenly the amusement arcades, tacky souvenir shops and worn-out boarding-houses were replaced with top-class restaurants, big-name hotels and glamorous casinos. This revamp did wonders for Atlantic City, and, along with providing over 45,000 jobs, succeeded in bringing in new and different types of visitors and, more importantly, restoring the city's reputation as a credible holiday destination.

Albeit with deteriorating credibility, this reputation continues today. Unfortunately, Atlantic City still experiences the problems common to similar seaside resorts. Having a city so dependent on a gambling culture brings a number of social problems. The majority of money brought into the area by huge numbers of tourists never benefits the local economy due to outside investment. The clear majority of the tourists it does attract are also Americans, and of an older age range. Like Las Vegas, Atlantic City is attempting to target the younger clientele after having little success marketing itself as a family destination.

Source: Various

Discussion questions

1 As it finds itself struggling in this industry yet again, can Atlantic City re-invent its image once more, or is a third chance too much to ask for?
2 Will the change in UK law with respect to casinos mean that some UK resorts, e.g. Blackpool, will look to re-inventing themselves as gambling destinations?

Two other influential theorists of this important early era of tourism management's development as an academic study need to be introduced at this stage. Miossec (1977), a French researcher, pointed out that the development of a destination was influenced not only by the behaviour of tourists but also by the destination's responses to that behaviour. The planning of facilities and infrastructure thus plays a significant role in shaping the eventual outcomes of tourism development. Second, Gray (1970) coined the expression 'sunlust' tourism to describe the motivation of those tourists who had begun flooding to the Mediterranean from northern Europe for their summer holidays.

Tourism flows

This large-scale flow of tourists from the United Kingdom, Germany and Scandinavia to Spain and Italy, and subsequently to Greece and Turkey, is one of the most obvious tourism flows if you are a native of one of those generating countries. The North–South flow is also prevalent in the United States and Canada. Residents of cities such as New York and Chicago move in large numbers to the sunlust destinations in Florida, and more recently to Caribbean island states and Mexico. The similarities to the major European flow are obvious, but it should be noted that movement from New York or Chicago to Florida is an example of *domestic* tourism, that is, tourism movement within the same country. The recent widespread introduction of the euro as the unit of currency in most European countries now means that tourism from Germany or The Netherlands to Spain or Greece has become economically domestic, but tourism from the United Kingdom or Sweden, who have not joined the European Monetary Union, to Spain or Greece, who are members, remains economically *international* tourism.

To identify tourism flows accurately it is essential to draw on accurate data for analysis. The most widely used data is that collected and published by the World Tourism Organization. While there are difficulties with all tourism data, an issue we will return to in the final chapter, most academics use this WTO data as a source, and the data in the following paragraphs is drawn directly from or derived from the WTO databases.

It is important to recognise which nations are the major tourism generators (i.e. where the visitors come from) and the major tourism recipients (i.e. where they visit). The major nations, measured by the parameter of international tourist arrivals, are listed in Table 1.2.

As we are studying tourism from a business perspective, an alternative parameter to consider is tourism spend. Table 1.3 gives the 'Top Ten' data on tourism spending by nation and tourism earning by nation.

Table 1.2	The world's top tourism destinations		
	2002 in millions	Market share (%)	Arrivals per 100 of population
World	703	100	11
1 France	77.0	11.0	129
2 Spain	51.7	7.4	129
3 USA	41.9	6.0	15
4 Italy	39.8	5.7	69
5 China	38.8	5.2	3
6 United Kingdom	24.2	3.4	40
7 Canada	20.1	2.9	63
8 Mexico	19.7	2.8	19
9 Austria	18.6	2.6	228
10 Germany	18.0	2.6	22

Source: Based on information derived from WTO (**www.wto.org**)

Table 1.3	The world's top tourism spenders and earners						
TOURISM SPENDING	International tourism expenditure (USbn$)	Market share (%)	Expenditure per capita (US$)	TOURISM EARNING	International tourism revenues (USbn$)	Market share (%)	Receipts per capita (US$)
World	474	100	76	World	474	100	76
1 USA	58.0	12.2	202	1 USA	66.5	14.0	231
2 Germany	53.2	11.2	646	2 Spain	33.6	7.1	837
3 UK	40.4	8.5	674	3 France	32.3	6.8	539
4 Japan	26.7	5.6	210	4 Italy	26.9	5.7	465
5 France	19.5	4.1	325	5 China	20.4	4.3	16
6 Italy	16.9	3.6	292	6 Germany	19.2	4.0	233
7 China	15.4	3.2	12	7 UK	17.6	3.7	294
8 Netherlands	12.9	2.7	804	8 Austria	11.2	2.4	1375
9 Hong Kong	12.4	2.6	1700	9 Hong Kong	10.1	2.1	1385
10 Russia	12.0	2.5	83	10 Greece	9.7	2.1	915

Source: Based on information derived from WTO (**www.wto.org**)

Discussion questions

3 What does the data in Table 1.3 suggest with respect to the idea of tourism being a means for rich countries to redistribute wealth to poorer countries?

4 Why might the figures for the USA be rather misleading in both Tables 1.2 and 1.3?

Both Tables 1.2 and 1.3 take no notice of the issue of how large a country is, and it is therefore not surprising that the USA appears high in each ranking (although there are other reasons for this as question 4 above implies). To see how significant tourism is in a particular country, we need to adjust the data to allow for the size of the population in each country. The world's top tourism destinations relative to population are given in Table 1.4.

Table 1.4	The world's top tourism destinations relative to population		
	Arrivals per 100 of population	International tourist arrivals (millions)	Population 2002 (thousands)
World	**11**	**703**	**6 228 395**
1 Andorra	4953	3.4	68
2 Macao	1422	6.6	462
3 British Virgin Islands	1338	0.3	21
4 Aruba	913	0.6	70
5 Turks and Caicos Islands	827	0.2	19
6 Monaco	822	0.3	32
7 Cayman Islands	743	0.3	41
8 Guam	659	1.1	161
9 Northern Mariana Islands	603	0.5	77
10 Bahamas	525	N/A	295

Source: Based on information derived from WTO (**www.wto.org**)

Quite a different picture emerges, one that will perhaps send you searching in an atlas! The nations which are most affected by, and dependent on, tourism are the tiny states. For the first time we see developing nations in the top ten. If the ranking were continued beyond ten, we would see a list dominated by small island states, especially those in the Caribbean and the Pacific. Only three bigger countries feature: Austria (ranked 21), Hong Kong (22) and the United Arab Emirates (23). The only sunlust destination for northern Europeans in the top twenty-five is Cyprus (ranked 17). For the countries which are the world's top tourism destinations by population, the business of tourism is a key industry, and although smaller in absolute size than in, for example, Spain or Greece, it has a greater relative significance in the countries' economies. Tourism flows into the countries may be more diverse than in the major destination countries, but they are large flows for the countries concerned. It is perhaps for this reason that much academic research has tended to be focused on small developing nations rather than on the mass-tourism destinations such as Spain.

The role of management in tourism businesses

The remaining chapters in this first part of the book continue to develop an understanding of the context of tourism business. Chapter 2 considers 'The structure of the tourism and travel industry', how the tourism industry is organised. Chapter 3 explores 'The role of the state in tourism'. The author, rather than simply describing the role of a particular state, takes a broader and more analytical view than is often taken in textbooks.

The second part, on business functions, opens with Chapter 4, which is on 'Organisational behaviour in tourism businesses', the study of how people behave individually and collectively within organisations, how they communicate, how they are motivated and how they exercise and react to different forms of leadership. The study of organisational behaviour is essential in understanding how organisations, whether state sector, private sector or voluntary sector, function.

A closely related field is that of 'Human resource management in tourism businesses', the subject of Chapter 5. This explores further the notion of motivation and explains how human resource management is a key factor in the development of a successful strategy for a tourism business.

The product of a tourism business is essentially different from conventional businesses: it involves a product which is not merely heavily services-oriented but one which is bought for consumption many months in the future and possibly thousands of miles away from the point of purchase. It follows that the marketing of such products will have very particular characteristics. Chapter 6, 'Marketing in tourism', outlines basic marketing principles as applied to the world of tourism. It looks at the subjects of tourist buyer behaviour and relationship building.

Chapter 7 introduces the key concepts for understanding 'Finance and accounting for tourism' in the tourism industry. Whether you work in the private sector, which is profit-driven, or in the voluntary sector, where an organisation must at least break even, you will need the skills and knowledge taught in this chapter.

The particular issues of 'Managing a small non-profit tourism organisation' are analysed in Chapter 8. Similarly, all tourism organisations have to worry about the business environment they operate in, at the mercy of political, economic, social and technological changes and developments. Chapter 9 explains the 'Analysis of the business environment and strategy in tourism'. This involves the integration of the business functions studied in the previous chapters.

'Quality and yield management in tourism businesses' are areas that managers must be familiar with if their businesses are to be successful, and are considered in Chapter 10. Today's businesses have been quick to take advantage of the possibilities which new technology has presented and Chapter 11 covers 'Information technology and management information systems in tourism'.

The third section of the book explores and develops themes raised in the first and second sections of the book. The three major impacts of tourism that have been introduced earlier in this chapter are investigated at length in three key chapters – 'The economic impact of tourism' in Chapter 15, 'Managing sociocultural impacts of tourism' in Chapter 16 and 'Managing the environmental impacts of tourism' in Chapter 17. Developing the work of Chapter 2 ('The structure of the tourism and travel industry') are chapters on 'The accommodation subsector' (Chapter 18), 'Tour operators' (Chapter 19), 'Travel agents' (Chapter 20) and 'Managing the transport subsector in tourism' (Chapter 21). The discussion on the role of the state, discussed in Chapter 3, is developed with a specialist look at 'Tourism businesses and the law' (Chapter 12). The final sub-theme in the third part is the review of specialist subsectors of the tourism industry from a management perspective – 'Visitor attraction management' (Chapter 13), 'Sports tourism' (Chapter 14), 'Developing mass tourism in developing nations' (Chapter 22) and 'The management of heritage and cultural tourism' (Chapter 23).

The book concludes with a look at 'The future of the tourism industry' (Chapter 24).

Discussion question

5   How might the study of tourism from a business or management perspective be different from studying it from a geographical or a sociological perspective?

Conclusion

Studying the business of tourism management can be challenging. If you come to this book with a background of tourism studies, it will be hard to take on board that management is at the core of tourism business – the sociology of tourism will help to explain the social environment which influences the development of tourism business, but will in itself prove totally inadequate to explain tourism business strategy, for example.

If on the other hand you approach this book with a basic understanding of business principles, you may feel that you come with a flying start. Be careful! While the idea that tourism management (the application of general management to tourism organisations) underpins this book (Chapters 4 to 11), it is also clear that the *distinctiveness* of tourism business – the 'industry recipe' – is also at the core (Chapters 12 to 23).

Tourism management has been widely researched, both from European and North American perspectives. Often research has focused on less common destinations but increasingly academics are investigating more popular destinations and the various dimensions of mass tourism. By developing a range of business skills which you will have developed in a range of applications, this book should help you not only with tourism management studies, but with your personal development regarding a career in tourism management. Large tourism companies, such as the big tour operators and travel agents, tend to place more emphasis when recruiting on applicants' management skills rather than on their knowledge of tourism.

Guided reading

As Jafar Jafari suggests, the study of tourism can be made from a range of academic perspectives. For the study of tourism from a business or management perspective, it will probably come as no surprise that this is the recommended book! You are, however, recommended to review how tourism can be studied from other perspectives. Peter Burns and Andrew Holden offer an excellent introduction to the study of tourism from the perspective of anthropology (Burns and Holden, 1995). For the study of tourism from a geographical perspective, try Shaw and Williams (2004). There is no better approach to an understanding of tourism from the sociological perspective than to read the classic texts such as Urry (1990) and MacCannell (1999).

For an excellent account of the social history of British seaside holidays see Walton (2000), and also Inglis (2000) who covers a wider theme. Barker (2002) offers a good insight into how Scarborough was at its zenith during the 1920s and 1930s.

Recommended websites

Two websites have been developed specifically to support this book:

- The Companion Website – **www.pearsoned.co.uk/beechchadwick** – which provides additional internet resources, clickable links to all the websites mentioned in the book and a link to the lecturers' resources (password protected – lecturers can apply for a password online from this website).
- The BOTM Blog – **www.businessoftourismmanagement.blogspot.com** – which provides regularly updated news of developments in tourism management and tourism businesses.

For a wide-ranging resource for tourism management students, see John Beech's Tourism Management Information Gateway – **www.stile.coventry.ac.uk/cbs/staff/beech/tourism/index.htm** .

Other large resources designed for students include Altis (**www.altis.ac.uk**) and HTSN (**www.hlst.heacademy.ac.uk/**).

The WTO publishes tourism data regularly (see its website at **www.world-tourism.org**). Your university may subscribe to its databases at **www.wtoelibrary.org**, and a brief summary is downloadable from **www.world-tourism.org/facts/highlights/Highlights.pdf** .

To see how Scarborough currently presents itself, see the Scarborough Borough Council's website for visitors – **www.scarborough.gov.uk/content/visitors/visitors_ home.html** . The Capri Tourist Board website is at **www.capritourism.com/en/index.php** and Atlantic City's is at **www.cityofatlanticcity.org/** (see under 'Visitor Info').

Key words

Allocentric; evolutionary theories; lifecycle; midcentric; psychocentric; sunlust; tourism flows.

Bibliography

Barker, M. (2002) *The golden age of the Yorkshire Seaside*. Great Northern, Ilkley.

BBC (1996) *The Sun, the Sea and the Spanish*. BBC, London, broadcast on 21 January 1996.

Berndt, R. and Berndt, C. (1964) *The World of the First Australians*. Ure Smith, Sydney.

Burns, P. and Holden, A. (1995) *Tourism: A New Perspective*. Prentice Hall, Hemel Hempstead.

Butler, R.W. (1980) The Concept of a Tourist Area Cycle of Evolution: Implications for Management of Resources, *Canadian Geographer*, vol. 14, no. 1, 5–12.

Gray, H.P. (1970) *International Travel – International Trade*. Lexington Books, Lexington Heath MA.

Inglis, F. (2000) *The Delicious History of the Holiday*. Routledge, London.

Jafari, J. and Ritchie, J.R.B. (1981) Towards a framework for tourism education, *Annals of Tourism Research*, vol. 8, no. 1, 13–34.

Krippendorf, J. (1987) *The Holiday Makers*. Heinemann, Oxford.

Leech, M. and Shales, M. (2003) *Naples and Sorrento*. New Holland, London.

MacCannell, D. (1999) *The Tourist*. University of California, Berkeley.

Miossec, J.M. (1977) Un Modèle de l'Espace Touristique, *L'Espace Géographique*, vol. 6, no. 1, 41–48.

Plog, S.C. (1974) Why Destination Areas Rise and Fall in Popularity, *Cornel Hotel and Restaurant Quarterly*, vol. 14, no. 4, 55–58.

Pritchett, V.S. (1964) *The Offensive Tourist*. Alfred Knopf, New York.

Shaw, S. and Williams, A.M. (2004) *Tourism and Tourism Spaces*. Sage, London.

Thurot, J.M. (1973) Le Tourisme tropical Balnéaire: le modèle caraibe et ses extensions, PhD thesis, Aix-en-Provence.

Turner, L. and Ash, J. (1975) *The Golden Hordes*. Constable, London.

Urry, J. (1990) *The Tourist Gaze*. Sage, London.

Vichas, R.P. (1994) Club Med Inc., in P. Wright, C.D. Pringle and M.J. Kroll (eds) *Strategic Management*. Allyn & Bacon, Boston MA, 575–588.

Walton, J.K. (2000) *The British Seaside: Holidays and resorts in the twentieth century*. Manchester University Press, Manchester.

Chapter 2

The structure of the tourism and travel industry

David Litteljohn and Ian Baxter Glasgow Caledonian University

Learning outcomes

On completion of this chapter the reader should be able to:

■ understand and differentiate between the terms *market, industry* and *industry structure* and use them to better understand trends in tourism supply;

■ understand the full complexity of tourism supply and recognise the main components of the tourism industry;

■ consider the role of mass tourism and the evolving role of tourism suppliers;

■ consider the role of support organisations in contemporary tourism;

■ take a supply view of the current structure of tourism by applying concepts of vertical and horizontal integration.

Overview

Tourism is often quoted as being one of the world's largest industries. Certainly, tourism is found, in different forms, in both affluent and in developing economies. Some commentators (for example, as reported in Eadington and Redman, 1991) see it not as a single industry but as a collection of service-based activities spread across a wide number of industries, which share little in common. It is the overall aim of this chapter to analyse the nature, structure and development of tourism and travel. It is accepted that there is variability in tourism: variety amongst the organisations that serve tourists and in the types of tourism activity in different regions. The general level of analysis adopted here will allow an understanding of the functions, structures and developments in tourism. The analysis does not intend to provide a detailed investigation of individual elements, organisations or issues in tourism. These aspects are covered in subsequent chapters. While the focus of the chapter is on supply-side factors, other factors, particularly demand, are selectively included to allow a full appreciation of tourism contexts.

An understanding of underlying concepts will provide future tourism managers with a foundation to judge the functions and performance of tourism organisations in their changing environments. The approach taken in this chapter acknowledges the breadth of tourism activity. Simply stated, tourism involves the temporary travel of people away from home. Given this breadth it is not surprising that its study embraces a number of approaches, as outlined in Chapter 1. Most business-orientated studies of tourism draw heavily on economics, and apply general economic concepts to the particular situation of tourism. This chapter maintains an economics-oriented approach and draws on the work of commentators who write in this area. The main method underpinning this chapter borrows significantly from Scherer's (1980) industrial economics approach. For the reader, however, previous study of economics is not necessary. The chapter does not burden the reader with a battery of statistics on tourism. Instead, through examples and case studies, readers are encouraged to explore a number of key issues of industry development. European case studies concentrate on supply trends in tourism and, additionally, apply an analytic approach to examine industry structure at a destination.

Conditions of demand and supply are explored and related to the characteristics of tourism organisations and the ways in which they operate. Sometimes situations have to be simplified to make the general point with impact. In doing this the authors accept, as the Organization for Economic Co-operation and Development (OECD) does, that: 'Tourism has been relatively difficult to measure and analyse in any meaningful way. It is an "industry" with no traditional production function and no common structure or organisation across countries . . . . [and] cuts across a number of conventional economic sectors . . .' (Organization for Economic Co-operation and Development, 2002). Thus the chapter hopes to encourage an appreciation of the complex and varied nature of tourism.

Introduction: foundations of analysis

A comprehensive analysis of an industry covers three main elements. The first two relate directly to the major groups that interact directly in the marketplace: on the one hand those that generate demand and, on the other, those that provide products and services to meet this demand. Thus it is important to understand:

- consumer conduct: a focus on the behaviour of purchasers – usually households and individuals – when making decisions to consume (or not) tourism products and services, e.g. what they buy, how much they buy and what price they buy at.
- supplier conduct: the approaches that suppliers take to offering (or not) products or services, e.g. what to put on the market, at what quantities and at what prices.

There is a third element, often seen as an individual actor: the government. Governments set the background against which consumers and suppliers interact. They have an immediate and direct influence on markets through legislation, licensing/operating conditions and level of duties they may place on particular products/services. Similarly, governments may provide economic incentives and support for favoured industries (e.g. in terms of employment generation) or business types (e.g. small- or medium-sized enterprises). Governments also take decisions which can affect the economy at large – for example, on levels of taxation and on minimum wage rates. Direct government involvement at central or local levels is emphasised though the section on organisations indicates how this may be supplemented through different arrangements.

Applying industrial economics concepts to particular situations requires an element of rigour in use of terms, particularly if they are in general usage but subject to different meanings. Thus the terms 'market' and 'industry' are often poorly defined and used interchangeably. Here the terms have specific meanings.

A *market* denotes the overall mechanism that equates what consumers demand with what organisations will supply. Thus it covers both consumer conduct and supplier conduct. For any given good or service, therefore, an understanding of a market involves understanding the interplay between demand and supply as circumstances affecting them change. Markets are often thought about in a general way – such as the market for package holidays in the UK or in Sweden, where an understanding of the market would examine aspects such as the preferences of consumers, prices of packages on offer, the numbers of suppliers, movement of input costs and their effect on final prices and the availability of other types of holiday.

Modern economies possess many markets. These include markets for private and public transport, markets for housing, markets for education and markets for financial services (affecting, for example, the amount of capital for investing in tourism enterprises). The ways in which demand and supply interact in each market will also vary. The latter point was mentioned previously when the terms 'consumer conduct' and 'supplier conduct' were introduced. For example, how would consumer behaviour change if the price of a good (or part of a good) were to change? Would consumers purchase less of the good, or would they be prepared to pay the increased price?

If the good in question was aircraft fuel and this increased the cost of the price of all package holidays would (i) the demand for all package holidays decrease or (ii) would consumers be prepared to pay the extra or (iii) would they divert demand from higher-cost package holidays towards cheaper packages?

An important factor to take into account is the spatial dimensions of tourism. Any basic understanding of tourism shows a requirement for travel and, hence, consumption away from home where goods and services are usually purchased and used. Leiper's (1979) landmark work usefully explains this difference by proposing three different 'geographies' or spatial components: (i) tourism in the generating or home region of the traveller; (ii) tourism at the destination region; and (iii) the transit routes – the 'area' or supply of travel and transport facilities between the two regions. While all three are naturally highly interconnected in terms of an individual's trip, each of these 'areas' possesses different supply and demand characteristics. Resorts such as Blackpool and Benidorm or cities such as Paris all cater for tourists but possess different market conditions in terms of consumer and supplier conduct.

Industry is a term that relates directly to suppliers. For example, Begg *et al.* define industry as 'the set of all firms making the same product' (Begg, Fischer and Dornbush, 1987: 40). This implies a high degree of similarity among suppliers with strict boundaries between one industry and another. Finally, there is the need to understand the term industry structure or *industrial organisation*. This relates to the ways in which individual firms are owned, organised and managed. In this chapter the terms cover both commercial and non-commercial operations. Given the breadth of tourism any approach which requires rigid boundaries between industries and organisations is dangerous. Spatial dimensions of industries should also be considered as they may range over many organisations, functions and national borders.

Taking all these factors together, the Organization for Economic Co-operation and Development's (OECD) conclusion on the difficulty of analysing tourism is shown in sharp relief: because tourism involves many different suppliers working across different locations and countries in different industries it will be difficult to analyse in terms of defining markets, industries and industry structure. As indicated above, the main approaches used to tease out the nature of these issues derive from economics, though more holistic ways, such as that advocated by Leiper (1979), will also be used where appropriate.

Applying industry analysis to contemporary tourism

To understand the nature of tourism more fully two differing approaches are employed. These should be considered as complementary. The first approach stresses the nature of tourists and elements of tourism consumption. The second method approaches the nature of tourism by classifying suppliers into different categories. The section ends with an integration of these two perspectives.

1 Demand-led understanding of tourism

The World Tourism Organization (WTO) defines tourism as 'the activities of persons travelling to and staying in places outside their usual environment for not more than one consecutive year for leisure, business and other purposes not related to the exercise of an activity remunerated from within the place visited' (World Tourism Organization, 2004). This approach concentrates on the nature of tourism consumption in a way that is easy to understand and relatively easy to track over time. The definition differentiates between tourism and other travel: thus tourism excludes trips during one's usual, day-to-day activities or in one's home environment. In other words, tourism travel is non-routine, in non-routine environments.

It may be noted, however, that tourism statistics produced nationally and internationally may differentiate between day visitors (e.g. cruise-liner passengers staying for less than 24 hours) and visitors who stay for one night or longer. The WTO recommends that to understand the nature of markets that of tourism visits may be classified as follows:

- purpose of the visit;
- duration of the trip (days/nights);
- origin and destination of the trip;
- area of residence and destination;
- main means of transport used;
- type of accommodation used.

This is shown in Figure 2.1, which plots relatively technical aspects of demand and classifies trip by technical details of consumption. It concentrates on tourism consumption rather than more abstract aspects such as visitor motivations. An understanding of the factors shown in the diagram thus provides an excellent snapshot of tourism consumption at one time. If reliable statistics are collected on these dimensions a picture of tourism (e.g. to a region) may be built up. To this 'frozen' picture may be added statistics of the same factors over several years to provide trends and highlight changes. While this step may provide deeper understanding of tourism behaviours, too great a reliance on consumption characteristics underplays more fundamental determinants of tourism conduct such as the desire for holidays, the propensity of consumers to prioritise spending on holidays and the changing popularity of destinations. The WTO approach does stress the wide number of components that make up tourism consumption, a point that is developed in Table 2.1.

An understanding of the intangible nature of tourism helps to differentiate between tourism and many other purchases that are made more routinely. Purchase of a holiday or a decision to take a business trip involves a commitment to something that cannot be pre-tested. In this sense consumers are purchasing an intangible service. Tourism purchases often include elements of novelty (e.g. visiting a new place) and, indeed, this may be one of their major appeals. For example, a family planning a safari-type holiday in game reserves in southern Africa may never have visited that part of the world or been on safari before. For this purchase intangible elements include not only which reserves

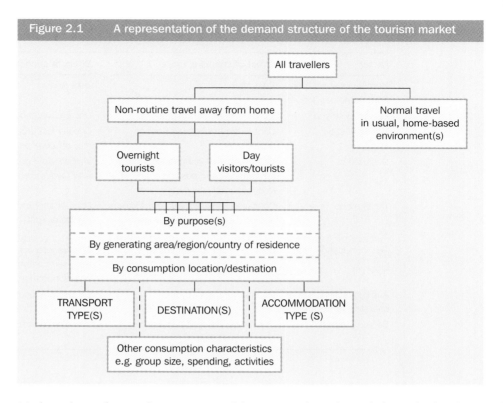

Figure 2.1   A representation of the demand structure of the tourism market

to visit but also safety and security; confidence may be achieved through the choice of operators of high reputation or through personal recommendations. Similarly, a business traveller may choose a branded hotel that s/he knows provides a particular standard of service. Independent travellers may use travel guides, grading systems, tourist information centres as well as word-of-mouth recommendations to help deal with intangibility. Past travel experience is also important because, as tourists become experienced travellers, so they may feel confident in their own judgements.

Many tourism purchases are also relatively large, involving a significant proportion of annual income. For example, in 2004 the total cost of a European holiday for four for, say, up to a fortnight could easily cost from £2000. This contrasts to a cost of, say, £12,000 for a mid-range family car or £2000 for a plasma screen television or £400 for a dishwasher. While compared to a car the cost of a holiday may seem small and, indeed, in absolute terms on a par with the new TV, the family might be taking holidays every year while the lives of consumer durables will stretch over several years. Of course, a short holiday could cost less than the example given nevertheless, holidays could still appear comparatively costly given the holiday cost per night. How short-term changes in consumer conduct may impact on consumption are shown in Table 2.1. For example, if a family that normally take holidays are economising, they need not sacrifice holidays; they may choose to travel at cheaper times of the year and use cheaper accommodation.

Thus, for many well-off consumers in economically developed societies, holiday decisions revolve around what types, where, when and how much to consume. Business tourism may also be subject to short-term change. While travel destinations may be greatly determined by centres of business and communications, business travel may be varied by other factors such as shortening/lengthening trips as well as changing the numbers of trips taken. For business conferences and conventions, even the destination is variable.

In summary, tourism consumption may be changed by many elements. Tourism choices for households and for business employers are wide. Intangibility in tourism emphasises the importance attached to ensuring confidence in the consumption process while often, and paradoxically, including a search for novelty. Underlying this

Table 2.1	Some examples of choices in varying overnight tourism trips	
Factor	**Effect of spending more**	**Effect of spending less**
Number of stays away from home per annum	*Take more*	*Take fewer*
Length of stay(s)	*Increase number of nights*	*Decrease number of nights*
Timing of stay	*Choose expensive/busy periods of year*	*Choose less expensive periods (i.e. off-peak periods)*
Destination	*Visit expensive destinations, foreign destinations and possibly those with less favourable exchange rates*	*Visit cheaper destinations (possibly those with favourable exchange rates)*
Travel mode	*Choose expensive mode of transport and/or categories of passenger comfort*	*Use cheaper modes of travel and/or lower grades of customer comfort*
Accommodation type	*Choose better appointed/more expensive accommodation types*	*Choose less well appointed/cheaper types (e.g. self-catering rather than serviced accommodation)*
Ancillary activities and spending at destination	*Do more and spend more*	*Do less and economise*
Booking method	*Use full-service and personalised booking methods*	*Use electronic/internet methods*

consumption analysis is a web of demographic, social and psychological factors which interlink with economic conditions to shape consumer conduct.

2 Supply-led understanding of tourism

This second approach provides supply-based views of tourism and emphasises aspects of industry structure. First, a functional view of industry structure is taken. This is followed by a tourism-income approach for classifying suppliers.

Holloway (1998) is one of many authors who analyses tourism comprehensively from a functional perspective. Given the diverse nature of supply, businesses are classified as either direct suppliers (producers of services which interact directly with travellers as part of the decision/consumption process) or indirect suppliers (e.g. where a business supplies another organisation which caters for holiday markets, classified as support services) as follows:

- **Producers** – which are grouped into transport carriers, accommodation providers and the suppliers of man-made attractions. Also in the class of producers, but more in an integration/intermediary role, Holloway places tour operators and brokers and travel agents.
- **Support services** – both private sector (e.g. transport, travel guides) and public sector (e.g. national/regional/local tourism-destination promotional bodies, public educational and training establishments, public ports and services and visa and passport offices).

Under this schema, producers are, in the main, those organisations that have direct contact with tourists. They cover a number of specific functions which range from providing services at a destination (e.g. accommodation, restaurants); air, sea and land passenger services; and those organisations which focus on a more retail and intermediary role – sometimes by combining the elements of the whole tourism experience into a standardised, easily purchased package.

The second category, support services, provides either direct or indirect services to tourists. For example, an airport provides direct and indirect services to travellers. Direct services come in the shape of security, car parks, catering and other retail services. Indirect services are services provided for airlines and tour operators that use the airports (e.g. aircraft servicing and re-fuelling).

A different supply-side approach may be adopted by an examination of the economic impact of tourism to specific suppliers. In contrast to a focus on function, this approach centres on the impact of tourism on the business. This approach was used by the European Union when it examined employment in tourism (European Commission, 1998). Here organisations were put into one of three groups according to the proportion of their income derived from tourism. The results of this work are represented in Figure 2.2, and Figure 2.3 shows the full listing of organisations by category.

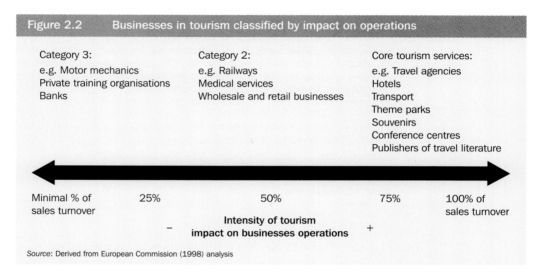

Figure 2.2   Businesses in tourism classified by impact on operations

Category 3:
e.g. Motor mechanics
Private training organisations
Banks

Category 2:
e.g. Railways
Medical services
Wholesale and retail businesses

Core tourism services:
e.g. Travel agencies
Hotels
Transport
Theme parks
Souvenirs
Conference centres
Publishers of travel literature

Minimal % of sales turnover   25%   50%   75%   100% of sales turnover

−   **Intensity of tourism impact on businesses operations**   +

Source: Derived from European Commission (1998) analysis

The first category contains those organisations that derive 50%–100% of their income from tourism, and are classified as 'core tourism services'. All other organisations are classed as complementary and ancillary services. They are divided into those that derive between 25%–50% from tourism and, finally, those where tourism makes a contribution of less than 25% of income.

This approach underplays the role of the public sector as it does not take full account of public bodies involved in tourism. It also assumes that it is always possible to identify the contribution that tourism income makes to a business: however, this is not always the case. This may be illustrated by two relatively clear-cut cases. For example, a casino in a provincial English town may gain nearly all of its custom from people who live close by. Hence, in impact terms it is not an important tourism attraction. On the other hand, casinos in Las Vegas provide an important tourist attraction, both functionally (entertainment) and in impact (economic) terms because many tourists will gamble when they visit. It is thus impossible to classify all 'similar' businesses neatly into the same category.

Both functional and income-impact approaches recognise the wide variety of organisations that make up tourism. Examination of the products, services and operations will show organisations to be dissimilar (heterogeneous) rather than similar (homogeneous). This provides an important contribution to understanding market structure/organisation in tourism. Many economic definitions of the term 'industry' see them made up of similar firms/organisations. Therefore they are inappropriate for tourism. Both functional aspects (what an organisation does) and impact factors (how much an organisation relies on tourism) need to be taken into account when understanding tourism supply.

Figure 2.3	Economic impact of tourism on businesses

In the first category were placed those organizations that derive most of their income (50%–100%) from tourism. These were classed as 'Core tourism services', which are listed as:

Travel agencies, tour operators, hotels and other accommodation, restaurants and other food and beverage services, transport companies, incoming agencies, health and spa enterprises, tourist information centres, leisure, theme adventure parks, sports facilities, associations of the tourist industry, souvenir industry, travel equipment outfitters, meeting/incentive/convention etc., event industries, airports, travel insurance, artisans (i.e. craftworkers/producers of art items), culture and entertainment enterprises, global distribution and reservation systems, publishers and distributors of travel literature and maps, bureaux de change.

All other organisations where classed as complementary and ancillary services.

The secondary category has those organizations which derive between 25%–50% of their income from tourism. Included here are:

Railway stations, sports goods industry, electronic entertainment, photo industry, transport manufacturers, doctors and other medical service suppliers, journalists, writers, artists, bands, wholesale and retail businesses, professions and self employed (tax, legal and business consultancies), advertising agencies, paper manufacturers, printing works, planning agencies, information/communication technology, landscape maintenance/farming.

Finally there are organisations which gain some income because of tourism, but where it makes a contribution of less than 25% of their income. These include:

Port companies, pharmaceutical and cosmetic industry, motor mechanics, universities, technical high schools and private training institutes, architects/developers, electrical engineering and music industry, banks, building industry.

Source: European Commission (1998)

Tremblay (1998) points out that it is important to understand the nature of relationships between suppliers in tourism. This is achieved by comparing a stylised view of supplier relationships to a more complex tourism application. First, Figure 2.4 illustrates a conventional view of the supply chain.

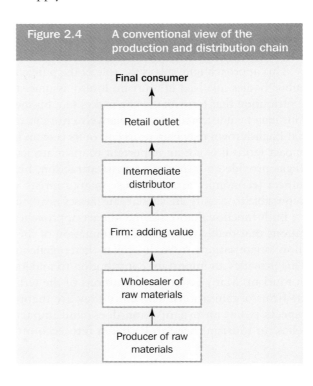

Figure 2.4	A conventional view of the production and distribution chain

At the start of the supply chain is the producer of raw materials and at the end there is the final consumer or customer. The model identifies distinct stages of transformation from raw materials to final consumer goods available for sale. Separate functions are carried out at these different stages. It is, of course, possible that one organisation could carry out all these functions, though the stages are differentiated. Thus whether there is one or there are many organisations in the supply chain, there will always be a standard sequence of activities as materials move towards the final consumer.

Supplier relationships may be different in tourism. This is shown in Figure 2.5, where the supply of holiday golf packages is taken as an example. Here there is not a clear flow from producer to final consumer, as there is in Figure 2.4. On the contrary, it shows that there may be a variety of paths between suppliers and the consumer. In one case, represented by the solid line, relationships between suppliers are similar to those in Figure 2.3. Here sets of suppliers who supply 'raw materials' (golf playing facilities and services, transport and accommodation). These are packaged together by an operator, who then distributes the holidays through retail outlets, in this case, travel agents.

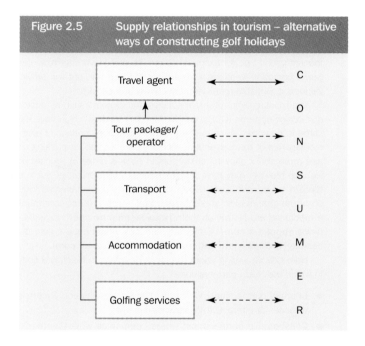

Figure 2.5 Supply relationships in tourism – alternative ways of constructing golf holidays

The dashed lines represent other representations of relationships between suppliers and consumers. One shows a situation where the consumer (the holidaymaker in this example) decides to organise a holiday herself. Here she contacts each of the main producers (e.g. hotels, rail and golf facilities) and makes arrangements directly, customising her own package. This excludes wholesale (operator) and retail (travel agent) functions. The variety of relationships that exist among suppliers is further complicated when it is remembered that some businesses – such as transport operators or accommodation providers – may, on their own initiative, offer packages which they have assembled and offer directly to consumers. Indeed, a hotel could produce golf packages and promote them nationally while, additionally, using a specialist incoming tour operator specialising in sports holidays to market the hotel in international golf markets. As the hotel will also cater for tourists who book accommodation and golfing facilities independently, the organisational/functional boundaries which are so clearly presented in Figure 2.4 are not always clear in tourism. Thus, relationships between tourism organisations and sectors may often be characterised, at a general level, as fuzzy. It is this potential of multiple relationships that exist in tourism–industry organisational networks that Figure 2.5 tries to capture. To an extent this approach allows, in tangible form, a simplified, supply-side application of the systems approach to tourism offered by Gilbert (1990) and Laws (1991).

Case 2.1	Info-mediaries, e-mediaries and the harnessing of ICT by the tourism industry

The information revolution, spearheaded by changes in forms and diffusion of information and communication technologies (ICT), has introduced changes to structures of tourism and functions of suppliers. The information below will assist you to analyse how these changes impact on the consumer choice in tourism.

Much ICT change since the 1970s is associated with functional management issues such as flight scheduling, reservation and check in, and communications between travel agents and tour operators, with the bundling of various services together (e.g. air travel, car hire and hotel bookings). The period witnessed the establishment and growth of Global Distribution Systems (GDSs) such as Galileo and Amadeus (see Chapter 11). Development of the systems has allowed management to refine yield management policies, so as to vary the price of a hotel room or an airline seat, for example, in line with market characteristics. Taken together these changes can help ensure efficiency – hence lower prices – and allow better alignment to individual customer requirements.

Tourism and travel have also used ICT for marketing and information dissemination about destinations and travel services. The term 'info-mediaries' has come to be used for this. It usually appears as a website providing an information resource, sharing other resources such as web links to organisations that do sell tourism/travel. See for example: Smart Traveler [**www.smarttraveler.com**]; Yahoo Travel [**www.yahoo.co.uk**]. Some company websites have a more focused role but will provide information which their users will also value: e.g. British Airports Authority [**www.baa.co.uk**].

The meeting point of info-mediaries and systems such as customer reservation systems (CRSs) or global distribution systems (GDSs) can be found in services which have developed since the early 1990s, that have come to be known as 'e-mediaries'. This combines notions of electronic commerce and the traditional intermediary role of travel agents. E-mediaries are less about pushing a product or pre-designed tourism package and more about allowing customers to book a range of tourism and travel services from one website. The website provider may have no experience in tourism/travel but is able to focus knowledge of ICT to bridge tourism 'producers'. Dale (2003: 110) defines e-mediaries as 'organisations offering services via a network of virtual channels to stakeholders, and which are not constrained by geographical boundaries.' Typical e-mediaries are lastminute.com [**www.lastminute.com**], expedia.com [**www.expedia.com**] and eBookers [**www.ebookers.com**]. E-mediary services which have grown out of an organisation's services include easyJet [**www.easyjet.com**] and Ryanair [**www.ryanair.com**].

Dale (2003) writing about the strategic role of e-mediaries suggests that there are five kinds of network in which they form partnerships:

- Channel partnerships, which link Central Reservation Systems/Global Distribution Systems through to websites or interactive TV services directly.
- Collaborative partnerships, where companies work together to provide a combined online presence, even though they may be competitors.
- Communicative partnerships, that link info-mediary services with the e-mediary's e-commerce service.
- Complementary partnerships, which involve cross-selling where relationships are developed between particular service providers and the e-mediary (often referred to as 'preferred providers').
- Converse relationships, which are developed where e-mediaries begin to distribute unrelated products of another e-mediary (such as an airline site offering banking).

Discussion questions

1 What advantages do e-mediaries and info-mediaries provide consumers who are considering trips away from home? What are their disadvantages?
2 What is necessary for the long-term survival of e-mediaries and info-mediaries?
3 How could e-mediaries affect industry structure in tourism and travel in the next five years?

Conclusions of complexity in tourism demand and supply

This section's appraisal of tourism demand and supply has emphasised its diverse nature. Tourism is a customer-led, malleable set of activities and expenditures affected by many different factors. The review of demand confirms a variety of tourism consumption modes, as well as the ease with which tourism may be quickly altered. While tourism motivations were only briefly referred to, the importance of taking a broad view in relation to overall consumption decisions and consumer preferences was made.

Supply-led examination showed that there are suppliers who conform to a simple model of industry structure where distinct functions are provided at different stages of the supply chain. However, when characterising operations by reliance on tourism income it was confirmed that this extends the number of organisations and functions included in tourism into an 'industry' which is so varied that it defies easy analysis. It was also shown that there may be a subtle interplay between organisations and the functions they undertake, with some organisations operating multiple producer functions.

Thus tourism activity may be characterised as being complex. Complexity arises from the recognition of the underlying factors that shape the market and how they interrelate to each other. Such factors include: levels of main and additional holiday-taking; (changing) popularity of destinations; impact on travel preferences of availability of different travel modes. Complexity further arises from the varied nature of supply – coming from the variety of functions across tourism, the variety of functions that organisations choose to undertake and the degree of financial reliance that organisations have on tourism. This understanding helps to build the following definition:

> Tourism markets are complex systems where a variety of demands for non-routine travel are met by a large number of for-profit and non-commercial organisations, based in the home and destination regions, which possess different orientations, including travel between the regions, and degrees of financial reliance on these types of demand.

To aid analysis it is useful to group organisations which exhibit similar characteristics into different sectors, e.g. hotels, air, cruise sectors. It is recognised that this definition largely omits the direct influence that governments may directly and indirectly exercise on tourism.

Development of mass markets

This section examines the development of the large and complex contemporary tourism markets. The first point to make is that not all countries have reached levels of mass tourism. Even where large travel markets exist, their presence is relatively recent in historical terms. For a long time travel was confined to small sectors of the population. Only since the middle of the twentieth century have conditions for mass tourism evolved in affluent societies. A prime model for the development of modern tourism is rooted in the change that Western European economies have passed through in their evolution from feudal, agrarian societies, through industrialisation and urbanisation to service-led economies.

In feudal times travel outside the vicinity of one's neighbourhood for pleasure or business was extremely limited. Travel was confined mainly to the aristocratic elite and traders, who had the wealth and/or motivation for travel. There were others who, for reasons of rank or employment, might travel, e.g. people in the legal profession or the Church, and entertainers. Exceptions to this elite, like the pilgrims (sacred tourism, in current terminology), are visible because they were exceptions. On the whole, subsistence-level economies and localised social and cultural horizons precluded travel for the masses. Even as industrialisation began, travel did not immediately flourish. Travel and emergent pleasure destinations were reserved for a social and economic elite, albeit one which was expanding slowly. Poor working conditions for most meant income just met basic needs. Also communities often retained local markets and travel was often difficult, time consuming and expensive. It was only when urbanisation grew and the expanding towns and cities encouraged investment in transport infrastructure that the possibility of affordable travel appeared. Given some rise in incomes and improvements in working conditions during the later nineteenth century the transformation of a small travel elite to large-scale markets began to develop. As discussed in Chapter 1, in many Western European societies the first mass destinations were seaside resorts with strong regional markets (e.g. Blackpool for the English North West). It was only gradually that changing social and economic conditions, along with cheaper travel, presented international options and more varied types of destinations.

Not all societies, even in the West, followed similar patterns of early change in demand and supply. For example, the USA developed differently. Here an element of travel was embedded into society, as eighteenth-century and nineteenth-century USA expanded towards the Pacific. Hotels, for example, sprang up to deal with transient 'residents' and commerce and industry developed in tandem with agriculture more than had been the European experience. In addition, North American populations showed differences in attitudes and lifestyles that show themselves in the amount and type of leisure and travel they engage in. As societies become more affluent, so certain underlying factors become important for generating mass tourism demand:

- Increasing levels of affluence that allow individual households/consumers sufficient discretionary income to consider travel consumption as part of their leisure expenditure. Discretionary or disposable income is that income which remains once all normal outgoings such as taxation, housing and other 'basics' of clothing, education, feeding have been paid. In the short term, it may be supplemented by consumer credit.
- Increasing availability of cheap, reliable and safe transport alternatives (including private and public transport systems) which has greatly assisted in changing spatial dimensions of tourism as it changes from a regional system to one where many travel long distances and internationally, as a matter of course.
- Social acceptability of recreation and time off work to pursue personal interests. Minimum periods for holidays are often codified in legislation. For example, in the UK the Holidays with Pay Act (1938) was passed. As previously indicated, attitudes to leisure and travel are a mix of many factors. Historically, for example, the elites and feudal populations would not have distinguished greatly between work and play but would have considered their way of life holistically. In the modern world, societies have different, culturally rooted work ethics; e.g. industrialised Asian countries will, on the whole, take shorter annual holidays than European countries.
- For business travel, the growth of companies across countries and internationally, with consequential requirements for employee travel to set up and operate businesses as well as to train and for more general communication/coordination purposes.

This list is by no means exhaustive, but provides a general background to factors that facilitate growth of domestic and international tourism. However, even in affluent societies not all travel. For example, while typically 80% of the Swedish population regularly took a holiday in the 1990s, UK participation rates in holidays remain, to date, stubbornly around 60% (Jansen-Verbeke, 1995). The growth of international tourism over the past 50 years is very impressive. From 1950 to 2000 international tourist arrivals increased from 25 million to nearly 700 million (World Tourism Organization, 2001), some 28-fold.

This is a period that has been typified by economic growth as well as a gradual spread of tourism-generating countries outside the established regions of North America and Europe to encompass Japan, Southeast Asia and China, for example.

Analysing changes in tourism over the past half century Poon (1993), who concentrates on leisure markets, sees an initial period of growth (roughly from the 1950s to the early 1980s) as fuelled by the supply of standardisation; for example, packaged holidays. The period was typified by a change in preference from national destinations to greater interest in locations further away. New packages, developed by tour operators usually from demand-generating regions, fed desires for sunlust holidays, though operators also diversified into other packages such as skiing holidays. Availability of cheap transport over longer distances was provided through air transport, especially by wide-bodied, economical jet planes, introduced in the 1960s. Motivations for travel during this period were often 'escape' from the working and social routines of the home environment. Tour operators sold packages that were convenient to buy and through the development of brands grew confidence in the holiday purchase. Because the new tour operator packages utilised economies of scale their low prices attracted new consumers to the market. By virtue of the large number of holidays they sold, tour operators held strong bargaining power over other tourism organisations. Thus they were able to keep prices competitive. Sometimes tour operators operated their own airlines and accommodation establishments. Thus tour operators who glued the fragmented parts of tourism supply into easily purchased packages, heavily promoted to their home markets, reigned supreme because they were able to tap into new and growing markets. Standardisation of the experience meant standardisation of development. Thus many of the Mediterranean resorts developed at this time are similar.

This type of growth formula is unlikely to be replicated in the future. Future leisure demand from existing mass markets is likely to become more diverse as more consumers become experienced travellers and more sophisticated in their tastes. On the other hand, markets in the newly industrialised areas may well exhibit many of the characteristics of the Western tourism markets as they advance to mass tourism. For business travel markets key determinants of growth are the nature of companies in the economy and the extent to which supply areas successfully promote themselves as conference/convention destinations. Naturally, the existence of good transport and communications infrastructure is a prerequisite for this.

This concludes the demand-led discussion of mass tourism development. It described the growth of demand, where tourism has been based on the trends in domestic markets, while showing that developments in travel have allowed greater numbers to journey further away. More recently, however, some other societies (particularly developing world communities in island or remote locations) have exhibited a very different path of tourism development. They are associated with incoming, foreign-based tourism and low levels of local tourism demand. In this path of tourism development, destinations may see the co-existence of low levels of economic activity and affluence for indigenous populations with a tourism industry that caters predominately for wealthy incomers, providing a stark comparison between the needs of local populations and those of the 'imported' and (comparatively) wealthy tourists. While many Mediterranean countries exhibited this pattern in the 1960s and 1970s, cheaper travel has meant that longer-haul destinations are now subject to this type of development.

Further organisational analysis of operators in tourism

This section will differentiate between three types of supplier. These are: public (government and government-funded organisations); commercial operations; and voluntary organisations. They are shown in Table 2.2.

Table 2.2	Major stakeholder types in tourism	
Stakeholder type	**Direct operator**	**Other operation types**
Public	Central government: government department (e.g. departments dealing with tourism industry, arts and sports, economic development, physical planning, travel, passports and immigration)	Government agencies
		National tourism organisations
		Heritage, sports, culture organisations
		Subcontracting
		Public/public partnerships
	Local government: cultural and recreation facilities and services, physical planning	Private/public partnerships
		Use of voluntary organisations
Commercial	Public limited company (plc)	Franchising
	Partnerships and sole proprietor businesses (usually privately owned)	Management contracting
		Private/public partnerships
		Strategic alliances
		Joint ventures
		Consortium-type
Voluntary	Charitable associations and trusts at national and local levels, including business/professional, sports, heritage and community groups	

Central government departments and government-funded organisations may be directly or indirectly involved in tourism. The rationale for government involvement often revolves around notions of the public good, i.e. because society benefits through provision of the good/service which would not exist unless the government intervened. In other cases government has decided to regulate an activity and sets up some way of doing so. For sponsored museums and sporting facilities there is a direct relationship between the public and the good or service. Other examples of grant-supported agencies in the UK include the Arts Council of England and English Heritage. A direct connection with the public good may be less direct for national tourism organisations and/or economic development agencies. In these cases the rationale for involvement may be that this necessary coordinating function could safeguard and enhance tourism as a source of income and employment.

Government also operates locally, usually on a city and/or a regional basis. These act as a second tier of government, determined by national policies and funding. Public/public partnerships relate to situations where public agencies work together, e.g. some development projects and planning areas where it is better to have an umbrella organisation. Similarly, private/public partnerships are where government combines with private enterprise for a development project such as the development of a conference centre and hotel complex. Governments and their public agencies may also enlist the help of voluntary organisations. Thus, for example, a heritage organisation with special skills may be contracted to run an attraction. Good examples of this are the unoccupied Royal palaces in London (including the Tower of London and Hampton Court Palace) which are conserved and opened to visitors by the Historic Royal Palaces Agency (**www.hrp.org.uk**).

Commercial operators or for-profit operators may be publicly or privately owned. A public limited company (plc) is an organisation which issues shares traded on a stock exchange. Thus, ownership is spread among organisations, such as pension funds, and individuals. Private operations are usually run by a sole proprietor or through a partnership, often with a family focus. Private operations that want to grow may change their status to plcs.

While many commercial organisations retain complete direct control over their operations, several alternative formats to direct control are used, for example:

- Franchising – where a business concept including a proprietary trademark/license, an operations 'recipe' and backup management training and support systems, is franchised to another operator in exchange for a set-up fee and an annual royalty;
- Management contracting – where the owner of capital resources (e.g. buildings) agrees that another firm will run a defined area of operations in exchange for a fee;
- Strategic alliance – an arrangement where two or more organisations share resources to pursue a joint aim. For example, a joint venture refers to a project where partners pool resources to set up a new, jointly owned enterprise. A consortium is a looser arrangement where individual businesses retain autonomy while engaging in activities such as joint purchasing and joint promotion.

There are many examples of successful consortiums among hotels. Some are locally based and jointly promote occupancy at periods of low demand. Others provide comprehensive backup reservations technologies with associated international branding and marketing benefits. Similarly, airline code sharing and marketing agreements by *Star Alliance* and *Oneworld* provide marketing benefits to their members.

Voluntary organisations may also have a tourism involvement. These cover local sports, historical and museum trusts and, at a national level, organisations such as the National Trust and the National Trust for Scotland in the UK. In addition, voluntary organisations across a spectrum of professional and leisure fields provide help in promoting destinations, interpretation services for visitors and administration and staffing for sports and arts events festivals, for example.

Conclusion: trends in tourism industry structure

Industries change their structure in response to many demand and supply factors. Conventionally, economists analyse changes in the relationships/arrangements between organisations in an industry by the following means:

- horizontal growth or integration: where firms in the same sector (stage of the production process) join together;
- vertical growth or integration: where firms from different sectors but in the same industry join together;
- conglomerate growth or integration: where two firms from different industries join together in single ownership.

In her seminal work Poon (1993) indicated the possibility of a fourth form of integration – 'diagonal'. This describes situations where firms in 'unrelated industries' (such as finance and travel) may join together because they find they both deal with tourists.

There is no guarantee that yesterday's business models will be successful in the future. Firms that were previously independent may generate benefits by joining together. Advantages may spring from cost savings as, for example, through amalgamating administrative functions and by gaining greater bargaining power with suppliers. Other benefits may positively affect income, e.g. by stimulating brand loyalty and offering new services to customers. Also, in the case of vertical integration, there may be greater reliability on sole suppliers of goods and services creating barriers to market entry for other competitor firms reliant on increased scale and/or the control of suppliers.

The structure of tourism markets has changed significantly since Thomas Cook organised his innovative railway excursions in the 1840s. He created a company which integrated the diverse elements of tourism into reliable packages that could be marketed to the growing middle class. Hotels have seen fashions in ownership over the last century. While retaining aspects of a sector which is largely run independently, the nineteenth century saw the involvement of railway companies, while the mid-twentieth century witnessed investment by a number of airlines in the sector. In the long term, however, the most distinctive feature has been horizontal growth rather than vertical integration. The largest hotel chains are, in the main, North American but include InterContinental Hotels (UK owned, though based on USA hotel brands), Accor (France), and Marriott (USA). Diagonal growth may be seen where travel, finance (e.g. currency exchange) and insurance services come together in one organisation. Examples of vertical integration include tour operators of which the example of TUI in Case 2.2 is provided for analysis.

Case 2.2   Preussag – integration and diversification

Mergers, acquisitions and demergers form a key feature of contemporary European tourism and travel. One area of change has been among vertically integrated travel groups where smaller competitors have been bought in an attempt to reach a critical mass at the Europe-wide level.

A particularly interesting case is the 'World of TUI'. The creation of the large company emerged from Preussag, a German steel-manufacturing company, which, following the re-unification of Germany, recognised that manufacturing industries in Germany showed signs of decline and steel bore the brunt of these economic trends. In little more than five years Preussag turned itself into one of the leading European travel groups.

The process started in 1998, when Preussag acquired Hapag-Lloyd and a majority stake in Touristik Union International GmbH (TUI). It also acquired First Reisebüro, a travel retail chain. Developing an international presence, Preussag purchased a stake in the UK tourism and financial services group Thomas Cook (*circa* 25%) which was merged with Carlson UK. In 2000, Preussag's complete takeover of the Thomson Travel Group (UK) was approved by the EU Commission on condition that all shareholdings in Thomas Cook were sold off. In the event, by early March 2001 Thomas Cook was acquired by C&N Touristic.

By the end of 2002 Preussag had built up an interest in the leading French tour operator Nouvelles Frontières and had acquired an involvement in Alpitour, an Italian tour operator, as well as extending interests into other tourism sectors including a cruise and holiday club company and a charter airline.

Discussion question

4 Through concepts of vertical, horizontal and conglomerate growth, assess Preussag's growth strategy during the period 1998–2002. Update the information by accessing details of the company's operations through its website. Discuss implication of any changes observed to the organisation of tourism sectors and organisations.

The logic that a profit imperative and a belief that competition among firms are the most important forces that shape the tourism industry must be tempered by the following:

- Privately owned business may be lifestyle type businesses where the owner/operator is running a business for non-commercial as well as commercial reasons.
- On the one hand this may help destinations have a spectrum of businesses which they otherwise might not possess.
- On the other, these businesses may stifle innovation and change because they are not necessarily market-oriented.

Cooperation may be seen as a substitute for competition, for example, when large businesses form alliances to develop costly technological infrastructure. Consortia are another example, as are destination marketing organisations where public and private organisations work together.

Regulatory frameworks enforced by governments may determine aspects of market structure (e.g. airline ownership and landing rights). These are usually nationally based, but may also be controlled at supranational levels. In the European Union, for example, many aspects of airline competition (though not landing rights) are now dealt with by the European Commission.

While tour operators have been in ascendancy in Europe during much of the latter part of the twentieth century their power has been diminished since the mid-1990s through the entry of low-cost air carriers who now are very influential in determining change. As the industry proceeds into the twenty-first century it is faced with the twin factors of more experienced travel markets and the internet, or 'e-tourism'/'e-mediaries', in its affluent markets. Combined with changing economics in supply this is likely to create a need for innovation in the search for new ways to change consumers into 'captured' tourists. In the emerging markets of the East, models of tourism development may initially share some resemblance with the demand phases in the West. However, different cultures and the changing role of technology will also have a significant impact on the development of the industry structure in the east, and as their influence grows, globally.

Case 2.3	The structure of Scotland's tourism industry

The structure of tourism within a country may be explored by examining the roles of major supply stakeholders: government; public sector agencies; corporate sector-related businesses and services; small and medium enterprises; and other service providers (where tourism is not the core business). These broad groups may be further sub-divided according to their activities, e.g. accommodation providers; tourist attractions; tour operators. To illustrate this the situation in Scotland will be explored.

VisitScotland (**www.visitscotland.com**; **www.scotexchange.net**) suggests that tourism is worth around £5 billion annually and supports 9% of all employment.

The structure of Scotland's tourism industry is typical of a developed industrial nation with a high number of small- and medium-sized enterprises employing less than 50 people, with the majority employing between 1–20 people.

Scotland's devolved government has responsibility for tourism issues, and has a Minister for Tourism, Culture and Sport whose job is to provide an overarching tourism strategy for the country. This is driven through a national policy framework for tourism (*Tourism Framework for Action 2002–2005*, Scottish Executive, 2002), developed in association with the other major stakeholders. Specialised units linked to particular strands of government interest, particularly VisitScotland, the national tourism organisation, support the ministerial department. VisitScotland provides logistical support for government policy and practical industry coordination through promotional activities, quality standards schemes and research. It is the national 'face' of the industry, promoting the country as a whole, and facilitates a regional network of industry marketing and support.

There are a number of other national public agencies which have some tourism remit though it may be subsidiary to other functions. Typical of these is Historic Scotland, which looks after the national estate of historic buildings and monuments, and is the biggest operator of visitor attractions in the country. It conserves and presents sites such as Edinburgh Castle and Skara Brae and caters for over two million visitors each year (**www.historic-scotland.gov.uk**). Other similar organisations include the national nature conservation agency, Scottish Natural Heritage, which is responsible for countryside protection and enhancement (**www.snh.org.uk**) and the Forestry Commission, responsible for opening woodlands to the public (**www.forestry.gov.uk**).

Business support falls under the remit of an Enterprise Minister. Ministers here are responsible for business development agencies (see **www.scottish-enterprise.com** and **www.hie.co.uk**). These agencies provide support with training and development within general economic strategies for their areas. Other national high-level organisations comprise groupings of public sector or private sector agencies, working together for a common purpose. Environmental issues pertinent to tourism are considered within the Tourism & Environment Forum (**www.greentourism.org.uk**). Private sector tourism businesses are represented through organisations such as the Scottish Tourism Forum (**www.stforum.co.uk**) or professional and membership organisations for specific sector groups (e.g. British Hospitality Association, The Association of British Travel Agents). These are supplemented by voluntary and charitable trusts with tourism interests, including the National Trust for Scotland (**www.nts.org.uk**); the Royal Society for the Protection of Birds (**www.rspb.org.uk**) and the Woodland Trust (**www.woodlandtrust.org.uk**). Key elements of tourism infrastructure have their own representative groupings to feed into local tourism issues and national policy and business development concerns – examples of these are local hoteliers' associations, and individual Chambers of Commerce (**www.scottishchambers.org.uk**).

▶

Case 2.3   Continued

It is important to note that focus on any particular geographic area (such as Scotland), reinforces the notion of a fragmented and variable structure for tourism. Tourism in Scotland can thus be characterised by some very broad groupings, as above, or at the micro-level through identification of operating units/suppliers (hotels, visitor attractions, etc.).

Discussion question

5 Using the national tourism industry website (**www.scotexchange.net**) to investigate the structure of tourism in Scotland, discuss the role of the public sector in tourism and the changing relationships between the public and private sectors.

Discussion questions

6   To what extent is a demand view of tourism necessary to understand the structure of tourism travel?

7   Assess the view that mass tourism is no longer an important factor for tourism organisations globally.

8   Assess the functions and importance of different types of organisation in tourism to the following:

- a European capital city of your choice or any other urban tourism destination;
- a major sporting event such as a world championship series;
- a Mediterranean resort.

9   To what extent do you agree that cooperation is just as important as competition when considering the nature of tourism markets?

Guided reading

MacLellan, R. and Smith, R. (eds) (1998) *Tourism in Scotland*. Thomson Learning, London.

Competition Commission (1997) *Foreign package Holidays: A Report on the Supply in the UK of Tour Operators' Services and Travel Agents' services in Relation to Foreign Package Holidays*, Cm 3813. Competition Commission, London.

Recommended websites

The chapter includes a number of references to websites. The following provide a good overview:

Info-mediary
Smart Traveler: **www.smarttraveler.com** .

e-mediaries
lastminute.com: **www.lastminute.com** .
expedia.com: **www.expedia.com** .
eBookers: **www.ebookers.com** .

In-company e-mediaries
easyJet: **www.easyjet.com** .
Ryanair: **www.ryanair.com** .

State agencies
VisitScotland (industry website): **www.scotexchange.net** .
VisitBritain (industry website): **www.tourismtrade.org.uk** .
Scottish Enterprise: **www.scottish-enterprise.com** .
Historic Scotland: **www.historic-scotland.gov.uk** .

Environmental issues
Tourism & Environment Forum: **www.greentourism.org.uk** .

Private sector
Scottish Tourism Forum: **www.stforum.co.uk** .

Key words

Discretionary income; e-mediaries; industry structure; info-mediaries; suppliers.

Bibliography

Begg, D., Fischer, S. and Dornbush, R. (1987) *Economics*, 2nd edn. McGraw-Hill, Maidenhead.

Dale, C. (2003) The competitive networks of tourism e-mediaries: New strategies, new advantages, *Journal of Vacation Marketing*, Vol. 9, No. 2, 109–118.

Eadington, W.R. and Redman, M. (1991), Economics and Tourism, *Annals of Tourism Research*, Vol. 18, 41–56.

European Commission (1998) *High Level Group on Tourism and Employment, European Tourism – new partnerships for jobs*. European Commission, Brussels.

Gilbert, D.C. (1990) Conceptual issues in the meaning of tourism, in C.P. Cooper (ed.) *Progress in Tourism, Recreation and Hospitality Management, Volume 2*, Belhaven, London, 4–27.

Holloway, J.C. (1998) *The Business of Tourism*. Addison Wesley Longman, Harlow.

Jansen-Verbeke, M. (1995) A Regional analysis of tourist flows within Europe, *Tourism Management*, Vol. 16, No. 1, 73–82.

Laws, E. (1991) *Tourism Marketing*. Stanley Thornes, Cheltenham.

Leiper, N. (1979) The framework of Tourism, Towards a definition of Tourism, Tourist and the Tourist Industry, *Annals of Tourism Research*, October/December, 390–407.

Organization for Economic Co-operation and Development (2002) *Household Tourism Travel: Trends, Environmental Impacts and Policy Responses*. Organization for Economic Co-operation and Development, Paris.

Poon, A. (1993) *Tourism, Technology and Competitive Strategies*. CAB International, Wallingford.

Scherer, F.M. (1980) *Industrial market structure and economic performance*, 2nd edn. Rand Mcnally, New York.

Tremblay, P. (1998) The Economic Organisation of Tourism, *Annals of Tourism Research*, Vol. 5, No. 4, 837–859.

World Tourism Organization (2001) *Trends in tourism markets*. World Tourism Organization, Madrid.

World Tourism Organization (2004) Tourism Satellite Accounts in Depth: Analysing Tourism as an Economic Activity. **www.world-tourism.org/statistics/tsa_project/TSA_in_depth/index.htm** (accessed 25 June 2004).

Chapter 3

The role of the state in tourism

John Jenkins, The University of Newcastle, New South Wales, Australia

Learning outcomes

On completion of this chapter the reader should be able to:

■ define the concept of the state with respect to tourism;

■ describe different theories of the state and explain their relevance to contemporary tourism policy;

■ identify the different forms of state involvement in tourism;

■ explain the need to integrate tourism into a broader political economy context;

■ explain the development of public sector tourism organisations in selected countries;

■ assess the current roles of various state sector tourism organisations.

Overview

This chapter defines the concept of the state, briefly examines different theories of the state, and explains the significance and role of the state with respect to tourism. References are made to case studies concerning protected area management in Australia, the United States federal tourism administration, sex tourism and child prostitution, and government and tourism in Italy to the mid-1990s.

Introduction

It is argued that the concept of the state is central to understanding tourism in modern capitalist society. While there is no consensus in definitions of the state, it is widely acknowledged that the state is much more than simply government. Almost all human activity is influenced by the state, which comprises a very varied and extensive range of institutions. As Ralph Miliband (1973: 3) put it, 'More than ever before men now live in the shadow of the state. What they want to achieve, individually or in groups, now mainly depends on the state's sanction and support. . . It is possible not to be interested in what the state does; but it is not possible to be unaffected by it.'

What is the state?

The state has been defined as:

> an ensemble of agencies of legitimate coercion and . . . an amalgamated set of collective resources which intentionally and unintentionally produce policy outcomes. It is a structure of different political forces and institutions which attempt to justify chosen policy directions and objectives. In policy terms, the state is a contingent political entity which reflects the interchanges of values, the outcomes of interest clashes, and accumulated patterns of resource usage. . . . The state is a complex structure which defies precise definition, but which remains of crucial importance in understanding the contours of public policy.
>
> Davis *et al.*, 1993: 18–19

According to Heywood (1997: 85) the origins of the modern state can be identified 'in the emergence in fifteenth-century and sixteenth-century Europe of a system of centralised rule that succeeded in subordinating all other institutions and groups, spiritual and temporal'. Heywood (1997: 85) adopts an organisational approach to defining the state and identifies five key features of the state:

- The state is sovereign, exercising absolute and unrestricted power in that it stands above all other associations and groups in society . . .
- State institutions are recognisably 'public', in contrast to the 'private' institutions of civil society. Public bodies are responsible for making and enforcing collective decisions, while private bodies such as families, private businesses and trade unions, exist to satisfy individual interests.
- The state is an exercise in legitimation. The decisions of the state are usually (though not necessarily) accepted as binding on the members of society because, it is claimed, they are made in the public interest or for common good; the state supposedly represents the permanent interests of society.
- The state is an instrument of domination. State authority is backed up by coercion; the state must have the capacity to ensure that its laws are obeyed and that transgressors are punished . . .
- The state is a territorial association with its jurisdiction geographically defined and encompassing all those who live within its borders, 'whether they are citizens or non-citizens. On the international stage, the state is therefore regarded (at least in theory) as an autonomous entity'.

Whether or not you broadly agree with Heywood's above summary, the state, and government itself, has many responsibilities, including defence, education, health, regulation of property rights, environmental protection and management, collection of taxes, supply of infrastructure and essential services, regulation of investment, and law and order. The main institutions of the state include: the elected legislatures, government departments and authorities and the bureaucracy and civil servants, the judiciary, enforcement agencies, other levels of government, government-business enterprises, regulatory authorities, and a range of para-state organisations, such as trade unions as well as a plethora of rules, regulations, laws, conventions and policies (Davis *et al.*, 1993, in Hall and Jenkins, 1995). In other words, the concept of the state includes a relatively permanent set of *political institutions* operating in relation to civil society (Nordlinger, 1981, in Hall and Jenkins, 1995). Institutions of the state sometimes pursue conflicting directions, and rarely work in concert (McFarlane, 1968, in Davis *et al.*, 1993). Different state levels will tend to have different tourism objectives 'because the aims of the local state may diverge from those of the central state' (Williams and Shaw, 1988: 230). This is quite apparent in federal political systems where there are several levels of government: national, state/provincial, regional and local. As Anderson states (1984: 18) states:

> . . . in a federal system, which disperses power among different levels of government, some groups may have more influence if policy is made at the national level; other groups may benefit more if policy is made at the state or provincial level . . . In summary, institutional structures, arrangements, and procedures can have a significant impact on public policy and should not be ignored in policy analysis.

At a more micro- (or decision-making and action) level, some people move easily and deliberately between institutions in the public and private spheres, or undertake functions which simultaneously serve both spheres (e.g. think about the potential for conflicts of interest for someone who works for the civil service or bureaucracy, holds strong ecocentric views about human society and the environment and is also a member of a conservation group). We don't know where the state begins and ends; it has no definable edge, and we don't have a ready-made theory of the state.

The role of the state is significant for tourism. Without an understanding of the role of the state, we cannot fully comprehend the historical and contemporary dimensions of tourism (see Case 3.1, which highlights how government intervention changes over time). For example, to explain the existing institutional arrangements and principles and practices for the management and use of protected areas, a major plank of the resource base for tourism in many countries, it is necessary to develop our explanatory frameworks and modes of analysis to include the role of the state. Australia is one of any number of good case studies we can analyse.

Case 3.1   Government and tourism in Italy to the mid-1990s

Italy has long possessed a wealth of tourist products, from cultural tourist attractions based on art, culture, music and religion, to coastal tourism, mountains, hot springs and spas, natural resources, theme parks and special events (Bonini, 1993: 302, 321). It was estimated that 'more than 50% of the global cultural and historical heritage is concentrated in Italy' (UNESCO, in van de Borg and Costa, 1996: 215). Such concentration, however, presents the Italian government, the tourism industry and other affected interests (including conservation groups, archaeologists and local communities) with a conundrum. Italy's cultural heritage will inevitably help to maintain that country's attractiveness to domestic and international travellers. Simultaneously, large numbers of tourists put at risk the sustainability of tourism resources, especially if visitor management policies and programmes are inadequate (e.g. see Bonini, 1993; Glasson and Godfrey, 1995).

Tourism in Italy is concentrated geographically. Northern Italy contains the leading tourist destination regions in terms of visitor arrivals and bed-nights, reflecting the economic differences between the wealthy north and the poorer south. The main destination areas in Italy continue to be Rome, Florence and Venice. During the 1990s, these cities, with lengthy tourism histories, experienced declines or stagnation in their tourist market shares because, among other things, their hotels were old and overly expensive, restaurant prices were excessive, transportation was inefficient, and many cultural attractions kept irregular hours (e.g. opening only in the morning or in the afternoon), or were closed on Sundays and public holidays, or were open only on special request (Bonini, 1993: 304). In addition, the Naples–Capri–Sorrento area was one of Italy's largest tourist destinations until the mid-1970s, when social problems, pollution and degradation led to declines in its share of tourist travel (Bonini, 1993: 304). Conversely, former minor historical and cultural sites (attributes which appeal to the growing numbers of discerning tourists) concentrated in central and northern Italy (e.g. Assisi, Pisa, Siena, Verona) steadily increased their shares of the tourist market (Bonini, 1993: 304). This area, too, however, suffered extensive physical damage in the September-October 1997 earthquakes, especially the Umbria-Marcha region, the consequences of which were quite severe and widespread.

Italian tourism itself has had a long and significant but turbulent history. During the Roman Empire, 'state official travel offices' provided travel permits incorporating maps with information on accommodation

▶

and transportation services. With the fall of the Roman empire and the coming of the 'dark ages' tourism was largely restricted to pilgrimages. From the seventeenth century onwards Italy regained its position as one of the world's leading tourist destinations, with the Italian peninsula the core destination within the 'Grand Tour'. In the nineteenth century, Thomas Cook's career as a travel agent began when increasing numbers of English people took an active interest in travelling to the beaches of the Italian Riviera (for more detailed discussions see Formica and Uysal, 1996; Bosworth, 1996). In brief, from 1860 to 1960, tourism was Italy's biggest and most lucrative industry (Bosworth, 1996).

In 1912, Bonaldo Stringher made dubious claims that tourism contributed invisible assets which kept the national balance in budget and thereby contributed to Italy's development and prosperity (see Bosworth, 1997). However, the onset of, and economic, social and physical destruction associated with, the First World War created a sense of urgency to develop a national tourism policy. Although many Italian tourist resources were either destroyed or extensively damaged in the two world wars (e.g. during the Second World War 40% of hotels were destroyed and another 20% were damaged), there was recognition that the management of post-war tourist attractions/sites (e.g. battle sites) would require public sector intervention and planning (Bosworth, 1997). Subsequently, the Ente Nazionale per le Industrie Turistiche (ENIT) (the first National Tourist Office) was established in 1919, mainly as a result of F.S. Nitti's commitment to rational economic planning (Bosworth, 1997). By October 1922, as Fascism came to power, 'this body was, inevitably, still feeling its way', and the fascist regime, beginning in 1923, thus had the 'major responsibility for developing a detailed policy on ENIT's future, and, thus on international (and national) tourism' (Bosworth, 1997: 4). Despite the well documented failings of ENIT, a second government tourist agency (the Compagnia Italiana Turismo – CIT) was established in 1927, followed by the Direzione Generale per il Turismo (DGT, which fell under the authority of the Ministry of Press and Propaganda) in 1934, and then the Ente Provinciale per il Turismo the following year. The charters of these and other independent agencies (e.g. the Royal Italian Automobile Club – RIAC) created considerable overlap in tourism policy and administration, thereby generating much debate about which administration/s should be retained and how it/they should be structured domestically and internationally (Bosworth, 1997).

The problems in the public administration of Italian tourism aside, by 1950 Italy had become the world's third most popular tourist destination after the United States and Canada. Between 1951 and 1965, tourism growth in Italy averaged 11.5% per annum, and tourism's share of exports rose from single figures to 19.3% (Formica and Uysal, 1996: 326). However, during and shortly after this period the international tourism scene changed dramatically as population growth and demographic changes (e.g. the baby boom), technological innovations (e.g. jet aircraft) and socio-economic developments (e.g. reduction in working hours) encouraged international travel and competition, and as tour operators began to invest heavily in the comparatively cheap coastal areas of the Mediterranean (e.g. Greece, Spain, Turkey and Yugoslavia). These areas competed successfully with Italy mainly on the basis of price and sustained marketing and promotion programmes (Formica and Uysal, 1996: 326).

This competition was all the more damaging since the public organisation of tourism in Italy had long been ineffective. Public tourist organisations lacked both a strategic focus and an appropriate institutional framework. The Ministry of Tourism and Performing Arts, abolished in April 1993, was transformed into a Tourism Department of the Presidency of the Council of Ministers and was charged with the responsibilities of formulating and implementing international tourism policy and, in partnership with tourism regions, coordinating the development and promotion of Italy as a tourist destination (Formica and Uysal, 1996; Francescone, 1997).

Until the early mid-1990s, most public sector activity had been concerned with funding large events such as the 1990 World Soccer Championships and the 1992 500th anniversary of the discovery of America. Simultaneously, the Ente Nazionale Italiano del Turismo (ENIT) (Italian National Tourism Board) performed poorly. Among other things, ENIT promoted Italy using images that had been in use for more than 50 years. The tasks of tourism marketing and promotion were handed over to a network of 20 regional tourist and promotion boards which discharged their responsibilities with mixed success (Formica and Uysal, 1996: 326–327).

In an important and recent turnaround in tourism planning and promotion, ENIT established foreign partnerships, regularly participated in international travel, trade fairs and congresses, and launched a series of interregional projects with diverse cultural and environmental themes, mainly by way of providing regional authorities with financial backing. These projects demonstrated a more coordinated approach within and among the different levels of tourism public sector administration in Italy, and reflected a wider concern with the broad relations and global dimensions of the tourism industry (Francescone, 1997).

It is also worth noting other negative factors limited Italy's ability to attract tourists from the 1970s to the 1990s. These factors included: Italy's lack of quality accommodation and transport services; negative publicity stemming from natural disasters and pollution (e.g. an oil spill in the Ligurian Sea off the coast of Liguria); crowding and congestion in major tourist centres; petty crime; and the algae problem in the Adriatic Sea, which discouraged seaside visitation from the late 1980s. As a result, domestic travel numbers, international visitor arrivals and visitor bed nights in Italy stagnated, and in some years declined quite dramatically, during the 1980s and early 1990s (for more detailed discussions see Bonini, 1993; Formica and Uysal, 1996; Francescone, 1997).

The 1992 recession and continued stagnation of the Italian economy created inflation in tourism services and hotel prices, thereby compounding problems outlined above, and further threatening the competitive position of Italy's tourist industry. However, the devaluation of the lira in September 1992, and the unstable political situations in the former Yugoslavia, the Middle East, Egypt, Turkey and Spain had positive impacts on international travel to Italy. These factors combined to allow the Italian peninsula to re-establish itself as a major tourist destination in 1993 and 1994, and led to a significant rise in international visitor bed nights (see Formica and Uysal, 1996; Francescone, 1997). By 1995, Italy was fourth in the list of the world's top ten tourist destinations (29.2 million visitors – a 9.2% rise on 1994), and was the world's third largest tourism earner, with international tourism receipts rising 13.1% in 1994/95. In 1994, the main origins of international visitors were European Union residents (approximately 50%, around half of whom were Germans), followed by the United States (approximately 10%) and then the Japanese (approximately 5%). In 1996, approximately 4.5% of Italy's workforce (1,063,000 people) was employed directly and indirectly in tourism. At that time, it was suggested that 'These results seem to augur well for the future of tourism, although Italy is prone to periodic economic, political, social and even meteorological vagaries which have repercussions on the sector' (Francescone, 1997: 5).

Clearly many domestic and global factors have impacted upon the development of the Italian tourist industry, and that country's competitiveness as a tourist destination. Interestingly, as suggested above, global forces largely beyond the control of the Italian government and the local tourism industry contributed to Italy regaining its status as a leading international tourist destination. Projections for the period 1994–2000 were promising, indicating that Italy would receive an average annual rise of 5.2% per annum in international tourists (Francescone, 1997). It was believed that increasing arrivals from Eastern Europe and Asia would help offset successful competition from the Caribbean, African and Asian markets. The greatest growth potential in tourist attractions was to be likely to come from the cultural, health, rural, and sport tourism sectors (Francescone, 1997: 25).

The sustainability of Italy's tourism industry has been threatened not only by large visitor numbers, ageing infrastructure and facilities, but also by inadequate and poorly coordinated government action. This is a curious situation given the lengthy history of tourism in Italy and indeed the lengthy history of government intervention, especially in its development, marketing and promotion. Public sector policies and programmes and the publication of extensive information dealing with many aspects of the Italian tourist industry by the Department of Tourism, ENIT, and several public and private agencies in the 1990s have proved to be a start in the right direction. By the middle to late 1990s, some of the major challenges for industry and government included: (1) the conservation of heritage and managing visitors at heritage sites; (2) the coordination of public and private sector tourism planning, development and promotion; (3) the geographical dispersion of visitors and overcoming of seasonal concentrations of visitors who put tremendous demands on resources; and (4) providing appropriate standards of facilities (for a discussion of these factors, see Formica and Uysal, 1996; Francescone, 1997).

Discussion questions

1 This case study deals with tourism administration and related issue to the mid-1990s. Briefly review developments in Italian tourism administration since the mid-1990s.
2 Has the optimism for a revival in tourism in Italy been realised?
3 How critical has been the role of the state to tourism development in Italy?

In Australia, most protected areas are managed by state and territory governments, reflecting land management responsibilities under the Australian constitution and the federal system of government. There are approximately 60 categories of protected areas encompassing an estimated 6755 terrestrial and 192 marine sites in Australia (Environment Australia, 2002). As many protected areas experience increasing tourism demand pressures, and use becomes more intense, the potential for conflict between maintaining environmental quality, maximising recreational accessibility and satisfaction, and promoting economic development is enhanced (e.g. Pigram and Jenkins, 1999; DISR, 2001). The current trend for tourism and recreation developments in protected areas is one of the major threats to the sustainability of national parks identified by environmental groups such as the National Parks Association, the Australian Conservation Foundation and the Wilderness Society (e.g. Figgis, 2000; see Jenkins and Wearing, 2003). The state is not a cohesive entity when it comes to protected area management and tourist use of resources.

Conservation agencies lobby against tourist use in some parks, and lobby for use in others, especially where consumptive resource uses (e.g. mining, forestry) either exist or are anticipated. In the case of the latter, there may be some compromise by conservation lobbies, as they support the potential for tourism rather than some vigorous consumptive activity (such as mining). These groups may even use some economic justification in addition to environmental protection for declaring national parks. That said, they will oppose certain activities in almost all national parks. Conversely, recreational groups (e.g. four-wheel drive clubs/associations; horse riding associations) lobby long and hard for supply of recreational opportunities in sensitive areas such as coastal dunes, as conservationists argue vociferously against such use. The fact is, we know very little about the environmental impacts of many recreational activities and conservation groups will seek the adoption of the precautionary principle in the management of protected areas. Political parties, parliamentarians, tourism industry representatives, and a host of interests have a stake in the management of protected areas. Even within these groups, however, views are not united. There are often strong differences of opinion within interest or lobby groups, political parties and resource management agencies as to what recreational and tourism, developments should be permitted within or adjacent to particular protected areas, and, ultimately, the levels, timing, extent and nature of recreational access and tourist use.

In Australia, no one piece of legislation or over-riding common law right exists with respect to tourist access to nature-based resources. Access provisions are scattered among many pieces of legislation across the continent and its six states and two territories; recreational access arrangements also vary greatly among individual protected areas in the same state. Even single Acts prescribing legislation for protected areas are often the responsibility of more than one government department. This legal and administrative complexity is reflected in the range of mechanisms by which protected areas are declared and managed, and by which rights of access for nature-based tourism are legitimated (a similar situation has been previously described in New Zealand in McIntyre *et al.*, 2001). The implementation of joint management regimes, which are intended to provide opportunities for aborigines to remain on their land and to 'exercise political and cultural power over decisions affecting their lives and land', are a recent development in Australian national park management which are proving to be a contentious Western cultural model (Craig, 1993: 137, in Wearing and Huyskens, 2001: 182). Pitts's (1983: 7) summary of the situation more than 20 years ago still rings true:

> The management of outdoor recreation resources and facilities in Australia is characterised by a myriad of government departments, authorities and agencies operating in apparent isolation of each other. Outdoor recreation has rarely been recognised, on its own, as a legitimate function of government in this country. Rather, it has been allowed to develop as a secondary function associated with more traditional government activities such as forestry, conservation, water supply and town planning. This approach has inevitably led to problems of coordination, conflicts in connection with overlapping responsibilities and doubts about the effectiveness of the whole delivery system in meeting community [and tourist] needs.

The role of the state is clearly salient to our understanding and study of tourism. The state is central to politics, and 'A citizen encounters politics in the government of a country, town, school, church, business firm, trade union, club, political party, civic association, and a host of other organisations . . . Politics is one of the unavoidable facts of human existence. Everyone is involved in some fashion at some time in some kind of political system' (Dahl, 1965: 1). The role of the state and its elements (institutions) could be central to studies concerning:

- government decisions and actions affecting recreation and tourism developments in protected areas;
- the domination of the corporate economy by relatively few companies and significant individuals (e.g. the proliferation of multinational companies);
- high market concentration in transport and other areas of the tourism industry;
- industry structures, pricing mechanisms and barriers to entry in areas such as the airline industry;
- the relationships between tourism businesses/entrepreneurs and the public sector (e.g. the development of networks and alliances between public and private enterprise in tourism development and marketing);
- the distribution of power in tourism policy making;
- the influence of pressure (or interest) groups on public sector decision-making;
- the political economy of tourism;
- the history of tourism organisations and public administrations (from national to local organisations to pressure groups);
- international comparisons of national tourism policies;
- organisational behaviour and tourism policy making;
- tourism policy and indigenous people;
- intergovernmental relations and tourism policy formulation. (For a discussion of these issues in a public policy context with references to the role of the state, see *Current Issues in Tourism*, 2001, 4(2–4).)

Many theories have been put forward to explain the role of the state. Some of these are discussed below.

Theories of the state: a brief introduction

Theories of the state derive from a number of theoretical perspectives. Liberal democracy is the key context in which we analyse the role of the state (Dunleavy and O'Leary, 1987: 4). Democracy, simplistically, means rule or government by the people (e.g. Heywood, 1997: 66). Various models of democracy have been described and variously praised and criticised. Models include classical, liberal, protective and developmental democracy. A broad consensus of democracy (liberal democracy) holds that represented governments are duly elected at regular intervals. Liberal democracies are characterised by electoral choice (which may be very wide) and political parties (of which there may be few or many) (Heywood, 1997: 27–8, 75). Nonetheless, in most democratic states far less than 100% of eligible voters lodge their votes, and large segments of the population may decide not to vote. In countries such as Australia, a rare exception, voting is compulsory.

Any discussion of the state requires that the discussion be contextualised within society. Different views on the state (its roles and responsibilities) are important statements about, among other things, society, systems of government and the historical development of a nation. Key questions for exploring the role of the state in any political decision or action that is taken include:

- Why should government and the wider state intervene?
- How should government and the wider state intervene?

■ Who has influenced public policy and with what effect?

■ What policies or programmes are foregone in any decision or action (i.e. what are the opportunity costs)?

■ What are the likely impacts of the decisions and actions taken?

■ Who benefits or wins?

■ Who loses?

■ What interests (perhaps business interests) are being served?

■ What are the implications for society generally?

So, with respect to tourism, the development of legislation concerning visas, environmental assessment, the allocation and distribution of resources, such as national, regional and urban parks, walking trails, and the construction of transport infrastructure such as airports and roads can be highly political issues. Choices and decisions are made to allocate funds and other resources to particular policies, programmes and projects at the expense of others, and these are generally made in response to competing claims from affected individuals and agencies, consideration of related programmes, party political ideology and resource constraints. There are winners and losers, and the distribution of power in democratic societies has been the subject of lengthy historical debate.

Rival theories of the state are rather plentiful and varied. Theoretical perspectives include pluralist (and neo-pluralists), elite, Marxist (and neo-Marxist) and Weberian (and neo-Weberian). In the space available, we will briefly describe and compare each of these theories of the state.

■ Pluralism

The origins of **pluralist theories** of the state 'can be traced back to the writings of seventeenth-century social-contract theorists such as Thomas Hobbes and John Locke' (Heywood, 1997: 87). Pluralists, of which Dahl and Polsby were major exponents, argue that 'power in western industrialized societies is widely distributed among different groups' (Ham and Hill, 1984: 27), and that the state is a more or less neutral body that arbitrates between the competing interests of society (Heywood, 1997: 98). Pluralism is society-centred. The state, then, is considered a referee, with much attention given to government. It is not uncommon in the pluralist tradition 'for "the state" to be dismissed as an abstraction, with institutions such as the courts, the civil service and the military being seen as independent actors in their own right, rather than as elements of a broader state machine' (Heywood, 1997: 86).

In recent works under the labels of 'reformed pluralism' and 'neo-pluralism', a more critical analysis of the state has been adopted. It is acknowledged that government and interest group relationships are frequently institutionalised and that certain groups may be excluded from policy agendas and debates. This is a more 'realistic' and applied perspective or view of the political system, because business, for example, is a powerful political force, with a firm and extensive foothold in influencing government decision-making, especially in modern capitalist societies. In addition, there is an influential state elite, which, ironically, includes government agencies and staff. Government itself, then, is viewed as a political actor and indeed a powerful interest group.

Since the 1970s, pluralism has been subjected to very intensive criticism. Pluralist explanations neglect the persistent and sometimes powerful influence of business and corporate elites on policy making, and have a limited or narrow view of state action. Brian Head (1983: 27) described several weaknesses of the traditional pluralist perspective:

Apart from the recognition of the importance of group interest and electoral politics as central to the policy-making process, there is little to recommend the pluralist theory . . . There is no analysis of the systemic or structural constraints under which (governments) operate in an advanced capitalist society, no theory of the state apparatus as a set of structures distanced from both the government and from the economic groups, no theory of historical change in state/economy relations, and no account of the international context of public policy . . .

Despite its limitations, pluralism's strong focus on the role of interest (pressure) groups in public policy processes is also something of a strength. Such a focus directs our attention, for example, to the extent and nature of political organisations in politics, to interest group competition, and to the ways in which groups coalesce around a particular policy issue. However, pluralist perspectives of decision- and policy-making processes generally fail to explain adequately how governments and the wider state actually work. Pluralist-based accounts are inadequate, for example, in explaining the adoption of particular economic theories or ideas (and hence ideology) to drive political action, the power of multinational corporations in developing countries, or why sex tourism is such an economically 'respected' and 'successful' industry in several countries in South East Asia.

Elite theory

Elite theory is based on the premise that power (political or economic) is concentrated in a minority of the population. Public policy, then, reflects 'the values and preferences of a governing elite' (Anderson, 1984: 16). Elitism is a belief in, or practice of rule by an elite or a minority. 'Gaetano Mosca (1857–1941), Robert Michels (1876–1936) and Vilfredo Pareto (1848–1923) are widely credited with developing the concept as a central idea in the social sciences in the late nineteenth century' (Green, 2003: 144). The term elite 'has been used in conjunction with Marxist analyses of class and economic power, as well as in accounts of corporatism as a form of state and/or government/interest group intermediation. It is, therefore, difficult to provide one clear definition of elitism with which all would agree' (Green, 2003: 144).

Power may be gained from one or more sources, including technical expertise (e.g. scientists), wealth (e.g. wealthy entrepreneurs), access to information or knowledge (businessman with good networks and alliances in government), formal appointment to an office or executive position (e.g. chief executive officers) (Green, 2003: 144). Thomas Dye and Harmon Zeigler (in Anderson, 1984: 16–17) summarise elite theory as follows:

> Society is divided into the few who have power and the many who do not . . . The few who govern are not typical of the masses who are governed. Elites are drawn disproportionately from the upper socioeconomic strata of society . . . Elites share a consensus on the basic values of the social system and the preservation of the system. Public policy does not reflect demands of the masses but rather the prevailing values of the elite . . . Elites influence masses more than masses influence elites.

'Whereas classical elitists strove to prove that democracy was always a myth, modern elitist theorists have tended to highlight how far particular political systems fall short of the democratic ideal' (Heywood, 1997: 76). In developed and developing countries, elite positions are closely linked to ownership of resources and the formulation and implementations of public policy. Readily identifiable examples of people in elite positions include members of large and powerful government agencies, including the military, and multinational corporations (e.g. see Mills, 1956; Ham and Hill, 1984). Elite theory is 'an important alternative to pluralism' (Ham and Hill, 1984: 32). In recent times, neo-Marxists take the comparisons further. Miliband in his treatise on the role of the state in capitalist society based on the ideas of Marx, seeks to show that the powerful elite is little more than a ruling or dominant class (Ham and Hill, 1984).

Marxism

In the mid-nineteenth century, Karl Marx wrote *The Communist Manifesto* (with Friederich Engels), *Capital* and other works. For Marx, history was a story of struggle between social classes produced by the way a given society reproduces its existence from day to day. **Marxism** is very concerned with 'who gets what'. It asks questions about how a capitalist society allocates labour and other resources and how consumption regulates and perpetuates differential relations within society. 'The relationship between capitalists and workers is an exploitative one – capitalists minimising the wages they pay and retaining maximum profits for themselves. The state in capitalist countries merely plays the role of propping up the exploitative system by curbing and regulating some of the worst excesses of capitalism and providing it with a "human face"' (Veal, 2003: 300).

For Marxists 'the capitalist state's main function is to assist the process of capital accumulation' (Ham and Hill, 1984: 33). Marxists (such as Ralph Miliband and Poulantzas, who, incidentally, do not agree on certain assumptions) argue essentially that the state 'is an instrument for class domination' (Ham and Hill, 1984: 32), maintaining 'the class system by either oppressing subordinate classes or ameliorating class conflict' (Heywood, 1997: 98). The state is thus considered to be acting largely on behalf of the capitalist class. 'In terms of its world view, the Marxist perspective sees the antagonistic relationship between classes as the central fact of politics in all societies . . . The overall pattern of public policy supports the general interests of capital' (Brooks, 1993: 41). The Marxist critique has been applied to leisure provision. 'It argues that by providing those leisure services which the market is incapable of delivering – such as parks, sports facilities, children's play facilities, quality arts output and conservation of the natural and historic heritage – the state provides capitalism with a civilized face. Not only does the state provide capitalism with a human face, it provides basic infrastructure at the public expense upon which the private sector builds profitable enterprises . . .' (Veal, 2002: 43). Unfortunately, especially given the salience of Marxist accounts to studies of political economy, tourism studies has grossly neglected this complex view of the state writ large.

Corporatism

Corporatism, like pluralism, recognises bargaining between competing interests. However, there is an important distinction in that corporatism sees the implementation of public policies and programmes through interest groups, and especially through corporate interests (e.g. corporatisation of government business enterprises) so that there are intricate and very direct links between business and the state. Max Weber argued that the notion of democracy known to Ancient Greeks could not be delivered in modern times, as politics and government were dominated by the professional elite of politicians and bureaucrats. He considered the modern era to be 'one of "party machine politics", in which the degree of participation of the ordinary citizen in the forging of political policies is strictly limited' (Giddens, 1982: 91).

One way of understanding the ways in which corporate power is exercised and unfolds is to focus on an aspect of business interaction with government (e.g. see Richter, 1989; Hall, 1994; Jenkins, 2001a). What analysts might find are that there are many dimensions of economic or corporate power: the domination of the corporate economy by relatively few companies; high market concentration in specific industries; trade practices (e.g. price-fixing arrangements); interlocking company directors; and, ultimately, the extent and nature of the relationship between big business and the governmental processes (or in other words, the relationships between economic and political power) (Wheelwright, 1974). The brokering of deals around policies concerning taxes, subsidies and resort developments and other projects in developed and developing countries has been questioned in these countries (e.g. see Richter, 1989; Hall and Jenkins, 1995: 61–3; Doorne, 1998; Jenkins, 2001).

The field of tourism studies is giving greater consideration to the role of the state (e.g. Richter, 1989; McMillan, 1991; Hall, 1994; Hall and Jenkins, 1995; Elliott, 1997; Jenkins, 2001b).

Clearly, the state merits attention and critical analysis because it is a very central aspect of tourism planning and policy making in developed and developing countries. The state performs many functions (developer, interest protector, regulator and arbitrator, redistributor, facilitator and organiser) (Davis *et al.*, 1993: 26–7). Indeed, as Minogue put it, 'any satisfactory explanatory theory of public policy must also explain the inter-relations between the state, politics, economy and society' (Minogue, n.d.: 5, in Ham and Hill, 1984: 17).

Tourism and the state

More than a decade ago, Stephen Britton (1991) argued, 'We need a theorisation that explicitly recognises, and unveils, tourism as a predominantly capitalistically organised activity driven by the inherent and defining social dynamics of that system, with its attendant production, social, and ideological relations'. Many modern capitalist states have long been interventionist (e.g. Australia, Canada, UK) and very involved in a range of enterprises designed to promote their country's physical, economic and social development (e.g. roads, railways, communications, electricity). In Australia, for example, dominant considerations in state intervention, and particularly government intervention, were the inadequacy of private resources of capital, labour and technical competence, and the challenges of 'taming' a harsh physical environment (Wettenhall, 1990). Australia's national development ethos has had a special place for the state as an undertaker of works to support private enterprise (e.g. see Ward, 1958; Head and Bell, 1994), and hence the expansion of capitalism.

Government and broader state intervention in tourism and other policy arenas is generally linked to some form of market failure, market imperfection and social need. According to Hula (1988: 6), 'implicit in each justification for political action is the view that government offers a corrective alternative to the market'. For instance, the market often fails to protect adequately the environment on which much of the tourist industry depends for its survival; it is often difficult to get private tourism interests to pool their resources; and tourism often impacts adversely on some sections of the community. Moreover, governments often necessarily find themselves as the main provider of various forms of infrastructure – roads, airports, railways, power supply, sewage and water supply (Hall and Jenkins, 1998).

Policies of deregulation, privatisation, the elimination of tax incentives, and a move away from discretionary forms of macroeconomic intervention, have been the hallmarks of a push towards 'smaller' government in the UK, US, New Zealand and Australia (Hall and Jenkins, 1997). Such changes in political philosophy have significant implications for tourism policy making, planning and development. Calls for smaller government in Western society have increased the demands from conservative national governments and economic rationalists for greater self-sufficiency in many industries, including tourism. Public sector involvement in tourism marketing and promotion has been characterised by the privatisation or corporatisation of tourism agencies or boards (Jeffries, 1988, in Jenkins and Hall, 1997). On occasions, governments have decided to withdraw industry support by abolishing entire tourism departments and corporations (e.g. the Swedish Tourist Board in 1992) or by reducing or terminating their funds (e.g. the United States Travel and Tourism Administration [USTTA] in 1995). Then, as circumstances change, as states and governments revise their roles, or if there is a change in government after an election, the nature or extent of intervention will change.

The US *National Tourism Act* 1996, alluded to some of the reasons for the abolition of USTTA – lack of resources, a failure to increase the US share of international travel, and the idea that the private sector could more effectively manage international travel and tourism promotion at far less cost to taxpayers (Jefferies, 2001). The Act, nonetheless, authorised the Secretary of Commerce to continue several vital federal functions, through the National Tourism Office (then Tourism Industries Office). The Act specified the purposes of the new body as:

- Seek and work for an increase in the share of the United States in the global tourism market;
- Work in conjunction with Federal, State, and local agencies to develop and implement a coordinated United States travel and tourism policy;
- Advise the President, the Congress, and the domestic travel and tourism industry on the implementation of the national travel and tourism strategy and on other matters affecting travel and tourism;
- Operate travel and tourism promotion programs outside the United States in partnership with the travel and tourism industry in the United States;
- Establish a travel and tourism data bank to gather and disseminate travel and tourism market data;
- Conduct market research necessary for effective promotion of the travel and tourism market; and
- Promote United States travel and tourism, including international trade shows and conferences.

> United States Code as of 26 January 1998, Section 2141a: United States
> National Tourism Organization; also see Jeffries, 2001: 183–4.

Various functions and resources of the USTTA were thus transferred to the International Trade Administration in the US Department of Commerce, within which the Tourism Industries office was established. The mission of this office was 'to foster an environment in which the US travel and tourism industry can generate jobs through tourism exports' (Goeldner *et al.*, 2000: 109). It was originally staffed by only 12 employees under a Deputy Assistant Secretary and organised into three groups: (1) Deputy Assistant Secretary for Tourism Industries, (2) Tourism Development, and (3) Tourism Policy Coordination, including the Tourism Policy Council, which comprises 'nine Federal agencies and the President of the US National Tourism Organization' (Goeldner *et al.*, 2000: 110–11).

The terrorist attacks on the United States on September 11 severely disrupted international and domestic travel in the United States. Subsequently, there were rushed and determined efforts to recharge the tourism industry. The Tourism Policy Council was revitalised on 29 October 2001. 'The TPC coordinates national policies and programmes related to travel and tourism, recreation, and national heritage resources that involve federal agencies. The TPC also provides a forum to ensure that US government agencies work together to enhance consumer confidence in the safety and security of travel, while taking into account the needs of tourists and business travellers' (Baker, 2002: 3). The US government, then, dramatically revised its interventionist role because of threats to the industry's sustainability; threats with which the market itself could not cope.

More than a generation ago, the IUOTO argued that the extent of the state's role in tourism varies according to the conditions and circumstances peculiar to each country (politico-economic-constitutional system, socio-economic development, degree of tourism development) (IUOTO, 1974: 67). This remains the case. However, IUOTO (1974: 71) did suggest that tourism was such a key sector that in order to foster and develop tourism 'on a scale proportionate to its national importance and to mobilise all available resources to that end, it is necessary to centralise the policy-making powers in the hands of the state so that it can take appropriate measures for creating a suitable framework for the promotion and development of tourism by the various sectors concerned'. The actions with respect to tourism administration in the United States appear to support IUOTO intentions. Whether IUOTO would have anticipated or supported developments in the marketing and promotion of the sex tourism industry in several countries, however, is unlikely.

Promoting sex tourism: what role for the state?

Case 3.2	Sex tourism and the state

In 1998, Canberra Tourism and Events Corporation [CTEC, Australia] chief executive, David Marshall, said that the corporation was happy to provide information and assistance to the sex industry on tourism promotion.

> What's happened is that they [the industry] are running their own tours aiming at clubs and so forth – and they have had tremendous success in this. . . They are finding that there are organisations coming to Canberra on bus tours who are adding their tours to their itinerary. They show people a brothel, take them out to a sex supermarket, the video distribution channel and so on. . . We have found – and the sex industry has confirmed to us – that when there are major activities in Canberra . . . that there is a boost to visitations in Fyshwick. We also get people coming to the visitors centre and asking where Fyshwick is, and we are quite happy to direct people out there. . .

> Canberra Tourism Backs Sex Industry's Brothel Tourism Campaign, *Canberra Times*, 8 March 1998: 1

In the same article, Marshall's view was endorsed by the spokesman for Australian Capital Territory (ACT) Chief Minister Kate Carnell, who said the [ACT] Government acknowledged the role of the sex industry in Canberra's tourism and had no problem with that. 'It is a valid industry, regulated and taxpaying and is undeniably a part of Canberra's industry', the spokesman said. 'That is not to say it would be appropriate to be out there actively promoting this as part of Feel the Power of Canberra.'

Clearly, there have been people in positions of great public responsibility and power (or an elite) in key institutions in the ACT, who are willing to support sex tourism. Prostitution and brothels in the Act are in fact legal (Prostitution Act 1992). Prostitution is, supposedly, a regulated industry involving people at least 18 years of age, who pay taxes, undergo health checks and are required to undertake careful and responsible practices. Given the sex industry's general conduct, reputation and association with criminal activity, however, there are those who, with good reason, will continue to question the industry's ability to regulate and address issues such as drug addiction, underworld and organised crime, trafficking of women and children, and sexually transmitted diseases. That said, decriminalising and regulating the sex industry is one thing; government representatives promoting sex tourism is a very different and questionable matter warranting scrutiny.

An analysis of prostitution and sex tourism in the ACT could be undertaken within a neo-Marxist framework, emphasising power relations among classes in society and the relationships between economic and political power. 'In the neo-Marxist view of the state, public policies are portrayed on a large canvas, and the key to understanding the actions of the state is to recognize that the capitalist class enjoys certain structural advantages. These advantages derive from the fact that in a capitalist system investment decisions (what is to be produced and how resources are to be allocated) are decisions made in large measure by business' (Atkinson and Chandler, 1983: 4). Matsui (1987: 9, in Hall, 1992) very astutely describes tourism prostitution in south-east Asia as 'a multinational sex industry'. The tourism industry has a demonstrated vested interest in sex tourism and prostitution and profits from it! David Marshall's (see above) reactions in a neo-Marxist account probably come as no surprise given the explicit links between tourism growth and prostitution, and the close relations between business and government so characteristic of tourism statutory corporations, one of which he represented.

The spokesman for the ACT's Chief Minister indicated the ACT government's support for sex tourism, but exhibited constraint in the extent to which her government would be prepared to promote it. As a 'regulated' industry in the ACT, then, it seems the sex tourism industry is not too contentious, especially as there is public policy and legislation which supports its 'healthy' operation. As a matter of interest, though, we might raise the matter that the World Tourism Organization (WTO), which functions as a global forum for tourism matters and whose members total approximately 140 countries (including Australia) and more than 350 public and private sector affiliate members, adopted a Global Code of Ethics for Tourism in 1999 in which Article 2 states:

> The exploitation of human beings in any form, particularly sexual, especially when applied to children, conflicts with the fundamental aims of tourism and is the negation of tourism, as such. It should be energetically combated and penalised without concession by the national legislation of both the countries visited and the countries of the perpetrators.

Conceptual problems abound, too. The question of how we define a child (or adult) is complex. In the United States, The Child Protection Act 1984 defines a child as anyone younger than the age of 18, yet in many industrialised nations (including the US), people under 18 years of age attend University, travel alone, work, pay taxes and live away from home 'working' in the field of prostitution. People under the age of 18 are entitled to marry. Another interesting turn in the promotion of sex tourism and the roles of the state might be uncovered in investigations of destinations, including Kenya, Gambia, and the Caribbean islands, where female sex tourists are likely to outnumber their male counterparts (see Oppermann, 1999).

Sex tourism takes an ugly turn when we direct attention to the commercial exploitation of children in Australia and overseas. The Australian federal government, with the support of a wide range of institutions, including state and territory governments, has been very active in enacting legislation which outlaws paedophilia and child pornography for Australians travelling abroad. Nonetheless, child sex tourism has been around for a very long time, and only recently has it become the centre of academic, media and government interest. At a conference on the child sex trade in June 1994, Chuan Leekpai, Prime Minister of Thailand stated:

> . . . this problem has not arisen just in the last year or two. It started long ago, but in the past it was not taken as a serious matter. The world didn't pay much attention to it; there was no organization working on this problem; there was no governmental policy, either written or spoken, regarding this problem and there was no international traffic of prostitutes from one country to another. However, all these things have now occurred and Thailand (like other countries in the region) must face the problem.
> Szadkowski, 1995

ECPAT, the organisation to End Child Prostitution in Asian Tourism was created in 1991 and became a central institution in this task. It took only a couple of years for ECPAT to spread its wings to almost thirty countries, but its energies have been directed mainly to Sri Lanka, the Philippines, Taiwan and Thailand.

Conclusion

The viability and role of the state in different countries varies. Different nations and local states possess different capacities to confront contemporary problems and issues. The fact that states often appear to be engulfed in conflicts, contests and fragmented or disjointed responses to societal problems is not at all unusual; in fact it is quite normal. Indeed, when we discuss 'state' action, what we will inevitably be referring to is the action of a particular state institution or a limited number of institutions. So, problems of policy coordination stem from the fact that different policies operating in different policy arenas, or being sponsored by different parts of the state, may often be in conflict. The limits to state intervention in economy and society are a key concern. W. Arthur Lewis (in Wheelwright, 1978: 171) argued that 'economic development depends on what people do; what people do depends on what they believe.' And, although the role of the state is an issue that often brings about negative ideas and perspectives, the state has broad roles and responsibilities that seek to protect, provide, defend and support people and society. The big question is, to what extent and how?

Discussion questions

4 Briefly describe the institutional arrangements for tourism policy and planning in a country of your choice.

5 Should tourism development be permitted in protected areas such as national parks? Explain your answer with reference both to your values and interests concerning national parks and protected areas and your views on theories of the state.

6 What are the roles of each level of government in your country with respect to tourism planning and policy making?

7 What factors or forces might impede the coordination of tourism planning and policy making between different levels of government in a country?

8 Critically reflect on your studies and readings in this course. How might your personal values and interests affect your perspectives of tourism public policy?

9 How important do you think community and individual attitudes to, and perceptions of, tourism development are to tourism planning processes in your local area?

10 'Power is clearly a key element in understanding how decisions are made and why certain values are excluded from tourism policy. The challenge for many involved in tourism studies is to acknowledge the centrality of power in tourism policy . . .' (Hall and Jenkins, 1995: 79). Discuss this statement with reference theories of the state and your perceptions of tourism policy in your local or regional area.

Guided reading

For an overview of tourism politics, public policy and the role of the state, students should consult: Richter (1989) which traverses diverse terrain on the politics of tourism in Asia; Hall (1994), Hall and Jenkins (1995) and Elliott (1997) which provide accounts of, among other things, tourism policy making and the roles of institutions of the state; *Current Issues in Tourism* (2001, vol. 4: 2–4) contains a recent editorial update on studies in tourism policy and thirteen insightful case studies including the role of the French state in supporting large tourism projects, the roles of interest groups, and tourism policy in Jamaica. In addition, students should be prepared to expand their understanding of issues raised in this brief chapter by acquiring references referred to in the discussion. This chapter is too brief to hope to provide a comprehensive account of theoretical and applied knowledge of the role of the state.

Recommended websites

Most states are members of the World Tourism Organization (WTO): **www.world-tourism.org** . Its website is rich in material relevant to this chapter.

The Tourism Offices Worldwide Directory (TOWD): **www.towd.com/** TOWD is a searchable directory for official tourism resources including government tourism offices.

Australia	Tourism Australia: **www.atc.net.au/** .
Europe	European Travel Commission: **www.etc-corporate.org/** . Visit Europe: **www.visiteurope.com/** .
New Zealand	Tourism New Zealand: **www.newzealand.com/travel/** . and **www.tourisminfo.govt.nz/** .
UK	Department for Culture, Media and Sport: **www.culture.gov.uk/ tourism/default.htm** . Visit Britain: **www.visitbritain.com/** . Visit Scotland: **www.visitscotland.com/** . Wales Tourist Board: **www.visitwales.com/** . Northern Ireland Tourist Board: **www.discovernorthernireland.com/** .
USA	USA Office of Travel and Tourism Industries, Department of Commerce: **http://tinet.ita.doc.gov/** .

Note: At the national, regional/provincial and local levels, official state websites vary considerably in their content, some being essentially promotional websites while others provide useful material such as policy statements and tourism data.

Other organisations which contain relevant policy and planning information include:

Pacific Asia Travel Association: **www.pata.org/** .

United Nations Environment Program – Tourism: **www.uneptie.org/pc/tourism/ home.htm** .

The International Ecotourism Society: **www.ecotourism.org/** .

Key words

Institutions; discretionary income; politics; public policy; the state.

Bibliography

Anderson, J.E. (1984) *Public Policy Making*, 3rd edn. CBS College Publishing, New York.

Askew, M. (1997) The business of love: Writings on the socio-cultural dynamics of Thailand's sex industry, *Journal of Southeast Asian Studies*, 28: 2.

Atkinson, M.M. and Chandler, M.A. (1983) Strategies for policy analysis, in M.M. Atkinson and M.A.

Chandler (eds) *The Politics of Canadian Public Policy*. University of Toronto Press, Toronto, 3–20.

Australian Territory Government (2004) *Prostitution Act 1992*, Republication No. 9, 27 May, **http://www.legislation.act.gov.au/a/1992–64/20040 527–13551/pdf/1992–64.pdf/** .

Baker, D. (2002) Helping the tourism industry recover, *Export America* at **www.export.gov/exportamerica/NewOpportunities/no_tourismrecov.pdf** (accessed 18 July 2004).

Bonini, A. (1993) Tourism in Italy, in W. Pompl and P. Lavery (eds) *Tourism in Europe – Structures and Developments*. CAB International, Wallingford.

Bosworth, R.V.B. (1996) *Italy and the Wider World*. Routledge, London (see Chapter 8, Visiting Italy: Tourism and Leisure 1860–1960).

Bosworth, R.V.B. (1997) Tourist planning in fascist Italy and the limits of a totalitarian culture, *Contemporary European History* 6,1, 1–25. (This work of Bosworth is a truly excellent piece of historical research.)

Britton, S.G. (1991) Tourism, capital and place: towards a critical geography of tourism, *Environment and Planning D: Society and Space*, 9(4), 451–478.

Brooks, S. (1993) *Public Policy in Canada*. McClelland and Stewart, Toronto.

Current Issues in Tourism (2001) 4, 2–4.

Dahl, R.A. (1965) *Modern Political Analysis*. Prentice-Hall, Englewood Cliffs, NJ.

Davis, G., Wanna, J., Warhurst, J. and Weller, P. (1988) *Public Policy in Australia*. Allen and Unwin, North Sydney.

Davis, G., Wanna, J., Warhurst, J. and Weller, P. (1993) *Public Policy in Australia*, 2nd edn. Allen and Unwin, North Sydney.

Department of Industry, Science and Resources (2001) *Ecotourism: Facts Sheet*, March **www.industry.gov.au/content/publications.cfm#results** (accessed 31 January 2002).

Doorne, S. (1998) Power, Participation and Perception: An Insider's Perspective on the Politics of the Wellington Waterfront Redevelopment, *Current Issues in Tourism*, 1(2), 129–166.

Dunleavy, P. and O'Leary, B. (1987) *Theories of the State*. Macmillan, London.

Dye, T. (1992) *Understanding Public Policy*, 7th edn. Prentice Hall, Englewood Cliffs, NJ.

Elliott, J. (1997) *Tourism Politics and Public Sector Management*. Routledge, London.

Environment Australia (2002) **www.environment.gov.au/bg/protecte/intro.htm** (accessed 30 March 2002).

Figgis, P. (2000) The double-edged sword: tourism and national parks, *Habitat Australia*, October, 28(5), 24.

Formica, S. and Uysal, M. (1996) The revitalization of Italy as a tourist destination, *Tourism Management* 17, 5, 323–331.

Francescone, P.M. (1997) Italy, in G. Todd (ed.) *International Tourism Reports, Travel and Tourism Intelligence*, 1, 5–25.

Giddens, A. (1982) *Sociology: A Brief But Critical Introduction*. Macmillan Press, London.

Glasson, J. and Godfrey, K. (1995) *Towards Visitor Impact Management*. Avebury, UK.

Gouldner, C., Brent Ritchie, J.R. and McIntosh, R.W. (2000) *Tourism: Principles, Practices, Philosophies*. John Wiley & Sons, New York.

Green, M. (2003) Elitism, in J.M. Jenkins and J.J. Pigram (eds) *Encyclopedia of Leisure and Outdoor Recreation*. Routledge, London, 143–144.

Hall, C.M. (1992) Sex tourism in South-East Asia, in D. Harrison (ed.) *Tourism and the Less Developed Countries*. Belhaven Press, London.

Hall, C.M. (1994) *Tourism and Politics: Policy, Power and Place*. Belhaven Press, London.

Hall, C.M. and Jenkins, J.M. (1995) *Tourism and Public Policy*. Routledge, London.

Hall, C.M. and Jenkins, J.M. (1997) Tourism planning and policy in Australia, in C.M. Hall, J.M. Jenkins, and G.W. Kearsley (eds) *Tourism Planning and Policy in Australia and New Zealand: Cases Issues and Practice*. McGraw-Hill, Sydney.

Hall, C.M. and Jenkins, J.M. (1998) The policy dimensions of rural tourism and recreation, in R.W. Butler, C.M. Hall and J.M. Jenkins (eds) *Tourism and Recreation in Rural Areas*. John Wiley & Sons, Chichester.

Hall, C.M. and Jenkins, J.M. (2004) Tourism and public policy, in A.A. Lew, C.M. Hall and A.M. Williams (eds) *A Companion to Tourism*. Blackwell, Maldan M.A.

Ham, C. and Hill, M. (1984) *The Policy Process in the Modern Capitalist State*. Harvester Wheatsheaf, New York.

Head, B. and Bell, S. (1994) Understanding the modern state: explanatory approaches, in S. Bell and B. Head (eds) *State, economy and public policy in Australia*. Cambridge University Press, Cambridge, 25–74.

Head, B.W. (1983) State and economy: theories and problems, in B.W. Head (ed.) *State and economy in society in Australia*. Oxford University Press, Melbourne, 22–54.

Head, B.W. (1984) Recent theories of the state, *Politics*, 19(2), 36–45.

Heywood, A. (1997) *Politics*. Palgrave, New York.

Hula, R.C. (1988) Using markets to implement public policy, in R.C. Hula (ed.) *Market-Based Public Policy*. St. Martin's Press, New York.

IOUTO (1974) The role of the state in tourism, *Annals of Tourism Research*, 1(3), 66–72.

Jeffries, ? (1988) **Details wanted.**

Jeffries, D. (2001) *Governments and Tourism*. Butterworth-Heinemann, Oxford.

Jenkins, J.M. (2001a) Statutory Authorities in Whose Interests? The Case of Tourism New South Wales, the Bed Tax, and 'The Games', *Pacific Tourism Review*, 4(4), 201–219.

Jenkins, J.M. (2001b) Editorial, *Current Issues in Tourism*, 4(2–4), 69–77.

Jenkins, J.M. (2003) Pluralism, in J.M. Jenkins, and J.J. Pigram (eds) *Encyclopedia of Leisure and Outdoor Recreation*. Routledge, London, 376–377.

Jenkins, J.M. and Hall, C.M. (1997) Tourism policy and legislation in Australia, in C.M. Hall, J.M. Jenkins and G. Kearsley (eds) *Tourism Planning and Policy in Australia and New Zealand: Cases, Issues and Practice*. Irwin, Sydney, 37–48.

McFarlane **XX** (1968) **Details wanted.**

McIntyre, N., Jenkins, J.M. and Booth, K. (2001) Recreational access in New Zealand, *Journal of Sustainable Tourism*, 9(5), 434–450.

McMillen, J. (1991) The politics of tourism in Queensland, in P. Carroll, K. Donohue, M. McGovern and J. McMillen (eds) *Tourism in Australia*. Harcourt Brace Jovanovich, Sydney.

Miliband, R. (1973) *The State in Capitalist Society: The Analysis of the Western System Power*. Quartet Books, London.

Mills, C.W. (1956) *The Power Elite*. Oxford University Press, New York.

Nordlinger, E. (1981) *On the Autonomy of the Democratic State*. Harvard University Press, Cambridge, MA.

Opperman, M. (1998) (ed.) *Sex Tourism and Prostitution: Aspects of Leisure, Recreation, and Work*. Cognizant Communication Corporation, Cammeray, NSW.

Pigram, J.J. and Jenkins, J.M. (1999) *Outdoor Recreation Management*. Routledge, London.

Pitts, D. (1983) Opportunity Shift: Development and Application of Recreation Opportunity Spectrum Concepts in Park Management, unpublished PhD thesis, Griffith University, Nathan Campus, Queensland.

Richter, L.K. (1989) *The Politics of Tourism in Asia*. University of Hawaii Press, Honolulu.

Szadkowski, J. (1995) *Taking a Stand for Children*. Originally published in *The Washington Times*, 16 December 1995, **www.vachss.com/av_articles/wash_ times_95.html** (accessed 19 July 2004). (Speech of Prime Minister Chuan Leekpai of Thailand, as reported in End child prostitution: report of an international consultation on child prostitution held in Bangkok, 13 and 14 June 1994. Published by ECPAT 1994.) United States Code, Section 2141a: United States National Tourism Organization as of 26 January 1998 at: **www.washingtonwatchdog.org/ documents/usc/ttl22/ch31A/sec2141a.html** .

Van de Borg, J. and Costa, P. (1996) Cultural tourism in Italy, in G. Richards (ed.) *Cultural Tourism in Europe*. CABI, UK, 215–231.

Veal, A.J. (2002) *Leisure and Tourism Policy and Planning*, 2nd edn. CABI, Wallingford.

Veal, A.J. (2003) Marxism, in J.M. Jenkins and J.J. Pigram (eds) *Encyclopedia of Leisure and Outdoor Recreation*. Routledge, London, 300–301.

Ward, R. (1958) *The Australian Legend*. Oxford University Press, London.

Wearing, S. and Huyskens, M. (2001) Moving on from joint management regimes in Australian national parks, *Current Issues in Tourism*, 2–4(4), 182–209.

Wettenhall, R. (1990) Australia's daring experiment with public enterprise, in A. Kouzmin and N. Scott (eds) *Dynamics in Australian Public Management: Selected Essays*. Macmillan, South Melbourne, 2–16.

Wheelwright, E.L. (1974) *Radical Political Economy: Collected Essays*. Australia and New Zealand Book Company, Sydney.

Wheelwright, E.L. (1978) *Capitalism, Socialism or Barbarism? The Australian Predicament: Essays in Contemporary Political Economy*. Australian & New Zealand Books, Brookvale, NSW.

Williams, A.M. and Shaw, G. (1988) Tourism policies in a changing economic environment, in A.M. Williams and G. Shaw (eds) *Tourism and Economic Development: Western European Experiences*. Belhaven Press, London, 230–239.

Part 2
Business functions applied to tourism

- This part examines tourism businesses from a functional perspective, considering the roles, operations and challenges facing a range of departments typically found in a tourism business. The reader should note that the activities of all of these departments will be found inside every tourism organisation even if the departments do not exist with the explicit names used in chapter titles.

- The purpose of this part is to help the reader become familiar with business functions, and to ensure that the importance of managing the organisation, human resources, marketing, finance, information, quality and performance are all recognised. The part also embraces a longer-term perspective and considers a range of strategic challenges facing tourism businesses.

- The part contains chapters on organisational behaviour, human resource management, marketing, finance, managing small and non-profit tourism organisations, strategy and environmental analysis, managing performance and quality, and information technology and management information systems.

- Cases included in the part are on Cathay Pacific, the Scottish Football Museum, P&O Ferries, Majorca and the Finnish Tourist Board.

Chapter 4

Organisational behaviour in tourism businesses

John Old, Coventry Business School

Learning outcomes

On completion of this chapter the reader should be able to:

- identify the internal aspects, functions and processes of organisations;
- examine different group behaviours;
- examine individual behaviours within a group;
- explain different models which classify organisational culture;
- recognise the features of different communications systems.

Overview

The success of managers and management are measured not in terms of what they achieve in a personal capacity, but what they can coordinate others to do. This requires an understanding of how organisational structures and systems function, of the behaviour of groups of people in an organisational setting, and how effective leadership and communication contribute to these processes.

Organising and organisations

By its very nature tourism is an activity that requires the coordination of a large number of separate activities – travel, accommodation, catering, financial services and so on. In a developed economy and society we take this for granted: the huge range of goods and services we have available to us not from the genius or extraordinary efforts of individuals, but from the coordinated activities of many different people.

However, it is worth noting that this coordination can come about in a number of ways. Compare, for example, travel agents and tour operators. As far as the holiday-maker is concerned, the 'package' that they buy from either may appear identical, but whereas a travel agent may 'organise' a holiday for a client by dealing with separate airlines, hotels, car hire firms, and so on – work that the final customers could, and, especially in these days of internet access, increasingly do, take on for themselves, the tour operator organises and offers a complete package to the customer. The tour operator typically 'bulk buys' flights, hotel spaces, and so on from providers, and then organises these into attractive retail packages. Some of the larger operators go further still and operate their own hotels or even airlines. More and more of the final product is actually produced 'in-house' rather than being bought in from outside and independent suppliers.

This is essentially a variation on the 'make/buy' decision which is as old as business (any business) itself. As soon as people began to trade, a decision had to be made: what things do you do for yourself, and what things do you buy in from the market – or in modern jargon, 'outsource'? This is not an 'either-or' question, but one of degree. No commercial organisation does everything for itself, no matter how self-sufficient it attempts to be. For example, you could run your own generators, to avoid reliance on an intermittent power supply – but then you would need to buy in the oil.

So *organising* can take place in a number of ways:

- by trading – buying and selling – through *markets*;
- by conscious planning, coordination and control within an *organisation*.

There are various other ways in which human activity is organised – for example, by laws, traditions, culture, and self-organisation. We shall refer to some of these later, but for now let us concentrate on the distinction between 'markets' and 'organisations'. There are crucial differences between organising through markets and organising through organisations, and two of these are the ways that people behave, and why.

Here is a simple example: a tourist attraction, such as a theme park, might alternatively hire in contractors to undertake cleaning (outsourcing: coordination through the market) or have cleaners on its own payroll. You may want to stop reading for a moment and reflect upon what the differences would be between these two arrangements, especially for the way in which the managers of the theme park manage the cleaning operation.

When outside contractors are employed, it will rapidly become clear that what is required is a 'service-level agreement', setting out in detail what is to be cleaned, and to what degree, and how frequently. In the event of a disagreement, there will probably be some sort of dispute-management procedure, either formal or informal. If this does not work, either side might take recourse to law, and/or they would simply cease to trade with each other – the theme park would hire new contractors, and the original contractors move to new customers. In all this, the theme-park managers would find themselves negotiating with the contractors, rather than simply directing them what to do.

Contrast this with the position of cleaners directly employed by the theme park, and the managers responsible for them. It is rare to find any contract of employment which would spell out in as much detail as a service-level agreement precisely what is expected from the employee, or the obligations of the employer. Employment contracts are, by their nature, deliberately 'fuzzy'. At one extreme, employees cannot do what they like, but at the other an employment relationship is not one (and in most countries, by law, cannot be) of voluntary slavery, where the employee undertakes to do anything that the employer requires. Most people find that the nature of their job changes over time without a formal change in their contract of employment, and would also accept that from time to time it is reasonable for their manager to direct them what to do – e.g. stop doing one task and move to another – rather than negotiate with them about it.

Again, consider the 'motivation' of people who are contractors, compared with employees. It is often taken for granted that 'you get what you pay for'. If we buy something, we accept that, in general terms, if we want better quality or quantity, we have to pay more for it. So, we reason, if we are paying people to do a job, then the best way to get better performance is to offer more money – for example a bonus – for successful completion. The prospect of more money is the best way of influencing people's behaviour.

Now this is very likely to be true when dealing with contractors. Again, both sides will carefully agree what is to be done: the more challenging or arduous the task the higher is likely to be the agreed contract price. And again, both sides will probably want the terms of what is required, and what is to be paid, set out in unambiguous terms. But we have already seen that this is unlikely to be the case with employees, and their 'fuzzy' contracts. And look what would happen if a manager tried to 'incentivise' better performance from employees by simply offering more money.

If the employee is told simply 'Do a better job and you'll get more money', they may reasonably ask (themselves, if not their manager) 'What does "better" mean?'. If they don't know, then it is difficult for them to improve. And if they do know, or think they know, and want the money, then they will quite reasonably concentrate on the aspects of the job that they think will be noticed, and therefore rewarded, and ignore the others. Managers may find that what started as an apparently simple idea – to offer a bonus for good performance – starts distorting the way people work. They in turn may have to increase their supervision to correct this.

And who is to judge if the job has been done 'better'? With a contractor, and a service-level agreement, this should be fairly clear, but an employee will probably depend upon the judgement of a manager. Will the manager be trusted? Furthermore, if I am a contractor, and undertake to do a job on the basis of payment by results, if I can't deliver due to circumstances beyond my control, I can hardly expect the customer still to pay up – unless that's written into the contract. But most employees are in just this position – all they can offer is increased effort; they can't guarantee increased performance. If they fear that they won't actually be able to deliver – for example because other people in the organisation may let them down – they won't be incentivised by the bonus.

All this means that effort by employees is likely to be affected by factors other than simply the amount of money on offer. This specific issue is explored in more detail in Chapter 5 on Human Resource Management, but the point here is that people's behaviour inside organisations is likely to be affected, and different, precisely because they are inside organisations. So managers need to understand some of the key features of what organisations are, how they function, and how they affect the people inside them.

What is an organisation?

We have seen that human activity can be organised in many ways, of which formal organisations are only one. So what are the features of organisations – what sets them apart? See Table 4.1 and the following sections.

People

It may seem obvious, but managers need to remember that, first and foremost, organisations comprise *people*. So much emphasis can be placed on systems and structures that this simple fact can be overlooked. Organisations are made up of *people*, and managers only achieve their ends by working through other people. Furthermore, these people can in some sense be said to be *members* of the organisation – whether as managers, workers, shareholders, or whatever. An organisation is more than simply a collection of people, even if they have a common purpose. People visiting a theme park, or staying in a holiday hotel, or flying on a charter air flight share a common purpose, but they are not 'members' of the theme park, hotel, or airline. Membership of the organisation implies that to some extent at least your behaviour is governed by its rules.

Rules

By 'rules' we mean all the structures, systems and procedures that govern the way the people within the organisation interact with each other – who does what when, how, and so on. Sometimes these may be laid down formally, for example in job descriptions

Table 4.1	Features of organisations
People	Who are the 'members' of the organisation?
Rules	Tasks, responsibilities and roles
	Patterns of communication
	Patterns of authority
Purpose	What is the official, or overt, purpose of the organisation?
	Is there an unofficial or covert purpose?
	To what extent do the members share the purpose?
Continuity	Over what time frame does the organisation operate? Is it intended to operate indefinitely?

and 'reporting lines'; sometimes they emerge informally. Either way they determine, among other things:

- the *tasks, responsibilities and roles* to be undertaken by each member. In all organised human activity, the key to efficient and productive activity is specialisation, rather than everyone trying to do everything for themselves. Sometimes this specialisation emerges in response to 'market forces', sometimes as a result of custom and tradition. In an organisation it is planned out among the members – often by way of formal *job descriptions*.
- how people *communicate* with each other – for example, verbally or in writing – or whether everyone can communicate with each other, or must go 'through channels'. This may be associated with:
- *patterns of authority* – in simple terms, who can give orders to whom – who is whose superior or subordinate. It is related to communication channels as we often refer to 'reporting lines'. In some, very 'tall' organisations there may be many layers of authority, with information having to pass through many levels to go from top to bottom of the organisation (or vice versa) while in other, very 'flat' structures one manager may be responsible for many subordinates (there is a large 'span of control') and few layers of authority. In a flat organisation there is typically much more lateral communication between people, and managers must *delegate* more, as it is more difficult to directly supervise the work of many people, rather than few.

The 'boundaries' of an organisation may be seen as between the people who are members and those who are non-members. Members are those who accept the 'rules', as defined here, and operate within their framework. Members do; non-members don't. One very practical implication of this distinction for managers is that they should remember that the rules don't bind non-members. We have already seen that, when dealing with contractors rather than employees, managers will have to negotiate their requirements rather than direct people what to do. Similarly, customers are not bound by the rules of the organisation. They feel they are due what they think they have paid for, and there are few more effective ways of antagonising, and therefore losing, customers than to insist, for example, that they must stand in line, or go to another department, or do anything else that is really for the benefit of the internal workings of the firm rather than the customer.

Acceptance of the 'rules' of the organisation is one of the most striking ways in which people's behaviour is affected by being in an organisation. They do things that can only be explained by their membership. For example, in our private lives many if not most of us would, as responsible adults, resent being told what to do by someone else; in an organisation we take it for granted. So why do we accept this, and behave this way? One reason is that to some extent we share, or at least are prepared to cooperate with, the *purpose* of the organisation.

Purpose

Organisations exist to achieve something. All these rules and structures exist for a purpose, and it is the responsibility of managers to ensure that the efforts of all the members contribute to the achievement of that purpose. The members do not necessarily have to share that purpose, but are prepared to 'go along with it' – for example, because they are paid enough, or can satisfy their own objectives through the organisation. A travel company may have objectives of corporate growth, or of becoming a major international supplier of tourism services, or quite simply of making profits. Some of its employees may not share these lofty aims, but are happy to work within the firm because of the pay on offer, or because the job offers opportunities for travel. Remembering that they can only achieve the ends of the company through other people, managers must ensure that the aims of every member of the organisation are satisfied. If people's own aims are not satisfied by their membership, they will leave; and, as already noted, an organisation without people is meaningless.

So people's behaviour in organisations is also affected by the extent to which they share the purposes of the organisation, or at least are prepared to cooperate in the achievement of those purposes, and are therefore prepared to compromise their own aims and purposes to achieve it.

Continuity

Most organisations, certainly commercial ones, do not exist for a purpose that can be completed in a given time frame – their purpose, and therefore the organisation, is ongoing. Take the most simple and stark of corporate objectives – to make profits. This usually means to make profits continually over an indefinite period ahead. Only a small minority of organisations is set up to pursue and complete a particular venture, and then disbanded. This is also likely to affect the behaviour of organisational members, as they may have an expectation that they will be associated with the organisation for a considerable period ahead – perhaps indefinitely – and therefore adjust their current behaviour accordingly. (As a crude example, your attitudes towards your work, your co-workers, your managers (and their 'authority') and the organisation itself are likely to be very different if you are employed on a very short-term contract, as compared with a permanent appointment with the prospect of working with the firm for years to come.)

Bureaucracy

It is beyond the scope of this chapter, or indeed book, to go into detail about the wide variety of forms that formal organisations may adopt; but a major influence on the behaviour of people within organisations is the extent to which the organisation is *bureaucratic*. In common parlance, the term 'bureaucracy' is usually used in a disparaging way, as it has connotations of people working slowly and inefficiently, and in a 'rulebound' way that frustrates both the customers of the organisation and its own goals. However, in the context of organisations and the behaviour of people who work in them, it simply refers to particular ways of working that may or may not contribute to efficiency. It is probably true to say that *all* organisations are bureaucratic to a greater or lesser extent, and it is difficult to imagine an organisation that does not employ some methods that can be described as 'bureaucratic'.

The simplest way to think of a bureaucratic organisation, and a metaphor that is often employed, is to imagine it as a *machine*. A machine is carefully designed to achieve a particular purpose. Each part is carefully designed to fit with every other, and (and in the context of organisations, this is a key point) if a part is faulty it can be replaced. How does this translate into organisational design?

- *Jobs and responsibilities are precisely defined.* In a bureaucracy, everyone will have not only a job title, but also a job description which clearly specifies what is expected of them. This allows the organisation to benefit to the greatest extent from the division of labour and the use of specialised skills. Individuals can concentrate on their own job, and doing them well.
- A *clear pattern of authority relationships is also clearly defined.* In simple terms, clearly defined *authority* relationships lay out who is whose superior and subordinate, or what is often now referred to as 'reporting lines'. These are usually represented as a *hierarchy*, from top management, through middle and junior management, down to clerks, operatives, and so on, and is often depicted in a formal organisation chart or 'organogram' of the type shown in Figure 4.1. Communication in this type of organisation tends to be a vertical exchange of information and instructions between superior and subordinate, rather than lateral between people at the same level, and tends to be formal – in writing, and with records kept of what was communicated to whom and by whom.
- *Impersonality.* If you look again at Figure 4.1, you will notice that the boxes contain job titles rather than people's names. Bureaucracy is based upon an impersonal approach to work, in the sense that people are supposed to relate to each other in terms of their job functions rather than their personalities. This is reinforced by the use of set procedures to carry out the work of the organisation.

These features of bureaucracy can be a major source of organisational efficiency. For example:

- Work, and especially decisions, can be speeded up, as everyone knows clearly what is expected of them, and there are rules, routines, and procedures to cover most if not all of the problems they come across.
- With clearly defined responsibilities and a clear reporting line – a superior to refer to if in doubt – people can feel confident in exercising their competence and initiative

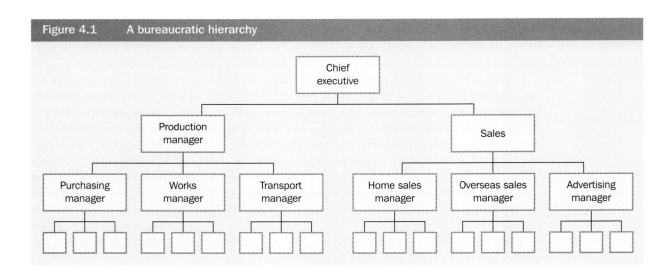

Figure 4.1   A bureaucratic hierarchy

within the defined bounds of their job. It is a mistake to think of a bureaucracy as an organisation in which 'bosses' are forever giving orders to 'underlings'. Here we can see the likeness to a machine again. If it is well designed, there is no need for the operator – or in this case, the senior manager – constantly to intervene. Bureaucracy can facilitate real delegation, as people with clearly defined jobs, and the competence and training to carry them out, can be trusted to get on with them without constant supervision. It is in the non-bureaucratic organisation that there may be a constant need for intervention. This, in turn, means there may be positive motivational effects for people working in bureaucracies, in that they feel they are trusted to do their job and are not continually being told what to do. For senior management, there is the benefit that they feel they have day-to-day control over the organisation, through its design, and have more time to spend on other matters without being constantly diverted by having to make petty interventions and decisions.

- This is particularly important where it is essential that minimum standards are achieved, all the time, and without exception. It is often said that this cramps the ability of the individual to deliver exceptional performance, but often this is not required. Flying an aeroplane is a highly skilled job, but what the organisation – and the passengers! – require is not outstanding performance 99% of the time, at the expense of a possible disastrous 'off day', but the same competent level of performance, day in and day out.

- The impersonality of the bureaucratic system can smooth interpersonal relations. You do not have to like, or even get on with, the people you work with for the organisation to function smoothly; as long as everyone performs their allotted functions, the bureaucracy should work. In superior–subordinate relations, the 'authority' of superiors does not come from their personal attributes but because of the greater responsibilities they carry, so there is a 'logic' in following their directions, and subordinates do not feel personally demeaned in doing so. Subordinate X does not carry out the instructions of manager Y because the latter is a better, or more important, person but because it is necessary for the smooth operation of the business. If their jobs were reversed, then Y would as easily follow the instructions of X. Furthermore, in many cases people do what they do not because any individual tells them what to do, but because the *rules and procedures* of the organisation require it. Rules represent the ultimate in impersonal authority in an organisation, and are the easiest type of authority for people to subject themselves to.[1]

- A further advantage of tight job descriptions and an impersonal approach to work is that when people leave an organisation they can be readily replaced (just as, again, it is easy to replace a broken part in a machine). All that is required is to find someone of equal competence (which bureaucratic recruitment and appointment procedures should ensure) and train them to be aware of their job responsibilities and the relevant rules and procedures.

- Communication is improved in a number of ways. If a problem arises that an individual does not know how to deal with, only one person needs to be consulted – the superior. And the superior has a responsibility to sort it out – or refer it still further up the organisation. Contrast this with the extreme alternative, where there are no clear reporting lines and responsibilities. Faced with such a problem, an individual may end up resorting to emailing everyone in the company. Not only is everyone then confronted with barrages of irrelevant communications, but the likely result is that the person whose problem it is receives either a number of suggestions – very likely contradictory – or none, because everyone assumes that

---

1 Provided that the rules are seen to be binding on everyone in the organisation – that no-one is viewed as 'above the law'. If there is a no-smoking policy, or dress code, or rules about private use of phones or computers, it must apply, and be seen to apply, to everyone, including senior management.

someone else will be handling it. Bureaucracies are a very good way of avoiding this, and of pinpointing responsibility.

It should be clear from this that bureaucratic working methods can be very attractive to organisations. Indeed, whenever people say 'We need to get organised' they probably mean 'we need to be more bureaucratic', at least in the sense defined here. In addition, bureaucracy *can* be very advantageous for customers and other people dealing with the organisation – run well, a bureaucracy can provide them with a smooth, efficient (and cheap!) service, deal with them impartially, and make sure any problems they have are dealt with quickly and efficiently.

However, common experience tells us that bureaucratic systems are not always efficient. The 'machine' as a whole often does not run as intended, and there can also be unfortunate effects on the behaviour of the people that work in them – in fact many of the problems with bureaucracies can be traced back to the behaviour that they give rise to. Some of the problems are the result of the system not working as intended – for example, it is badly designed, with poor or vague job descriptions or obsolete procedures. These can be addressed by a re-think and re-design, but possibly more serious problems arise not because the bureaucracy is not working as intended, but, perversely, because it is working too well. Bureaucratic methods are having their desired effect on people's behaviour and the way the organisation functions, but these effects, carried too far, have damaging consequences. For example:

- People are encouraged to concentrate on a narrow range of functions, defined by their job descriptions, and to become experts in that area. The problem with this is that this affects the way they look at problems. For example, problems with catering in a hotel are likely to be seen differently by the chef, the front desk, and an accountant, all of whom are likely to come up with different, but plausible, answers to the problem of dissatisfied guests. People are not encouraged to think 'outside the box': by definition, what is outside the box is someone else's area of expertise and responsibility. Bureaucracies emphasise the importance of doing your own, narrowly defined, job well.

- A related problem is that people working in bureaucracies are encouraged, and tend, to see 'success' in terms of the success of their own department rather than of the organisation as a whole. Again, we see the similarity to a machine: if each part functions well, then the whole will perform well. But this is not true in organisations: marketing may generate too many potential customers for the rest of the firm to handle, resulting, for example, in over-booking at a resort hotel. Subsequent customer dissatisfaction is then likely to be blamed on the failure of these other parts to keep up, rather than over-optimistic marketing.

- Just as people may come to focus on the success of their own section or department rather than that of the organisation as a whole, so they may come to pursue the rules and procedures of the organisation for their own sake rather than any benefit they confer. Different parts of the organisation then respond to each other in a ritualised and inefficient way, and customers and suppliers are dealt with as 'categories' rather than human beings with individual requirements.

Anyone who has dealt with, or worked in, a bureaucratic organisation will be familiar with such problems, and sensible management is rarely unaware of them. So why do they so commonly recur? Why isn't there, for example, more application of 'common sense'?

The problem is that the advantages and disadvantages of bureaucratic methods are, to a large degree, inseparable. Indeed, in terms of what they require of the behaviour of people in organisations, they are in many ways simply the same thing looked at in different ways. For example, people are encouraged to concentrate on their own job and become more expert at it; we cannot simultaneously require them to take a broader perspective *and* develop expertise in other areas. If we stress the use of rules to speed up decision-making and make the outcome of decisions more predictable, it would defeat the object to ask people to decide, in every instance, whether the rule should be applied or not. If a rule becomes discretionary, it ceases to be a rule.

What can make things even worse is that the 'bureaucratic' response to problems in the system is to 'apply more of the same'. For example, if the application of a rule appears to be giving rise to problems, the response will typically be to draft new, 'improved' rules. If specialists seem to ignore each other's contributions and problems, the solution may be sought in arranging meetings at which they can 'get to know each other'. It is rarely suggested that if the application of rules, or specialised job descriptions, are the problem, then the solution is to abolish rules and specialisation. So the 'solution' to the problem often simply reinforces it.

Alternatives to bureaucracy

Many organisations have sought alternatives to bureaucratic ways of doing things. As noted above, it is probably impossible to abandon bureaucratic ways of working completely, at least in modern commercial organisations, but many modern business practices show marked differences from bureaucratic 'norms'. However, in applying these the managers of organisations should be aware of what is being abandoned, and the likely effects on the performance of the organisation and the people working within it. If not, there is often an unfortunate tendency to try to recapture what has been 'lost' by the re-imposition, even unconsciously, of bureaucratic systems – which is then likely to mean that the benefits of the alternative working methods are then lost. Here are some examples:

■ *Bureaucracies emphasise hierarchy: alternatives may emphasise networks.* This means that instead of information flowing up and down the organisation through predetermined channels (and, crucially, orders flowing down) people are encouraged and expected to seek and pass information and advice to anyone else in the organisation, regardless of their departments or 'rank'. This has become particularly important in recent years, first, as firms have come to realise that their crucial competitive advantage is likely to lie in the people they employ, and, in particular, in the knowledge of these people.[2] Allowing free communication between organisational members may help maximise the use that can be made of this knowledge. Second, developments in electronic communication – email, organisational intranets, etc. – have made it more possible than ever before for this type of communication to take place. In consequence, many approaches to 'knowledge management' go beyond simply trying to identify lists of 'internal experts', or capturing and codifying the knowledge of organisational members – these are typically 'bureaucratic' approaches – and encourage this sort of network interaction.

However, recall what hierarchies can do and networks cannot. In particular, hierarchies help pinpoint responsibility. It is clear who has done something or taken a

---

2 It is rather beyond the scope of this chapter to discuss this but the argument is that with the development of markets and the increasing use of outsourcing, virtually everything that a firm needs to produce what it sells to its customers has been, or can be, 'commoditised'; that is, a competitor can go to the market and buy it. The unique skills and knowledge of the members of the organisation – including 'tacit knowledge' that people may not even be aware that they have – may be the only assets that a competitor cannot readily duplicate.

decision, and, if they have sought formal written advice, what the basis of their actions was. In a network actions and decisions tend to emerge from a process of continuous and often informal interaction that is often virtually impossible to disentangle after the event, and this may encourage people to act irresponsibly. A further problem with networks is that they only work effectively if people are comfortable with this way of working. By definition, networks take little account of people's formal status within an organisation: you are encouraged to communicate freely with others, however 'senior' or 'junior' to you they may appear to be. This way of working may run counter to the culture of the organisation. People may be inhibited in giving advice to others who appear to be their superiors, or seeking it from those who appear to be subordinate. We return to the influences of culture later in this chapter.

■ *Bureaucracies fit people to jobs: an alternative is to fit jobs to people.* As noted earlier, every position within a bureaucracy typically has not only a title, but a job description which sets out what is expected of the post-holder. Appointment or promotion to such a post then usually depends on having the skills and attributes necessary to carry out those tasks. (This is epitomised by modern recruitment procedures, which often involve drawing up both a 'job description' and a 'person description' of the type of applicant sought – in other words the characteristics of the person likely to be successful have been determined in advance.) An alternative approach is to recruit people who appear to have interesting characteristics or abilities, and then try to find ways of using them effectively.

Such an approach can appear attractive as a way of maximising the amount of internal expertise available to the organisation, which, as we have already noted, may be its greatest source of competitive advantage. In addition, by offering people the greatest chance to contribute to the success of the organisation, it can have very strong *motivational* effects (see Chapter 5). One of the strongest criticisms of bureaucracies is that they are too restrictive on the individual – they prevent people from being creative, and can leave them feeling like 'small cogs in a big machine'. Even people who are initially well disposed towards their work and the organisation, may feel they are being controlled to such an extent that they may become apathetic or even hostile towards their work. On the other hand, as the similarity of the organisation to a machine is undermined various benefits are lost; for example, the departure of a single individual who cannot be smoothly replaced by someone identical, or at least very similar, can be very disruptive.

■ *Bureaucracies rely on written communication and formal records: alternatives may emphasise verbal communication and informality.* There are advantages and disadvantages to the different types of communication, and we deal with these separately below.

■ *Bureaucracies emphasise the individual: alternatives might emphasise groups and teamwork.* Bureaucratic structures are based on the duties and responsibilities of the individual – which is why it is so important to understand the responses of the individual to working in this sort of environment. But many organisations rely on teamwork to achieve their ends, and this can have a profound effect on people's behaviour. This is explored more fully in a later section of this chapter, but at this stage a couple of examples will suffice: there may be a *positive* effect on people's motivation as a result of 'team spirit', but on the other hand there may be a *negative* effect, as working in a team gives people the opportunity to put in less than full effort, secure in the confidence that they can 'free-ride' on the backs of others and/or that their shirking will not be detected. The important point to note at this stage is that groups of people do not behave simply as collections of individuals – they have a psychology and behaviour of their own.

When bureaucracy may be appropriate and when it may not

It is impossible to be dogmatic and say when a more, or less, bureaucratic way of working may be more appropriate. It depends on a variety of factors, such as:

- the type of work;
- the size of the organisation;
- the environment of the organisation.

Bureaucratic methods and structures tend to be most effective when the job to be done is predictable and/or repetitive and/or can be reduced to routines. So, for example, the work of mass-catering restaurants is often set up this way, as are the procedures for the booking of package holidays. In contrast, an effective tour guide on a safari holiday must have the flexibility to adapt to changing conditions, to be responsive to the changing needs of travellers, and so on.

Research has indicated that the larger the organisation, the greater is likely to be the relationship between 'bureaucracy' and business success, and that, conversely, smaller firms tend to be able to use non-bureaucratic approaches more successfully.[3]

The 'environment' of the organisation includes the type of customer, the competition and the technology of the industry, as well as the legal and regulatory framework in which it operates. If this is very stable, or is expected to change only slowly, then it is possible to plan ahead, anticipate problems and challenges, and reduce much of the working of the organisation to literally predictable routines. If not, then greater flexibility is required, and the advantages of bureaucratic approaches are fewer, and the disadvantages greater.

Of course, all these are likely to be related. An industry with a highly predictable environment, and predictable and routine types of work, is likely to be one dominated by large and more bureaucratic organisations. And the opposite is likely to be true where change is rapid and unpredictable, and people are expected to work in flexible ways.

It is apparent that there is no single 'right' way to structure and run an organisation; both bureaucratic and non-bureaucratic approaches have their attractions and drawbacks. Many organisations try to capture the advantages of both ways of working, for example, by:

- *Organising different departments in different ways* – for example, in cleaning and safety maintenance activities it is imperative that at least minimum standards are maintained all the time, so here emphasis is placed on rules, routines and standards. In other activities – particularly 'front-of-house' jobs where one is coming directly into contact with the customer or where rapid responses to changing circumstances are required – it is important to adopt more flexible working methods.
- *Splitting a large organisation into smaller units*, each of which can have their own distinct methods of working.
- *Varying the degree of control over different functions in the organisation.* In their 1980s best seller *In Search of Excellence* Peters and Waterman identified one of the characteristics of 'excellent' organisations as 'simultaneous tight–loose properties', that is they kept very tight control over certain key activities while allowing much

---

3 People whose work experience has been with larger organisations tend to have seen the advantages of routines, clear job descriptions, defined reporting lines, and so on, and therefore make the (to them) quite reasonable assumption that this is the 'right way' to do things, whatever the size of the organisation. In contrast, people whose experience is of smaller organisations often hold the opposite view. Both, of course, are partially right – but it is often the former who write the textbooks!

greater freedom to others. A problem for the individual working in such circumstances is that sometimes they can find themselves expected to adhere strictly to procedures – for example, in recording financial transactions – whereas at other times they are expected to use their own initiative. Psychologically, this may be very difficult, and instead they may find themselves either looking to apply rules where none exist or ignoring them when they do. Once again, the *culture* of the organisation is likely to be important here.

A 'systems' perspective on organisational design

The fact that in reality we come across a number of different types of organisation, some more bureaucratic, some less, and yet they can all be successful, does not mean that any type of organisation can be successful in any situation – that organisational design is irrelevant. As we have just seen, there are a number of different factors that could make more (or less) bureaucratic structures appropriate. The problem is trying to decide which factors are more important in which circumstances. It is all very well being able to explain after the event why one approach was successful and another failed – managers need some sort of framework, or aid to decision-making, which helps them make a sensible decision about organisational design in advance.

This is where *systems theory* can help. One of the lessons of the systems approach is that you cannot understand a system simply by analysing all its parts, and you cannot design an effective system simply by aggregating a load of parts, or subsystems, that look effective or efficient in isolation – you have to examine how what happens in one part affects the others. This is true, for example, in automobile design – a car is much more than a chassis, power train, and body shell designed independently and welded together.

The same is true in organisations. You cannot design, for example, the 'reporting lines', the rewards system, and the technical systems in isolation from each other. (For example, you cannot simply bolt together a reward system based upon purely individual performance-related pay schemes, an organisation structure that stresses teamwork, and a technical production process whose output is actually largely independent of effort, whether by individuals or teams, but is governed more by the laws of physics.)

But managers taking a systems perspective also need to be aware of *feedback* within their systems. *Positive* feedback tends to reinforce effects, *negative* feedback damps them down. You can design your system to encourage behaviour which helps the organisation reach its objectives, and discourage that which deflects or diverts it. As we saw in the discussion of compliance with rules, the more impersonal a rule, and the more that the rule appears simply to be the product of logic, rather than the whim of a manager, the more likely it is to be followed. And sometimes it is not necessary to articulate rules at all, but simply to design a system in a way that makes certain patterns of behaviour appear more sensible, or simply easier. So, for example, rather than order people to do something in a particular way, or lay down rules about how it should be done, if a system is designed so that one way makes things very easy, and others make it difficult, then people will tend to take the easy route. It is when orders, rules, and organisational structures seem to conflict with the intuitive or easiest ways of working that they are likely to run into resistance and cease to be effective.

This can be seen in the design of manufacturing systems: rather than order people to do a job in a particular way, the design of the tools and the workspace may simply make that the easiest way to do the job, and others much more difficult, or even impossible. Offices and other workplaces can be designed in such a way that people naturally move through them in an efficient way, without the need for instructions about which doors or stairs to use, and no-one gives it a second thought. It is when such 'control' appears arbitrary, and the worker feels he or she can do the job much more effectively another way, that dissatisfaction grows and performance drops. It is at this point that management should consider, for example, allowing workers to take more control over not just the performance but the design of their work, or at least open up meaningful two-way *communication* (see later in this chapter) to help workers understand the logic of the way they are being required to work.

Open systems and customers

One interesting extension of systems thinking is that it can be extended to take into account people who are not formally members of the organisation, such as customers. Organisations are not 'closed systems' – they are 'open systems' which interact with their environment, affecting and being affected by it. We saw earlier that one of the problems with the 'rules' of an organisation – any organisation, not just bureaucracies – is that there is a tendency to try to enforce these rules on non-members (such as customers) or at least to expect the latter to comply with them. And, of course, very often non-members don't see why they should, and become irritated at this – for example, at insistence that they deal with a particular department or official, or stand in line, when they cannot see the point of this.

But if the customer can see that there are personal benefits in going along with the 'rules' (or doesn't even recognise that there are rules), then this resistance disappears, and the customer can be integrated into the system. For example, modern airport terminal designers are increasingly learning the lesson about attention to layout in managing passenger flows through terminals. If the 'flow' through appears logical to the customer (e.g. they don't find themselves doubling back) they go along with it; they, and their behaviour, have been integrated into the system.

In contrast, consider the example of call centres. For many companies, their call centres are the most important way that they come into contact with prospective or existing customers. Yet a report in the UK (Citizens Advice Bureau, 2004) found that a third of all customers were dissatisfied with the service they received from call centres. This is a literally frighteningly high level of customer dissatisfaction for any business. Yet one of the original competitive reasons why firms introduced call centres was to provide a *better* level of service – to give the customer access to a 'one-stop shop' for all their enquiries at the end of a telephone line. Unfortunately, it appears that many organisations have lost sight of this and can see only the potential cost savings, especially when allied to technological devices such as 'option menus'. Among the most frequent complaints found by the Citizens Advice Bureau were inability to talk to a person (as opposed to a machine) and the number of options on menus, along with the concomitant increase in time taken to resolve an enquiry. This is an example of where firms are attempting to impose systems designed for internal 'efficiency' on outsiders – customers – and the latter at best feel irritated and resentful, and at worst take their business elsewhere. Firms in a competitive environment that rely on call centres need to ask: what does the customer get out of this?

Compare this with (well-designed) websites that allow customers to browse, compare options and make choices. They serve the same purpose as call centres of contributing to internal efficiency, and similarly integrate and to an extent control the customers, but the latter actually welcome them, and even enjoy using them, as they can see something of benefit to themselves and not just the firm.

The same logic can be applied in other areas where it is helpful to control customer behaviour. For example, if a theme park finds it necessary to have customers park a considerable distance from the attraction, the trek from the parking space can be turned into a pleasurable experience in itself by providing an exciting transfer, for example by monorail or themed shuttle. The tedium of queuing can to some extent be reduced or even removed if the queue itself becomes a pleasurable experience – with plenty to look at, or other entertainment.

Groups and teams

So far we have tended to concentrate upon how organisations, and the people who work in them, are likely to behave when the emphasis is on coordinating the activities of numbers of individuals. But we have noted that many organisations now emphasise groupwork and teams, and that it is important to understand that groups are more than simply collections of individuals, and often display their own characteristics and even 'psychology'. An example of this which drew popular attention in the media in 2004 is 'groupthink'. This is a phenomenon in which people who, *as individuals,* may entertain doubts about the correctness of a particular course of action, the accuracy of information, etc., abandon these doubts when they come together through a process of mutual reassurance – if everyone else thinks it's right, then it must be – mustn't it?

■ Characteristics of work groups and teams

It is useful to think of a group as a collection of people whose behaviour affects each other in some way – who are *interdependent*. This interdependence leads to a number of effects – some of them (known as 'process gains') are helpful for the effectiveness of the group and its work. Others (known as 'process losses') detract from it. For example, most organisations hope that working in groups will build 'team spirit' or *'esprit de corps'*, in which people mutually motivate each other; but there is also a danger that people may feel inhibited when working with others.

Some effects may lead to both process gains and process losses. For example, a group, especially if it has been working together for some time, will develop *norms* – standards of behaviour which are expected from the group members. These can be more powerful than formal rules established by the organisation. They can help maintain and improve performance – people don't want to let down the other members of the group – but they can also undermine or deflect it. For example, if the group has views about how work should be done which differ from those of the organisation, the group norms may be so strong that its members persist in doing what they want rather than what the organisation requires.

This is why some organisations emphasise the individual rather than the group – for example in the use of incentive schemes based upon individual performance related pay (PRP) and performance management. Similarly, a high degree of group *cohesiveness* is not necessarily beneficial from the point of view of the organisation. Cohesiveness reflects how much the members value their membership of the group and the extent to which they share its norms. It tends to be stronger the more similar the members of the group are – for example in age, culture, or experience. It tends to make group norms more extensive and powerful, which might be beneficial to the organisation if these are aligned with what the organisation wants – but not if they conflict.

Cohesiveness also tends to instil a degree of *conformity* among group members – people tend to moderate their behaviour, and even their thought processes and beliefs, to come in line with those of the group as a whole. This can help with organisational discipline, but sometimes a degree of *deviance* is actually desirable; for example, to counter the 'groupthink' mentioned earlier, someone has to be prepared to challenge the accepted views of the group. *Creativity* rarely arises in a situation where people are encouraged to think the same.

There are various degrees of interdependence in groupwork, which in turn influence the development of group cohesiveness, group norms, and so on. The simplest form of interdependence is *'pooled interdependence'* (see Thompson, 1967). Each member of the group can work as an individual, but the outcome depends upon them all performing their own work satisfactorily when it is all brought together. Much of the work of a hotel is of this nature – cleaning, front desk, catering, laundry, etc., can all to some extent work on their own, but the satisfaction of the guests will be dependent on the totality of their experience of their stay. It is not, of course, necessary for people actually to work together as a group at all to reap the benefits of pooled interdependence, but there may be process gains if having them work together – for example, in an open-plan office – helps motivate each other, if only by discouraging slacking. If nothing else, groupwork can help save management costs, as people are watching each other and are likely to be aware before the boss if someone is not 'pulling their weight'.

The social interaction involved in working together can also have both its advantages and disadvantages. Time could be wasted on gossip; inefficient group norms may develop – more reasons why some organisations have deliberately avoided groupwork. But, on the other hand, preventing this interaction can cause problems: for example, people may be simply duplicating each other's work without knowing it, or trying to solve similar problems. Bringing them together physically can not only help overcome or avoid such problems, but can also remove feelings of social isolation. Many organisations whose staff typically work on their own, or are dispersed geographically, make a point of trying to bring them together on a regular basis. Teleworkers can be brought into the office, while organisations such as those involved in the tourism industry, whose workers may be scattered round the world, arrange periodic company meetings.

With pooled interdependence, one person's work does not directly depend upon that of another. But often one individual must complete his or her work before another can start or complete theirs. For example, a charter package flight cannot operate effectively unless the passenger bookings have been made, the airport slots booked, and so on. This is termed *'sequential'* interdependence. There are many process gains to be had from sequential interdependence – for example, the ability of people to specialise – but a potential loss is that the whole system is only as effective as its 'weakest link' – slow or inefficient work by one affects all.

The highest degree of interdependence is *'reciprocal interdependence'*, where everyone's performance depends on everyone else's. This, of course, is the essence of true teamwork, where success depends on the performance of everybody, and especially their willingness to support and cover for colleagues who are underperforming. Reciprocal interdependence offers the greatest opportunities for process gains, through mutual support and motivation, but the possibilities of process losses are also at their greatest. The most striking arise from *'social loafing'* – people taking it easy and relying on the efforts of others to cover for them. This can actually be rational behaviour if team spirit is weak – after all, as success depends on the efforts of the whole group, and individual slacking is (by definition) virtually undetectable, if the rest of the group is performing, why should any individual bother to try hard? And if they aren't – again, why should they be the only one trying? It is very easy for such groups to give rise to frustration, ill feeling and poor motivation. You might note that the potential for, and hence likelihood of, social loafing increases the less the chances of it being detected. This in turn depends on the size of the group, and it is doubtful if very large groups can really be organised as true teams.

Much of the research on effective groups and teams has highlighted two further key variables that affect their performance and the behaviour of their members:

- *the stage of development of the group;*
- *the roles played by group members.*

Work on the stages of group development was popularised by Tuckman and Jensen (1977), who suggested that very different performance and behaviour would be expected as a group moved through stages from its formation, through interpersonal conflict before norms and roles became clearly established, through to a period of effective performance, before (in some cases) the group outlived its usefulness, and 'adjourned' – but its effects could still be felt as former members carried over the norms, beliefs and working practices of the group to their future work. (A cycle described as 'forming' – 'storming'– 'norming' – 'performing'– 'adjourning' – 'mourning'.) Other researchers differ in their views on the nature of group development – for example, groups with different cultures may behave differently – but the general point remains that a group, and its members, may behave very differently over time. In a newly formed group, norms have not yet had a chance to develop and can be strongly influenced by group members and their managers as they develop, whereas in a long-established group, powerful norms may have been developed years before and continue to influence the behaviour of members, even if few (if any) of the original members are left.

There is also no universal agreement on the range of roles that need to be undertaken in an effective group (despite the popularity with some firms of psychometric tests which purport to show the role with which one would feel most comfortable). But there is widespread agreement that an effective group does depend on people undertaking a balance of roles – for example, people who are good at planning, people who are good at seeing that deadlines are met, people with good interpersonal skills who can help the social interaction of the group, and so on. One problem for the individuals involved can be if they are involved in more than one group and are expected to perform different roles in each. A natural reaction may be to try to take on a similar role in different groups, giving rise to friction – or alternatively becoming psychologically confused by these conflicting requirements and lapsing into ineffectiveness in both groups.

Leadership

One role that may be required in many groups is that of a leader – someone to influence and direct the activities of the group members (but not in all groups; some groups, for example of skilled and dedicated individuals, may not need a leader, but every leader needs a group of followers!). The traditional view of leadership was that leaders were a particular 'type', or possessed particular characteristics such as confidence or intelligence that set them apart, while later research suggested that effective leaders were those who paid high and equal attention to both organising the work, and motivating the group members. However, today emphasis tends to be put on finding an appropriate style of leadership for a particular situation. Different types of group member ('followers') or different tasks may require quite different types of leader, if indeed they require active leadership at all. (Recall that a well organised bureaucracy can both organise the work, and encourage people to exercise their initiative, without the active intervention of a manager, or 'leader' at all.) John Adair (1984), for example, has argued that the leader's role will vary according to what is most important for the success of the group – is it motivating or directing the individual members, helping the group as a whole to function, or organising and shaping the job to be done?

Much modern leadership theory analyses which leadership style is appropriate for which contingencies (type of follower, work, etc.). Typically it considers where leaders should pay high attention to the people in the group, or to the work, or to both, or to neither. Consider these four situations:

Group 1. A group of young and inexperienced employees brought together for the first time. They are unfamiliar with the work, and probably lack confidence in their ability to do it. (Perhaps a group of young people brought together on short-term contracts to work in a tourist resort over a peak season.)

Group 2. A group of more experienced employees, reasonably well motivated, but confronted with unfamiliar problems. (Perhaps experienced workers on permanent contracts, brought together at the opening of a new resort attraction.)

Group 3. A similar group of skilled and experienced workers, but now working on problems that are familiar and to a large extent routinised. (Perhaps the technical crew of a cruise ship.)

Group 4. A group of highly skilled employees brought together to work on a new project. They probably know more about all aspects of the job to be done than their manager, find their work highly challenging and motivating, and are strongly committed to the success of the project.

A style of leadership appropriate and successful for one group is unlikely to work as well with another. Before looking at the suggestions below, you might find it useful to consider which way you would attempt to 'lead' these different groups.

Group 1 might respond best to a 'task-oriented' or even fairly authoritarian leader, who would personally take all the responsibility and clearly direct the subordinates in what to do. *Group 2*, while still welcoming clear directions, would probably respond well to a leader who paid high attention to the 'human' aspects of the job, expressing interest and concern for their individual needs and the effective functioning of the group. This latter is also probably true for *Group 3*, though they would need much less direction about the job itself. *Group 4* probably don't require 'leadership' from their manager at all – they are more concerned that their manager gets them the resources to do their job.

There are other 'contingencies' which can make a particular style more appropriate – for example:

- the *power* of the leader to get compliance with their ideas (e.g. the power to reward, or the respect in which they are held by their subordinates);
- the existing *relationships* of leader and followers (if these are poor, the leader may feel they need to spend time on improving these; if good, the leader may feel there is more chance of followers trusting them);
- the *speed* with which decisions need to be taken – is there time for a leader to consult with subordinates, or do they have to act quickly?
- and, when *decisions* have to be taken, will involving subordinates in decision-making improve the quality of the decisions – either because they make useful suggestions or because, having been involved, they feel more committed to seeing the decision through?

Some modern research on leadership draws an interesting distinction between '*transactional*' and '*transformational*' leadership. 'Transactional' leaders, it is argued, tend to work with the followers – their needs, hopes, abilities, etc. – as they are, and then try to clarify the goals to be achieved and provide the followers with what they need by way of guidance, encouragement, reward, and so on. The 'transformational' leader, in contrast, tries to build up the self-esteem of the group, inspire its members to achieve outcomes that they would not previously have thought possible, to transcend their own self-interest for the sake of the group, and to share a vision of what the organisation can achieve and become. Transformational leaders try to build up relationships, especially of trust, with their followers, and then seek to inspire them, for example, by taking personal risks, engaging in unusual activities, and so on. The two styles are not exclusive, but it has been suggested that transformational leadership may augment what is achieved through transactional approaches. In addition, there may be circumstances where it performs much better, for example, in seeing through a major organisational change, though in other circumstances it could be less effective or even dangerous (for example, because attention to necessary short-term detail is sacrificed to pursuing the long-term 'vision').

One further key variable that affects not only the appropriate style of leadership but also the behaviour of people in groups, and indeed in organisations generally, is the *'culture'*, both of the organisation, and of the wider environment and society in which it operates.

Culture

Most of us are familiar with the way that even simple things, such as the way people greet each other, or eat, or the importance they attach to punctuality or exchanges of gifts, can vary between different countries, and 'culture' is often defined as 'the way things are done round here'. However, this is a great over-simplification. The most significant differences between cultures are not the obvious 'practices' that can be directly observed, but the thought processes – especially the subconscious thought processes – that underlie these. Geert Hofstede (1991), one of the best-known researchers on differences between national cultures, at least as far as they affect organisational behaviour, has compared culture with the software on computers, likening it to a collective programming that then distinguishes groups of people from each other.

It is now widely accepted that both organisations and countries can exhibit variations of culture that can have a powerful influence on the way people behave. There may also be 'occupational' cultures; for example, an engineer, accountant, or doctor may have similar working practices and ways of thinking in different organisations and countries. As tourism businesses, by their nature, tend to operate in a number of different countries, both national and organisational cultures are likely to be significant factors in shaping their organisational behaviour.

National culture

Hofstede has identified five largely independent 'dimensions' of national cultures:[4]

'Individualism'. In some societies (e.g. the USA and the UK) emphasis is placed upon individual achievement and responsibility. In others (e.g. Japan, Colombia and Pakistan) much more emphasis is given to collective efforts.

'Uncertainty avoidance'. To what extent do people in a particular culture feel comfortable with risk or the unusual, including unconventional ideas or behaviour? Hofstede rated countries such as Sweden and Singapore as being 'low' on this dimension, that is members of those national cultures were fairly tolerant towards uncertainty. Greece, Mexico and Japan were rated 'high'.

'Power distance'. All societies have inequalities of wealth, power, and so on. A culture 'high' on this scale not only accepts these differences but also pays respect to them. People with power are expected to use it, and others defer to this authority. Status, titles, and rank are highly regarded. Hofstede classified countries such as France, India and Hong Kong high on this scale; Australia, Israel and Denmark low.

'Masculinity'. Hofstede found that, across all 40 countries in his work, there were beliefs and values that were more commonly held by men than women – for example that assertiveness is a virtue, that performance and achievement rather than the quality of life are important, and that men should take the lead in society rather than there be equality of the sexes. The 'masculinity' dimension then measures to what extent these views were held by *both* sexes in a particular national culture. In simplified terms, a

---

4 'Independent' in the sense that they do not vary directly with each other, and therefore any combinations of them are at least theoretically possible.

national culture that is rated 'high' on this dimension (e.g. Japan, Ireland, USA) tends to place a high value on the acquisition of material wealth; a country rated 'low' (e.g. Sweden, Thailand) places more value on personal relationships and the 'quality of life'.

'*Long term v. short-term orientation*'. Long-term orientation cultures typically value long-term commitments and respect for tradition. East Asian cultures typically score much more highly on this than Europe or North America.[5]

One of the implications of Hofstede's research is that management ideas and techniques that may work well in one country do less well in another. Schemes for performance-related pay that emphasise the individual are more likely to succeed in cultures that are high on individualism and masculinity than those which are low on these characteristics; a 'participative' style of leadership that involves people and invites them to put forward their ideas is likely to be less successful in a culture that has high power distance, where authority is respected and bosses are expected to take the responsibility for making decisions. Bureaucratic systems appeal to cultures with a strong uncertainty avoidance; more fluid structures may be appropriate elsewhere.

Organisational culture

There are several well-known theories of organisational culture. As with models and theories of national cultures, the common theme of these theories is that culture is more than simply what you can observe or 'how things are done round here'; for example, whether people wear business suits to work, or are commonly on first-name terms. Rather, these practices arise from a common shared mindset among the members of the organisation. As with national cultures, the practices and the mindsets are self-reinforcing; things are done a certain way because the organisational members assume that is the way to do things, and the more they are done that way the more people come to assume that it is the right way. But in addition, there is a further reinforcement that does not apply to national cultures. People can *choose* which organisations to belong to, so an organisation with a particular culture will attract people whose existing mindset is suited by it.

Miles and Snow (1978) argue that the objectives, strategies and systems of an organisation all reflect its underlying corporate culture. They distinguish between '*Defenders*', '*Prospectors*' and '*Analysers*'.

'*Defender*' cultures find change threatening and therefore pursue strategies that promise continuity and security. They seek to perfect and protect existing products and market positions. These strategies are underpinned by bureaucratic systems and methods.

In contrast '*Prospector*' cultures seek out change, looking to exploit new markets and opportunities. Internally there will be an emphasis on flexibility and decentralisation.

'*Analysers*' fall somewhere in between, seeking to match new opportunities to the existing shape of the business. Internally there is likely to be a strong emphasis on planning, and complex integrating mechanisms (such as product managers) to coordinate the different parts of the firm.

Two of the important points made by Miles and Snow are:

- *There is no 'best' culture*. Different cultures work best for different product and market strategies. The culture has to fit with the strategy, and vice versa.
- *Culture is often self-reinforcing*. Successful pursuit of a particular strategy (underpinned by a suitable culture) will tend to lead to the further pursuit of the strategy and solidification of the culture in the future, while the organisational systems and routines – e.g. what sort of person to recruit – will be confirmed by the success of the strategy.

---

5 British readers may be interested to know that Hofstede rated the UK as high on individualism and masculinity, low on power distance and long-term orientation, and moderate on uncertainty avoidance.

Charles Handy (1991) has popularised the idea (originally put forward by Harrison (1972)) that organisational cultures can be typified as:

'Power' (e.g. the small entrepreneurial firm). Here the organisation revolves around one or a few people who control all its resources and there is little emphasis on formal procedures and job descriptions. People act on the basis of direct instructions from the 'power-holders' or, in their absence, on the basis of what subordinates know, or believe, the power-holders would want. Jobs are ill-defined; decisions are made quickly. Speed is often possible as people are often able to decide what to do on their knowledge of 'the boss' and what he or she wants, so formal communication and instructions are not necessary. This type of culture is typical both of small businesses – for example small hotels – and also of some political dictatorships!

'Role' (e.g. the classic bureaucracy). Here the emphasis is on doing your own job in the correct way, following the laid-down procedures of the organisation. There is an emphasis on rationality, order and predictability. This culture fits well with 'bureaucratic' structures and procedures.

'Task' (e.g. emphasis on new technologies, project teams). The emphasis is on problem solution, and harnessing human and other resources to tackling a succession of new and unpredictable challenges. You do not expect to concentrate simply on your own role, but bring your skills to bear wherever they help solve the problems of the organisation. This culture is often found in organisations where teamwork and project-based operations are common, for example where there is a continual emphasis on developing or improving markets and products.

'Person' (where individuals have a high degree of autonomy). In the first three cultures the individual is subordinate to the organisation. Here the picture is reversed – the organisation is there to support the work of (typically highly-skilled) individuals. Examples include medical general practices and some University departments.

Case 4.1	A party game – what does someone do for a living?

Ask someone what they do for a living. Suppose they work at a local hotel, 'The Beeches', proprietor Mr Chadwick. How do they reply to your question?

'I work for Mr Chadwick' = Power culture
'I work at The Beeches' = Role culture
'I'm in catering' = Task culture
'I'm a chef, and a ****** good one' = Person culture

Communication

'Why won't people do what we want?' is a common complaint of management about their workforce, with the implicit answer that this is due to wilful disobedience or even stupidity. More often the answer lies in a 'failure of communication', but what does this actually mean?

A basic model of communication

Communication comprises a *sender*, a *message* and a *recipient*. 'Failure to communicate' could have its source in any or all of these. For example, if I am attempting to talk to someone, the message may not get through because I am not talking loudly or clearly enough, because the message is unclear, or because they are not listening or misinterpret the message.

In organisations today, there is a previously unparalleled number of lines of communication – written, spoken, visual, paper, electronic, etc. The problem is that often this proliferation of 'media' has meant that, far from becoming clearer, communication has become more confusing. As an example, when all communication had to be written, it was customary to use very standard forms to transmit information. This may have seemed slow and bureaucratic, but could have the advantage that the information was recorded in an unambiguous way – with a standard wording, both sender and receiver would know what the message meant. Voice communication or rapidly-composed emails increase the possibility of confusion as to the content of messages and what action the receiver is supposed to take.

Take a very simple message from a manager to a secretary – a verbal request to 'check the mail'. What is the receiver supposed to do? See if the mail has arrived? Report back whether it has? Open it? If so, are they supposed to respond to the contents? And if so, how?

Ways to improve communication

Let us take the original request to 'check the mail'. There are a number ways in which this piece of 'communication' can be improved:

- Include the context in the message. By 'context' we mean the situation in which the recipient receives the message. Sometimes the context is so clear that the recipient knows what to do. For example, in bureaucratic organisations there may be a requirement that on receiving a particular message (e.g. bookings for next month) a particular individual (e.g. the catering manager) is expected to place orders for certain quantities of food. Here it is not necessary to include the 'context', as the recipient knows what to do when the figures are communicated. But often it is not clear, so the message can be clarified by indicating what needs to be done. In the case of our 'check the mail' message, it might be expanded to: 'Please check the mail – I'm looking out for that confirmation from the coach company – if it's not there, please phone them and ask what is going on'.
- Allow, or even encourage, two-way communication. Do not be tempted to say 'Just do it!' Allowing people to query or clarify the message helps them to understand what is required of them, and might, for example, evince the information that the bus company confirmation has just been received.
- Consider using face-to-face communication. We do not just communicate through what we say but also how we say it. Not only our tone of voice, but our 'body language' can convey, for example, the urgency of a message.
- Communicate to several people at once, for example through a group meeting. For example, 'If Zak would check the post and check if the confirmation is through from the bus company, and then let Ash know, Ash can get on to the hotel and confirm the itinerary with them.' Everyone is then made more aware of the context, and in addition can share ideas and problems.

Appropriate types of communication

Some methods and media of communication are better suited to some purposes than others. For example, detailed information is probably better transmitted in written form – either a memo or an email so that both sender and recipient have an exact copy (though it might be followed up by a verbal inquiry to check that it has been received, understood and acted upon). Alternatively, verbal communication might use very precise technical terminology – not for the sake of using 'jargon' but because this has a precise meaning for both sides (as with air traffic control instructions to pilots). If two-way communication is important, then small face-to-face meetings are probably best; if it is enough that a message is made quickly available to all then a round-robin email or notice might suffice.

The pattern and form of communication needs also to be appropriate in the wider context of the organisation. For example, people working in a bureaucracy are likely to expect, and be more comfortable with, written communication through set channels. Two-way communication is likely to be inhibited if managers are used to employing a directive style of leadership. Open two-way communication is more likely to flourish in a task-oriented rather than role-oriented culture.

Structure, behaviour, culture and communication – how they all come together

It should be clear from the last paragraph that organisational structure, culture, leadership, communication and so on are all interdependent and cannot be dealt with in isolation. For example, a bureaucratic and hierarchic organisation is likely to go hand-in-hand with a role culture, formal written communication, and one-to-one communication between people as office-holders. In contrast, a project-based organisation is likely to have a task culture, to emphasise groups and teams, and exhibit a high degree of face-to-face verbal communication.

Either of these combinations, and others, may be equally appropriate, but in different situations. The important point is that, as management 'fads' come and go, managers realise the importance of seeing how these different aspects, determinants and outcomes of organisational behaviour fit together. For example, it is meaningless and probably counter-productive to announce that the organisation is to take a team approach to work and problem solving if there is still an emphasis on hierarchy, strict job descriptions and formal written communication.

Case 4.2 Managing a cruise liner in the twenty-first century

The cruise industry has changed dramatically from the days when a cruise was seen as a holiday only for the very rich. While some cruise companies still attempt to recreate the ambience of those days, with an emphasis on opulence and formality, the market has now developed greatly in terms of both the target customer and the product on offer. Whereas in the 1970s, a typical cruise ship would carry up to 800 passengers, and weigh 20,000 tons, today vessels over 70,000 tons and carrying more than 2000 passengers are becoming common. In addition, the product on offer has changed: whereas once the emphasis had been on the exotic nature of the ports-of-call, today as much emphasis or more is placed upon the on-board experience, and the modern cruise liner is best viewed as a floating self-contained resort.

For example, one such liner, at a relatively modest 40,000 tons, accommodates over 1500 passengers and employs some 500 crew who are organised into a number of departments, all reporting ultimately to the captain:

Technical: this is primarily the bridge and engine room, responsible for the actual safe running and navigation of the ship. Officers are seamen with considerable experience, often in other branches of civil and/or military seafaring. Senior officers are mainly British and North American, with some Eastern Europeans. This department also handles technical activities peculiar to cruise liners, such as maintaining and cleaning the ship's pools, and also safety and security, as well as general maintenance. This includes maintaining the ship's appearance externally, such as by touching up the external paintwork, at every port-of-call.

Hotel department: as its name suggests, this department handles the functions that would be associated with a large hotel on shore – guest relations, catering and bars, and cabin services.

Entertainment: today's passengers expect a wide range of on-board entertainment (shows, games, etc.) as well as the opportunities for organised visits to ports-of-call. This department is headed by the cruise director, who has extensive experience in the entertainment industry, as do many of his staff (musicians, dancers, etc.).

Medical: the ship has its own medical centre, with qualified doctors and nurses.

Business: this department liaises with all others and also with the head office of the cruise company, chiefly with regard to financial matters (for example weekly running costs and expenses, budgets, etc.). The chief business officer has onshore business and accountancy experience.

Crew typically work (during the summer months) eight-week tours of duty, during which time they work, or are at least nominally available for work, seven days a week and for over 12 hours a day. From spring to autumn the ship operates cruises in the Mediterranean; at other times of the year it undertakes cruises in the Caribbean and off South America.

The organisation structure that coordinates all these activities is very hierarchical, with all reporting lines leading back to the captain, who retains overall responsibility for all activities on the ship. For example, even when a local pilot is used for entering or exiting port, the status of the pilot is only as a temporary senior officer with the role of advising, not directing, the captain. A great deal of the ship's activities is reduced to routines which are captured in formal procedures, rotas and rosters. For example, catering and entertainment both work to a 14-day plan (to cover both one-week and two-week cruises). There are daily inspections for routine and emergency maintenance. Daily and weekly budgetary control and reconciliations take place. Navigation from port, once plotted, is formally committed to paper, with either the captain or deputy captain giving instructions, while the other checks these from the written plan and a third officer monitors them both.

The ship employs people from over 30 nations, including significant numbers of Britons, North Americans, Eastern Europeans, and Filipinos. However, in the view of the captain at least, there are remarkably few culture clashes, which he ascribes to them all having adopted to a great extent the 'culture' of the cruise-liner industry, and of this ship in particular, and the disciplines that go with it. Greater problems, he considers, are to be found in culture clashes between passengers with different national cultures. For example, on South American cruises, there are problems between South American and European (and North American) passengers arising from different attitudes towards such matters as queuing and the level of noise at night which is acceptable – problems which the crew have to manage without causing undue upset to either group of customers.

It is one thing to expect the crew of a ship (whatever their specialism and background) to accept the disciplines of shipboard life, but quite another to expect this of holiday-making passengers, many of whom are unfamiliar with the environment.

Source: Personal interviews

Discussion questions

1   How would you describe the organisation structure of the ship described? Why is this appropriate in this situation? Are there any circumstances when it could cause problems?

2   Why do the differing national cultural backgrounds of the crew pose less of a problem than those of the passengers? Can you suggest any ways in which the latter problems could be overcome?

Conclusion

Human activity is at its most productive when the activities of many are coordinated. This coordination, or 'organisation', may take place in a number of ways, such as markets, laws, and customs, as well as formal organisation. An organisation involves a deliberate arrangement of rules, procedures, communication patterns, and so on, for various people to achieve a common purpose. Most formal organisations involve some features of bureaucracy, such as basic job descriptions and reporting lines. However, the strengths of bureaucratic systems, such as the reduction of complex problems to routines, can also be a source of weakness and, according to such factors as the size of the organisation or the type of business in which it is involved, it may adopt other organisational structures and systems which diverge from the model of full bureaucracy.

Many organisations today emphasise teamwork. It is important to recognise that groups are more than simply collections of individuals, and that people's behaviour in groups is likely to be affected by key characteristics of the group, for example its size, cohesiveness, stage of development, and the degree of interdependence between group members. Leadership is essentially a group function; different groups require leading in different ways.

Countries, occupations, and organisations may all exhibit different cultures, which are more than simply patterns of the way things are done, but these different cultures also reflect different ways of thinking.

Communication within organisations takes a number of forms – for example verbal and written, one-to-one or within groups. Which is appropriate may depend on a variety of factors, such as the nature of the information and the context in which it is being sent and received.

Structure, behaviour, style of leadership, culture and communication cannot be viewed independently of each other. Their effects can be mutually reinforcing, or can work against each other. They need to be mutually consistent.

Discussion questions

3   Consider the booking details requested for a cruise holiday in Figure 4.2.

   ■   Why is the information asked for required?

   ■   Who, within the organisation arranging the package holiday, would require each piece of information?

   ■   Which departments or activities within that organisation would have to work closely together, and which could operate at 'arm's length'?

   ■   How might this affect the way the different departments or activities are organised and coordinated, and how they might communicate with each other?

4   Consider the following groups of people working within the tourism industry:

   ■   The staff, mainly in their twenties, of a local branch of a travel agency.

   ■   A number of qualified accountants working in the finance department of the head office of the travel agency.

   ■   The cleaning and catering staff, largely temporary workers, of a resort hotel.

   ■   The entertainments team responsible for all entertainment at an all-inclusive holiday resort in the Dominican Republic.

   What similarities and differences might you expect to encounter between the various groups? Would a different approach to leadership be appropriate for the different groups? Why?

Figure 4.2   Extract from a P&O cruises brochure

How to Book

Booking a cruise couldn't be easier. Once you've decided which cruise you'd like to travel on, simply book in one of these ways:

 ONLINE at www.pocruises.co.uk
Available 24 hours a day; follow the user-friendly steps and book from the comfort of your home

 BY PHONE ON 0845 3 555 333
Monday – Friday: 8.30am – 6.00pm   Saturday: 8.30am – 5.00pm.
Calls are charged at local rate and may be recorded for training purposes.

 IN-STORE at ABTA travel agents
Call into your local travel agent to discuss your holiday requirements.

When you're ready to book, please ensure that you have the following information to hand:

1. Cruise Details
2. Cabin Details
3. Passenger Details
4. Age At Time Of Sailing
5. Address Details
6. Flight & Hotel Details
7. Dinner Seating Request
8. Insurance Details
9. Special Requirements
10. Mobility
11. Celebration Packages
12. Honeymooners & Anniversary

FULL DETAILS OF THE INFORMATION REQUIRED ARE OUTLINED BELOW

Please note that by making a reservation and paying a deposit, you will be deemed to have read and accepted our Booking Conditions (as set out on pages 73 – 74) and all other information relevant to your holiday.

1. Cruise Details
When making a booking we will ask for the ship name, holiday number and UK departure date. The holiday number and departure date are shown in the price panel on the itinerary pages.

2. Cabin Details
We will need to know what grade of cabin you have chosen to travel in and how you'd like the cabins to be set up ie twin or double bed. All ships offer a choice of twin or double beds. However some cabins on Arcadia and Oceana are not convertible to double beds and some suites and mini-suites are not convertible to twin beds. Please check at time of booking. Further information can be found on the cabin details and deck plan pages 48 - 59.

www.pocruises.co.uk

3. Passenger Details
We will request the full name, title (Mr, Mrs, Miss etc) and sex of each passenger as it appears in their passport. We will also ask for each passenger's date of birth. We also need the ages of any children (maximum age is 16) or infants travelling.

4. Age At Time Of Sailing
We will need to know how old each passenger travelling in your group will be at the time of sailing.

5. Address Details
We require the full private postal address of all passengers travelling with your party (including postcode) and at least one contact telephone number.

6. Flight & Hotel Details
For fly cruises we will need to know which of our UK airports you wish to fly from and, if you're flying from London Gatwick or Manchester, whether you'd like to take the option of a hotel stay at the airport the night before your flight at our special rate of £99 per room. Airport options are shown on the relevant itinerary page and hotel details can be found on page 64. If you're travelling on one of our fly cruises and wish to take our scheduled flight option please let us know at the time of booking. Scheduled flight information can be found on page 65.

7. Dinner Seating Request
Please indicate which sitting you would prefer for dinner (first sitting is at 6.30pm and second sitting is at 8.30pm) and any requests for a specific table size. Please note that tables for 2 are limited on all ships and that we cannot guarantee allocation of any of the table sizes requested. Table allocation is done in booking date order. All restaurants are non-smoking.

8. Insurance Details
For details of the P&O Cruises Travel Insurance policy (arranged with Fortis Insurance) please see page 71. If you would like to take the P&O Cruises Travel Insurance, please let us know.

If you do not wish to take this insurance the following details are required: the name of your insurance provider and the policy number. We also require the name of the Emergency Assistance Company attached to the policy and its emergency phone number.

9. Special Requirements
If you or any individuals travelling with you have any special dietary or medical requirements this should be made known to us at the time of booking. Please see page 66 for further information on the special services we can help with.

10. Mobility
Passengers who are not fully mobile and use either a wheelchair or a motorised wheelchair/ scooter (whether permanently or periodically) must let us know at the time of booking. We will then contact you to obtain further information. See page 73 for details.

Failure to inform us may result in us refusing boarding and/or your insurance being invalidated.

11. Celebration Packages
Please let us know if you would like to book one of our Occasion packages or gifts. Further details can be found on page 69.

12. Honeymooners & Anniversary
If you are celebrating a honeymoon or joining one of our special Anniversary cruises please ensure you let us know at time of booking. For further details of these complimentary packages please see page 69.

Deposits

When you are happy with the accommodation offered and the fare quoted you will be given a booking reference number. You will then need to pay the deposit of 10% per person plus the full insurance premium where applicable, or for bookings made within 56 days of departure, the full balance. For passengers booking direct with P&O Cruises, deposits are only payable by credit or debit card. Deposits are not returnable in the case of cancellation but may be recoverable subject to the terms and conditions of your travel insurance.

Please note that passengers under the age of eighteen must travel with a parent or companion over the age of twenty one.

Source: P&O Cruises, *Caribbean 2005/6*, p.68

Guided reading

Robbins (2003) gives a very readable introduction to all of the topics covered in this chapter. Mullins (2005) and Robbins and Coulter (2005) give further management perspectives, explanations of relevant research and a wealth of examples.

For a really in-depth view of modern thinking about organisations, see Morgan (1997). This is a deliberately challenging book, but for someone who wants to study organisations it provides a stimulating variety of different perspectives on what organisations are and how they work.

For further reading on corporate culture, see Handy (1991). The latter uses a metaphor (which has become quite famous) of four Greek gods to represent the four cultures, and explores what the 'worship' of these four gods means for an organisation.

The website 'businessballs.com' contains a wealth of short, punchy definitions, articles, and activities on business topics, many of which are relevant to this chapter. A more conventional source of material is to be found at 'theworkingmanager.com', while for in-depth reading and research, the Social Science Information Gateway links to articles, case studies, biographies of management writers, and so on. Especially worthwhile for this chapter are the pages for Organisational Management (**www.sosig.ac.uk/roads/subject-listing/World-cat/orgman.html**) and Organisational Behaviour (**www.sosig.ac.uk/roads/subject-listing/World-cat/orgbehav.html**).

The tourism sector is not generally very well served with respect to specialist organisational behaviour texts. An early exception was Carmouche and Kelly (1995), which is focused on the hospitality subsector, and more recently Lashley and Lee-Ross (2003) have written a text covering organisational behaviour in the leisure industries.

Recommended websites

Businessballs.com: **www.businessballs.com/** .

Theworkingmanagercom: **www.theworkingmanager.com/** .

Social Science Information Gateway: **www.sosig.ac.uk** .

Key words

Bureaucracy; control; culture; delegation; group norms; leadership; organisation.

Bibliography

Adair, J. (1984) *The Skills of Leadership*. Gower, Aldershot.

Carmouche, R. and Kelly, N. (1995) *Behavioural Studies in Hospitality Management*. Chapman & Hall, London.

Citizens Advice Bureau (2004) *Hanging on the Telephone: CAB advice on the effectiveness of call centres*. Citizens Advice Bureau, London.

Handy, C. (1991) *Gods of Management*, 3rd edn. Business Books, London.

Harrison, R. (1972) Understanding Your Organization's Character, *Harvard Business Review*, vol. 50, May/June, 119–128.

Hofstede, G. (1991) *Culture and Organisations: Software of the Mind*. McGraw-Hill, London.

Lashley, C. and Lee-Ross, D. (2003) *Organization Behaviour for Leisure Services*. Butterworth-Heinemann, Oxford.

Miles, R.E. and Snow, C.C. (1978) *Organizational Strategy, Structure and Process*. McGraw-Hill, London.

Morgan, G. (1997) *Images of Organization*, 2nd edn. Sage, London.

Mullins, L.J. (2005) *Management and Organisational Behaviour*, 7th edn. FT Prentice Hall, Harlow.

Peters, T.J. and Waterman, R.H. (1982) *In Search of Excellence*. Harper and Row, London.

Robbins, S. (2003) *Organizational Behavior*, 10th edn. Prentice Hall, Upper Saddle River NJ.

Robbins, S. and Coulter, M. (2005) *Management*, 8th edn. Prentice Hall, Upper Saddle River NJ.

Thompson, J.D. (1967) *Organizations in Action*. McGraw-Hill, New York.

Tuckman, B.W. and Jensen, M.C. (1977) Stages of Small-Group Development Revisited, *Group and Organizational Studies*, Dec., 419–427.

YOU DON'T HAVE TO KNOW THE ROPES

FULL AND PART-TIME POSITIONS AVAILABLE NO EXPERIENCE NECESSARY

ASK INSIDE FOR DETAILS OR CALL GRAHAM OR LEANNE ON 02920 450947

terra nova

Chapter 5

Human resource management in tourism businesses

Claire Haven-Tang and Eleri Jones, Welsh School of Hospitality, Tourism and Leisure Management, University of Wales Institute, Cardiff

Learning outcomes

On completion of this chapter the reader should be able to:

■ identify and explain human resource management issues relevant to tourism businesses;

■ explain the key human resource management functions;

■ relate the main motivational theories to different tourism scenarios;

■ assess the importance of human resource management to the overall strategic position of an organisation;

■ explain and assess the key human resource management processes within an organisation.

Overview

The chapter begins with a brief overview of the origins of human resource management and goes on to explain the critical contribution of employees to the competitive advantage of tourism organisations and why human resources (HR) are an important issue for the industry. Following an outline of the major HR functions involved in the hiring and firing of employees, the focus turns to understanding motivational issues and how managers can inspire employees. The chapter then considers how the holistic integration of HR into organisational strategy can ensure business success. The chapter concludes with a summary of best practice approaches for recruiting, retaining and motivating employees. The chapter includes two real-life case studies to illustrate the contribution of flexible employee benefit packages in recruitment in a multinational tourism company and best practice in HR for small tourism businesses. The chapter also refers to a 'Head of HR' vacancy in a fictitious tourism organisation and uses the job description, person specification and advertisement to demonstrate the HR function in an organisation. The learning outcomes are reinforced by the use of discussion questions that draw on case material and other topics covered in the chapter.

Introduction

Human resource management (HRM) is about managing people and their interrelationships within organisations. It aims to ensure that organisations benefit from their employees' abilities, while ensuring that employees gain concrete and psychological rewards from their employment. Globally, in any particular destination, the tourism industry comprises a range of different-sized public, private and voluntary sector organisations which operate across different elements of tourism supply (accommodation; attractions; food and drink; intermediaries; transport), yet regardless of the nature or size of tourism operations, they are all reliant on the quality of their human resources, i.e. their employees. To achieve competitive advantage in an increasingly competitive marketplace, the success of an individual organisation or destination is dependent upon employee contribution and commitment.

Historically, the personnel role in the UK was linked to the values of the social reformist movements of the nineteenth century. High-profile social reformers exerted influence upon the '*factory system*' before personnel emerged as a specialist management activity (Hall and Torrington, 1998). Although the industrial revolution created urbanisation and a shift away from rural poverty, the factory system was exposed for its poor working conditions and treatment of employees. Thus, the origins of personnel management are class-based and can be attributed to philanthropic employers, e.g. the Quaker-owned company Cadburys, who towards the end of the nineteenth century developed a sense of social responsibility and appointed 'Welfare Officers' to dispense '*benefits to the deserving and unfortunate employees*' (Hall and Torrington, 1998: 12). As government took more social responsibility and the welfare state emerged in the UK, the 'welfare' role changed to incorporate other functions. Some (e.g. Torrington, 1989; Boella, 2000) argue that contemporary personnel management still retains the welfare tradition, while others (e.g. Monks, 1996) suggest that its motive is cost-effectiveness, in terms of minimising absenteeism and labour turnover, rather than a genuine concern for employee welfare.

The increasing emphasis on effective employee relations and on the importance of securing the involvement of employees and their commitment to organisational aims have led to the increasing use of the term '*human resource management*' (HRM) to replace '*personnel management*'. The term HRM originated in the United States of America, where it was used interchangeably with personnel management. Bratton and Gold (1999: 9) suggest that this is not simply a 'matter of semantics', but a concept adopted by organisations as a strategic response to the more competitive environment, with employees being a means of creating and maintaining competitive advantage in the global marketplace. Therefore, while personnel management is concerned with the administration and implementation of policies, HRM adopts a more focused and integrated strategic dimension than personnel management, in terms of achieving organisational objectives and maintaining costs by engaging strategic management techniques to utilise human resources. HRM is principally business-oriented, centred on the management of people to enable the businesses to gain added value, ensure competitiveness and focus on long-term perspectives.

Why is HR such an important issue in the tourism industry?

Worldwide tourism employment is estimated at 214,697,000 jobs or 8.1% of total employment (WTTC, 2004). Employees are the most important assets in a tourism organisation and are key to the success of service-sector companies, because of their critical role in customer interactions. Baum (1997) asserts that the management of the customer–employee encounter is one of the most difficult but crucial tasks for tourism managers with major implications for service quality. While the industry offers well-qualified individuals, e.g. graduates, exciting, dynamic and rewarding international career opportunities, the industry also needs a vast number of operational staff. Low entry barriers and high turnover pose particular HR challenges to tourism managers.

HR implications for service quality

Service quality is dependent on employee–customer interaction at the point of service delivery. However, this interaction is potentially problematic and difficult to control, with responsibility for high-quality service provision falling on front-line staff (Schaffer, 1984; Mattsson, 1994). Therefore, employees must understand and be committed to service quality goals, as well as being in possession of the skills, knowledge, attitude, authority and access to information necessary to be able to provide a high-quality service tailored to specific customer needs. The establishment of appropriate customer–host relationships is critical to the delivery of a quality service and Evans *et al.* (2003) state that in labour-intensive service industries important factors include not just an individual's ability and knowledge but also his/her ability to learn and adapt to change.

Characteristics of tourism employment

Although the development of the tourism industry creates new employment opportunities, critics contend that tourism employment provides predominantly low-paid and low-skilled demeaning jobs (e.g. Choy, 1995). The negative aspects of tourism employment focus upon the physical demands of the job, poor conditions of work, job insecurity, low pay, long working hours, high labour turnover and lack of training. Many tourism students will be aware of the opportunities for seasonal employment in operational roles in the tourism industry. Reports of poor pay, attempts to circumvent national minimum wages and exploitation of asylum seekers do little to promote the image of employment in the industry as a worthwhile career choice (Hayter, 2001). Additionally, there are equality issues – despite the large number of women working in the tourism industry, research (White and Jones, 2002) found that unsociable hours make it difficult for women to return after maternity leave and employees often regard family-friendly policies as '*cosmetic*'. Emotional labour (see Hochschild, 1983; Chappel, 2002) is also an important part of tourism employment. In many cases, the display of certain emotions is a job requirement and without displaying the required emotion, the job may not be seen to have been carried out effectively. Where emotional expression is inherent for role performance, the manner in which emotions are expressed is often prescribed, through the use of scripts, such as '*Have a nice day*' and '*Missing you already*'. Generic customer care training for tourism employees often dictates the expected emotions of staff in order to convince guests that they are enjoying their roles, convey positive emotions to visitors and promote the corporate image.

Labour turnover

Labour turnover in the tourism industry is generally accepted as an inevitable and natural process. According to a survey published by the CIPD in 2004, the overall employee turnover rate for the UK in 2003 was 16.1% and for Ireland was 15.7%, although turnover levels varied considerably from industry to industry. The highest levels of labour turnover (over 50%) are found in the private sector, e.g. retailing, hotels and restaurants. The lowest levels (below 10%) are found in the public sector. Deery (2002) reports variable turnover rates in the hotel sector in Australia, ranging from 20% in central business district hotels to 300% in remote resort hotels, while Lashley (2000) found an average of 188% in the licensed retail sector in the north of England. Some perceive labour turnover to be beneficial as it enables manipulation of workforce size according to demand and thus enables the control of labour costs (Lashley and Chaplain, 1999; Torrington *et al.*, 2002). Additionally, new recruits can bring new ideas and experiences to make organisations more dynamic and innovative. Those who do not perceive labour turnover to be dysfunctional argue that staff mobility facilitates skills acquisition.

Nevertheless, labour turnover is a cost to tourism businesses and can create severe operational difficulties. High labour turnover affects the quality of services and goods. It also incurs high replacement, recruitment and selection costs as well as training costs, which can subsequently reduce profitability and affect organisational morale (Johnson, 1981; Deery and Iverson, 1996; Torrington *et al.*, 2002). Labour turnover can be symptomatic of a poorly managed organisation leading to a poor image and recruitment difficulties. Research (HtF, 2001) has shown that high staff turnover militates against investment in employee development and training.

Many employers are unwilling to invest money in training post-induction, unless required by legislation, as they are unlikely to recoup the advantages of employee development and training. Employers faced with high labour turnover and skills shortages often 'deskill' jobs, so that lower skilled staff can be recruited. When an employer has adjusted to a lack of skilled workers by adapting their product and thus the job so that highly skilled staff are not required, a 'skills trap' is apparent. In the long term, deskilling reduces the demand for particular skills and thus the incentive for their acquisition. Ultimately, this impacts on visitor experiences and destination competitiveness.

Flexible employment

The tourism industry provides a labour-intensive service at the customer interface and, while demand is fairly steady and predictable, peaks and troughs in demand do occur. These peaks can only be met through temporary increases in labour at the point of contact, via functional or numerical flexibility (see later section). Part-time employment is the usual solution to uneven work distribution, providing employers with a reserve of peripheral (casual, part-time or seasonal) workers, to supplement core (full-time) workers. However, the predictability of seasonal fluctuations is pivotal in maintaining regular part-time employment and the availability of part-time employees. An alternative response to fluctuations in small and family-run businesses, e.g. small hotels and guesthouses, is self-exploitation – '*rhythmic fluctuation in demand will be met by a willingness to work very long hours*' (Shaw and Williams, 1994: 148). Fredena Burns, the owner of a well-established bed and breakfast in west Wales, reports that her day begins at 5.30 a.m. and ends whenever her guests retire to bed (BBC, 2004).

While labour flexibility may be a positive attribute, it can also be detrimental. Although labour markets are increasingly flexible, occupations requiring a flexible workforce may not be identified as viable career choices – in the UK part-time tourism and hospitality employment is significantly higher (with a poorer image) than in other European Union countries (Keep and Mayhew, 1999). The high proportions of casual and part-time staff employed within the industries may be less inclined to view the tourism industry as a long-term career option, perceiving it to be a transient job. Subsequently, part-time and casual employees may be unwilling to invest in industry-related qualifications.

Qualifications and professionalism

One factor likely to contribute to poor qualification attainment within the tourism industry is the willingness of employers to recruit people without the necessary qualifications. Although this approach is often linked to the problem of labour shortages, it may dissuade relatively highly qualified students from considering tourism as a career option. The selection procedures for entry into particular careers convey different levels of image and status, with higher status and professionalism attributed to careers with high entry thresholds. A clear career structure is also important and the tourism industry generally suffers a lack of clearly defined routes to supervisory and managerial positions.

Baum (1995) argues that in other European countries tourism employment, in particular, has a stronger tradition of perceived professionalism than the UK. The concept of professionalism is closely associated with status but may incorporate personal attributes, such as career aspirations, progression and attitudes – Switzerland, for example, requires qualifications to access employment in particular management and skill areas (Baum, 1995). Furthermore, the traditions of tourism management education and training in other European countries serve to illustrate the importance awarded to the development of practical skills. Lack of professionalism in the UK tourism industry exacerbates the trend towards deskilling resulting from skills shortages.

The low entry threshold for tourism entrepreneurship leads to a dominance of microbusinesses (less than ten employees) in the tourism industry. Some owner-managers are seriously deficient in management skills, notably financial management and HR skills. This affects the viability of small tourism businesses as well as impacting on their ability to offer an attractive career package for ambitious employees.

Although globally the industry faces skills shortages in key operational, technical and managerial areas, the context varies between developed and developing countries. In developed countries, Baum (1997) argues that demographic trends, better education and low industry image and status combine so fewer young people enter the industry. In developing countries it is educational, technical, cultural and language barriers that raise entry thresholds to tourism employment and make tourism employment less accessible. Jobs deemed to be low-skilled in developed countries are not perceived as such in developing countries. For example, in Cuba tourism employment is highly desirable as tourism employees earn highly-prized US dollars rather than local currency resulting in a 'brain drain' (Pax Christi, 2000) from professional and academic sectors into tourism.

Pay

Remuneration is linked to professionalism. Levels of pay are often dependent upon the market demand for particular skills. Industries that have weak internal labour markets, such as the tourism industry, often demand generic skills accessible cheaply within the marketplace. The tourism industry does little to counteract the perception of low pay and low-skilled employment. The introduction of a national minimum wage (NMW), e.g. in the UK in 1999, has to some extent addressed pay issues. However, employer reaction has been to offset increased costs by minimising the use of full-time employees; increasing the use of flexible labour and distributing the workload among existing employees (Rowson, 2000). Many tourism organisations are recognising the importance of retaining good performers and seek reward packages to increase retention (see Case 5.1 on Cathay Pacific on p.102).

Equality and diversity issues

While legislation facilitates equality implementation and promotes diversity, major problems can emanate from local interpretation of the legislation and how policies are implemented in individual workplaces. Many tourism organisations are microbusinesses and too small to be required to have an equality and diversity policy. The transparency of human resource management practices in an organisation can have a major influence on perceptions of equality throughout all phases of the employee lifecycle from the recruitment and selection of staff to their retention.

HR challenges facing the tourism industry

There are a number of reasons why HR presents the tourism industry and tourism managers with significant challenges and poses a threat to future expansion of the industry (see Figure 5.1). Demographic trends coupled with a negative image has resulted in reduced numbers of young recruits to the tourism industry. Managers must seek to recruit from non-traditional labour sources and from overseas. Traditional reactive HR practices, conditions of work and lack of a career structure contribute to high labour turnover and skills shortages which ultimately impact on visitor experience, product quality and destination competitiveness. An effective HR function will intervene to address issues, maximise employee performance and achieve business objectives.

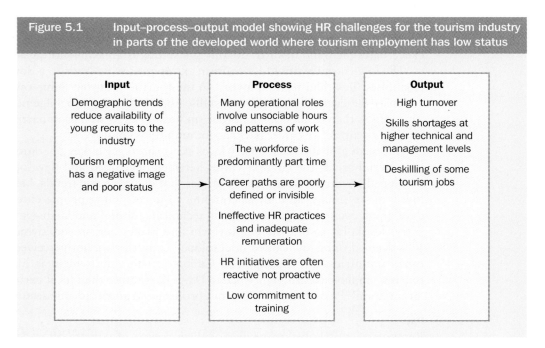

| Figure 5.1 | Input–process–output model showing HR challenges for the tourism industry in parts of the developed world where tourism employment has low status |

Input

Demographic trends reduce availability of young recruits to the industry

Tourism employment has a negative image and poor status

Process

Many operational roles involve unsociable hours and patterns of work

The workforce is predominantly part time

Career paths are poorly defined or invisible

Ineffective HR practices and inadequate remuneration

HR initiatives are often reactive not proactive

Low commitment to training

Output

High turnover

Skills shortages at higher technical and management levels

Deskillling of some tourism jobs

Hiring and firing employees

Regardless of whether a tourism business is a large multinational or family-run microbusiness it will still need to recruit, train, retain, motivate and reward staff, and comply with employment legislation. All tourism organisations need an effective HR function, even if not all justify a specialist HR department. The understanding of HR issues by all managers in the tourism industry is a key to its success.

Employee resourcing

Employee resourcing strategies are often reactive and detached from wider business strategies, rather than planning flexibly for a range of external influences. These may include competition, economic climate, government policy, technological developments, socio-demographics and skill shortages, all of which can affect business organisation and management. Torrington *et al.* (2002) identify three responses to flexibility:

- numerical flexibility (using different employment contracts – part-time, seasonal and casual – to supplement core full-time employees in response to demand);
- temporal flexibility (varying the pattern of hours worked by individual employees through job share and part-time employment);
- functional or task flexibility (involving employees in a wider range of tasks).

Recruitment and selection

Staff recruitment and selection is fundamental to effective organisational functioning – inappropriate selection decisions impact negatively, reducing effectiveness and performance. Recruitment attracts suitably qualified applicants for consideration, whereas selection reduces the number of applicants and matches the right applicant to the job.

Internal recruitment can be quicker and cheaper – candidates understand the organisational culture and offering promotional opportunities can impact positively on motivation and demonstrate a career structure. However, it can demotivate employees who are not promoted and limit the inflow of 'new blood'. Although external recruitment is expensive and time consuming, it accesses a wider pool of potential candidates through: advertisements; job centres; executive search or employment agencies; educational establishments and unsolicited applications. Online recruitment allows cost-effective advertising, although its indiscriminate nature and ease-of-response may attract many unsuitable applications and effective filters are needed.

Job analysis

Job analysis provides the information to identify job and candidate profiles in the job descriptions and person specifications, as well as being valuable for job design. There are a number of ways to undertake job analysis, e.g. direct or participant observation, interview with the current job holder or supervisor, work diaries, or questionnaires. As a result of the HR challenges facing the tourism industry, well-designed jobs are increasingly important in attracting and retaining a motivated workforce with the ability to produce and deliver quality products and services.

Job description

Job descriptions are complete statements of the duties and responsibilities required of specific jobs and underpin job evaluation, recruitment, training and performance appraisal. While job description contents vary, there is consensus that they should not refer to post-holders. A job description for a fictitious vacancy is shown in Figure 5.2.

Figure 5.2   Job description for the Head of Human Resources, Taith Travel International

Taith Travel International

JOB TITLE: Head of Human Resources
DEPARTMENT: Human Resources
LOCATION: Cardiff, Southeast Wales
REPORTING TO: Managing Director
RESPONSIBLE FOR: HR and Training Teams

SUMMARY OF POSITION
To operate as a member of the Senior Management Team (SMT), producing, implementing and developing a HR strategy, ensuring adherence to current employment legislation and best practice policies. To be responsible for a large team of HR and training professionals focused on maintaining our competitive advantage in the marketplace.

MAIN RESPONSIBILITIES
- Review existing HR practices
- Produce and deliver a performance-led, people-sensitive, professional HR strategy, consistent with organisational values
- Update and maintain HR policies and procedures in line with EU/UK employment legislation and best practice
- Ensure the development of EO policies and culture
- Manage HR and training teams
- Maintain and report HR departmental budget and participate in strategic budgetary discussions
- Maintain and develop trade union relations
- Work with SMT on recruitment, retention, organisational development, employee relations, reward and communication activities
- Participate in identification of the strategic direction and objectives of the organisation and promote organisational effectiveness through HR frameworks

Figure 5.2	Continued

■ Facilitate effective individual management and team-working skills within SMT

WORKING CONDITIONS
New office development on the outskirts of Cardiff, within easy reach of the M4. Free on-site car parking. 25 days holiday per year plus statutory holidays.

Person specification

A person specification is generated from the data gathered during the job analysis, complements the job description and is useful for short listing (see below). The person specification clarifies the *essential* and *desirable* education/qualifications, skills/abilities, attributes, experience and knowledge required and how these criteria will be measured (i.e. by application form, interview, presentation, references, test). The criteria will vary according to the job. For example, essential criteria for direct contact positions will include very good communication and interpersonal skills. A person specification for our fictitious vacancy is shown in Table 5.1.

Table 5.1	Person specification for the Head of Human Resources, Taith Travel International	
Factor	**Essential**	**Desirable**
Qualifications	Degree or equivalent[1] Graduate CIPD by examination[1]	Postgraduate Management Qualification, e.g. MBA, Diploma in Management Studies[1] MCIPD[1] Qualified in psychometric assessment[1]
Experience	Knowledge of employment legislation[1, 2] Six years HR management experience at a senior level within a service-orientated environment[1, 2] Experience of employment tribunals[1, 2] Experience of Investor in People and other quality models[1, 2] Knowledge of NVQ and Modern Apprenticeship schemes[1, 2]	Experience of dealing with trade unions[1, 2] Understanding of wider commercial issues[1, 2, 3] Experience of coaching and/or mentoring[1, 2]
Leadership	Ability to lead change and introduce new HR practices in line with the strategic aims of the organisation[1, 2, 3]	
Communication	Effective communication skills, both verbal and written[1, 2, 3] Acute questioning and listening skills[1, 3] Analytical ability to inform decision-making at Board level[2, 3]	Knowledge of a European language[1]
Interpersonal skills	Ability to relate to people at all levels within the organisation[1, 3, 4] Ability to represent the organisation at local level with external bodies[1, 4] Ability to adapt to the culture of the organisation and facilitate change[1, 2]	
Planning	Ability to assist the Board of Directors in HR planning to meet the constantly changing needs of the business[2, 4] Evidence of devising and implementing HR solutions with tangible impacts on business performance[1, 2, 3, 4]	

Technical	Knowledge of HR computer packages[1,2]	Awareness of alternative IT packages available to meet the future needs of the organisation[2,3]
	Experience of Word; Excel and PowerPoint IT packages[1]	
Special aptitudes	Self-motivated[1,4]	
	Enthusiastic[2,4]	
	Flexible and resourceful[1,2,4]	
	Good time management[1,4]	
	Valid driving licence[1]	
	Good medical record[1,4]	

Evidenced by: Application form[1]; interview[2]; presentation[3]; references[4]

Job advertisements

Well-designed advertisements should attract suitably-qualified candidates cost-effectively, while deterring unsuitable candidates. Ideally, they should include details of the organisation, the job and the person required, as illustrated for our fictitious vacancy in Figure 5.3.

A number of factors will determine the appropriateness of the publications in which the vacancy is advertised, including: job role, seniority and salary, labour supply issues. To advertise their Head of Human Resources vacancy, Taith Travel International might consider advertising in national newspapers, tourism sector and HR specialist journals. Lower status positions in the company may be advertised more locally, e.g. in local or regional newspapers. Careful records should be kept to monitor the effectiveness of the advertisement and different advertising channels to inform future recruitment.

| Figure 5.3 | Job advertisement for the Head of Human Resources, Taith Travel International |

Taith Travel International

Head of Human Resources
£55,000 to £65,000 + benefits Cardiff, Southeast Wales

Taith Travel International is currently one of the UK's leading tour operators, with a turnover in excess of £600 million and over 1200 employees. We operate within a vertically-integrated structure, covering: Mass and Specialist Tour Operating, High Street Distribution, Internet Sales and Foreign Exchange. We are seeking to appoint as Head of Human Resources, a dynamic and proactive professional with the ability to inspire and develop our employees in line with the strategic aims of the organisation.

The Position
- Review existing HR practices
- Produce and deliver a HR strategy that is performance-led, people-sensitive, professional and consistent with organisational values
- Deliver an outstanding HR service and contribute to strategic and commercial goals and enhanced business performance
- Work with the Senior Management Team on recruitment, retention, organisation development, employee relations, reward and communication activities
- Drive HR policies on Equal Opportunities and implement new policies on recent employment legislation

The Person
- Graduate, CIPD-qualified with a minimum of 6 years' proven HR management experience in a service environment
- Knowledge of employment legislation and demonstrable employee relations experience
- Understanding of wider commercial issues and evidence of devising and implementing HR solutions that have had a measurable impact on business performance
- Ability to lead change and introduce new HR practices in line with the strategic aims of the organisation
- Enthusiastic, self-motivated, flexible, resourceful, excellent communication and interpersonal skills with the ability to lead and motivate a team

For an application pack, please contact: C. Haven-Tang, PA to the Managing Director, Taith Travel International, (029) 123 456, chaven-tang@taithtravelinternational.co.wales

Application forms

It is preferable to ensure that candidates complete an application form for the selection process, as it collects candidate information in a logical manner. The following headings usually apply:

1 Job applied for/post number.
2 Personal details (name, address, email, telephone number, date and place of birth, nationality).
3 Education, training and qualifications.
4 Employment history (names and addresses of previous employers, dates of employment, job description and reasons for leaving).
5 Medical history.
6 Additional information as a '*supporting statement*' written with reference to the job description, person specification and previous experience.
7 Referee details.
8 Candidate's signature under '*This information is correct to the best of my knowledge*' (because application forms have legal implications for employment contracts).
9 Date.

Short-listing

The essential criteria from the person specification that can be evidenced by the application form (see Table 5.1) should be used to short-list candidate applications using a short-listing matrix form. Systematic recording facilitates selection and eliminates bias and subjectivity. An individual not meeting all the essential criteria should not be short-listed. Where a large number of applications meet the essential criteria, scores against desirable criteria can be used to reduce the number of applications to an appropriate number for interview. Interviewing is a time-consuming process and numbers should be sufficient to allow for 'no-shows' and to give the interviewers reasonable choice without being overwhelmed.

Interview

Face-to-face interviews are a popular selection method as they evaluate characteristics such as self-confidence and communication skills. Interviews may involve a phased process including aptitude and psychometric tests as well as presentations. An interview panel needs to be sufficiently large to evaluate the candidate. Typically a panel comprises the line manager to the post being interviewed for, a HR manager and another colleague. Larger panels can be difficult to coordinate and may intimidate the candidate. Before the interview the panel should agree and allocate questions relating to the person specification criteria to be evidenced at interview. Records for each candidate should be completed by each interviewer of the candidate's performance to score candidates and enable an objective decision to be reached. These records can be important if unsuccessful candidates appeal or request feedback on their performance.

References

Reference checks verify the credentials of a candidate. A factual check just asks a referee to confirm candidate details, whereas a character reference asks for an opinion about the candidate. Legal issues may arise if the character reference contains knowingly false information. It is important to check the legal status of references in particular international contexts.

Final selection

The final decision involves assessing each candidate against the selection criteria, to ensure that the best person for the job is selected. It is usual to make a verbal offer which, if accepted, is followed by a written offer, including: salary; job title and any special conditions; essential conditions of employment (hours, holidays, bonuses, etc.); any stipulations, e.g. '*subject to satisfactory references/medical examination*'; clarification of the next stage(s) in the process.

Employee records
The application form, letter of job offer and employee acceptance letter initiate an employee's record (see Graham and Bennett, 1998). Employee records are a legal mine-field, e.g. data protection and confidentiality arrangements. It is good practice for an organisation to communicate its document retention policy and monitoring programme via its staff handbook.

Employee relations

Employee relations involve the regulation of workplace activities and include setting standards, promoting consensus and managing conflict. More employers now appreciate the contribution positive employee relations can make to profitable and effective organi-sational performance.

The employment contract
Internationally, written employment contracts may not be a requirement. However, best practice employers issue written statements outlining the main terms and conditions of employment to avoid contractual misunderstandings/disagreements. Core information should be given in a single written statement – the '*principal statement*' – that may refer to additional documentation, such as organisational rules and HR policies. UK law requires a contract of employment to include: names of the employer and employee; start date; the nature of employment; end date if fixed term; normal place of work and alternative work locations, employer's address; details of collective agreements; rate of pay, method of calculation and payment interval; hours of work and normal working hours; holiday entitlement and holiday pay; arrangements for sickness and sick pay; pension arrangements; length of notice periods (on both sides); job title; and disciplinary and grievance arrangements and procedures.

Communication
Organisations pay increasing attention to employee communication to reflect apprecia-tion of the key role of employees in understanding and achieving business objectives and recognition of employee expectations of involvement in communication processes. Effective managers understand the needs, motives and desires of employees and will use formal and informal methods of communication. Organisations without effective formal communication networks are likely to experience communication problems.

Grievance and disciplinary procedures
It is good practice for employers to have formal grievance and disciplinary procedures (see the Arbitration and Conciliation Advisory Service or ACAS website). Employer failure to meet employee expectations may result in grievance, while employee failure to meet employer expectations may result in disciplinary action. Both require HR intervention. In the UK, failure to operate a reasonable grievance or disciplinary procedure will be taken into account by employment tribunals when considering cases, e.g. of unfair dismissal.

Resignation and dismissal
The employee or employer giving notice of the date on which the contract will end may terminate employment contracts. Resignation is when an employee gives notice to termi-nate, and, while an employee may not legally have to disclose his/her reasons for resignation, it is good practice for an employer to organise exit interviews to clarify any workplace issues contributing to resignation. Dismissal is when an employer gives notice to terminate or fails to renew a fixed-term contract or an employee resigns as a result of

an employer's unreasonable behaviour (see Torrington *et al.*, 2002; EmpLaw website, see Recommended websites, p.111).

Employee development

Training has two functions. First, better use can be made of employees if they are more competent and multi-skilled. Second, more competent employees are more likely to gain management recognition, increasing job satisfaction and motivation. When planning a training programme for an employee, managers should consider: the relevance to the employee, the department and the organisation as a whole; staff cover; de-briefing sessions immediately and one month post-training. In addition to planned training schedules, training may be reactive in response to employee promotion or transfer, labour shortages, new equipment installation, new legislation, amended company policies and quality enhancement programmes.

Some organisations are now moving towards learning (Reynolds and Sloman, 2004). This often requires a shift in organisational culture to create an environment promoting employee confidence and commitment. The use of technology, e.g. e-learning, expands delivery methods and promotes flexibility.

Appraisals

Appraisal may focus on reward, performance or assessing an employee's potential within an organisation. Appraisal is an important element in an integrated organisational communication and performance management strategy, allowing managers to disseminate business objectives and clarify individual roles in their achievement. Managers should provide individual feedback on performance and encourage employees to reflect on their performance. Through the appraisal process development needs and individual objectives are identified. These may be linked to individual reward and motivation. However, to avoid negative issues relating to appraisals, organisations should separate reward appraisal from performance or potential appraisals. A typical appraisal form is shown in Figure 5.4.

Career development

While individuals are obviously responsible for managing their own careers, organisations can facilitate career development (see Torrington *et al.*, 2002) and enhance employee commitment and motivation; this in turn will reduce staff turnover and improve the image of the organisation. Opportunities for internal promotion make explicit organisational career structures and demonstrate commitment to existing employees.

Employee rewards

An organisation's pay and reward strategy should be integrated into the wider organisational philosophy and strategy and reflect and complement the organisational structure. Apart from statutory minima, pay levels will be affected by the value of the job to the organisation, the value of the person to the organisation and the value of the job or person in the marketplace. Both financial and non-financial rewards should be used for individuals who add value to the organisation and help it achieve competitive advantage. Effective pay and reward systems should aim to attract and retain employees, encourage commitment and motivation, meet employee expectations and reward effort, expertise and output.

'*New pay*' (see Lawler, 1995) focuses on integrating pay with corporate strategies to achieve organisational objectives and on managing financial reward to communicate the right messages about performance and corporate values to employees. Conversely, '*old pay*' is detached from strategic organisational objectives, focuses on rewarding seniority and is characterised by organisational hierarchies and incremental progression.

Figure 5.4   Sample appraisal template

Personal details:

Name of reviewee:

Department:

Job title:

Length of time in post:

Name of reviewer:

Date of previous review:

Date of current review:

Job description:

Training activities undertaken in past 12 months:
(How have these helped to improve your performance?)

Self appraisal:

Which areas of your job do you feel you performed particularly well over the past 12 months and why?

Which areas of your job do you feel you could have performed more effectively and how?

Have you encountered any particular difficulties in achieving your key objectives? If yes, please explain.

To improve your performance, what suggestions can you make regarding yourself, your manager, the business?

Do you have any experience, skills or interests that are not currently being used which could benefit the business?

Key objectives:	**Training and other support required to achieve key objectives:**
	What training would you like to undertake in the next 12 months and how will this help you to achieve your objectives and enhance your performance?
Signature of reviewee:	**Signature of reviewer:**

However, in addition to financial rewards, employee reward strategies should also include non-financial rewards or intrinsic elements, e.g. a sense of achievement, recognition, responsibility, personal growth and self-actualisation (see the section below on inspiring employees, p. **103**), all of which serve as motivational tools.

Performance-related pay

Performance-related pay (PRP) is associated with new pay and should provide a flexible approach to distributing rewards fairly among employees. It can attract and retain; reward without promoting; and achieve business objectives through improved employee performance. However, PRP can undermine teamwork; encourage employees to focus narrowly on specific, PRP-related, tasks; and demotivate if employees are not awarded the PRP they believe they deserve.

Pensions

Pension arrangements are a complex area of employee reward which HR specialists need to understand in order to communicate company pension schemes to employees. Pension schemes can demonstrate that the organisation is a good employer and concerned about the long-term interests of its employees, as well as attracting and retaining high-quality employees.

Benefits

The detail of any particular benefits scheme will depend on local circumstances (see Case 5.1), but core benefits often include: holidays; life assurance; private medical insurance; critical illness insurance or long-term disability insurance; and personal accident insurance. Examples of additional benefits include: company car schemes; childcare vouchers; dental insurance; financial planning; Give-As-You-Earn charitable contributions; health screening; home or mobile telephone package; legal expenses insurance; pet insurance; retail vouchers; travel season tickets; live-in accommodation; parking facilities; relocation expenses; subsidised sports and crèche facilities; travel insurance; and concierge benefits (e.g. laundry services). Some businesses enhance statutory rights, e.g. to maternity, paternity and sickness leave, as part of their benefits scheme.

Total reward

Some organisations are moving towards more integrated reward packages of 'total reward' encompassing pay; flexible benefits; the working environment; career and personal development. Total rewards encourage positive employee commitment by empowering employees to tailor their work and surroundings to meet their own needs, without incurring open-ended uncontrollable operational costs for the company. However, some rewards are easier to provide than others and some are more quantifiable, so ensuring parity among employees is a challenge.

Case 5.1	*RightChoice*, Cathay Pacific's flexible benefits package, attracts and retains employees

Founded in 1946 and with a long-term commitment to service excellence and almost 14,000 employees worldwide, Hong Kong based Cathay Pacific Airways Ltd (CPAL) is recognised as one of the best airlines in the world. Although CPAL is a private-sector company, it positions itself as Hong Kong's airline negotiating traffic rights with other countries. In Hong Kong, CPAL's multinational workforce comprises cabin crew, cockpit crew and ground staff.

Like most good employers, CPAL recognises the importance of a benefits package to its employees. However, in the mid-1990s, a CPAL employee survey demonstrated that, despite representing a significant proportion of their remuneration package, employees took benefits for granted and did not fully understand or appreciate the benefits CPAL provided.

In benchmarking its benefits scheme against other large and medium-sized multinational companies, CPAL found that most had Flexible Benefits Plans (FBPs) to attract and retain employees. FBPs, also known as a cafeteria approach to benefits, are formalised schemes allowing employees to vary pay and benefits packages according to individual requirements. FBPs allow employees autonomy in selecting benefits from menus rather than receiving standardised packages. FBPs adopt a formulaic approach, factoring in seniority, salary, age and family size, to allocate benefit points to individual employees. Using a points tariff for benefits, employees select benefits, paying the difference if they exceed their allocation. FBPs represent a cost-effective approach to benefit provision so money is not wasted on unwanted benefits.

In 1997, CPAL introduced *RightChoice*, one of the first FBPs in Hong Kong, to respond better to employees' individual needs and align benefits with corporate strategy. *RightChoice* matches basic benefits points to Hong Kong's statutory benefits. The *RightChoice* menu includes opportunities to buy or sell annual leave; insurance options (travel, life, accident, critical illness and income protection); medical care options (outpatient, hospital, preventative and dental); and retirement schemes. Unspent benefit points can be taken as cash, an option favoured by younger employees.

RightChoice is complex and the internet plays an important administrative role. Customised benefits software calculates benefits points and employees track their used/unused points online. Online enrolment worksheets instruct employees to select benefits annually.

Educating employees is key to successfully implementing FBPs. Even the best FBP in the world will not work if employees do not understand it. Good two-way communication enhances employee understanding and appreciation of the benefits. *RightChoice* communication channels include: briefing sessions; a benefits service centre manned by well-trained advisors; a website and printed materials to enhance transparency and accessibility, while building employee trust.

More than just being cost-effective, *RightChoice*, plus concessionary travel benefits, makes CPAL an attractive employer. It improves employee attitudes towards benefits; better meets the needs of a diverse workforce; and encourages employees to take an active role in selecting their benefits coverage and taking ownership of their well-being.

Thanks are due to Bob Nipperess (Employee Services Manager) and Toby Tang (Compensations Manager) of Cathay Pacific Airways Ltd for their invaluable help in compiling this case study.

Inspiring employees: motivation

The role of managers is to create a transparent and supportive environment in which individual employees can contribute to the achievement of organisational objectives and fulfil their potential. Anyone who works as a manager must understand what motivates and demotivates employees, but nowhere is this more important than in customer-facing roles in the service sector, where employees are a critical factor in the service encounter and thus in customer satisfaction. There are a number of different theories of motivation and they are divided into two broad perspectives: content and process theories.

Content theories of motivation

Content theories focus on what motivates individuals at work and includes: Maslow's hierarchy of needs and Alderfer's ERG theory; McGregor's Theory X and Theory Y; Herzberg's two factor theory and McClelland's achievement motivation.

F.W. Taylor

F.W. Taylor (1911), an American engineer, expounded a theory that employees are basically lazy and have to be motivated by pay, a view later described by McGregor as Theory X. Taylor, who focused on factory work, was interested in productivity and turned the study of work into a science, e.g. through the use of stopwatches to time tasks and sub-tasks. The management response to Taylor would be treat employees like machines and devise payment methods that maximise productivity, e.g. piecework and payment by results, and, arguably is the approach adopted by some tourism operations, e.g. hospitality franchises.

Maslow's hierarchy of needs and Alderfer's ERG theory

Maslow's hierarchy of needs (Maslow, 1943) suggests that people are motivated by a number of factors at work which can be arranged into a hierarchy of needs, with physiological needs (food and shelter) at the bottom of the hierarchy moving through safety needs, to love/social needs, esteem needs and, at the top of the hierarchy, to self-actualisation or growth needs (see Figure 5.5). According to Maslow, needs lower down the hierarchy must be satisfied before those higher up are pursued. Money is clearly important in helping people to meet their fundamental needs but becomes less important once these are satisfied. Maslow's theory has important management implications. To

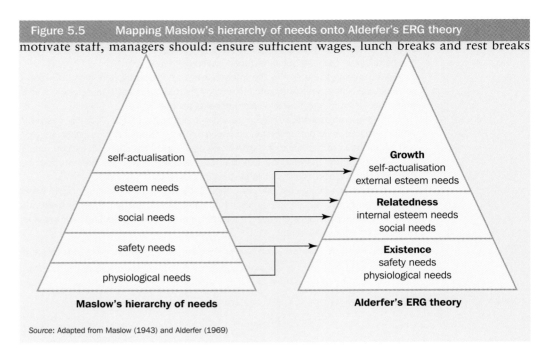

Figure 5.5   Mapping Maslow's hierarchy of needs onto Alderfer's ERG theory

Source: Adapted from Maslow (1943) and Alderfer (1969)

resolve physiological needs; provide a safe working environment and job security to satisfy safety needs; promote team building to meet social needs; recognise achievement to enhance esteem; and provide challenging work with opportunities for innovation and creativity to encourage self-actualisation. Maslow is widely criticised because there is no scientific evidence to support his strict hierarchy.

In contrast to Maslow's theory, Alderfer's ERG theory (Alderfer, 1969) is supported by empirical evidence. It collapses Maslow's five levels into three levels – existence, relatedness, and growth (see Figure 5.5) which different people prioritize differently. Existence relates to requirements for basic material existence; relatedness refers to a desire for interpersonal relationships; growth refers to a desire for personal development. The ERG theory introduces the *frustration–regression principle*, i.e. that an individual may regress to increase the satisfaction of a lower-order need that is easier to satisfy if a higher-order need is frustrated. For example, if growth opportunities are not provided an employee may satisfy relatedness needs more by socialising with fellow employees or by demanding more pay. The management message is that employees need to satisfy multiple needs simultaneously and a manager must take steps to ensure that employees are able to satisfy frustrated needs.

McGregor's Theory X and Theory Y
Maslow is reflected in McGregor's Theory X and Theory Y – characterisations of the way managers view workers rather than objective characterisations of workers. As suggested above, Theory X assumes employees to be lazy and motivated by pay. In contrast, Theory Y assumes they are motivated by goals of self-esteem; want to do a good job; seek responsibility and will be committed to the organisation if a job is satisfying. McGregor's message for management is simple – staff contribute more to an organisation if they are treated as responsible and valued employees.

Herzberg's two factor theory
Herzberg *et al.* (1959) found that the factors causing satisfaction – motivators – were different from the ones causing dissatisfaction – what he termed 'hygiene factors', and that employees could be dissatisfied with particular aspects of their work while still being satisfied with the job overall. Motivators associated with good feelings include achievement,

responsibility, recognition, advancement and the work itself. Hygiene factors included company policy and administration, working conditions, supervision and relationship with the supervisor, and pay. Unless the hygiene factors are satisfied then the motivators are of little use. Pay is categorised as a hygiene factor and employers must find an appropriate level of remuneration to meet expectations; no motivation will be achieved by paying more than this level, although hourly-paid staff are a notable exception to this rule (Weaver, 1988). Herzberg's theory helps to explain why it is necessary for managers to consider job design in providing employees with satisfying work, as true motivation comes from the extent to which a job enables achievement, involvement and recognition.

Job design (rotation, enlargement and enrichment) can be used to enhance individual satisfaction derived from work and ensure the most effective utilisation and performance of people within the organisation. Job rotation entails moving an employee from one job to another in order to add variety and relieve boredom, although this may only suffice in the short term. New skills may be acquired, but not necessarily skills at a higher level. Job rotation is a useful form of training to help employees identify with the complete product or service, e.g. graduate training programmes: restaurant staff working in the kitchen, and vice versa. Job enlargement increases the range of tasks to be completed by combining a number of same-level operations and provides more variety rather than improving intrinsic satisfaction. Job enrichment increases the complexity of the job and focuses on intrinsic satisfaction by incorporating motivators into the job and allowing more employee autonomy in the planning, execution and control of their work.

McClelland's achievement motivation

McClelland emphasises the importance of achievement in motivation among three main needs: affiliation (a sense of organisational belonging), power and achievement. He emphasises the importance of feedback by managers in maximising employee performance and retention. McClelland's focus on the individual can be at odds with the team approach which is essential for business success.

Process theories of motivation

Process theories, e.g. expectancy theory and equity theory, focus on how motivation takes place and why particular behaviours are initiated and sustained once they have attained their goals.

Expectancy theory

Developed by Victor Vroom (1964), expectancy theory suggests that motivation is based on how much we want something and how likely we think we are to get it – motivation plus effort leads to performance and outcomes. Outcomes are split into two levels – first-level outcomes, e.g. performance, and second-level outcomes, e.g. positive feedback, higher wages or promotion. Vroom identifies three key variables – valence (the attractiveness of a particular outcome to an individual); instrumentality (the extent that first-level outcomes lead to second-level outcomes); and expectancy (the likelihood that a particular behaviour leads to the desired outcome).

Porter and Lawler (1968) extended Vroom's expectancy model by suggesting that performance should be matched to rewards. Extrinsic rewards include satisfaction, achievement, responsibility and recognition. Intrinsic rewards include salary and working conditions. Rewards are evaluated against the effort expended and the level of performance attained and individuals are generally satisfied if the rewards seem fair.

To apply expectancy theory, managers must understand the outcomes individual employees want and the levels of performance required to meet organisational goals, making sure that the desired levels of performance are achievable and that the outcomes and performance are linked with sufficient rewards.

Equity theory

Equity theory, developed by Adams (1979), focuses on how fairly employees think they have been treated in comparison with others. Under-reward or over-reward results in inequity and a review of behaviour, e.g. reduced effort, absenteeism, resignation. Managers must understand that to motivate employees rewards must be seen to be fair.

Reinforcement theories

Rewards are important in producing particular required behaviours and causing such behaviours to be repeated. Managers can use positive reinforcement to reward and strengthen particular behaviours and punishments to eliminate undesired behaviour. Ignoring and not reinforcing inappropriate behaviour should result in extinction of that behaviour.

■ Motivation in practice

This list of different motivational theories might seem daunting. However, it is important for a manager to realise that no one theory reflects the complexity or sophistication of individuals. An awareness of the different theories is an important part of a manager's toolkit. 'Carrots', i.e. treating people fairly, clear goals and an understanding of individual motivation, are much more effective than 'sticks', i.e. disciplining and punishing, in enabling a manager to maximise employee contribution to the overall success of the business.

Holistic HR integration for tourism business success

The customer interface is totally reliant on employee performance so employees are vital to the success of tourism organisations and their competitive advantage. There are some implicit assumptions about how HR contributes to tourism business success:

- Satisfied and motivated employees perform better and add value to the organisation by enhancing customer perceptions of quality.
- Shared organisational values aid the development and achievement of business objectives.
- Good employee relations promote a positive image of the organisation.
- Effective recruitment and training ensures organisational resources are used efficiently.
- Motivated employees are more adaptable to change.

■ Performance management

Effective managers understand the 4Cs – commitment, competence, congruence and cost-effectiveness (Beer *et al.*, 1984) – and are able to integrate them holistically into business strategy to achieve organisational competitiveness.

- **Commitment:** awareness of business objectives and understanding how they can contribute to their achievement enhance staff commitment to the organisation. Managers have a critical role in communicating business objectives to staff – it is counter-productive if staff do not understand what the organisation is trying to achieve.
- **Competence:** managerial and employee competence are both critical to the achievement of business objectives and organisational competitiveness. Remedial action must be taken to address skills gaps.
- **Congruence:** managers and staff must pull in the same direction and share the same vision to collaborate in achieving business objectives. Transparency and good com-

munication will enhance working relationships and identify any obstacles to achieving business objectives and how these may be overcome.

- **Cost-effectiveness**: managers must be both proactive and responsive to use human resources effectively and efficiently and maximimise productivity. Job enrichment, for example, may retain valued employees dissatisfied in their current roles and avoid incurring unnecessary recruitment costs while increasing competence and developing a multi-skilled and more flexible workforce.

Performance management integrates employee development with results-based assessment aligned to strategic business objectives to achieve the 4Cs. The effective management and execution of appraisals is an integral part of performance management, as they encourage continuous improvement and development. The model of performance management adopted by an organisation must be customised to meet individual business and employee needs. HR audits can be used to identify key strategic issues and define the role of HR in achieving competitive advantage (see Lynch, 2000).

Human resource planning

Human resource planning (HRP) forecasts how many and what type of employees will be required in the future and whether this can be met within the current workforce or whether there is a need to hire, train, redeploy or dismiss employees. HRP will shape the development of the organisation by integrating a HR strategy holistically into the wider business strategy to achieve organisational objectives. Effective HRP should investigate and analyse internal and external environments, identify HR imbalances or 'employee gaps' through forecasting, manage staff deployment through effective HR policies/procedures and develop strategies for staff retention.

Training needs analysis

Training is critical to business success – training and development needs can be identified at organisational, job/occupational and individual levels. This triangulation of information forms the framework for training needs analysis (TNA). To ensure the effectiveness and efficiency of training, a systematic approach should be adopted (see Graham and Bennett, 1998):

1 Analyse and define the job in terms of its composite tasks.
2 Establish reasonable standards of performance for individual tasks.
3 Measure employee performance against reasonable standards of performance in (2) for each task.
4 Training gaps exist where employee performance in (3) is less than the reasonable standards of performance established in (2).
5 Develop training programmes to fulfil training needs.
6 Deliver training and update employee training records.
7 Assess post-training performance. Successful training will achieve the requisite performance standards identified in (2).
8 Compare the cost of training with the financial benefits achieved by improved employee performance (cost–benefit analysis).
9 Modify the training, as necessary, in the light of (7) and (8).

Training demonstrates organisational commitment to employees. Thus, the benefits of training may extend beyond improved performance of a specific task due to enhanced motivation and commitment. In many tourism jobs success relates to customer perceptions of the quality of the experience of the service interaction and it is often difficult to quantify cost–benefits – assessment is easier for more tangible and quantifiable tasks.

Case 5.2   Signposts to success

In many parts of the world the tourism industry is dominated by small and microbusinesses – many with less than ten employees. In developed countries there are few handicaps to becoming the owner/manager of a small tourism business. This coupled with an 'anyone can do it mentality' results in many tourism businesses lacking management skills, particularly HRM skills, and consequently these businesses underperform. Lack of HRM skills sets up a downward spiral with impacts on staff recruitment; motivation; job satisfaction; and ultimately staff retention. High labour turnover militates against investment in training and many businesses suffer from *warm body syndrome*, i.e. they opt to run underskilled rather than understaffed, deskilling their product to match labour market skills. Low employee skills impact on customer interaction and reduce customer perceptions of quality, which reduces competitiveness, restricts profitability and limits the opportunity for re-investment at an individual business level.

Many tourism destinations, e.g. Wales and a number of other European countries, are dominated by small and microbusinesses and quality at a business level impacts upon competitiveness at a destination level. 'As a rule the extent of political involvement is directly related to the importance attached to tourism as an economic activity' (Wanhill, 2004: 54), and correlates with the vigour with which public-sector agencies responsible for strategic destination development pursue tourism microbusiness development. One agency involved in destination development with a focus on tourism microbusiness development through human resource development (HRD) is the Tourism Training Forum for Wales (TTFW)[1], which has produced a range of business support materials, including the *Success Through Your People Toolkit*[2] that integrates HRM into strategic business development.

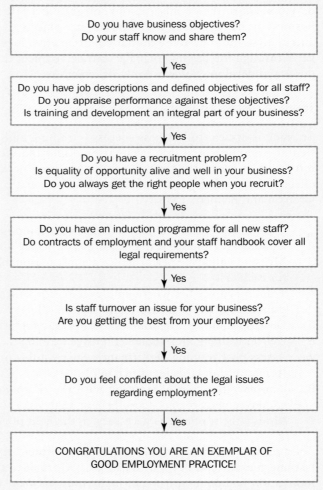

Do you have business objectives?
Do your staff know and share them?

↓ Yes

Do you have job descriptions and defined objectives for all staff?
Do you appraise performance against these objectives?
Is training and development an integral part of your business?

↓ Yes

Do you have a recruitment problem?
Is equality of opportunity alive and well in your business?
Do you always get the right people when you recruit?

↓ Yes

Do you have an induction programme for all new staff?
Do contracts of employment and your staff handbook cover all legal requirements?

↓ Yes

Is staff turnover an issue for your business?
Are you getting the best from your employees?

↓ Yes

Do you feel confident about the legal issues regarding employment?

↓ Yes

CONGRATULATIONS YOU ARE AN EXEMPLAR OF GOOD EMPLOYMENT PRACTICE!

Source: TTFW and WTB

Success Through Your People provides comprehensive support on employment issues for tourism employers. The toolkit uses an auditing flowchart to enable tourism managers to pinpoint key areas of underperformance in relation to their employment practices. It showcases successful examples of good employment practice and provides templates of documents, e.g. contracts of employment, induction programmes, and appraisal forms, that can be customised for individual business needs. Thus, *Success Through Your People* demonstrates how to achieve transparency in employment practice.

© Tourism Training Forum for Wales and Wales Tourist Board

1 Tourism Training Forum for Wales (TTFW) was established in 1998 to coordinate key stakeholders and enhance professionalism in the Welsh tourism industry by developing a culture of education and training to provide a higher value tourism product and enhanced visitor experience.

2 *Success Through Your People* is available in printed and CD-ROM format and can be accessed on **www.whodoiask.com**, which provides hotlinks to key UK-based support agencies including the Health and Safety Executive, ACAS and the Inland Revenue.

Thanks are due to Diana James and Anna Chapman of TTFW for their invaluable help in compiling this case study.

Conclusion: future HR challenges for the tourism industry

The success of the tourism industry and ultimately of the destination depend on the quality of employees. The real HR challenge for the tourism industry is recruiting and retaining employees with the right skills, knowledge and attitudes to their work. There are a number of approaches to recruiting, retaining and motivating employees:

- positively targeting recruits from groups under-represented in the workplace (e.g. women returners, ethnic minorities, people with special needs and mature workers);
- providing career development opportunities;
- ensuring competent line management;
- considering job design and job roles, including: job enlargement, job enrichment, job rotation, job satisfaction and job sharing;
- providing a better deal than employees perceive they can get from alternative employers;
- providing training and development opportunities and ensuring that the organisation views training as an investment rather than a cost;
- considering levels of pay and non-financial rewards on a regular basis;
- managing employee expectations;
- ensuring all new recruits complete a well-planned induction programme;
- addressing equality issues, e.g. through the implementation of family-friendly HR practices.

Discussion questions

A visitor attraction with a large food and beverage operation is located in a former industrial area of the UK and attracts approximately 500,000 visitors annually. It has traditionally recruited from the younger end of the local labour market through government employment agencies and word-of-mouth. The attraction is currently experiencing recruitment difficulties in key operational areas and the senior management team (SMT) is considering other sources of labour, specifically mature local employees and overseas employees, to fill these vacancies and ensure that the visitor attraction maintains its competitive advantage.

Discussion questions continued

1 Using supporting evidence, identify possible reasons for the recruitment difficulties facing this visitor attraction and discuss how HR can enhance service quality and enable the visitor attraction to maintain its competitive advantage.

2 Explain how you would advise the visitor attraction's SMT to adapt its recruitment, selection and training programmes in order to attract and retain (a) mature local employees and (b) overseas employees.

3 Devise three flexible benefits packages – one aimed at overseas employees, one at employees aged between 16–19, and one for those aged over 45 – explaining why each package is suitable for these different employees.

Guided reading

HRM issues may be explored through a range of sources. A variety of topical HR issues relevant to students, academics and practitioners, is covered in *People Management* – the magazine of the Chartered Institute of Personnel and Development (CIPD), and their website is a further source of information (**www.cipd.co.uk**).

HRM-specific academic journals include *Employee Relations*, *Human Relations*, *Human Resource Management Journal*, *International Journal of Human Resource Management*, *Training and Development*, *Journal of Human Resources*, *Education + Training*, *Personnel Management*, *Journal of Human Resources in Hospitality and Tourism* and the *Journal of European Industrial Training*. These provide a rich source of information on all aspects of HRM and HRD.

HR issues are also addressed in mainstream tourism journals, such as *Annals of Tourism Research*, *Journal of Tourism Studies*, *Journal of Travel Research*, *Tourism Economics*, *Tourism and Hospitality Research*, *Journal of Hospitality and Tourism Management* and *Tourism Management*.

There are a number of generic HRM textbooks, including *Human Resource Management: a contemporary approach* (Beardwell and Holden), *Human Resource Management* (Graham and Bennett), *Human Resource Management* (Torrington, Hall and Taylor) and *Contemporary Human Resource Management* (Redman and Wilkinson).

The Institute for Employment Studies (**www.employment-studies.co.uk**) covers all aspects of employment policy and practice, undertakes research and consultancy for UK and international organisations and can provide a further source of valuable information.

Recommended websites

4Hoteliers: information for international hoteliers and travel trade executives, providing current industry news and a research library covering topics such as human resources and training, **www.4hoteliers.com** .

Arbitration and Conciliation Advisory Service: employment information and practical help to tackle workplace issues, **www.acas.org.uk** .

Business Link: practical advice for businesses, including employees, sales and marketing, and finance, **www.businesslink.gov.uk/bdotg/action/home** .

EmpLaw: online British employment law information, **www.emplaw.co.uk** .

European Employment Observatory: contributes to the development of the European Employment Strategy through the provision of information and research on employment policies and labour market trends, **www.eu-employment-observatory.net** .

The HR Portal: includes: HR hot topics; industry indicators; financial and academic viewpoints and workplace legislation, **www.hrportal.com** .

HRMGuide: a series of linked websites containing HRM-related resources covering all the basic subject areas. The UK site **www.hrmguide.co.uk** contains direct links to HRM Guide Australia (**www.hrmguide.net/australia**); HRM Guide Canada (**www.hrmguide.net/canada**) and HRM Guide USA (**www.hrmguide.com**).

International Labour Organization: a source of information on: vocational training; employment policy; labour administration; labour law and industrial relations; working conditions; management development; labour statistics; and occupational safety and health, **www.ilo.org** .

World at Work: Professional Association for Compensation, Benefits and Total Rewards, **www.worldatwork.org** .

Your People Manager: aimed at helping the managers of small businesses deal with the everyday issues of managing staff, **www.yourpeoplemanager.com.**

Key words

Employee relations; Human Resource Management (HRM); labour market; motivation; recruitment difficulties; personnel; skills gaps; skills shortages.

Bibliography

Adams, J.S. (1979) Injustice in Social Exchange, in L.L. Berkowitz (ed.) *Advances in Experimental Social Psychology*, Volume 2. Academic Press, New York, 267–299.

Alderfer, C.P. (1969) An Empirical Test of a New Theory of Human Needs, *Organizational Behaviour and Human Performance*, 4: 142–175.

Baum, T. (1995) *Managing Human Resources in the European Tourism and Hospitality Industry: A Strategic Approach*. Chapman and Hall, London.

Baum, T. (1997) Managing People at the Periphery: Implications for the tourism and hospitality industry, in N. Hemmington (ed.) *Proceedings of 6th Annual CHME Hospitality Research Conference*, Oxford Brookes University, 86–97.

BBC (2004) *Pillow Talk* [online]. Available from: **www.bbc.co.uk/wales/overnightsuccess/casestudies** (accessed 2 September 2004).

Beer, M., Spector, B., Lawrence, P.R., Quinn Mills, D. and Walton, R.E. (1984) *Managing Human Assets*. Free Press, New York.

Boella, M.J. (2000) *Human Resource Management in the Hospitality Industry*, 7th edn. Stanley Thornes, Cheltenham.

Bratton, J. and Gold, J. (1999) *Human Resource Management: Theory and Practice*, 2nd edn. Macmillan, Basingstoke.

Chappel, S. (2002) Hospitality and Emotional Labour in an International Context, in N. D'Annunzio-Green, G.A. Maxwell and S. Watson (eds) *Human Resource Management: International Perspectives in Hospitality and Tourism*. Thomson, London, 225–240.

Choy, D. (1995) The quality of tourism employment, *Tourism Management*, 16(2), 129–137.

CIPD (2004) Recruitment, retention and turnover 2004: a survey of the UK and Ireland, London, Chartered Institute of Personnel and Development.

Deery, M.A. (2002) Labour turnover in International Hospitality and Tourism, in N. D'Annunzio-Green, G.A. Maxwell and S. Watson (eds) *Human Resource Management: International Perspectives in Hospitality and Tourism*. Thomson, London, 51–63.

Deery, M.A. and Iverson, R.D. (1996) Enhancing productivity: intervention strategies for employee turnover, in N. Johns (ed.) *Productivity Management in Hospitality and Tourism*. Cassell, London, 68–95.

Evans, N., Campbell, D. and Stonehouse, G. (2003) *Strategic Management for Travel and Tourism*. Butterworth-Heinemann, Oxford.

Graham, H.T. and Bennett, R. (1998) *Human Resources Management*, 9th edn. Pitman, London.

Hall, L. and Torrington, D. (1998) *The Human Resource Function: the dynamics of change and development*. Pitman, London.

Hayter, R. (2001) The 'hospitality' branding: a question of impact on the industry's image, *The Hospitality Review*, 3(1), 21–25.

Herzberg, F., Mausner, B. and Snyderman, B.B. (1959) *The Motivation to Work*. John Wiley and Sons, New York.

Hochschild, A.R. (1983) *The Managed Heart: commercialization of human feeling*. University of California Press, Berkeley.

HtF (2001) *Labour Market Review 2001 for the Hospitality Industry*. Hospitality Training Foundation, London.

Johnson, K. (1981) Towards an understanding of labour turnover, *Service Industries Review*, 1, 4–17.

Keep, E. and Mayhew, K. (1999) *The Leisure Sector. Skills Task Force Research Group: Paper 6*, Oxford and Warwick Universities: ESRC Centre on Skills, Knowledge and Organizational Performance.

Lashley, C. (2000) Up against the wall: the cost of staff turnover in licensed retailing, *The Hospitality Review*, 2(1), 53–56.

Lashley, C. and Chaplain, A. (1999) Labour Turnover: hidden problem – hidden cost, *The Hospitality Review*, 1(1), 49–54.

Lawler, E. (1995) The new pay: a strategic approach, *Compensation and Benefits Review*, July–August, 14–22.

Lynch, R. (2000) *Corporate Strategy*, 2nd edn. Financial Times Management, London.

Maslow, A. (1943) A theory of human motivation, *Psychological Review*, 50, 370–396.

Mattsson, J. (1994) Improving service quality in person to person encounters: integrating findings from a multidisciplinary review, *Service Industries Journal*, 14(1), 45–61.

McGregor, D. (1960) *The Human Side of Enterprise*. McGraw-Hill, New York.

Monks, K. (1996) *Roles in Personnel Management from Welfarism to Moderism: Fast Track or Back Track?* [online]. Available from: **www.dcu.ie/dcubs/ research_papers/no17.htm** (accessed 1 April 2004).

Pax Christi (2000) *The European Union and Cuba: Solidarity or Complicity?* Pax Christi Netherlands, Utrecht, The Netherlands.

Porter, L.W. and Lawler, E.E. (1968) *Managerial Attitudes and Performance*. Irwin, Homewood, IL.

Reynolds, J. and Sloman, M. (2004) In the driving seat, *People Management*, 10(3), 40–42.

Rowson, B. (2000) Much ado about nothing: the impact on small hotels of the national minimum wage, *The Hospitality Review*, 2(1), 15–17.

Schaffer, J. (1984) Strategy, organization structure and success in the lodging industry, *International Journal of Hospitality Management*, 3(4), 159–165.

Shaw, G. and Williams, A. (1994) *Critical Issues in Tourism: a geographical perspective*. Blackwell, Oxford.

Sisson, K. (1995) Human Resource Management and the Personnel Function, in: J. Storey (ed.) *Human Resource Management: A Critical Text*. Routledge, London, 87–109.

Taylor, F.W. (1911) *Principles of Scientific Management*. Norton and Co, New York.

Torrington, D. (1989) Human Resource Management and the Personnel Function, in: J. Storey (ed.) *New Perspectives on Human Resource Management*. Routledge, London, 56–66.

Torrington, D. and Hall, L. (1998) *Human Resource Management*, 4th edn. Prentice Hall Europe, London.

Torrington, D., Hall, L. and Taylor, S. (2002) *Human Resource Management*, 5th edn. Financial Times Prentice Hall, Harlow.

Vroom, V.H. (1964) *Work and Motivation*. John Wiley and Sons, New York.

Wanhill, S. (2004) Government Assistance for Tourism SMEs: From Theory to Practice, in R. Thomas (ed.) *Small Firms in Tourism: International Perspectives.* Elsevier Ltd, Oxford, 53–70.

Weaver, T. (1988) Theory M: Motivating with Money, *Cornell Hotel and Restaurant Administration Quarterly*, 29(3), 40–46.

White, A. and Jones, E. (2002) *Gender Equality in the Tourism Workplace.* Tourism Training Forum for Wales, Cardiff.

WTTC (2004) *Travel and Tourism Forging Ahead: the 2004 Travel and Tourism Economic Research.* World Travel and Tourism Council, London.

Chapter 6

Marketing in tourism

Beulah Cope, Bristol Business School

Learning outcomes

On completion of this chapter the reader should be able to:

- identify the challenges of marketing a business that is essentially based on the provision of services rather than products;

- review the strategies available to address those challenges and assess their suitability for particular tourism operations;

- apply theoretical and conceptual knowledge and understanding to practical tourism marketing situations;

- assess tourism buyer behaviour both at individual and corporate level;

- assess the value of relationship-building within tourism and review the methods used to achieve this;

- apply elements of the services-marketing mix to a range of tourism contexts;

- outline the elements of a marketing plan for a tourism organisation.

Overview

The chapter explores a range of key topics within the marketing arena and relates them to different types of organisation within the tourism sector. It begins with an explanation of the challenges posed by the services nature of tourism businesses, looking in turn at intangibility (which encompasses perishability and lack of ownership), inseparability and variability. Potential solutions to each challenge are examined, using suggestions from general services-marketing theorists as well as from tourism-marketing specialists, and demonstrating how the elements of the services-marketing mix can be used separately or in combination to address the challenges identified. There is particular focus on the importance for tourism managers of understanding buyer behaviour, of identifying and using the most appropriate distribution and promotional methods for their particular products and services, of anticipating critical incident points during service delivery, of integrating physical evidence into the service offering and of developing and managing relationships. The chapter concludes with a résumé of the processes involved in marketing planning and sets them within the context of tourism.

Introduction

Marketing tourism is not for the faint-hearted! A range of factors ensures that it is extremely challenging and that, even when one challenge is overcome, there are always new ones to be faced, new decisions to be taken. Every tourism organisation encounters its own set of ongoing challenges. Take an international airline for example. To ensure profitability it needs to sell as many seats on its flights as possible, especially since, once a flight has taken off, the opportunity to sell seats on it has gone forever. How can it differentiate its flights from those of other airlines? How can it convey the message to potential passengers and persuade them to use its flights? Indeed, who are its potential passengers and how can it find out what matters to them in choosing an airline? Is it the ticket price, comfort on board, availability of connecting flights, location of airport, timing of flights, etc? If it is a mixture of all those things, which is most important? Should the airline pay travel agencies to ensure as wide a distribution of its flights as possible or should it sell directly to passengers and so keep the ticket price in its entirety? How can it ensure that its passengers enjoy their flight and are inspired to use the airline again and recommend it to others? How does it respond when another airline introduces a new idea to tempt passengers onto its flights? And what happens if there is some unfavourable publicity about its own flights or destinations? The challenges are seemingly unending, and while they are very practical in nature, it is through understanding and applying marketing theory that solutions are normally to be found and, equally important, that the implications of new and innovative ideas can be fully considered before implementation so that costly mistakes can be avoided.

While tourism has many features which distinguish it from other industries, an understanding of general marketing principles is essential for any manager involved in tourism marketing. More specifically, the increasing volume of services marketing literature is particularly useful for tourism managers, given that tourism offerings tend to be either pure services or a combination of services and goods or products. Effectively, successful tourism marketing involves adapting and applying general- and services-marketing strategies and techniques to the specific needs of individual organisations and operations.

While definitions of marketing are plentiful, and lifetimes could be spent debating their relative merits, this chapter will use as its basis the one provided by the Chartered Institute of Marketing (Blood, 1976) in which marketing is summarised as:

> The management process which identifies, anticipates and supplies customer requirements efficiently and profitably.

Whereas some marketing texts focus on those marketing activities which are conducted 'pre-consumption' by a marketing department, this chapter adopts a wider perspective and explores the role of marketing before, during and after the consumption of the tourism service or product. This approach is based on the premise that marketing should not simply be the province of a marketing department. Rather, it is something that needs to permeate the whole organisation and its operations, ensuring that the business has a 'marketing orientation' rather than a 'product orientation', with each and every employee having a role to play in its marketing (Narver and Slater, 1990; Palmer, 2001).

The services-marketing approach

When applying marketing theory to specific tourism operations, managers need to be aware of the position of their operation along the goods–service continuum. Is what they are marketing a pure service or is it a mixture of goods and services? Their marketing activities will need to be adapted accordingly. For the marketing of goods, the key elements which managers must have correct in their 'marketing mix' are known as the 'four Ps' of: Product, Price, Place and Promotion. For the marketing of services, three extra Ps are added to the list: People, Processes and Physical evidence.

Whereas a good is a physical entity that, once purchased, can be taken away, eaten, drunk or used, a service in contrast has no physical existence; it is an experience. For example, in a restaurant that offers a take-away service, the good is the food to be consumed, and the service is the experience of purchasing that food, including elements such as the ambience in the waiting area, the customer care provided by the staff, the clarity of the menu, the length of time taken for the order to be processed and the interaction with other customers. In many tourism operations, it is the service which constitutes the greater part or all of the offering, thus obliging tourism managers to focus more and more on services-marketing principles. The theatrical metaphor (Figure 6.1) often used by services-marketing theorists is applicable to a greater or lesser degree to the entire tourism sector, where customers judge the whole organisation by what they see and experience of it, oblivious to the work that needs to go on behind the scenes before, during and after the 'performance'.

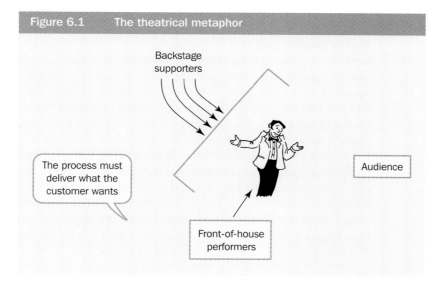

Figure 6.1   The theatrical metaphor

The three characteristics that distinguish services from goods and that have obliged marketing managers to incorporate the three extra Ps of People, Process and Physical evidence into their marketing mix are intangibility (which embraces two further characteristics of perishability and lack of ownership), inseparability and variability (sometimes referred to as heterogeneity).

Intangibility

Services are intangible. Unlike goods, they cannot be inspected before purchase, so customers are unable to check them before they buy them to make sure that they are exactly what they want and of the right quality. Buying goods can be seen as relatively straightforward in comparison with buying services. Taking shoes as an example, customers can compare what is on offer in the various footwear outlets. They can select any pair of shoes on sale, look at them, touch them, even smell them if they choose to, try them on, see what they look like on the feet, walk around in them to check how well they fit. If there is anything they do not like about them, they can keep looking and trying on pairs until they find exactly what they want. It is only if and when they finally decide on a particular pair that they will delve into their wallet and produce payment, for which they will receive the shoes to take away with them. By contrast, someone wanting to buy a service such as a holiday can only imagine what the holidays on offer will be like, assisted admittedly by brochure and/or screen images. The customer is likely to say to herself: 'Yes, the hotels all look very welcoming in the pictures and the beaches seem idyllic, but will they be like that all the time? Will the rooms be clean, how good will the service be? How crowded are the pools likely to be in high season? It's really important that I find the right thing, as this is my main holiday this year and I'm looking forward so much to going somewhere nice, meeting new people and enjoying myself. How on earth can I choose between all these seemingly very similar holidays? And whichever I do choose, I have to pay for it weeks before I go and won't find out if it's okay until I'm there and it's too late.'

The above scenario illustrates several of the challenges faced by tourism managers in trying to market something intangible. From the customer's perspective, buying a tourism service involves risk, as she is paying for an experience which it is impossible to sample in advance. In her efforts to reduce that risk, she is likely to adopt one or more of the following strategies.

To seek tangible cues

In this case, she would study the holiday brochures, comparing the descriptions of resorts, hotels, excursions and activities. Because the tangible evidence to which she has access is so limited, however, she would be likely to be influenced by much more than just the written word and the images of the hotel and landscape. The photographs used on the cover and in the brochures become highly significant, particularly if the holiday-makers shown in those photographs look like people she would either like very much or not like at all to meet! Even the paper quality and the colours used in the artwork are likely to influence her perception of the holiday company and its suitability for her. Such points show just how important it is for tourism managers to identify their target markets, so that they can ensure that any tangibles they produce will be attractive to those target markets. A quick inspection just of the front covers of holiday brochures on a travel agency shelf will provide a strong indication of the impression each tour operator is trying to convey of its holidays and its clients.

To seek personal and third-party recommendations

The would-be holiday-maker, anxious to make the right decision over her choice of holiday, is likely to seek the advice of others from whose knowledge and experience she may be able to benefit. In the purchasing of services, personal recommendations understandably become particularly important. If someone whose judgement is respected passes on advice or recommendations about a service and/or service provider, then the risk factor involved in the service purchase decision will be alleviated. Of course, it is a brave, even foolhardy person who dares tell someone else that they will definitely enjoy a particular holiday, but nevertheless they can provide information on their own perceptions of the experience. The would-be holiday-maker is likely to look beyond just personal friends and acquaintances for advice and guidance. She may refer to any third-party guidance, including reports on television, in magazines and newspapers; she may even ask the travel agent the loaded and extremely dangerous question: 'What would you choose if you were me?'

Thus, from the perspective of tourism managers, it is essential to ensure that any 'word-of-mouth' or third-party information about their operation is positive, and that their customers enjoy their experience so much that they recommend the company to their friends and acquaintances.

To use price as a basis for assessing quality

One criterion to measure quality used, understandably, by buyers of goods as well as of services is to assume that quality is related to price and that the more one pays, the better will be the product or service provided. The challenge for the tourism manager is to set prices at levels which will be seen by the customer as 'worth paying' and appropriate for the type of experience they are purchasing, in other words, which will fit with their quality expectations, ensuring above all that on consumption those customers will feel that they have received value for money.

The challenge of price-setting is exacerbated in tourism by the issue of perishability and its associated seasonality. Tourism services are perishable – they cannot be stored and used at a later date. They are also usually seasonal, either because their offering is dependent on the season – summer-sun destinations or winter-sports resorts, for example – or because their market is seasonal – dependent on school-holiday periods, perhaps. From a financial perspective, tourism managers use price as a mechanism to generate as much profit as possible from an operation where demand is uneven. Package-holiday prices, for example, are varied (or 'flexed') throughout the year, with prices lowered at times of low demand in order to stimulate sales, and increased at peak times to capitalise on high demand. These changing prices are likely to create a measure of confusion for those customers who are trying to use price as a basis for quality measurement. Further, yield management, explored fully in Chapter 10, has emerged in many tourism operations, particularly in the transport sector, as a management response to fluctuating demand and has the potential to create a certain amount of dissatisfaction among customers, should they be tempted into a discussion comparing how much each has paid for the same service.

Tourism managers' responses to the challenges of intangibility

The intangibility of tourism often results in potential customers:

- perceiving high levels of risk in the buying process;
- finding it difficult to distinguish between competing services;
- seeking third-party advice and/or relying on word-of-mouth recommendation;
- using price as an indicator of quality.

To address these challenges, several responses are used, including:

- creating a reassuring buying process, with a focus on tangible, physical evidence;
- creating a strong brand image which is attractive and reassuring in itself to potential customers;
- ensuring that current customers enjoy their experience so that they will provide word-of-mouth recommendation to future customers;
- establishing and maintaining links with those current customers so that they will book again as well as generate word-of-mouth recommendation;
- engaging the support of those third parties who could influence the purchasing decisions of new customers, such as the travel media and travel agencies;
- including and publicising something in their service offering which distinguishes them from and provides a competitive advantage over other tourism services, at least until their competitors 'catch up' through imitation.

Underpinning all these responses is the need for the services organisation to undertake continuous research into its potential clientele, to identify their preferences for the service itself, the tangibles which would appeal to them, the sources to which they would refer for recommendations, and so on.

The subtleties of intangibility

The impact of intangibility varies between both customers and services. In the example quoted earlier, the customer's perception of risk over her holiday purchase was great. For some tourism purchases, however, the fact that they are intangible may appear to be utterly insignificant. For seasoned business travellers, who see a flight as a means of transport from one place to another and who have experience of all the airlines operating on a particular route, there would be no perception of risk in booking a flight and no desire to refer to a third party for help in making the purchasing decision. In fact, as the travellers feel confident that they know exactly what to expect, the service has become more or less tangible to them. Interestingly enough, however, such seasoned travellers do present a serious challenge for transport managers. If they, or the person who books the flight on their behalf, always buy a service they know, how will competing airlines or even railways, who may offer a more suitable service, ever find the opportunity to suggest this to them?

Corollaries of intangibility: perishability and lack of ownership

Perishability

Mentioned earlier was the challenge to profitability created by the perishable nature of tourism services. If only 20 of the 50 rooms in a hotel are used one night, then the potential income from the remaining 30 rooms that night is lost forever. An additional challenge produced by uneven demand for services is its impact on operations and quality of customer experience. Visiting a theme park on a busy day, for example, may mean waiting in long queues for the ride of choice, whereas on a quiet day there may be no queues, but equally not much atmosphere. Lovelock (2001) talks of four conditions for a service which has a fixed capacity:

- **excess demand**, where some customers have to be turned away and conditions are likely to be crowded and rushed;
- **demand exceeds optimum capacity**, where even though no-one is turned away, conditions are likely to be crowded and rushed;
- **demand and supply are well-balanced**, the optimum level of capacity, where staff and facilities are fully used yet not overworked and customers feel well served;
- **excess capacity**, where resources are under-used and customer experience may be disappointing.

Clearly the goal of tourism managers is to achieve the optimum level of capacity, for the sake of profitability as well as service quality. A range of possible strategies is explored in services-marketing theory to achieve this balance, and tourism managers select and apply those strategies which best fit their particular operation. Essentially the strategies involve either or both adjusting supply to meet demand and adjusting demand to meet supply.

Methods of adjusting supply to meet demand

Some tourism operations may be able to increase their capacity at peak times and reduce it at quiet times. For example, trains may carry extra coaches at commuter times, holiday operators usually recruit extra staff to cope with the busy periods and restaurants regularly squeeze in extra tables and chairs for their peak times. Because such adjustments do pre-suppose advance knowledge of peaks and troughs in demand, integral to operational planning must be effective booking systems, analysis of previous usage patterns and awareness and anticipation of external influences on demand. Further, some flexibility in the workforce is essential, managers opting perhaps to have a core of permanent staff and in addition recruit seasonal, temporary, and peripheral staff.

Case 6.1   Some of the Eden Project's strategies to address seasonality

The Eden Project in Cornwall has become 'an internationally renowned destination, . . . described as the 8th wonder of the world, . . . a gateway into the fascinating world of plants and people and a vibrant reminder of how we need each other for our mutual survival.' (**http://www.edenproject.com/3567.htm**) As a tourist destination it is fairly unusual as 'price' is not its key mechanism to address the challenges of perishability and seasonality. Rather, it addresses them by adapting its supply to attract visitors all year round, actually making use of the different possibilities afforded by the different seasons. Even though much of the thirty acre 'global garden' is outside, much of it is also under cover and heated, so its visitor numbers will not be reduced dramatically by inclement weather. Strategies mentioned in this chapter which are in current use by the Eden Project include the following:

Increasing the versatility of the attraction

- its use as a venue for concerts, hosting high profile bands and most notably its participation in the 2005 global Live 8 concerts, showcasing as it did the best of black African music;
- its development of an Education Centre to host events, exhibitions and learning activities;
- the inclusion of a large floodlit covered ice-rink in the winter months;
- the availability of some of its facilities for private functions.

Increasing capacity at peak times

- extending opening hours throughout the summer, with even longer opening hours in school holiday periods;
- evening activities in school holiday periods, in 2005 for example, tempting visitors with spit roast barbecues and the chance to experience the jungle rainforest as night fell. (Entrance prices for evening events are lower than for full day visits, which may well serve to 'even out' demand, by persuading local visitors to come later in the day than they may ordinarily have done.)

Adapting the servicescape

- paying particular attention to traffic and customer management, the Eden Project was able to limit the number of queues on site in 2004 to one!

Source: Reproduced with permission of the Eden Project

As well as increasing and reducing capacity to meet demand, tourism businesses may also increase the versatility of their capacity to suit a range of markets. An excellent example of this is the Lakeside Holiday Centre in Hayling Island, where complementary markets are catered for all year round; groups of bowls players stay during the week, enjoying playing and watching this, the UK's most popular team sport, in the multi-rink undercover bowls centre, and over the weekend short-break holiday-makers enjoy themed weekends during which the bowls hall is transformed into a ballroom or a stage and auditorium, according to the needs of the particular theme for the weekend. Again, in developing such versatile services there is a need for flexible staffing; in this case some members of staff would also need to be multi-skilled.

Tourism managers may also consider other adaptations to accommodate greater numbers of customers at busy times. These could involve redesigning the 'serviscape' (the place in which the service occurs), increasing the role of the customer in the service process and industrialising that service process. All three techniques will be explored later in this chapter, as they serve to respond not just to the challenges of perishability, but also to the challenges of inseparability and variability.

Methods of adjusting demand to meet supply

Common in tourism is the marketing technique of manipulating price to smooth demand. Room prices in some city-centre hotels, for example, are high during the week, when business demand is strong, and then much reduced at the weekend, when the business market largely disappears. Additionally, promotional efforts are increased when tourism services are 'chasing demand'. Remaining with the example of the city-centre hotel, different 'weekend' markets will be targeted and packages offered that provide free use of the hotel's fitness club or a 'kiddies' club, for example. Tourism providers working through agencies are also likely to offer increased incentives to their agents during periods of low demand. In some cases the most practical incentive may be a free experience for the agent, especially since there is likely to be spare capacity at this time of low demand. Such an incentive has the advantage of providing the agents with first-hand knowledge of the service so that they can recommend it with authority when they return to the agency.

Lack of ownership

When customers buy goods, they can take them away with them or consume them; when they buy a service, nothing actually changes hands. Neither the buyer nor the seller can claim to 'own' the service. One key implication of this for service businesses is that they are unable to patent the service they provide. Should they be resourceful enough to include a new and attractive service element into their offering, the competitive advantage it brings them will only last until others copy their idea and integrate it into their service. The tourism industry is well served with examples of this. The winter sports operator, Neilson, was the first to introduce a 'snow guarantee' in the 1980s, which compensated clients in the event of insufficient snow, taking some of the 'risk' from the holiday purchase and thereby providing Neilson with a competitive edge. By 1990, all winter-sports operators offered snow guarantees and it no longer provided a competitive edge for any one company. The concept of the low-cost airline, pioneered by Southwest Airlines, has now spread worldwide and competition between low-cost carriers is becoming intense.

For tourism managers the phenomenon of lack of ownership has both advantages and drawbacks. On the positive side, because there is no physical product to sell, tourism businesses do not experience the same practical problems of distribution and storage as businesses selling goods. They do, however, have to convince their potential customers (and intermediaries if they use them) that their service is the one to buy. One way of doing this is to create a 'unique selling point' or USP which sets them apart from their competitors. Thanks to lack of ownership, that USP, should it be worthy of imitation, will only be temporary. Further, the cost of innovation is high compared with the cost of imitation.

Inseparability

Whereas goods are usually produced, then sold, and finally consumed or retained, services are sold first and then produced and consumed simultaneously. To illustrate the comparison, a pair of shoes is made in a factory, using a specific design, then checked for quality before being transported to a sales environment. If there was a fault in either shoe, it would be corrected at the factory or the shoes would be labelled and distributed as 'seconds' or even thrown away. The ultimate buyer of those shoes can be sure that they are correctly sized and that the shoe manufacturer has authorised them for sale. A customer going on a cruise, on the other hand, books and pays for it before it is 'produced' and then is present throughout its production. Like a theatre performance, no matter how many rehearsals there have been, the cruise is produced 'live' for the consumer. This means that any errors or problems which may occur during the production are seen by the customer and that these need to be resolved there and then. Also, as most tourism services involve more than one customer, the interactions are not simply between the tourism supplier and one person at a time; other customers are involved in the service process. On a cruise, for example, customers eat, socialise on board and undertake shore excursions together. Effectively, customers are simultaneously interacting with the tourism providers and one another and this 'live' situation presents the cruise company with great challenges, not the least of which is to attempt to achieve some measure of standardisation so that the promises articulated in the brochure are systematically met on each cruise undertaken. Bateson and Hoffman's 'Servuction System' model (1999), shown in Figure 6.2, encapsulates the merging of production and consumption within a services environment, where each customer's experience of an organisation in a particular service encounter is a combination of the visible environment, the service staff and any other customers who happen to be present.

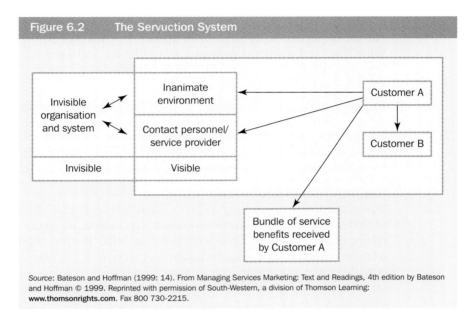

Figure 6.2   The Servuction System

Source: Bateson and Hoffman (1999: 14). From Managing Services Marketing: Text and Readings, 4th edition by Bateson and Hoffman © 1999. Reprinted with permission of South-Western, a division of Thomson Learning: **www.thomsonrights.com**. Fax 800 730-2215.

The inseparability between service production and consumption means that each and every service encounter is likely to be different, which contributes to the last service characteristic, namely, variability. Because the services-marketing solutions to inseparability are inextricably linked with those to variability, they will be discussed together once the full implications of variability have been explored below.

Variability

As the Servuction System model (Figure 6.2) shows, the customers' perceptions of the service organisation will be heavily influenced by the service encounter. A successful service encounter will produce satisfied customers who will use the organisation again or recommend it to friends; an unsuccessful one will alienate the customer, who will probably not use the organisation again and may well pass on negative word-of-mouth information to other potential customers. It has been suggested that while every satisfied customer recommends a service provider to, perhaps, two or three friends and acquaintances, a dissatisfied customer will announce that dissatisfaction to around a dozen people (Palmer, 2001). Thus, managing the service encounter has become a major challenge for tourism managers, with all staff involved in the encounter effectively working as marketers for the organisation. The ideal is for service encounters to be consistently successful. It is most unlikely that they could ever be exactly the same as one another, and indeed in many cases this would be undesirable. Nevertheless in some service businesses managers do strive to create as much uniformity as possible. However, people are involved in services – suppliers, customers and co-customers – and this inevitably creates variability between service encounters. Further, in tourism, other factors lead to variation of experience – factors over which an organisation's management often has neither direct control nor influence, such as the weather, mechanical failure and air traffic control strikes.

That the service encounter is likely to be variable is largely a result of two service characteristics discussed above: the inseparability between service production and consumption, which means that each 'performance' is live; and the perishability of the service itself, which means that service encounters can occur at times of both heavy and slack demand. Add to these two characteristics the intangible nature of the service and the challenges to management become even more demanding. Because a service is not an object, rather an experience, each and every customer is likely to view it differently. What one customer may view as a fast, efficient and professional service, another may interpret as brusque, impersonal and unfriendly.

Tourism managers' responses to the challenges of inseparability and variability

Tourism managers can adopt, adapt or reject the following techniques, explored in services-marketing literature, to suit the needs of their particular operations. Some of the ideas will suit certain operations; some would be utterly inappropriate!

Targeting of like-minded customers
Other customers consuming a service simultaneously can affect each others' enjoyment of that service both positively and negatively. Indeed, for many people the tourism experience is inextricably linked with meeting other people and sharing enjoyment. The tourism organisation's priority is thus to ensure that any interaction between customers is positive and any negative encounters are avoided. For some operations it is possible to target a particular clientele who should 'get on' together, either overtly, like the tour operator Club 18–30, or more subtly through images in advertising and placing of advertisements in particular publications. Many tourism organisations, however, whose markets are more general, must develop other means of ensuring harmony between customers, avoiding, for example, the unease created by people refusing to take their turn or behaving in a way which upsets others.

Rule setting
This is a precarious task for tourism managers, who risk antagonising at least some of their clients by dictating how they should behave. At one end of the scale there is the classic seaside landlady who posts up the house rules on the bedroom wall; at the other end of the scale are the gentle reminders from company staff to be considerate to other customers and the locals. As well as being a promotional activity for a tour operator and a means of selling excursions, the welcome party provided at the beginning of many package holidays serves as an induction to the guests where behaviour norms are established and exemplified. The physical setting of the tourism service encounter is also often used to set rules and facilitate the service encounter, theme parks, for instance using queue-management installations, visitor attractions controlling the flows of tourists with direction signs and headset recordings that move them on from one part of an exhibition to the next.

Identification of the critical incident points (CIPs) in the service encounter
Defined as events between the customer and service organisation (or sometimes more than one organisation) which lead to the customer changing service provider (Bateson and Hoffman, 1999), critical incident points or 'moments of truth' embrace any event which occurs when the customer has (or even perceives that he has) contact with a service organisation. Critical incident technique, developed by Bitner, Booms and Tetreault

(1990), was used to identify, retrospectively, the moments which persuaded customers to change service providers, either through dissatisfaction or satisfaction experienced. Managers can use this technique, not just to identify CIPs that have already occurred, but also to anticipate those which may occur in the future. The service process can be broken down into separate events, at each of which the customer may be satisfied or dissatisfied with the encounter. Further, unplanned events can be anticipated, the response to which will affect the customer's perception of the service received. Hence a hotel, for example, can identify every moment at which customers may be (or believe themselves to be) in contact with it. The managers can then devise the optimum method of handling each CIP. CIP identification is lengthy and complex. The first contact point for a customer with a hotel, for example, may be its internet site, it may be its entry in a hotel directory or it may be the person in the tourist information office who recommends it. While it may be regarded as fairly straightforward to identify such moments of contact in an 'ordinary' service process, it is much more challenging to anticipate 'out-of-the-ordinary' events and devise responses. Records need to be kept of every incident that occurs which has not been anticipated, so that in future, should something similar re-occur, a coping strategy will be available.

Blueprinting

Shostack (1984) represented graphically how organisations can break the service process down into separate stages, effectively the CIPs, and provide guidelines for each one, indicating standards expected and allocating responsibilities and resources. This should take the uncertainty out of handling service encounters, so that employees know how to react and to whom they should refer if the situation demands it. Service personnel will usually be provided with either or both written 'blueprint' instructions and practice through role play in training sessions. A good example of blueprinting is the holiday representative's manual, updated every season as new and different CIPs are encountered, where the writers attempt to anticipate all possibilities for the service process and then blueprint the company's responses. The major tour operators also have a backup emergency centre at Head Office for those situations which are not blueprinted. This means that a consistent approach is adopted. It is surprising to what extent potential encounters have already been blueprinted within the tourism industry. For example, disaster routines are in place, with a comprehensive sequence of actions initiated once the alert is received.

Industrialising the service encounter

This strategy reduces the scope for error in the service encounter by some or all of the following:

- Simplifying the range of services available. Some travel agencies, for example, may choose to delete services which are rarely sold and whose complexity may lead to mistakes and slow, faltering service. Alternatively, they may choose to centralise particular services so that expertise can be developed and a fast, accurate and efficient service offered.
- Standardising encounters, by, for example, using flow charts where staff responses are scripted according to customer reactions. Telesales staff often have scripts on screen, which act as prompts to move the customer towards making a purchase. Role-plays in training are also used to act out scripted service encounters.
- Systematising procedures and/or substituting automation for human inputs, for example, the use of internet reservation systems.
- Separating production from consumption, often adopted by tourism managers, reduces the risk of error in the 'live' performance. Elements of the service are identified which can be produced before service consumption. Business travel agencies, for example, maintain 'profiles' of their regular travellers, containing information such as preferences for smoking/non-smoking accommodation, passport expiry date, any

visas held, and, perhaps most important of all, any limitations imposed by the company which pays for the travel on which airlines may be used, class of travel, hotel price or grade of car rental. As soon as the traveller or the booker contacts the agency to make a booking, the consultant can refer to a computer held profile which will save the time and tedium of establishing basic details and preferences at the same time as reassuring the client of the professionalism of the operation.

Case 6.2   Customer profiling at Ian Allan Travel

The booking process for any trip can be much simplified if a traveller profile is used. The example in Figure 6.3, from Ian Allan Travel, shows how both the travel consultant and business-travel booker can save time and possible error through the former having ready access, electronically, to key details about a traveller and his or her travel preferences. The consultant will refer to such a profile every time a booking is requested and relevant details from it will be used for all reservations effected.

Traveller profile

Figure 6.3   Ian Allan Travel customer profile form

Full name: (as passport):....................   Nationality: ....
....   Job title: ....

Date of birth: ....
Company: ....   Passport no(s): ..../.....................
Home address: ....   Expiry date(s): ..../.....................
....   Credit card no.: ....
....   ***Personal***
Postcode: ....   o Visa o MasterCard o Amex o Other Exp date
Home tel: ....   ***Company***
Mobile: ....   o Visa o MasterCard o Amex o Other Exp date
Email: ....   Visas held: ....
Travel booker: ....   Travel insurance required?   oYes   o No
Cost centre: ....

Airline frequent flyer memberships
    Company: ....   Card No: ....
    Company: ....   Card No: ....
    Company: ....   Card No: ....
    Company: ....   Card No: ....

Preferred seating
    o Window   o Aisle   o Smoking   o Non-smoking
    o Other preferences ....
(Note: Bulkhead and emergency seats can only be allocated at check-in)

Special meal requirements
    o Vegetarian   o Low calorie   o Salt free   o Kosher
    o Other   ....

Hotel/car rental loyalty traveller card(s) held
    Company: ....   Card No: ....
    Company: ....   Card No: ....
    Company: ....   Card No: ....
    Company: ....   Card No: ....

Signature: ....   **Date:** ....

Source: Ian Allan Travel Ltd

Increasing the role of the customer in the service process

This technique, usually highly dependent on equipment quality and performance as well as on clarity of instructions, can be used to reduce the risk of problems within a service encounter at the same time as improving operational efficiency. Examples include the use of self-service ticket machines, automated check-in for some airlines, tourist information points, and automated check-out in hotels using computers in the guests' rooms.

Role adoption

Given that the service encounter is seen as a 'performance', the appearance and manner of any tourism organisation's employees should 'fit' the expectations of its customers. Those tourism operations with a clearly identified target market enjoy great advantages here. For example, Club 18–30, targeting young people who seek lively, fun-packed, highly social holidays, can select, train and even dress its resort staff to suit its clientele, as can other specialists. Companies appealing to a wider audience need to be much more circumspect. Uniforms of airline staff, for instance, are decidedly conservative! Some tourism managers develop the notion of role adoption to the extent that they train their front-line staff in transactional analysis, equipping them with techniques to assess the role subconsciously being enacted by the customer – whether it is the role of an adult, parent or child – and then to select and adopt the most appropriate of those three roles in response to that customer. The tension between this approach, where high levels of responsibility are entrusted to front-line staff, and the other approach, which requires staff to follow scripts when dealing with customers, will be explored later in this chapter.

Managing large customer numbers

Where large numbers of customers cannot be avoided, or indeed where they are a desirable element of the overall experience, strategies to cope and provide customer satisfaction for all must be implemented. Using 10 principles of waiting time (see Table 6.1) Lovelock (2001) gives examples of strategies used to reduce any negative impacts of queuing, which include redesigning the servicescape to accommodate high numbers and to facilitate their movement. He emphasises the need for customers to be given accurate forecasts of time to be spent in queues, a clear view or understanding that progress is being made along the queue and the integration of some form of distraction from the boredom of queuing – which could even provide a sales opportunity for the organisation.

Table 6.1	Principles of waiting time
1	Unoccupied time feels longer than occupied time
2	Pre- and post-service process waits feel longer than in-process waits
3	Anxiety makes waits seem longer
4	Uncertain waits seem longer than known, finite waits
5	Unexplained waits seem longer than explained waits
6	Unfair waits seem longer than equitable waits
7	The more valuable the service, the longer people are prepared to wait
8	Lone waits feel longer than group waits
9	Physically uncomfortable waits feel longer than comfortable waits
10	Unfamiliar waits seem longer than familiar ones

Source: Based on Lovelock, Christopher, *Services Marketing: People, Technology, Strategy*, 4th edition, © 2001. Adapted by permission of Pearson Education, Inc. Upper Saddle River, NJ

Managing quality control with any third parties involved in the service

Where tourism companies are often interdependent, communications, training and support must be effective. Relationships between tourism organisations are often symbiotic.

For example, a customer's perception of a travel agency may well be affected by the performance of the tour operator or airline it booked. Similarly, another customer's perception of an airline may well be coloured by the booking experience at the travel agency. One approach for organisations in such a complex situation is to link-up – as have the major tour operators with their own charter airlines and travel-agency chains. Where this is not possible, there is significant representation between companies. For example, airlines send representatives to travel agencies to update them on new services, fare deals and routes.

Recognising failures and resolving them

It is possible to turn a service failure to an advantage if an organisation's front-line staff follow two key precepts identified by Palmer (2001):

- show empathy to customers by recognising a failure and its impact on them;
- identify a way forward which is suitable to meet customers' needs and implement the solution.

Factors influencing a tourism organisation's approach in responding to inseparability and variability

The choice of how to address inseparability and variability in the tourism service encounter will depend on several factors, largely associated with the nature of the operation, the expectations of the customers, the staff employed and the management style. While some organisations may adopt an approach which attempts to standardise all processes, training personnel to adhere closely to a script, others may seek to provide a personalised service for each and every customer. Figure 6.4 offers a simplification of the approaches available. Management can empower staff, giving them the authority to act on their own initiative during the service encounter; they can control staff, training them to respond in a particular way at each critical incident point; they can automate some or all of the service process; and they can combine all three approaches, empowering some but not all staff. On the one hand, empowered staff are likely to be more motivated and are likely to provide high-quality customer service, (Kotler, Bowen and Makens, 2003), but that service may take longer to deliver as it is being individually designed for each client, and in some tourism operations, speedy, standardised service is what the customer seeks. Empowering staff is also likely to increase costs, since the high-calibre staff required are likely to need higher rates of pay. Further, fewer customers will be processed, service variability will increase and mistakes made by empowered individuals could lead to critical losses, as well as providing learning opportunities! The dilemma for tourism managers over which approach to adopt is more acute than in many other services. While

Figure 6.4   The choices for management

on the one hand, there is consensus among theorists that high-calibre, motivated, empowered front-line staff who can 'think on their feet' will best serve the interests of the clients and of the service provider, on the other hand, the nature of the tourism business mitigates against the practical application of such theory, with so many tourism operations constrained by low profit margins, low salaries and seasonal fluctuations creating the need to attract, employ and train a new, temporary workforce each year.

Understanding buyer behaviour

The key in both goods and services marketing is the understanding of buyer behaviour. It underpins an organisation's planning processes and informs its decisions on all elements of the services marketing mix, identified earlier as Product, Price, Place, Promotion, Process, Physical Evidence and People. By understanding its buyers and their decision-making processes an organisation can develop a service which is appropriate, accessible, appealing and at the right price.

First, it needs to get to know its customers. Working on a large scale, customers can be 'grouped' to a certain extent and then targeted as a group or market segment. This grouping is undertaken at two levels – simple (superficial) and subtle (psychographic). For simple segmentation, customer groups are established from demographic data, for example, by age, gender, occupation, income, location. This basic information can be obtained fairly easily from census statistics, electoral rolls, postal codes (the UK propensity for home ownership making these an effective indicator of household wealth!) and commercially produced market research surveys.

Many companies rely heavily on segmenting the market at this basic level, using only socio-demographic data. However, it is particularly difficult to categorise the tourism market using such simplistic information because:

- individual tastes within segments are likely to be very different;
- previous experiences of individuals within segments will differ;
- motives of individuals within segments for undertaking tourism will differ;
- individuals are likely to move from segment to segment depending upon particular circumstances.

Subtle (psychographic) segmentation is thus seen as more appropriate for tourism, customer groups being established according to personality, attitudes, opinions, self-concept. This more complex information can be gained from primary sources, such as questionnaires, focus groups, customer records, and from secondary sources, such as commercially produced market-research surveys and other companies' mailing lists. Advantage can also be taken of segmentation that has been adopted by other organisations. For example, a holiday company which places an advertisement for its gourmet holidays to France in the Sunday Times Wine Club magazine can be fairly confident that its advert will be seen by an appropriate market segment.

As well as identifying market segments, it is also vital that a tourism provider understands the purchasing decision processes. Palmer (2001: 90–99) identifies five key issues for the marketer to establish and provides useful models to assist in the process:

- Who is involved in making the purchasing decision?
- How long does the process of making a decision take?
- What is the set of competing services from which consumers make their choice?
- What is the relative importance attached by decision-makers to each of the elements of the service offer?
- What sources of information are used in evaluating competing service offers?

Figure 6.5 presents Palmer's decision-making unit (DMU) to enable the service provider to answer the first question above.

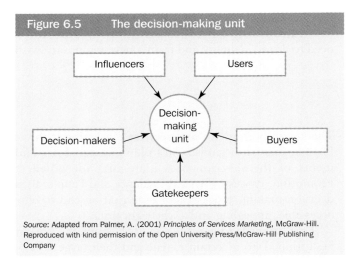

Figure 6.5   The decision-making unit

Source: Adapted from Palmer, A. (2001) *Principles of Services Marketing*, McGraw-Hill. Reproduced with kind permission of the Open University Press/McGraw-Hill Publishing Company

Some tourism purchasing decisions will be more complex than others and perhaps require the involvement of many different people before a final decision can be taken. Whereas in some decisions one person could probably combine the roles of buyer, user and decision-maker, for more complex purchases the number of people involved in the process is likely to be relatively high. If we take the example of a flight undertaken by an executive working for her employer in Paris, and adopt the perspective of the airlines wishing to sell their seats, the components of the DMU would be as follows:

- **User:** The traveller, whose priorities are likely to be convenience, comfort, reliability, and stress-free travel arrangements, since for most business travellers, travelling for work purposes soon becomes more of a burden than a pleasure.
- **Buyer:** The buyer is whoever has the authority to make purchases on behalf of the business and so may be the company accountant, a procurement manager, the managing director, or perhaps even the traveller herself.
- **Gatekeeper:** Gatekeepers are people who can limit the options available to decision-making units, and as such they are terribly important for suppliers to have 'on side'. In this case, the company's travel policy could act as a gatekeeper, precluding the traveller from selecting certain airlines or certain classes of travel. Further, the person booking the flight could limit the choice available to the DMU by, for example, specifying a particular airline or particular airport. The travel agent could limit the choice by favouring a particular airline, either as a matter of policy or thanks to the display layout of the reservation system, which in its turn is then acting as a gatekeeper.
- **Decision-maker:** For flight bookings, the final decision could rest with the company's buyer, the user or very often the booker. From the perspective of the airlines competing for that company's business, the need is to know who has the final say, what their priorities are in selecting airlines and by whom or what they are likely to be influenced.
- **Influencer:** Purchasing choices made by each of the four groups of people above – users, buyers, gatekeepers and decision-makers – will be subject to a range of influences, which will include their own personal experience, the recommendations and criticisms of others, media reporting, and the marketing activities of the airlines themselves.

By using models such as the DMU shown above, to understand the needs, wants and constraints of any tourism organisation's users, buyers, gatekeepers, decision-makers and influencers, marketers can attempt to anticipate client responses and ensure that their service offerings are appropriate and that they select the right distribution and promotional methods. It is important to recognise also that buying decisions are not simply made pre-purchase. Decisions on future purchases and indeed on whether or not to recommend a purchase will be being made during and after consumption.

Relationship management

Closely linked to buyer behaviour is relationship management – in its simplest form the creation of customer loyalty and an ongoing seller–buyer relationship. It is an approach that can contribute to overcoming some of the challenges of services marketing. Customers who feel a sense of loyalty to a tourism provider, for whatever reason, will have a reduced sense of risk when buying from that tourism provider, so intangibility and the lack of ability to patent become much less of an issue to deal with. Further, that sense of loyalty may help them overlook one-off errors. If they are regular users of the tourism service, they will also be familiar with the processes and so easier to cope with during the service encounter. Thus the potential dangers of inseparability and variability are reduced. Above all, loyal customers may pass on their recommendations to friends and acquaintances. Many more reasons for developing and nurturing customer relationships are provided by theorists (see particularly Christopher, Payne and Ballantine, 1991) such as the marketing costs saved in retaining clients rather than having to seek new ones, the extra income generated by having repeat and new purchases from loyal customers, insight gained into changes in consumer tastes thanks to regular contacts and the fact that long-term customers are generally less concerned about price than new ones. Reichheld and Sasser (1990) argue that an increase in customer retention of 5% can boost profits by anywhere between 25% and 85%.

Many tourism organisations practise relationship development and management, aided by ever-improving information systems. Examples includes frequent-flyer programmes and hotel-chain loyalty schemes. Key to the success of any relationship marketing initiative must be the identification of appropriate market segments with whom the supplier would wish to develop a long-term relationship. The ideal relationship progresses from a successful first-time purchase to repeat purchases and thereafter to commitment to a particular organisation. There are, however, some customers to be avoided! For example, some customers are inherently disloyal, so there would be little point in developing a relationship with them. This is the case with many package-holiday takers, whom the industry has inadvertently 'trained' to shop on price. Further, some customers are not profitable, such as late paying clients for business travel agents and the persistent holiday complainer who is looking for a free holiday next year.

There is a danger in tourism that organisations may waste money in their quest for loyalty. Airline loyalty programmes serve as an example of how the costs of relationship marketing may exceed its value to the organisation. Because so many airlines have frequent-flier programmes, they no longer offer a real competitive edge for any one airline, forcing each one to add incentives to its own programme in an attempt to regain that competitive edge.

| Case 6.3 | P&O Ferries frequent traveller and homeowners abroad scheme |

One of several market segments identified by P&O Ferries as appropriate for relationship development is the ever-growing number of Britons who are buying houses in mainland Europe, either as holiday homes or as places of permanent residence. Those who buy houses as holiday homes will inevitably be travelling to them on a regular basis, often carrying furniture, do-it-yourself tools and materials, pots, pans, bed-linen, curtains, etc. They will also require the use of the family car while on holiday, thus making them an ideal target market for a car-carrying service. By offering these homeowners abroad both discounts on fares as well as a points scheme which returns to them £1 for every £4 spent on a fare to offset the price of future bookings, the attraction for the customer is strong. Similarly, for those people who have already moved abroad, who may be travelling back to the UK from time to time as well as receiving friends and family in their home abroad (they may indeed find they had more friends than they had ever realised, all of whom are suddenly very keen to visit them in their home abroad!), discounts and a scheme which provides points for both their own travel and that of their friends are a very enticing prospect. The P&O Ferries homeowner traveller scheme, illustrated below, provides an excellent example of what Palmer (2001), describes as strategic relationship marketing, where the tie between customer and supplier is mutually beneficial.

Join homeowner traveller and save up to 50%

Homeowner Traveller is the P&O Ferries scheme dedicated to **Property Owners** overseas. If you own a holiday or second home abroad, you know how travelling back and forth can be expensive. That's why we have introduced a special scheme for you. It is designed to allow maximum convenience, comfort and value for money on travel across any of our routes. For you and for guests visiting your property, **Homeowner Traveller** offers amazing discounts on standard passenger and vehicle fares, for just £35/€50 annual membership fee. You can also **collect points** on any Homeowner Traveller bookings (made by yourself or your guests) to use against future crossings on all P&O Ferries routes. So you could soon save enough points for a free trip.

And the benefits go on and on

- Travel comfortably and enjoy the simple luxury of a **complimentary inside ensuite cabin on day sailings** to Le Havre and Cherbourg or **half-price Club chairs on the fastcraft** to Cherbourg and Caen (excludes Club cabins and rest chairs and must be pre-booked).
- Nominate a second account holder free of charge.
- On board all our ships, just show your card and ticket when requesting the bill to claim **10% off meals** (including drinks bought with a meal).
- **Commission-free bureau de change** (excludes North Sea routes) when you show your card on board.

Source: P&O promotional leaflet *homeowner traveller concessions*, available July 2004; offer subject to change

The concept of relationship marketing extends beyond the nurturing of seller–buyer relationships. Christopher *et al.* (1991) propose a 'Six Markets' model which embraces customers, suppliers, employees, internal departments, referral and influence markets. In the context of the Decision-Making Unit explored above, where it is clear that purchase decisions can depend on all six markets, the reasons for engaging the support of them all become clear. However, in practice, managing such multiple relationships becomes complex. Clearly, for example, if a supplier distributes through travel agencies, it is logical for that supplier to engage their commitment to selling its services through the establishment of a relationship. Does the supplier seek to engage all travel agents through, for example, higher commissions, familiarisation trips, training sessions and so on? If so, then the project is likely to be very expensive and, further, a competitor may offer more attractive incentives to some or all agents, any of whose loyalty to the first company may then evaporate. If, however, the supplier chooses to be selective over the agents with which it seeks relationships, perhaps identifying only their current best segments, there is a likelihood of antagonising those agencies excluded from the relationship, from whom all bookings would cease. Indeed, in recent years, large agency chains have very publicly de-racked certain tour operators seen to be favouring their competitors.

Branding

Like relationship marketing, branding depends on effective market segmentation. It can be used as a means of engaging a market when there is limited opportunity for formal relationship building, brands being chosen by customers when the image the brands create matches their needs, values and lifestyles. Loyalty is created to the brand, reducing the risk element in purchasing an intangible.

Distribution

The perishable nature of tourism services makes distribution decisions crucial to the immediate, short-term and long-term success of organisations. Technological changes are revolutionising the distribution choices available to tourism providers and in many ways reshaping the structure of the industry, as discussed in Chapter 11.

Some tourism organisations sell directly to the public; some sell indirectly, using intermediaries such as tourist offices, travel agencies, partner companies; and many sell both directly and indirectly simultaneously. Listed below are reasons why some tourism businesses decide to use intermediaries:

- They save suppliers the cost of dealing directly with the customers, specifically the costs of employing sales staff and the renting or buying of premises, allowing them to invest more in their core activities.
- They often provide pre- and after-sales support, saving the supplier time and thus costs.
- They collect individual payments and make consolidated payments to suppliers, again saving costs.
- Many customers feel more comfortable dealing with a local agency, where they have tangible evidence of the services offered by suppliers (in the form of brochures) and with whom they may also have developed a relationship and whose advice they perceive to be objective.
- They rationalise queries and ensure that contact with suppliers conforms with their systems and procedures.
- Finally, if suppliers choose not to work with them and their service offer is similar to that of others who do, then their competitors will get the bookings of all those buyers whose preferred booking method is via the intermediary.

The emergence of the internet as a means of promoting and distributing tourism means that much of the intermediary's contribution to the sales process, as articulated above, can be replaced by technology, at least for the increasing number of customers ready to shop and book via the web.

If tourism organisations do choose to work with intermediaries, they usually have a 'push' or 'pull' relationship with them (or a mixture of the two). **Push** is where the supplier (or principal) promotes strongly to the intermediary, encouraging it to sell equally strongly to the customers. In the tourism industry, examples of push from principals include sales teams visiting intermediaries to provide training; incentives such as increased commissions on sales (targeted at management) and personal rewards – from shopping vouchers to free trips (targeted at sales staff); organised events, either as a reward for sales or as a training mechanism; marketing support, for example window displays and point of sale material, such as free pens and mouse-mats; and finally, establishing links with particular agencies – through ownership, alliances, special relationships and franchises. **Pull** is where the supplier promotes strongly to the customer, ensuring that he or she will specify that company when booking via the intermediary. Branding, mentioned earlier, is an important tool in this respect.

Some tourism suppliers choose not to distribute via intermediaries, for a range of reasons, including:

- If the tourism product or service is highly specialised, the company may prefer to deal directly with its customers rather than rely on an intermediary with limited expertise.
- If profit margins are tight, the commission demanded by intermediaries may be more than the business can afford.
- If a company is in direct communication with its customers, the feedback mechanisms are much more effective.
- Relationships can be built up with customers if the organisation has direct contact with them. (A travel agency, for example, would not normally release customer contact details to a supplier.)
- Not only do suppliers usually have to pay intermediaries commission, they also often have to wait for payment of the net price from those intermediaries.
- The technology networks used by intermediaries charge fees to suppliers.

Many suppliers, however, distribute both directly and via intermediaries, a challenging balance to achieve as intermediaries may not recommend with enthusiasm those suppliers who blatantly deal directly with customers. Recent guidance to a hotel sales team suggested that they should be 'keeping their arm around the agents while embracing the corporate clients'. While the hotel company would be extremely pleased to enter into a direct relationship with its corporate clients, thus saving commissions and the need for expenditure on push activities with the agencies, at the same time it is aware that many corporates still insist that all their travel arrangements are made via a travel agency to save time spent by employees shopping around on the internet and to prevent deviance from the company travel policy.

One way for a supplier to manage direct and indirect distribution simultaneously is to have such a strong pull on the customers that the power of the intermediaries to influence choice is reduced. Another option is for a company to use separate names for direct-sell products.

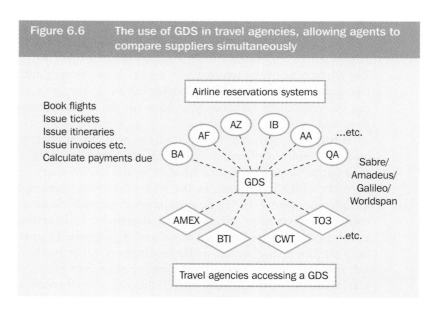

Figure 6.6 The use of GDS in travel agencies, allowing agents to compare suppliers simultaneously

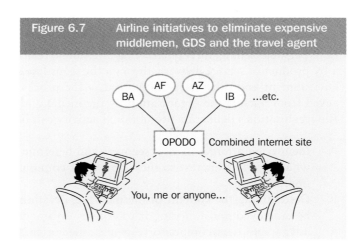

Figure 6.7   Airline initiatives to eliminate expensive middlemen, GDS and the travel agent

While advances in internet technology are providing great opportunities for companies to distribute directly, existing networks and their usage make developments more complex. For those airlines, for example, whose traditional distribution method has been via travel agencies where Global Distribution Systems (GDS) are used, the take-up of direct booking via their internet sites remains limited. Effectively, the GDS, linked as they are to most airlines, provide a much more efficient means for the travel agent – and indeed for the customer – of comparing airlines' times and prices than looking in turn at each airline's website. Figure 6.6 illustrates the process.

Many major airlines have recognised this as an issue and are now linking their websites to permit simultaneous comparisons using the internet. Figure 6.7 shows the principle of this, using the Opodo website as an example.

Physical evidence in selling tourism

The importance of the intermediary in tourism sales is linked to the need for tangible evidence in the tourism buying process. Tour operators, for example, have needed to make their brochures accessible to potential customers, and the location of travel agencies on the high streets of most towns has made them ideal dissemination points. With the emergence of the internet as a distribution tool, the debate is keen over the continued need either for the paper brochure or indeed for so many high-street agencies. For the moment, it would seem that in a strong position to move forward are those tourism suppliers whose target markets are ready and able to shop and book electronically. For Brilliant Weekends!! (the company illustrated in Case 6.4 whose target market is at ease with web bookings) there is no need for a paper brochure, the purpose of which is now served by the website.

Promotion

Extremely important for services whose intangibility so often renders them high-risk purchases for the consumer, promotion, or communication, is only one element of the marketing mix and it will be ineffectual if the other elements – price, product, distribution, physical evidence, process or people – are defective. It involves the transmission of messages to past, present and potential customers. However, messages are received about the service and the organisation both through deliberate promotional activity *and* by other means. Deliberate promotional activity can involve advertising, sales promotion, personal selling, direct marketing and public relations. Promotion can also occur as a by-product of service delivery, through the front-line staff, other employees, the service environment and third parties involved in the process. Further, messages can be conveyed from outside the organisation by the media and word-of-mouth communication. An organisation's deliberate promotional activity can be divided into several stages:

- **Identifying a target market segment** and determining who are the decision-makers, what is of key interest to them and what communication method is most likely to impress them.
- **Determining the content of the message**, defining the objectives of the message to be conveyed and tailoring it to convey an image of the service/organisation, its advantages over competitors, its customer orientation, its track record of satisfied customers and any selling points its research suggests would be of value to the target market.
- **Communicating the message**, developing a promotional mix which ensures that the desired message is understood by the recipients exactly as it was intended by its creators. Too often, there is 'interference' along the communication line, either through erroneous 'coding' of the message by the organisation or by misinterpretation on the part of the receivers. The promotional mix can include advertising through newspapers, magazines, journals, billboards, posters, television, cinema, commercial radio, teletext and the internet. Personal selling, whether it be directly to customers or to intermediaries, is also part of the promotional mix, as is public relations, the purpose of which is to enhance the public image of an organisation through press releases, lobbying, education and training, organising special events or sponsorship.

Case 6.4   Brilliant Weekends!!

Brilliant Weekends!! Taking the Hard Work Out of Having a Great Time!

You may know Brilliant Weekends as the UKs leading arranger of Stag Weekends and Hen Weekends, but for everyone else we also specialise in Beer Festivals, Ski Weekends, New York Christmas Shopping Breaks and New Years Eve 2005.

We provide short breaks and weekends away for many corporate, sports and social groups, Any of our Brilliant Weekends can be tailored specifically to your needs, with meeting rooms, private dinners or special activities & entertainment added as required, all managed for you by ourselves.

For pease of mind, we hold an ATOL license and are exclusive weekend break partners to Flybe and EasyJet. This means you can buy your low cost flights direct, then come to us for everything else!

An example of a tourism company distributing and promoting through the internet is Brilliant Weekends!!, based in Bristol, targeting customers who are 'at home' with shopping via the web. Whereas historically, tourism suppliers have needed to promote themselves via hard-copy brochures, whose production and distribution incur high costs, Brilliant Weekends!! capitalises on the ability of the web to provide tangible evidence of its products at relatively low cost, having identified both the key importance of featuring in the top five of search engines' links for its travel products and the value of having a web link from the site of a low-cost air carrier, in this case Flybe. Initially focusing on stag and hen weekends, the company has now expanded into corporate events, family reunions, golf breaks, New Year's Eve celebrations or simply groups of friends taking off for a fun-packed holiday which they have no time to organise themselves. Demonstrating the extent to which promotion is only one aspect of the marketing mix, Brilliant Weekends!! also exemplifies the integration of brand and relationship development into its marketing mix.

Source: **www.brilliantweekends.co.uk** as at 15 August 2004; offer subject to change

Marketing planning

In developing a marketing plan, tourism managers can draw on theory from at least two academic fields – strategy and marketing. The planning process in essence involves finding the answers to five key questions, the last of which will always bring managers back to the first, making the planning process a continuous as well as cyclical activity (see Figure 6.8).

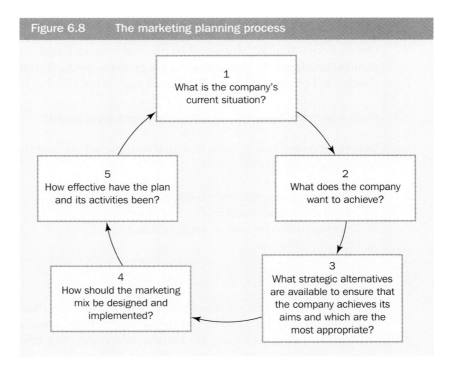

Figure 6.8   The marketing planning process

What is the company's current situation?

The startpoint for this analysis is usually an analysis of the environment in which the organisation operates, looking in turn at its political (including legal), economic, sociological and technological contexts. Known as PEST analysis (see Chapter 9), this framework allows managers to review what already influences or indeed is likely to influence their business. Organisations in mainland Europe, for example, needed to plan well before January 2002 for the change from their national currency to the euro. On a much smaller scale, proposed changes in laws can create both opportunities and difficulties for businesses and managers pay inadequate heed to them at their peril.

Having completed the PEST analysis, a second analysis is normally undertaken, the SWOT analysis, in which an organisation reviews its strengths and weaknesses from an internal perspective and then looks externally to assess its opportunities and threats.

What does the company want to achieve?

Many businesses, but by no means all, take the opportunity to articulate their mission and objectives at this stage of the planning process. While the mission statement expresses overarching aims, the objectives are much more clearly defined, often set out in order of priority, measurable and set within realistic time limits.

■ **What strategic alternatives are available to ensure that the company achieves its aims and which are the most appropriate?**

Both marketing and strategic management theory offer a range of alternatives for business development, and businesses assess the appropriateness of the alternatives discussed, including seeking to increase market share, to attract new markets, to develop new services, to differentiate through cost leadership or specialisation, or to grow through mergers, acquisitions and alliances.

■ **How should the marketing mix be designed and implemented?**

Once an organisation's strategic direction has been agreed, the design of the marketing mix should flow logically with decisions on product, price, distribution, promotion, people, process and physical evidence linked with each other and the company's objectives.

■ **How effective have the plan and its activities been?**

Implementation and control of a marketing plan are simultaneous, with three things happening concurrently:

■ the setting of targets of expected performance;
■ the measurement and evaluation of performance;
■ taking corrective action where necessary.

Conclusion

It is impossible in one book chapter to explore in great detail the business function of marketing in the context of the tourism industry. Indeed neither the discipline of marketing nor the scope of tourism can be fully addressed. Nevertheless, this chapter has been able to demonstrate that tourism, as part of the services sector, can benefit from the wealth of experience and learning available within general and services-marketing literature. Tourism, with its special blend of challenges, is particularly interesting when it comes to the application of services-marketing theory. So much is happening technologically, with the impact of the internet creating opportunities as well as threats across the industry. Customer sophistication continues to increase, with buyers more knowledgeable and demanding than ever, yet still conscious of the risk of buying the unknown. Services-marketing approaches, such as relationship marketing and service-quality management (explored later in Chapter 10), are being adopted and developed by tourism managers to tackle the challenges they face, and more and more services-marketing theorists are looking at the tourism industry as an exemplar of their discipline. Perhaps the most important concept that has emerged from this brief study is that tourism businesses should not see marketing in isolation from other business functions. Given the importance of the experience, and the priority given by buyers to third party and personal recommendations, tourism businesses must put the customer at the centre of all their activities. Everyone employed by the tourism provider has the potential to please or displease the customer, whether they work in the accounts, human resources or systems department. Thus if you work in tourism, or indeed any services business, think again if you, or worse, your employees, are tempted to say to a customer or potential customer: 'That's nothing to do with me: you need to contact the XYZ department'.

Discussion questions

1 Devise a list of CIPs for a low-cost airline and suggest what activities should go on 'backstage' to ensure that customers are satisfied.

2 Look at a seasonal attraction and review the mechanisms in place to cope with variable visitor numbers.

3 Discuss whether and to what extent a tour operator should empower its overseas resort representatives.

4 Using the decision-making unit model, review who contributes to the annual summer-holiday decision for a family including a parent, grandparent and three children of school age.

5 Conduct a PEST and SWOT analysis on behalf of a visitor attraction or tourist destination of your choice.

Guided reading

Palmer (2001) provides a comprehensive exploration of services marketing, often using examples from the tourism sector. In his chapter on services buyer behaviour, for example, he uses the annual holiday choice to illustrate his decision-making unit model and then looks at airline choice to explore how customers choose between competing services. Lovelock (2001) devotes two very helpful chapters to managing perishable services.

The empowerment versus control debate is tackled in depth by Bateson and Hoffman (1999) and they also consider the use of physical evidence in services marketing, something only touched on in this chapter.

Relationship management is related directly to tourism and hospitality by Kotler, Bowen and Makens (2003) and finally the marketing planning process is detailed by Holloway (2004), who illustrates each stage with examples from the tourism sector.

Recommended websites

Journal of Travel and Tourism Marketing: **www.haworthpress.com/store/product. asp?sku=J073** .

Journal of Vacation Marketing: **www.henrystewart.com/journals/hspindex.htm?vm/ index.html~mainFrame** .

Journal of Hospitality Marketing: **www.haworthpressinc.com/store/product.asp?sku= J150** .

Eye for Travel (a travel marketing practitioners' website): **www.eyefortravel.com/ index.asp** .

Journal of Travel Research: **http://jtr.sagepub.com/** .

Key words

Critical incident point (CIP); decision-making unit (DMU); Global Distribution System (GDS); inseparability; intangibility; intermediary; Opodo; perishability; physical evidence; seasonality; service encounter; servicescape; services marketing mix; variability.

Bibliography

Bateson, J. and Hoffman, K. (1999) *Managing Services Marketing*, 4th edn. Dryden Press, Fort Worth.

Bitner, M.J., Booms, B.M. and Tetreault, M.S. (1990) The Service Encounter: Diagnosing Favorable and Unfavorable Incidents, *Journal of Marketing* 54, January, 71–84.

Blood, P. (1976) *Chartered Institute of Marketing Annual Report*. Chartered Institute of Marketing.

Christopher, M., Payne, A. and Ballantyne, M. (1991) *Relationship Marketing*. Butterworth-Heinemann, London.

Holloway, J.C. (2004) *Marketing for Tourism*, 4th edn. Pearson, Harlow.

Kotler, P., Armstrong, G., Saunders, J. and Wong, V. (1999) *Principles of Marketing*, European edn. Prentice-Hall, Harlow.

Kotler, P., Bowen, J. and Makens, J. (2003) *Marketing for Hospitality and Tourism*, 3rd edn. Prentice Hall, New Jersey.

Lovelock, C. (2001) *Services Marketing: People, Technology, Strategy*, 4th edn. Prentice Hall, New Jersey.

Narver, J.C. and Slater, S.F. (1990) The Effect of a Market Orientation on Business Profitability, *Journal of Marketing*, October, 20–35.

Palmer, A. (2001) *Principles of Services Marketing*, 3rd edn. McGraw-Hill, London.

Reichheld, F.F. and Sasser, W.E.J. (1990) Zero Defections, *Harvard Business Review*, Vol. 68, Sept/Oct 1990, 105–111.

Shostack, G.L. (1984) Designing Services that Deliver, *Harvard Business Review*, January–February, 133–139.

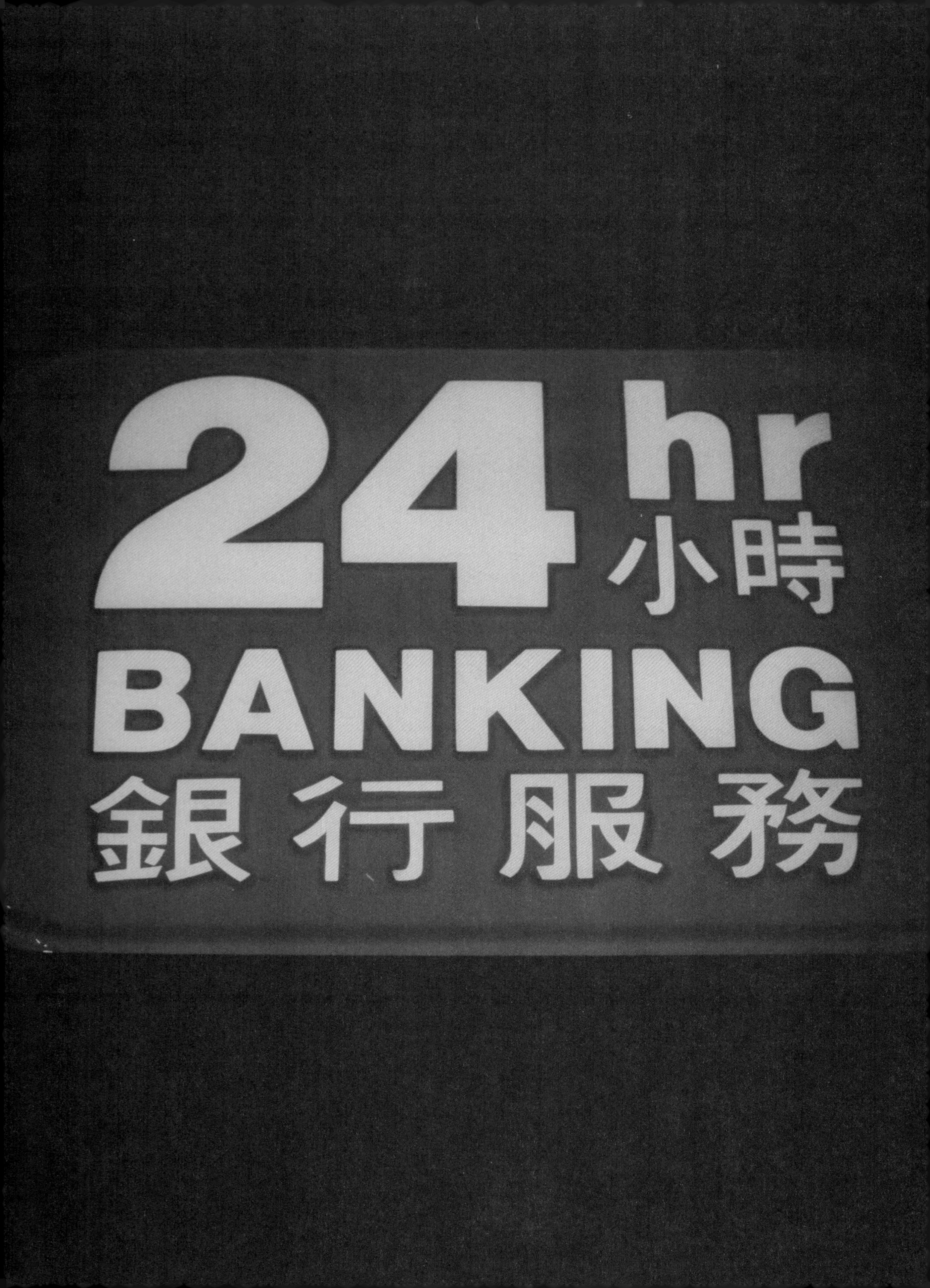
24hr
小時
BANKING
銀行服務

Chapter 7

Finance and accounting for tourism

Helen Atkinson, University of Brighton

Learning outcomes

On completion of this chapter the reader should be able to:

■ understand how tourism organisations generate profit and explain and interpret the main financial statements;

■ explain the basic cost concepts and analyse cost structure;

■ conduct breakeven analysis and identify the different approaches to pricing;

■ use a variety of ratios to evaluate financial statements;

■ be able to prepare and appraise a business plan.

Overview

This chapter provides an introduction to some of the important aspects of finance and accounting in relation to tourism management. It begins with an overview of the commercial domains of the tourism industry, including travel and transport, accommodation and provision of food, beverages and entertainment. Many of these businesses share the same key financial issues associated with high fixed costs, seasonal demand and the emphasis on revenue management. In the context of this commercial environment, a definition and explanation of the main financial statements used by tourism organisations is provided. The presentation of the *profit and loss account* and *balance sheet* is clarified and the key concepts and terminology underpinning them explained. The main costs incurred by different tourism organisations are considered and the concepts and conventions, which support clear analysis of expenditure, are explained. These cost concepts are applied to *cost volume profit analysis*, a technique that supports management decision-making, and to *pricing*. The chapter then continues to demonstrate how ratios can be used to evaluate the financial performance of a tourism organisation and to look at other methods of monitoring business performance. Finally, the process of business planning integrates the preceding topics and provides a simple case study example.

A number of numerical examples are used to demonstrate key points and examples from well-known companies are used to illustrate various financial aspects. Important learning points are reinforced by the use of discussion questions that draw on case studies or other issues and topics raised in the chapter. Throughout the chapter there is guidance on further reading for those who require a deeper understanding.

Introduction to the tourism business

Tourism is one of the most significant areas of the economic activity in many developed and developing nations worldwide, accounting for 10.4% of the GDP, generating 214,697,000 jobs or 8.1% of total employment (WTTC, 2004). Its importance is growing; for example in the European country of Croatia, tourism will be a significant source of regeneration and in African countries such as Kenya tourism is a very important source of foreign currency and invisible exports. The UK is a net[1] exporter of tourism and, although there are large volumes of inbound tourist spend, UK nationals spend even more on tourism abroad, resulting in a net outflow of currency. (For further discussion on the economic impact of tourism see Tribe, 1999.)

Types of tourism business

The provision of tourism services such as passenger transport, accommodation and the provision of food, beverages and tourist attractions are mainly supplied by commercial organisations. These profit-making organisations range from multinational and public limited companies such as The World of TUI and Hilton Corporation to nationally-based companies such as The Restaurant Group (formerly City Centre Restaurants) in the UK and Sol Meliá in Spain. However, a large proportion of tourist services are provided by small-to-medium-sized organisations (SMEs), some of which are described as micro-businesses, which only employ three to five people. This chapter will focus on the financial management concepts and factors that commercial profit-making organisations of all sizes must consider. The recognition of the profit motive is important and the examples in this chapter will be based on commercial companies whose primary motive is to make profit in the short, medium or long term.

In addition, there are a range of not-for-profit organisations operating in the tourism industry; the most high-profile in the UK are probably the London-based museums and art galleries, such as the British Museum, the Victoria and Albert Museum, the National Gallery and the relatively new Tate Modern, but there are many historical houses, monuments and churches which are also established as registered charities or not-for-profit organisations. Other key organisations are the tourist boards; these are government-funded organisations established on both a regional and a national basis to promote tourism. Examples include VisitScotland and the Welsh Tourist Board in Britain, the New Zealand Tourism Board and the Canadian Tourism Commission; these organisations provide important intermediary and information services, with offices and support staff in most tourist destinations. Financial management for these types of organisation is specialised and is not covered in this chapter; for a more focused reading on not-for-profit organisations see the recommended reading at the end of this chapter. Although specialised many of the concepts and frameworks presented in this chapter are applicable to such organisations as most operate trading divisions that generate much needed funds and cash.

Characteristics of tourism businesses

A key feature of tourism organisations is the nature of the cost base and the cost structure. Businesses involved with the provision of services such as passenger transport including airlines and passenger-train operators experience a high proportion of fixed costs. This means that most of the costs they incur do not change with the number of

---

1 'Net' is the term used to mean 'after deductions' – in this case, after the figure for UK outbound tourism have been deducted from the figure for UK inbound tourism (the pre-deduction or 'gross' figure).

passengers, so it will cost more or less the same to operate a service carrying one passenger, as it will to carry two hundred passengers. The same applies for the accommodation sector and to a large extent tourist attractions; most of the costs are relating to the provision of facilities, e.g. land and buildings, and the associated running costs are only moderately affected by the number of guests or visitors. (See the section on cost concepts later in the chapter for definitions of fixed and variable costs.) In addition to a high fixed costs structure many tourism services are *perishable*; this means that they cannot be stored or kept until later, so if a hotel room is not sold on one night or a plane takes off with empty seats, those sales are lost for ever. This means that the major priority for these organisations is to maximise the number of customers, to ensure the maximum amount of revenue is received to cover fixed costs. The notion of *revenue maximisation* is crucial to airline and hotel companies alike and they have developed sophisticated systems to achieve this. Chapter 10 deals with yield management in detail, but for the purposes of this chapter it is important to remember these underlying business realities.

Another key feature of the industry that stems from the cost profile is the importance of scale; generally larger organisations are more successful than smaller ones. The concept of economies of scale is important and results in significant amounts of integration within the industry (Tribe, 1999). As can be seen in Chapter 2, organisations engage in vertical integration and horizontal integration, which result in organisations like the World of TUI. Like other large companies, the World of TUI is a conglomeration of a range of businesses linked both horizontally and vertically. Businesses that are linked by the type of service they provide and the customers they serve are horizontally integrated. Those businesses that are linked by the supply chain in the business are vertically integrated. This chapter will look at how to evaluate the performance of these large organisations, using information from the published annual accounts to calculate basic financial ratios and understand operational and efficiency statistics.

Finally it should be noted that for many tourism organisations the theatre of operations and the country of origin are different; for example the World of TUI is a German-registered company which provides tourism services across the globe. This can expose companies to foreign currency risk and a major role of financial management for large multinational companies is the management of foreign exchange (for further reading on Financial Management see Brigham, 2001). In addition many such companies repatriate profit made overseas to the domestic parent company, which reduces the benefit for the host nation; these economic and political issues are addressed in Chapter 15.

These issues will provide the backdrop to this chapter on financial aspects of tourism, which will address questions such as:

- whether the business has made a profit;
- which part of the business generates the most revenue;
- which of the key costs are fixed and which are variable;
- what will happen to profit if prices are reduced;
- how well the business is performing compared to other organisations.

These and many other questions will be addressed in the following sections, starting with a review of profit and wealth expressed in the two key financial statements.

Understanding financial statements

Having established that most tourism organisations aim to make a profit, the key question to be addressed is, *what is profit?* Profit is one of the main financial metrics which is used to determine how successful an organisation has been. This section of the chapter will introduce profit and the key financial statement that presents and summarises a company's profit and loss. It is important to note that company accounting reports are produced on a periodic basis, i.e. set time frame, usually one year, usually called an accounting period and having implications for the financial statements.

Profit and loss account

The profit and loss account is one of the two most important accounting statements. It provides details of how many sales a company has generated over a period of time and what expenses have been incurred. Sales can be defined as the amount received from the provision of goods or services to customers in the normal course of business. The term sales is synonymous with revenue, income and turnover. Any of these terms can be found in common use; however, what is critical about defining sales is that they result from ordinary activities. Thus for a restaurant they result from the provision of food and beverage, for an airline they result from the sale of tickets for flights and for a tourist attraction they result from entry charges to a theme park. Funds received from the sales of belongings or property of these businesses, such as sale of a car, a plane or a computer, would *not* be considered sales.

In addition sales do not have to be received in the form of cash to be included; a business can include revenue and treat it as sales even if cash has not been received. Providing the service/product transaction is substantively complete and the customer is likely to pay, non-cash receipts can be included. It is normal for many businesses to allow customers, especially business customers, to pay after a set period of time e.g. 30 days. This means that value of sales and cash receipts are normally different. (For a deeper discussion on revenue recognition and the realisation principle see Berry and Jarvis, 1997.)

In tourism businesses sales revenue is generated through many different ways; for example, travel agents will generate income from the commission on the sale of all inclusive holidays, tickets, insurance and car hire. The accommodation sector breaks down sales into different income streams; for example the overall sales for a hotel will be made up of income from rooms, food and beverage and leisure departments. Case 7.1 demonstrates the different income streams enjoyed by the Go Ahead Group.

Case 7.1   Analysis of revenue for the Go Ahead Group

The Go Ahead Group provides passenger-transport services on both road and rail. An extract of the annual report for 2003 demonstrates the way a business generates sales from a range of business activities.

Year	2003	2002
	Turnover (£ millions)	
Bus	310.9	270.3
Rail	560.8	508.9
Aviation	211.7	150.0
Total	1083.4	929.2

Source: Go Ahead Group PLC Annual Report 2003

Discussion questions

1 How many different income streams does Go Ahead Group PLC have?
2 Which is the most important in terms of volume?

To generate sales a company will incur costs; to calculate the correct profit for an organisation and to determine how well a company has performed it is necessary to identify all expenses and deduct these from the sales. The next section will look at different types of expenses, explaining how they are incurred and which should be deducted from profit.

Expenses

The expenses that must be deducted are the cost of the resources an organisation has used up in the process of generating the sales. Here the word *resource* represents anything of value that has been *consumed* or *used up* in the process of delivering the service to the customer. The most obvious examples would be the food in a restaurant, the petrol in a bus and salaries for the flight crew in an airline. But there are also less obvious costs: the electricity in a travel agent and the landing charges for an airline; maintenance costs for a rail operator and laundry costs for a hotel. Companies also incur costs associated with managing and raising finance, for example interest on an overdraft or loan and fees for setting up large leasing agreements. Typical costs for tourism businesses are shown in Table 7.1.

Table 7.1	Typical costs for tourism businesses			
Typical businesses				
Airline	Coach operator	Hotel	Restaurant	Travel agent
Typical expenses				
Advertising	Airport taxes	Commissions	Depreciation	Electricity
Food costs	Fuel	Insurance	Labour	Loan interest
Maintenance	Rental	Road tax	Telephone	

This is an indicative list and what is important to understand is which expenses are significant for a particular business, as the significance of different types of costs will vary between different businesses and thus will be more, or less, important depending on the business context.

All the costs relating to the *accounting period* must be deducted from the revenue to calculate the true profit for the period. It is important to note that not all types of expenditure are deducted from the profit; it is only those items where the costs incurred have been fully used up or consumed which are deducted. For example, expenditure on long-term investments or assets such as the purchase of a coach or plane, the refurbishment of a hotel or the investment in a new computer system should not be deducted from profit in any single period. These types of expenditure relate to many years of trading (i.e. multiple accounting periods) and therefore should not be charged to any single period. Later it will be shown how (through depreciation) a small proportion of such long-term costs can be charged against revenue in a single accounting period. This approach to *matching* revenue and costs is fundamental to accurate calculation of the profit and is governed by the Accruals or Matching concept (see Berry and Jarvis (1997): Chapter 4).

Presentation of profit and loss account

Profit is generated when the revenue for a given period exceeds the expenses incurred in that period. The profit for a business is calculated by identifying all sales for the period and deducting all expenses that relate to those sales or that period. When all expenses have been deducted from sales the residual amount is profit. The profit and loss account provides a detailed report on the revenues and expenses and a simple example is presented in Table 7.2, which shows main line items and a two-column layout. This allows for the collection and subtotalling of similar items before inclusion in the right-hand column and adopts the convention of using brackets to denote items which are to be deducted.

Table 7.2	A simple profit and loss account

Profit and loss account for a hotel company for the period ending December 2005

	£000s	£000s
Sales		806
Less costs of sales		(262)
Gross profit		544
Less expenses		
Wages and salaries	197	
Utilities costs including gas and electric	50	
Advertising and marketing	90	
Administration, insurances and commission	33	
Depreciation	24	
Total expenses		(394)
Net profit (earnings) before interest and taxation		150
Interest		(12)
Net profit after interest before taxation		138
Taxation		(36)
Net profit after taxation		102
Dividends		(43)
Net profit retained		£59

The example shown in Table 7.2 illustrates some of the different types of expenses which must be deducted; it also shows the deduction of depreciation[2] and taxation, which are discussed below, and also what happens to the profit in the end. This level of detail regarding expenses is not normally provided in published financial statements but is used internally to help management to control the business.

Depreciation and other deductions

Depreciation is a charge made in the profit and loss account to take account of the use of, or loss in value of, fixed assets. As mentioned above expenditure on large fixed assets is not deducted from the profit in the period where expenditure is made but in the period when the asset is *used*. This is important to ensure that the resources used up or *consumed* are linked to the revenues that were generated in the same time period; it also avoids large variations in profit from year to year when large capital expenditure is incurred. Depreciation (which is also called amortisation in some contexts) is the mechanism for charging a share of the cost of fixed assets to the revenue in each accounting period. (For a more detailed look at depreciation and the various methods for calculating the annual charge see Berry and Jarvis (1997): Chapter 8.)

When all expenses have been deducted and the profit figure is known it is possible to calculate the taxation, which must be paid to government. Corporation taxation, as it is known in the UK, is paid by companies on the profit they make; however, the calculations are very complicated with various allowances and adjustments relating to complex

---

2 See following section for an explanation of *depreciation*.

rules, so for the purpose of this chapter it is sufficient to note that taxation must be deducted *after* expenses (for example, interest on a loan), but before dividends are paid to shareholders or owners. (Depreciation is a special case and must be added back before the calculation of taxation. For a more detailed exploration of taxation and financial reporting see Brigham, 2001.) Before leaving the issues of taxation it is worth pointing out that value added tax (VAT) is a completely different factor; this is not included in the revenue (sales) figures or the expenses for most large companies and is only considered in this chapter in the context of setting prices (for further discussion on Accounting for VAT see Owen (2000): Chapter 10).

Finally, dividends are deducted from the net profit after tax. Dividends represent a reward to the shareholders who risk their money to finance the business. Thus some of the profit after taxation is paid out to the shareholders (owners) as dividends and the remainder is *retained* in the business to help the business grow. This retained-profit figure is important for the business and is used to finance continued growth and development. It is very important to recognise though that profit is not the same as cash. The profit retained in the business (in Table 7.2 this amounted to £59,000) has been tied up in a variety of assets, including cash debtors; even fixed assets can be financed by retained profit.

To recap:

- *Sales* – revenue from ordinary activities – not necessarily cash.
- *Accounting period* – normally one year, the period for which accounts are drawn up.
- Revenue expenditure – the cost of resources consumed or used up in the process of generating revenue, generally referred to as expenses.
- *Profit* – the excess of revenue over expenses; if expenses exceed revenues in a given period the organisation will make a loss.
- *Capital expenditure* – the cost of long-term assets such as computer equipment, vehicles and premises. Importantly these are bought to use over several years and not to resell.
- *Retained profit* – the profit left in the business at the end of the accounting period after all deductions and appropriations have been made.

Case 7.2 provides extracts from the accounts of the Go Ahead Group PLC and shows how much profit is generated in this large public limited company.

Case 7.2	Go Ahead Group PLC profit and loss account	
Year	2003	2002
Operating profit (£ millions)		
Bus	43.9	33.3
Rail	25.0	17.5
Aviation services	1.0	3.4
Total	69.9	54.2
(Figures exclude goodwill and exceptional Items)		

Source: Go Ahead Group PLC Annual Report 2003

Discussion question

3 What proportion of the profit is earned by each of the business areas?

The balance sheet

The second key financial statement which is explained in this chapter is the balance sheet. The balance sheet is produced at the end of an accounting period and shows the position of the company after the year's trading. Importantly it is a 'snap shot' of the business and shows *at one particular moment* what the business is worth.

The balance sheet shows what the business owns (its assets) and what the business owes (its liabilities) and therefore provides a total of the wealth or net worth of the business. If a business is making a profit each year the wealth will grow; if the business is making a loss the wealth will shrink. Table 7.3 shows a typical balance sheet layout; this should be reviewed in conjunction with the definitions and explanations that follow.

Table 7.3	A simple balance sheet		

Balance Sheet for a Hotel as at the end of December 2005

	£ 000s Cost	£ 000s Accumulated depreciation	£ 000s Net book value
Fixed assets			
Land and buildings	850	000	850
Vehicles and equipment	350	250	100
Fixtures and fittings	181	150	31
	1381	400	981
Current assets			
Stock	65		
Debtors	11		
Cash at bank	180	256	
Less current liabilities			
Creditors	112		
Accruals	18		
Deferred taxation	91	(221)	
Net current assets (**working capital**)			35
Total assets less current liabilities			1016
Long-term liabilities			(364)
Capital employed /total net assets			£ 652
Financed by			
Share capital			200
Retained profits			452
Owners' equity			£652

Assets

Assets are things that a business owns, or can use for its benefit. The essence of an asset is that it will provide future benefit; for example, the stock of food in a restaurant which can be cooked and sold to generate revenue and a coach which can be used to transport customers to generate revenue. These assets last different lengths of time and are used in very different ways, but they are both useful to the business. Employees are arguably useful to the business, certainly in the service sector, but they cannot be treated as assets on the balance sheet, because, put simply, they are not owned by the business and as such are only treated as inputs to the business (see Expenses section (p. 147) earlier).

Assets are categorised according to the length of time they will last. Fixed assets are those assets that will be used over a long period of time in the business, such as land and buildings, vehicles, airplanes, coaches, computers, tables and chairs. All these assets will be useful for more than one year and will provide future benefit or utility to the business over many accounting periods. Current assets are those assets that have a short lifespan and will be used up quickly. Tangible examples are the stock of food in a restaurant and the stock of goods for resale in a tourist gift shop. Current assets will be used up or consumed within one year. Cash is considered a current asset, because you will spend it (and hopefully replenish it) to pay for expenses within one accounting period. There are other current assets that arise through the course of business including debtors (who are customers who have been invoiced for goods and services they have consumed but have not yet paid). Debtors rarely occur in most tourism businesses, as customers pay immediately (e.g. restaurant or bus service) or they pay in advance (e.g. travel agency and tour operations). They appear more in companies where business-to-business transactions occur (e.g. the hotel conference trade).

Liabilities

Liabilities can be defined as 'obligations to pay or provide value outside the business', e.g. bank overdrafts and creditors (who are suppliers to whom the business owes money). In these cases in the future the company will have to pay money out to the banks or the suppliers. In the former case it will be the repayment of monies borrowed, in the latter it will be payment for goods delivered. Liabilities are classified according to time and can be short-term or long-term liabilities in the same way as assets. A bank overdraft and creditors are examples of current liabilities, which will be paid off within one year. Bank loans, mortgages, finance agreements and commitments under finance leases are all examples of long-term or medium-term liabilities which will have to be repaid over a longer period of time.

Liabilities do not just involve making payments; they can arise when a company promises to provide a service. For example, in the tour operating businesses customers pay deposits and from the time the deposit is received the company has an obligation to provide a service (e.g. all-inclusive holiday) to the customers or return the deposit (depending on contractual details). Within about eight weeks of the holiday, customers will normally pay the full balance of the price of their holiday, which means that these liabilities can be substantial. These deposits and advance payments are shown on the balance sheet as a current liability called deferred income.

The current liabilities form part of the working capital of a business. Working capital comprises the operational assets and liabilities needed for everyday operation, e.g. cash or bank overdraft, stock and trade creditors. It is calculated by deducting current liabilities from current assets and shown in the balance sheet as net current assets (or liabilities when the value of current liabilities exceeds the value of current assets). Some businesses have more current liabilities than assets as a norm, for example tour operators (as seen above) and supermarkets (which have all cash sales and generous credit terms); other companies such as hotel companies normally have net current assets.

In addition to these current and long-term liabilities, which arise through the course of operating and financing the business, companies will also have a liability to the owners of the business. It is the owners who provide the original money (or capital) to start the business – this is called share capital (for companies) or owners' investment. This liability is very long-term; in fact it can be considered to be *permanent*, as it will exist as long as the business exists. In addition to the original capital invested in the business, the profits retained in the business also belong to the owners or shareholders. This is why the balance sheet shows the original capital invested and the retained profit together in the 'financed by' section; collectively these are called shareholders or owners' equity. The balance sheet is presented this way to enable the reader to see what assets and liabilities are being used in the business and how those assets and liabilities were financed. Some balance sheet layouts include long-term liabilities with owners' equity to separate *operational* aspects from *financial* aspects; either layout is 'correct'.

To recap:

- *Assets* – something of value that will provide future benefit or utility, and can be used to generate revenue. Usually owned, so simply described as 'things we own'.
- *Liabilities* – an obligation to pay money or provide service in the future. Simply described as 'things we owe'.
- Working capital – operational assets and liabilities needed for everyday operation, e.g. cash or bank overdraft, stock and trade creditors, known as net current assets/liabilities.
- *Net worth / total net assets* – the net value of all operational assets and liabilities and shows the amount of money invested in the operational capacity of the business. Calculated by deducting current and long-term liabilities from the value of fixed assets and current assets.
- Owners' equity – combines the original investment and any retained profit to show the total value of the owners' interest in the business.

In summary, the *balance sheet* provides details of the assets and liabilities in the business at one point in time, as at the end of the accounting period, whereas the *profit and loss account* shows what revenues and expenses occurred *during* the whole period, thus showing a summary of all that has transpired since the beginning of the accounting period, i.e. when the last balance sheet was prepared. These two statements are the key mechanisms for statutory (i.e. required by law in a specified format) financial reporting; in addition to these reports, companies must produce other statements and disclosures every year, such as cash flow statement and statement of gains and losses (for further details on financial reporting requirements see Horngren and Sundem (2002) or Alexander and Nobes (2001)).

For the purposes of this chapter it is sufficient to understand the profit and loss account and the balance sheet. These will be analysed and applied later in the chapter and the reader may benefit from reviewing this initial section a couple of times before moving on to look at cost concepts.

Case 7.3 shows the final accounts for Ryanair for the year ended March 2003. The aim of this case study is to show an example of published accounts from a real tourism organisation and help readers become familiar with the layout and terminology of the financial statements by answering the discussion questions.

Case 7.3	Ryanair

Consolidated profit and loss account for Ryanair for the years ended 31 March 2002 and 2003

	2003 Euros 000s	2002 Euros 000s
Operating Revenues		
Scheduled revenues	731,951	550,991
Ancillary revenues	110,557	73,059
Total Operating Revenues	**842,508**	**624,050**
Operating Costs		
Staff costs	(93,073)	(78,240)
Depreciation and amortisation	(76,865)	(59,010)

Fuel and oil	(128,842)	(103,918)
Maintenance, materials and repairs	(29,709)	(26,373)
Marketing and distribution costs	(14,623)	(12,356)
Aircraft rentals	–	(4,021)
Route charges	(68,406)	(46,701)
Airport and handling charges	(107,994)	(84,897)
Other costs	(59,522)	(45,601)
Total Operating Expenses	**(579,034)**	**(461,117)**
Operating Profit	**263,474**	**162,933**
Other Income/(expenses)	1,076	9,441
Profit on Ordinary Activities before tax	**264,550**	**172,374**
Tax on profit on ordinary activities	(25,152)	(21,999)
Profit for the financial year	**239,398**	**150,375**
Profit and Loss Account at beginning of year	439,230	288,855
Profit and Loss Account at end of year	**678,628**	**439,230**

Source: Extracted from Ryanair Annual Report and Financial Accounts 2003: 30

Consolidated balance sheet for Ryanair as at 31 March 2002 and 2003

	2003 Euros 000s	2002 Euros 000s
Fixed Assets		
Tangible assets	**1,352,361**	**951,806**
Current assets		
Cash and liquid resources	1,060,218	899,275
Accounts receivable	14,970	10,331
Other costs	16,370	11,035
Inventories	22,788	17,125
Total Current Assets	**1,114,346**	**937,766**
Total Assets	**2,466,707**	**1,889,572**
Current Liabilities		
Accounts payable	61,604	46,779
Accrued expenses and other liabilities	251,328	217,108
Current maturities of long-term debt	63,291	38,800
Short-term borrowing	1,316	5,505
Total Current Liabilities	**377,539**	**308,192**
Other Liabilities		
Provisions for liabilities and charges	67,833	49,317
Accounts payable due after one year	5,673	18,086
Long-term debt	773,934	511,703
Total Other Liabilities	**847,440**	**579,106**
Shareholders' Funds – Equity		
Called-up share capital	9,588	9,587
Share premium account	553,512	553,457
Profit and Loss account	678,628	439,230
Total Shareholders' Funds – Equity	**1,241,728**	**1,002,274**
Total Liabilities and Shareholders' Funds	**2,466,707**	**1,889,572**

Source: Extracted from Ryanair Annual Report and Financial Accounts 2003: 29

Case 7.3	Continued

Discussion questions

4 List the three most significant cost items for Ryanair in 2002 and 2003.

5 How many different sources of revenue does Ryanair have?

6 To what extent has the value of tangible assets increased between 2002 and 2003, what does this tell you about the company?

7 What is the value of working capital for 2003?

8 How much profit did Ryanair make in 2003, and how could you work this out from the balance sheet?

9 What differences do you notice about the layout of the Ryanair balance sheet compared to Table 7.3? Can you work out the value of total assets minus current liabilities and other liabilities for Ryanair.

Understanding and application of cost concepts

The expenses included in the profit and loss account can be analysed to help management decision-making; understanding these costs is a key skill and enables managers to plan and control tourism organisations more effectively. This section will look at the different ways of classifying costs and introduce some concepts and applications of this cost analysis.

Classifying costs

There is a variety of different methods of classifying and analysing costs which have been devised for different purposes and yield different types of information. Table 7.4 summarises the main approaches.

Table 7.4	Classification of costs	
Basis of classification	**Cost category**	**Purpose**
Basic elements	Materials	Preparation of profit and loss account
	Labour	
	General expenses	
Attributability	Direct and indirect	Budgeting and control
		Responsibility accounting
		Product/service pricing
Cost behaviour	Fixed and Variable cost	CVP analysis
		Flexible budgeting and variance analysis
		Analysing operational gearing
		Decision-making and pricing

Basic elements of costs

First, costs can be classified by type, i.e. all costs can be classified into materials, labour or general expenses. This approach comes from the manufacturing background of cost analysis and provides the main categories for financial reporting. Although convenient for financial reporting, it provides limited discrimination for management decision-making as it fails to identify what drives these costs and how they behave in different circumstances. It is, however, useful for higher level financial analysis carried out by investors and external analysts (see the Evaluating Business Performance section (p. 166) later in the chapter).

Direct and indirect costs

The second main approach to cost analysis categorises costs as direct or indirect. This approach focuses on whether the cost item can be attributed (or linked) to a single product or service, sometimes to a department. Direct costs can be linked or traced to one product or service. Indirect costs cannot easily or accurately be isolated in relation to a particular product or service, and are often called general expenses or overheads. Analysing costs this way can be useful for detailed product costing or for control and accountability. For example, costs such as food can be traceable to a particular menu item or meal, thus facilitating the analysis of the profitability of a single menu item. The analysis of food costs is an important part of menu planning – for further reading on this topic see Kotas and Jayawardena (1994). Direct costs form an important basis for cost-based pricing methods and are often, but not necessarily, variable (see definition of variable costs later). Indirect costs must be apportioned to products, services or departments on an appropriate basis, and this gives rise to absorption costing (see Berry and Jarvis, 1997). However, the larger the proportion of indirect costs in a business, the less useful this type of analysis can be. It is true that hotel companies, airlines and some tour operators endeavour to identify costs according to departments and/or product lines, however, the methods used to apportion indirect costs to each department or product/holiday are often arbitrary and negate any benefit to be gained from the analysis. Generally this form of analysis is used in businesses where there is a significant tangible product and the company operates at the goods end of the goods/services continuum.

Fixed and variable costs

A more powerful and useful method of classifying costs is according to behaviour; this means analysis of costs according to how they change in relation to activity or sales volume. All costs can be categorised by the way they behave. Costs either change in direct proportion to sales and are therefore *variable costs*, or they do not change and are thus *fixed costs*. For example, in a restaurant, food and beverages will be consumed every time a meal is served and will be classified as variable costs. On the other hand, overhead costs (like rent, insurance and often energy costs) do not change with the number of customers, so are categorised as fixed costs. Obviously it will depend on the nature and the size of the business. For example, the labour cost (salaries) for the cabin crew on a scheduled airline flight will be fixed regardless of the number of passengers on the flight, whereas in a fast-food outlet labour costs (for non-managerial staff) are variable, as staff are employed on a casual basis of hourly-paid contracts and can be employed on shift patterns linked directly to demand (i.e. the number of anticipated customers). The classification of costs therefore depends on factors such as operational flexibility, management information systems, and employment contracts in addition to the nature and size of the business concerned. Figure 7.1 shows how fixed and variable costs change with different levels of activity.

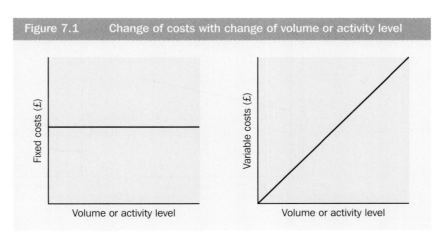

Figure 7.1 Change of costs with change of volume or activity level

These diagrams show the simplified cost functions for variable and fixed costs. The total fixed costs remain unchanged as volume increases and display a flat or horizontal cost function line. The total variable cost shows a straight diagonal line with a linear function (here the increase is constant, so the line is straight). The angle of the line is determined by the unit variable cost (the variable cost of one unit); the larger the unit variable cost the steeper the diagonal line will be. Figure 7.2 shows two cost functions: one for a business with high unit variable costs, and one for a business with low unit variable costs.

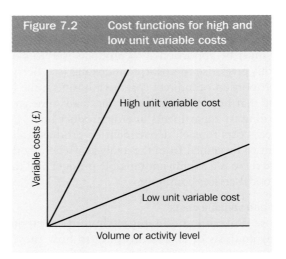

Figure 7.2   Cost functions for high and low unit variable costs

Later in this section the effect of these different costs profiles will be discussed. For a deeper discussion about costs functions see Berry and Jarvis (1997): Chapter 15.

This process of categorising costs is not an exact science and some costs combine a fixed and variable element – these costs are sometimes called semi-variable or semi-fixed. The following examples demonstrate how these can arise. The cost of labour can include both staff who are paid a salary and employed regardless of the number of customers and also hourly-paid staff who are employed at peak times as customer numbers increase. For businesses when demand can be reliably forecasted, hourly-paid staff can be treated as variable, therefore labour costs can display a semi-variable or stepped function. These costs functions are illustrated in Figure 7.3.

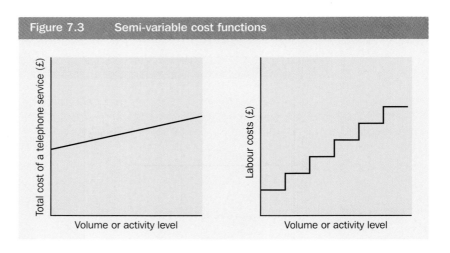

Figure 7.3   Semi-variable cost functions

Assumptions about cost behaviour are often based upon analysis of previous years' costs and industry norms. It is important to recognise that this analysis is limited to a specific range of activity, normally referred to as the 'relevant range'. This refers to a normal variation in sales activity within which the assumptions and forecasts of cost behaviour are reliable. For example, a coach operator can carry between 120 and 180 passengers per day operating a shuttle service from the airport to the town centre. However, to increase the number of passengers per day beyond this range an extra vehicle will need to be brought into service and this will change the cost assumptions and dynamics. Figure 7.4, with its discontinuities in the line, demonstrates this point.

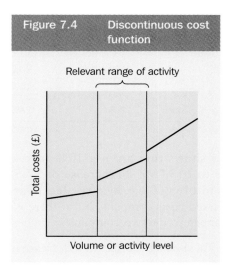

Figure 7.4   Discontinuous cost function

For a more detailed review of cost behaviour and estimation see Arnold and Turley (1996): Chapter 6 or Harris and Hazzard (1992): Chapter 5.

It is important to remember that all assumptions about costs and cost behaviour are context specific, thus it is not possible to generalise about whether a particular cost item will normally be fixed or variable; however, the majority of costs in tourism organisations are fixed and the next section explains why this is significant.

Application of cost concepts – cost structure

Cost structure is determined by the proportion of fixed and variable costs and is often referred to as *operational gearing*. A business that has a relatively high proportion of fixed costs, such as the Savoy Hotel Group or Quantas Airlines, is described as having high operational gearing. A business that has a high proportion of variable costs compared to fixed costs, such as McDonald's fast-food restaurants, is described as having low operational gearing.

Cost structure, or operational gearing, has an impact on *business risk* – the higher the fixed costs percentage, the more volatile profits will be when sales levels change. Table 7.5 shows how this works. In this example there are two companies that have exactly the same level of sales and the same overall profit percentage but one company has high fixed costs (high operational gearing) and the other has low fixed costs (low operational gearing). Both companies are exposed to the same fluctuations in sales, but, despite experiencing the same sales volume fluctuations the companies experience very different profit fluctuations.

Table 7.5	Cost structure and profit volatility example – sales increase	
	LoFix £	HiFix £
Sales	50,000	50,000
Variable costs	25,000	10,000
Fixed costs	15,000	30,000
Profit	10,000	10,000
Profit as a % of sales	20%	20%
If sales increase by 15%:		
Sales	57,500	57,500
Variable costs	28,750	11,500
Fixed costs	15,000	30,000
Profit	13,750	16,000
Profit as a % of sales	24%	28%

Table 7.5 shows that given a 15% increase in sales, the profit in LoFix Company increases to £13,750, an increase of 37.5%, whereas the profit in HiFix Company increases to £16,000, i.e. by 60%. It is clear that the increase in profit is much higher in the high fixed costs company, but if there were a recession and the sales decreased what would happen to the two companies?

Table 7.6 shows the effect of a decrease in sales.

Table 7.6	Cost structure and profit volatility example – sales decrease	
	LoFix £	HiFix £
If sales decrease by 10%:		
Sales	45,000	45,000
Variable costs	22,500	9,000
Fixed costs	15,000	30,000
Profit	7,500	6,000
Profit as a % of sales	16.6%	13.3%

In Table 7.6 the LoFix Company experiences a drop in profit of £2500 (25% reduction) whereas the HiFix Company has a large drop of £4000 (40%). As can be seen from this example the higher the fixed costs percentage the greater will be the profit volatility. In a recession (when there are falling sales) the business with high fixed costs will suffer more than businesses with low fixed costs. This means that when there is buoyant demand and sales are rising the high fixed cost business will do better and thus the potential returns are higher. It is normally the case that risk and return are related. As in this case, low fixed costs businesses generally face less risk than high fixed cost businesses although they do not have the same potential for high returns.

Cost structures are often germane to a particular sector. For example, hotels have higher fixed cost structures than restaurants. Airlines have much higher fixed cost percentages than travel agents. However, it is possible to observe differences within sectors, comparing luxury hotels to budget hotels and low costs ('no frills') airlines to flag-carrying ('full service') airlines. Table 7.7 summarises the cost profiles for a range of tourism businesses.

Table 7.7	Typical cost profiles

Examples of high-geared businesses (i.e. high fixed costs to low variable costs):

Airlines	– high fixed costs of fuel and crew for every flight
	– low variable costs per passenger for meals and other extras
Luxury hotels	– high fixed costs due to location, space and staffing levels
	– low variable costs of consumables
Leisure centres	– high fixed costs of premises and equipment and labour costs
	– low variable costs due to very few consumable resources/costs

Examples of low-geared businesses (i.e. low fixed costs to high variable costs):

Restaurants	– lower fixed costs as property is usually rented
	– higher variable costs of food and drink costs relative to prices
Retail outlets	– lower fixed costs as property is usually rented, flexible staffing
	– higher variable costs of goods relative to prices

Cost volume profit analysis

The second key application for cost behaviour analysis is that it enables the business to engage in cost volume profit (CVP) analysis (also known as breakeven analysis). This analysis is based on the ability to isolate fixed and variable costs and enables managers to evaluate pricing strategies and identify the breakeven point of a business or product or service within the business.

This section will explain the key concept of contribution and explain how to carry out CVP analysis and thus show how a range of management decisions can be supported applying CVP analysis. First though, it is important to recognise and understand the difference between unit and total cost.

Unit versus total cost

The term 'unit cost' refers to the cost of a single product or service event; for example, every burger which is sold in a fast-food restaurant will cost the same, so the variable cost per unit (that is, per burger) will also stay the same. Total variable costs, however, will increase as more sales are made: more unit costs will be incurred and the greater will be the *total* variable cost. The opposite is the case for fixed costs: total fixed costs remain unchanged (within the relevant range) regardless of the number of sales. However, if you were to calculate the fixed costs per unit this would gradually decrease as the volume of sales increase. The following simple example will illustrate this point.

Ice-cream for sale from a kiosk

The fixed costs of running a kiosk include electricity, insurance and labour costs of £560 per week. The number of ice-creams expected to be sold is 600. Therefore the fixed costs shared over 600 ice-creams would give £0.93 per ice-cream (i.e. £560.00 divided by 600). These simple calculations can show how the fixed cost per unit changes as the volume of sales change. Table 7.8 shows how the fixed cost per unit decreases as sales increase.

Table 7.8	Fixed costs per unit versus sales

No. of ice-creams	Fixed costs per ice-cream
200	£2.80
400	£1.40
600	£0.93
800	£0.70

It is important to remember this when considering what price to charge for a product or service and this is intrinsic to CVP analysis.

Breakeven analysis

Cost volume profit (CVP) analysis, sometimes called breakeven analysis, is a simple formulaic approach, which enables managers to understand the impact of a variety of options and decisions. For example, how many sales are required to cover costs and break even? Will it be worthwhile increasing advertising and increasing the price? What will be the effect on profit if prices are reduced to increase sales volume? These are questions that all tourism businesses should consider. The following section explains the key terminology, concepts and calculations involved.

The breakeven point is the point at which a business 'breaks even'; it makes neither a profit nor a loss and, in other words, this is the point at which total costs equal total revenue. This can be demonstrated using the kiosk example from above.

Ice-cream vendor

The fixed costs per week are £560 and variable costs per ice-cream are £1.20. If the selling price for the ice-cream is £2.60, how many ice-creams need to be sold to cover our costs? To answer this question it is important to understand the concept of contribution.

Contribution

In the example above every time an ice-cream is sold the customer pays £2.60 and the vendor incurs an expense of £1.20, so with the sale of each ice-cream the vendor earns £1.40. This is called *contribution* because, for each ice-cream sold, a small contribution is generated to help pay for the fixed costs of running the business. It is like an interim profit, but is called contribution because initially it will help to cover the fixed costs; after sufficient ice-creams have been sold and all fixed costs have been covered it will generate profit. There is a simple formula for contribution:

$$C = SP - VC$$ where C represents contribution per unit; SP represents selling price and VC represents variable costs per unit.

If every ice-cream sold makes a contribution of £1.40, the vendor will have to sell 400 ice-creams to make enough contribution to cover the fixed costs and hence break even. This is calculated by dividing the total fixed costs by the contribution per ice-cream as follows: total fixed costs per week £560, divided by contribution per ice-cream (unit) = £1.40.

£560.00 ÷ 1.40 = 400 ice-creams (units) must be sold

The formula to calculate this is:

$$FC \div C = B/E$$ where FC represents total fixed costs; C represents contribution per unit and B/E represents breakeven point in units.

Knowing the breakeven point of a business helps the manager not only to evaluate profit potential but also business risk. One of the risks a business faces is the chance that sales will drop to a point where the business is no longer profitable. The margin of safety measures the gap between the breakeven sales point and the normal operating (or budgeted) sales level to give an indication of how risky a business is. If a business is operating at its maximum capacity and yet is very close to the breakeven point, only a small change in volume or selling price could move the business into a loss-making situation. So the margin of safety is a useful tool for evaluating and comparing risk of different options. For further reading on CVP see Arnold and Turley (1996): Chapter 8 and for a more applied approach to CVP in a hotel context see Harris (1999): Chapter 5.

CVP formula

The relationship between cost, volume and profit can be presented in a formula, which is:

$$P = SP - (VC + FC)$$

where P represents profit; SP = selling price per unit; VC represents variable costs per unit and FC represents total fixed costs.

(All the formulae used above are derivations of this main CVP formula.)

This formula can be used to answer a range of questions with the application of simple algebraic rules; it can be manipulated to provide the answers to questions such as:

- How many sales are required to cover costs and break even?
- Will it be worthwhile increasing advertising and increasing the price?
- What will be the effect on profit if the price is reduced to increase sales volume?

Case 7.4 provides an example of how CVP can answer such questions.

Case 7.4   Costs at a theme park

A company is considering operating a concession in a popular theme park. They have developed two concepts, which have different menus, service formats and pricing structure. The forecasted costs and revenues for both options are shown below:

	Option one	Option two
Investment costs	€ 220,000	€ 340,000
Estimated monthly sales (covers)	16,000	36,000
Estimated average spend per cover	€ 4.40	€ 3.05
Variable costs	30%	40%
Monthly fixed costs	€ 27,000	€ 24,000

Discussion questions

10 Calculate the breakeven point, margin of safety and profit potential for each option.

11 Make recommendations as to which option would be best, justifying your decisions.

Case 7.4 shows how, through applying CVP principles, it is possible to make decisions about the best options in business, but this technique is for short-term decisions only. There are also many other techniques and concepts to consider in short-term decision-making, which are covered in detail in Atrill and McLaney (2003).

In relation to the cost concepts and their application the following terminology has been explained:

- *Variable cost* – a cost that increases in direct proportion to sales volume or output.
- *Fixed cost* – a cost that remains fixed for a period of time and does not change when sales increase or decrease.

◾ *Contribution* – the difference between selling price and the variable cost; it represents the money earned from one unit of sale which can contribute towards fixed costs and profit.

◾ *Breakeven point* – the level of sales where total cost equals total revenue.

◾ *Margin of safety* – the difference between current or expected sales and the breakeven sales point. Gives an indication of risk.

◾ *Relevant range* – the normal variation in activity or sales volume within which assumptions about cost behaviour are reliable.

Pricing

Setting prices is one of the most important decisions that managers in any business have to make since it is the main decision that influences the revenue side of the business. As explained in the introductory section of this chapter it is important for tourism businesses to maximise revenue, so pricing is particularly important. This emphasis on revenue maximisation has resulted in sophisticated systems for yield management and revenue management within which *price* is the single most important factor. (For a more detailed review of revenue management see Ingold *et al.* (2000); for a closer look at profit improvement see Harris (1999): Chapter 7.) Pricing is also important because it can have far-reaching effects, particularly in the tour operating business where brochure prices have to be determined up to 18 months prior to the actual booking and the holiday taking place. Pricing is also a complex matter because it brings together concepts from marketing, accounting and economics. The following section will firstly introduce the economic concept of elasticity and then continue to look at cost-based and market-based pricing methods. This section will close with a brief look at the process of price-setting in all-inclusive tour operations.

Elasticity of demand

Elasticity of demand is an economic concept that relates changes in demand for a product or service to a range of factors. The most important factor is price, known as price elasticity of demand, often abbreviated to elasticity of demand. There are, however, other factors of elasticity, income elasticity and cross-price elasticity, which are discussed in detail in Tribe (1999).

Price elasticity of demand describes the response in demand to a change in price. Demand is described as *elastic* when it changes in relation to change in price. *Unit elasticity* results in an equal effect on demand to a change in price, e.g. if price increased by 10%, demand would decrease by 10%. If demand is *inelastic* then an increase in price would not result in a decrease in demand. This effect happens when price is increased or decreased, so, if price was reduced demand would be stimulated to increase, assuming demand is price elastic; however, inelastic demand would not increase in response to a decrease in price.

In general terms, luxury goods tend to be more price elastic, because people can manage without them, whereas essential goods such as petrol and fuel, are often price inelastic. So for a similar percentage increase in sales, demand will be less affected in essential products and services. This is important to remember when setting prices and considering price changes – managers must consider the price elasticity or their pricing strategies may be ineffective in increasing revenue and hence profit. For a more detailed discussion of elasticity, see Tribe (1999) and for broader discussion on cost structure elasticity and pricing for hospitality services see Cullen (1997).

Approaches to pricing

There are two main approaches to pricing: cost-based pricing and market/competitor-orientated pricing. Although many textbooks show a range of different approaches they all in fact fall within these two broad categories.

Cost-based or cost-plus pricing **approaches**

This is the simplest and most widely used internally-orientated approach to pricing. It involves establishing the cost of producing a product or service and then adding on an amount to get the selling price. The amount added, often called the mark-up, will vary according to how much of the overall costs have been included. This can be expressed mathematically as follows:

$$P = C + f(C) \qquad \text{where P = price, C = costs and } f = \text{the \% mark-up required.}$$

So, for example, if C = £3.40 and the mark-up required was 30%, the price would be £5.59, as P = £3.40 + (30% × £3.40) = £5.59.

The main variations in cost-plus methods of pricing are effectively explained by Harris and Hazzard (1992) and shown in Figure 7.5.

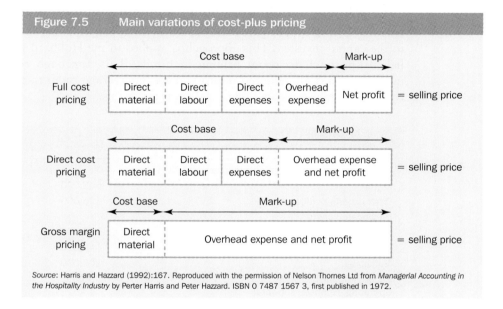

| Figure 7.5 | Main variations of cost-plus pricing |

Source: Harris and Hazzard (1992):167. Reproduced with the permission of Nelson Thornes Ltd from *Managerial Accounting in the Hospitality Industry* by Perter Harris and Peter Hazzard. ISBN 0 7487 1567 3, first published in 1972.

As can be seen from Figure 7.5 the size of the mark-up will depend on the amount of costs included. Where a full cost approach to pricing is operated the mark-up need only cover the required net profit, whereas with marginal or gross-margin pricing the mark-up needs to be large enough to cover overheads as well as net profit. The approach adopted will be dependent on the cost structure of the business and the quality of the management information systems to track costs accurately.

The *full cost pricing* approach endeavours to take account of all costs the business will incur. It requires the apportionment of overheads to specific products, services or departments and thus in the tourism context is often difficult to implement effectively due to the difficulties of accurately identifying, attributing and apportioning of costs.

The contribution margin pricing – often called marginal cost pricing – is a very useful approach to pricing for businesses where there are high fixed costs and it is not easy to apportion indirect costs. Price is based on marginal cost (marginal cost is often synonymous with variable cost, but for a detailed definition see Cullen (1997)). The mark-up in marginal pricing methods is larger to cover required profit and to contribute to costs, thus it allows manager more discretion to vary the price. This approach is also useful to consider when there is strict price competition, because it identifies the very lowest possible price a business could sell at. It should be used carefully as this approach can lead to insufficient revenue being generated to cover all costs. It is particularly useful when considering pricing strategies after breakeven sales have been achieved.

Another variation is breakeven pricing; where capacity is fixed *breakeven pricing* is useful, because a company will calculate the price that must be charged to break even, given a fixed sales-volume forecast. It is then clear that any market-based price assessment must exceed this breakeven price to ensure profit is generated (see discussions on CVP earlier).

Rule-of-thumb method of pricing has been established in the hotel industry. This states that the average room rate charged by a hotel should be equivalent to £1 for every £1000 invested in the hotel building (originally specified as per1000). The approach aims to take account of capital investment (including capital cost of building and furnishings) and operating structure of hotels, but is criticised for the lack of scientific underpinning; largely ignored in recent years, it has, however, been found to be reasonably accurate, depending on the class of hotel, in some new research carried out in North America (O'Neill, 2003).

Profit-orientated/Rate-of-return pricing takes account of the profit required by the business overall and in particular identifies an appropriate amount of profit in relation to the capital invested. This approach is applied in the Hubbard Formula, a long established approach to room pricing in hotels. This approach recognises the capital investment and the required return and sets an average room rate to generate sufficient revenue. The example in Table 7.9 demonstrates this.

Table 7.9	Example of Hubbard Formula		
Rooms department operating expenses			
Payroll	565,000		
Other departmental expenses	125,000	690,000	
Unallocated costs			
Utilities	75,000		
Administration	43,000		
Marketing	105,000		
Repairs and maintenance	86,000	309,000	
Operating expenses sub total		999,000	
Return on capital employed			
Capital employed	4,850,000		
10% return required after tax	10%	485,000	
Taxation			
Taxation at 25%	25%	161,667	
Fixed charges			
Interest and depreciation		115,950	
Deduct any profits from other departments			
Food and beverage	65,800		
Banqueting and conference	22,000		
Shop franchises	15,600	–103,400	
Total amount to be realised from room sales to			
cover costs and the required return on capital employed		£1,658,217	
Calculation to establish average daily room rate			
Amount realised from room sales (A)		£1,658,217	
Rooms available for sales		150	
No. of rooms available annually (× 365)		54,750	
Average expected occupancy (65%)		65%	
No. of room-nights to be occupied (B)		35,588	
Average room rate (A ÷ B)		£46.60	

This approach is a more sophisticated cost-plus approach to pricing and although it recognises the operational dynamics of a hotel, it is still internally orientated and suffers from the weaknesses of all cost-based methods. All cost-based methods fail to consider the market dynamics and competition – if the equivalent hotel across the road, for example, has set its prices at £35 per night per room, this hotel is not likely to sell many rooms at £46.60. So all pricing techniques must consider issues of supply and demand and competition, while remaining aware of the cost-based methods calculations and recommendations.

Market-based approaches

Market-based approaches to pricing are externally focused. A variety of factors are considered including issues of supply and demand, plus the structure and dynamics of the market. For example, if demand for a product or service exceeds supply then prices can rise. This can happen because of a one-off event (room rates for hotel accommodation in Athens rose prior to the Olympics) or regularly (as in the cruise industry where holiday prices increase in the high season as demand increases).

Marketing textbooks describe a range of approaches to pricing including prestige pricing, loss leader and psychological approaches to pricing (see Bowie and Buttle, 2004). All these approaches have to be based on knowledge of the company's costs. *Going-rate pricing* looks at the market to set a price according to the competition; this has implications for costs and requires organisations to reduce or cut costs, which can impinge on service standards and quality. A company must be aware if a market-based price is below full cost price and particularly the marginal cost price, it is likely that such tight pricing cannot be maintained for very long without serious financial implications.

In the light of this complexity and the demands of market-orientated pricing and the need to understand costs, the following process is often adopted by tourism organisations. Table 7.10 demonstrates a typical approach to pricing in a tour operating company.

Table 7.10	Setting prices in all-inclusive tour operations
Step 1	Identify supply-chain elements, transport, accommodation, excursions required for all-in package
Step 2	Break down costs into direct, indirect, fixed and variable
Step 3	Forecast expected volumes associated with those costs
Step 4	Calculate prices based on a range of load factors
Step 5	Benchmark prices against competitors
Step 6	Fix brochure price and pray

Tour operator pricing is a high-risk aspect of management decision-making which is why detailed forecasts are required. The level on uncertainty is a key factor and so Step 4 above, *calculating prices at a range of load factors*, is very important, as is the use of forward contracts for accommodation and transfers. In addition advance purchase of currency and forward contracts for currency sales are also a key aspect of financial management of the tour operator's businesses. Case 7.5 shows a simple numeric example.

Case 7.5	Olympic Tours Ltd – an example of price setting

Olympic Tours Ltd is developing a package holiday for sports fans. Designed to coincide with the Athens Olympics in Greece, the all-inclusive package includes:

- return flight to Athens;
- transfers from airport;
- hotel accommodation for fourteen days half board;

▶

Case 7.5	Continued

– tickets to key events including the opening ceremony;

– book of vouchers for use at attractions in the locality.

The basic cost information is as follows:

Fixed costs

- chartered planes – three return flights, seating capacity 250, cost £24,000 per return flight;
- coaches to transfer holiday-makers from airport to hotel and back (plus from hotel to opening ceremony): cost €2000 per coach per round trip, coach capacity 52 passengers.

Variable costs

- Hotel Metropolitan: cost €1680 per person (the contract with the hotel states that the tour operator will only pay for the number of rooms actually booked);
- tickets to the opening ceremony and five event sessions (including Athletics final night and marathon finish): total cost €1250 (packs of tickets are returnable up to two weeks before the opening ceremony);
- voucher book: €160 per book.

Discussion question

12 Calculate the final selling price for the tour assuming that the operator requires a mark-up of 30% and expects the load factor to be 80%. You can assume that the exchange rate will be €1.498 to £1.

This case study demonstrates the calculations for pricing a simple all-inclusive package. This type of calculation should be completed on a spreadsheet to enable quick recalculation under different assumptions of load factor and exchange rate to see the impact on price. Ultimately many small tour operators use a combination of research, calculations, competitor benchmarking and importantly the gut feeling of the country or product manager.

Summary of key pricing concepts

In relation to pricing the following concepts and terminology have been explained:

- *Price elasticity of demand* – a measure of the variability that can be expected in sales when prices are changed. *Unity elasticity* would see equal increase in sales in reaction to a decrease in price. *Inelastic demand* would not change when prices went down or up.
- *Cost-plus pricing* – a method of pricing where an amount to cover profit is added to costs to establish the selling price. This is an internally-orientated pricing method.
- *Marginal or contribution pricing* – a method of cost-plus pricing which focuses on the variable or marginal cost only and thus establishes the lowest possible selling price.
- *Market-orientated pricing* – a method of pricing that benchmarks prices against competitors when deciding on price.
- *Load factor* – the percentage of full capacity that is achieved on an aeroplane or packaged holiday. This is of critical importance in the high-fixed cost businesses. In the accommodation sector it is often based on rooms and is called *occupancy*.

Evaluating business performance

So far this chapter has addressed the main financial statements, analysed costs and reviewed approaches to pricing. Before continuing to look at how to prepare a business plan, this section of the chapter will focus on how to evaluate financial information.

A variety of techniques has evolved to evaluate company performance but they all involve comparison of at least two factors. Without something to compare it is not possible to make a judgement about a piece of data or a company. The illustrative example in Table 7.11 demonstrates the value of ratios and how they can put financial information into context.

Table 7.11	Evaluating company performance		
		Company A	**Company B**
Sales		£300,000	£1,125,000

Which company has performed better?
Company B has the higher sales but is that all that matters?

		Company A	**Company B**
Profit		£ 75,000	£ 112,500

Now which company has performed better? Company B still appears the better with higher profit, but it has much higher sales so profit should be even higher. By calculating a ratio of profit to sales it is possible to compare the companies

		Company A	**Company B**
Profit % (profit as a percentage of sales)		25%	10%

Now it is clear that Company A has a better profit margin. It is earning 25p from every £1 of sales generated, compared to 10p earned by Company B. So Company A is better.
But this does not tell us how much money is tied up in each business, so it is still not a full picture.

		Company A	**Company B**
Capital invested		£ 500,000	£ 750,000

It can be seen that Company B has more money tied up or invested than Company A. If the profit earned is presented as the percentage of the money invested, it is possible to compare the companies again.

		Company A	**Company B**
Return on capital employed (ROCE)		15%	15%

So both companies perform equally well when profit is related to money (or capital) invested.
So how can two companies achieve the same overall result, yet have very different profit figures?
This is due to their *productivity*; Company B is making its assets work harder than Company A. When comparing the sales generated from the assets invested, it is clear that Company B is more productive.

		Company A	**Company B**
Asset utilisation (times)		0.6	1.5

This shows that Company A is generating only 60p of sales for each £1 it has invested in assets, while Company B is generating £1.50 for every £1.

Table 7.11 shows that a range of ratios must be used to compare performance and that a similar overall performance can be achieved by different means. Overall performance is measured by return on capital employed (ROCE). This ratio gives an overview by comparing profit before interest and tax (PBIT)[3] to the capital employed. This gives an overall measure of operational performance; by excluding interest and tax and including all operating assets, this ratio excludes the effect of financing decisions and focuses purely on operational performance.

---

3 Also known as EBITDA: earnings before interest and taxation depreciation and amortisation.

■ Profitability and productivity

Table 7.11 demonstrated that overall performance is the result of two key aspects of performance, profitability and productivity. Table 7.12 shows the main ratios for each aspect and what they evaluate.

Table 7.12	Key ratios	
Main ratio		
Overall performance	ROCE (PBIT ÷ capital employed [CE] × 100)	Overall measure of performance; links profit generated to the value of assets employed to earn that profit. Excludes financing because PBIT is profit prior to interest and long-term liabilities are excluded in CE.
Subordinate ratios		
Profitability	Net profit % (PBIT ÷ sales × 100)	Key measure of performance; reflects all expenses and thus overall business performance. Shows what money is left to cover finance costs and fund growth. Expressed as a percentage.
	Gross profit % (GP ÷ sales × 100)	Reflects core profitability of product or service. Reflects pricing policy and basic cost control of prime costs. Expressed as a percentage.
	Expenses as % of sales (exp ÷ sales × 100)	Diagnostic ratio that can explain performance; can be calculated as total expenses or they can be broken down, for example: labour costs %; overhead %.
Productivity	Asset utilisation (sales ÷ capital employed)	Shows how many sales are being generated from the assets. Indicates the intensity with which assets are being used. Expressed as times utilisation, but can be interpreted as the value of sales generated per £ of assets.
	Sales to fixed assets and sales to current assets	Isolates the productivity by class of assets; usually only useful when reviewing a trend to see whether each class of assets is being managed effectively.

The definitions and explanations in Table 7.12 show that a range of measures must be used and interpreted together to establish a clear picture of company performance. It should be noted that although there are commonly used ratios there are no absolute rules about which ratios should be calculated and terminology varies – the only important thing to remember is that you must compare *like with like*. So compare expenses to sales of exactly the same period. Compare profit before tax to total net assets, excluding long-term finance; if long-term finance is included, then the interest relating to that finance should also be included in the analysis, and thus (as an expense) deducted from profit before the comparison is made. Also be aware that figures in any one year are not always representative, so ratios should be calculated for two or three years to give a clear indication of a trend and provide a reliable analysis of performance. Case 7.6 is extracted from the annual accounts of Whitbread plc and shows how company executives explain performance to shareholders.

Case 7.6	Whitbread hotel division performance

Whitbread Annual Report and Accounts includes a statement from the chief executive. Within this are the key operating ratios and statistics; the following mini-cases include these statistics and the commentary associated with them extracted from the accounts.

Marriott	2003/4	Change
Sales	£391 million	–0.30%
Operating profit	£71.5 million	–10%
Return on capital employed	6.20%	(0.3%)
Travel Inn	2003/4	Change
Sales	£230 million	12.00%
Operating profit	£74.0 million	11%
Return on capital employed	13.60%	1.00%

'It has been another good year for Britain's most popular hotel brand {Travel Inn}: a year of strong sales; and a year of double-digit profit growth. Occupancy dipped in the first six months as our London properties suffered from broad market pressure; but after a steady second half we finished the year at 80.2%.

Marriott has delivered another gritty performance in a market that remains tough. Operating profit has fallen and we have seen further erosion in return on capital employed, but we have performed better on profit per room than our peer group average. Occupancy has edged ahead to 71.5%.'

Source: Extracted from Whitbread PLC Annual Report and Accounts 2003/4 (Whitbread, 2004)

Case 7.6 demonstrates a series of points: first that within one operating division two companies can perform very differently and thus the level of analysis is important; if the whole of Whitbread hotels division results were looked at together the relatively different performance of these two companies would have been hidden. This also shows that as a relative novice in accounting it is possible to understand the commentary provided within the annual reports. It is also interesting to note that Whitbread have subsequently announced their desire to reduce the amount of capital invested in the hotel division.

Liquidity

Working capital or liquidity is another key area for investigation that underpins productivity, but also focuses on cash flow. The following ratios focus on working-capital management and the balance of current assets and current liabilities. This aspect of management is crucial in keeping the cash flowing in the business, especially for small businesses, where it can be the difference between success and failure. The main working-capital ratios are summarised below in Table 7.13.

The ratios presented in Table 7.13 are used in most industries but are less helpful when there is little or no stock, or where normal operating practices result in negative figures. For example, in retailing the current ratio is often negative because in the retail sector all sales are in cash, all purchases are on credit and stock is kept to a minimum, which results in more current liabilities than current assets. Tour operators also experience net current liabilities. This is due to the fact that customers pay deposits and pay for holidays some time in advance, which results in a liability called deferred income (see discussion earlier) and because there are also no stock holdings, current assets are normally less than current liabilities.

Table 7.13	Main working-capital ratios	
Current ratio	$\dfrac{\text{Current assets}}{\text{Current liabilities}}$	Main measure of liquidity; gives indication of the company's ability to pay immediate debts; reflects industry profile and ability to manage working capital. Expressed as ratio (x:1).
Stock turnover	$\dfrac{\text{Average stock}}{\text{Cost of sales}} \times 365$	Indicates the average length of time stock is held. Expressed in days.
Debtor collection period (DCP)	$\dfrac{\text{Debtors}}{\text{Credit sales}} \times 365$	Gives the average length of time it takes to collect money from customers. Expressed in days.
Creditor payment period (CPP)	$\dfrac{\text{Creditors}}{\text{Credit purchases}} \times 365$	Gives the average length of time it takes to pay for purchases; best observed as a trend. Expressed in days.
Cash operating cycle	Stock turnover + DCP − CPP	Measures the length of time between first payment to supplier for purchases to receipt of cash from customers.

Financial structure

The final aspect of performance is financial structure. This aspect of performance is associated with the financial management of the company and focuses on the balance of different sources of finance and the ability to cover the cost of finance, i.e. cover interest payments and dividends. Other investor ratios are not covered here but are discussed in detail in McKenzie (1998); also Vellas and Bécherel (1995: Chapter 7) discuss aspects of financial performance and finance. Table 7.14 presents three key ratios in this area.

Table 7.14	Key financial ratios	
Gearing ratio	$\dfrac{\text{Debt}}{\text{Equity and debt}}$	Shows what proportion of overall funding comes from debt finance; the higher the percentage debt the higher the gearing. This gives an indication of financial risk. Higher-geared firms are considered more risky.
Interest cover	$\dfrac{\text{PBIT}}{\text{Interest}}$	Shows the ability of the company to pay interest cover; the higher, the better.
Dividend cover	$\dfrac{\text{Profit attributable to shareholders}}{\text{Dividend}}$	Shows the ability of the company to pay dividends; as above, the higher, the better – the more funds will be available for retention and the faster the growth.

Case 7.7 demonstrates how this theory translates into practice with extracts from The Restaurant Group (TRG) showing how a successful company can have very different levels of debt to equity.

Case 7.7	The Restaurant Group financial structure					
		2003	2002	2001	2000	1999
Net (debt)/funds (£000s)		(38,163)	(44,600)	(53,261)	(56,853)	(41,396)
Gearing (%)		76.1	95.8	132.2	86.6	51.1
Interest cover before exceptional items (times)		8.6	6.1	4.9	5.2	8.8

TRG has funded expansion through borrowing which led to a gearing ratio of 132% in 2001, which has now started to reduce. Throughout this time TRG has been profitable and successful but obviously the levels of risk faced by the investors have been considerable, increasingly in 2001 and 2002. This case provides another example of the level of detailed information available in company annual reports.

Source: The Restaurant Group (TRG) Annual Accounts extracts from five-year review (TRG, 2003: 41)

Common-sized statements

The main approach to evaluating financial information is to use ratio analysis, but some authors advocate the use of common-sized statements (CSS). This involves presenting the main financial statements expressed as a series of ratios. This technique reduces the complexity of the financial statements by turning £ millions into simple percentages. It is useful for comparing companies of different sizes and provides a useful first round of analysis before key ratios are calculated. (See Berry and Jarvis (1997): Chapter 12, and also Harris (1992): Chapter 4, which reviews CSS to compare intra-company data in the profit and loss restaurant context.) However, calculation of key ratios is the most widely accepted method of evaluating company performance.

Having reviewed the main generic ratios it is useful to recognise that there are specialized industry-based ratios which are also regularly used. These are the subject of the next section.

Industry-based ratios

In addition to the generic ratios described above, there are several industry ratios that are commonly used and reported in annual accounts of major companies. The final table in this section (Table 7.15) shows the main measures used in two important tourism sectors, accommodation and airlines.

Table 7.15	Industry ratios	
Accommodation sector	Occupancy %	Key measure of productivity; demonstrates the utilisation of capacity. Critical measure monitored internally and benchmarked externally by all hotels.
	RevPar – revenue per available room	Combines pricing and productivity by dividing total revenue by the number of rooms available for sale. Key drivers of this measure are occupancy and average room rate.
	Yield	Focuses on total revenue achieved versus revenue potential expressed as a percentage. It combines the effects of occupancy and average achieved room rate to show relative performance in this key area of revenue maximisation.
Airline sector	Revenue per passenger kilometre (RPK)	Similar to RevPar in hotels. Shows how much revenue is generated on average from each passenger kilometre travelled. Expressed per kilometre.
	Load factor	The number of seats (or holidays) sold as a percentage of the full capacity. Key productivity measure, equivalent to occupancy in hotels.
	Available seats per kilometre (ASK)	Measure of capacity is the number of aircraft seats available multiplied by the kilometres flown.

The ratios included above are fundamental, quantitative, efficiency ratios. Companies also collect more qualitative data on performance through 'mystery guest' programmes and staff and customer questionnaires. This type of qualitative information is increasingly being used internally to monitor company performance with the development of performance measurement (PM) systems such as the balanced scorecard,[4] however this kind of data is not often found in the public domain or in annual reports.

Case 7.8 shows some operating ratios included in Lufthansa's Annual Report and includes a range of operating statistics and ratios.

Case 7.8   Industry statistics – Lufthansa AG

The following figures are extracted from the accounts of Lufthansa AG for the accounting periods 2002 and 2003:

Output data Lufthansa Group		2003	2002
Total available tonne-kilometres	millions	23,237.30	22,755.60
Total revenue tonne-kilometres	millions	16,226.50	16,080.80
Overall load factor	per cent	69.8	70.7
Available seat-kilometres	millions	124,026.60	119,876.90
Revenue passenger-kilometres	millions	90,708.20	88,570.00
Passenger load factor	per cent	73.1	73.9
Passengers carried	millions	45.4	43.9

Results for Lufthansa show a downturn in most key indicators in 2003, which reflects the difficult trading conditions and increased competition in the airline industry. This extract from the Chairman's statement reflects this:

'2003 was an extremely challenging year. It involved a great deal of hard work and strenuous effort. The threefold crisis – the war in Iraq and the latent fear of terrorist attacks, the SARS epidemic and the weak global economy – dented demand, exerted additional pressure on prices, and weighed heavily on our result.'

This example also shows a high level of detailed reporting now being included in annual reports. Such reports are usually freely available on the company website as .pdf files and provide a valuable source of information for investors analysts and students alike.

Source: Lufthansa AG Annual Accounts for 2003 (Lufthansa, 2003: 186)

Summary of evaluation of business performance concepts

In relation to the evaluation of business performance the following concepts, ratios and aspects of performance have been explained:

- *Profitability* – this aspect focuses on the core profit margins and the business operating profit, to understand where and how the company is generating profit from its sales revenue.
- *Productivity* – focuses on asset utilisation and efficiency to see how the company is using the assets and liabilities at its disposal to generate revenue.
- *Liquidity* – focuses on working-capital management and ability of the company to meet its immediate debts.
- *Financial structure/gearing* – concentrates on how the company is financed and how effectively it can meet its financial obligations. This aspect addresses finance risk and gearing.

---

4 The balanced scorecard is a multivariate model developed by Kaplan and Norton (1992); also see Adams (1997) for a discussion of this PM framework.

An understanding of business performance and how to evaluate it is a crucial element of preparing a business plan. The next section will show what other information should be included in the preparation and presentation of a business plan.

Preparing and evaluating a business plan

The preparation of a business plan is an essential part of starting up a business. Business plans contain information about the business, the business concept, the business mission, its markets and importantly its finances. Business plans are usually developed to help raise finance and so they are targeted towards potential investors and lenders. This should be remembered when the tone and style of the documents is considered. A typical business plan will include:

- business concept, description of the business idea, the product or service;
- market demand and justification, customer profile and sales forecasts;
- resources requirements, staffing and manpower requirements, capital investments and operating-capacity requirements;
- forecasted financial statements including cash budget and budgeted profit and loss account and balance sheet;
- other key issues, which may include legal requirements for licences, planning requirements and permissions, copyright, entertainment licences etc. in addition to health and safety requirements.

Preparing a business plan requires entrepreneurs to look carefully at their business model, i.e. the nature of their business and the cost structure, and forecast revenues and expenses. Most European banks provide packs for small businesses, but consultants and venture capitalists also provide guidance of what is required, so after an entrepreneur has carried out his/her research, he/she may have to rewrite the business plan to meet the needs of different investors and lenders. The following section provides a brief outline of the stages involved in writing a business plan.

To start with, identifying a business concept is the most important part of starting up a new business. Many businesses are born out of the hobbies and interests of the entrepreneur, or people have experience in a particular business as an employee and decide to set up their own business. Sometimes new businesses stem from redundancies or the need to change the quality of life. Whatever the stimulus to start a new business, an in-depth knowledge of the industry or sector of business is necessary. It is critical to understand the marketplace to be able to identify a unique selling point (USP). A necessary first step in preparing a business plan is a clear and detailed idea of the business concept, what makes the product or service attractive and different from others. At this stage it is helpful to demonstrate innovation and creativity.

Next it is important to carry out research into the marketplace, identify the main sources of competition and consider if it is direct or indirect (see Bowie and Buttle, 2004). Who are the customers for the product or service and are they sufficient in number to make a business viable, in the context of the other businesses competing for those customers? It is essential to have a detailed profile of the potential customers, including their spending habits and disposable income. How will these potential customers be converted into sales revenue and how much sales revenue will be expected in the first few months and the first year of trading? This process of forecasting sales is where the external perspective (understanding demand) meets the internal perspective (how can the business meet that demand). Issues of capacity and operations are important to consider here – this will start to raise questions about premises, capital equipment and other resource requirements.

Once there is a clear idea about the nature and the scale of the business, resource plans can be prepared. Answers will need to be found to the following questions:

- What premises, if any, will be required?
- What equipment and fixtures are needed?
- Will the business need vehicles for delivery of goods or transport of customers?
- What level of staffing is required, is the service 24 hours?

A schedule of manpower needs should also be prepared. This information can then be turned into a financial plan or forecast.

When preparing financial forecasts, it is critical not to be too optimistic – adopt the accounting principle of *prudence or conservatism* (see Berry and Jarvis, 1997), but be realistic. A clear understanding of cost structures and cost behaviour in addition to realistic costings for all purchases is important. A business plan should include forecasted financial statements including cash budget and budgeted profit and loss account and balance sheet. Figure 7.6 shows clearly how these processes interrelate.

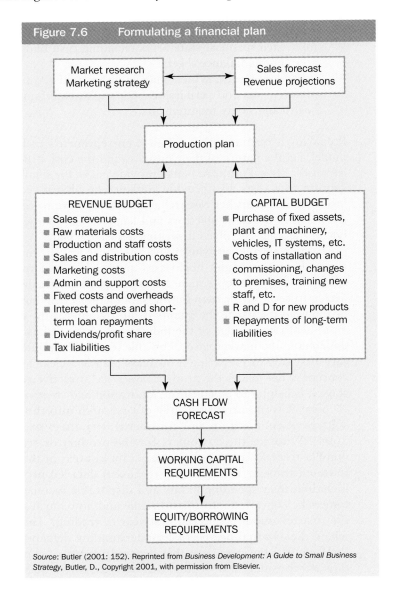

| Figure 7.6 | Formulating a financial plan |

Source: Butler (2001: 152). Reprinted from *Business Development: A Guide to Small Business Strategy*, Butler, D., Copyright 2001, with permission from Elsevier.

Finally, it is important throughout the planning process to recognise any legal requirements such as licenses, patents, planning requirements and permissions which might be required before the business can start trading. There is a range of legislation affecting how businesses operate, from employment legislation and rights to health and safety restrictions; these should be built into the planning process and a clear time plan for business opening should be prepared. (For more detail on preparing business plans see Butler (2001) or one of the guides produced annually by banks and lending institutions.)

Conclusion

Finance is an important aspect of managing a tourism business. Whether it is a small café or a multinational tour operator, the same concepts and issues apply. This chapter has provided an introduction to the main financial statements and looked at costs and cost structure. Cost behaviour has been applied to CVP analysis and to pricing to show how financial information can be used to support management decisions. The evaluation section of the chapter identified key areas for investigation and introduced the main ratios for external users in addition to key industry ratios. Finally, a brief introduction to business planning demonstrated how the concepts and techniques in this chapter should be integrated to prepare an effective business plan.

Discussion questions

The discussion questions in this chapter are designed to recap key learning points, test understanding and/or consolidate learning. In addition to the 12 questions linked to the cases wihin the chapter above, there are 24 further questions on the website. (**www.pearoned.co.uk/beechchadwick**) and in the Instructor's Manual. These consist of 21 additional shorter discussion questions, which help consolidate and apply the learning points from the chapter, and also three extended discussion questions, which provide an opportunity to apply concepts and techniques with more in-depth numeric activities. It is recommended that sudents and tutors use these questions as learning support as they work through the chapter.

Guided reading

Financial issues in not-for-profit organisations are covered in a range of textbooks focused on the UK active leisure industry, which has a high proportion of local government provision; such books as Wiseman *et al.* (1996) and Whitehouse and Tilley (1992) provide introductory coverage of financial issues. For those readers with a strong understanding of financial concepts, Engstrom (1996) provides an in-depth coverage of government and non-profit-making finance issues and concepts.

For more detailed coverage of financial management readers are directed to Atrill (2000). This textbook is designed for non-accountants and, although it does not specialise in service industries, it covers topics not covered in this chapter. For example, working capital management (here the emphasis on stock is not particularly relevant but details of management of debtors and cash is pertinent), capital investment appraisal and long-term decision-making are covered, plus the cost of capital and sources of finance, which are other topics useful to tourism managers.

This chapter does not cover budgeting and forecasting including the production of a cash budget. For coverage of this topic a range of texts is useful: Owen (2000) covers the production of a budget in detail with cash budget production included, also Atkinson, Berry and Jarvis (1995) provide detailed worked examples as does Atrill and McLaney (2002).

Recommended websites

British Association of Hotel Accountants: **www.baha-uk.org/** . This website includes news from the industry, events and information on how to join and how to carry out professional development.

Company websites: e.g. **Accor www.accor.com/** ; World of TUI **www.TUI.com/** .

Department of Trade and Industry: **www.dti.gov.uk** . This government site provides access to many useful reports relating to hospitality, tourism and the economy.

ehotelier.com: **www.ehotelier.com/** . News and information service for the global hotel industry.

European BIC Network: **www.ebn.be/** – EU website for business information and networking.

Financial Times: **www.ft.com** . *The Financial Times* site provides excellent free news coverage, lots of company results coverage and the opportunity for students to subscribe to the newspaper at a greatly reduced cost.

Hotel & Catering International Management Association: **www.hcima.org.uk/** .

Keynote: **www.keynote.co.uk/** . Keynote produces market and sector reports, usually available free for registered students through university and college libraries.

Mintel: **www.mintel.com/** . Mintel produces a range of reports similar to Keynote.

World Tourism Organization: **www.world-tourism.org** .

Accounts referred in the text are available online:

- Ryanair: **www.ryanair.com/investor/investor.html?id=1** .
- The Restaurant Group: **www.ccruk.com/html/investor.asp** .
- Whitbread: **miranda.hemscott.com/servlet/HsPublic?context=ir.access.jsp&ir_client_id=43&ir_option=RNS_HEADLINES&transform=ir_home&nav=home&d=1** .

Key words

Accounting period; assets; capital expenditure; cost-plus pricing; liabilities; marginal or contribution pricing; market-orientated pricing; net worth/total net assets; owners' equity; price elasticity of demand; profit; retained profit; revenue expenditure; sales; working capital.

Bibliography

Adams, D. (1997) *Management Accounting for the Hospitality Industry: a Strategic Approach*. Cassell, London.

Alexander, D. and Nobes, C. (2001) *Financial accounting: an international introduction*. Financial Times Prentice Hall, Harlow.

Arnold, J. and Turley, S. (1996) *Accounting for Management Decisions*, 3rd edn. Prentice Hall, Harlow.

Atkinson, H., Berry, A. and Jarvis, R. (1995) *Business Accounting for Hospitality and Tourism*, reprinted 2001. Thomson Learning, London.

Atrill, P. (2000) *Financial Management for Non-specialists*, 2nd edn. Pearson Education, Harlow.

Atrill, P. and McLaney, E. (2002) *Management Accounting for Non-specialists*, 3rd edn. Pearson Education, Harlow.

Atrill, P. and McLaney, E. (2003) *Accounting and Finance for Non-Specialists*, 4th edn. Pearson Education, Harlow.

Berry, A. and Jarvis, R. (1997) *Accounting in a Business Context*, 3rd edn, (reprinted 2001) Thomson Learning, London.

Bowie, D. and Buttle, F. (2004) *Hospitality Marketing: An Introduction*. Elsevier Butterworth Heinnemann, Oxford.

Brigham, E.F. (2001) *Fundamentals of Financial Management*, 9th edn. Harcourt College Publishers, London.

Butler, D. (2001) *Business Development: A Guide to Small Business Strategy*. Butterworth Heinemann, Oxford.

Cullen (1997) *Economics for Hospitality Management*. International Thomson Business, London.

Engstrom, J.H. (1996) *Essentials of Accounting for Governmental and Not-for-Profit Organizations*, 4th edn. Irwin, London.

GoAhead (2003) *Go Ahead Group Annual Review 28th June 2003*. Go Ahead Group PLC, Newcastle upon Tyne.

Harris, P. (1999) *Profit Planning*, 2nd edn. Butterworth Heinemann, Oxford.

Harris, P.J. and Hazzard, P.A. (1992) *Managerial Accounting in the Hospitality Industry*. Nelson Thornes, Cheltenham.

Horngren, C.T. and Sundem, G.L. (2002) *Introduction to Financial Accounting*, 8th edn. Prentice Hall, Upper Saddle River NJ.

Ingold, A., McMahon-Beattie, U. and Yeoman, I. (2000) *Yield Management*, 2nd edn. Continuum, London.

Kaplan, R.S. and Norton, D.P. (1992) The Balanced Scorecard – measures that drive performance, *Harvard Business Review*, Jan–Feb, v70, n1, 71–80.

Kotas, R. and Jayawardena, C. (1994) *Profitable Food and Beverage Management*. Hodder & Stoughton, London.

Lufthansa AG (2003) *Annual Report 2003*. Lufthansa, Frankfurt. Available from **www.lufthansa-financials.de/servlet/PB/menu/1024430_l2/index.html** .

McKenzie, W. (1998) *Financial Times Guide to Using and Interpreting Company Accounts*, 2nd edn. Pitman/Financial Times, London.

O'Neill, J.W. (2003) ADR Rule of Thumb: Validity and Suggestions for its Application, *Cornell Hotel and Restaurant Administration Quarterly*, Vol. 44, No. 3, 7–16.

Owen, G. (2000) *Accounting for Hospitality and Tourism and Leisure*, 3rd edn. Longman, Harlow.

Ryanair (2003) *Annual Report and Financial Statements 2003*. Ryanair, Dublin.

The Restaurant Group (TRG) (2003) Annual Accounts. Available from **www.trgplc.com/html/frameset1.asp?w=116** .

Tribe, J. (1999) *The Economics of Leisure and Tourism*, 2nd edn. Butterworth Heinemann, Oxford.

Vellas, F. and Bécherel, L. (1995) *International Tourism*. Macmillan Business, London.

Whitbread Annual Report and Accounts 2003/4 available from company website at **http://miranda.hemscott.com/servlet/HsPublic?context=ir.access.jsp&ir_client_id=43&ir_option=RNS_HEADLINES&transform=ir_home&nav=home&d=1** .

Whitehouse, J. and Tilley, C. (1992) *Finance and Leisure*. Longman in association with Institute of Leisure and Amenity Management, Harlow.

Wiseman, E., Edmonds, J. and Betteridge, D. (eds) (1996) *Finance in Leisure and Tourism*. Hodder & Stoughton, London.

WTTC (2004) *Tourism Satellite Accounting Report*. World Travel and Tourism Council, London. Available from **www.wttc.org/2004tsa/frameset2a.htm** .

Chapter 8

Managing a small non-profit tourism organisation

Lynn Parkinson, Independent training consultant

Learning outcomes

On completion of this chapter, the reader should be able to:

- define criteria for small and non-profit tourism organisations;
- explain the unique challenges of managing both small and non-profit tourism organisations;
- identify a range of revenue streams for small tourist attractions;
- make market targeting decisions;
- design low-budget promotional approaches;
- manage the fit between tourism and the organisation's aims.

Overview

Small organisations dominate the tourist supply sector in many geographical areas, spanning attractions, accommodation, transport and food/drink suppliers. Non-profit organisations have played an important part of this since the early days of tourism.

The chapter begins with a definition and explanation of small organisations and non-profit organisations. Examples of tourist attractions that match these criteria are identified. The chapter then identifies challenges in running these types of tourist attractions. The chapter focus then shifts to managing key areas: managing different revenue streams, market targeting for small tourist attractions and managing promotion of small tourist attractions with limited budgets.

Small non-profit tourism organisations are characterised by being driven by non-financial organisational objectives. These may be to celebrate achievements, to educate the community, or to preserve heritage or wildlife. It is rare that meeting tourist needs is the primary driver of these organisations, but rather tourism is the means of achieving part or all of their aims.

Unlike most profit-oriented businesses, such tourism organisations are not always located in areas that will attract many tourists. Rather, they are often sited in locations determined by history or as an 'accident' of their purpose. This adds to the challenge for the organisation. Traditional marketing theory would view this approach as lacking marketing focus. Yet examples of innovative marketing activity, customer satisfaction and best practice abound in these small non-profit organisations.

The organisations that match the profile for this chapter are characterised by diversity, and, by definition, small scale. The case studies in this chapter are all tourist attractions. This shows this diversity in one sector of tourism, and includes museums, arts, sport and wildlife organisations. In keeping with the characteristics of small organisations in this sector, these organisations are not the best known, but they are all highly regarded by industry experts, peers and visitors. These case studies illustrate each of the challenges for small non-profit tourist attractions.

What are small non-profit tourist organisations?

This chapter focuses on small non-profit tourist organisations, and in particular on tourist attractions. The foundation for this discussion is based on understanding three component aspects – 'non-profit', 'small' and 'tourist attractions' – which highlight issues that influence management priorities.

Non-profit

Non-profit organisations have played a long-established role in tourism. In the eighteenth and nineteenth century, travellers on the Grand Tour would often visit churches and stay at monasteries. In the twenty-first century their role is central to tourism in many areas. Non-profit organisations are those which do not return profits generated to owners, trustees or shareholders, and which are formally constituted to recognise their non-profit status according to prevailing national regulations. The most common form of registration is as a charity or charitable trust. In the UK, a charity is defined to include educational, religious and community organisations. The latter category encompasses organisations with interests in health, sporting, leisure, culture and education or which exist for social or welfare purposes. These often include organisations which are tourist attractions, or where an aspect of their operation is an attraction for tourists. Non-profit organisations have a non-commercial purpose that underpins their existence. For example, Sydney's Darlinghurst Theatre is a non-profit organisation that aims to 'present fresh and vibrant professional theatre with a focus on new Australian and international work . . . creating a theatrically diverse and appealing program' and The Alamo in Texas, run by The Daughters of the Republic of Texas (DRT), is 'dedicated to the preservation of the Alamo as a sacred memorial to the Alamo Defenders'.

The non-profit sector has grown markedly in the late twentieth century in many countries in response to changes in the economic, social and political environments (Salamon *et al.*, 1999). In the past non-profit organisations were viewed as inconsequential (Perrow, 1986), largely because of their relatively small scale in the economy, but their importance is increasing as they account for increasing levels of employment and they deliver more value. Often they are focusing on aspects that the state will not or does not undertake. For example, Thailand's Wild Animal Rescue Foundation trains wild animals currently held in captivity to survive in the wild. Just as many people seek advice for chronic illnesses from charitable bodies, people no longer expect that the state should manage preservation of cultural or historical artefacts or conservation of flora or fauna. The responsibility for these is shifting to the non-profit sector.

Non-profit organisations can have employees, who are often supported by volunteers. The organisations are generally run by trustees – the equivalent of board directors in a commercial organisation. Registered charities must conform to strict regulations that govern charities. Regulations often mean that trustees are volunteers who cannot achieve any direct or indirect benefits, whether financial or non-financial, for undertaking this role. Exemptions are possible for someone who is also working as an employee. Charitable status allows non-profit organisations to claim allowances from taxation and become eligible for targeted external funding. For example, Canada's TD Bank's Friends of the Environment Foundation offers grants for Canadian non-profit organisations with environmental projects.

Salamon and Anheier (1997) believe that non-profit organisations should be defined as those that are institutionally separate from the public sector. Associated with this, non-profit organisations are seen as autonomous and self-governing, so able to choose their own activities.

A further form of organisation falls between profit and non-profit organisations – that of cooperatives. A cooperative is:

> … an autonomous association of persons united voluntarily to meet their common economic, social, and cultural needs and aspirations through a jointly-owned and democratically-controlled enterprise.
>
> International Co-operative Information Center, 2004

Cooperatives can be non-profit or profit-seeking organisations. However, if the latter, the profits are shared between the members of the cooperatives rather than external parties.

Small

Formal definitions of small organisations focus on size, using criteria such as the number of employees, income or expenditure levels. For example, one US legal definition stresses that small organisations are those which have 'fewer than four hundred employees' (JCARR, 2004), and others define small organisations as having a turnover of less than £2m. Such broad definitions contrast with those for small businesses. Small businesses differ from small non-profit organisations through their legal status.

Other criteria are also often used to define small businesses, such as financial measures like revenue (turnover) and profit. Ownership is another distinguishing aspect.

Employees
Commonly, definitions distinguish between *microbusinesses*, with fewer than 10 employees, *small businesses*, with 10 to 49 employees and *medium-sized businesses*, with 50 to 250 employees. The latter two categories are commonly integrated and referred to as SMEs (small- to medium-sized enterprises). These criteria are used in assessing eligibility for funding or business support to generate employment.

Turnover
Bankers commonly use turnover to target small business financial services. Barclays Bank defines UK small businesses as being those with an annual turnover of less than £500k, for example. Government departments use turnover or revenue levels to classify small businesses for eligibility for grants, but these levels differ between and within governments.

Ownership
Small businesses are often defined by ownership. Some definitions state that no more than 25% of equity should be owned by another organisation (unless it is another small business). This identifies that small businesses need not be completely independent. These rules are not consistently used across or within countries.

Such definitions detail ownership characteristics of organisations, but small organisations – both profit-seeking and non-profit-seeking – differ from larger organisations in how they operate and in the challenges they face.

Ang (1991) identified that management and ownership are rarely separate in small businesses, contrasting with the separation of these roles in larger organisations. Often one or two people in a small business have control over its direction and operations. Hence small business managers work with relatively few stakeholders (Ang, 1992).

Small businesses need staff with general skills, rather than having a specialist functional workforce. Commonly, small businesses seek to do things in-house because of the high costs of buying-in services. Resources, including staff and money, are managed differently in small and large organisations.

Owners motivation

Small businesses may also be defined based on the owner's motivations for forming a small business. Typically, these motivations are either financial (e.g. to make money) or social/psychological.

Financial

Entrepreneurs often seek to exploit commercial opportunity. However, small businesses often lack efficiency (because of their scale and lack of management specialism), and so high levels of profit are uncommon. Typically, their management focuses on managing costs, which limits growth and reduces the subsequent returns. Common small businesses' financial goals are seeking stability in finances and/or breaking even, rather than performance goals such as to achieve specified levels of profit or return on investment.

Social and psychological

Small businesses are often formed by people with a desire for independence, possibly resulting from dissatisfaction with aspects of existing employment, a need for personal recognition or the need to have flexibility in work commitments and work patterns. Small businesses often have value-based reasons for formation and existence.

Small non-profit tourism organisations have much in common with the definitions for small businesses. Often, they have few employees (or volunteers) and a modest turnover, and are typically motivated by non-financial aims. They may have links to public or private companies, but tend to be autonomous, as the case studies in this chapter demonstrate.

Cooperatives are common in some developed tourist destination areas. These can be wholly involved in tourism, such as the rural women's cooperatives in Greece, which provide accommodation for tourists (Greek National Tourist Office, 2004), or partially involved in tourism, such as wine cooperatives, which supplement their business by offering tastings and direct sales to tourists.

■ Tourist attractions

The third component of the focus of this chapter is on tourist attractions. This category has been selected as it shows the diversity of organisations, and avoids overlap with other chapters of the book.

Terms such as leisure attractions, tourist attractions and visitor attractions have different interpretations and connotations. For example, the WTO definition of tourism implies that tourist attractions are those which attract only visitors who stay overnight, and that business people would not visit leisure attractions for anything that related to their work.

Such distinctions are often inappropriate and unhelpful, especially for small organisations. Commonly, tourist attractions appeal to several markets, both in terms of where visitors come from (i.e. residents and non-residents) and the reason for visiting (e.g. for a professional or a leisure interest). Tourist attractions also differ in the extent to which they encourage people to visit a destination, with some being visited only when the visitor is already in the area, while others are strong enough as attractions to encourage people to visit an area.

VisitBritain (2004) defines an attraction as:

> ... a permanently established excursion destination, a primary purpose of which is to allow public access for entertainment, interest or education rather than being primarily

a retail outlet or a venue for sporting, theatrical or film performances. It must be open to the public, without prior booking, for published periods each year, and should be capable of attracting day visitors or tourists, as well as local residents.

This definition excludes shopping, sport, cinema and theatre as tourist attractions on the 'primary focus' dimension, although studies in many countries show that shopping is a major tourist activity. Sports facilities are not tourist attractions using this definition, while sports events fail on two counts – their primary focus and their temporary nature – even though sport is a reason for tourism, and international sports events such as the Olympic Games or marathons are now significant drivers of tourism demand. Interestingly, art galleries or museums are included, even though temporary exhibitions are increasingly attracting tourists. These issues suggests that the definitions are not derived from what tourists consider to be attractions.

Tourist attractions come in many forms, and are classified by their characteristics, such as:

- fun attractions, such as theme parks, waterparks, recreation parks; steam railways, piers; other entertainments (e.g. wax museums);
- wildlife attractions, such as zoos, wildlife/safari parks, aquaria;
- cultural attractions, such as historic houses and monuments, cathedrals and churches; museums and galleries; science centres;
- other attractions, such as gardens; country parks; managed parks; visitor centres; events and exhibitions.

Finally, public or private or non-profit attractions are further categorised as paying or free attractions, as illustrated in Table 8.1.

Table 8.1	Types of visitor attractions in the UK	
	Paying	**Free**
Public	Windsor Castle and other royal residences, UK Stonehenge, and other English Heritage sites, England, UK Aberdare National Park, Kenya Wildlife Services, Kenya The Immigration Museum, Melbourne, Australia	British Museum, London, UK Golden Gate National Recreation Area, US Museum of the Jewellery Quarter, Birmingham, UK The Reichstag, Berlin, Germany
Private	Madame Tussauds, London, New York, Las Vegas, Amsterdam, Hong Kong Tjakupai Aboriginal Culture Park, Cairns, Australia Disney theme parks, Los Angeles, Florida, Tokyo, Paris, Hong Kong Night Safari, Singapore Zoo and Jurong Bird Park, Wildlife Reserves Singapore	Blackpool Pleasure Beach, England Luna Park, Victoria, Australia Jubilee Market, Covent Garden, UK Museum of Contemporary Art, Sydney, Australia
Non-profit	National Trust National Trust of Australia New Lanark World Heritage Site, Scotland, UK The Vatican Museum, Italy The Olympic Museum, Switzerland Melbourne Cricket Ground, Australia	Many cathedrals, mosques and other places of worship The Chartreuse Cellars, Voiron, France The Alamo, San Antonio, USA The Atomic Testing Museum, Las Vegas, USA Cable Car Museum, San Francisco, USA

These classifications are used to monitor tourist flows and track trends in tourism statistics. However, it is not easy to gather information on small non-profit attractions, as the larger organisations, whether public or private, dominate the visitor statistics and tourist-attraction investment data. Government data on small businesses commonly does not identify tourist attractions, although hotel and catering establishments are detailed.

Small non-profit tourist attractions

The definition of tourist attractions presented above may not be practical for small organisations. Many rely on volunteers or donations and have limited access. So these fail to meet some of the defining criteria. For example, the Harrogate International Festival is an event, and therefore non-permanent. The Scottish Football Museum asks for advance booking because of limited capacity and is closed whenever matches are held at Hampden Park. Many other small non-profit tourist attractions are subsidiaries of larger organisations (albeit with non-profit status). This accentuates the challenges for these organisations.

Small non-profit tourist attractions are valuable, adding richness and diversity to the range of tourist attractions for both local communities and staying visitors. For locals, they offer employment, income, education and often the chance to maintain local culture, wildlife or history. For tourists, they offer specialist insights into local life and culture, which provides a variety not provided for by the large, commercial, international tourist attractions.

Small non-profit tourist attractions also bring money and jobs into the community, making local residents more aware of their heritage and the importance of protecting it, and offering them additional leisure facilities. The stronger attractions may become a reason for tourist visits. For example, the Brontë Museum in Yorkshire has led to development of many local businesses catering for the needs of Brontë fans. Research shows that 48% of international tourists to Australia want to explore Aboriginal art or culture (ALII Council for Aboriginal Reconciliation, 2004).

These organisations provide offers that are unlikely to be provided either by the public sector or large companies. They are too specialist for governments, and not profitable enough for commercial concerns. They ensure the survival of activities, resources and environments that would not be retained or accessible without the involvement of smaller operators.

Case 8.1	The Scottish Football Museum

Football (soccer) is the world's most popular sport, and Scotland was a pioneer in developing the competitive and international sport that we know today.

The Scottish Football Museum is the world's first National Museum of Football. It is based in a 4000-metre space in the new South Stand at Scotland's national soccer stadium, Hampden Park, the oldest international football ground still in current use. (The downside of this location is that the museum is closed on match days.) Hampden Park is the home of Queen's Park, which is the oldest amateur league club in the world. It was thus at the heart of football in Scotland, and steeped in its heritage.

The museum is owned and operated by the Scottish Football Association Museum Trust (SFAMT), a limited company and registered charity, and any profits fund research and new exhibitions, or improve the museum's services. The museum is independent of the Scottish Football Association (SFA), although it has trustees from it. The museum attracted initial start-up funding and ongoing support from public funds. Over 40,000 visitors came to the museum in 2003.

Prior to the completion of its premises at Hampden Park, a temporary location was opened at Glasgow's Transport Museum. This involved local people with the museum, and encouraged them to bring donations for display in the museum. It also enabled the museum to gain feedback on what it should offer.

The museum displays collections on the history of the game, including football memorabilia, advertising related to football, football in the media and football lifestyles. Among its exhibits are the world's oldest international 'cap' and match ticket, dating back to the first international match in 1872, played in Glasgow, and the world's oldest national trophy, the Scottish Football Association Challenge Cup, made in 1873. The museum has many exhibits donated or loaned by the SFA, football clubs and private individuals. The original Scottish Cup resides in the collection and is only removed for presentation at the Scottish Cup Final. (The winners only get a replica.)

The museum offers stadium tours to complete the Hampden experience. These allow visitors the chance to follow in the footsteps of players, through the changing rooms, and down the tunnel to the pitch. They can visit the Royal Box and experience the climb to the presentation area where cup medals are awarded. Would-be stars can play in an indoor pitch area. The museum can be booked for events such as children's parties.

Discussion questions

1   What non-financial aims does the Scottish Football Museum seek to achieve that allow it to claim charitable status? How does this impact on the management of this venture?

2   If a commercial organisation were to set up a museum of football, what would its priorities be for the operation? How would this contrast with the priorities for the Scottish Football Museum?

3   What advantages does the Scottish Football Museum have over a commercial operation? What limitations does it face compared with a commercial museum?

Managing small non-profit tourist attractions

Anheier (2000) comments:

> . . . the management of non-profit organisations is ill understood because we do not understand these organisations well, and is frequently ill conceived because we operate from the wrong assumptions about how these organisations function.

The purpose of distinguishing between small v. large and non-profit v. profit-seeking tourist attractions is to understand management challenges for non-profit tourist attractions. Anheier identifies problems of academic review of non-profit management. Such criticism could be applied to the literature on small organisations. Tourism, with its multiple components, creates further challenges to the relevance of such theory. Accordingly, this chapter selects and chooses relevant themes, based on issues identified in the literature and current management practice in small non-profit tourist attractions. This section addresses the challenges of managing these attractions in a competitive environment.

Historically, non-profit management drew from public sector management, because of the focus on social purpose. However, increasingly non-profit organisations are looking to commercial management for models of business practice, in part because they compete, directly or indirectly, against commercial organisations.

A brief review of the UK tourism marketplace shows the pattern of competition in tourist attractions. The UK attractions market is characterised by intense competition, from existing attractions and from new entrants. There is also competition from other leisure activities, such as shopping or visiting the cinema. While visitor attractions are popular, they are not gaining market share against other leisure pursuits. Further, there is limited growth in the market, and long-established attractions dominate the market.

Accordingly, achieving success is difficult. High-profile developments, such as the National Centre for Popular Music in Sheffield (which closed in 2000) and the Millennium Dome project, show how hard it is to capture the interest of potential visitors. Small business generally is characterised by high closure rates (with studies reporting that around a third of businesses fold within three years), and research shows that many private-sector attractions are closing (Mintel, 2002).

Small non-profit organisations tend to be internally focused, yet this competitive marketplace requires them to be externally aware – of market needs and competitor offers – as well as being accountable to their trustees and non-profit status.

Large providers dominate the attractions sector in the public sector (e.g. English Heritage), the private sector (e.g. Merlin and Madame Tussauds) and the non-profit sector (e.g. The National Trust). Privately-owned attractions account for 56% of visits, while publicly-owned and -operated attractions account for 16% of all tourist attraction visits. The most successful attractions are museums, art galleries and leisure or theme parks, which together account for around a third of visits. Mostly these are long-established attractions, with only a few new attractions such as the Eden Project and the BA London Eye attracting large numbers of visitors (Mintel, 2002). Smaller attractions, whether public or private, compete against these giants. Arguably, the biggest difference in management comes from the scale of small organisations, rather than their non-profit status. New attractions clearly struggle against the attention and reputations of long-established ones.

UK figures show a Pareto-like distribution of visitor numbers for tourist attractions. Approximately 9% of attractions have more than 200,000 admissions (64% of total visits), while 72% of tourist attractions have fewer than 50,000 visits each year (11% of visits). Estimates indicate that 57% of all attractions receive less than 6% of all visitors while just 7% of attractions cope with 58% of total visits (Mintel, 2002). These figures show that small-scale organisations face pressure to survive.

Competing against larger organisations presents formidable barriers for small, value-driven organisations. Small organisations lack benefits from scale. Larger organisations can negotiate preferential purchasing prices and terms, while smaller organisations often buy at higher prices and receive less support from their suppliers. Larger organisations are often higher profile and often gain more media exposure from PR activity than smaller organisations. Mass promotional costs have to be borne by lower visitor numbers for the small organisations, which impacts adversely on creating awareness and stimulating demand. Further, smaller organisations lack specialist staff across management disciplines, so lack the time to focus on management issues and the sophisticated management systems that larger competitors have.

Small non-profit organisations are also at a disadvantage compared with commercial organisations when launching new initiatives. Commercial organisations evaluate the market potential before developing their offers, and reject those propositions that do not offer sufficient returns. Typically, these decisions create the gaps that small non-profit attractions fill. These include attractions with specialist, small markets, attractions where target customers are difficult to identify or reach, or where the profit margins are too low. Non-profit organisations need to identify additional revenue streams to overcome these challenges if they are to survive.

Several attributes of small non-profit organisations work in their favour. Smaller organisations can act faster and are more innovative in meeting customer requirements. They are not accountable to external investors, but to the trustees of the organisation, and decision-making can be swift and informal in order to match organisational aims and customer requirements. Decision-makers are often in close contact with their potential customers, and work with them to design services.

Small non-profit organisations tend to be more people-oriented inside the organisation, with 'family' organisation cultures and a shared pride in their work. This impacts on the interaction with customers, which is more personal and more involved. However, this may not happen automatically. While visiting one of the tourist attractions featured in this chapter, a visitor asked an employee in the café about whether it was worth going to see a specific exhibit area. The employee responded that she had only ever been in the café, and did not know if any part of the attraction was worth visiting. When the visitor recommended that she took the time as it was so enjoyable, the employee said 'I just want to go home when I've finished my work!'

Small business literature stresses the importance of networks as a means of business support and development. This extends the family culture to 'extended families' or networks of similar organisations between which resources can be shared and referrals made. This too is essential for attractions as it helps achieve better efficiency (such as through shared promotion) or more effectiveness (though sharing best-practice methods). Interestingly, these issues are entirely compatible with current thinking on relationship marketing.

Managing revenue streams

Organisations need money for routine activities and development initiatives. Commercial organisations predominantly raise funds for development initiatives from banks and investors, and use sales revenue for routine activities.

Seeking a range of revenue sources and streams is critical for non-profit organisations, as they often have difficulty in raising money from external investors and finance organisations because of their legal status.

Entrance fees are an important source of revenue for some attractions, but not all tourist attractions charge visitors. Blackpool Pleasure Beach, a commercial venture, has no entrance fees, which no doubt contributes to it being the UK's leading tourist attraction. Some churches and public art galleries do not charge admission fees either. In the UK, public art galleries found that demand fell when entrance fees were introduced, and complained that this created a barrier to access, which was against their aims. Admissions grew when the charges were dropped. Churches and other religious institutions are facing similar challenges of reconciling fees for tourists with their role as places of worship. Similar debates about fees have taken place in other countries, with interesting results. For example, in Australia the Museum of Contemporary Art in Sydney has secured a sponsorship deal from Telstra, a telecoms supplier, that enables it to waive entrance fees.

Increasing attention is being focused on augmenting visitor spending per visit rather than just on entrance fees. Attractions seek to increase revenue through additional visitor spending, such as at gift shops, catering facilities, parking, guided visits or other related (and chargeable) services. This is a double-edged sword for many though. These can generate cash, but often such facilities are expensive to maintain – stock for gift shops may tie up cash and require additional staff, even when the attraction is not busy. These facilities move away from the core purpose of the organisation. Some organisations lease shops or catering to external parties, thus ensuring a regular return without increasing operating costs. However, attractions need to generate a reasonable volume of customers for this to be a viable proposition.

Statutory national and local organisations help share information on new forms of revenue-earning activities, often bringing new ideas from international markets or commercial sectors. Many attractions rent out facilities for weddings, parties, meetings, conferences and other events. The nature of the attraction will dictate or limit its potential options. The Robert Burns National Heritage Park in Scotland might be more attractive for wedding receptions than the Irish Famine Museum, for example. Equally, the resources of the attraction will also influence potential applications – fireworks parties may be fine at a theme park, but not at a wildlife park.

Small non-profit organisations seek to find continuity in their revenue, to give them stability and iron out the seasonality that is inherent in many tourist areas. Increasingly, non-profit organisations seek to achieve this by increasing visitors' commitment to the organisation, moving visitors up the 'ladder of loyalty' from casual involvement to more active involvement. These initiatives run along a continuum from one-off payments such as benefactor donations to ongoing contributions such as regular sponsorships or as 'friends' of the organisation.

A 'friend' of the organisation normally makes a regular (either annual or monthly) payment to the organisation in return for additional benefits such as newsletters, events and other member privileges. These packages are generally targeted at individuals, although increasingly they are offered to companies. Corporate packages include free tickets or hospitality events for staff or customers. This has an additional advantage of creating referrals within the corporate friends' organisations. Many governments offer tax benefits on these regular donations or subscription payments to non-profit organisations. Some organisations help prepare wills to achieve legacy donations. These forms of income are aided by the financial benefits offered to charities.

Individual sponsorship is another form of gaining longer-term commitment. Often this is linked to specific parts of the organisation, such as a collection or an exhibit in a museum, or an animal in a wildlife park. Such approaches are linked with services marketing theory principles, where satisfaction is improved by making services more tangible and specific.

Commercial organisations and individuals can be major sponsors for tourist attractions too, as in the Telstra and Museum of Contemporary Art agreement mentioned earlier. Sponsorship can also be towards assets of the organisation, such as Pepsi's sponsorship of a rollercoaster at Blackpool Pleasure Beach. Often, lower visitor numbers at smaller attractions tend to mean this concept can be difficult to sell, except where there is direct link or relevance between the attraction, its visitors and the sponsoring organisation.

Government and public sector support for tourism is common due to its income and employment generation benefits. This allows attractions to apply for grants or other financial incentives.

Grants for tourism projects can come from:

- international or transnational organisations and initiatives, such as those from the United Nations and the European Union;
- national government initiatives;
- regional or local government initiatives, which may in turn be supported by either national or international organisations;
- grant awarding bodies from the public and private sector, such as a national lottery, or specialist trusts.

Small non-profit tourist attractions are not always well-placed to take advantage of these initiatives. Comparatively few initiatives are specifically targeted at non-profits and, of those that are, many are defined more in terms of 'public benefit' groups such as hospices rather than tourism-related organisations.

The general, rather than specialist, management competences of small organisations often mean that they lack the awareness of and skills in applying for such funds. Indeed, the time taken to prepare such applications can stretch small organisations, as this may take people away from their roles within the organisation without any guarantee of success. Government applications, especially those involving collaboration between several parties, can be especially time-consuming. However, specialist agencies are available to help, and often local government offices will also help with the applications.

Case 8.2	Harrogate International Festival

Harrogate International Festival, a limited company and a registered charity, organises an annual two-week multi-arts festival. The festival has a very small core – with less than eight full- and part-time staff – supplemented by volunteers, especially in the festival period.

The festival encompasses several genres, such as orchestral and classical music, jazz, dance, and comedy. A Crime Writing Festival was added in 2003. This four-day event on murder and mystery writing has visits from the world's top crime authors. The music parts of the festival have a predominantly local market, with only about 30% of visitors coming from outside the Yorkshire area. However, the Crime Writing Festival has a different appeal, with around 80% of visitors being non-local. The jazz and world music events have a growing international stature.

Ticket sales are a major source of revenue, but the festival has several ways of generating income, including:

- **Individual friends** – at varying levels related to fees, who are offered benefits including a priority booking period and a festival newsletter.
- **Benefactors** – who make a more substantial payment to the festival and receive additional benefits to those offered to friends, including a Benefactors Dinner hosted by the Festival Director.
- **Corporate friends** – who are offered free tickets, an exclusive interval-drinks area, complimentary festival programme books and discounted advertising.
- **Sponsors** – who support the festival in various ways. Sponsorship is for events, such as KPMG sponsoring an orchestral event and Mercedes-Benz of Harrogate sponsoring a jazz event; for venues, such as the Majestic and the Old Swan Hotels; and providers, such as GNER rail and Harrogate Spa Water.

The festival also seeks support from public funds and trusts. In particular, Harrogate Borough Council and the Arts Council England give considerable support to the festival. Various smaller charitable trusts support events, although these vary depending on the programme. The festival organises a series of Sunday concerts in spring to generate funds and to further support the aims of the festival.

Discussion questions

4 Identify all the sources of income for the Harrogate Festival.

5 Given the small number of staff, how can the Harrogate Festival best manage the process of generating income from all these sources?

6 If you were responsible for raising more money from corporate sponsorship for a small non-profit tourism organisation, which companies might you approach and why?

Market targeting decisions

Tourist attractions commonly attract people of different ages, genders, occupations and nationalities. However, people differ in the benefits they seek from attractions, as identified by Kotler and Kotler (1999) in their review of experiences sought by museum visitors:

- recreation;
- sociability;
- learning experience;
- aesthetic experience;
- celebrative experiences;
- enchanting (delightful) experience.

This list is arguably not comprehensive but it suggests the diversity of reasons for visiting attractions. Customers with different needs require different propositions, and different marketing mixes for satisfaction.

Traditional marketing theory focuses on managing the segmentation, targeting and positioning process to manage decisions about customers. Non-profit tourist attractions face challenges in this apparently simple task.

- **Segmentation** opportunities are often limited because of the geographical location of the attraction or its specialist nature. While tourists may travel to go to a major theme park like Disneyland, the market for and the pull of small attractions is comparatively limited. A geographically isolated attraction may be limited to considering people who are visiting the area, rather than detailing the ideal prospective marketplace. Further, many tourist segments are difficult to identify and reach through promotional media, thus failing the tests of effective segments detailed in most marketing textbooks.

■ **Targeting** decisions may be constrained by organisational factors such as resources, the organisation's aims and objectives or indeed the views of the organisation's trustees. Further, the desired target markets may not be compatible with each other. For example, school trips may bring in substantial visitor numbers, but these may reduce the number of children that visit attractions with their families and also may lessen the enjoyment of individual visitors.

■ **Positioning** may be difficult to communicate effectively with multiple markets and limited budgets. Being 'top of mind' is hard enough for big-budget organisations, but almost impossible for smaller ones. Further problems include spreading the promotional budget both in local and more distant geographical markets and presenting consistent positionings that appeal across different segments.

Understanding customer requirements is critical to success. However, customer needs vary, and so, in order to achieve customer satisfaction, management must recognise the distinct requirements of priority segments of the market and deliver these through an amended marketing mix.

Small organisations more commonly start by profiling, rather than segmenting, markets. This can be based on questionnaires of existing visitors. Many tourist boards are working with geodemographic segmentation organisations to enable the visitor bases of hotels and attractions to be profiled more precisely. This information can then guide future promotional activities.

Choosing segments is an active decision. The balance of segments needs to be considered, for example, to manage demand and capacity levels. Low-income visitors or parties should be encouraged to come at times when the capacity is under-utilised. This approach can also be used to manage segments prioritised in the organisation's goals with those of low priority but which are attractive financially. Understanding the resources required for the different segments and the potential returns is essential for targeting decisions.

Matching segment requirements is essential for satisfaction. Satisfaction drives repeat business. An example of how understanding segments can guide the adaptation of the attraction's offer is in the market for school visits. Schools have requirements for the generic facilities offered (in terms of safety and security), the focus of the visitor attraction and its presentation. The attraction must not only communicate with children, but also meet the subject needs of the teachers. The former encourages the pupils to behave and learn; the latter increases teachers' willingness to visit the attraction, and also impacts on funding for such visits.

Tourist attractions can substantially enhance the value of visits through the development of interactive activities to engage the children. Larger organisations commonly employ educational specialists; smaller attractions may seek assistance from teachers or volunteers in developing such materials.

Meeting requirements is necessary for each targeted segment as competition for each of these customers is high. A 'one-size-fits-all' approach is not effective in the long term. Once again, small organisations often lack valuable specialist expertise. Non-competitive organisations may share understanding and resources of 'best practice' (or things that work) and tourist boards also provide general market research about the visitor base. This needs to be supplemented by market research based on visitor perceptions, suggestions and comments from the attraction.

Visitor comments help understand gaps between expectations and perceptions, and the reasons for such gaps. Models of service quality identify that these are likely to arise from the failure to understand visitor needs, inappropriate service design, failing to deliver the service in the manner expected and how communications present the service to the visitor in advance of the visit. Identifying reasons for dissatisfaction can help in designing, delivering and communicating services that satisfy visitors.

Case 8.3   Thackray Museum, Leeds

Who wants to visit a medical museum? Who is interested in the history of medicine? Or historical medical instruments? And diseases? Over 50,000 people in 2002. This unusual museum was the idea of Paul Thackray, whose grandfather Charles Thackray founded a medical company in Leeds in 1902. The museum was located in a building adjacent to St James's Hospital, the largest teaching hospital in Europe. The museum shows how changes in public health and in health care have changed people's lives over the last 150 years. The rather specialist topic is made 'real' by interactive displays.

Thackray Museum has a large conference and corporate entertainment centre, which includes an auditorium for up to 120 delegates, a large room for dining or receptions, and smaller rooms for meetings. The museum actively seeks corporate bookings for these.

The Thackray Museum was one of the first museums to design exhibitions to meet the specific curriculum needs of teachers. Teachers can build a term of class-based work from one visit to the museum. Teachers were actively involved in developing museum exhibitions and education support materials for schools.

Teachers are offered free familiarisation visits to allow them to check out the suitability of different exhibits for their needs. Some exhibits are rather gruesome, such as one which details the amputation of a young girl's limb before anaesthetic was developed. Bookings are essential for school trips. The museum requires 1 adult to every 10 pupils. Teachers accompanying groups are admitted free. The museum makes rooms available for class sessions or lunch breaks and helps schools prepare risk assessment documents required by their education authorities in advance of the visit. Resource packs for pupils can be bought in advance of the visit or at the Museum. The museum staff also train teachers in topics related to the museum's content. As education markets are critical for the Thackray Museum, it encourages teachers to work with the museum in consultation groups on future development plans.

Since opening, the museum has gained several awards, including a Museum of the Year Award, and was nominated for European Museum of the Year. It also achieved a Sandford Award for Excellence in Education.

Discussion questions

7 Identify the factors that show the Thackray Museum has applied the principles of effective market targeting.

8 In what ways does the Thackray Museum show understanding of diverse visitor requirements?

9 What activities are Thackray Museum undertaking to reduce gaps between customer expectations and perceptions?

10 Given the content of the Thackray Museum, what markets are likely to rent the meetings and conference rooms?

Designing low-budget promotional approaches

This chapter has stressed that small non-profit tourist attractions have limited funds. Spending on promotion reduces the funds available for other areas of the organisation. However, creating market awareness is critical to achieving visitor numbers and generating income.

Promotion is the part of the marketing mix addressing communications between an organisation and its existing and potential customers. The traditional view of the promotional mix comprises advertising, sales promotion, personal selling and publicity. Over time, increasing attention has been given to activities such as exhibitions, merchandising, direct marketing and sponsorship in addition to the core promotion elements. Online versions of promotional approaches, using websites, email, banner advertising and referral sites, are also now gaining attention. The range of options is high, but the challenge for small tourist organisations is to create awareness and interest to stimulate visits from the target markets – all at minimum cost.

Many tourist attractions use a fairly limited and conventional range of promotional approaches. Research shows that local advertising can be effective in generating visits, but its high costs mean that this can only be used occasionally. Personal selling is important for corporate sales and sponsorship deals, but puts pressure on management time. Publicity can be very effective and at a low cost, but it needs to be managed well to create impact. Leaflets are used extensively to provide more detailed information. Exhibitions such as Berlin's Internationale Tourismus-Börse [International Tourism Exchange] or the UK's World Travel Market are used by destinations and large attractions to sell to the travel trade, but these are usually beyond the budget of small organisations. Even if these are used by small organisations, they require professional management which is not always available.

Typically, smaller tourist attractions work with other organisations in promotion in order to gain professional expertise and a good return on their investments. These include themes of offers, such as tourist trails, to encourage visitors to more tourist attractions. Early examples of this were the Mission Trail in San Antonio, Texas and the Paraffin Young Heritage Trail in Scotland in the 1970s; more recently The Orange Routes in Tel Aviv and the Freedom Trail in Boston (USA) have proved popular. These trails can be specifically designed to help specific types of organisations. For example, the English city of Bradford formed a very successful programme based round 'The Flavour of Asia'. Bradford has a substantial Asian population, and this local authority-initiated scheme benefited local Asian food and textile businesses as well as local tourist attractions.

As these examples indicate, there are many bases for such trails – cycling trails, food trails, wine trails, whisky trails, religious trails, historical trails, literature trails, etc. Packages offer more benefits to consumers (through signposting, information and discounts) and the integrated effort helps the offer rise above the 'clutter' of competitors' offers. For example, Bradford's Flavour of Asia trail achieved national TV coverage, which resulted in substantial benefits for the town, its attractions, its restaurants and its shops.

Cooperative or collaborative activities can be led by small organisations, profit-seeking organisations or by statutory tourist organisations. Small organisations are realising that they need to collaborate to compete. By working together to develop a higher profile and clearer positioning, they can compete more effectively. They also deliver more value to visitors.

These ideas build on the concept of networks that are so important for small businesses. Networks create many opportunities for destinations, marketing consortia and individual businesses to participate in and promote themselves. For example, Museums Month operates in many countries, often in May. The UK initiative involves over one thousand UK museums, which organise events and exhibitions, supported by television advertising and high-profile publicity activities. These activities create awareness of museums in a wider, non-traditional audience and encourage repeat visits from museum visitors. Events programmes like these increase attendances at attractions.

The suitability of promotional approaches depends on the markets sought. For visitors to an area, direction signs to tourist attractions and having stocks of leaflets in tourist information centres, hotels, and other local attractions may increase awareness and reach people when they are looking for 'something to do'. Direct marketing approaches, including referral approaches (introduce a friend), can be effective at targeting local residents, and can help inform about events at the attraction. Local media contacts should also be developed so that they include coverage in 'What's on' guides, and possibly competitions with small prizes, such as tickets for an attraction, can generate additional media coverage. These also stimulate local awareness and interest.

Much of this discussion has focused on why people visit attractions. However, a key to promotion of small attractions lies in understanding the reasons why people do not visit. Major barriers include natural factors such as weather. Visitor numbers tend to have seasonal variations. However, new (and often collaborative) successful events or products, can overcome these barriers. For example, Finland has developed a market for Santa Claus snow holidays in the cold winter months, attracting visitors in what was previously an off-peak period. The Finnish Tourist Board is working with local organisations to develop a new 'wellness' package which will also iron out seasonality. Often it is easier to achieve awareness and media coverage at off-peak periods, because of the limited competitive activity.

Case 8.4   The Highland Wildlife Park

The Highland Wildlife Park is a nature reserve in the Cairngorm National Park, at the heart of the Scottish Highlands region. The park opened in 1972 to protect, and to educate people about, Scotland's wildlife.

Visitors to the Cairngorms come from all over the world. Overseas visitors are strongly encouraged to visit by friends and relatives, but their decision to visit is also influenced by guidebooks, films and TV programmes. The internet is an increasingly important source of information for them. Advertising is of little importance in encouraging their visits. Scottish visitors are also strongly influenced by recommendations from friends and relatives, but are also motivated by newspaper articles and advertising. Travel agents are of little importance for visitors, and only a few visitors report that they visit the region as a result of a visit to a tourist information centre. More than half of all visitors say that a previous visit to the area is the major reason for their visit.

The Cairngorms is a popular destination for walkers, who generally appreciate the region because of its wildlife and scenery. In winter, the area is at the heart of Scotland's skiing market. The park opens year-round, but only about 10% of the annual 65,000 visitors come in the peak skiing months of January to March.

The park's promotional expenditure is limited, but leaflets are distributed throughout Scotland. Occasionally, other organisations have events linked with the park, such as the Scottish Wildlife Trust Week, where Trust members are given free access to the park. Local initiatives are set up to encourage visits especially when the local weather conditions change. Indeed, many visitors visit when the ski runs are closed.

The park's attractions include familiar animals such as red deer and highland cattle, but there are also mouflon (a form of sheep), capercaillie, wild horses and bison. Several trails focus on different wildlife habitats, such as forest, moorland, tundra, wetland and woodland. A highlight is the Wolf Territory, which is recognised by international zoo architects as having the world's leading design for a wolf enclosure. It appears on the ZooLex website, which is one of the sites that zoo designers, directors and curators explore when they are starting to plan a new enclosure. This has brought inquiries from zoos as far afield as South Korea.

People want different levels of involvement in their visits to the park. Volunteer roles are available, but visitors who are especially keen on wildlife can buy a 'day as a warden' package at the park. Working with park staff brings real insight into the animals and their care, although this is an expensive offer.

The park is used as a location for filming for various television companies. Commercial photographers and keen amateur photographers are encouraged, where possible, although often these need to be accompanied by a warden for safety. Additional fees are charged for this service.

Discussion questions

11 Based on the information here, what promotional approaches would be cost effective for the Highland Wildlife Park in targeting each of the different types of customer?

12 To what extent should promotional plans for the Highland Wildlife Park be prepared in advanced?

Discussion question

13 Read the chapters on strategy (Chapter 9) quality and yield management (Chapter 10). How should the key theories and assumptions be adapted to (a) a non-profit organisation of your experience, (b) a small organisation, (c) a small, non-profit organisation?

Conclusion

Whether they are commercial organizations, such as hotels or restaurants, or non-profit organisations, including charitable trusts, small organizations provide local flavour and character to tourist destinations.

Small, non-profit tourist attractions organizations are commonly set up for non-commercial reasons, such as preservation of an archive or resource, educating or informing the public rather than for meeting tourist needs. Their success as tourist attractions is often required to realise or continue their wider ambitions.

Small, non-profit tourist attractions are disadvantaged in this competitive tourist market compared to the larger non-profit and commercial organizations. Often limited specialist skills and/or access to the resources required for generating demand in a wider marketplace hinder smaller organisations.

Managing revenue streams is essential for their viability. Historically, many have relied on grants from public organisations or charities, especially for new developments and structural works. However, regular revenue is needed to cover operating costs. Increasingly these organisations are moving beyond admission fees to earn money from other revenue sources, such as retailing, catering, publications, etc. New forms of regular payments, such as membership schemes, are increasingly important, both for corporate and individual support. Sponsorship opportunities are created for the attraction or components of the attraction. Hosting corporate and personal events generate income for some attractions, although this may not be suitable for all attractions because of their location or focus. Cash flow gives stability to the organization.

Managing revenue builds on an understanding of the needs of different market segments. Targeted offers create propositions for different types of customers and supporters and help manage visitor flows. More visitors may not always be better for small attractions as too many visitors can ruin the visitor experience – queuing is frequently cited as a major reason for dissatisfaction at tourist attractions. The varied segments can be managed to reduce problems and maximise revenue. Understanding of the different segments helps add value to the experience of the targeted customers through interpretation and presentation of the attractions.

The effectiveness of promotional activity relies on reconciling revenue generated and promotional spend. Targeted and measurable promotion guides activity, and so many small organisations are using more direct marketing methods, such as direct mail. Cooperative or collaborative arrangement with other organisations or associations with a common interest, such as topic, geography or target market, shares costs and offers the chance to create impact in a cluttered market.

Many of these points may seem obvious, but they are difficult to manage given the constraints on resources (human and financial) in these organisations. All these activities are compatible with a relationship marketing approach, with priority areas being managing relationships with customers, influence markets (including the media), referral organisations, staff and volunteers, as well as forming networks and alliances with other organisations. Historically, many small attractions have followed this approach intuitively. However, this needs to be better managed to survive in the future.

Recent research reports on the attractions sector show slow growth in developed markets, coupled with increasing competition from tourist attractions and other leisure activities. The gap between the skills and resources of the large international players and that of small, non-profit tourist attractions will undoubtedly continue to widen. The challenge is immense for these small players.

Guided reading

The following books are recommended:

Rose, A. and Lawton, A. (1999) *Public Services Management*. Pearson Education, Harlow.

Beaver, G. (2002) *Small Business, Entrepreneurship and Business Development*. Pearson Education, Harlow.

Stutely, R. (2001) *The Definitive Business Plan*. Pearson Education, Harlow.

There are few readings specifically on small, non-profit tourist attractions, but many articles address aspects of the topic. Occasionally articles appear on these topics in tourism and leisure journals, such as *Annals of Tourism Research, Tourism and Hospitality Research, Journal of Travel and Tourism Marketing, Journal of Travel Research, Journal of Vacation Marketing, International Journal of Contemporary Hospitality Management, The Tourism Review, Tourism Management* and *Managing Leisure*.

However, the broad scope of this area means that articles in other more specialist publications also help add understanding of challenges and current issues and practice. Examples of these specialist journals include:

- **Managing in small organisations:** *Entrepreneurship: Theory & Practice, Entrepreneurship & Regional Development, International Journal of Entrepreneurship & Innovation, Journal of Developmental Entrepreneurship, Journal of Business Venturing*, and the *Journal of Small Business Management*.
- **Management of non-profit organisations:** *Fundraising Management, International Journal of Nonprofit & Voluntary Sector Marketing, Journal of Nonprofit & Public Sector Marketing*.
- **Different types of tourist attractions:** *Attractions Business, Attractions Management, Event Management, International Journal of Heritage Studies, Museums Journal*.

Some of these are practitioners' publications.

Finally, many research sources are available from national and international tourism bodies, including the WTO, and commercial research agencies, such as Mintel, which has a range of tourism and travel related research publications, or Global Market Information Database (GMID), which offers country specific reports on tourist attractions. These may be available through academic or commercial libraries.

Recommended websites

This section is separated into three categories – general and academic sites, websites related to the case studies, and examples of tourist organisations or events mentioned in this chapter.

General and academic
Charity Commission: **www.charity-commission.org.uk** .

International Co-operative Information Center: **www.wisc.edu/uwcc/icic** .

leisuretourism.com is a subscription-based online resource with a range of information on leisure, recreation, sport, hospitality, tourism and culture. Some free content is also available. **www.leisuretourism.com** .

World Tourist Attractions Travel Guide, a detailed online resource featuring a range of tourist attractions throughout the world: www.worldtouristattractions.travel-guides.com/ .

Case study organisations
Harrogate Festival: www.harrogate-festival.org.uk .
Highland Wildlife Park: www.highlandwildlifepark.org .
Scottish Football Museum: www.scottishfootballmuseum.org.uk .
Thackray Medical Museum: www.thackraymuseum.org .

Tourist organisations mentioned in this chapter
Alama: http:www.thealamo.org .
British Museum: www.thebritishmuseum.ac.uk .
Cable Car Museum: www.cablecarmuseum.org .
Chartreuse Cellars: www.chartreuse.fr .
Darlinghurst Theatre: www.darlinghursttheatre.com .
English Heritage: www.english-heritage.org.uk .
The Finnish Tourist Board: www.mek.fi .
Freedom Trail: www.nps.gov/bost/freedom_trail.htm .
Golden Gate National Recreation area: www.nps.gov/goga .
The Greek National Tourist Organisation (Women's Rural Cooperatives): www.greektourism.com/travel_guide/rural/cooperatives.stm .
Internationale Tourismus-Börse [International Tourism Exchange]: www.itb-berlin.de .
Irish Famine Museum: www.strokestownpark.ie/museum.html .
Melbourne Cricket Ground: www.mcg.org.au .
Museum of the Jewellery Quarter: www.birmingham.gov.uk .
New Lanark World Heritage Site: www.newlanark.org .
Olympic Museum: www.olympic.org .
Reichstag, Berlin: www.reichstag.de .
Robert Burns National Heritage Park: www.burnsheritagepark.com .
San Antonio Missions Recreational Area: www.nps.gov/saan .
Singapore Zoo: www.zoo.com.sg .
TD Friends of the Environment Campaign: www.td.com/fef/index.jsp .
Tjakupai Aboriginal Culture Park: www.tjapukai.com.au .
Wild Animal Rescue Foundation of Thailand: www.warthai.org .
Vatican Museum: www.christusrex.org/www1/vaticano/0-Musei.html .
Windsor Castle: www.royal.gov.uk/output/Page557.asp .
World Travel Market: www.worldtravelmart.co.uk .

Key words

Market segmentation; non-profit; relationship marketing; revenue management; small business; tourist attractions.

Bibliography

ALII Council for Aboriginal Reconciliation (2004) Valuing cultures – the features of the indigenous arts and crafts industry, accessed at **www.austlii.edu.au/ au/special/rsjproject/rsjlibrary/car/kip3/11.html** .

Ang, J. (1991) Small Business Uniqueness and the Theory of Financial Management, *The Journal of Small Business Finance*, 1(1), 1–13.

Ang, J. (1992) On the Theory of Finance for Privately Held Firms, *The Journal of Small Business Finance*, 1(3), 185–203.

Anheier, H.K. (2000) Managing non-profit organizations: towards a new approach, Civil Society Working Paper 1.

Greek National Tourist Organisation (2004) Women's cooperatives, accessed at **www.greektourism.com/ travel_guide/rural/cooperatives.stm** .

Joint Committee on Agency Rule Review (JCARR) (2004) accessed at **www.jcarr.state.oh.us/ man_affect.cfm** .

Kotler, N. and Kotler, K. (1999) *Museum Strategy and Marketing*. Jossey Bass, San Francisco.

Mintel (2002) Visitor Attractions – UK, Mintel International Group, accessed at **www.mintel.co.uk** .

Perrow, C. (1986) *Complex Organizations: A Critical Essay*, 3rd edn. Random House, New York.

Salamon, L.M. and Anheier, H.K. (eds) (1997) *Defining the Non-profit Sector: A Cross-National Analysis*. Manchester University Press, Manchester.

Salamon. L.M., Anheier, H.K., List, R., Toepler, S., Sokolowski, S.W. and Associates (1999) *Global Civil Society: Dimensions of the Non-profit Sector*. Johns Hopkins University, Institute for Policy Studies, Baltimore, Maryland.

VisitBritain (2004) *Visitor Attraction Trends England 2003*, VisitBritain, 20 September.

Chapter 9

Analysis of the business environment and strategy in tourism

Resham Sandhu, Coventry Business School, Coventry University

Learning outcomes

On completion of this chapter the reader should be able to:

- appreciate the global nature of tourism and the significance of domestic tourism;
- understand the structures of the markets in which tourism businesses operate;
- demonstrate the significance of consumerism issues in tourism;
- conduct PESTEL and SWOT analyses and demonstrate their use.

Overview

The purpose of the chapter is to develop a systematic and integrated approach to environmental analysis and strategy development for tourist organisations by providing an introduction to environmental scanning and analysis, and developing an understanding of the strategy development process. It then identifies the importance of strategic thinking to tourism management strategists and emphasises the need to plan for the unexpected and for complex and uncertain situations.

Introduction

The chapter progresses by discussing the importance of tourism as a global industry and why strategy is important for the future success of tourism businesses using case studies. This is followed by an examination of procedures (PESTEL; Porter's forces and value chain analysis and SWOT) for environmental scanning and methods for developing strategies (such as TOWS). Further examples are used as supporting evidence.

The scale and importance of tourism

The importance of tourism to the global economy and national economies cannot be over-estimated. The World Tourism Organization (2001) in its report *Tourism 2020 Vision* suggested that international arrivals could reach over 1.56 billion, of which 1.18 billion would be intra-regional and 377 million would be long-haul travellers. Their general assumption is that the post 9/11 (11 September 2001) events (wars in Afghanistan and Iraq; instability in the Middle East and other parts of the world) will not appreciably slow down this forecast growth in an industry with the fastest growth rate. The WTO (2003) published a follow-up report *Tourism Highlights 2003* in which it wrote:

> Although 2002 was certainly not an easy year, international tourism held up fairly well. According to data collected by the WTO from the vast majority of destination countries, the number of international tourist arrivals grew by 2.7 per cent in 2002 after a decrease of 0.5 per cent in 2001. For the first time, the 700 million mark was surpassed and compared to the previous record year 2000 almost 16 million more arrivals were counted.

By comparison, in 1990, the number of international arrivals was 456 million, so over the twelve-year period, there has been a significant increase of 54% in international arrivals. In 2002, this was worth $474bn in international tourism receipts. However, as the WTO acknowledges, tourism has shown itself prone to downturns due to significant events such as wars, disasters and economic instability and economic crises. The 1991 Gulf War, earthquakes in Turkey, the 2001 UK foot and mouth epidemic and the SARS epidemic in 2003 have all resulted in reduced visitor numbers. But the timescale for recovery varies, depending on the event and the responses (strategies) to aid recovery.

So what factors are fuelling this large forecast expansion in tourism flows?

Underhill (2004) writing in *Newsweek*, attempts to provide the answers:

> Tourism, once the privilege of the wealthy, is becoming available to more people than ever before. Led by Asia's burgeoning middle class, the industry is poised to prosper – all the while helping travellers gain a new, deeper understanding of their world. Imagine you're Chinese and in search of once-forbidden thrills. Your country's super-charged economy means easier access to money. And its more relaxed politics means a passport is on offer for the first time. But where to go for that once-in-a-lifetime holiday and a chance to spend some of that cash? Head for the other hemisphere and you won't be alone.

The tourism industry, dominated by North American and West European players, is gearing up to enter China, with a population of 1.3 billion people, and therefore a vast potential for outward-bound tourists. But this is a two-way flow; there is also a big growth in travel to China and the Far East: 'Industry experts predict a new era of mass globe trotting, in which Beijing will feature alongside Barcelona as a must-see destination' (Underhill, 2004).

In addition to China, India, with another population of over one billion people, is also opening up; together they represent a combined market of some 2.5 billion people.

China's contrasting experiences of tourism

However, while the Chinese experience of modern tourism is positive, it has not always been the same. In the eighteenth and early nineteenth centuries, China was visited by European business tourists in search of tea and other products. In exchange, they began dumping opium and heroin by bribing corrupt Chinese officials. By the late 1830s, this illegal 'drugs tourism' was having serious effects on the Chinese population. In 1842, Britain and France, backed by superior touring naval military forces armed with the latest guns and cannons, demanded acceptance of even bigger quantities of heroin. When the Chinese refused, superior European naval power quickly demolished their defences (Hooker, 1996), marking the economic decline and colonisation of the country from which it took over 150 years to recover.

However, today, China and India with growth rates of 10% are experiencing an economic miracle through which they will overtake the western economies, which in turn will fuel the massive expansion of inward and outward tourism from these and other 'tiger' economies as envisioned by the WTO and others.

The moral of this preamble is that countries and organisations cannot ignore the changes in their environments, otherwise they will be bypassed and even face economic meltdown. Another useful example is the experience of tourism in the USA after 9/11.

Data from the Travel Industry Association of America (2004) illustrates the economic importance of tourism to the world's largest economy, generated by 41.9 million international visitors and 1,127 million total domestic person trips. In 2002, the US travel industry received more than $545.5 billion from domestic and international travellers (including international passenger fares). These travel expenditures, in turn, generated nearly 7.2 million jobs for Americans, with nearly $157 billion in payroll income. Approximately one out of every 18 US residents in the civilian labour force was employed due to direct travel spending in the US during 2002. However, the number of international visitors had reduced from 44.9m in 2001 to 41.9 in 2002 and 40.4 in 2003 as a result of the pre-9/11 economic slowdown and the 9/11 attacks in 2001, followed by the invasions of Afghanistan and Iraq. By contrast, domestic travel in the USA has continued to rise from 1123.1 million domestic person trips in 2001 to 1140.0 million in 2003. Travel to the USA has been affected by the fear factor.

Changes in the travel and tourism environment are an important factor influencing people's propensity to travel. However, this is not a new phenomenon to travel and tourism. Political and economic instability, climate change, natural disasters, etc. have all been factors deterring travel.

Wilson (2004) suggests that:

The Global travel and Tourism market is expected to achieve turnover of US$2,295 billion this year, representing a growth of 3.7% over 2003, according to the latest Tourism Satellite Accounts produced by the World Travel and Tourism Council (WTTC). The forecast promises blue sky for a sector beset by heavy unpredictable storm clouds for the last 3 years. It places the industry on track to return to the long-term historical growth trend of 4% growth per annum that was knocked off course . . . by an unprecedented combination of external events affecting the sector including war, terrorism and SARS.

Tourism organisations and providers do not exist in a vacuum, but in an environment consisting of other entities and individuals, which in turn influence their direction, organisation, plans, operations, and the goods and services they provide. The environment of tourism is not stable; instead it regularly manifests chaotic and complex behaviour in response to other inputs, and this in turn influences both the scope for strategy development and the processes by which strategy is developed.

This chapter will conclude that, because of the ongoing uncertainty and change in travel and tourism, strategy development based on a stable business environment model is not appropriate; instead that models based on, and accounting for, chaos and complexity provide a more fruitful approach.

However, there are two essential ingredients for successful strategy development. First a capacity for strategic thinking and second models, methods and techniques for developing strategies. These are to be discussed in detail in this chapter.

The context of strategy in travel and tourism

The word strategy has its origins in warfare: the need to have a plan to defeat the enemy. Clausewitz (1982) wrote that 'war is the continuation of policy by other means, and, conversely, policy is the continuation of war by other means'. The Chinese, in 1842, discovered they could not ignore the demands of Britain and France. However, today, neither in the wider business world nor in the tourism sector, is it acceptable for one travel agent to send an armed group to demolish a competing travel shop to prevent potential holiday-makers from booking holidays with them. It is a criminal offence. Therefore alternative ways need to be found to ensure one travel agent attracts more customers than the competition. This harnesses human creativity and ingenuity for developing ways of winning customers. Therefore tourism strategy should be concerned with ways of acquiring wealth but without stealing it.

How is this to be done? Shortly before the Wall Street crash of 1929, Alford (1924) recommended selling and selling to customers, to make profits in expanding markets. In his book on management of nearly 2000 pages, Alford has little or no discussion of changes in the business environment and how they impact back on businesses, despite the fact that economists and business leaders were aware of ups and downs in the business cycle, leading to economic downturns and recessions in the nineteeth and early twentieth centuries. However, there was a general belief that markets would continue growing, often by colonial expansion. The 1929 Wall Street crash and ensuing economic collapse clearly proved them wrong. Ansoff (1984: 10–15) puts environmental challenges in a historical perspective, and suggests that the growth in environmental turbulence in the twentieth century has influenced the evolution/revolution in management systems and thinking. Consequently, by contrast to Alford, current management textbooks emphasise the need to build relationships with customers and fulfil their value expectations (Piercy, 2002), and to retain them in a world where competition is around every corner and many markets are at saturation point.

Organisations exist in their environment, interact with it, and deal with the problems and challenges that are thrown up. This requires thinking about the business environment and developing strategic responses. Case 9.1 illustrates how one leading tourism company interacted with its environment and changed over time.

Case 9.1	Thomas Cook

Tourism has developed into one of the most important branches of trade and industry in the world. On the basis of positive growth prospects Thomas Cook has set themselves the ambitious objective of further expanding their position among the world's leading tourism companies.

Thomas Cook have undergone substantial changes in its approach to serving tourists, as revealed by a historical overview. Its strategic direction has been closely linked to its changing ownership, changes in the travel and tourism sector, and changes in social and cultural expectations in potential travellers and tourists. Its success has largely hinged on its capacity and willingness to make strategic innovations.

Early beginnings

Thomas Cook, a committed Baptist and a Temperance man, organised a successful train journey in 1841 from Leicester to Loughborough for 500 people to attend a Temperance meeting. This was a success. Recognising an opportunity, he followed with tours to other British cities. An early success was to arrange for over 165,000 people to attend the Great Exhibition in 1851. He followed by tours to continental destinations, Egypt and the USA, making these destinations accessible to the middle classes, providing them with 'wholesome experiences'. This was complemented by other strategic innovations such as the hotel voucher, travel agent shops, credit vouchers (later travellers cheques), cruises, travel catalogues and the first airline tickets in 1921.

By 1900, this company was the market leader in international travel.

The family sold the company in 1928 to Wagons-Lits, a competitor. In 1948, it was nationalised under British Rail, during which period it continued its travel operations. It was privatised in 1972 and bought by Midland Bank, Forte and the Automobile Association. The bank saw this as an opportunity to develop its financial activities and expand into traveller's cheques and related financial products and, by 1990, was the world's largest foreign exchange dealer. In 1992, the company was taken over by Westdeutsche Landesbank (WestLB), a German Bank, and LTU, a German holiday airline company. In 1994, Thomas Cook became the world's largest supplier of traveller's cheques outside the USA by taking over the traveller's cheques subsidiary of Barclays Bank, while selling off its business travel service to American Express. In 1995, WestLB became sole owner.

Thomas Cook was the first British leisure group to offer holidays, traveller's cheques, foreign exchange, guide books and flights via the internet.

The company continued its acquisition programme to broaden its portfolio by taking over:

- Sunworld, a British short-break supplier, and Time Off, a European city tours specialist in 1996;
- Flying Colours Leisure Group including the Flying Colours airline in 1998;
- Sunset and Club 18–30 brands in 1998 (the latter acquisition causing quite a stir in view of Thomas Cook's Temperance and Baptist origins).

Also in 1998, a 'Global Services' division was created to offer comprehensive service packages worldwide to business and leisure travellers. Thomas Cook became the UK's third-largest joint travel group and airline in 1999 with the creation of the umbrella brand JMC (John Mason Cook) encompassing Sunworld, Sunset, Flying Colours, Inspirations and Caledonian Airways.

Preussag AG, owner of TUI, a continental competitor, bought 24.9% of the shares in Thomas Cook in 1999, but sold them in 2000 after its purchase of Thomson, Thomas Cook's competitor. The European Union agreed to the merger between Thomas Cook and Carlson Companies Inc. (the British arm of Carlson Leisure Group's travel division).

In 2001, Thomas Cook was taken over by German-based C&N Touristic AG, which was in turn owned by Deutsche Lufthansa AG (50%) and Karstadt Quelle AG, to form an international tourism company trading as Thomas Cook AG and building on its traditions. The combined international leisure group worked across the travel value chain – airlines, hotels, tour operators, travel and incoming agencies, providing its customers with the right product in all market segments across the globe. The group encompassed 32 tour operators, about 3600 travel agencies, a portfolio of 76,000 controlled hotel beds, a fleet of 87 aircraft and a workforce numbering some 28,000. The company operated in Germany, Great Britain, Ireland, France, Belgium, Luxembourg, The Netherlands, Austria, Hungary, Poland, Slovakia, Slovenia, Egypt, India and Canada.

By 2002, it was apparent that JMC was not a successful brand. The company decided to trade under the Thomas Cook name, the new brand giving its holiday airlines a new design. However, the transition to a common brand was not at the expense of the brands of subsidiary companies.

JMC continues for the families and young adults market, with Sunset reintroduced as the budget brand replacing JMC Essentials. The Thomas Cook brand targets confident or frequent travellers. The other brands in the Thomas Cook (UK) portfolio – including Style Holidays, Club 18–30, Neilson, and Sunworld Ireland – continue.

Case 9.1 Continued

Thomas Cook after 11 September 2001

In common with other tour operators, Thomas Cook was affected by the decline in travel after 11 September 2001 as shown by this data:

INDICATOR	10/2002–11/2003	10/2001–11/2002
Sales (million euros)	7241.5	8058.6
Transported customers (thousands)	12,484.6	13,334.1
Sales per customer (euros)	580.0	604.4
Average travel price	523.0	539.0
Average trip duration	9.7	10.7
Gross profit (euros)	2155.4	2490.4
Gearing (%)	163.1	121.7
Number of employees	25,978	27,906
Travel agencies	625	759

The Thomas Cook Annual Report for 2002–03 identifies these factors for the company's difficulties:

● the Iraq war and the SARS epidemic;
● unusually hot weather in northern and central Europe encouraged people to stay at home;
● rationalisation/shortening of school holiday season in Germany.

Thomas Cook's co-owner, Lufthansa AG, has also suffered from the loss of tourism business, and could not declare a dividend in 2003–04. Lufthansa's Chairman and CEO Wolfgang Mayrhuber (2004) stated 'Thomas Cook's priorities must be to minimise the losses, put in place a competitive cost structure and return to profitability'.

This led to short-term responses such as price-cutting and last-minute deals; but it was not always possible to pass on these losses further down the line to service partners, airlines and hotels.

Thomas Cook also concluded there would be longer-term consequences of the Iraqi war, which required a more thorough rationalisation, through 'downsizing of corporate structures' and travel agency closures; generating more income from the sales markets, reducing capital spending; and a cutback on flights in Germany. The company also implemented a focus on the Thomas Cook brand across all markets. The expectation is for a medium-term recovery.

Source: Thomas Cook website; Thomas Cook Annual Reports; **www.traveldailynews.com/**; **www.travelmole.com**

Discussion questions

1 During the last 165 years, has Thomas Cook remained true to its founding principle of offering 'wholesome experiences' in tourism?
2 Discuss the environmental factors responsible for changes in ownership and strategy.

So what is strategy and why is it important?

Strategy is defined by Johnson, Scholes and Whittington (2005: 10) as 'the direction and scope of an organisation over the long-term, which achieves advantage for the organisation through its configuration of resources within a changing environment and to fulfil stakeholder expectations'. This contrasts with an earlier view by Ansoff (1969: 7) as a set of management guidelines which specify the firm's product-market position, the directions in which the firm seeks to grow and change, the competitive tools it will employ, the means by which it will enter new markets, the manner in which it will configure its resources, the strengths it will seek to exploit, and conversely the weaknesses it will seek to avoid. Strategy is a concept of the firm's business which provides a unifying theme for all its activities.

Coulter (2002: 7) has a narrower view of strategy as 'a series of goal directed decisions and actions that match an organisation's skills and resources with the opportunities and threats in its environment'. Kotelnikov (2004), echoing Ansoff, also suggests that strategy is the way in which a company orients itself towards the market in which it operates and towards the other companies in the marketplace against which it competes. 'It is a plan that an organisation formulates to gain a sustainable advantage over the competition.'

Piercy (2002: 273) says strategy is really about 'being best at doing the things that matter most to our customers; building shareholder value by achieving superior customer value; finding new and better ways of doing things to achieve the above'.

By contrast, Stacey (2003: 319–20), drawing on complexity theory, views strategy in a radically different way as the 'emergence of organisational identity', that is

> . . . what an organisation does, what it is . . . the community the organisation serves . . . and how this recognition evolves. Strategy as the identity of an organisation is continuously constructed and enacted in the interaction of the organisational practitioners . . . how human futures are perpetually constructed . . . in the ordinary, everyday relating between human bodies in local situations in the living present.

The power of the unexpected to influence not only tourism but the global economy has been dramatically illustrated by the extremely severe earthquake (rated 9.0 on the Richter scale) off the coast of Sumatra in the Indian Ocean and the subsequent tsunamis of 26 December 2004. The effect has been the death of over 300,000 people in at least eleven countries, including tourists, and the destruction of local economies and infrastructure, which will cost over $7bn and many years to repair. With the possibility of follow-up earthquakes and tsunamis, planned recovery remains problematic.

Because complexity assumes unpredictability, uncertainty and paradox, it implies that a long-term strategy is problematic as the future cannot be known; that strategy development is an emergent and organic process involving all the participants who are active agents. Hence, the organisation contributes to the making of its own future. In this approach, the idea of copying others to achieve success is nonsensical because the unfolding future cannot repeat the past. Therefore, past excellence models can lead to failure as much as success. However, chaos and uncertainty do not mean a tourist organisation or destination is doomed to failure. Schurmann (1995) suggests there is a 'key scientific principle – that, while there is chaos in all order, there is also order in chaos' when discussing how inward investment, including for tourism projects, was changing African countries previously riven by war. So out of the chaos of the 1990s Balkans conflicts, tourism is leading the drive to economic recovery as people seek to improve themselves.

In the same way, President Chandrika Kumaratunga of Sri Lanka stated 'we can certainly welcome tourists in three months, maximum four' in this fashion leading the way to recovery following the wholesale destruction caused by the Indian Ocean tsunami of 26 December 2004 (Sukarsono, A. and Eaton, D., 2005)

Drawing on these themes, Edgar and Nisbet (1996) conclude that hospitality organisations should place greater emphasis 'on adopting, implementing and facilitating the innovative and creative organization'. Shelton (1999) suggests that organisations can use:

▪ stretch – the assumption that nothing is impossible; the striving to achieve goals or targets that may appear hard to achieve,

- speed – being better through being faster,
- boundarylessness – willingness to find a better idea or way by going beyond established boundaries or frameworks

to respond to uncertainty and change, by developing them as sources of competitive differentiation.

These debates about chaos, uncertainty and complexity are not new. Drucker (1985: 50) suggested seven sources of innovative or strategic opportunity in descending order of importance for organisations:

- The unexpected – unexpected success, failure or outside event.
- Incongruity – between reality as it actually is and reality as it is assumed to be or 'as it ought to be'.
- Innovation based on process need.
- Changes in industry structure or market structure that catch everyone unawares.
- Demographics.
- Changes in perception, mood and meaning.
- New knowledge, both scientific and non-scientific.

A good example of the unexpected is the opportunity created in the aftermath of the 11 September 2001 attacks for low-cost airlines such as Ryanair and easyJet. The reduction in air travel meant that the large carriers with massive overheads were faced with substantial losses in business which they could not sustain for long; this forced them to ask their governments for financial assistance. By contrast, low-cost carriers with lower overheads were able to make a profit.

Case 9.2   Encouraging people to fly – an incongruity-led change

Vance Packard (1960: 60–1) recounts how airlines in the USA encouraged people to fly more. He begins with a quote from Ernest Dichter, President of the Institute for Motivational Research: 'One of the main jobs of the advertiser in this conflict between pleasure and guilt is not so much to sell the product as to give moral permission to have fun without guilt' (p. 54).

Then he proceeds to explain as follows: 'When the jet engine plane began to be used for commercial flights, people had doubts about flying.' Packard says that Dr Dichter was asked to develop strategies for encouraging people to fly more.

American Airlines became disturbed by the fact that many of its passengers flew only when it was imperative. The airline hired a conventional research firm to find out why more people didn't fly. The answer came back that many people didn't fly because they were afraid of dying. A lot of money was spent, carrying the emphasis on safety to great extremes; and according to Dr Dichter, it didn't pay off with the increase in traffic that might be expected. Then Dr Dichter was called in. He went into the problem in depth and even used projective tests that permitted potential travellers to imagine themselves being killed in an air crash. His investigators found that the thought in men's minds at such times was not death at all, but rather the thought of how their family would receive the news. Dr Dichter concluded that what these people feared was not death but rather embarrassment and guilt feelings, a sort of posthumous embarrassment. The husband pictured his wife as saying 'The darned fool, he should have gone by train'. The airline took this diagnosis seriously and began aiming its campaign more at the wife, to persuade her that her husband would get home to her faster by flying, and to get her in the air through family flying plans. In this way, Dr Dichter explains, the man was taken off the spot through the symbols of family approval of flying.

Meanwhile, all the airlines began going to great extremes to preserve a 'psychologically calm environment' for passengers up in the air.

Airlines began schooling their hostesses in how to treat customers who got excited when they saw sparks flying from an engine. One airline official said the main reason the hostesses of his airline ask the name of each passenger and write it down on a sheet is to give the hostesses a chance to talk to the passenger and reassure the passenger through the calmness of their voice that all is well. Several of the airlines require that hostesses practise talking in a calm, soft manner into tape recorders and listen to the playbacks of their voices for correction.

The pilots, too, in some airlines are trained to have a voice that exudes confidence. One airline says that it wants pilots who can talk over the loudspeaker 'like they could fly an airplane'. Another airline indoctrinates its pilots to talk with the 'voice of authority from the flight deck'.

Source: Packard, V. (1960: 60–1)

Discussion questions

3   How did the airlines give 'moral permission to have fun without guilt' to air passengers?

4   How did these strategies contribute to the growth of mass air travel?

Case 9.3   Strategic responses to an ageing population in Europe

Scenario planning for understanding and forecasting the holiday market

TUI, the world's largest travel and tourism company, commissioned the Swiss Prognos Institute to develop a picture of future developments and trends in European tourism and to prepare alternative scenarios, because instead of reacting to changes, the company wanted to be pro-active and pre-empt and shape future change. Prognos confirmed that changed customer needs, a highly differentiated product offering and new entrants to the market have led to a structural change. Customer demand for modular products, the trend towards late-bookings and low-cost flying are here to stay. Customers are no longer willing to commit themselves to their holiday dates at the start of the year, because many have more choice over organising their leisure time much more spontaneously and freely. Consequently people may go away on holiday more frequently but for shorter periods.

In Europe the gap between rich and poor is continuing to widen. Consumer price sensitivity is a combination of consumers thinking it is 'cool' to find a bargain and a change in social structures and values. The expectation is that growth in coming years will take place mainly on the margins of the tourism product offering, the low-price and luxury segment. The low-cost carrier sector will gain considerable market share by 2006, with the annual rate of growth levelling out at around 4% to 5%.

The study also suggests growth in demand for modular products (flexibly and individually packaged travel components) from around 5% to 40% or 50% by 2010, driven by internet familiarity, information and marketing. The main reason for this shift in the market, from which new low-price travel products will benefit in particular, can be found mainly in the increasing affinity that people have with the internet. Prognos estimates that by 2007 at least 25% of holiday-makers will have had experience of booking their holidays online. Today the figure is just 10%. Some 60% of all households in Scandinavian countries already have internet access accelerating the advance of online travel companies and low-cost carriers. Is northern Europe therefore providing a window onto the future of the tourism industry? As internet tourism sites become safer and easier to use, the demand for online products will increase; TUI is advised to give more weight to expanded internet presence.

Sunny prospects – Europeans are loosening their purse strings

Demographic change is driving people's desire for a new type of holiday content. In other words, the age pyramid is shifting upwards in the West. Tourism products need to reflect this. Big-selling holidays on the beach and in the sun will tend to show below-average growth, i.e. stagnate and become 'cash cows'; the future belongs to holiday products connected with health, fitness, culture, etc. Luxury tours, cruises and holidays for ramblers could also be major winners.

In future, spending on holidays will rise from the present low point. In 2003, Germans were rather subdued in holiday spend, spending altogether 52.5 billion euros on foreign holidays – a decrease of 5% compared with 2002, but this is expected to change in coming years. The study anticipates that by the year 2010, spending on holiday travel will rise by 4% annually to over 72 billion euros, driven by a combination of Germans and British, who are among the world champions for holiday spending.

However, rates of 10% to 20% annual increase in holiday spending are expected in Russia and Eastern and Southern European countries providing their economic growth continues into the future.

Source: Adapted from *TUI Times*, 2004 (newspaper for all TUI staff members)

Case 9.3	Strategic responses to an ageing population in Europe continued

Discussion questions

5 What challenges does an ageing population create for tour operators?

6 What are the risks inherent for tour operators in concentrating on the market of older people?

Therefore, how an organisation conducts its business and develops strategic responses is influenced by the external environment and by its resources and competences, but environmental uncertainty and chaos do not mean a destination is impotent to act.

There are different ways of developing strategies. Common approaches are the rational choice and decision-making methods. Rational choice assumes that people and organisations are purposive, seeking to achieve a desired state or outcome, and goal-oriented with a hierarchy of preferences, or benefits, as suggested by Coulter (2002) above. In making choices, rational calculations are made to assess the:

■ usefulness and benefits of alternative options and choices based on the preferred hierarchy of preferences and benefits;

■ costs of each alternative assessed against alternative benefits foregone;

■ the best way to maximise benefits.

The development of a strategy can be conceptualised in terms of inputs, processing and outputs. This can be done in two distinct ways: visioning and problem solving.

The first approach is driven by a desire to achieve a future position or state, i.e. a vision. From this flows the 'strategy pyramid' approach shown in Figure 9.1.

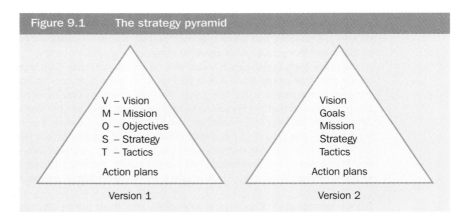

Figure 9.1	The strategy pyramid

Porth (2003: 4–5) suggests that mission comes before vision as it is a statement of the present, of current markets and customers, as opposed to vision which is about the future direction, aspirations, 'what do we want to become'. For example, Thomas Cook used to provide middle-of-the-road family-oriented package holidays. Then, recognising the spending power of the 18–30 generation, it changed direction and bought Club 18–30 well known for youth holidays driven by an excess of sex and alcohol.

At other times, the two terms get combined; Thomas Cook's annual report (2003) refers to their 'vision/mission'.

These approaches to the strategy process have some key components in common:

■ a vision or perspective of where the organisation is, could be, or wants to be;

■ an assessment of the organisation's competences, resources and sources of competitive advantage;

- an assessment of the external opportunities, threats and competition;
- developing strategic options and evaluating them;
- making final strategy choices;
- developing tactics;
- determining timescales for implementation;
- marshalling resources and winning support for them;
- implementing agreed strategies;
- monitoring, reviewing and evaluating;
- re-assessing strategies in light of experience and modifying as necessary.

This model assumes feedback loops at each stage to allow for changes in thinking. Hence the re-assessment of strategies after implementation might involve a re-examination of the organisation's vision; resource base and competences. This backward influence is called feedback.

The second approach is to start with problems facing the organisation that need to be dealt with or solved, and this requires the development of strategies and action. Here inductive logic takes over, beginning with:

- an assessment of the problem/issue;
- identification of the causes;
- generating options for dealing with it;
- deciding on the right way forward, i.e. strategy for dealing with it;
- implementing/taking action;
- reviewing progress and evaluating and taking further action to improve performance.

Again, there are feedback loops for reviewing thinking at each stage.

From different starting points, both approaches facilitate rational thinking by generating options and choosing between them to maximise benefits in a step-by-step manner. They are examples of strategic choice models which lead to short-, medium- and long-term plans, and are the dominant approach in management theory. They use a range of fairly common methods and techniques.

Who develops and implements strategies will depend on the organisation, its culture and traditions and the level for which the strategy is intended, and more importantly will also influence the outcome. Porth (2003: 183) quoting Pfeffer (1992) suggests that 'the inability to get things done, to have ideas and decisions implemented, is widespread in organisations today. It is moreover a problem that seems to be getting worse in both public and private sector organisations'. Some of the recent big corporate crises and failures on both sides of the Atlantic – Enron, WorldCom and Parmalat – are less about the inability to get things done, and more about the total secrecy and lack of communication of strategic decisions made by top management, raising concerns about corporate governance as well as strategy. These prompted investigations such as those by Smith (2003) and Higgs (2003) in the UK, by Congress in the USA, by the Italian government and the European Union, leading to tighter regulation such as the UK's new Combined Code of Conduct for Corporate Governance (Financial Services Authority, 2003). They also confirm Stacey's (2003) suggestion that the conduct of management and workers at all levels itself contributes to organisational complexity and uncertainty, which in turn influences organisational efficacy.

The importance of strategic thinking

Workers in tourism need to be both ethical and have a capacity for problem solving to meet the challenges of an unpredictable, highly volatile and competitive marketplace. Graetz (2002) says that a capacity for innovative, divergent strategic thinking at multiple organisational levels is seen as central to creating and sustaining competitive advantage. Liedtka (1998), echoing Drucker (1985), identifies five major attributes of strategic thinking:

- a holistic view of how different parts of the organisation influence and impinge on each other and on their different environments;
- a focus on intent, to create a misfit between existing resources and emerging opportunities;
- continuous, ongoing thinking to link past, present and future;
- the generating and testing of hypotheses; asking 'What if?' and 'If . . . then?' questions;
- a capacity for intelligent opportunism, to recognise and take advantage of newly emerging opportunities.

Therefore strategic thinking requires a capacity for divergent, creative, intuitive and innovative ways of looking at the business environment, and a capacity for synthesising the important issues.

Shelton and Darling (2003) attempt to pull together environmental challenges and the skills and behaviour needed to deal with them, as shown in Table 9.1.

Table 9.1	The relationship of quantum skills to key workplace challenges		
Challenge	**Quantum skill**	**Definition**	**Behaviour**
Quality	Quantum seeing	The ability to see intentionally	Focused
Innovation	Quantum thinking	The ability to think paradoxically	Creative
Motivation	Quantum feeling	The ability to feel vitally alive	Energetic
Empowerment	Quantum knowing	The ability to know intuitively	Confident
Social responsibility	Quantum acting	The ability to act responsibly	Ethical
Change/chaos	Quantum trusting	The ability to trust life	Flexible
Teamwork/diversity	Quantum being	The ability to be in a relationship	Compassionate

Source: Shelton and Darling (2003). Republished with permission, Emerald Group Publishing Limited

The strategic planning process

This begins with environmental scanning and analysis by capable people; and then developing and selecting strategies. What is environmental scanning and analysis and how is it carried out? After an extensive review of the literature, Teare *et al.* (1997: 7) identify the main functions of environmental scanning to be to:

- learn about events and trends in the external environment;
- establish relationships between them;
- make sense of them;
- extract the main implications for decision-making and strategy development.

Every organisation has three types of environment to deal with: internal, external (general), and external (industry-specific). Tourist organisations have an interactive relationship with them. A useful framework for understanding environments is PESTEL (Political – Economic – Social – Technological – Environmental – Legal), which is commonly used to understand external and industry changes. However, it can be used equally well to understand changes internal to the organisation. This is not as confusing as it may seem. Internally, the organisation has to:

■ deal with different ideas of what problems it faces and how to deal with them (political);

■ have income to meet its commitments (economic);

■ ensure best use of its workers taking account of demographic changes and cultural and diversity factors (social);

■ continuously review its use of technology to ensure effective use of resources (technological);

■ carry out its activities in a way that minimises impacts on the physical environment (environmental);

■ carry out its activities in an ethical manner, taking account of existing law and industry codes of conduct (legal).

■ Using PESTEL to understand the external environment of tourist organisations

The purpose of environmental scanning is to identify the drivers of change, and to prioritise these in order of importance.

■ **Political** – driven by government and quasi-autonomous government agencies. Government policies can influence the capacity to travel. In 1950s Britain, there was a limit on how much money could be taken for travel abroad; later, this limit was abolished, facilitating travel. Many countries still have such controls. In tourism, many international and national bodies exist to promote the interests of tourism to government. Some of these are extensions of national governments, such as the European Union (influences travel and tourism through treaties, regulations, directives and policies), and the WTO set up under the aegis of the United Nations. Others represent the interests of the tourism industry and exercise substantial influence on governments, such as the International Air Transport Association (IATA) representing the airline industry, the European Tour Operators Association (ETOA), the Association of British Tour Agents (ABTA) representing tour operators, the International Association of Tourism Professionals, and the British Resorts Association representing local authority-sponsored tourism.

   Early in 2004, Davies (2004) suggested that comments by London Mayor Ken Livingston and the Metropolitan Police Commissioner about the lack of preparedness of London and UK to deal with terrorist attacks had an impact on consumer confidence, resulting in group cancellations from North America, Italy and Scandinavia.

■ **Economic** – the performance of the economy generates income for people to afford to travel. In the early 1980s, there was a significant loss of jobs in the UK, which reduced demand for tourism. The current economic slowdown in Germany has likewise curtailed German travel abroad and the spending of money on second homes. In a similar way, the currency exchange rate can encourage or discourage travel. At the time of writing (summer 2004), the American dollar is weak against the euro, and this is encouraging European travel to destinations such as Florida. Conversely, economic growth in the Far East is encouraging outward travel from the region, benefiting American, British and other European destinations; however, only five years ago, the Far East experienced an economic downturn, leading to a reduction in outward travel.

■ **Social** – this includes changes in demography (make-up of a country's population), a population's well-being (health, education, potential to earn money, amount of free/leisure time) and its knowledge and cultural development which inform awareness of, and a motivation to visit other places. Case 9.3 shows that the ageing of the European population is a key driver in TUI's willingness to develop tourism resources for older people. Likewise, people's curiosity and willingness to learn about other places is driving the expansion of cultural tourism, for example to the Far East or India, and remote tourism, such as to Antarctica, the Himalayas or the rain forests.

Previously, people's desire for the familiar drove the expansion of mass tourism destinations offering the same as what they had at home, such as the costas in Spain, which have been compared to UK resorts like Blackpool or Scarborough.

■ **Technological** – changes in technology which have driven developments in tourism. Both the train and the aeroplane have revolutionised travel. The potential of train travel provided an opportunity for Thomas Cook. More recently, the internet has created new opportunities through online bookings, with TUI expecting 20% of booking from the internet. However, other technological innovations have proved less significant – commercial plane speed is set to remain below the sound barrier, for example. In 2002, Boeing scrapped plans for a new Sonic Cruiser, arguing that their airline customers wanted planes which were more economic rather than faster. Instead, it is developing the Boeing 7E7 with a range of some 8000 miles and between 15% and 20% more fuel-efficient. This confirms a prediction by Naisbitt (1994: 138) that 'the gains in aviation for the next couple of decades will be in capacity, not speed', based on the assumption that 'the power required to propel an airplane increases with the cube of its speed; . . . to go twice as fast as a 747, you would need eight times as much power . . . current thinking . . . is . . . in the direction of subsonic speed, but . . . extremely large passenger capacity'.

■ **Environmental** – protection of the physical environment has become an international concern. Tourism has contributed substantially to environmental damage through chemical and noise pollution, loss of habitats and often poor quality urbanisation. Even remote places such as Antarctica and the Himalayas have experienced environmental degradation and litter caused by human activity. The environment has become a battle ground between protectionists and the doubters. Even ecotourism has impacts. Campaigners such as Friends of the Earth and Greenpeace have raised awareness of the negative impacts. Tour operators, destinations, hotels and airlines are being forced to develop initiatives to protect environments, confirming Naisbitt's (1994 : 181) view: 'while issues involving labour, transportation, health, security, and safety are critical, probably the single greatest concern for every country is the impact tourism will have on its environment'. Boeing's 7E7 plane is partly aimed at placating the environmental lobby.

■ **Legal** – tourism in the UK is controlled and regulated by laws from the European Union and the British government and by policies and regulations from tourism industry organisations. The EU's package holiday directive has provided protection for holiday-makers. The increased post-9/11 security at US airports has had a significant impact on visitor numbers to the USA. Colin Powell (2004), US Secretary of State, testifying before the House Judiciary Committee of the US Congress, argued for a postponement of passports with embedded biometrics (to include a digital image of the bearer's face and biographic information on the electronic chip embedded in the passport to facilitate verification of identity through facial recognition), to November 2006 to provide more time for Visa Waiver Participating countries to introduce the new technology. Otherwise visitors numbers to the USA would decline either because of delays in obtaining visas or potential travellers not having the new documentation.

Using a similar STEP approach, Feather (1990) identified 35 'G-Forces' (global forces) driving environmental change.

PESTEL analysis is then used to identify potential threats and opportunities, and the key drivers of change. For example, the nearly US$2 rate to a British pound and the euro at the start of 2005 means that it is a big opportunity for European tourists to visit the USA. Conversely, it is a big threat to European manufacturers of products, such as sailing boats, used by the US tourism industry because they cost nearly twice as much as they did in 2001. Consequently a company like Clyde Marine, producing products for the sailing sector, will lose sales in the USA.

7   Choose a tourist company or destination and carry out a PESTEL analysis of the external environment.

8   From this, identify potential threats and opportunities, and the key drivers of change.

Analysing industry environments

Michael Porter (1985) proposed a five forces framework (Figure 9.2 Porter's Forces), extended by others to six forces, to assess the industry environment.

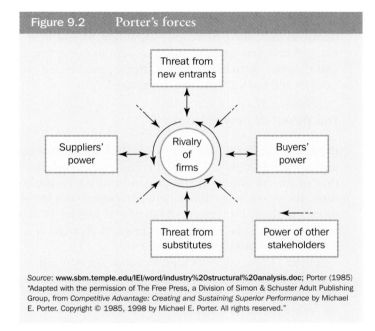

Figure 9.2   Porter's forces

Source: **www.sbm.temple.edu/IEI/word/industry%20structural%20analysis.doc**; Porter (1985)
"Adapted with the permission of The Free Press, a Division of Simon & Schuster Adult Publishing Group, from *Competitive Advantage: Creating and Sustaining Superior Performance* by Michael E. Porter. Copyright © 1985, 1998 by Michael E. Porter. All rights reserved."

The interaction of these forces provides the basis for an analysis of the tourism industry and the specific sectors within it. By analysing these forces, it is possible to assess the potential for profit; the strength of a force limits the firm's ability to set prices and make profits. Strong forces pose a threat because they can reduce profits. Weak forces create opportunities because they provide a chance to make more profit. These forces can be evaluated to determine the scale of their threat or opportunity. Strong forces suggest lower prices and higher costs, or both; and weak forces suggest lower costs and increased prices, or both.

How can each force influence tourism?

Competitive rivalry among firms

An organisation can face both direct and indirect competitors. In tourism, direct competitors will depend on the sector of activity. In hotels, there are companies providing an economy, mid-range or top-level service, for which they charge an appropriate price. They compete within their own segment. Similarly for airlines, there are low-cost/budget airlines and high-cost airlines. Prior to 11 September 2001, the high-cost and low-cost airlines were serving relatively different segments of customers. However, the increased costs and drop in travel after 11 September 2001 imposed severe pressures on the high-cost airlines as long-distance travel, especially across the Atlantic, was much reduced. By contrast, low-cost airlines operating short hauls, were better able to survive and grow. Consequently, the high-cost airlines were forced to engage in price cutting and competing with low-cost airlines to retain business. Since then, the long-haul airlines have learnt to reduce turnaround times between flights, reduce operating costs and become leaner and meaner. By contrast, the low-cost airline sector is more competitive, with about 50 firms in Europe alone. In addition there is the threat of high-cost carriers competing in the 'no-frills' sector as British Airways is threatening to do.

How can an organisation decide who its competitors are? One approach is strategic group analysis, based on the assumption of similar use of strategies and resources. Hence they are most likely to compete directly.

By this analysis, Lufthansa, Air France and British Airways etc. form one strategic group, and easyJet, Ryanair and BmiBaby form another. In the same way, the mass destinations appealing to hedonistic, single, young people such as Palma Nova/Magaluf, Faliraki and San Antonio in Ibiza form one strategic group, and Rome, Athens, Venice and Florence form a different strategic group based on cultural assets targeting different tourists and having different resources.

The threat of new entrants

Prior to 9/11, there were only a handful of low-cost carriers in the UK, flying mostly to holiday destinations. After 9/11, the market valuation of Ryanair became more than that of British Airways, the valuation of which declined dramatically. However, since then, there are many more new entrants in the low-cost carrier sector, posing major threats to the front runners, Ryanair and easyJet. A major shake-out of the low-cost segment is taking place. The share price of Ryanair has begun to decline because of the threat of new entrants.

Porter (1985) suggests that the scope for new entrants into a market segment is influenced by existing barriers to entry and the responses from competitors. Barriers to entry are influenced by factors (Coulter, 2002 and Parker, 2004) such as those detailed under the following subheadings.

Economies of scale

This involves savings that can be made by increasing volume and forcing down unit costs. New entrants have to match, or have lower prices than, existing providers to be able to survive and grow. That means having a comparable or lower cost base; if they cannot, then entry is less likely. One appeal for new airline entrants is the forecast increases in UK air travel from around 200 million at present to an estimated 500 million journeys in 2030 (Department for Transport, 2003). Worldwide, the WTO estimates doubling of air journeys over the same time period. Therefore, simply by matching the cost base of existing carriers, new entrants could command a share of the air journeys. Within this long-term trend, there are likely to be slowdowns and reductions caused by events such as 9/11 and the subsequent wars in Afghanistan and Iraq. The 1991 Gulf War showed that air travel took several years to recover. This can lead to consolidation through takeovers and mergers or failures, as has happened through the merger of KLM and Air France, TUI taking over Thomson and Thomas Cook merging with German-based tour operators. These have led to companies with a global presence in the tourist market.

Product differentiation

A new entrant has to have a unique selling point to attract customers. In tourism, there is a significant propensity among tourists to be tempted by special offers in the form of discounts, add-ons and novelty value. Tourists have changed destinations, or chosen different offerings in the same destination, depending on what was on offer and at what price and quality, or have moved from high-cost to low-cost carriers for their travel. Alongside this, there are also companies that seek to develop a distinctive product and branding, such as Thomas Cook (offering Club 18–30) and Saga (providing holidays and other products for the 50+ age group), and ecotourist holidays by TUI.

Switching costs

These are one-time costs for the customer in switching from one supplier to another. In booking a holiday, these are a relatively small factor as most travel agents' shops tend to be in close proximity to one another, and can now also be easily accessed by the internet and the telephone. Customers are used to shopping around and, especially in a culture driven by bargain hunting, this is a relatively small psychological barrier. Selecting which country to visit is also influenced by whether it offers value for money.

KPMG (2003) commissioned a recent survey from YouGov on people's holiday preferences. This concluded that '63 per cent feel the UK doesn't offer value for money as a family holiday destination' despite 'the prospect of holidaymakers getting fewer euros to the pound, higher prices on the continent, and continued airport delays owing to the French strikes'.

Capital investment and working capital

This can be a substantial entry barrier. For example, Iberostar are expanding by creating resorts in Croatia and the Caribbean. These require substantial capital investment and operating costs, and therefore a long-term commitment, which in turn is predicated on an assessment of economic and political stability in these destinations. Existing resorts will also need renewed investment to maintain their competitiveness.

The returns on some investments will require a long time horizon and a conviction that tourists will keep coming. The Al Maha Resort in the Dubai Desert combines hospitality with conservation management of wildlife and natural habitats. Opened in 1999, it cost US$28m, and after 5 years had attracted 38,000 business and first-class visitors. The aim is a payback over ten years. Guests pay as much as $1300 a night per couple (FT Business, 2004). The aim is to have a cumulative cashflow of US$57.5m over 20 years (Wilson, 2004). In 2004, it was one of twelve projects nominated for the World Legacy Awards for recognition of excellence in environmental, social and cultural travel. While airlines and hotels in other countries have suffered from the effects of the 9/11 attack, wars in Afghanistan and Iraq and SARS, in Dubai business travel has grown, trade shows and conferences have kept hotels open and the Al Maha Resort has continued to attract visitors.

Access to distribution channels

A good tourism product will not succeed without distribution channels to ensure its sale. Consolidation in the holiday market means that organisations such as Thomas Cook and TUI have substantial vertical integration involving hotels, airlines and travel agents and by market development have expanded their distribution channels. Independents have to develop their own networks. However, telesales and internet intermediaries have created new opportunities for new entrants to sell their services, particularly for niche markets.

Government policy and regulation

Laws passed by governments can act as a disincentive to new entrants. Some governments, such as India, require inward investment to be linked to a local partner. By contrast, the Maastricht Treaty of 1991 freed up the free movement of capital from one member state to another within the European Union, facilitating new entrants. In the Mallorcan resort of Palma Nova/Magaluf, the local organisation of tourism businesses is lobbying municipal and regional government not to allow the development of all-inclusive resorts because their members will lose sales to these tourists.

■ Bargaining power of buyers

Buyers can have tremendous power and can influence profitability. Tour operators such as Thomas Cook and TUI purchase large volumes of hotel accommodation at the lowest prices. A common complaint by hoteliers is that, if they do not comply, tour operators threaten to take their custom elsewhere. In the same way, tour operators identify and promote a new destination with low start-up costs, and therefore in competition with existing destinations, which are then forced to lower their prices. Holiday-makers in turn make choices based on quality at the lowest price, and consequently choose destinations different from the previous year.

■ Bargaining power of suppliers

When suppliers have bargaining power, they can vary prices and quality of their services. In tourism, suppliers include providers of raw materials, equipment, financial services, and sources of labour. Coulter (2002: 89–90) suggests supplier power is influenced by:

- domination by a few companies;
- availability of substitute products;
- whether the industry is unimportant;
- the importance of supplier products and services to the industry;
- the situation when suppliers' products are differentiated or if customers are switching costs.

Tour operators have been bypassing travel agents by selling direct to holiday-makers through telesales and the internet. Richer (2004) suggests that travel agents are challenging operators at their own game – he says that the Global Travel Group is 'one of several travel agency groupings that are contracting, packaging and selling their own products, therefore taking an extra chunk of profit from the value chain'.

TravelMole (2003) has also reported consolidation in the business of air flight bookings with the creation of EasySell Flight Travel technology by market leaders Comtec and Datalex.[1] This is the industry's first-ever system allowing agents to search and book every available category of airfare.

■ Substitute products

The British mostly took their holidays in UK resorts before the 1960s. However, since the late 1950s, the development of jet travel has opened up travel to European destinations and further away, leading to the decline of UK resorts. However, following the downturn in international travel after 9/11, there has been the potential to develop sales to UK destinations.

■ Power of other stakeholders

External stakeholders include government, unions, environmental groups, and other NGOs. They can limit a firm's freedom of action. In tourism, NGOs include the World Tourism Organization and the World Travel and Tourism Council, which have an influential role. Wilkening (2004) writes that the WTTC has a 2004 forecast, in which 'global tourism is set to grow 3.7%, almost matching its historical 4% growth a year prior to

---

1 Comtec is the retail travel industry's leading agency software provider and one of the fastest-growing e-commerce pioneers. Datalex provides technology to leading global travel industry suppliers and distributors that enable them to aggregate and package a broad range of travel components for distribution across multiple sales channels.

war, terrorism and SARS'. Wilson (2004) further writes that to help the tourism industry reach its potential, the WTTC has launched 'Blueprint for New Tourism', a strategy to provide a framework for improving partnership between private and public sectors.

The aims are:

- governments to recognise travel and tourism as top priorities;
- business to balance economics with people, culture and environment;
- a shared pursuit of long-term growth and prosperity.

These aims are to encourage more sustainable tourism.

At a local level, local authorities can also contribute by encouraging conditions for the development of tourism and the development of partnerships between the public and private sectors.

Internal analysis

Having discussed frameworks for understanding the external environment, it is also necessary to analyse the internal environment of the organisation; from this, the strengths and weaknesses of the organisation can be identified. David (2003: 121) suggests the internal audit should consider functions such as the products/services operations, marketing, finance/accounting, HRM, management and information systems, and research and development. From this, the organisation's distinctive competences can be identified; these are the organisation's strengths which cannot be easily matched or copied by the competition. Competitive advantage can be built on these competences (David, 2003: 120). These factors can also be assessed for tourism destinations. However, it is possible for a destination to be perceived in different ways. Young people see Magaluf as a clubbing destination, with a good supply of bars and clubs open into the early hours; whereas families perceive it as a place with a good range of daytime attractions and activities. Some people find the drunken scenes in summer a turnoff, while others see it at the *raison d'être* for their holiday. So exactly what are Magaluf's distinctive competences? Are they the bars/clubs or the daytime amenities OR its attraction as a place to visit again and again? We have to start by asking 'what do tourism organisations or destinations produce and sell?' Given the intangible nature of tourism, it can be difficult to assess competences.

In Chaplin's Bar in Magaluf, what 'pulls in the punters'? Is it the drinks? Late opening? Music and dance? The people who frequent it? The ambience? Or is it the synthesis of these components which makes it a good night out?

Despite the intangibility of the tourism product; it is important to identify its distinctive, or core, competences. Several analytical methods and models can be used for this.

Tourism lifecycle (TLC) analysis

The lifecycle concept assumes that like living organisms (birth, childhood, adolescence, adulthood, child rearing, old age and death), organisations and places/destinations experience a similar process. Drawing on Butler (1980), a tourism lifecycle for understanding the evolution of destinations comprises these stages: discovery, exploration, involvement, development, consolidation, stagnation, decline and possible recovery.

Cooper (1993: 147) suggests that the TLC can be used to understand both the 'physical development of a destination, but . . . also its market evolution'. A destination tends to progressively adapt to its customers. As Plog (1974) suggests, initially allocentric adventurers visit a new place, followed by midcentrics (people preferring novelty combined with home comforts) to be succeeded by psychocentrics (mass tourists). Combining these two typologies results in:

- exploration and involvement = allocentrics;
- development and consolidation = midcentrics;
- stagnation and decline = psychocentrics.

Supporters of the lifecycle approach argue it can be used to identify development and managerial strategies best fitting the stage of the lifecycle. However, Cooper (1993: 156) concludes the TLC is 'an excellent descriptive tool . . . for integrating the disparate factors . . . involved in developing a resort', but less suitable as a prescriptive tool. Basically the TLC contributes to an understanding of the existing position and how that has been arrived at, from which strengths and weaknesses can be identified and assessed as part of the process of developing future strategies using other methods.

Case 9.4   Majorca

As an example, Majorca as an island destination is perceived to be a mature destination, at the stagnation stage, and facing threats from new entrants such as Turkey, the Caribbean and the Far East. It had rapidly developed for the tourist market in the 1960s and 1970s, often with poor quality buildings displacing picturesque landscapes. However, the island continues to have a range of tourist offerings for different segments of tourists. New destinations in the Caribbean and the Far East are open all year, while Majorca closes for the winter. To forestall a decline and initiate a recovery, new initiatives have been developed, such as Winter Calvia (so that hotels, bars and restaurants stay open during the winter months, catering mostly for the senior citizens market) promoting Palma city as a shopping destination and a push to quality tourism based on sustainable principles. Local government has adopted policies to control the building of new hotels, protect the environment, limit noise from bars and clubs and discourage alcoholism and anti-social behaviour by tourists.

Source: Author's personal experience

Discussion questions

9   Is quality based sustainable tourism leading to a better tourist experience in Majorca?

10   Can this strategy be sustained against the threat of low-cost entrants?

Assessment of value creation

The performance of a tourist organisation or destination depends on its ability to create value, which is the use of a 'resource to exploit external circumstances . . . to bring in revenue, or . . . to neutralise external situations . . . likely to keep revenue from flowing in' (Coulter, 2002: 38–9).

Resources need to be combined or processed in a way to get value out of them, and therefore they are the inputs for capabilities, that is, how things get done to deliver a tourism product or service. Therefore how, and how much value is created by a tourist company or destination will depend on the resource inputs and their processing and sale for end-consumption by tourists. Porth (2003: 81) suggests the value chain helps managers to 'visualise and analyse value-creating activities' and to pursue strategies which offer 'lower prices than competitors for equivalent benefits or provide unique or differentiated benefits that more than offset a higher price'. Therefore, Porter's (1985) value chain model, shown in Figure 9.3, can be used to assess value creation in tourism. The assessment of value added by a tourist organisation's activities cannot be ignored. Piercy

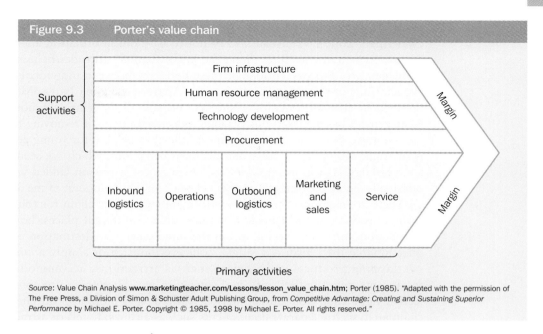

Figure 9.3   Porter's value chain

(2002: 75–7) goes further to suggest 'we are in an era of value driven strategy' through 'value innovation' based on three assumptions:

- operational excellence – reliable products/services at competitive prices, delivered with minimal difficulty and inconvenience, e.g. an airline that flies people to destinations at realistic prices and with few or no delays;
- customer intimacy – precisely tailored offerings for niches, e.g. 18–30 holidays which do not interfere with the enjoyment of families or senior citizens;
- product leadership – offering leading-edge products and services that competitors have difficulty catching up with.

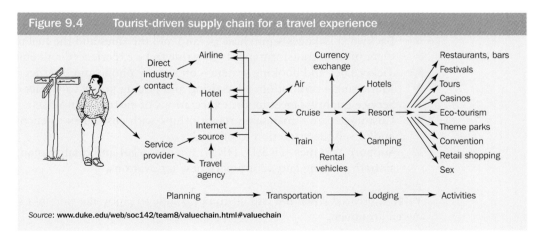

Figure 9.4   Tourist-driven supply chain for a travel experience

As Figure 9.4 shows, the tourist has to go through many stages from the decision to take a holiday to experiencing it at the destination. At each stage, the tourist can have a negative or positive experience which can contribute to a gain or loss in perceived value.

How easy is it to apply the value chain concept to tourism? Tourism is experienced at the point of consumption, i.e. the destination; therefore, it cannot be brought back home. The tourist product is experienced at the personal, subjective and individual level, and where there is a wide choice in the marketplace. The 'value added' by a tourism product is likely to be manifested by an increase in enjoyment of the experience for a tourist (Weiermair, 2000). Value can also be added by more information about the destination, the experience of travelling there, the local weather; attitudes/behaviour of locals, the ambience, etc. *But* perceptions of these will vary between individual tourists and their expectations of the visit. The Portonova Apartos in Palma Nova, Mallorca has a high number of low-term senior residents, because it is relatively noise free at night. Management has achieved this through a declared policy of removing hotel guests if they are too noisy. For senior residents, this is 'added value', but for young people 'added value' is the right to engage in noisy and drunken behaviour, which are seen as essential for a good holiday. As this example shows, having a consensus on 'added value' of the tourist offering is highly problematic and will depend on the standpoint of the different actors.

There are significant problems with mapping a value chain for tourism. In manufacturing, production and consumption are often in different places; however, in tourism, production and consumption are in the same place, the destination or resort. It is also questionable if tourism is a single, cohesive industry or simply a convenient label for overlapping products and services such as attractions, accommodation, bars/clubs, restaurants, retail outlets, gifts and souvenirs, etc. Therefore, attempts to develop a collective value chain for tourism may be flawed. It is more appropriate to develop value chain analysis for separate components such as airlines, hotels or attractions.

The following example, which examines a ride, demonstrates how value can be achieved through the examination of the structure of and the supply chain for an attraction.

Structure of the attraction (ride)
- Line personnel – maintenance and engineers, marketing and sales staff – all are involved in producing and selling the attraction's services.
- Operators of rides – ensure rides run smoothly, within health and safety guidelines, to provide a positive experience.
- Support staff – finance and accountants, personnel, public relations to support the work of the line personnel, so that the attraction runs smoothly.

The combined activities of these workers can ensure the creation of value for the tourist.

Supply chain for the attraction (ride)
- Backward linkages – purchase of land and the rides and the fuel to run them.
- Operations – transform inputs to a ride to be experienced and enjoyed.
- Ticket sales and booking system – on site, by phone and internet.
- Marketing – promotion, advertising and pricing policy to attract customers.
- Service quality – meeting the expectations of customers/tourists.
- Customer care – managing relationships with customers to encourage repeat visits and/or sell the attraction to others.
- Support activities – R&D, HRM, finance, legal and quality management to ensure smooth running and adoption of new innovations.

Value is created when the end customer is able to enjoy the ride in a safe and encouraging environment.

Assessment of capabilities and competences

The creation of value requires staff who have the capabilities and competences required to create the experience desired by the tourist.

Coulter (2002) suggests a framework for identifying and assessing an organisation's distinctive capabilities and competences which contribute to creating customer value, are difficult for competitors to copy and are capable of multiple uses. For the existing products and markets, sources of competitive advantage and disadvantage are identified. Next, capabilities and competences are identified and sorted according to strategic importance. Finally, the key capabilities and competences are agreed. Therefore, in the example of the ride discussed above, value for the tourist is delivered when the tourist enjoys a unique thrilling ride in a pleasant and safe environment, with helpful and friendly staff, after minimal queuing time.

SWOT analysis

This brings together, in a summary form, a tourist organisation's or destination's main strengths and weaknesses as generated by the internal environmental assessment, and the threats and opportunities and competitor analysis from the external environmental assessment.

A SWOT analysis is only as good as the tourism strategists who prepared the preceding environmental analysis. Based on their assumptions, biases, experiences and judgements, they may come up with a similar or different SWOT. As Simon (1960) suggests, people have limited, differing capacities for processing information. They need the ability and scope to balance the bigger picture with commitment to delivering customer value to their organisation. As Stacey (2003) suggests, the organisation and its staff contribute to the complex and uncertain environment in which it operates.

TOWS matrix for generating strategies

Following David (2003: 200), the information from the SWOT can be transferred to the Threats–Opportunities–Weaknesses–Strengths (TOWS) matrix, and through a process of matching, can be used to develop four broad types of strategies:

1   Strengths–Opportunities (SO) strategies (using internal strengths to take advantage of external opportunities).
2   Weaknesses–Opportunities (WO) strategies (using external opportunities to reduce internal weaknesses).
3   Strengths–Threats (ST) strategies (using internal strengths to reduce the effects of external threats).
4   Weaknesses–Threat (WT) strategies (reducing internal weaknesses and also avoiding external threats).

An example of this for Southwest Airlines, a well-known US airline, is given in Table 9.2.

Table 9.2   Example of TOWS matrix for Southwest Airlines

	Strengths	Weaknesses
	S1 Won Triple Crown S2 Great company to work for S3 Excellent public reputation S4 Very strong financially S5 Strong culture S6 Experienced and strong management S7 Only newer 737s S8 Easy personnel substitution S9 Loyal/committed employees S10 Innovative marketing S11 Fourth largest domestic airline S12 Highly rated website S13 30% of bookings online S14 Lowest cost airline in its market S15 Fastest turnaround time for aircraft S16 Flexible union work rules S17 Great low-term growth/orientation S18 Only profitable airline in 2001 S19 24-hour emergency medical service	W1 Few long-haul flights W2 No international flights W3 Operating/net income fell in 2001 W4 Delayed purchase of new aircraft
Opportunities O1 20% capacity cutback by competitors O2 Possible federal aid O3 Internet ticket sales are accepted by public O4 Passengers want low prices and frequent departures O5 They only fly to 58 cities leaving lots of room for expansion in US O6 International routes	**S–O Strategies** Take over routes abandoned by other airlines (O1, O4, S4, S6, S10, S14) Use federal aid to expand current operations (O2, O4, S10, S15, S17) Add more coast-to-coast flights (O2, O4, S3, S4, S6, S10, S15, S17) Enter Midwest Market (O2, O5, S3, S4, S10, S15, S17) Add flights to Mexico and Canada (O2, O6, S3, S4, S6, S10, S15, S17) Increase marketing efforts in current markets (O4, S1, S3, S5, S10, S17)	**W–O Strategies** Add more coast-to-coast flights (O3, W3) Enter Midwest market (O2, O4, O5, W1) Add flights to Mexico and Canada (O2, O4, O6, W2)
Threats T1 Persistent losses in airline industry T2 Terrorism threats add costs and make people afraid to fly T3 Economic downturn T4 New security and ticket tax regulations T5 Uncertain fuel prices T6 New direct point-to-point competitors T7 Existing competitors – United, Delta, America West T8 Large competing online airline reservation systems	**S–T Strategies** Hedge fuel prices (T5, T3, S3) Increase marketing efforts (T1, T2, T3, T6, T7, S1, S3, S7, S10, S12, S17) Abandon unprofitable routes (T1, T2, T3, S16, S17) Acquire America West (T6, T7, S4, S11, S18) Join other online agencies (T8, S13)	**W–T Strategies** Join other online agencies (T8, W3) Lease aircraft from others (T1, W4) Joint venture with other airlines (T1, T6, T7, W1, W2) Add cargo hauling (W3, T3)

Source: The Arrowhead University Consortium of Northeast Minnesota, USA (2004) **www.arrowheadu.com/site/files/breaker/2004springbuad4556southwestairlines.doc**
© 2004. Reprinted by permission of the author: Martin T. Breaker, Bemidji State University, Bemidji, MN 56601

Conclusion

The strategic process should be central to the management of tourism and draws from mainstream strategic planning theory. As the December 2004 tragic disasters in the Indian ocean and the September 2001 attacks on the USA have demonstrated, the environment of tourism is highly complex and dynamic, in which unexpected events occur and have dramatic consequences for tourists, tourism providers and future investment in tourism. Following the 2001 attacks the US Federal, state and local governments actively promoted tourism to domestic and overseas markets to assist recovery. Likewise, the World Tourism Organization (2005) seeks to assure governments and the tourism sector that 'the (December 2004) tsunami will not sink world tourism'. It suggests that it is safe to plan for long-term tourism growth as the overall impact of the disaster will be limited. Others such as Stacey suggest that long-term planning is problematic as the future remains unknown. Until the December 2004 tsunami, the main threats to tourism in the Far East were the re-emergence of SARS, bird flu and terrorist attacks. There is now the possibility of further earthquakes as the Far East is a hot spot area for seismic activity.

Therefore, tourism recovery may be problematic in the coastal areas even combined with an early warning system and better designed buildings and rigorous planning controls. But it may create opportunities for inland tourism. This will depend on environmental analysis to assess the current situation and to facilitate consideration of alternative future scenarios for tourism. This in turn requires encouraging a capability for divergent, strategic thinking, which goes beyond day-to-day operational issues to take a wider strategic view. Tourism businesses which fail to do so will be inadequately prepared to meet the threats from competitors and complex and often unpredictable environmental forces giving rise to the unexpected.

Guided reading

The standard textbook on corporate strategy is Johnson, Scholes and Whittington (2005) which now has a new section by Richard Whittington exploring the context for strategy development. Drucker (1985) discusses the sources for innovation and entrepreneurship which can be applied to tourism businesses. Piercy (2002) discusses the importance of not only developing relationships with customers, but also the need to deliver value. Weaver and Lawton (2002) provide a broad based introduction to tourism management.

Recommended websites

For trends in commercial/business aspects of the tourism industry, visit:

TravelMole.com: **http://www.google.com/www.travelmole.com** .

Travel Weekly: **www.travelweekly.co.uk/** .

Hospitality Net: **www.hospitalitynet.org** .

For strategic planning in tourism, visit:.

World Travel and Tourism Council: **www.wttc.org/** .

World Tourism Organization: **www.world-tourism.org/** .

Key words

Chaos theory; environmental scanning; Porter's forces; PESTEL analysis; strategy pyramid; SWOT analysis; TOWS matrix.

Bibliography

Alford, L.P. (1924) *Management's Handbook*, 5th edn. Machine Publishing Group, Ronald Press, New York.

Ansoff, I. (1969)(ed.) *Business Strategy*. Penguin, Harmondsworth.

Ansoff, I. (1984) *Implanting Strategic Management*. Prentice Hall, Harlow.

Arrowhead University Consortium (2001) 'TOWS Matrix for Southwest Airlines', The Arrowhead University Consortium of Northeast Minnesota, **www.arrowheadu.com/site/files/breaker/2004 springbuad4556southwestairlines.doc** . Prentice Hall/FT.

Butler, R.W. (1980) The concept of a tourist area cycle of evolution, *Canadian Geographer*, vol. 24, 5–12.

Clausewitz, K. von (1982) *On War*. Penguin, Harmondsworth.

Cooper, C. (1993) The Life Cycle Concept and Tourism, in P. Johnson and B. Thomas (1993) *Choice and demand in tourism*. Mansell Publishing, London.

Coulter, M. (2002) *Strategic Management in Action*. Prentice Hall, Harlow.

David, F. (2003) *Strategic Management: Concepts and Cases*. Prentice Hall, Harlow.

Davies, P. (2004) *UK inbound tourism prospects improve*. Available from **www.travelmole.com/ news_detail.php?news_id=100170** .

Department for Transport (2003) *The Future of Air Transport*, Annex A. Department for Transport, London.

Drucker, P. (1985) *Innovation and Entrepreneurship*. Harper & Row, New York.

Edgar, D. and Nesbitt, L. (1996) A matter of chaos – some issues in hospitality businesses, *International Journal of Contemporary Hospitality Management*, 8(2), 6–9.

Feather, F. (1990) *G-Forces: The Thirty-Five Global Forces Restructuring our Future*. William Morrow & Co., New York.

Financial Services Authority (2003) *Combined Code of Conduct for Corporate Governance*. Financial Services Authority, London.

FT Business (2004) *Destination Dubai*. Available from **www.fdimagazine.com/news/fullstory.php/aid/293/ Destination_Dubai.html** .

Graetz, F. (2002) Strategic thinking versus strategic planning: towards understanding the complementarities, *Management Decision*, 40(5), 456–462.

Higgs, D. (2003) *Review of the role and effectiveness of non-executive directors*. Department of Trade and Industry/Stationery Office, London.

Hooker, R. (1996) Ching's China: the Opium Wars. Available from **www.wsu.edu:8080/~dee/CHING/ OPIUM.HTM** .

Johnson, G., Scholes, K. and Whittington, R. (2005) *Exploring Corporate Strategy*. Prentice Hall, Harlow.

Kotelnikov, V. (2004) *YourEnterpriseStrategy*. Available from **www.1000ventures.com/business_guide/ mgmt_inex_stategy.html** .

KPMG News (2003) Boost for UK tourism on the horizon but it must convince holidaymakers on value for money. Available from **www.kpmg.co.uk/news/ detail.cfm?pr=1756** .

Liedtka, J.M. (1998) Linking strategic thinking with strategic planning, *Strategy & Leadership*, 26(4), 30–35.

Mayrhuber, W. (2004) Lufthansa on course but still a long way to go, *Travel Daily News*, March 26.

Naisbitt, J. (1994) *Global Paradox*. Avon, New York.

Packard, V. (1960) *The Hidden Persuaders*. Penguin, Harmondsworth.

Parker, C. (2004) Strategy and environmental analysis in sport, in J. Beech and S. Chadwick *The Business of Sport Management*. Pearson, Harlow.

Pfeffer, J. (1992) *Managing with Power*. Harvard Business School Press, Boston, MA.

Piercy, N. (2002) *Market led strategic change*. Butterworth-Heinemann, Oxford.

Plog, S.C. (1974) Why Destination Areas Rise and Fall in Popularity, *Cornel Hotel and Restaurant Quarterly*, vol. 14, no. 4, 55–58.

Porter, M.E. (1985) *Competitive advantage: Creating and sustaining superior performance*. Free Press, New York.

Porth, S. (2003) *Strategic Management: A Cross-Functional Approach*. Prentice Hall, Harlow.

Powell, C. (2004) Passports and Visas with Embedded Biometrics and the October Deadline, Prepared Testimony by the US Secretary of State, House Judiciary Committee, US Congress, 21 April.

Richer, G. (2004) Travel agents fighting back, *TravelMole*, 21 May.

Schurmann, F. (1995) *The World in Chaos: Chaos Theory Teaches That Things Come Together Even as They Fall Apart*, Pacific News Service. Available from **www.pacificnews.org/jinn/stories/columns/heresies/950627-chaos-theory.html** .

Shelton, C. (1999) *Quantum Leaps: Skills for workplace re-creation*. Butterworth-Heinemann, Boston MA.

Shelton, C. and Darling, J. (2003) From theory to practice: using new science concepts to create learning organizations, *The Learning Organization*, 10(6), 353–360.

Simon, H.A. (1960) *The New Science of Management Decision*. Harper, New York.

Smith, R. (2003) *Audit committees: Combined Code Guidance*. Financial Reporting Council, London.

Stacey, R. (2003) *Strategic Management and Organisational Dynamics: the Challenge of Complexity*. Prentice Hall, Harlow.

Sukarsono, A. and Eaton, D. (2005) *Indonesia reassures aid workers after gunfire*, Reuters. Available from **newsbox.msn.co.uk/article.aspx?as=article&f=uk_-_olgbtopnews&t=11881&id=531794&d=20050109&do=http://newsbox.msn.co.uk&i=http://newsbox.msn.co.uk/mediaexportlive&ks=0&mc=5&lc=en&ae=windows-1252** .

Teare, R., Canziani, B.F. and Brown, G. (1997) *Global Directions: New Strategies for Hospitality and Tourism*. Cassell, London.

Thomas Cook (2003) *Annual Report for 2002–03*. Available from **www.thomascook.info/tck/de/en/car/0,2773,0-0-307571,00.html** .

Travel Industry Association of America (2004) *Economic Research: Economic Impact of Travel and Tourism*. Available from **www.tia.org/Travel/EconImpact.asp** .

TravelMole (2003) *Comtec Announces New Holiday And Flight Content On Easysell*, TravelMole.com, available from **www.travelmole.com/news_detail.php?news_id=97557** .

TUI (2004) Scenario forecasting of trends in the holiday market, *TUI Times*, March.

Underhill, W. (2004) Tourism: The new golden age, *Newsweek*, 19 April, 46.

Weaver, D. and Lawton, L. (2002) *Tourism Management*. Wiley, Hoboken, NJ.

Weiermair, K. (2000) Tourists' Perceptions Towards and Satisfaction With Service Quality in the Cross-Cultural Service Encounter: Implications for Hospitality and Tourism Management, *Managing Service Quality*, 10(6), 397.

Wilkening, D. (2004) Travel and tourism: 'robust growth ahead', *TravelMole*, 1 March.

Wilson, J. (2004) *Global tourism set to grow 3.7% in 2004*, available from **www.wttc.org/blueprint/EUreporter.pdf** .

World Tourism Organization (2001) *Tourism: 2020 Vision*. WTO, Madrid.

World Tourism Organization (2003) *Tourism Highlights 2003*. WTO, Madrid.

World Tourism Organization (2005) *The tsunami will not sink world tourism: Seven reasons that the disaster of 26 December will have only a limited impact on world tourism*, available from **www.world-tourism.org/newsroom/Releases/2005/january/sevenreasons.htm** .

Chapter 10

Quality and yield management in tourism businesses

Peter D. Dewhurst University of Wolverhampton and Marcjanna M. Augustyn, University of Hull

Learning outcomes

On completion of this chapter the reader should be able to:

■ define the term 'operations management' and explain the nature of the operations management function within tourism organisations;

■ explain the significance of quality and quality management within an operations management context;

■ profile the initiatives that can be implemented in order to enhance the quality of tourism organisations;

■ demonstrate an understanding of capacity management and especially yield management;

■ highlight key contemporary issues that are of relevance to those managers that are responsible for the operational performance of tourism organisations.

Overview

This chapter discusses quality and yield management from a tourism operations management perspective, with particular attention being paid to their role in ensuring high levels of customer satisfaction. The chapter begins with an explanation of the background context to operations management within tourism organisations and goes on to provide a definition and classification of the operations management function. The importance of quality to operations managers is then discussed with an emphasis on the need to build quality into tourism services. Consideration is given to managing supplier relationships and the role of the ISO 9001:2000 standard in this process. The discussion then proceeds to focus on process management tools that can be used to enhance the quality of processes within tourism organisations, with particular attention being paid to process design, process improvement and performance measurement. In the case of process improvement, the chapter focuses on Ishikawa's seven basic tools, together with the 'conceptual model for service quality and benchmarking'. An explanation of what is meant by capacity management is then provided, together with an exploration of the significance of capacity management to operations managers seeking to ensure customer satisfaction. An insight is also provided into yield management, which is regarded as a key facet of capacity management. The chapter concludes with a profiling of some major contemporary issues that are of relevance to those managers that are responsible for the operational performance of tourism organisations.

Operations management

The operational function of any organisation is essentially concerned with the production of goods and/or services for sale or delivery to an intended market. The production process has frequently been described within a systems context as involving the transformation of a series of inputs into outputs (Krajewski and Ritzman, 1999). This process is most easily understood in respect of manufacturing businesses, where raw materials are transformed via the manufacturing process into a series of finished goods. However, the transformation process is just as relevant to the service sector, in which organisations develop a service product that is then offered to and consumed by the organisation's customers, who receive both a tangible outcome and an intangible experience (Johnston and Clarke, 2001). For example, in the case of an airport, the transformation process encompasses those activities including baggage-handling, aircraft maintenance, air traffic control and catering provision, that, as a minimum, enable the airport's human and physical resource base to provide customers with the tangible outcome of travel to their destination of choice, while also delivering a variety of less tangible customer-care related experiences.

An overview of the operations process in an organisation is given in Figure 10.1.

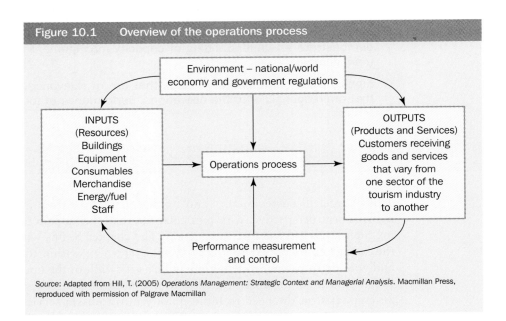

Figure 10.1   Overview of the operations process

Source: Adapted from Hill, T. (2005) *Operations Management: Strategic Context and Managerial Analysis*. Macmillan Press, reproduced with permission of Palgrave Macmillan

The operations function within a tourism organisation is therefore concerned with the full spectrum of activities that combine to meet both the tangible and intangible needs of customers. Such activities fit within what has been termed the '6Ps' of the operations mix (Bicheno and Elliott, 1997). The 6Ps represent the common features of all organisations' operational activities and include: product; process; place; programmes; procedures and people. These are set out in Table 10.1.

Implicit within this categorisation is a sense that operational activities have a temporal dimension. Indeed, certain operational activities take place only periodically, e.g. those related to process design and product development, while others are required to occur continually, e.g. quality-assurance monitoring procedures (Certo, 2000). The 6Ps categorisation also reveals the interrelationships that exist between the operational functions of organisations and those associated with marketing, financial management,

Table 10.1	The 6Ps operations mix of Bicheno and Elliott
Product	Within a tourism context, the *product* element refers to the design and development of facilities and includes consideration of issues of interpretation and quality.
Process	The full range of operational processes, including those geared towards quality assurance, product purchasing and financial monitoring, are the focus of the *process* element.
Place	*Place* refers to the physical location and layout of facilities and may include consideration of visitor flows, capacity and yield management issues.
Programme	The *programme* element of the 6Ps refers to the schedules and plans that are established to structure and direct operational activities, these include maintenance programmes and development plans.
Procedures	*Procedures* are developed by organisations as the means for communicating what are considered to be the ideal means of operating, especially in a particular circumstance or environment.
People	*People* refers to the human resource base within an organisation, which many regard as the most critical in ensuring the success of service sector operations.

Source: Bicheno and Elliott (1997)

human resource management, etc. Indeed, Slack *et al.* (2004) have developed a model that demonstrates the interrelationships for both service and manufacturing sector organisations (see Figure 10.2).

Operations management can therefore be defined as 'that function of an organisation which is concerned with the design, planning and control of resources for the production of goods and the provision of services' (Bennett *et al.*, 1988). Within the service

Figure 10.2 Some interfunctional relationships between the operations function and other core and support functions

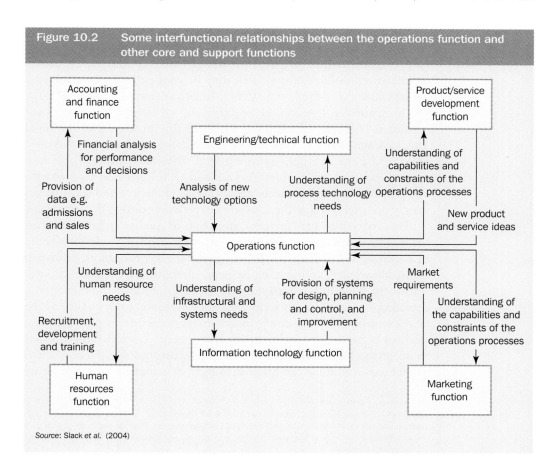

Source: Slack et al. (2004)

context, operations management entails 'the ongoing activities of designing, reviewing and using the operating system to achieve service outputs as determined by the organisation for customers' (Wright, 1999).

Consequently, the key priority for operations managers[1] working within tourism organisations is to deliver a product to their customers that balances the need to meet customer requirements with the need to ensure an effective and an efficient operating system. Achieving such a balance is crucial to the long-term competitive success of any organisation (Evans and Lindsay, 2002; Kimes, 2000). Indeed, the focus on meeting customer requirements is essential in contemporary operations management, as it helps to ensure the attainment of high levels of customer satisfaction. The focus on ensuring the effectiveness and efficiency of an operating system is necessary for achieving high performance levels. The securing of high performance levels is especially challenging to tourism organisations, which are typically characterised as experiencing continuous fluctuations of demand for what is essentially a perishable product. However, over the last twenty years quality management and yield management have emerged as mechanisms for achieving high levels of customer satisfaction within the context of effective and efficient tourism operations and so these two management processes serve as the key focus for the rest of this chapter.

Quality management in tourism: an operations management perspective

From the operations management perspective, quality may be regarded as the degree to which a set of *inherent* characteristics of a product fulfils customer requirements (ISO, 2000a). Within this context, a product is defined as the 'result of a process' (i.e. output), which may be a service, goods (hardware or processed materials) or software (e.g. information), or a combination of the above (ISO, 2000a: 7). Processes within a tourism organisation produce outputs that may be used either by external customers or by internal customers (i.e. employees within the organisation).

Consequently, meeting the requirements of external customers as well as of internal customers is crucial to achieving a high quality product that is offered for consumption. This indicates that a quality service results from an ability of everyone in the organisation to recognise the internal and/or external customers and for them to ensure that all customers' requirements are met. As Oakland (2003) stresses, failure to meet requirements in any part of a quality chain creates problems elsewhere and leads to more failure and ultimately poor service that the consumer experiences during the service encounter.

The operations management approach to quality enhancement emphasises the need for building quality into the service at every stage of its development, from the moment of acquiring the necessary inputs (e.g. materials, procedures, information, specifications, skills, knowledge, training, equipment, methods) throughout all internal processes that transform these inputs into outputs. In this approach the managerial focus shifts from detecting non-conformance (by means of evaluating the quality of the service delivered) to preventing such non-conformance from occurring in the first place (by means of the efficient organisation of the inputs and process control). This approach ultimately leads to achieving high performance levels and customer satisfaction with a service. A range of methods and tools can assist managers in achieving this, among which supplier man-

---

1 The term 'operations manager' can refer within a small organisation to an individual who has responsibility for overseeing an organisation's entire operational activities, while in larger organisations the term can refer to the variety of individuals who collectively share operational responsibility, these may include site managers, duty managers and even to a certain extent HR managers and marketing managers.

agement and process management, discussed below, are of particular importance to tourism operations managers.

Supplier management

Many tourism organisations operate with narrow profit margins and attempt to reduce their operating costs by acquiring low-quality inputs (e.g. labour, materials, equipment, technology) from a variety of suppliers who offer the lowest price. In the short term, this may lead to temporary cost reductions. However, in the longer term such an approach can result in significant losses being incurred by tourism organisations due to the increasing costs of the non-conformance of such inputs. These costs of non-conformance may include costs of repairing the equipment, costs of frequent product redesign, development and promotion, costs of service failure and recovery, and costs associated with the loss of customer trust.

To avoid such costs, building quality into the service should begin with ensuring that the inputs into the processes are of a high and consistent quality. However, controlling the quality of inputs before they are acquired from various suppliers may not be simple, particularly within the context of complex tourism products. It is therefore seen as good practice to develop partnerships with a limited number of suppliers. This approach can be particularly beneficial to tourism organisations that operate within tourism destinations, such as visitor attractions, hotels and other accommodation units, tourism information centres and restaurants. Indeed, one of the leading authorities in quality management, W. Edwards Deming, stresses that the establishment of long-term relationships with fewer suppliers who share common values leads to greater certainty, loyalty and opportunities for mutual improvement (Walton, 1989). There are many examples of strong partnership relationships between tourism organisations and their suppliers. For example, many visitor attractions operate catering services or gift shops that are perceived by the consumers to be an integral part of the visitor attractions' product offering, but which are run by independent organisations (i.e. suppliers).

The development of partnerships with suppliers may also contribute to improving the quality of complex services offered by tour operators. Although the great number of suppliers that tour operators have to deal with across the globe makes this task extremely difficult, they can at least seek to ensure that every supplier is chosen on the basis of its conformance to a clear set of stipulated requirements. This may seem to be a difficult task for tour operators to accomplish, given the variety of (a) industry-specific and country-specific standards that each supplier will need to conform to and (b) the variety of management styles adopted within the supplier organisations that may either stimulate or inhibit positive behaviour on the part of employees. One way in which tour operators may reduce the burden of selecting suppliers that conform to their requirements is by acquiring inputs (i.e. components of a holiday package) from those suppliers who have obtained a quality standard certificate such as ISO 9001:2000.[2] There are a number of reasons why tour operators and other organisations can be certain that the inputs purchased from such suppliers are likely to be of a high and consistent quality.

First, organisations that are ISO 9001:2000 certified must conform to the ISO 9001:2000 requirements, which represent the state-of-the-art approach to managing quality. To obtain such a certificate, an organisation has to demonstrate that it has an established quality management system, that it focuses on customers and identifies their

---

2 ISO 9001:2000 constitutes an important part of the ISO 9000:2000 series of international voluntary standards that have been developed by the International Organization for Standardization and which provide a framework for developing quality management systems within organisations. It should be noted that ISO 9000:2000 is the latest version of the ISO 9000 family of standards that was first published in 1987 and then revised in 1994. At the time of writing, the latest version of the standard was published in December 2000.

requirements (including industry and legal requirements), that adequate human and physical resources are provided and continuously developed, that all processes are planned and appropriately designed, that the relationships with suppliers are managed and that the organisation continually measures its performance and analyses and improves its operations (ISO, 2000b). Thus the ISO 9001:2000 standard does not refer to the quality attributes of a particular product but to the way in which quality is *managed* within an organisation, adherence to the ISO 9001:2000 requirements should result in the production of quality outputs.

Second, an independent certification body (e.g. in the UK the British Standards Institute – BSI) assesses the conformance of an organisation's quality management system to the ISO 9001:2000 requirements. This process, known as the conformity assessment process, constitutes the first step in the certification process. Subject to fulfilment of the requirements by the organisation, the certification body then issues a certificate of conformance to the ISO 9001:2000 standard, which is verified on a regular basis (ISO, 1999). This prevents organisations from allowing their systems to become obsolete.

Organisations can therefore trust suppliers who are ISO 9001:2000 certified to manage quality appropriately, which saves time and money that would otherwise be spent on checking the credibility of potential suppliers. Furthermore, the international nature of the ISO 9001:2000 standard facilitates the establishment of effective supplier relationships across the globe. As a standard, ISO 9001:2000 is an important common reference for quality requirements, since conformance to this standard carries a recognisable message about the ways in which an organisation is managed.

In spite of the system's merits, certification to ISO 9001:2000 is not yet widespread within the tourism industry, mainly due to the lack of awareness of the standard among tourism businesses or due to the lack of appreciation of the potential benefits that such a system may bring to a tourism business (Augustyn and Pheby, 2000; Augustyn, 2002). Consequently, the scope of using this tool for managing suppliers within the tourism industry is currently very narrow and will remain so until a greater number of tourism businesses develop systems that conform with ISO 9001 requirements. Examples of hotels and other tourism-related organisations that have developed quality management systems based on ISO 9001 requirements and which have obtained the ISO 9001 certificate clearly indicate that this is a worthwhile activity that produces a range of direct and indirect benefits for an organisation, particularly if the ISO 9000 systems embrace all aspects of a firm's activity. Case 10.1 provides a further insight into the benefits that can be derived from this process.

Case 10.1 Westons Cider Company and ISO 9000

Westons Cider Company in Herefordshire, England, was established as a family-owned business in 1880. It is one of the oldest cider producers in the world and has always been committed to delivering high-quality products. This has enabled the company to enjoy a highly competitive market position. However, since the Second World War cider has generally experienced a decline in popularity as other alcoholic beverages, such as lager, have become increasingly popular. Several increases in the duty payable on cider production during the 1990s placed the consumption of cider under still more pressure.

In response to such market changes, Westons took the decision to build its market position upon its strong commitment to quality. The quality culture of the company needed a formalised system to bring about (a) the potential benefits that other quality-led companies have enjoyed and (b) market recognition as a trusted supplier. Westons therefore decided to develop and implement a quality management system that conforms to the ISO 9000 family of standards. Despite some initial resistance from the workforce, Westons successfully introduced the ISO 9000 quality management system into their operations and obtained an ISO 9001 certificate in 1990. The benefits of this approach included increased sales, both at home and internationally, as well as an increased sense of empowerment within the workforce.

To ensure further growth, Westons decided to extend the scope of their activities. Building upon their heritage, the company developed a visitor attraction product, which included tours of the factory, a souvenir shop and a themed licensed restaurant. However, some of these activities were not originally included in the organisation's ISO 9000 quality management system, which led to some inconsistency in the level of quality that visitors experienced. While the tours and the shop provided visitors with a highly satisfying experience, which was reflected in the customers' comments included in the company's guest book, the restaurant initially offered a significantly lower level of service quality, as its operations were excluded from the quality management system. Indeed, during the restaurant's first year of operation, up to 80% of customers expressed dissatisfaction with at least one aspect of its operation. The difficulties could at least partly be attributed to the fact that the organisation did not initially hire specialist staff to run the restaurant, but instead relied on a rotation system involving staff from other parts of the organisation's operation. This resulted, for example, in customers waiting for long periods for their orders and becoming both disgruntled and disillusioned with their total experience. Not surprisingly, this quality-oriented company soon took steps to rectify this situation. With their appreciation of the benefits that the ISO 9000 quality management system has produced within other parts of the organisation's operations, Westons included the activities of the restaurant within a revised quality management system that fully conforms to ISO 9001:2000 requirements. Westons believe that a quality management system has to be consistently and rigorously applied across the whole range of the company's activities if it is to be successful and ensure customer satisfaction with their total experience. Indeed, high levels of customer satisfaction and loyalty have combined with high levels of operational performance to enable Westons to expand the range of their tourism-related activities. A cider museum and Edwardian Gardens have recently been opened and extensive car parking and picnic facilities built. The company is considering a further expansion of its tourism-related activities with plans to open rural craft workshops on the site.

Further reading: Augustyn (2000); Augustyn and Pheby (2000)

Process management

Building quality into tourism services that are offered to customers for consumption requires effective process management, which involves design, control and improvement of key business processes. Process management is concerned with the creation of value for the customers. The value-added approach can be either explicit or implicit. Explicit value can be measured and can be clearly defined. Implicit value is related to perceived performance and image. Central to value creation and ensuring high levels of performance within tourism organisations are process design, process improvement and performance measurement.

Process design
Process design involves all practices needed to deliver an output that meets the requirements of the customer (Rao et al., 1996). A tool that facilitates process design is called process flow mapping. It allows organisations to gain an understanding of what is done within a process, i.e. what the inputs are and what the flow of the process is. It eliminates inconsistencies, makes employees realise how they fit into the process and who their customers and suppliers are. It also improves internal communication (Ho, 1995).

While all processes have to be properly designed, careful design of tourism services is of critical importance, as the service specifications that result from this exercise should strike a balance between the requirements of all stakeholders and the operational capability of an organisation. These issues are further explored later in this chapter within the context of capacity and yield management. Certain tools can assist tourism organisations in undertaking the service design process and these include the quality function deployment (QFD) technique, also known as the 'development of product characteristics' or the 'house of quality' (Rao et al., 1996). This tool allows service designers to consider all factors that influence the design of a service, e.g. customer, technical, human and statutory requirements, the organisational capabilities, as well as the characteristics of products offered by competitors. A service blueprint is another tool used in service design, which requires service designers to define the service concept, consider issues of resource allocation, coordinate service functions, develop promotional techniques, design the service encounter, monitor and evaluate performance and provide appropriate feedback information to product managers (Williams and Buswell, 2003).

Process improvement

Process improvement is a proactive task of management 'aimed at continual monitoring of a process and its outcome and developing ways to enhance its future performance' (James, 1996: 359). Process improvement involves the solving of problems, i.e. changing the state of what is actually happening to what should be happening (Evans and Lindsay, 2002). Thus, 'Could we do the job better?' is the key improvement question (Oakland, 2003). This question, however, cannot be answered without the continual monitoring of a process and its outcomes, which is facilitated by a range of tools that enable organisations to identify and analyse the problem.

Although more sophisticated tools for process monitoring have been developed by quality management scholars (e.g. statistical process control), Ishikawa's seven basic tools, Parasuraman *et al.*'s (1985) 'conceptual model of service quality and the process benchmarking' technique together constitute a useful set of diagnostic tools that can be utilised by tourism organisations in their efforts to identify opportunities for quality improvement.

Ishikawa's seven basic tools

Ishikawa, one of the leading authorities in quality management, proposed a set of seven tools that enable organisations to identify and analyse internal problems and opportunities for their rectification (Ho, 1995). The key features of each of these tools are summarised in Table 10.2.

Table 10.2	Key features of Ishikawa's seven basic tools		
Tool	**Purpose**	**Procedure**	**Benefits**
Process flow mapping	To understand what is done within a process (what the inputs are and what the flow of the process is)	Map the process using standard symbols and answer questions: – Is the process doing what it is supposed to do? – Does every step in the process add value? – Is there any overlap of activities? – Where/how can the process be improved?	– Eliminates inconsistencies – Makes employees realise how they fit into the process and who their customers and suppliers are – Improves internal communication
Control charts	To continuously control variations within a particular process, e.g. variations in number of customer complaints per day, customer satisfaction indexes, staff turnover, costs, etc.	Establish measures for each activity to be controlled including upper control limit (UCL) and lower control limit (LCL), e.g. for customer complaints per day: UCL=6; LCL=0 – Collect data (e.g. using check sheets), plot the points on the chart and connect them – Compute the process mean and draw horizontal line. If the values fall outside the control limit or if a non-random pattern occurs, the process should be examined and corrective actions taken	– Can be used to trace variations and detect special causes of variations in the process – Minimises product non-conformance as quality problems can be identified as they occur

Tool	Purpose	Procedure	Benefits
Check sheets	To find how often something occurs due to pre-determined reasons, e.g. errors in service delivery	– Select and agree on event to be observed – Decide on time period – Design a simple form – Observe how often an event occurs due to specified reasons – Record data on the form	– Indicates the most common cause of a particular problem – Results can be interpreted directly – Ensures the gathering of facts rather than opinions
Histograms	To discover patterns in data collected on a continual basis, e.g. number of complaints	– Collect numerical data within a specified time – Present the data graphically with values presented on the vertical axis and the number of times on the horizontal axis	– Show directly the frequency with which a certain value occurs over time
Pareto analysis	To separate the most important causes from the many trivial	– Present the data collected via check sheets in the form of a histogram from the largest to the smallest frequency – Draw a cumulative frequency curve based on the percentage of a particular cause of problem occurrence in relation to all problems	– Clearly shows the magnitude of a particular problem
Cause-and-effect analysis	To find out possible causes of problems	– Brainstorm all possible causes of the problem under analysis and present the problem (effect) at the end of the horizontal arrow – Classify the major causes under relevant headings and then show as labelled arrow entering the main cause arrow. Each arrow may have other arrows entering it as the sub-causes	– Presents a chain of logical causes and effects – Identifies the most likely causes of a problem – Allows a problem to be considered fully before a solution is chosen
Scatter-diagram	To allow the relations (if any) between two factors to be established, e.g. customer satisfaction and levels of training	– Collect data about the causes and effects – Draw the cause on the horizontal axis – Draw the effect on the vertical axis – Draw the scatter diagram	– Simple to construct and interpret – Shows whether there is a relationship – Provides a basis for further causal analysis

Source: Authors own work based on Ho (1995); Kanji and Asher (1996); Oakland (2003); Evans and Lindsay (2002)

The generic nature of these tools makes them applicable to every process within an organisation. Many of the current quality problems that tourism organisations face can be identified, analysed and solved with the use of these tools, which produce factual information on which decisions can be based. Ishikawa's tools also stimulate cooperation between functions and departments and encourage the involvement of people in ensuring the quality of the processes, as with some training they can be used by every employee to monitor the performance of those processes for which they are directly responsible. The simplicity of these tools also allows operations managers to use them on a daily basis.

The conceptual model of service quality

The conceptual model of service quality developed by Parasuraman *et al.* (1985) is one of the main tools that can be used to identify quality improvement areas within service organisations. The model assumes that customer expectations of a service are influenced by four factors: word-of-mouth communication, the personal needs of the customers, their previous experiences and external communications, i.e. information provided by the service providers. Furthermore, the model assumes that the discrepancy between customer expectations and perceptions of a service results from the existence of four gaps in what is termed the internal customer–supplier chain. These gaps include:

1   The gap between customer expectations and management perceptions of customer expectations, which may be caused by a lack of marketing research, the inadequate use of research findings, the lack of interaction between management and customers, inadequacies in the upward communication channels, or possibly too many levels of management.

2   The gap between management perceptions of customer expectations and service quality specifications, which may arise from inadequate standardisation, an inability to achieve the standard, inadequate management commitment to service quality, or the absence of goal setting.

3   The gap between service quality specifications and service delivery, which may be caused by role ambiguities and conflict, poor employee–job fit, poor technology–job fit, inappropriate supervisory control systems, as well as a lack of effective teamwork.

4   The gap between service delivery and external communications to customers, which may arise through inadequate internal communications (e.g. between advertising and operations, between salespeople and operations, between management and marketing), or the propensity to promise too much.

The model thus provides a framework for undertaking a study of the operations within an organisation with a view to identifying the major causes of the discrepancy between customer expectations and their perceptions of the service.

Process benchmarking

Benchmarking as a tool for identifying areas for improvement was formally developed by Xerox in 1979 and since then it has been widely used across a range of manufacturing and service industry organisations. An exception to this is generally within tourism, where the benchmarking practice has historically been under-utilised, mainly due to a limited awareness of this tool amongst industry practioners.

Pryor (1998) defines benchmarking as 'the process of measuring organisational performance against that of the best in class companies'. It requires a determination as to *how* the best-in-class achieve high performance levels. The results of a benchmarking exercise constitute a basis for setting improvement targets. Thus, through benchmarking, companies discover their strengths and weaknesses and learn how to incorporate the best practices into their own operations. This tool facilitates the transfer of knowledge between organisations, with ideas external to an organisation serving as the platform for internal change (Zairi, 1996).

There are three major types of benchmarking that literature and practice recognise: competitive benchmarking, which focuses mainly on comparing product design and costs; process benchmarking, which is concerned with comparing a particular process; and strategic benchmarking, which is undertaken with a view to creating and implementing a new strategy (Rao *et al.*, 1996). Within the tourism industry the majority of benchmarking exercises undertaken by tourism organisations fall within the competitive benchmarking category, with a particular focus on product features. However, from the operations management perspective, process benchmarking is crucial.

The effectiveness of undertaking a process benchmarking exercise depends on various factors. First, a process benchmarking project team should be established and include a mix of people who have knowledge of benchmarking and legal issues associated with the use of this tool. They should also have knowledge of the process to be benchmarked and understand the requirements of the customers of the process. Second, the project team should be able to appropriately focus the benchmarking topic. The process that will be benchmarked has to be clearly defined with the use of the process flow-mapping technique. Appropriate critical success factors and performance benchmarks need to be set. Third, suitable benchmarking partners should be selected. Such partners do not necessarily have to represent the same industry as long as one of their processes is the same as the process that will be benchmarked and as long as they perform better than the organisation that initiates the benchmarking exercise. Fourth, once relevant data has been collected and the performance gaps identified, the benchmarking team should develop recommendations for improvement. The practice of many organisations that use separate teams for specifying recommendations should be avoided as such an approach frequently results in misinterpretation of the benchmarking results (Rao *et al.*, 1996; Zairi, 1996).

Approaches to enhancing future process performance

Once the diagnosis of the performance of processes has been completed and the areas for quality improvement have been identified, an organisation needs to decide on the type of improvements that will best address any identified weaknesses. Two possible approaches to enhancing future process performance are open to tourism organisations.

First, if the processes require only minor changes, then the Kaizen philosophy for improvement can be adopted. This approach is concerned with the introduction of continual improvements in all areas of business to enhance the quality of the organisation (Evans and Lindsay, 2002). Continuous process improvement requires a commitment to the systematic use of process-control tools (e.g. Ishikawa's seven basic tools).

Second, if the processes are fundamentally flawed, they should be subjected to a complete redesign. Business process redesign (BPR) is a radical step towards improvement and may require fundamental changes in process structures and associated management systems to deliver improvements in performance. BPR involves managers in rethinking their traditional operating methods with a view to designing effective and efficient customer-focused processes. Evidence suggests that many organisations that choose BPR as a means of process improvement have made rapid and marked improvements in both their performance and levels of customer satisfaction (Oakland, 2003).

Many tourism organisations, especially small- and medium-sized enterprises (SMEs), operate traditional processes that do not regularly produce outputs that the tourists require. These processes can be inflexible and they may not be supported by the latest technological developments. In such circumstances, changes to the external environment that are beyond the control of the tourism providers may hit the organisations so hard as to jeopardise their continued existence. BPR offers such organisations an opportunity to create flexible processes that would allow them to switch to other activities if the external environment within which they operate changes.

Performance measurement

Since the early 1990s the use of the SERVQUAL scale, as developed by Parasuraman *et al.* (1988), has dominated the process of measuring service quality in tourism. The SERVQUAL scale has been used to evaluate the levels of consumer satisfaction with certain aspects of service quality and has been deployed in various tourism business contexts including hotels (Knutson *et al.*, 1991; Saleh and Ryan, 1991; Akan, 1995) and historic houses (Frochot and Hughes, 2000).

However, it has been argued that a range of other measures needs to be employed in order to gain a more comprehensive and objective picture of quality levels achieved within organisations (Augustyn and Seakhoa-King, 2004). For example, the European Foundation of Quality Management recommends the use of four groups of measures in evaluating the levels of quality (EFQM, 2000). These groups of measures include customer results, people results, society results and performance measures. The first three groups comprise perception measures and performance indicators, while the fourth comprises performance outcomes and performance indicators. Within the group of customer results, the range of perception measures includes customer satisfaction, overall image, relevance of products, perceived value, and loyalty. Thus measures of consumer satisfaction, that may include the SERVQUAL scale, only partly contribute to the evaluation of the quality levels being achieved within organisations. This is particularly true from an operations management perspective where there is the need not only to ensure conformance to the requirements of both internal and external customers, but also to ensure the effective and efficient performance of operational processes.

Capacity management

The need to ensure an effective and efficient operating performance is especially challenging to tourism organisations given their tendency to experience significant and repeated fluctuations in demand for a product that exists in a moment of time. The essential perishability of the tourism product is evidenced within the airline industry, where an unsold seat represents permanently lost revenue. It is within this context that tourism managers have sought to implement capacity management techniques, which seek to ensure that their organisations operate at optimum capacity while maintaining customer-satisfaction levels. In order to achieve this the first priority is to set in place accurate demand-forecasting measures.

■ Demand-forecasting techniques

Demand-forecasting techniques may be classified as either qualitative or quantitative in nature. Qualitative techniques involve the analysis of background information by selected individuals or groups of individuals, as well as the collation and comparison of their findings. These techniques, which include subjective probability assessments, executive consensus and Delphi techniques, as well as consumer intentions surveys, are judgement based and are often used to produce best- and worst-case scenarios. Qualitative methods tend to be used in instances where there is unreliable or insufficient historical data, where the macroenvironment is experiencing significant change, where major disturbances are expected, or where long-term forecasts are required (Frechtling, 1996).

Quantitative techniques involve some form of mathematical analysis and can be classified as either extrapolative or causal (Frechtling, 2001). The extrapolative methods seek to identify patterns or trends in existing demand data, which are then used as the basis for predicting future demand levels. Causal methods, such as structural econometric models, use 'what if' questions in order to establish cause-and-effect relationships, thereby identifying key determinants of demand. Some of the quantitative approaches, especially the noneconomic systems models, have been criticised for providing simplistic insights, while others including the structural econometric models are highly complex, reliant upon a vast range of data and costly to use.

Capacity planning and management

Once managers have been able to establish the likely future demand for their product, there is a need for them to determine the capacity levels for their facility and then seek either to adjust their product supply in order to meet demand levels, or to introduce measures to match demand to supply. Within the tourism industry most organisations have relatively fixed customer-capacity levels that are determined by a variety of factors including the size of the facility and health and safety requirements. Capacity management within the tourism industry is consequently focused primarily on the manipulation of demand via a range of marketing initiatives, which are addressed in Chapter 6. However, one technique has emerged in recent years which sets demand manipulation within a more operational context and so it is appropriate that yield management is given consideration here.

Yield management

According to Kimes (2000) the ideal environment for the successful application of yield management techniques is one in which:

- capacity is relatively fixed but demand is variable;
- the market can be readily segmented;
- the product is perishable and can be sold in advance of consumption;
- the marginal cost of making the sale is low.

These factors characterised the 1980s airline industry in the United States, where airline operators first introduced yield management techniques as a response to the increasing levels of competition that followed the US Government's deregulation of the domestic air travel industry. The techniques, which were soon adopted by hotel chains, rely on the ability of organisations to accurately forecast likely demand levels from across their range of customer groupings and to implement variable pricing strategies that will maximise both the income from bookings as well as the actual number of bookings. Yield management can therefore be defined as 'a revenue maximization technique which aims to increase net yield through the predicted allocation of available . . . capacity to predetermined market segments at optimal price' (Donaghy *et al.*, 1997a).

Yield management techniques include the *over-booking of capacity* to counter the damaging effects of 'no-show' customers. This approach is normally adopted following a careful assessment of the number of 'no-shows' during an equivalent time period and any miscalculation is likely to result in an excess of demand leading to high levels of customer dissatisfaction as well as the very real potential for adverse publicity. *Differentiated pricing mechanisms* are a second option; these provide variations in prices at particular times to identified target markets as a vehicle for encouraging certain customer groupings and possibly discouraging others. Examples of this include the use of free child places to encourage early booking. *Differentiated product packages* may also be offered to the different customer groupings, these may deliver different service standards partly as a mechanism for justifying the differentiated pricing structures, or they may offer diversified packages at the same or different times as a means of attracting different target groupings.

McMahon-Beattie and Donaghy (2000) have identified a ten-stage process for the successful deployment of a yield management system, which is of generic relevance although nominally oriented towards hotels. The process, as presented in Figure 10.3 recognises the human dynamic that is essential to all successful capacity management systems, by emphasising the need to inform and educate employees via effective training programmes about the purpose and merits of the process. There follows an information-gathering phase, which seeks to identify both demand levels and key market segments. This phase should incorporate both an historical demand analysis and a prediction of future demand levels, which together make use of past booking and enquiry details including booking cancellations, denials (enquirers who could not be accommodated), declines (enquirers who chose not to purchase the product), no-shows (customers who failed to consume the product, i.e. booked a ticket to fly but did not then take the flight, or made a hotel reservation that they then failed to honour) and previously recorded levels of overbooking (Jauncey *et al.*, 1995; McMahon-Beattie and Donaghy, 2000). This information needs to be available for each existing market grouping and should include not only expenditure figures for the core product components, i.e. the flight in the case of airlines and the room in the case of hotels, but also supplementary expenditures on refreshments, etc. (Jones, 1999). Without such information managers will not be able to determine the true value of different market groupings to their organisation. Additional consideration needs to be given to the capacity of the product and the overhead costs associated with each customer grouping, together with the duration of use by customers, the arrival times of customers and the range of acceptable prices that can be charged to the identified market segments at specified times (Kimes, 2000). The link between operational and strategic considerations is then made with optimal segmented capacity levels being established that are aligned to the organisation's strategic objectives. The yield management system is then introduced which offers a differentiated price regime to selected market groupings at designated times. In order to optimise performance, the system includes measures to reduce the time between customers and manage customer arrivals. Many of the budget airlines have been able to reduce the time

---

Figure 10.3   Key stages in a formal yield management system

Stage 1: Personnel
- Develop employee understanding
- Highlight the customer/organisational interface
- Appoint forecasting team/committee
- Collate and analyse customer and market data

Stage 2: Analyse demand
- Identify competitiors and sources of demand
- Define own organisation's strengths and weaknesses
- Predict demand levels and booking patterns
- Constantly monitor external factors

Stage 3: Market segmentation
- Identify existing and potential market
- Segment market (demographic, psychographic, geographic)

Stage 4: Determine optimal customer mix
- Based on volume usage and propensity to spend

Stage 5: Analyse trade-offs
- Extensive calculation of monetary leakages
- Avoid displacing higher spending customers

Stage 6: Establish capacity levels
- Set capacity to meet the demands of the various market segments

Stage 7: Introduce YM system
- Large organisations introduce tailor-made systems
- Smaller organisations adopt off-the-shelf versions that may be derived from large organisations' tailor-made systems

Stage 8: Customer reorientation
- Training comes into practice to achieve the organisation's YM objectives while meeting customers' needs

Stage 9: Operational evaluation
- Review resource allocation
- Evaluate changing patterns of demand
- Identify additional factors which determine demand

Stage 10: Action
- Implement any required changes immediatly

Source: Adapted from McMahon-Beattie and Donaghy (2000)

between customers by reducing the time that their aircraft spend on the ground between flights; this has been achieved by streamlining the product offering, e.g. by removing or reducing the on-board catering services. Customer arrivals can be managed through the establishment of check-in times together with well-publicised strict penalties for those failing to comply with such times. These systems have been widely introduced especially within the airline industry, in spite of the potential for customer dissatisfaction, as they help to minimise the uncertainties associated with late arrivals and 'no-shows' (Barlow, 2004). The next stage is for organisations to manage customers' expectations so as to minimise the likelihood of customer dissatisfaction, while implementing monitoring procedures that facilitate the evaluation of performance against set targets, which may in turn lead to operational adjustments.

Case 10.2   Holiday Inn reservation optimisation (HIRO)

To achieve Holiday Inn's corporate objectives of ensuring that maximum occupancy and revenue are realised in each hotel and that guests, franchises, and internal staff are experiencing the highest level of customer satisfaction, Holiday Inn installed HIRO. The goal of maximising occupancy and revenue means renting as many rooms as possible for the best price that the market will bear. With more than 500,000 rooms in the equation, a yield management optimisation system could increase revenue tremendously.

HIRO, which is similar to American Airlines' SABRE, uses historical and current booking behaviour to analyse room requests for each hotel. The yield management optimisation equation includes seasonal occupancy patterns, local events, weekly cycles and current trends to develop a hurdle price (i.e. the lowest point at which rooms should be booked at that particular hotel). The system predicts full occupancy at hotels and filters out discounted requests. HIRO even uses overbooking to account for cancellations and no-shows. As with any yield management system in the service industry, HIRO helps the hotel manager balance the ability to charge full price for a room and still maintain satisfaction from its loyal customer base.

Source: Leibmann (1995)

Implementing yield management systems

In a survey of three and four star UK hotels undertaken in 1997, 15% of the respondents who claimed to be operating a yield management system were found not to be collecting the data needed to operate such a system (Jones, 1999). This is indicative of a lack of industry understanding of yield management, which is best addressed at an organisational level via training programmes that provide conceptual and practical insights to managers and operational staff (McMahon-Beattie and Donaghy, 2000).

The complexity of yield management systems encourages many organisations to deploy computer-based technology (Jones, 1999), which enables managers quickly to receive a great volume of information that is then used to manage sales on a day-to-day and even hour-by-hour basis. The introduction of such computer-based yield management systems frequently leads to the establishment of integrated management teams (Jones, 1999) that play a central role in the entire ten stage yield management process as presented in Figure 10.3. Moreover, the significance of yield management systems to both the operational and strategic performance of organisations means that the integrated management teams are placed at the centre of the organisation's entire decision-making process. Research undertaken by Donaghy, McMahon-Beattie and McDowell (1997b) has suggested that an organisation's recognition of the importance of such teams is likely to impact upon the management structures being deployed and even the physical working locations of those involved in the management teams. A failure to engage staff at the initial stage of the yield management implementation procedure could mean that such changes are met with resistance from middle managers and operational staff, who may not recognise the need for structural change and may resent the imposition of what could be regarded as complex systems. Strategies to overcome this in addition to effective training programmes may include incentive schemes for sales staff to encourage revenue maximisation (McMahon-Beattie and Donaghy, 2000). Such schemes inevitably require the introduction of effective performance monitoring systems, which may be computer-based and should be used to inform regular reviews of the yield management system at both a strategic and operational level. Through such an approach it should be possible to ensure an effective and efficient operating system, while simultaneously maintaining customer satisfaction levels.

Conclusion

The key priority for operations managers working within tourism organisations is to deliver a product to their customers that provides a balance between meeting customers' requirements and the need for an effective and efficient operating system. Central to achieving high levels of customer satisfaction within the context of effective and efficient tourism operations are two processes: quality management and yield management.

The operations management view of quality management stresses the need for building quality into tourism services through effective and efficient supplier management and process management procedures, which recognise the importance of responding to the needs of both internal and external customers. This requirement represents a particular challenge for tourism organisations that frequently struggle with extreme variations in demand and so there has emerged a focus on capacity management techniques, especially that of yield management.

Fundamental to the success of quality management, capacity management and yield management systems and procedures is a recognition of their role in both strategic and operational decision-making, which in turn requires senior management commitment and support, as well as the active involvement of all employees. Staff training and empowerment are therefore crucial in developing successful quality management and yield management programmes.

Discussion questions

1   In the process of managing quality in tourism organisations, why should the strategy of *prevention* replace the strategy of *detection*?

2   Read Case 10.1 *Westons Cider Company and ISO 9000*, as well as the two articles recommended as further reading for the case study. How did the adoption of the ISO 9000 quality management system benefit the company? Why is it important to include all organisational activities within this system?

3   Define process management and its main component. Why is process management important to tourism organisations?

4   Can yield management potentially be in conflict with the goal of achieving customer satisfaction?

Guided reading

A valuable insight into operations management is provided in the work of Slack, Chambers and Johnston (2004), while Johnston and Clark (2001) focus more explicitly on service operations management.

A helpful overview of quality management and associated systems is provided in the work of Evans and Lindsay (2002), while Williams and Buswell's book (2003) provides an excellent insight into quality management from a tourism perspective. Useful sources that will assist in providing an enhanced understanding of the ISO 9000 family of standards include the ISO website (**www.iso.ch**), while publications that discuss the application of the standard to tourism organisations include those of Augustyn and Pheby (2000) and Augustyn (2002).

The work of Evans and Lindsay (2002), Oakland (2003) and Rao *et al.* (1996) provide a greater understanding of issues relating to process management. Information on quality measures can be found on the website of the EFQM (**www.efqm.org/**).

Finally, an excellent examination of yield management from a tourism perspective is provided in the work of Ingold, McMahon-Beattie and Yeoman (2000), while Yeoman and McMahon-Beattie's book (2004) includes some interesting case studies of yield management systems within tourism organisations.

Recommended websites

EFQM: **www.efqm.org/** .

ISO 9000: **www.iso.ch** .

Juran, J.M. *Quality Control in Service Industries*: **www.juran.com/research/articles/SP7316.html** .

Juran, J.M. *Quality Control of Service*: *The 1974 Japanese Symposium:* **www.juran.com/research/articles/SP7517.html** .

Operations Management Center: **www.mhhe.com/business/opsci/pom** .

The Teachings of Dr. Deming: **deming.org/deminghtml/techings.html** .

Key words

Benchmarking; benchmarks; capacity management; customer; operations management; performance measurement; process; process control; process design; process improvement; process management; product; quality; requirements; yield management.

Bibliography

Akan, P. (1995) Dimensions of service quality: a study of Istanbul, *Managing Service Quality*, 5(6), 39–43.

Augustyn, M.M. (2000) From decline to growth: innovative strategies for small cultural tourism enterprises – Westons Cider case study. *Tourism, Culture and Communication*, 2(3), 153–64.

Augustyn, M.M. (2002) Can Local Tourism Destinations Benefit From Employing the ISO

9000:2000 Quality Management System? in N. Andrews, S. Flanagan and J. Ruddy, (eds) *Tourism Destination Planning*, 330–345. Dublin Institute of Technology, Dublin.

Augustyn, M.M. and Pheby, J.D. (2000) ISO 9000 and performance of small tourism enterprises: a focus on Westons Cider company, *Managing Service Quality*, 10(6), 374–388.

Augustyn, M.M. and Seakhoa-King, A. (2004) Is the SERVQUAL scale an adequate measure of quality in leisure, tourism and hospitality? *Advances in Hospitality and Leisure*, 1(1).

Barlow, G. (2004) easyJet: an airline that changed our flying habits? in I. Yeoman and U. McMahon-Beattie, (eds) *Revenue Management and Pricing: Case Studies and Applications*, 9–23. Thomson Learning, London.

Bennett, D., Lewis, C. and Oakley, M. (1988) *Operations Management*. Philip Allan, London.

Bicheno, J. and Elliott, B.B. (1997) *Operations Management. An Active Learning Approach*. Blackwell Learning, Oxford.

Certo, S.C. (2000) *Modern Management*, 8th edn. Prentice Hall, New Jersey.

Donaghy, K. and McMahon, U. (1995) Yield management – a marketing perspective. *International Journal of Vacation Marketing*, 2(1), 55–62.

Donaghy, K., McMahon-Beattie, U. and McDowell, D. (1997a) Yield management practices, in I. Yeoman, and A. Ingold (eds) *Yield Management: Strategies for Service Industries*. Cassell, London.

Donaghy, K., McMahon-Beattie, U. and McDowell, D. (1997b) Implementing yield management: lessons from the hotel sector, *International Journal of Contemporary Hospitality Management*, 9/2, 50–54.

EFQM (2000) *The EFQM Excellence Model*. **www.efqm.org/** .

Evans, J.R. and Lindsay, W.M. (2002) *The Management and Control of Quality*, 5th edn. South-Western, Cincinnati, OH.

Fitzsimmons, J.A. and Fitzsimmons, M.J. (2001) *Service Management: Operations, Strategy and Information Technology*, 3rd edn. McGraw-Hill Higher Education, New York.

Frechtling, D.C. (1996) *Practical Tourism Forecasting*. Butterworth-Heinemann, Oxford.

Frechtling, D.C. (2001) *Forecasting Tourism Demand: Methods and Strategies*. Butterworth-Heinemann, Oxford.

Frochot, I. and Hughes, H. (2000) HISTOQUAL: The development of a historic houses assessment scale, *Tourism Management*, 21, 157–167.

Hill, T. (2005) *Operations Management. Strategic Context and Managerial Analysis*. Macmillan Press, Basingstoke.

Ho, S.K. (1995) *TQM: An Integrated Approach. Implementing Total Quality Through Japanese 5-S and ISO 9000*. Kogan Page, London.

Ingold, A., McMahon-Beattie, U. and Yeoman, I. (2000) (eds) *Yield Management*, 2nd edn. Continuum, London.

ISO (1999) *Introduction*. **www.iso.ch/infoe/intro.htm** .

ISO (2000a) *Quality Management Systems – Fundamentals and Vocabulary*. ISO, Geneva.

ISO (2000b) *Quality Management Systems – Requirements*. ISO, Geneva.

James, P. (1996) *Total Quality Management: An Introductory Text*. Prentice Hall, Hemel Hempstead.

Jauncey, S., Mitchell, I. and Slamet, P. (1995) The meaning and management of yield in hotels, *International Journal of Contemporary Hospitality Management*, 7(4), 23–26.

Johnston, R. and Clark, G. (2001) *Service Operations Management*. Pearson Education, Harlow.

Jones, P. (1999) Yield management in UK hotels: a systems analysis, *Journal of the Operational Research Society*, 50, 1111–1119.

Kanji, G.K. and Asher, M. (1996) *100 Methods for Total Quality Management*. Sage Publications, London.

Kimes, S. (2000) A Strategic Approach to Yield Management, in A. Ingold, U. McMahon-Beattie and I. Yeoman (eds) *Yield Management*, 2nd edn, 3–14. Continuum, London.

Knutson, B., Stevens, P., Wullaert, C. and Patton, M. (1991) LODGSERV: A service quality index for the lodging industry, *Hospitality Research Journal*, 14(7): 277–284.

Krajewski, L.J. and Ritzman, L.P. (1999) *Operations Management Strategy and Analysis*, 5th edn. Addison-Wesley Longman, Reading, MA.

Leibmann, L. (1995) Holiday Inn Maximises Profitability with a Complex Network Infrastructure, *LAN Magazine*, June, vol. 10, no. 6, 123, quoted in Fitzsimmons and Fitzsimmons (2001), 385.

McMahon-Beattie, U. and Donaghy, K. (2000) Yield Management Practices, in A. Ingold, U. McMahon-Beattie and I. Yeoman (eds) *Yield Management*, 2nd edn, 233–255. Continuum, London.

Oakland, J.S. (2003) *Total Quality Management. Text with Cases*, 3rd edn. Butterworth-Heinemann, Oxford.

Parasuraman, P.A., Zeithaml, V.A. and Berry, L.L. (1985) A conceptual model of service quality and its implications for future research, *Journal of Marketing*, 49 (Fall), 41–50.

Parasuraman, A., Zeithaml, V.A. and Berry, L.L. (1988) SERVQUAL: a multiple item scale for measuring consumer perceptions of service quality, *Journal of Retailing*, 64(1), 14–40.

Pryor, L.S. (1998) Benchmarking: a self-improvement strategy, *Journal of Business Strategy*, Nov/Dec, 28–32.

Rao, A., Carr, L.P., Dambolena, I., Kopp, R.J., Martin, J., Rafii, F. and Schlesinger, P.F. (1996) *Total Quality Management: A Cross Functional Perspective*. John Wiley & Sons, New York.

Saleh, F. and Ryan C. (1991) Analyzing service quality in the hospitality industry using the SERVQUAL model, *The Services Industry Journal*, 11(3), 324–343.

Slack, N., Chambers, S. and Johnston, R. (2004) *Operations Management*, 4th edn. Pearson Education Ltd, Harlow.

Walton, M. (1989) *The Deming Management Method*. Mercury Books, London.

Williams, C. and Buswell, J. (2003) *Service Quality in Leisure and Tourism*. CAB International, Wallingford.

Wright, J.N. (1999) *The Management of Service Operations*. Continuum, London.

Yeoman, I. and McMahon-Beattie, U. (2004) (eds) *Revenue Management and Pricing: Case Studies and Applications*. Thomson Learning, London.

Zairi, M. (1996) *Benchmarking for Best Practice. Continuous Learning Through Sustainable Innovation*. Butterworth-Heinemann, Oxford.

Chapter 11

Information technology and management information systems in tourism

Dimitrios Buhalis, University of Surrey and Carlos Costa, Universidade de Aveiro

Learning outcomes

On completion of this chapter the reader should be able to:

- appreciate the effects of information technology on tourism;
- understand the most significant information communication technologies (ICTs) in tourism;
- explore ICT applications and identify technological enablers for the tourism industry;
- understand the issue of technological convergence in the tourism field;
- identify critical strategic decisions and directions for tourism organisations empowered by ICTs;
- explore the sources of competitiveness for tourism organisations and explore how technology affects them.

Overview

This chapter begins by demonstrating that tourism and information communication technologies (ICTs) have a symbiotic and dynamic interaction. ICTs are critical for both tactical and strategic tourism business management and without ICTs the tourism industry could not function at the scale and reach that it currently has. The chapter demonstrates the ICT needs and requirements of tourism business and identifies what are the most critical functions for technology. It identifies the hardware, software and network currently used in tourism businesses and demonstrates that there is a certain degree of convergence already evident. Computer Reservation Systems (CRSs) and Global Distribution Systems (GDSs) are presented as the backbone of tourism distribution and management. In addition the internet and its contribution to tourism businesses are examined. Finally, the chapter concludes that ICTs can be critical for tourism businesses to achieve strategic advantage in the global marketplace.

Introduction: eTourism – ICTs and tourism dynamic interaction

Information technology has revolutionised both the global economy and tourism management. The development of powerful personal computing systems in the 1980s provided individuals with reliable, powerful and affordable machines that improved personal effectiveness. Mainframes or mini-computers supported corporations in automating a number of internal processes and in expanding their operational capacity. The automated industrial production enabled a greater total output as well as better planning and quality control. This led to the manufacturing of sufficient products to cover the increasing demand, on top of the development of new standardised and consistent commodities, which could be traded at a global level. Productivity was increased dramatically by taking advantage of the emerging tools and gradually workers were able to concentrate on 'lighter' but more intelligent work, leaving hard labour to machinery. The proliferation of the internet in the 1990s enabled the networking of computers globally and access to multimedia information and knowledge sources. As a result, the way we live and work in most societies around the globe was significantly altered. As a whole range of organisational capabilities changed rapidly during the technological revolution, organisations were forced to re-engineer their processes in order to take advantage of the new potentials and improve their competitiveness (Buhalis, 2003).

Information Technology (IT) is one of the external environment elements for tourism, travel and hospitality, although in recent years technological developments have supported tourism innovation and vice versa. ICTs have become an imperative partner and they increasingly offer the interface between consumers and suppliers globally. Tourism and technology therefore go hand in hand together. The tourism system is inevitably influenced by the new business environment created by the diffusion of ICTs. Poon (1993) has argued 'Tourism is a very information intensive activity. In few other areas of activity are the generation, gathering, processing, application and communication of information as important for day-to-day operations as they are for the travel and tourism industry'. Communications and information transmission tools are indispensable to the marketing of the tourism industry (Sheldon, 1997).

Tourism business ICT needs and requirements

Tourism businesses need to enhance their competitiveness by employing the emerging tools and re-engineering all processes. Tourism businesses need to become more flexible, more efficient and quicker in responding to consumer requests. The ICT revolution offers a variety of tools and mechanisms that allow innovative and dynamic players to take advantage and strengthen their competitiveness.

The tourism industry has long been regarded as a labour-intensive industry following traditional processes and practices. The continuous development of ICTs during the last decade has had profound implications for the whole tourism industry. Innovative ICTs provide the tools and enable the evolution of tourism demand and supply. Technology is often used for the operational management of tourism businesses (O'Connor, 1999; Inkpen, 1998; Marcussen, 1999a, 1999b). ICTs incorporate not only software, hardware and netware but also information, management and telecommunication systems to enable the processing and flow of tourism information within and between organisations. The use of ICTs in tourism businesses digitises all processes and value chains in the tourism, travel, hospitality and catering industries. All business functions – sales and marketing, finance and accounting, human resource management, procurement, research and development, and production, as well as strategy and planning for all sectors of the tourism industry, including tourism, travel, transport, leisure, hospitality, principals, intermediaries and public sector organisations – are influenced by the emerging capabilities of ICTs.

At the tactical level, this includes e-commerce and applies ICTs for maximising the efficiency and effectiveness of the tourism organisation. In addition to data processing and automation requirements, technological innovations enable the use of ICTs for strategic and tactical management and purposes. ICTs enable tourism organisations to have a global presence as well as to formulate partnerships with organisations around the world in an efficient and cost-effective manner. Constant interactivity with consumers and partners supports flexible and competitive pricing, which can maximise the yield of enterprises. Monitoring sales by the minute allows marketers to undertake the appropriate adjustments to the product and price or/and to initiate promotional campaigns in order to maximise sales. ICTs can also assist the reduction of operation and communication costs. In addition, ICTs offer unique opportunities for research and development, which enable the industry to provide specialised products to niche markets, thus achieving competitive advantage through differentiation.

Case 11.1   Fidelio's OPERA Hotel Property Management System

Fidelio is one of the leading international systems integrators for the hospitality industries, changing the way hotels computerise and operate. Fidelio allows hotels and chains of any size and type, restaurants, cruise ships and catering and conference operations to computerise their operations and to integrate major industry software products through analysing individual requirements and appreciating their uniqueness. The Fidelio OPERA Enterprise Solution is a fully integrated suite of products consisting of modules that can be easily added or expanded allowing effective and easy deployment from smaller operations to global, multi-branded hotel chain environments. The OPERA Property Management System (PMS) is designed to scale according to the requirements of any size hotel or hotel chain. The OPERA Back Office provides a powerful financial software suite that empowers hotels with a fully integrated, flexible financial and e-business solution. The OPERA Reservation System (ORS) manages the hotel inventory efficiently as it is integrated with the OPERA Property Management System and OPERA Sales and Catering System. The system emulates traditional CRS functionality, while at the same time integrating the bold new technologies shared in the OPERA Enterprise Solution, including system access via web client or any Java-enabled browser. With the power of the internet, ORS is easily deployable and globally accessible. The OPERA Revenue Management System provides both property-based and centralised yield management and is interfaced with the OPERA Sales and Catering System to analyse the value of particular group business and maximise revenue. The Customer Information System collects and manages guest, travel agent, source, group, and company profile information from designated hotel properties in a centralised database. OPERA can be deployed in any size environment, from a single property with just Front Office to a large, full-service hotel with Sales & Marketing, Catering, Revenue Management, Quality Management, Back Office, and Materials Management. In addition, the OPERA Enterprise Solution offers products for a hotel chains corporate office, including a Central Reservations System for both centralised guestroom and function space sales, and an Enterprise Information System, the Customer Relationship Management (CRM) package specifically designed for the hotel industry. Its software is adaptable to changing business requirements and integrates both the ongoing technological developments of industry standard computer and software systems and the organisational change experienced. All of these systems are interrelated and interconnected, enabling hotels to use the system internally (intranet), externally with partners (extranet) and as a window to the world (internet).

For more information see **www.fidelio.com**

Discussion questions

1 Examine the relationship of PMSs with Yield Management
2 Discuss why fully interoperable PMSs are critical for eCommerce
3 Explain how PMSs can embrace Intranet Technologies

At the strategic level, eTourism revolutionises all business processes – the entire value chain as well as the strategic relationships of tourism organisations with all their stakeholders (Buhalis, 2003). As with other industries, ICT's penetration into tourism should provide strategic tools for the networking of the industry, for adding value to products and for enabling organisations to interact with all stakeholders in a profitable way. In addition, ICTs can improve the managerial processes in order to ameliorate control and decision-making procedures, and to support enterprises to react efficiently to environmental changes and consumer behaviour trends. Increasingly ICTs play a critical role in customer relationship management as they enable organisations to interact with customers and continuously alter their product for meeting and exceeding customer expectations. Managing customer relationships on a continuous (365/24) and global basis is of paramount importance for the successful tourism organisation of the future. The strategic dimension gradually propels the business process re-engineering of tourism businesses, changing all operational and strategic processes. Innovative ICTs therefore transform the best operational practices and provide opportunities for business expansion in all geographical, marketing, and operational senses.

Case 11.2   The Finnish Tourist Board infostructure

ICT is used as an integral part of its operations by the Finnish Tourist Board (FTB). FTB has pioneered the use of the internet for developing a network for managing tourism in Finland as well as a tool for cross-industry and coordination. The system includes three main elements:

- MIS: the FTB's Market Information System offers a data management and distribution system. Launched in 1992 and updated in 1997, this is the internal system for FTB and is distributed to all its offices internationally. The system allows FTB staff to manage and organise sales and marketing campaigns, to coordinate their marketing and branding activities, as well as to distribute documents and administrate the tourism board globally. Access is also allowed to other professionals.
- RELIS: the Research, Library and Information Service provides the backbone to the national travel research and product documentation. The service connects the travel industry to research and education organisations.
- PROMIS: the national database of Finnish travel products and services provides a wide range of up-to-date information on travel products, services and contact information. External PROMIS partners provide and update data and include regional and city tourism organisations and other tourism professionals. Most of the information and images are copyright free and can be used for brochures and other promotional campaigns. The professional Marketing Information Service offers a tourism database covering the whole of Finland.

In summer 2000, services for the tourist industry were improved considerably by opening an internet connection to the PROMIS information system, which the FTB has developed together with the industry. The number of cooperation partners in the PROMIS information system exceeded 130 at the end of the year. The amount of information in the PROMIS system consequently rose by over 40% from spring to autumn, to more than 5000 tourist products. Over 20 new information producers joined the system. Cooperation partners can now add and update information online. Internet service was expanded, with eight new languages being added to the site. At the end of the year the site presented tailored pages on Finland as a tourist destination in thirteen languages. Product information in the PROMIS system was used increasingly in brochures and information is also available on the internet. Christmas pages were also produced, along with extranet pages for participants in the Savotta Travel Market and a site for arranging sales events complete with registration procedures. During the year the structure and content of traditional marketing tools were developed intensely. Development focused especially on electronic marketing tools (web and wap). FTB aims for all its information to be accessible via internet protocol systems for its employees (intranet), partners (extranet) and the general public (internet).

Source: Based on WTO (1999 and 2001) and Finnish Tourism Board (**www.mek.fi**)

Discussion questions

4   What will be the future role of destination management organisations (DMOs)?
5   How will ICTs be critical in allowing them to achieve this role?
6   Do DMOs have to develop destination management systems or will the industry portals suffice?

Information communication technologies used in tourism businesses

The tourism industry uses the full range of ICTs to facilitate its operations and management and to facilitate the value system (Werthner and Klein, 1999). As demonstrated in Table 11.1 these include a combination of:

- hardware;
- software and computer applications;
- communications (including telecommunications) and networking.

Table 11.1	Information technologies used in tourism
Hardware	
Computer systems	Mainframes, mini-computers and personal computers (PCs)
	Central processing unit (CPU)
	Input devices (keyboards, mouses, touch screens)
	Storage devices such as hard disks, CD-ROMs and magnetic tapes
	Output devices, such as display terminals, printers and audio output
Mobile devices	Mobile phones
	Personal digital assistants (PDAs)
	Tablet computers
Software	
Standard software	Operating systems such as Windows and UNIX, programming languages with graphical programming tools, and databases used in tourism for generic business functions
Applications	Business applications supporting human and business functions, such as property management systems or computer reservation systems. These include expert systems and artificial intelligence
Software process	The process of designing and implement software, software engineering, such as workflow procedures, Computer Supported Cooperative Work (CSCW)
System architectures and networks	Worldwide distributed systems accessible from remote locations such as the internet with its TPC/IP protocol. These support extranets and internet representations
Media	Handling of text, graphics, sound and video in a comprehensive way. They enable the development of multimedia presentations
User interfaces	Development from character-oriented terminals to window-based and graphical user interfaces (GUI). Virtual-reality applications enable users to be part of the digital world
Communications and telecommunications	
Telecommunications	Telephone
	Mobile communications such as citizens' band (CB) communications, bleepers, pagers and message pagers
Communications	Telex
	Telefax
	Teletext
	Videotext
	Electronic data interchange (EDI)
	Integrated services digital networks (ISDN)
	Digital subscriber lines (DSLs or IDSL or HDSL)
Computer networks	
Inter- and intra-organisational networking	Local area networks (LAN)
	Wide area networks (WAN)
	Metropolitan area networks

Table 11.1	Continued
Internet protocol based networks	Internet
	Intranets
	Extranets

Source: Based on Werthner and Klein (1999), Beekman (2001), Laudon and Laudon (2002)

Technological solutions are normally incorporated to increase efficiency and reduce the cost and time required for undertaking particular activities and processes. Based on the technologies given in Table 11.1 a wide range of information technologies applications are used in the tourism and hospitality industries, as illustrated in Table 11.2. Although each of these systems may be standing alone, it is their integration to a comprehensive information management system that can maximise their operational effectiveness and enable them to contribute to the organisational strategic competitiveness.

Table 11.2	Information technology systems and applications used in tourism

- Internet/intranets/extranets
- Office automation, reservation, accounting, payroll and procurement management applications
- Internal management tools such as management support systems, decision support systems and management information systems
- Tailor-made internal management applications
- Databases and knowledge management systems
- Networks with partners for regular transactions (EDI or extranets)
- Networking and open distribution of products through the internet
- Computer reservation systems (CRSs)
- Global distribution systems (GDSs) (e.g. Galileo, SABRE, Amadeus, Worldspan)
- Switch applications for hospitality organisations (e.g. THISCO and WIZCOM)
- Destination management systems (DMSs)
- Internet-based travel intermediaries (e.g. Expedia.com, Travelocity.com, Preview Travel, Priceline.com, etc.)
- Wireless/mobile/WAP based reservation systems
- Traditional distribution technologies supporting automated systems (e.g. Videotext)
- Interactive digital television (IDTV)
- Kiosks and touch screen terminals

Source: Buhalis (2003); O'Connor (1999)

Traditionally technological solutions have been used as standalone entities and until recently a fairly low level of technological integration was evident. However, the use of ICTs in tourism and hospitality has been pervasive as information is essential for both the day-to-day operations and the strategic management of tourism. As demonstrated in Table 11.3, technology supports vital everyday functions and enables organisations to communicate and cooperate with other tourism and hospitality enterprises, their consumers as well as their partners and suppliers.

These functions are not only part of the core business of the organisation but also inform strategic considerations as they determine competitiveness and the ability to grow. It is evident therefore that the entire range of business functions has been changed dramatically as a result of the ICT revolution.

Table 11.3	Critical tourism and hospitality functions supported by ICTs

- Front office: reservations, check-in, payments
- Back office: accounting, payroll, human resources management, marketing
- Customer entertainment and service
- Communication with consumers and partners
- Marketing research and industrial espionage
- Reaction and management of unexpected events
- Flexible and dynamic pricing through yield management
- Differentiation and personalisation of products
- Monitoring performance indicators and building feedback mechanisms
- Control of business processes and personnel

Computer Reservation Systems (CRSs) and Global Distribution Systems (GDSs) as the backbone of tourism distribution

The rapid growth of both tourism demand and supply in the last decades has demonstrated that the industry could only be managed by powerful computerised systems. CRSs are often used as an umbrella term, which includes the entire variety of systems used. Various CRS categories and types will be examined. CRSs are essentially computerised systems which assist tourism enterprises with handling and distributing their inventories profitably. They normally use mainframes and extensive networks to support many remote terminals. CRSs are normally operated by tourist producers such as airlines, hotels and tour operators and are distributed nationally or globally, via computerised or videotext systems. The instant update of the information and the ability to provide specific information and support reservation/confirmation/purchase of a wide range of tourism products are the greatest advantages of a CRS. However, the installation and usage costs, lack of user-friendliness and bias in favour of their vendors are significant disadvantages. CRSs originally appeared in the early 1960s, aiming to offer airlines an efficient tool for handling and managing inventory. Airlines were the pioneers to introduce this technology, as they replaced their manual booking systems with electronic databases. Soon, international hotel chains and tour operators realised the potential and followed by developing centralised information and reservation systems. CRSs can provide important strategic tools for tourism enterprises, while they can also form autonomous strategic business units (SBUs) and act as a new independent tourism distribution industry (Sheldon, 1997).

Since the 1980s, airline CRSs have experienced a great expansion, which affects almost all tourism enterprises. Airline CRSs emerged to become Global Distribution Systems (GDSs), incorporating a comprehensive range of services and products and providing a global distribution infostructure for the entire industry. As demonstrated in Table 11.4 the need for GDSs arises from both the demand and supply sides as well as from the expansion of the tourism industry in the last decades. CRSs and GDSs were the most important facilitators of tourism industry changes until the arrival of the internet, as they provided a comprehensive travel marketing and distribution system and were often called 'travel supermarkets' (Go, 1992).

GDSs were utilised to facilitate and manage the drastic expansion of tourism enterprises and destinations globally. GDSs comprise the backbone of the tourism industry as they connect the vast majority of the tourism suppliers with the travel trade and tourism intermediaries. They enable immediate itinerary building and reservation confirmations

Table 11.4   Drivers which have supported the use of CRSs and GDSs as part of tourism and hospitality globalisation

Cost drivers	Market drivers
• Increase efficiency	• Satisfy sophisticated demand
• Low distribution cost	• Flexibility in time of operation
• Low communication cost	• Support specialisation and differentiation
• Low labour cost	• Provide last-minute deals
• Minimisation of waste factor	• Accurate information
• Facilitator of flexible pricing	• Support relationship marketing strategies for frequent flyers/guests
	• Quick reaction to demand fluctuation
	• Multiple/integrated products
	• Yield management
	• Corporate intelligence
	• Marketing research
Government and regulatory drivers	**Competitive drivers**
• Deregulation	• Managing networks of enterprises
• Liberalisation	• Value-added skill building
• Government support	• Flexibility
	• Knowledge acquisition
	• Strategic tool
	• Barrier to entry

Source: Adapted from Go (1992). Reprinted from *Tourism Management*, vol. 13, no. 1, Go, F., 'The role of computerised reservation systems in the hospitality industry', pp. 22–26, Copyright 1992, with permission from Elsevier.

while offering a comprehensive mechanism for commission settling and legal documentation. Therefore GDSs are often characterised as the 'circulation system' of the tourism product in the international market. Table 11.5 demonstrates the main GDS benefits for different stakeholders.

Table 11.5   GDS benefits for different stakeholders

Consumers	Tourism suppliers	Travel trade intermediaries
• Accurate, timely and relevant information access transparent and easy to compare information	• Inventory control	• Support quick and firm responses
	• Demand forecasting and management	• Make tourism products accessible
• Immediate confirmation of bookings	• Capacity manage	• Reliable, comprehensive, adequate and accurate information
• Speedy reservation documentation	• Inventory distribution	
	• Expansion of business	• Reduce communication/ reservation costs
• Information on attractions and travel formalities	• Inexpensive communication with partners and distributors	• Facilitate commission payments
	• Promotional tool	• Printing documents and information for consumer
	• Flexible pricing	
	• Facilitate commission payments	
	• Tool for capacity alterations	
	• Reduction of distribution and communication costs	
	• Tool for managerial information	

The internet and tourism business

The rapid development of the internet in the late 1990s revolutionised the tourism industry in general. The sheer growth of e-commerce and consumer acceptance means that companies which do not embrace this new way of doing things will be left out in the cold. Consumers who cannot find their favourite company on the internet will simply go somewhere else. Organisations can raise a number of key benefits by adopting an enterprise-wide internet and e-commerce strategy. These benefits can be classified as: growth, protection, differentiation, management of change and developing trust. It is critical to integrate online tools and strategies with the offline world though and particularly to re-engineer all processes and practices in order to maximise benefits. Synergies between functions, processes and practices can enable organisations to redesign their value-added chain and enhance their competitiveness.

Implications are evident in the distribution of products and services, while revolutionary methods of interactivity between producers and consumers are initiated. Information, speed and interactivity become part of the core product for all enterprises worldwide and their competitiveness will be assessed according to their ability to outperform both traditional competitors and newcomers. The internet enables business to deliver real-time information to the point of customer contact without any regard for geographical boundaries. This frequently reduces the buying cycle and improves the time-to-market of new products and services. As these developments are extremely dynamic, strategic planners need constantly to follow the major trends in the new environment and assess how they can benefit from the new opportunities emerging (Turban *et al.*, 2002; Porter, 2001).

In tourism, the internet instantly bridged the gap between consumers and businesses enabling interactive communication and trade. The proliferation of e-commerce enabled electronic trading, both from enterprises to consumers (B2C) and perhaps more importantly between businesses (B2B). It also enabled consumer-to-consumer (C2C) services and communities to emerge providing a wide range of tourism information services online. Not only did it enable tourism businesses to increase their reach but also intensified online trading and globalised the market of all types of products and services.

B2C transactions incorporate the trading and delivery of commodities and services to consumers as well as the entire support information and mechanisms required for these transactions. This category includes the ability of consumers to search for information online and to make reservations for tourism products and services. A number of tourism businesses took advantage of the ability to communicate directly with consumers and developed comprehensive mechanisms to serve customers directly, disintermediating travel intermediaries. Perhaps the most successful examples of these tourism organisations are low-cost airlines, such as Southwest, Ryanair and easyJet. No-frill or low-cost carriers emerged in the 1990s primarily for low-budget, independent, leisure travellers. They provide a fairly limited service on-board. No-frill airlines normally fly national and short-haul international routes, with a high percentage of both leisure and business travellers. Most of their traffic is based on simple A-to-B itineraries. Therefore, being able to communicate with their clientele directly, reducing commission fees and enabling consumers to purchase their products, there and then, were critical for their business models. As demonstrated in Case 11.3 by the end of 2001 more than 90% of easyJet's seats were booked online on the internet.

Case 11.3   easyJet online

easyJet in the UK is one of the internet pioneers and has capitalised fully on the potential. Stelios Haji-Ioannou was persuaded to invest an initial £15,000 on the internet and monitored the growth of the bookings to the dedicated telephone number. Having seen the increasing number of bookings taken on that particular number he was persuaded to invest in e-commerce and to develop the transaction side of the site. The airline sold its first seat through the internet in April 1998. In 1998, easyJet sold 13,000 seats via the internet in 24 hours following a campaign in *The Times* newspaper and for most of the year it achieved 10% of its bookings electronically. In just three-and-a-half years it reached 12 million seats sold, selling almost 90% of all its inventory through its website by September 2001. The airline uses the 'web's favourite airline' phrase to promote its own online offering. Booking online is quick, easy and secure and the airline offers a £5 discount for passengers booking online.

Online sales have seen an impressive growth as easyJet now sells around 95% of its tickets online, reinforcing its position as the 'web's favourite airline'. This has been acheived by the following initiatives:

- easyJet is the first low-cost airline to offer customers the opportunity to view their bookings online, and make flight transfers and name changes online for a transfer fee;
- passengers booking online receive a discount of £5.00 for each leg of a journey. They can also request duplicate confirmation emails;
- any easyJet promotions are exclusive to the internet;
- the best fares are first available to those who book via the internet.

For more information see **http//www.easyJet.com/EN/About/Information/Inforpack_internet.html**

Tourism has always been a complex industry that is based on partnership between individual organisations within a loosely defined value system. The distribution channel of tourism includes a number of distributors, including travel agencies, tour operators, and incoming handling agencies, that have traditionally been responsible for putting together tour packages and distributing them at their national markets (Buhalis and Laws, 2001). These linkages have traditionally been facilitated by manual systems and processes, which, although robust, often slow down the system and allow minimum flexibility. Therefore, B2B internet trade enabled many tourism businesses to refocus their operations and to expand their business models. B2B transactions include both trading between producers and intermediaries and also transactions between producers towards the final production of a product. In this case, the internet is used to add value and to support the functions at each stage of the value chain before the final product or service reaches the consumer. Although B2B e-commerce transactions have a lower profit margin, it is normally the volume of trading and the relatively low level of information and support required that make them profitable and desirable for organisations. The latter type of transaction is, in fact, the fastest growing section of the internet and generates a considerable amount of trade (Turban *et al.*, 2002).

Hospitality organisations have benefited dramatically from B2B trade as intermediaries have been able to collaborate in exchanging bed stock and enhancing the overall supply. Hotel aggregators and intermediaries such as Worldres.com, Active hotels, Hotels.com, Octapustravel.com and Pegasus benefit by developing B2B networks backwards (with hospitality suppliers) and forwards (with distributors such as online travel agencies and portals). This enables them to increase their customer reach and at the same time to support their hospitality suppliers in the global marketplace.

The electronic-business revolution gathers momentum everyday and transforms communication, collaboration and commerce. E-business replaces some of the offline business transactions, but more importantly it enhances the total transaction volume as both organisations and consumers take advantage of the new tools to purchase products and services that many were unable to purchase before. Although the internet is

Case 11.4	WorldRes.com the hotel reservation network

Built specifically for the internet, WorldRes uses the latest technology to provide a cost-effective alternative to hotel reservation services that rely on the Global Distribution System (GDS) and other legacy systems. WorldRes offers comprehensive property pages with photos, detailed information, and real-time, confirmed reservation capabilities and empowers SMTEs to achieve a presence – including real-time reservation capabilities – on all applicable websites and call centres in WorldRes' international partner network. With just a PC and internet access, any property can join WorldRes – from independent one-room B&Bs to international hotel chains. WorldRes offers an effective, low-cost way to market and sell accommodations via the internet.

There are no costs for hotels to join the system but WorldRes charges a 10% commission/transaction fee for each reservation made via a WorldRes partner site and a 4% commission for a reservation made via the hotel's own website. The system has more than 20,000 member properties and over 2000 distribution partner websites and call centres through which reservations are made. Membership in WorldRes is non-exclusive so properties that already participate in other online marketing and distribution services can also join WorldRes.

As key distribution points, WorldRes also owns the consumer travel website, PlacesToStay.com, and operates a wholly owned subsidiary, BedandBreakfast.com, the leading supplier of information about B&Bs. Therefore WorldRes provides a cost-effective way for all properties to create a worldwide internet sales and marketing strategy, or to supplement an existing one.

For distribution partners, WorldRes offers rich content on a range of unique properties, plus a share of revenues generated by room reservations that are made through partner websites and call centres. WorldRes is a typical example of B2B organisations that emerged to take advantage of the internet and to reintermediate the tourism system.

For more information see **www.WorldRes.com**

more suitable for trading services, since they do not require the transportation of products, it is increasingly evident that no organisation can escape its impacts. To the degree that producers develop their presence in the global marketplace and offer their products in favourable terms in comparison with intermediaries, they will be able to attract consumers and sell directly, saving commissions and distribution costs. On the other hand, traditional retailers and intermediaries (e.g. Thomas Cook) as well as electronically-empowered newcomers (e.g. Expedia.com) fight back to increase their global market share. They develop their presence in the electronic marketplace by adding value to the needs of the customer, by providing a trusted one-stop-shop, by attracting better deals from producers due to the volume of their business, and by using information collected for marketing research and promotion. Only organisations that have a clear and valuable business proposition and offer value on top of an easy and accessible service using all possible platforms will be able to survive and grow in the future. Expedia.com, marriott.com and easyJet.com are some of the brighter examples of using the internet strategically to increase market share and to interact profitably with clients. These companies clearly offer value to the customer, have efficient web pages and achieve 'e-Fulfilment', i.e. deliver what they set to do in a consistent and hassle-free manner.

Conclusion: using ICTs for tourism businesses' strategic advantage

The emerging ICT developments have direct impacts on the competitiveness of enterprises, as they determine the two fundamental roots to competitive advantage, i.e. differentiation and cost advantage. On the one hand, ICTs enable tourism businesses to differentiate and specialise their products to each consumer. By unwrapping the tourism product and by enabling consumers to put together all the elements for their individual needs, ICTs offer the opportunity to target the market segment of one, i.e. each individual customer. This is only possible because ICTs support flexible and responsive value-added chains and empower consumers to repackage products through endless combinations. On the other hand, ICTs become instrumental to cost management in the industry and particularly for the distribution and promotion costs. Organisations around the world have reduced their costs by reducing commission to intermediaries, whether by trading directly from their web page, by paying lower distribution fees to electronic intermediaries, or by cutting commission levels and fees. In addition, redesigning processes and eliminating repetitive tasks reduced labour costs and increased efficiency (Buhalis, 1998).

As the vast majority of the wealthy people in the Western world are cash-rich and time-poor a new source of competitive advantage is emerging. Perhaps more importantly for tourism, ICTs can support value for time and generate time-related competitive advantages. Technology assists organisations to share information internally and with partners rapidly. Hence it maximises their efficiency and their ability to interact constantly with consumers and tourism suppliers. Consumers can interact, trade and communicate with tourism businesses from their office or home using the internet, on a 24-hour, 365-day-a-year basis. Instant confirmation and purchasing means that consumers can also maximise their own efficiency, and as a result, appreciate the competitive advantage of organisations based on time. Increasingly consumers will be able to interact through mobile devices and interactive digital television, developing their capabilities further. Timely and instant connectivity through simple equipment and interfaces will therefore be critical for achieving time-competitive advantage (Puhretmair *et al.*, 2001; Zipf and Malaka, 2001).

The rapid increase of the reliability, speed and capacity of ICTs, in combination with the decrease of their cost, propels tourism business enterprises to adapt and use these new organisational tools heavily. Innovative organisations throughout the industry, such as easyJet, Marriott Hotels and the Tyrolean Tourism Board, have already strengthened their competitiveness, increased their market share and enhanced their position by using advanced ICTs and by driving their sector towards a higher level of ICT utilisation. However, tourism organisations that fail to incorporate the new tools in their strategic and operational management will increasingly be left behind and will lose market share, jeopardising their future prosperity. The paradigm shift experienced illustrates that only dynamic and innovative organisations will be able to survive in the future.

Guided reading

The following books are suggested for further reading:

- Buhalis, D. (2003) *eTourism: information technology for strategic tourism management*, Pearson (Financial Times/Prentice Hall), London, for comprehensive coverage of eTourism from a strategic perspective.
- Werthner, H. and Klein, S. (1999) *Information Technology and Tourism – A challenging relationship*, Springer, New York, for comprehensive coverage of eTourism from a technology and management techniques perspective.
- Sheldon, P. (1997) *Information Technologies for Tourism*, CAB, Oxford, for an overview of systems used in the tourism industry.
- Poon, A. (1993) *Tourism, technology and competitive strategies*, CAB International, Oxford, for strategic thinking and vision towards new tourism.
- O'Connor, P. (1999) *Electronic Information Distribution in Tourism & Hospitality*, CAB, Oxford, which focuses on the internet and emerging trends.

Recommended websites

Technological developments
Siemens information and communications: **www.siemens.convergence-advantage.com** .
Nua Statistics: **www.nua.com** .

Tour guides
Lonely Planet: **www.lonelyplanet.com** .
Rough Guides: **www.travel.roughguides.com** .

eTravel Agencies
Bargain Holidays: **www.bargainholidays.com** .
Ebookers: **Ebookers.com** .
Expedia: **expedia.com** .
Lastminute.com: **Lastminute.com** .
Priceline.com: **Priceline.com** .
Thomas Cook: **www.thomascook.com** .
Travelocity: **www.travelocity.com** .

Airlines
Aer Lingus: **www.aerlingus.ie** .
Air France: **www.airfrance.fr/** .
Austrian Airlines: **www.aua.co.at/** .
British Airways: **www.ba.com** .
British Midland: **www.iflybritishmidland.com** .
easyJet: **www.easyjet.com/** .
Lufthansa: **www.lufthansa.com/** .
United Airlines: **www.ual.com/** .
Virgin Atlantic Airways: **www.fly.virgin-atlantic.com** .

Railways
Deutsche Bahn AG: **www.bahn.de/index_e.html** .
Rail Europe: **www.go.raileurope.com** .

Car rental
Avis: **www.avis.com** .
Eurodollar: **www.eurodollar.co.uk/** .

Cruises
Cunard line: **www.cunardline.com** .
Seabourne Cruise Line: **www.seabourne.com** .
Stena Line: **www.stenaline.co.uk** .

eTour operators
Airtours: **www.airtours.co.uk** .
Bridge Travel Services: **www.bridgetravel.co.uk** .
Cosmos: **www.cosmos-holidays.co.uk** .
Cresta: **www.crestaholidays.co.uk** .
Crystal Holidays: **www.crystalholidays.co.uk** .
Kuoni: **www.kuoni.co.uk** .

Hotels – Hospitality
Hilton Hotels Corporation: **www.hilton.com** .
Holiday Inn Worldwide: **www.holiday-inn.com/** .
Hyatt Hotels & Resorts: **www.hyatt.com** .

Inter-Continental: **www.interconti.com/** .
Last minute rooms: **www.LastRoom.com** .
Thistle Hotels : **www.thistlehotels.com** .

Destinations
Great Britain: **www.visitbritain.com/** .
Netherlands: **www.Holland.com** .
New Zealand: **www.purenz.com** .

International organisations
World Tourism Organization: **www.world-tourism.org/** .
World Tourism Travel Council: **www.wttc.org** .

Key words

Competitive strategies; computer reservation systems (CRSs); disintermediation; e-commerce; information systems; strategic information systems; virtual organisation.

Bibliography

Beekman, G. (2001) *Computer Confluence: Exploring tomorrow's technology*, 4th edn. Prentice Hall, New Jersey.

Buhalis, D. (1998) Strategic Use of Information Technologies in the Tourism Industry, *Tourism Management*, 19(5), 409–421.

Buhalis, D. (2000) Tourism and Information technologies: Past, Present and Future, *Tourism Recreation Research*, 25(1), 41–58.

Buhalis, D. (2003) *eTourism: information technology for strategic tourism management*. Pearson (Financial Times/Prentice Hall), London.

Buhalis, D. and Laws, E. (2001) *Tourism Distribution Channels*. Continuum, London.

Go, F. (1992) The role of computerised reservation systems in the hospitality industry, *Tourism Management*, 13(1), 22–26.

Inkpen, G. (1998) *Information technology for travel and tourism*, 2nd edn. Addison Wesley Longman, London.

Laudon, K. and Laudon, J. (2002) *Management Information Systems: Managing the digital firm*, 7th edn. Prentice Hall, New Jersey.

Marcussen, C. (1999a) *Internet Distribution of European Travel and Tourism Services*. Research Centre of Bornholm, Denmark.

Marcussen, C. (1999b) The effects of Internet distribution of travel and tourism services on the marketing mix: No-frills, fair fares and fare wars in the air, *Information Technology & Tourism*, Vol. 2(3/4), 197–212.

O'Connor, P. (1999) *Electronic Information Distribution in Tourism & Hospitality*. CABI, Oxford.

Poon, A. (1993) *Tourism, technology and competitive strategies*. CAB International, Oxford.

Porter, M. (2001) Strategy and the Internet, *Harvard Business Review*, March, Vol. 103D, 63–78.

Puhretmair, F., Lang, P., Tjoa, A.M. and Wagner, R. (2001) The XML-KL Approach: XML-based integration of tourism and GIS data for HTML and WAP clients, in P. Sheldon, K. Wober and D. Fesenmaier (eds) *Information and Communication Technologies in Tourism*, 73–82. Springer, Vienna.

Sheldon, P. (1997) *Information Technologies for Tourism*. CABI, Oxford.

Turban, E., Lee, J., King, D. and Chung, H. (2002) *Electronic Commerce: A Managerial Perspective*. Prentice Hall, New Jersey.

Werthner, H. and Klein, S. (1999) *Information Technology and Tourism: A challenging relationship*. Springer-Verlag, Wien.

WTO (1999) *Marketing Tourism Destinations Online*. World Tourism Organization, Madrid.

WTO (2001) *eBusiness for Tourism: Practical guidelines for destinations and businesses*. World Tourism Organization, Madrid.

Zipf, A. and Malaka, R. (2001) Developing location based services for tourism: the service providers' view, in P. Sheldon, K. Wober and D. Fesenmaier (eds) *Information and Communication Technologies in Tourism*, 83–92. Springer, Vienna.

Part 3
Management issues specific to tourism businesses

■ This part considers some of the current issues facing tourism business managers. Readers should be aware that the content of this part, more than any other, is likely to change rapidly. Changes in technology, developments in the law and general shifts in tourism management practice are likely to be such that readers will need to remain vigilant of the impact these may have for the chapters in this section.

■ The first purpose of the part is to highlight key factors currently facing tourism businesses. In particular, the law and the issues of economic, sociocultural and environmental impact. Second, subsectors of tourism which constitute the main components of holiday packages are considered: accommodation, transport, visitor attractions, package-builders and package-retailers. Third, the management of particular tourism niches is considered; these are sport tourism, tourism to developing nations and cultural tourism. Fourth, the part considers the future for tourism businesses and reflects upon many of the observations made in this book as the basis for making predictions about what might happen in the future in tourism.

■ The part contains chapters on tourism businesses and the law, visitor attraction management, sports tourism, the economic impact of tourism, managing sociocultural impacts of tourism, managing the environmental impacts of tourism, the accommodation subsector, tour operators, travel agents, managing the transport subsector in tourism, developing mass tourism in developing nations, the management of heritage and cultural tourism and the future of the tourism industry.

■ Case studies presented include studies on Vietnam, the Greek island of Samos, Arctic tourism, Machui Picchu, Thomas Cook and MyTravel.

Chapter 12

Tourism businesses and the law

Karen Bill and Alice Pepper, University College Worcester; University of Wales Institute Cardiff

Learning outcomes

On completion of this chapter the reader should be able to:

- identify when and how different types of tourism business may become subject to litigation and the actions that may be taken against them;

- discuss the principles of contract and tort and relate them to a range of typical tourism cases;

- consider possible defences in cases where tourism businesses are subject to litigation;

- develop legal study skills to anticipate the legal outcome of cases;

- discuss legal management strategies to reduce the risk of becoming involved in litigation and understand the alternative options available for resolution of disputes when they arise;

- highlight sources of legal advice and help available to tourism businesses engaged in more complex litigation.

Overview

This chapter provides an overview of a range of legal management issues relevant to the travel and tourism industry. The chapter concentrates upon those topical legal issues surrounding the interface between tourism businesses and their customers, as it is this relationship that gives rise to the majority of legal cases affecting the industry. It provides a basic understanding and application of aspects of a number of principles of contract and tort law and relates them to tourism cases and also explores dispute resolution methods.

The law used in this chapter is that currently in force in England and Wales at the time of writing. However, much of the relevant English law derives from European Directives, such as the Package Travel Directive 1990. Readers are directed to the guided reading section (see p. 282) in order to familiarise themselves with the structure and the role of institutions within the legal system in England and Wales and the European Union.

Problem solving as a mode of assessment is applied extensively within the domain and the chapter provides study skills and legal cases, with discussion questions, in order to promote the interpretation and analysis of case law.

The chapter concludes with a report (Case 12.4) on Nicholson Graham & Jones, one of the UK's leading law firms to the travel and leisure industries. It discusses the mechanisms for legal advice and support to tourism businesses.

Finally, this chapter should not be treated as a source of definitive legal advice and as such the authors, editors and publishers do not accept responsibility for any advice inferred.

Introduction

While it is relatively straightforward to define tourism, it is not so easy to illustrate the relationship between law and tourism. Lonnfors (2001) states '. . . Travel and Tourism law. There is a general lack of awareness of it, which is as a result of the inertia of the legal profession.' Perhaps one of the best cases which depicts the relationship is that of *Cowan* v. *Tresor Public* (1990) 2 CLMR 613 (pp. 621–623),[1] which attempted to define a tourist. Whether or not a person is a tourist, depends on the general manner of the services received during the journey, which is determined at the beginning of the journey.

However, tourism businesses and litigation have grown at an unprecedented level over the last thirty years. Awareness of consumer rights has been fuelled by media interest in the broadcasting of holiday-disaster programmes such as 'Airport' and 'Holidays from Hell' and tabloid headlines such as 'Holiday claims set to soar' (Macefield, 2003), as well as the academic interest reflected in articles such as 'Stranded Abroad: your rights' (Grant, 2004b). Moreover, according to the Association of British Travel Agents (ABTA) in 2000 approximately 5% of annual package holiday-makers were, to some extent, dissatisfied with their holidays. This in turn has led to improved standards as obligations on tour companies, hotels and airlines become greater.

Whether a tourism business is a large tour operator dealing in the mass market of package holidays or whether it is just a small hotel in the countryside, many of the legal principles affecting it will be the same. Typical legal issues could affect many different types of business, including:

- large tour operators (mass tourism);
- small tour operators (niche markets);
- travel agents;
- hotels;
- visitor attractions (e.g. wildlife or theme parks);
- miscellaneous businesses such as caravan/campsites, chalet resorts, outdoor adventure centres, etc.).

Similarly, although the laws in different countries may vary, in large parts of the world the broad legal principles and outcomes will be similar.

Common examples of legal problems are listed below.

- Breach of contract, e.g. inadequate service; delay; facilities or services not provided.
- Use of exclusion clauses to reduce liability.
- False description of holidays: brochure inaccuracy; misleading statements by travel agents.

---

1 There is a section explaining how court cases are referenced at the end of this chapter, see page 281.

- Disruption to holidays for various reasons, such as aircraft delay; hurricane; civil unrest; building works.
- Theft from hotel rooms.
- Discrimination in the provision of a service on grounds of disability or race.
- Personal injury arising from the possible negligence of tour operators or from natural hazards such as dangerous sea conditions, steep cliffs and wildlife.
- Illness arising from food poisoning, contaminated swimming pools, communicable diseases.

The following section deals with some of the basic legal principles the tourism manager needs to consider when putting systems in place to reduce the risk of legal problems.

Legal principles

Contracts and breach of contract

A contract is an agreement which legally binds the parties (Abbott, Pendlebury and Wardman, 2002).

To be valid, most contracts need not be in writing, although some contracts must be in a special written form to be valid, for example consumer credit contracts and contracts for the sale of land.

Usually it is clear whether or not a contract exists, but where parties disagree about the existence of a legally binding agreement, the courts will look for the existence of a clear, firm and certain offer that has been unconditionally accepted by the other party. The terms of the contract should be clear and there should be a meeting of minds between the parties concerning the essential terms of the contract. Also, both parties should give something of value to the other. This is called giving 'consideration'. Money, goods, services and promises to supply goods or services in the future are all examples of consideration.

Unfair contract terms

Tourism businesses will commonly operate on their own standard terms and conditions. These are often shown at the back of brochures or other printed material given to customers. Care should be taken in drafting such contracts, as there are a number of legal factors to be considered.

In particular it is important to make sure that the contract is clear and reasonably fair to both parties as the Unfair Terms in Consumer Contract Regulations 1999 provide that any term of a contract with a consumer that creates a significant imbalance in the rights and obligations of the parties can be disregarded by the court. According to the Commission's report on the implementation of the Package Travel Directive (1999), of the 6673 decisions of unfair contract terms in the database, 273 of those concerned the tourism sector.

Many businesses also try to limit or even avoid their contractual liability altogether by putting exclusion clauses (sometime called exemption clauses) into their standard conditions.

Under the Unfair Contract Terms Act 1977 (UCTA) such 'get-out' clauses are either void or subject to a test of reasonableness. A term will be reasonable only if it is fair and reasonable taking into account all the relevant circumstances affecting the parties at the time the contract was made.

Clauses that attempt to exclude liability for negligence are governed by section 2 of UCTA 1977:

> *s2*   A person cannot by reference to a contract term or to a notice seek to exclude or limit his liability for personal injury or death caused by negligence.
>
> In the case of other loss or damage a person cannot so restrict or exclude his liability for negligence unless the clause is reasonable.

This section applies to business occupiers of premises, so if, for example, a hotel proprietor were to display a notice saying:

> 'The management will take no responsibility for injury to guests howsoever caused'

this would be automatically void. It would also be a criminal offence to display such a notice as it could give the misleading impression to customers that they have been deprived of their legal rights.

Clauses trying to exclude or limit liability for other acts of negligence will only be valid if they are reasonable.

For example, under the Hotel Proprietors' Act 1956 a hotel may display a statutory notice at the reception desk limiting the hotel's liability for the property of guests to £50 per item or a maximum of £100 per guest. If the notice, which should be in the prescribed form, is not displayed, the hotel proprietor will be strictly liable for the property of guests staying overnight. Terms of a contract can also be implied so that a court will say that the term exists even if it has not been expressed. An example of an implied term would be that a contract for an overnight stay would include the provision of a bed!

Breach of contract

Breach of contract is a very common cause of legal action in the tourism industry. It occurs where a party to a contract fails to perform the contract properly or at all.

The nature of a contract is that it gives rise to rights and obligations on both sides, so that in a contract for a package holiday the following examples would amount to a breach of contract:

- The customer arrives in a resort to find that her hotel is overbooked and she is placed in a different hotel.
- The customer fails to pay the balance due on his holiday by the due date.

Where there is a breach of contract, the innocent party is entitled to claim damages (compensation). Where the breach of contract is serious, the innocent party might also have the right to reject the contract altogether. There are other remedies for breach of contract, which include rescission (the cancellation of a contract by mutual agreement of the parties) and rectification (where relief is granted in relation to mistakes made in the recording of the agreement).

Remedies for breach of contract

The objective of damages in contract is to place the innocent party in the position they would have been in had the contract been properly carried out. The most common contract remedy is damages.

Liquidated damages are awarded where the parties have agreed a clause in their contract pre-estimating the damages to be paid in the event of breach. For example, a tour operator might put in their brochure a clause showing the damages to be paid to consumers in the event of any delay to their holiday.

Unliquidated damages are awarded by the court and include such things as financial loss, damage to property, personal injuries, distress, disappointment and upset.

Damages will only be awarded in respect of loss, damage or injury that is reasonably foreseeable. This is sometimes known as the 'remoteness test'. Loss, damage or injury will be reasonably foreseeable (or not too remote) if it:

- arises naturally from the breach of contract, and
- is in the contemplation of the parties as the probable result of the breach at the time the contract was formed.

This is known as the rule in *Hadley* v. *Baxendale* (1854):

> The plaintiff's mill shaft broke and had to be sent to the makers in Greenwich to serve as a pattern for a replacement. The defendant agreed (for payment) to transport the shaft to Greenwich. The delivery was delayed, causing several days' loss of production for the mill. The plaintiff claimed £300 for loss of profit. The court held that the defendant was not liable, on the grounds that the parties did not foresee the loss at the time the contract was made. The plaintiff did not explain to the defendant that delay would stop production and the defendant had no way of knowing that the plaintiff did not have a spare shaft.

Damages for distress, upset and disappointment

Such damages are frequently claimed for breach of holiday contracts. This is because the main purpose of such contracts is usually enjoyment, so that the court will say that where the contract has not been properly carried out, loss of enjoyment is a clearly foreseeable result.

The case of *Jarvis* v. *Swan Tours* (1973) 1 All ER 71 was one of the first cases to award substantial damages for disappointment in a holiday case:

> Mr Jarvis had booked a winter holiday in 1969. The holiday was for two weeks in Switzerland with Swan Tours Ltd. The brochure described the holiday as having a house-party atmosphere in a hotel with an Alpine bar, English-speaking host and set among a wide variety of ski runs. There were to be a number of social functions including a welcome party, Swiss candlelight dinner, fondue party and a yodeller evening. The brochure also said that there would be a local representative. Mr Jarvis was very disappointed with his holiday. The ski runs were quite a long way from the hotel and skis were not always available for hire. The host spoke no English and in the second week he was the only guest, so that a party was out of the question. The bar was in the annexe and was only open one evening a week, and even the yodeller evening was a disaster. Mr Jarvis sued for damages for breach of contract and was awarded £63.45, which was the cost of the holiday, plus £125 damages, including damages for disappointment.

Note that where the claimant has not suffered as a result of the breach of contract, the court will only award nominal damages, so that if a holiday-maker's enjoyment of a holiday is not in fact spoiled by changes, no significant damages are payable.

The package travel regulations

In practice, huge numbers of breach of contract cases in the tourism industry concern customers making claims for breach of contract against tour operators. In such cases, the rights and remedies arise from the <u>Package Travel, Package Holidays and Package Tours Regulations 1992</u>.

The Package Travel Regulations came about as a result of the <u>European Community Directive on Package Travel, Package Holidays and Package Tours Directive 1990</u>. The directive obliges every member state of the European Union to implement a range of stringent rules to regulate its package travel industry. The result is that any consumer buying a package from any organiser (tour operator) or supplier (travel agent) based in a member state can expect the minimum standard of legal protection laid down in the regulations. Tourism managers operating in Europe therefore need at least a basic knowledge of these regulations or the directive.

First, then, it is important to know how the regulations define a package.

'Package' means the pre-arranged combination of at least two of the following components when sold or offered for sale at an inclusive price and when the service covers a period of more than twenty-four hours or includes overnight accommodation:

- transport;
- accommodation;
- other tourist services not ancillary to transport or accommodation and accounting for a significant proportion of the package.

It is not possible for the organiser to prevent a holiday being a package by splitting up the services and invoicing them separately. Also, tailor-made packages are still covered by the regulations. The result of this is that the organiser will still be liable for all the components of the package even where it has been specifically tailor-made to the customer's requirements.

The Package Travel Regulations cover a wide range of issues the most pertinent of which are discussed below.

<u>Regulation 4</u> is a key provision, as it states:

No organiser or retailer shall supply to a consumer any descriptive matter concerning a package or any other condition applying to the contract which contains any misleading information.

A consumer who has been misled by a brochure is entitled to treat this as a breach of contract and sue for damages (Regulation 6). It is also potentially a criminal offence to provide misleading information in a brochure or other advertising material (<u>Regulation 5</u> and Trade Description Act 1968).

<u>Regulation 14</u> contains some important rules about what should happen if, after the departure of the consumer, a significant proportion of the services contracted for are not supplied. If this happens, the tour operator should:

- make suitable alternative arrangements at no extra cost to the consumer;
- provide compensation for any difference in the services provided and those contracted for.

If suitable alternative arrangements cannot be made, or if the consumer reasonably rejects these, then the organiser must arrange for the consumer to be transported back to the place of departure or to some other place agreed by the consumer. The transport must be equivalent to that originally contracted for.

An important principle of contract law is that the innocent party has a duty to mitigate loss. In other words, a claimant cannot claim losses that ought to have been avoided. For example, a tourist on a package holiday should complain promptly to the tour operator about any breaches of contract, allowing the operator a fair chance to rectify the problem. The court would be reluctant to award damages to an aggrieved holiday-maker who failed to inform the tour operator of his or her grievances. This is particularly important if a consumer wishes to rely on the provisions of <u>Regulation 14</u> as the organiser might, in some circumstances, be unaware that there is a problem.

<u>Regulation 15</u> makes the tour operator liable to the consumer for improper performance of the contract, whether this is committed by the tour operator or by other providers of the component services. So, for example, where a holiday-maker arrives in a resort to find her hotel is overbooked, she will be able to sue the tour operator for breach of contract, even though the fault might lie with the hotel proprietor.

Other circumstances that often give rise to claims under <u>Regulation 15</u> include building works, flight delays, unavailability of advertised services and poor standards of safety or hygiene.

From a legal management point of view, this means that the tour operator should enter into robust contracts with those who will supply the component parts of the package. Enforcing these contracts could be the only way for the tour operator to recoup these kinds of losses.

The case of *Halpern* v. *Somak Travel Limited* (1997) provides a good illustration of the impact of <u>Regulations 14 and 15</u>.

Miss Halpern and her friend booked a ten-day package to Goa with Somak Travel Limited at a cost of £730 each. When they arrived, they were kept waiting at the hotel reception for three hours, after which they were told that the hotel was overbooked. They were offered accommodation at a two-star hotel. When they objected to this they were offered a place in a five-star hotel which was an hour's drive away. They were also offered a free dinner, £50 in compensation and free telephone calls. They had to wait a further three hours before they were driven to the new hotel, only to find on arrival that they were not to be given the £50 or the free dinner after all. The following morning, the representative was an hour-and-a-half late arriving to collect them. Before they could drive back to the original hotel, they waited for about an hour in a van, without air-conditioning, while the rep argued with the manager about the dinner bill. On arrival at the original hotel they were once again told that there were no rooms available. Eventually the hotel allocated them a small, dark room for the remainder of the holiday, during which they felt that the staff of the hotel were mocking them.

The court awarded the claimants £250 each for the diminution in value of their holiday and a further £1000 each for distress and disappointment. The total award against the defendant was £2754 including interest.

A more recent case, *Minhas* v. *Imperial Travel Ltd* (2003) 2 CL 263, illustrates the relationship of an agent and holiday company under <u>Regulation 4</u> and <u>Regulation 15</u>.

Minhas sued Imperial Travel, a travel agent, for supplying misleading information and substandard accommodation. The information originated from a tour operator, S. It was misleading, first, in that it described an apartment as suitable for three occupants when it was too small to accommodate this number. Second, Minhas were informed that there was a roof-top swimming pool when, in fact, it was 400 yards away down a busy main road. Third, there were problems with plumbing.

Imperial contended that as they were only agents they were not liable for the misdescriptions. It was held that under <u>Regulation 5</u> they were a 'retailer' and liable and, as they were 'the other party to the contract' under <u>Regulation 15</u>, they were liable under that Regulation.

Damages of £743 were awarded: £418 for alternative accommodation; £25 for travel and telephone expenses; and £300 for inconvenience and distress.

Breach of contract: defences

Under <u>Regulation 15</u>, the tour operator is potentially responsible for a wide variety of losses that could befall its customers so that it is important for the manager to know where the boundaries of his or her contractual duties lie. <u>Regulation 15</u> goes a little way towards limiting these boundaries by saying that the tour operator will not be liable where:

- the failure which occurred in the performance of the contract was the fault of the consumer;
- the failure was attributable to a third party unconnected with the provision of the services contracted for and was unforeseen and unavoidable;
- the failure was due to unusual and unforeseeable circumstances beyond the control of the organiser, the consequences of which could not have been avoided even if all due care had been exercised;
- the failure was due to an event, which the organiser or the supplier of the services, even with all due care, could not foresee or forestall (often described as 'force majeure').

Despite the strictness of the regulations, the tour operator is not inevitably liable to the consumer if something goes wrong with a holiday.

Case 12.1   Scott Jennings *versus* Rayburn Tours Limited 2001

Scott Jennings was 15 when he and his school went on a music tour to Italy organised by Rayburn Tours. In July 1998, he and the rest of his group took part in a sung mass in the basilica of St Mark's Square in Venice. When the mass finished, the party boarded a vaparetto for the return trip to Punta Sabbioni, which was near where the group was staying. As Scott disembarked, the vaparetto suddenly moved away and his leg was crushed between the boat and the quay. He alleged that his injury was caused by the negligence of the Master and the crew of the vaparetto and that, as the vaparetto journey formed part of the package holiday, Regulation 15 of the Package Travel Regulations meant that liability rested with Rayburn.

The judge accepted that the holiday was subject to the Package Travel Regulations because it involved the prearranged combination of transport and accommodation. However, the judge ruled that the vaparetto journey was not 'prearranged' within the meaning of the Package Travel Regulations 1992 because it was not pre-booked or included in the price paid to Rayburn. The group had to purchase the tickets locally to travel on the vaparetto, so the journey did not form part of the contract purchased by the school when it booked the music tour with Rayburn. He therefore held that the 1992 Regulations did not apply to the vaparetto journey and consequently the claim against Rayburn failed entirely.

Discussion question

1 Discuss the relevance of Regulation 15 to the scenario.

Although this particular claim did not succeed, it shows how Regulation 15 can potentially result in the tour operator being liable to the consumer, not only for failure to provide facilities or services, but also for personal injury or even death. These claims are made on the basis that the tour operator owes the consumer a duty of care, because of the contract between them. Where this duty of care has been breached, a potential case for negligence arises.

Many cases each year use Regulation 15 as the legal basis for a wide range of less serious claims than personal injury, for example, delays. Two recent cases that illustrate this are *Hone* v. *Going Places* (2001) EWCA Civ 947, which clarified the liability of tour operators when things go wrong with a package holiday, and *Brunton* v. *Cosmosair plc* (2003) 4 CL 43.B.

The tort of negligence

A *tort* is a civil wrong. As in other civil law areas, the claimant (or plaintiff, as she/he used to be known) bears the burden of proof. The claimant must show on a balance of probabilities that the defendant is liable.

To prove that a defendant is liable in negligence, the claimant must show that:

- a **duty of care** was owed by the defendant to the claimant;
- the duty of care was **breached** (that not enough care was taken); and
- the breach of duty **caused** the loss, injury or damage; and
- the loss, injury or damage was **reasonably foreseeable**.

Defences to negligence

Even after the claimant (plaintiff) has proved these matters, it still might be possible for the defendant to raise a valid defence.

The most common defence to negligence is **volenti non fit injuria** ('volenti' for short), which means that **no injury is done to one who consents**.

A case that illustrates the defence of consent is *Morris* v. *Murray* (1990) 3 All ER 801:

> Two friends, having had a good deal to drink, decided to go for a flight in the defendant's light aircraft, despite adverse weather conditions. The plane crashed, but the court held that the passenger had no claim in negligence against the pilot, knowing that the pilot was drunk, as he had clearly consented to run the risk of injury or death.

Where the defence of 'volenti' fails, a claimant might be successful in pleading contributory negligence. In such cases, the court attributes some of the blame for an accident or its consequences to the claimant and reduces the claimant's damages accordingly.

The case of *Griggs* v. *Olympic Holidays*, Lincoln County Court (1996), illustrates the way in which a tour operator can find itself liable for a personal injury that is essentially the fault of a third party.

> Mr and Mrs Griggs were on holiday in Cyprus in October 1993. Mr Griggs, owing to the collapse of a railing, fell 20 feet from the veranda of their apartment into the street below. He broke an arm and a leg. He spent six days in hospital in Cyprus before being flown home, where he spent a further six weeks in hospital. He was able to return to work after four months. He made a good recovery and was awarded £24,109.
>
> Mrs Griggs claimed damages for stress. She had grabbed her husband's hand, but had been forced to let go or be dragged over the drop herself. She ran down into the street below where she saw her husband lying. She thought he was dead. She had been left to cope with the situation more or less on her own while her husband was in hospital and had developed a fear of heights and intense anxiety. The court awarded her £14,925.

Not all similar cases will succeed and it is important to realise that the court will look at each case in the light of its particular facts. Where a death or personal injury arises from the existence of a natural hazard, like the sea, the court is often reluctant to find the tour operator liable.

In such cases, tour operators should take reasonable care to warn the consumer of known hazards. For example, most airlines now warn passengers about deep-vein thrombosis and advise them on exercises they can do to minimise the risk of it.

Liza Jones married John Jones in August 1998 and flew to Fun Island in the Maldives for a two-week honeymoon provided by Sunworld Limited (JMC). Tragically, Mr Jones drowned and Liza Jones brought a claim.

They were enjoying a walk in the lagoon about 50 yards from the shore when Mrs Jones alleged that she suddenly felt as though they had stepped off a steep step and that the seabed had dropped away, pulling them into a deep hole. She was able to get herself out but not her husband.

JMC disputed Mrs Jones' account of her husband's death. The water in the lagoon was clear, still and shallow and although there were three deeper areas in the lagoon, these were clearly identifiable from the shore, as a much deeper blue. There was a notice on site which warned customers not to try to swim to neighbouring islands.

Mrs Jones alleged that the natural pool was a hazard and that JMC was under a duty of care to warn them of it. She argued that the lagoon formed part of the package provided by JMC and was the key attraction of the holiday from the brochure pictures. The brochure referred to 'a long narrow island paradise with two neighbouring uninhabited islands (which you can reach at low tide!)'. To Mrs Jones this gave the impression that it was safe to walk in the lagoon, when, in her view, it was not.

Mrs Jones relied on Regulation 4 of the Package Travel Regulations, which provides that tour operators who supply misleading information in any brochure are liable for breach of contract and on Regulation 15. In the ten years before Mr Jones' death, 75,000 visitors had stayed at Fun Island and none had reported any difficulty or danger about the lagoon. JMC's expert carried out a site visit and confirmed that, in his opinion, the lagoon and its pools were not hazardous.

Mr Justice Field accepted on the facts of this particular case that the lagoon was an integral part of the resort and formed part of the package holiday. He did not accept that JMC was obliged to assess the safety of the lagoon in the same manner as it assessed a building. He concluded that the death was a tragic accident and Mrs Jones's claim against JMC was dismissed.

Discussion question

2 Comment critically on this case and discuss JMC's defence in relation to Mrs Jones' claim and recommend practical measures that tour operators might take to amend their booking conditions and brochures in response to the concerns raised by the scenario.

Developing legal study skills to anticipate the outcome of simple cases

The following approach is recommended to help students to write a thorough and well-structured answer to case studies of this kind. Students should avoid reaching conclusions or attempting to apply the law before they have explained the relevant legal theory.

- Analyse the scenario to *identify* clearly the legal issues affecting the parties.
- Explain (briefly accurately and clearly) the legal principles and *rules* of law relevant to the issues.
- Cite appropriate legal source of principles, preferably a statutory provision or case as appropriate.
- *Apply* the law to predict the likely outcome.
- Evaluate the legal outcome and discuss any management issues arising before reaching any *conclusion*.
- Remember – issues, rules, application and conclusion.

Discrimination law

Modern tourism businesses cater for a diverse society and need to take steps to avoid committing unlawful discrimination on the grounds of sex, marital status, race, colour, ethnic origin, disability or sexual orientation. Without careful management, such unlawful discrimination can all too easily take place either in the workplace or in the provision of services, as employees cannot necessarily be relied upon to do 'the right thing' without proper guidance and training.

Disability discrimination

Disability is one current topic of crucial importance in the travel industry. Ethical considerations may make some in the industry aspire to make the tourist experience as socially inclusive as possible, but such idealism can be a scarce commodity in any industry hard-pressed to make a profit in the face of ferocious competition. However, as disabled tourists account for a significant segment of the market, it makes both commercial and legal sense to pay attention to their needs.

The Disability Discrimination Act (DDA) 1995 is:

> 'an Act to make it unlawful to discriminate against disabled persons in connection with employment, the provision of goods, facilities and services or the disposal or management of premises; to make provision about the employment of disabled persons. . . .'
>
> Preamble to the Act

Disability is defined by section 1 as:

> 'a physical or mental impairment, which has a substantial and long-term effect on his ability to carry out normal day-to-day activities'.

The impairment must be (or be likely to be) of at least 12 months' duration, before it will qualify as a disability. An otherwise healthy person who breaks a leg would not usually be disabled within the meaning of the Act, as most fractured limbs will heal within a few weeks or months.

Many disability cases have foundered because claimants are unable to show that they are disabled within the meaning of the Act.

Some important provisions of the Disability Discrimination Act 1995 are:

- to make it unlawful to discriminate against a disabled person in the workplace (both as applicants for work and as employees);
- to impose a duty on employers to make reasonable adjustments to accommodate disabled employees;
- to give employment tribunals power to compensate victims;
- to make it unlawful to discriminate against a disabled person in the provision of goods, facilities or services;
- to impose a duty on service providers to make reasonable adjustments to make the service available to disabled people.

In October 2004 Part 3 of the DDA 1995 became effective, specifically requiring a range of adaptations by service providers to make their facilities and services more accessible.

The Disability Rights Commission began its work in 2000, replacing the National Disability Council. Its job is to promote the rights of disabled people. Many feel that this is a step in the right direction as the Commission has many more powers than the old Council, putting it on a similar footing to the Equal Opportunities Commission and the Commission for Racial Equality.

Legal management strategies

Where accidents occur, tourism businesses need to be in a position to answer detailed questions that are asked by the various stakeholders. They can only do so if they have properly developed and implemented health and safety policies and procedures for the well-being of staff and clients. The same is true for other organisations such as schools, where over the years there have been a number of tragedies involving young people.

> ### Case 12.3   The Smith family on holiday (fictional)
>
> A family, Mr and Mrs Smith and their two daughters Emily (7) and Susan (9), booked a two-week holiday in Spain, using a travel agent in London. The agent provided them with a wide range of brochures from different tour operators. Mr and Mrs Smith spent a long time considering the different holidays available, as Mrs Smith is disabled and uses a wheelchair. They chose a four-star hotel from the 'Happitours' brochure because it appeared to offer good family facilities, including a specially adapted groundfloor apartment suitable for a wheelchair user. On booking, they specifically asked the agent to reserve the special apartment. The agent also agreed to inform the airline of Mrs Smith's special needs.
>
> The hotel was also described as being set in its own extensive gardens with a large swimming pool, a children's holiday club and a courtesy minibus service every half-hour to and from the local beach.
>
> Mr and Mrs Smith had a disappointing holiday in a number of ways. First, they arrived at the hotel to be allocated an apartment on the third floor, with difficult access. The hotel manager apologised, but said that the agent had not informed her of Mrs Smith's disability. (The travel agent has since produced a fax showing that the hotel in resort was asked at the time of booking to provide the special room.) The manager did change her arrangements to give them a groundfloor apartment, but it was much less convenient for Mrs Smith than the specially adapted room would have been. She had to rely more on help from her husband and children than she otherwise would have done, making it a less relaxing holiday for them all.
>
> To add to their disappointment, the hotel's swimming pool was closed for repairs during six days of their two-week holiday. On those days they went to the beach, using the courtesy bus service. Although the minibus was not specially adapted for wheelchair use, the driver was more than willing to help, so they were able to manage. This did help to make up for the disappointment at the lack of the swimming pool.
>
> **Discussion question**
>
> 3 Advise the Smith family on any rights they might have in relation to the scenario.

School trips

The conviction of schoolteacher Paul Ellis of manslaughter on 23 September 2003 has highlighted the need for proper safety systems to be in place before any school trip is undertaken.

> The conviction arose out of the tragic death of 10-year old Max Palmer on a school outing to the Lake District. Paul Ellis was described by the judge as 'unbelievably foolhardy and negligent' for allowing Max to jump into a mountain pool following heavy rain.

At the end of 2003, the Department for Education and Science (DfES) issued new guidelines entitled 'Standards for Local Education Authorities in overseeing educational visits'. These guidelines recommend that LEAs should list questions which schools should ask contractors, such as tour operators, relating to safety management, and what to look for in the replies. Further, teachers should obtain assurances from service providers that risks have been assessed. It is good practice to seek details of any independent inspection based on external verification. For example, outdoor recreation in the UK that is designed for children or young people under the age of 18 is likely to be regulated by the <u>Activity Centres (Young Persons' Safety Act) 1995</u>. The effect of the Act is that 'persons providing facilities for adventure activities' for young people will, in most cases, need a licence. Therefore, it would be important for teachers to ask to see a copy of this license where applicable.

The <u>Health and Safety at Work Act 1974</u> provides that employers of five or more people must have a written health and safety policy and a written assessment of risks. Even where there are fewer than five employees it is good practice to write these down and review them regularly. A good policy should ensure the highest reasonable standard of safety. Although it is not mandatory for organisers of overseas holidays to have a

Safety Management System in place for the services and facilities which they provide to consumers, it is good practice and may provide a defence to a charge of gross negligence. This means:

- ensuring that the component parts of tours comply, where applicable, with local national and or/international standards, and maintaining records;
- actively promoting safety awareness, continual assessment and improvement, both in the UK and overseas;
- ensuring that the training provided to staff equips them to give accurate advice, and to carry out their duties;
- ensuring that all directors and members of staff are trained to respond quickly and efficiently in the event of an emergency;
- monitoring safety standards and reporting matters of concern for the immediate attention of the directors of the company.

However, prevention is not always possible. Tourism is a sector that is, by its very nature, likely to suffer a higher-than-average level of litigation claims, so that tourism businesses, particularly tour operators, need some basic knowledge and expertise in dispute resolution.

Managers of smaller enterprises also need to recognise when they need outside legal help. Larger tourism businesses will often have in-house legal departments, but even these will sometimes need the help of a specialist.

Dispute resolution

Despite best management efforts, most tourism businesses of any size will inevitably find themselves involved in legal disputes from time to time. The effect of the Package Travel Regulations makes it likely that any tour operator business will have a steady flow of small claims. Other types of business might hope to have fewer problems, but will still need to develop a protocol for dealing with any disputes that do arise.

Legal disputes can be settled in a number of ways, namely inaction, negotiation, mediation, arbitration or litigation. Each of these methods has its advantages and disadvantages, which have to be considered in the light of the facts of each individual dispute.

Inaction
This is appropriate in some circumstances. For example, it is usually not worth pursuing a debt if the debtor is bankrupt or has not the money to pay. Inaction also has the advantage of being trouble-free. The obvious disadvantage is that a claimant who does nothing to pursue a debt usually receives nothing.

A potential defendant need not act until a claim has been formalised in writing. However, once a formal written complaint has been made, a tourism business should at that point respond to the complaint, since if the defendant ignores the complaint completely until court proceedings are issued, this could lead to the court making the defendant pay the costs that could otherwise have been avoided.

Negotiation
Often, tour operators have a policy of offering a modest amount of compensation to discontented holiday-makers in resort, or soon after their return home as appropriate, as a way of promoting goodwill and hoping to fend off a justified claim for a larger amount. When reaching a negotiated settlement, the parties should agree that it is in full and final settlement of the dispute.

A major advantage of successful negotiation is that it avoids court action, which can be expensive and time-consuming. A disadvantage is that the claimant might receive less than his or her full legal rights. Also, poor negotiating skills can make the situation worse.

Discussion question

4 Consider other benefits and possible drawbacks to negotiation and think about the various techniques a person might use to negotiate successfully.

Mediation (also known as conciliation)

Mediation is an attempt to settle a dispute using a neutral third party. The conciliator (or mediator) does not have the power to impose a solution. Mediation is inappropriate for simple debt actions, as the mediator's fees must be paid, making it relatively expensive, without any guarantee of a settlement at the end. Also, if money is owed, then really there is nothing to discuss!

Many tourism organisations, for example ABTA, have a mechanism for hearing complaints against its members by consumers, following which they will do what they can to help the parties reach a negotiated settlement by way of mediation. At this stage ABTA will look at any complaint in the light of its own code of conduct rather than the law.

The Chartered Institute of Arbitrators, in cooperation with ABTA, has also set up a cost-controlled mediation scheme to help to settle personal injury and illness disputes in the travel industry. If the conciliation process fails, the customer may choose to use the arbitration service run by the Chartered Institute of Arbitrators as an alternative to going to court.

Arbitration

Arbitration shares many of the characteristics of mediation in that it is informal and requires the consent of both parties. The arbitrator does, however, have the power to impose a solution, in the same way as the court. The decision of the arbitrator is binding on the parties. The court is very reluctant to interfere with any arbitration decision and will only do so if it can be shown that the arbitrator has made a significant mistake in the law in reaching a decision.

In the context of tourism, small claims are often settled using the independent arbitration services used by organisations like ABTA and the Association of Independent Tour Operators (AITO). These schemes are appropriate for straightforward holiday claims, as they are conducted by post, but they cannot be used in cases of personal injury.

Other sectors of industry offer arbitration services as an alternative to litigation. For example, a person who is not happy with the way an insurance company has dealt with a holiday insurance claim can refer the matter to the Financial Ombudsman Service.

Arbitration is often a good choice for consumers, as it is quicker, cheaper and less formal than litigation, but still has a definite and enforceable outcome. Disadvantages of arbitration are that without a hearing, it might not be as fair as litigation. Another potential disadvantage for the consumer is that most arbitration schemes allow a relatively short period, typically nine months, in which to start proceedings. The court allows six years for breach of contract claims to be started.

Litigation

In April 1999, the new Civil Procedure Rules were introduced. These were the result of the so-called 'Woolf Reforms'. The rules were formulated to try to eliminate some of the problems of the civil justice system, in particular those of delay and cost. The court encourages disputing parties to see litigation as the last resort only to be used when alternative dispute-resolution methods have failed or are inappropriate.

One of the reasons why people fear litigation is the cost involved. The general rule in civil cases is that the loser must pay all the costs of the case. This includes the court fees and the loser's own and the winner's legal bills. However, the rule for small claims is different.

Small claims

Breach of contract claims under £5000 will normally be placed in the 'Small Claims Track' of the County Court, where the basic rule is that each party pays their own legal costs. The claimant, if successful, may reclaim court fees, up to £200 for an expert's report and up to £50 for loss of wages lost through attending the court hearing. As solicitors' costs (usually the largest part of the cost of litigation) are not awarded in small claims, a tourism business must either have the necessary expertise itself to bring and defend small claims or be prepared to pay someone else to do it for them. As the cost of employing a solicitor for this purpose is likely to outweigh the value of the claim itself, it is usual for larger tourism businesses to develop the necessary expertise in-house and to try to avoid time-consuming small claims litigation, by enabling the use of postal arbitration schemes as an alternative where a settlement cannot be reached.

> ### Discussion question
>
> Mr and Mrs Jones, an elderly couple, are upset at the levels of noise at the hotel where they are staying and have made a complaint to reception about what they describe as 'yobbish behaviour' late at night. They are threatening legal action.
>
> 5 Discuss ways to resolve this dispute and explore management strategies for avoiding such problems in future.

Claims over £5000 will generally be allocated to the 'fast-track' or the 'multi-track' procedure, in which case professional legal advice is normally recommended, although 'litigants in person' are allowed. Personal injury claims exceeding £1000 cannot go into the small claim track, so legal advice and representation for these is also recommended.

Claims for a fixed amount of money up to £100,000 can now be claimed through 'MCOL', which stands for 'Money Claims On-line'. This procedure is very suitable for collecting debts where it is not anticipated that a defence will be filed. MCOL is not suitable for complex claims, as the system will not allow the particulars of the claim to exceed 1080 characters. MCOL can only be used against defendants in England and Wales and there must be no more than two defendants in any one case.

Advantages of litigation are that it is thorough, with a definite outcome that is fair and enforceable. Disadvantages include cost, time, stress, possible adverse publicity and risk of losing the case. A party who fails to use an appropriate Alternative Dispute Resolution (ADR) technique risks a costs penalty in court.

In situations where litigation will go beyond the scope of arbitration or the small claims track of the County Court, tourism businesses will need the benefit of professional legal advice and representation. Larger businesses may be able to afford to employ solicitors to run specialist legal departments, but many other businesses will seek the services of an independent solicitor.

Case 12.4	Nicholson Graham & Jones, Solicitors, London

Nicholson Graham & Jones (NGJ) is regarded as one of the UK's leading law firms to the travel and leisure industries. The Travel and Leisure group within the firm was formed in 1991. Cynthia Barbor, Head of the group, joined in 1993. The publication of *Travellers' Checks*, which is a very informative legal publication on aspects of travel and leisure law, has been ongoing since 1993. *Travellers' Checks* can be viewed online at the firm's website at **www.ngj.co.uk**.

As a market leader in travel and leisure legal services NGJ acts for over 100 tour operators and allied companies within this growing business sector. Their client base consists of some of the best known and most prestigious names in the travel and holiday industries, including some of the top tour operators (e.g. Kuoni Travel Limited, Thomas Cook Tour Operators Ltd, hotels (e.g. Peel Hotels), airlines (e.g. Air Jamaica), car rentals (Holiday Autos), niche market holidays (Abercrombie & Kent), and travel trade associations (ABTA, Confederation Passenger Transport, Federation of Tour Operators). In recent times the Travel and Leisure team has been at the leading edge in a number of high-profile international assignments as well as defending numerous consumer class actions involving around 600 claimants. They also represented ABTA in its successful action against the Office of Fair Trading (OFT) concerning the General Insurance Standards Council.

Nicholson Graham & Jones offers a one-stop shop for clients' legal needs. The services include company formation, regulation (since the UK travel industry is more heavily regulated than any other jurisdiction) for companies selling flight-inclusive packages to comply with the Air Travel Organisers Licensing Regulations (CAA), contract documentation, suppliers and employment law.

Ongoing legal needs are also met, such as contract disputes with suppliers, consumer and public liability insurers; new investment and the Alternative Investment Market (AIM) as well as issues such as data protection and website terms. Although most of their work is cyclical, perhaps the biggest practical area of advice that they give is to do with health and safety, 'due diligence' actions and risk-assessment systems and strategies in order to reduce risk and improve quality. Robust systems and monitoring are a priority to avoid any possible allegations of recklessness or gross negligence, which can even lead to charges of manslaughter.

Note: The contents of this section are the author's own work and do not necessarily express the views or legal opinion of Nicholson Graham & Jones, nor do they constitute legal advice and are solely a general guide to the particular subjects referred to.

Source: An interview with Head of Travel and Leisure Industry Group, Cynthia Barbor, with respect to highlighting sources of legal advice and help available to travel and tourism organisations and legal management strategies.

Discussion question

6   Develop a clear set of criteria or a flow chart to help a tourism manager to decide whether or not to seek professional legal help in any given set of circumstances.

Conclusion

The tourism industry no doubt will have further obstacles ahead as it grapples with poor economies, increased competition and the threat of war, which can cause disappointment and disruption to its customers, creating additional liability issues. The mounting regulatory framework, as illustrated in this chapter, typified by the Package Travel Regulations 1992 and Disability Discrimination Act 1995, together with escalating consumer protection, imposes increasing obligations on tourism providers.

This has often led to a culture of disclaimers becoming more prevalent and the recommendation of internal 'liability audits' (Miller, 2003) as precautionary measures to try to reduce or eliminate risk. This chapter specifically looks at legal management strategies to reduce the risk of becoming involved in litigation and illustrates health and safety processes in relation to school trips and 'due diligence' and risk-assessment systems and strategies. The chapter also reviews the differing mechanisms for dispute resolution when faced with litigation.

While travel journalists may feel that the tourism industry is well regulated, there is no room for complacency as there are still aspects that are clearly not. For instance,

Grant (2004b) reports the need to extend consumer protection where flights are bought direct from the airlines and not bought as a 'package'. As precedent cases materialise, further obligations and practical implications ensue, e.g. the Gerona decision and its implication for air traffic accidents (Rees, 2004). Finally, the impact of European legislation must not be underestimated in terms of its impact on tourism businesses, e.g. the introduction to the UK of the <u>Montreal Convention 1999</u>. This chapter has discussed European Community directives and contends that it is critical that tourism managers operating in Europe keep abreast of any new directives.

Legal research – case citations

The law which is valid in England is established in one of the following:

- EU law.
- Cases.
- Statutes.
- Statutory Instruments.

Law Reports – case law

There are various different Law Reports and often cases are reported in more than one of these.

The cases are referred to by their name, e.g. *Jarvis* v. *Swan Tours*. Some of the main reports and their abbreviations are:

All England Law Reports	(All ER)
Appeal Cases	(AC)
King's Bench Division	(KB)
Panastadia International Quarterly Report	(PIQR)
Queen's Bench Division	(QB)
Weekly Law Reports	(WLR)
England and Wales High Court (Administrative Court)	(EWHC)

How to cite cases correctly

Cases are referred to by the names of parties to the action. In addition, because there may be several versions of a case reported, the case name is followed by a sequence of numbers and letters which identify where the report is published.

Cases contain five elements:

1 The names of the parties (in italics).
2 The date – the year in which the case was reported.
3 The number of the volume of the law report.
4 The abbreviation of the category of law report.[2]
5 The page number where the case is located.

---

2 Help in expanding fully the abbreviation of the title of the law report is available in publications such as:
Current Law Case Citator (any issue)
Legal Journals Index (any issue)

Here is how a case would be cited:

1		*2*	*3*		*4*	*5*
Jarvis v. *Swan Tours*		(1973)	1		All ER	71

The case is to be found in Volume 1 of the All England Law Reports for 1973 at page 71.

Guided reading

In order to assist non-law students with the necessary legal knowledge on the essential institutions, practices and principles that together make up the English legal system, Slapper and Kelly (2004) is a useful text, as is Elliott and Quinn (2004). The internet site of the UK Parliament at **www.parliament.uk/index.cfm** provides a brief guide to the history and procedure of the UK Parliament with links illustrating how legislation is made. With respect to the institutions of the European Union and the Community law-making process, Craig and de Búrca (2002) is a very thorough, challenging book that combines textual commentary with extracts from judgments and other academic literature. However, a more basic text would be that of Douglas-Scott (2002). There are also a large number of sites, both official and unofficial, devoted to the topic of EC Law. Europa is the portal site of the European Union (**europa.eu.int/**). It provides up-to-date coverage of European Union affairs and essential information on European integration.

A general textbook on the area of contract law is that of Koffman and Macdonald (2001); however Abbott, Pendlebury and Wardman (2002) also provides a good and comprehensive overview not just of the law of contract, but of the general area of business law. Elliott and Quinn (2005) provides an up-to-date and student focused approach to this area of law, while more about the subject of formation of contracts can be found in Adams (2004). An article in *Consumer Law Today* (2002) reviews the issue of unfair contract terms and fairer deals for consumers by the holiday companies. An article written by David Grant (2004a) 'Unfair terms sent on vacation' in the *New Law Journal* discusses the OFT guidance on unfair terms in package holiday contracts.

For more information in relation to the Hotel Proprietors' Act 1956, Pannett, Boella, and Pannet (1999) is a useful text dedicated specifically to hospitality law.

Suggested further reading, for those wishing to know more about the Package Travel Regulations, would be Downes and Paton (2003) which provides a very detailed analysis of the regulations in relation to travel and tourism law in the UK. Furthermore, a full copy of the Regulations, together with explanatory notes, can be viewed at **www.hmso.gov.uk**. Another text is that of Grant and Mason (1995) *Holiday Law*.

There are endless examples of cases which refer to issues related to the Package Travel Regulations, and as such an increasing number of articles have been written which draw out such legal issues. For instance, Mead (2002) discusses the impact of European harmonisation legislation on holiday-makers injured abroad, while Martin (2002) provides a brief discussion of liability on holiday claims and Jeffrey Goh (2002) looks at what constitutes a package holiday.

The law of negligence is a vast area of study in itself and there are many excellent reference books on the subject. Suggested further reading is that of Cooke (1997), while Deal (2003) in 'All Inclusive' in the *New Law Journal* reports on the scope of tour operator's duties in assessing safety and reviews the implications of *Jones* v. *Sunworld Ltd*, which is illustrated in the chapter.

Further information and discussion can be found concerning disability discrimination at the Disability Rights Commission website at **www.drc-gb.org** while, although a study on the provision of American tour operators for passengers with disabilities, Takeda and Card

(2002) look at the problems encountered when providing package tours for those that have difficulty in walking, which may have some resonance with aspects of UK provision.

More information about ADR and more specifically mediation can be found at **www.arbitrators.org.uk**, which is the mediation scheme set up by the Chartered Institute of Arbitrators, in cooperation with ABTA, designed to help settle personal injury and illness disputes in the travel industry. Full details about the ABTA arbitration scheme can be seen at **www.abta.com/benefits.html#arbitration**, while an article by Jason Munro 'Arbitration Review Procedure: Fear of the Unknown?' can be found in the *International Travel Law Journal* 9(4) 2002. A series of articles within the *New Law Journal* entitled 'The A–Z of ADR by Michaelson (2003) also provides a guide to ADR.

Journals include *International Travel Law Journal* (University of Northumbria Travel Law Centre), *New Law Journal* and *Travellers' Checks* for lawyers to the travel and leisure industry (Nicholson Graham & Jones).

Recommended websites

The guide to internet resources in hospitality, leisure, sport and tourism: **www.altis.ac.uk/index.html** .

AITO (The Association of Independent Tour Operators): **www.aito.co.uk** .

African Travel and Tourism Association: **www.atta.co.uk/** .

BBC Holiday Disabled Traveller: **www.bbc.co.uk/holiday/disabled_traveller/index.shtml** .

Chartered Institute of Arbitrators: **www.arbitrators.org.uk** .

Disability Rights Commission: **www.drc-gb.org** .

Europa – the portal site for the EU: **europa.eu.int/,** a resource to current and historical European Union (EU) full text documents. Key EU documents can also be accessed at **eurotext.ulst.ac.uk:8017/** .

The Financial Ombudsman Service: **www.financial-ombudsman.org.uk** .

Field Fisher Waterhouse specialist travel site: **www.ffwtravellaw.com/** .

FTO (Federation of Tour Operators): **www.fto.co.uk** .

Holiday Travel Watch – Package holidays pressure group: **www.holidaytravelwatch.com/htw/welcome.htm** .

International Forum of Travel & Tourism Advocates (IFTTA): **dbs.tay.ac.uk/iftta/** .

Package Travel Regulations: **www.hmso.gov.uk** .

University of Northumbria Travel Law Centre: **tlc.northumbria.ac.uk/** .

International Bar Association: Travel, Tourism and Hospitality Law Committee: **www.ibanet.org/general/CommHome.asp?section=SBL&Committee=SBL-Y** .

UK Parliament: **www.parliament.uk/index.cfm** .

Useful links to EU Policy and regulations: **www.bileta.ac.uk/01papers/lonnfors.html** .

World Tourism Organization (Tourism Legislation Database – LEXTOUR): **www.world-tourism.org/doc/E/lextour.htm** .

Key words

Case; class action; contract; discrimination; due diligence; exclusion clause; force majeure; litigation; mediation; negligence; negotiation; statute; statutory instrument; tort.

Bibliography

Abbott, K., Pendlebury, N. and Wardman, K. (2002) *Business Law*, 7th edn. Continuum, London.

Adams, A. (2004) *Law for Business Students*. Pearson, Harlow.

Consumer Law Today (2002) Holiday Firms change unfair terms, Vol. 25, part 12, December, 6.

Cooke, J. (2005) *Law of Tort*, Pearson, Harlow.

Cooke, J. (2003) *Law of Tort*, 6th edn. Pearson, Harlow.

Craig, P. and de Búrca, G. (2002) *EU Law – Text and Materials*, 3rd edn. Oxford University Press, Oxford.

Deal, K. (2003) All Inclusive, *New Law Journal*, 6 June.

Douglas-Scott, S. (2002) *European Union Law (Law in Focus S.)*. Longman, Harlow.

Downes, J. and Paton, T. (2003) *Travel and Tourism Law in the UK*, 3rd edn. ELM Publications, Huntingdon.

Elliott, C. and Quinn, F. (2004) *English Legal System*. Pearson, Harlow.

Elliott, C. and Quinn, F. (2005) *Contract Law*, 5th edn. Pearson, Harlow.

Goh, J. (2002) *New Law Journal*, Vol. 152, No. 7047, 13 September, 1338–1339.

Grant, D. (2004a) Unfair terms sent on vacation, *New Law Journal*, 2 April 2004, 486–487.

Grant, D. (2004b) Stranded Abroad: your rights, *New Law Journal*, 14 May 2004, 722–723.

Grant, D. and Mason, S. (1995) *Holiday Law*. Sweet & Maxwell, London.

Koffman, L. and Macdonald, E. (2001) *The Law of Contract*, 4th edn. Tolley, Surrey.

Lonnfors, M. (2001) 16th BILETA Annual Conference, University of Edinburgh, Scotland, 9–10 April.

Macefield, S. (2003) Holiday claims set to soar. Travel companies braced for more lawsuits after £25,000 award. *Daily Telegraph*, 21 June, 5.

Martin, G. (2002) *Law Society Gazette*, 99(20), 16 May, 35.

Mead, P. (2002) *Journal of Personal Injury Litigation*, 2, 119–123.

Michaelson, J. (2003) The A–Z of ADR – Pt 1, *New Law Journal*, 24 January 2003.

Miller, J. (2003) Limiting Liability (Travel Law), *Travel Agent*, 10 February 2003, v311 i6, 21(1).

Pannett, A., Boella, M. and Pannett, M. (1999) *Principles of Hospitality Law*. Cassell, London.

Rees, J. (2004) The sky's the limit? *New Law Journal*, 16 January 2004, 62–63.

Slapper, G. and Kelly, D. (2004) *The English Legal System*, 7th edn. Cavendish Publishing, London.

Takeda, K. and Card, J. (2002) U.S. Tour Operators and Travel Agencies: barriers encountered when providing package tours to people who have difficulty walking, *Journal of Travel & Tourism Marketing*, Vol. 12, part 1, 47–61.

Westlaw UK (2004) various case citations, Sweet & Maxwell, London. **http:west.thomson.com/store/ product.asp?product%5Fid=Westlaw&catalog% 5Fname=wgstore** .

Chapter 13

Visitor attraction management

Peter D. Dewhurst and Helen Dewhurst, University of Wolverhampton

Learning outcomes

On completion of this chapter the reader should be able to:

- define and classify visitor attractions;

- identify and profile the sector-wide issues that confront the managers of visitor attractions, both now and in the future;

- explain the strategic- and operational-level management approaches that can be used to address these sector-wide issues successfully.

Overview

The chapter begins with a brief explanation of the significance of visitor attractions, followed by a statement of definition and a consideration of key classifications. A profile of the issues that confront attraction managers is then presented, with particular attention being paid to changing patterns of demand and supply. The chapter proceeds to explore the various strategic and operational level management approaches that are available to attraction operators, including those concerned with product development and diversification, marketing and promotion, visitor management, human resources and revenue management.

Introduction

Visitor or tourist attractions, as they are sometimes termed,[1] are a vital component of any country's tourism industry, as they stimulate travel to destinations (Cooper *et al.*, 2005) and engender customer satisfaction (Gunn, 1994). Indeed, they have been cited as providing 'the *raison d'être* for tourism' (Boniface and Cooper, 2001: 30) as 'for the majority of tourists, the attractions at a destination are the reason for visiting' (Page *et al.*, 2001: 117). In other words, they have been recognised as the primary component or 'first power' (Gunn, 1988) in what Leiper (1990) has termed the 'tourism system'.

Yet, in spite of the widespread acceptance of their significance, it is noteworthy that the attractions' sector of the tourism industry remains under-researched and relatively poorly understood (Leask, Fyall and Garrod, 2002; Swarbrooke, 2002; Benckendorff and Pearce, 2003; Prideaux, 2003). Indeed, there remains a lack of consensus as to the definition of visitor attractions.

---

1 Refer to Swarbrooke, J. (2002:9) for a brief discussion of the two separate terms.

Definition of visitor attractions

In the broadest sense visitor attractions may be defined as anything that serves to attract visitors, including a locality's climate and scenic beauty, as well as distinctive cultural patterns, the friendliness of local residents, special events and retail outlets (Inskeep, 1991). However, such a broad definition inhibits a detailed comparative analysis and so academics (e.g. Middleton, 1988) and industry bodies (e.g. Scottish Tourist Board, 1991) have sought more precise definitions. This quest for a shared understanding has led the UK's national tourist boards to agree a definition that they use as the basis for an annual survey of the UK's attractions. This states that a visitor attraction is:

> A permanently established excursion destination, a primary purpose of which is to allow public access for entertainment, interest or education; rather than being primarily a retail outlet or a venue for sporting, theatrical or film performances. It must be open to the public without prior booking, for published periods each year, and should be capable of attracting day visitors or tourists as well as local residents. In addition, the attraction must be a single business, under a single management . . . and must be receiving revenue directly from the visitors.
>
> ETC, 2001: 8

This definition, which reflects terminology used by the World Tourism Organization (WTO) and the World Travel and Tourism Council (WTTC), has been cited by many commentators who value its capacity to narrow the focus of attention to managed sites, while simultaneously accommodating a wide range of attraction products. However, this is not to say that the definition has received universal acclaim. It has been criticised by some as being restricted and outdated (Stevens, 2000), while others have expressed doubts as to its relevance within different national contexts (Leask, 2003). Yet in spite of calls to develop a more contemporarily relevant and universally apposite definition, it remains that which is currently used by most industry commentators when seeking to explain what is generally understood by the term 'visitor or tourist attraction'.

Categorisation of visitor attractions

A similar level of debate exists over the categorisation of visitor attractions, with different commentators proffering varied listings of attraction types. One of the most broadly cited categorisations, as presented in Table 13.1, is utilised by the English national tourist board as the basis for their annual survey of visitor attractions. However, this listing has been criticised for being restrictive and outdated, and attempts have been made to develop a more contemporarily relevant categorisation.

Table 13.1	Categories of visitor attractions – basic	
Cathedrals and churches	Other historic properties	Wildlife attractions and zoos
Country parks	Leisure and theme parks	Workplace attractions
Farms	Museums and art galleries	Other attractions
Gardens	Steam railways	
Historic houses and castles	Visitor centres	

Source: ETC (2001) Sightseeing in the UK 2000

A more comprehensive categorisation emerged from an investigation into England's most visited attractions (Dewhurst, 1996). This identified visitor attractions as belonging to three distinct groupings each of which contains a number of sub-groupings, as shown in Table 13.2. The enormous diversity of visitor attractions, as indicated by these classifications, is also reflected in such matters as their physical characteristics, nature and scale of operation, ownership profiles, product offerings and market orientations. An example of this is provided by Leask, Garrod and Fyall (2004), who chose to classify visitor attractions according to whether they were built or natural, with the former grouping being divided into those that had been built specifically for tourism and those that have been built for purposes other than tourism. Similarly, Yale (1998) referred to work that classifies attractions according to whether they charge admission fees or offer free entry. A useful conceptualisation of the various options for attraction categorisation is provided by Leask (2003) and is presented in Figure 13.1.

Table 13.2	Categories of visitor attractions – comprehensive	
Attraction category	**Attraction types**	**Constituent attractions**
Historico-cultural	Religious sites	Abbeys, cathedrals, chapels, priories
	Museums and galleries	Art galleries, open air museums, traditional museums, science centres
	Historic sites	Castles, landmarks, monuments, palaces
	Interpretative heritage sites	Interpretative centres, heritage sites
	Multi-faceted historic sites	Castles, docklands, historic houses, palaces
Environmental	Animal attractions	Safari parks, wildlife parks, zoos, rare-breed farms, nature centres, aquaria
	Parks and gardens	Botanic gardens, outdoor activity parks, public parks
	Country parks	Country parks, reservoirs
Entertainment	Leisure and recreation complexes	Leisure centres, leisure pools, recreation centres, water parks
	Amusement parks	Pleasure beaches, pleasure parks
	Theme parks	Indoor parks, outdoor parks, beach resorts
	Themed retail outlets	Antique centres, garden centres, retail and leisure parks
	Workplace industrial visit centres	Craft workshops, factory shops
Miscellaneous other		Arboretums, piers, themed transport

Source: Adapted from Dewhurst (1996)

The constituent parts of visitor attractions have also been categorised, perhaps most notably by Swarbrooke (2002), who adapted Kotler's (1994) three-category classification of product components. The *core* element of a visitor attraction is regarded as whatever serves as the central appeal for customers and is likely to be intangible, for example, a sense of excitement associated with a theme park. The *tangible* component comprises attraction features that the customer purchases in order to satisfy their needs;

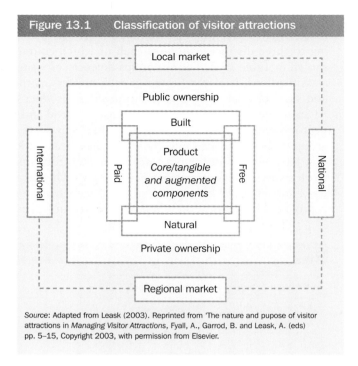

Figure 13.1   Classification of visitor attractions

Source: Adapted from Leask (2003). Reprinted from 'The nature and pupose of visitor attractions in *Managing Visitor Attractions*, Fyall, A., Garrod, B. and Leask, A. (eds) pp. 5–15, Copyright 2003, with permission from Elsevier.

these include the product components associated with the core appeal of the site, as well as the quality of service, presentation and product interpretation. The *augmented* component includes the tangible and intangible features that are peripheral to the core appeal of the attraction, but which contribute to satisfying customer needs. Included in this category are car parking facilities, toilets, catering and retail outlets.

Inevitably, the size, significance and diverse nature of the visitor attractions' sector of the tourism industry make it both a complex and fascinating area of study, but also one where few broad generalisations are appropriate. Indeed, it could well be this latter point that has served to deter commentators from focusing on visitor attractions as a topic for research investigation. This, coupled with the fact that many national governments and industry bodies do not gather reliable data on visitor attractions (Market Assessment International, 2000; Leask, Fyall and Garrod, 2002), means that there tends to be a heavy reliance on the relatively few sources of information that do exist. A review of these sources has revealed a variety of challenges confronting many visitor attractions (Stevens, 2000). It can be argued that the challenges are greatest in countries such as the USA (Robinett, 2003), the UK and Germany (Market Assessment International, 2000) where there are mature markets and where there have already been instances of prominent attractions being forced into closure. However, the attractions in these countries are merely the first to face a series of challenges that are set to increase in significance for attraction operators in all countries that experience a maturing in the levels of leisure provision and demand. These challenges, which serve as the focus for the next part of this chapter, include rapidly shifting patterns of demand, the pressures of a highly competitive and ever more commercially orientated marketplace and the need to align multiple stakeholder interests with management priorities.

Pressures facing visitor attractions

It is clear from an analysis of industry reports that many of the challenges confronting the world's visitor attractions vary both in scale and nature according to their location and the subsector to which the individual attractions belong. However, there is also evidence to show that maturing markets bring with them a series of pressures that are common to many visitor attractions and it is these that will be discussed in this section.

Shifting patterns of demand

Most commentators agree that a combination of structural changes in the population, rising consumer expectations and changing leisure patterns are the key factors behind a general slowing and shifting of the demand for those attractions that operate in a mature market (ETC, 2000; Mintel, 2002a; Mintel, 2002b; Fyall, 2003).

1 Structural changes in the population

Changes in the demographics of the population can have a varying impact on visitor attractions. The ageing population of many of the developed countries (Mintel, 2004a; Office for National Statistics, 2004) is leading to a growth in demand for family-oriented entertainment (Market Assessment International, 2000; Milman, 2001). Also, a growth in the number of citizens belonging to ethnic-minority groupings (Milman, 2001; Office for National Statistics, 2004), together with an increase in the number of single-parent households and pre-family and no-family adults (Mintel, 2004a), is serving to diversify the demand for leisure activities. These changing patterns of demand can prove challenging to the operators of visitor attractions, especially those that are long established and have limited resources with which to effect changes in product content, presentation and/or promotion.

2 Rising consumer expectations

The time available for leisure activities is increasingly being regarded as a precious commodity to which those in employment are prepared to commit a growing proportion of their personal disposable income (PDI). The leisure industry is also becoming more competitive and these factors, combined with recent technological advances that have brought higher standards of in-home entertainment products, are working to increase the expectations of leisure consumers (Morgan, 1998). As expectations have risen the public has become more critical of poor products and services and this has led to a more discriminating and discerning customer base, which is increasingly prepared to vote with its feet.

Research has shown that quality of product, ease of access and value for money are of key importance to the leisure consumer (Morgan, 1998). Yet these priorities can in themselves represent a major challenge to attraction operators, especially those faced by plateauing or falling demand. Indeed, the evidence from a market survey of customers to UK attractions in 2001 suggested that many attraction operators were failing to meet these needs satisfactorily, with it being reported that the major factors limiting attendances at attractions were over-crowding and over-charging (Mintel, 2002b). However, failure to meet customer expectations is increasingly not an option for those wishing to survive.

3 Changing leisure patterns

It is no coincidence that the emergence of leisure time as a precious commodity has occurred at a time when there are increasing work-related pressures being experienced by the citizens of many developed countries. These pressures, which are manifested in the increasing prevalence of weekend and evening working, have combined with the growing variety of leisure provision to encourage consumers into seeking 'bite-sized' leisure activities that they can accommodate at times before and after work (Key Note, 2001a). This development has been exacerbated by the growth in the number of well-paid working women, which itself has led to a shift in the relative peaks and troughs of leisure demand (Mintel, 2004a), as well as a diversification of leisure provision and a requirement for the more traditional leisure facilities to re-package and even re-invent themselves so as to better cater for their customers' needs (Key Note, 2001b).

An increasing amount of leisure time is also being spent in often sedentary, home-based activities that Milman (2001), reporting on previous work by Popcorn (1991), has cited as evidence of 'cocooning'. This phenomenon has emerged as a consequence of the increasing amount of time that the more affluent are having to spend in work (Morgan, 1998), the growing concern over personal safety in public areas and increasing difficulties associated with regional travel and parking (Key Note, 2001a). An additional contributory factor has been the recent advances in the quality and variety of in-home leisure products. Evidence that supports this trend includes the recent growth in expenditure on home computers and entertainment equipment, audio-visual technology, garden-based leisure products and even DIY materials (Key Note, 2001a).

Unfortunately, these trends have all served to increase the pressure confronting visitor attractions, many of which are located some distance from their intended markets, with most typically requiring their customers to commit to an out-of-home leisure experience of between a couple of hours' and a week's duration. Many attractions also find it difficult to respond to shifting patterns of demand with their operational activities being geared towards more traditional family markets.

Increasing competition

An increase in personal disposable income (PDI) has been experienced in many developed countries and this has led to a growth in expenditure on leisure activities, which has in many instances outstripped the growth in spending on such essentials as education, clothing and footwear (Office for National Statistics, 2004). Within the UK the share of total consumer spending on leisure activities increased from 24% in 1990 to 27% in 2000 (Key Note, 2001a). This growth in leisure spending might reasonably be expected to have benefited visitor attractions, and evidence does indeed exist to show that many attractions have experienced significant increases in both visitor admissions and visitor expenditure.

Table 13.3 provides a listing of visitor attendance figures for a variety of English attractions and it reveals that over the ten years from 1990 to 2000 a number of both large and small attractions experienced significant increases in demand. The ETC's UK annual *Sightseeing in the UK* survey in 2000 also confirmed that visitor expenditure increased in one year by an average of 2% in England and Scotland and 4% in Wales (ETC, 2001). However, these indicators do not present a universally positive profile, with Table 13.3 also listing a number of attractions that experienced a reduction in visi-

Table 13.3	Annual admission figures at selected English visitor attractions		
	1990	**2000**	**Percentage change 1990–2000**
Alton Towers	2,070,000	2,450,000	+18.36
Chester Zoo	904,000	1,118,000	+23.67
Flamingo Land, Yorkshire	1,138,000	1,301,000	+14.32
Imperial War Museum, London	413,701	575,651	+39.16
Ironbridge Gorge Museum	330,376	230,743	−30.16
Kew Gardens, Greenwich	1,196,346	860,340	−28.09
Natural History Museum	1,534,298	1,577,044	+2.79
Severn Valley Railway, Bewdley	213,029	227,204	+6.65
Stonehenge, Amesbury	703,221	799,742	+13.73
Thorpe Park, Surrey	974,000	925,000	−5.03
Tintagel Castle, Cornwall	145,651	192,528	+32.18
Tower of London	2,298,193	2,303,167	+2.16

Source: Various, including English Tourist Board (1991); English Tourism Council (2001)

tor numbers, while the proportion of UK adults visiting attractions fell from 26.2% in 1996 to 23.6% in 2000 (Key Note, 2001c). Furthermore, the modest increases in visitor expenditure reported for English and Scottish attractions in 2000 actually represents a decline in spending once account is taken of a 3% average inflation rate.

The tremendous variation in performance of attractions, as indicated by the attendance profile data in Table 13.3, has at least partially been caused by a series of competitive pressures that have emerged both from within and outside the attractions' sector of the leisure economy.

1 A growing attractions sector

The increasing emphasis on leisure activities and a growth in PDI have persuaded many individuals and organisations to move into the attractions sector. Within the UK the government has also contributed to an 'explosion in the number of visitor attractions' (Mintel, 2002a), especially in the period up to the millennium celebrations of 2000, by directing income secured from the National Lottery into new attraction-development schemes. It has been reported that as many as 47% of all UK visitor attractions have opened since 1980 and 21% since 1990 (Key Note, 2001c). Further evidence of this rapid growth in the number of attractions is provided by Mintel, which found that 78 new attractions opened in the UK in 2000 (Mintel, 2002b).

This increase in the number of visitor attractions, which as a consequence of the UK Government's interventions has not been entirely demand driven, has led to a growth in competition for customers at a time when the market has been faced by an increasing variety of leisure products. Attraction operators have therefore experienced increased competition from other attractions for a shrinking customer base, a situation that has been exacerbated by a reduction in the cost of overseas travel. This has resulted in the competition for customers being extended across international frontiers, especially in regions such as Europe where barriers to international travel have also been reduced (Market Assessment International, 2000). The present position is therefore one of expanding provision and largely stagnating or falling demand. In such circumstances there are bound to be winners and losers and within the UK it is estimated that around 60% of all attractions receive less than 6% of all visitors, while the top 7% of attractions receive around 60% of total visitors (Mintel, 2002b).

2 A growing leisure economy

Over the past twenty years leisure provision has expanded in four significant ways. First, technological innovations have been harnessed to support the introduction of new leisure activities, with the internet possibly representing the most important of these innovations. Second, traditional leisure pastimes have developed in innovative ways that have seen them being re-invented either physically or within the perceptions of the public. Prominent examples include interactive television, online betting and computer-based games, as well as multi-leisure parks that provide mixed packages of leisure activities (Mintel, 2004b). The third trend has been for a growth in the provision of traditional leisure activities, with examples including the expansion in the number of golf courses and leisure centres (Key Note, 2001b). Finally, a growing recognition among many politicians of a need to reduce state control has led to the deregulation of many leisure activities including gambling, alcohol consumption and international air travel. This in turn has provided a further boost to certain leisure activities including overseas short breaks.

In the light of such a growth in and diversification of leisure provision, it is hardly surprising that the level of demand for visitor attractions has failed to match the level of provision. Indeed, Mintel (2002b) has reported that, in spite of the burgeoning year-on-year growth in the number of UK visitor attractions, the size of the UK visitor attractions' market increased by just 2% (by volume) between 1999 and 2000, showing a real-term fall in value.

■ Government legislation/regulations

The seasonal fluctuations in demand experienced by most visitor attractions means that many operators rely on their ability to recruit temporary staff to address their operational needs at their busiest times. This places a requirement on attraction operators to pay close heed to changes in employment legislation (Key Note, 2001c). Within the UK the British Government has, since 1998, introduced a range of new employment laws that have regulated the length of the working week, introduced a minimum wage and set in place enhanced individual and collective rights for employees. New regulations for part-time employees and a new Code of Practice on Disciplinary and Grievance Procedures were introduced in 2000 (Harris, 2000), as was the Race Relations Amendment Act.

In most developed countries there has been a movement towards preventing discrimination against disadvantaged groups and to this end legislation has been passed to ensure that disabled people have the same rights to access facilities as able-bodied people. Within the UK attractions have been required to comply with the requirements of both the Special Needs and Disability Act (SENDA) and the Disability Discrimination Act (DDA), which requires the providers of services to make reasonable adjustments to ensure that their products are made more accessible to disabled visitors. Such developments can prove a major challenge to visitor attractions, a majority of which are small businesses with limited resources and consequently limited capacity to either monitor legislative developments or ensure rapid compliance.

■ Multiple expectations of different stakeholder groupings

It is clear that the need to satisfy visitor expectations is of critical importance to all visitor attraction operators, as dissatisfied customers will tell their friends, relatives and neighbours about their poor experience and in so doing help dissuade them from visiting, while they themselves will be less inclined to return for a repeat visit. Customer satisfaction is itself dependent upon the quality of the service encounter with staff at the visitor attraction and so it is vital that employees are recognised and treated by the attraction operators as a stakeholder grouping whose needs and requirements must be addressed and satisfied. Unfortunately, many attraction operators have historically failed to recognise this requirement and so the attractions sector continues to be dogged by a perception that the only employment opportunities are for low-paid and low-skilled staff. Within the UK, training sponsored by government and EU initiatives is beginning to address the training needs of such staff, but such initiatives must be fully embraced by the sector if they are to be effective in improving employee skills, thereby further 'professionalising' the sector.

Other stakeholder groupings that attraction operators must also seek to engage and satisfy include investors, local residents and special interest groups such as wildlife conservation bodies in the case of zoos and safari parks and heritage conservation bodies in the case of castles and stately homes. The disparate range of such stakeholder groupings and the very real potential for them to hold conflicting views makes the attraction operators' task of securing their support or at least consent for their activities and developments, an extremely challenging one. However, failure to achieve this brings with it the potential for bad publicity, conflict and even business failure.

Perhaps the most extreme stakeholder-related pressures exist in the case of those attractions that benefit from investment programmes that form part of broader strategies to encourage the economic development or regeneration of regions. Within the UK the Millennium Commission contributed £15.65 million to The Lowry Art Gallery at Salford Quays as part of a plan to regenerate an area to the west of Manchester that had suffered from a lengthy period of industrial decline. In this and other instances, including the development of the Guggenheim Museum in Bilbao, Spain, the National Museum in Wellington, New Zealand, the Royal Armouries Museum in Leeds, UK, and the

Millennium Dome in Greenwich, UK, the developments have brought with them an expectation of a growth in visitor numbers both to the attraction and the host environment, leading to an increase in spending, economic activity and employment opportunities.

The pressures associated with such an approach are twofold. First, at the development stage, there is a danger that the externally imposed strategic priorities that serve as the rationale for the development take precedence over sound business planning, thereby contributing to the ultimate failure of the attraction. Second, once the attraction is in operation the burden of the external pressures serves to undermine its performance. The London Millennium Dome provides an example where both of these pressures came into play. The Dome was developed as the centrepiece of the UK's millennium celebrations and was intended to serve as a vehicle for the economic regeneration of the eastern side of London. During its one year of operation the Dome succeeded in attracting 6.5 million visitors, making it the most visited admission-charging attraction in the country. Yet in spite of this it fell almost 50% short of its visitor target of 12 million customers. A subsequent Parliamentary review concluded that the management lines of responsibility were confusing and that politicians and not just business people were involved in the early decision-making processes, which contributed to a loss of business-planning focus. A lack of attraction related management experience further compounded the Dome's problems and led to claims that the attraction offered a mundane and generally uninspiring product that lacked cohesion and which had set for it unrealistic visitor-admission targets. The review also concluded that the site had been inadequately promoted, with a reliance being mistakenly placed on free press coverage (Select Committee on Culture, Media and Sport, 2000). The expectations, not least of attracting 12 million visitors, were readily seized upon by the media, which provided an overwhelmingly negative coverage of the Dome (Wickens *et al.*, 2000), which in turn helped undermine the efforts of the Dome's management team in striving towards their business targets.

Case 13.1   Earth Centre

Examples of attraction failure are one unfortunate by-product of the significant recent investment in new attraction development in the UK. Millennium projects sponsored by the Heritage Lottery Fund that are now closed include the National Centre for Pop Music in Sheffield, the Centre for the Visual Arts in Cardiff and the Earth Centre near Doncaster in South Yorkshire (Wanhill, 2003). The latter was one of fourteen 'landmark' projects and was conceived and built as an 'eco-friendly' discovery centre and country park attraction that combined indoor and outdoor exhibition space, gardens and wetlands, with an education and conference centre. Described by some as a premier visitor attraction for South Yorkshire (Rich primary sITes, 2004), it was intended to provide a working example of sustainable development; to inspire visitors to consider possible solutions to environmental problems while enjoying a day out. The centre itself provided an example of landscape regeneration as it was built on approximately 400 acres of former coal-mining land and its buildings were designed to be exemplars of low energy and sustainable design.

The attraction was one of the first millennium projects to open in 1999 and it did enjoy some success. By the time of its final closure in October 2004, it had succeeded in attracting around 130,000 visitors annually and its conference centre and education programmes were growing in popularity. It was hailed by the local press as a modern, quality facility of the kind needed to support Doncaster's desire to develop as a visitor destination (*Doncaster Today*, 2001) and was located within two hours' journey time for over 17 million potential visitors. Furthermore, with a product designed to appeal to the reported desire of many western consumers for environmentally friendly visitor experiences, how could it fail?

Fundamentally, the Earth Centre failed to attract enough visitors. Original predictions of visitor numbers in excess of 500,000 per year, were always considered overly optimistic by industry analysts (Mathiason, 1999; Wanhill, 2003) and many discerning visitors found key features to be in a constant state of disrepair and the centre to be dull and lacking vibrancy (Dollard, undated). The centre was also accused of basic operational and layout mistakes, such as the siting of the restaurant and shop after the pay points, and of failing to develop a marketing strategy that communicated effectively and directly with consumers (*Yorkshire Business Insider*, 2003) who, consequently, had a limited perception of the sustainable development theme

Case 13.1   Continued

(Townsend, 2004). A major refurbishment and re-opening in 2001, with a clearer focus on visitor entertainment, came with high hopes for improved visitor numbers but these did not materialise.

It is possible to argue that, given its social agenda, the Earth Centre should not have been judged solely on commercial criteria. Some have suggested that it should never have been presented as a popular visitor attraction but supported and developed as a national educational asset (*Yorkshire Business Insider*, 2000). The reality of UK lottery-grant funding is that projects have to secure matching funds from the commercial sector. The Earth Centre was a recipient of £50 million, but in an area not associated with tourism and with the restriction that matched funds must come from sources also demonstrating a commitment to a sustainable development agenda, the attraction struggled financially from the outset. The result is that the Earth Centre is no longer operating and its future as a possible business park is in the hands of local government.

The case raises some interesting and important issues for attraction developers and operators. Was the Earth Centre simply located in the wrong place to become a popular attraction or should such developments be afforded greater levels of public funding if they are to change visitor habits thereby assisting the regeneration of post-industrial areas? Was the theme of the attraction simply ahead of its time or was its downfall caused by basic operational and marketing failures? An answer to these questions comes in part from Wanhill (2003), who noted that while redundant land should be used for such developments, this should only occur if the high level of risk involved in attraction regeneration strategies is understood and new visitor attraction developments are not based on inflated predictions of visitor numbers.

Summary statement

The operators of visitor attractions are therefore confronted by an increasingly competitive environment, in which demand is stagnating and market expectations are both growing and shifting. Within this context it is hardly surprising that even some prominent visitor attractions within the UK have been forced into closure, recent casualties including Tussauds Rock Circus in London, the Centre for Popular Music in Sheffield, the National Glass Centre in Sunderland and the Earth Centre near Doncaster (see Case 13.1). This picture of plateauing levels of demand and a growing number of business failures has been cited along with employee recruitment and retention difficulties, a reliance on subsidies and grants and an inability to fund product developments independently, as evidence of a 'management deficit' (ETC, 2000). In other words, organisations such as the English Tourism Council have at least in part attributed the difficulties being experienced by many attractions to the deficiencies of their management teams. However, there are many examples of good management practices and it is these that will serve as the focus of the next section.

Management responses

The following section will concentrate on six key areas of management responsibility, with consideration being given to product investment programmes, strategic partnerships, promotional activities, visitor management, revenue management and human resource management. In each instance, examples will be used to demonstrate how attraction managers are seeking to employ effective management techniques to address the challenges that currently confront them.

Product investment programmes

Increasing levels of competition in static markets has meant that attraction investment programmes have frequently been supply- rather than demand-driven. Such programmes have generally focused on product developments, diversifications and product acquisitions.

Product development and diversification strategies

Product developments are recognised as a key means of boosting market demand (Key Note, 2001c) and so many attraction operators recognise the need to engage continually in development programmes that are concerned with both core and ancillary activities. Theme parks such as Blackpool Pleasure Beach in the UK, provide an example of both forms of investment, with a new white-knuckle ride entitled 'Bling' and a £5m investment in a new food court, both taking place during 2004 (Mintel, 2004a). Technological innovations are also used to improve the core-product offering, with an increasing emphasis on providing visitors with a high-quality interactive experience (Milman, 2001).

Many product development programmes are also used to diversify the product offering in order to better engage with existing markets, while also extending their appeal to new markets. This in turn has led to a blurring of the boundaries between previously distinct categories of attractions. This trend is typified by initiatives that have seen the introduction of theme-park style rides at zoos and educational resource centres at theme parks (Market Assessment International, 2000). Indeed, as the traditional distinctions between attractions have diminished, so there has emerged new terminology with attractions that used to offer an educational or entertainment oriented product increasingly being recognised as providing 'edutainment' (Hannigan, 1998; van Aalst and Boogaarts, 2002). In addition, a number of operators have sought to diversify by introducing new customer services. The Tussauds Group, for example, has developed a themed hotel at Alton Towers, which mirrors similar developments at attractions in The Netherlands and Germany (Mintel, 2002b).

Yet in spite of current demand related pressures facing visitor attractions in mature markets and industry calls for widening access (ETC, 2000), there is evidence to show that product development and diversification programmes have not yet begun fully to embrace the needs of a diverse market (BBC News, 2003). Consequently, there remain both an opportunity and a need for attraction operators to develop their products to appeal to a broader customer base.

Product repositioning and acquisition strategies

A trend that seemingly runs counter to that of product diversification is exemplified by the Tussauds Group, which in 2004 chose to embark on a strategy to differentiate their Chessington World of Adventures and Thorpe Park theme parks with a view to targeting two separate and more narrowly-defined markets. The product components of the sites, which had both formerly catered for a family market, were reviewed with a view to developing the Chessington site for young families and Thorpe Park for a young-adult market (Attractions Management, 2004a).

The expansion of many physically constrained sites has in many areas been limited by the high cost of land acquisition and so the operators of theme parks and other private-sector attractions have frequently sought to expand through the purchase of other attractions (Market Assessment International, 2000). In the case of Legoland's acquisition of Windsor Safari Park, the site was re-opened in 1996 with a fundamentally different product offering. More recently the French attraction operator Grèvin and Cie acquired the New Pleasurewood Hills Park in Great Yarmouth.

This trend towards attraction takeovers and the implementation of repositioning strategies is likely to increase in significance; indeed attraction managers in North America have predicted that consolidation, merger and acquisition activity among attraction operators will intensify to a point where regional oligopolies emerge (Milman, 2001).

Strategic partnerships

Where consolidation through acquisition does not take place, many attraction operators choose to develop strategic partnerships with other businesses. Such alliances are usually centred on marketing and promotional activities, but on occasion have extended to the sharing of resources. Madame Tussauds provides a valuable example of the former with its operators having developed strategic brand partnerships with Coca Cola, Fuji, Disney, Universal, Columbia (Attractions Management, 2004b) and United Biscuits (Attractions Management, 2004c).

In some instances strategic marketing alliances have been established between attraction operators that in the past were viewed as competitors. Research conducted in Scotland has revealed a willingness for attraction managers to work together, as well as with transport and accommodation providers, in order to develop joint brands, themes and packages (Fyall, Leask and Garrod, 2001). Indeed, the managers of many rural attractions regard such approaches, which can include the development of shared advertising, printed promotional material and websites, as being essential for their very survival.

Another manifestation of collaboration and collaborative working is provided within urban centres where cultural quarters have been established which have at their core clusters of historico-cultural attractions. This developmental approach has emerged as a popular vehicle for raising the profile of districts and thereby increasing the numbers of visitors accessing the attractions and adjacent shops, bars and restaurants (van Aalst and Boogaarts, 2002). An additional benefit of such a collaborative approach can be the emergence of a deeper working relationship, which can be manifested in the shared use of resources and even shared management practices.

Promotional activities

Many attractions have utilised the internet to develop sophisticated websites that are used to attract visitors. A notable example is provided by New York's Museum of Modern Art, which offers a virtual tour of the museum, as well as online booking and retailing services. Other initiatives, including the development of computerised booking systems and the promotion of attractions via tour operators, are also designed to improve the channels of distribution thereby increasing market penetration (Market Assessment International, 2000). Attraction operators such as Disney have also developed sophisticated databases that facilitate a more effective targeting of potential customers in campaigns designed to attract additional first-time visitors and to encourage more repeat visitors via the introduction of a variety of customer loyalty schemes.

Visitor management

Visitor attraction operators are faced by the conflicting demands of having to safeguard and protect their sites and exhibits, while at the same time encouraging as many visitors as possible to access their sites. The tension created by these two demands inevitably places a requirement on the operators to manage their customers effectively at the same time as ensuring that they enjoy a satisfying visit experience. A failure to implement effective visitor management techniques is likely to lead to congestion outside and over-crowding inside the attraction, with the former resulting in the alienation of local residents and the latter resulting in increased wear and tear of the product components within the attraction. Even more significantly, a lack of effective visitor management will undermine the visit experience and contribute to a sense of dissatisfaction among visitors, who will be less inclined to make a repeat visit and more inclined to make negative comments about the attraction to their friends, neighbours and relatives, thereby reducing the likelihood of them choosing to visit the attraction.

Effective visitor management techniques, which are essential if customers are to enjoy their visit experience, address issues of demand and supply. Demand-related management techniques such as differentiated pricing and de-marketing, can be used to control and manipulate the peaks and troughs in demand, while product interpretation and presentation can be used to inform and educate visitors thereby influencing their behaviour. Supply-oriented visitor management techniques are used to manipulate capacity levels in such a way as to avoid the physical degradation of the site while ensuring customer satisfaction. These techniques include queue management, site-hardening initiatives and capacity-raising schemes that may involve new product developments that extend the existing site (Garrod, 2003).

The FastPass at Disneyland Paris (Market Assessment International, 2000) is an example of a queue-management technique that has grown in popularity in recent years. This involves visitors reserving a time when they can access a particular attraction component, thereby enabling the visitors to enjoy other facets of the attraction at the same time as they are 'virtually queuing' for their booked activity.

Revenue management

An increasing level of competition for a plateauing or in some cases shrinking market, combined with a growing emphasis on commercial priorities even among long-established historico-cultural attractions (van Aalst and Boogaarts, 2002), has meant that there is increasing pressure on attraction operators to ensure that they optimise the earnings potential of their sites. This can be achieved through the introduction of revenue management techniques that provide 'a systematic approach to maximising revenue from the sale of intangible tourist services and facilities through pricing, market segmentation and service enhancement' (Leask, Fyall and Garrod, 2002). The key revenue management options available to managers include the varying of admission prices according to (a) the time and duration of the visit, (b) the category of visitor, (c) the volume of visitors and (d) the number of resources being accessed by the visitors (Leask, Fyall and Garrod, 2002). Many attractions are also developing additional income streams through the introduction of conference and events programmes, while they seek to maximise their return from secondary-spend activities associated with enhanced customer services, such as catering and retail outlets (Leask, Fyall and Goulding, 2000).

Human resource management

In an increasingly competitive mature market, a growing number of attraction operators are required to deliver an efficient and effective operating performance at the same time as ensuring customer satisfaction. These demands can only be met through the professional management of staff, which is best achieved through the development and implementation of effective human resource strategies (Graham and Lennon, 2002) that comprise human resource planning, recruitment and selection, induction orientation, training and development, as well as performance monitoring (Taylor, 2004).

Unfortunately, such strategies are not that common among visitor attractions, many of which have struggled to set in place effective HR strategies. Indeed, the challenges that many operators face include a workforce that largely comprises part-time, seasonal and/or voluntary staff and a management team that is frequently under-resourced and potentially lacking in key management skills. This latter point is emphasised in a research investigation into managerial competency requirements, which revealed that the managers of Scottish visitor attractions attached relatively little significance to either strategic or people-management skills (Watson, McCracken and Hughes, 2004). Yet it is just such skills that need to be demonstrated by the managers of attractions, who are increasingly required to take a lead in innovative developments as a response to the rapidly evolving and increasingly competitive marketplace. The RAF Museum Cosford in the UK (see Case 13.2) provides a good example of an attraction that effectively employs many of the management approaches discussed in the latter part of this chapter.

Case 13.2	RAF Cosford Museum

Opened in 1979, this attraction, the only national museum in the West Midlands, is home to one of the largest aviation collections in the UK, with over 70 aircraft spanning 80 years of aviation history. The museum also includes a conference and visitor centre and art and exhibition galleries. Situated in the rural English Midlands county of Shropshire, the museum strives to preserve an important part of Britain's aviation heritage while also entertaining visitors with interactive displays and a dynamic events programme, incorporating the hugely successful annual air show. Voted Regional Tourist Board Visitor Attraction of the Year 2003, the museum receives in excess of 200,000 visitors per annum and in November 2004 announced its largest ever development project. Costing £13 million, this will develop the site into one of the foremost visitor attraction and aviation research centres in Europe.

The attraction's status as a national museum means that customers benefit from free admission and visitor numbers have risen substantially since the entrance fee was removed in 2001. However, the cost of visiting an attraction is just one element of customer decision-making and a wide variety of factors ultimately contribute to the success of such attractions. Increasing customer expectations make constant product innovation and development a necessity and this requires the museum's management team to continually seek to secure funding to support this work. In this respect, management understanding of the availability of contemporary funding sources and the importance of expertise in preparing bids to external agencies cannot be underestimated.

The museum's management also recognises the importance of a continuous focus on quality management and improvement. They demonstrate this to customers by displaying their achievement of externally approved standards, including the public-sector sponsored 'Charter Mark' and the national tourist board-assessed 'Quality Assured Visitor Attraction' marque. Involvement in these standards also provides the attraction with access to a range of management insights from other participating attractions for benchmarking purposes. At a more local level, the museum has long understood the value of working collaboratively with other attractions as a founder member of the Shropshire's Star Attractions group. This ensures the attraction is perceived by potential customers as part of a coherent regional attraction package and enables the museum to benefit from valuable collective promotional activity.

Like many contemporary attractions, the museum actively targets a range of market segments. For example, it offers support to many local schools through its structured education programmes based on science and history and provides an increasingly popular corporate events facility for business. The management of the museum believes it is critical to understand the perceptions of such customer groups and engage in effective market positioning. In this respect, the RAF Museum Cosford identifies itself as a four-hour visit attraction and uses promotional efforts to position itself as such in the mind of potential customers, alongside other attractions in the area that can together provide a full day out.

Conclusion

The growing variety of pressures that are confronting an increasing number of visitor attractions, many of which are operating as small businesses at the margins of viability, inevitably raises the spectre of large-scale business failure. However, while such failures are considered by many to be inevitable, every effort must be taken to support the attractions sector of the visitor economy, for a shrinking attractions sector may well serve to dissuade the public from participating in tourist and day-trip travel. This would in turn help to undermine one of the key vehicles for economic development and regeneration that is increasingly being deployed by governments around the world.

The principal measure for assisting attractions must inevitably focus on what has been termed the 'management deficit'. To this end the onus is on academics to engage more fully in attractions-oriented research that can be of direct benefit to attraction operators. There is also a need to further develop benchmarking schemes and training-support packages that provide attraction operators with enhanced and applied insights into best business practices. Such insights should address in detail the management areas covered within this chapter and in doing so demonstrate how individual attraction operators might maximise their opportunities for both business survival and success.

Discussion questions

5 Is it important to be able to define what constitutes a visitor attraction?

6 How might visitor attraction operators define success?

7 What factors are likely to contribute to the success of visitor attractions?

Guided reading

The work of John Swarbrooke (2002) provides an excellent overview of visitor attractions and their management. A more detailed consideration of specific aspects of the development, management and marketing of visitor attractions is provided in the work of Fyall, Garrod and Leask (2003). Anna Leask and Ian Yeoman (1999) have also produced a compelling text that is concerned with the management of heritage visitor attractions, while Myra Shackley (2001) has focused on the management of sacred sites. In addition, individual chapters in a number of more generic management texts (McMahon-Beattie and Yeoman, 2004; Yeoman and McMahon-Beattie, 2004; Cooper *et al.*, 2005) provide valuable insights into particular aspects of visitor attractions management.

There are also a number of journal articles that provide key insights into visitor attractions. These include considerations of managerial competences (Watson, McCracken and Hughes, 2004), revenue management (Leask, Fyall and Garrod, 2002), human resource management (Graham and Lennon, 2002), management collaborations (Fyall, Leask and Garrod, 2001) and future prospects (Stevens, 2000; Milman, 2001).

Finally, market and industry intelligence data can be obtained from a variety of sources including Mintel and Key Note.

Recommended websites

Amusement Business magazine: **www.amusementbusiness.com** .

Association of Leading Visitor Attractions: **www.alva.org.uk** .

Attractions Management magazine: **www.attractions.co.uk** .

Institute for Theme Park Studies: **www.themeparkcity.com** .

International Association of Amusement Parks and Attractions: **www.iaapa.org** .

Key words

Collaboration; diversification; mature markets; personal disposable income (PDI); positioning; stakeholder; tourism system.

Bibliography

Attractions Management (2004a) Tussauds repositions Chessington and Thorpe Park. **www.attractions . co.uk /newsdetail.cfm?codeID=7498** , 7 April.

Attractions Management (2004b) Tussauds looks to strategic partners. **www.attractions.co.uk/ newsdetail.cfm?codeID=8691**, 5 August.

Attractions Management (2004c) Hula Hoops team up with theme parks. **www.attractions.co.uk/ newsdetail.cfm?codeID=7529** , 13 April.

BBC News (2003) *Free museums pull in 'well off'*. **news.bbc.co.uk/1/hi/entertainment/arts/ 2812167.stm** , 2 March.

Benckendorff, P.J. and Pearce, P.L. (2003) Australian tourist attractions: The links between organisational characteristics and planning, *Journal of Travel Research*, 42, 24–35.

Boniface, P. and Cooper, C. (2001) *Worldwide Destinations: The Geography of Travel and Tourism*, 3rd edn. Butterworth-Heinemann, Oxford.

Cooper, C., Fletcher, J., Fyall, A., Gilbert, D. and Wanhill, S. (2005) *Tourism: Principles and Practice*, 3rd edn. Pearson Education, Harlow.

Dewhurst, P. (1996) *England's most visited tourist attractions: an evaluation of success and taxonomic review*. Unpublished PhD, Manchester Metropolitan University, Manchester.

Dollard, R. (undated) *The Earth Centre: Green is fun!* **www.bbc.co.uk/southyorkshire/culture/venues/a_f/ earth_centre.shtml** (accessed 18 November 2004).

Doncaster Today (2001) Town calls on tourism experts. **www.doncastertoday.co.uk** (accessed 24 October 2004).

ETB (1991) *Sightseeing in the UK 1990*. English Tourist Board, London.

ETC (2000) *Action for Attractions*. English Tourism Council, London.

ETC (2001) *Sightseeing in the UK 2000*. English Tourism Council, London.

Fyall, A. (2003) Marketing visitor attractions: a collaborative approach, in A. Fyall, B. Garrod and A. Leask (eds) *Managing Visitor Attractions*, 236–252. Butterworth-Heinemann, Oxford.

Fyall, A., Garrod, B. and Leask, A. (eds) (2003) *Managing Visitor Attractions*. Butterworth-Heinemann, Oxford.

Fyall, A., Leask, A. and Garrod, B. (2001) Scottish visitor attractions: a collaborative future? *International Journal of Tourism Research*, 3, 211–228.

Garrod, B. (2003) Managing visitor impacts, in A. Fyall, B. Garrod and A. Leask (eds) *Managing Visitor Attractions*, 124–139. Butterworth-Heinemann, Oxford.

Graham, M. and Lennon, J.J. (2002) The dilemma of operating a strategic approach to human resource management in the Scottish visitor attraction sector, *International Journal of Contemporary Hospitality Management*, 14(5), 213–220.

Gunn, C. (1988) *Vacationscape: Designing Tourist Regions*, 2nd edn. Van Nostrand Reinhold, New York.

Gunn, C. (1994) *Tourism Planning: Basics, Concepts, Cases*, 3rd edn. Taylor & Francis, New York.

Hannigan, J. (1998) *Fantasy City: Pleasure and Profit in the Postmodern Metropolis*. Routledge, London.

Harris, L. (2000) Employment regulation and owner-managers in small firms: Seeking support and guidance, *Journal of Small Business and Enterprise Development*, 7(4), 352–362.

Inskeep, E. (1991) *Tourism Planning*. Van Nostrand Reinhold, New York.

Key Note (2001a) *UK Leisure and Recreation: 2001 Market Review*. Key Note, Hampton.

Key Note (2001b) *Trends in Leisure Activities: 2001 Market Assessment*. Key Note, Hampton.

Key Note (2001c) *Tourist Attractions: 2001 Market Report*. Key Note, Hampton.

Kotler, P. (1994) *Principles of Marketing*, 6th edn. Prentice Hall, Englewood Cliffs.

Leask, A. (2003) The nature and purpose of visitor attractions, in A. Fyall, B. Garrod and A. Leask (eds) *Managing Visitor Attractions*, 5–15. Butterworth-Heinemann, Oxford.

Leask, A. and Yeoman, I. (eds) (1999) *Heritage Visitor Attractions*. Cassell, London.

Leask, A., Fyall, A. and Garrod, B. (2002) Heritage visitor attractions: managing revenue in the new millennium, *International Journal of Heritage Studies*, 8(3), 247–265.

Leask, A., Fyall, A. and Goulding, P. (2000) Revenue management in Scottish visitor attractions, in A. Ingold, U. McMahon-Beattie and I. Yeoman (eds) *Yield Management*. 2nd edn, 211–232. Continuum, London.

Leask, A., Garrod, B. and Fyall, A. (2004) Managing visitor attractions – comparisons of international management practice, in *State of the Art II Conference proceedings*. The Scottish Hotel School, University of Strathclyde, Glasgow.

Leiper, N. (1990) Tourist attraction systems, *Annals of Tourism Research*, 17, 367–384.

Market Assessment International (2000) *European Tourist Attractions 2000*, July. Market Assessment International.

Mathiason, N. (1999) Cultural revolution's cul-de-sac. *The Observer*, 4. 31 October 1999.

McMahon-Beattie, U. and Yeoman, I. (eds) (2004) *Sport and Leisure Operations Management*. Thomson Learning, London.

Middleton, V.T.C. (1988) *Marketing in Travel and Tourism*. Heinemann, Oxford.

Milman, A. (2001) The future of the theme park and attraction industry: A management perspective, *Journal of Travel Research*, 40, 139–147.

Mintel (2002a) *Visitor Attractions – Pan-European Overview*, April. Mintel International Group Limited.

Mintel (2002b) *Visitor Attractions – UK*, March. Mintel International Group Limited.

Mintel (2004a) *Theme Parks – UK*, March. Mintel International Group Limited.

Mintel (2004b) *Multi-leisure Parks UK*, March. Mintel International Group Limited.

Morgan, M. (1998) Market trends in leisure, in J. Buswell (ed.) *ILAM Guide to Good Practice in Leisure Management*. ILAM/Pitman, London.

Office for National Statistics (2004) *Social Trends 34*. HMSO, London.

Page, S.J., Brunt, P., Busby, G. and Connell, J. (2001) *Tourism: A Modern Synthesis*. Thomson Learning, London.

Popcorn, F. (1991) *The Popcorn Report*. HarperCollins, New York.

Prideaux, B. (2003) Creating visitor attractions in peripheral areas, in A. Fyall, B. Garrod and A. Leask (eds) *Managing Visitor Attraction*, 58–72. Butterworth-Heinemann, Oxford.

Rich primary sITes (2004) *Earth Centre – Doncaster*. **www.richprimarysites.com/doncaster/ earth_centre.htm** (accessed 18 November 2004).

Robinett, J. (2003) Scouting the track: Economic outlook for tourism and attractions. Presentation to the Florida Attractions Operators Association, 29 May 2003.

Royal Botanic Gardens Kew (2002) *Annual Report and Accounts*. The Stationery Office, London.

Scottish Tourist Board (1991) *Visitor Attractions: A Development Guide*. Scottish Tourist Board, Edinburgh.

Select Committee on Culture, Media and Sport (2000) *Marking the Millennium in the United Kingdom*. Eighth Report. **www.publications.parliament.uk/ pa/cm199900/cmselect/cmcumeds/578/57802.htm** , 1 August.

Shackley, M. (2001) *Managing Sacred Sites*. Continuum, London.

Stevens, T. (2000) The future of visitor attractions, *Travel and Tourism Analyst*, 1, 61–85.

Swarbrooke, J. (2002) *The Development and Management of Visitor Attractions*, 2nd edn. Butterworth-Heinemann, Oxford.

Taylor, T. (2004) Managing human resources in sport and leisure, in U. McMahon-Beattie and I. Yeoman (eds) *Sport and Leisure Operations Management*, 58–74. Thomson Learning, London.

Townsend, M. (2004) Flood sweat and tears. *The Observer Magazine*, 24–31. 7 November 2004.

van Aalst, I. and Boogaarts, I. (2002) From museum to mass entertainment, *European Urban and Regional Studies*, 9(3), 195–209.

Wanhill, S. (2003) Economic aspects of developing theme parks, in A. Fyall, B. Garrod and A. Leask (eds) *Managing Visitor Attractions*, 39–57. Butterworth-Heinemann, Oxford.

Watson, S., McCracken, M. and Hughes, M. (2004) Scottish visitor attractions: managerial competence requirements, *Journal of European Industrial Training*, 28(1), 39–66.

Wickens, E., Paraskevas, A., Hemmington, N. and Bowen, D. (2000) The Dome – The perception and the reality, *ETC Insights*, A137–A142. English Tourism Council, London.

Yale, P. (1998) *From Tourist Attractions to Heritage Tourism*, 2nd edn. Elm Publications, Huntingdon.

Yeoman, I. and McMahon-Beattie, U. (2004) (eds) *Revenue Management and Pricing*. Thomson Learning, London.

Yorkshire Business Insider (May) (2000) Lottery land. **www.2ubh.co.uk/features/lottery.html** (accessed 18 November 2004).

Chapter 14

Sports tourism

Mike Weed, Loughborough University

Learning outcomes

On completion of this chapter the reader should be able to:

- illustrate the intertwining of the development of sport and tourism in both historical and contemporary contexts;

- identify the range of activities that comprise sports tourism and the products developed to cater for them;

- identify the global sports events which result in large-scale tourism and the provision issues and impacts associated with such events;

- assess the impacts of different sports tourism types;

- outline the areas in which collaborative polices and strategy might be developed for sports tourism.

Overview

This chapter examines the growth of sports tourism in the industrial age and notes those factors that have helped shape its contemporary form. It discusses the concept of sports tourism as arising from the interaction of activity, people and place before outlining five key areas of sports tourism provision, namely: tourism with sports content, sports participation tourism, sports events, sports training and luxury sports tourism. It assesses the main impacts of sports tourism, focusing particularly on sports events and sports participation tourism. Finally, policy development for the sport-tourism link is examined and those areas in which sport and tourism agencies might reasonably be expected to collaborate are discussed.

Introduction

While interest, particularly academic interest, in sports tourism has been a relatively recent development, sports tourism has not suddenly arrived in the tourism marketplace in the last 20 years or so. However, the classification of many aspects of sports tourism as such is a rather recent development. At the start of this chapter it is useful to examine both the historical development of sports tourism, and those aspects of the histories of sport and of tourism that have impacted upon sports tourism development.

Weed and Bull (2004: 3) identify the ancient Olympic Games, dating back to 776 BC, as the earliest documented example of sports tourism, also noting that the games at Olympia were the most prestigious of more than a hundred such festivals. However, it is largely the developments of the industrial age in which the antecedents of modern day sports tourism can be found.

The industrial age brought with it advances in transport that impacted significantly on both sport and tourism, and specifically enabled sport to develop through travel. Vamplew (1988: 11) describes how railways 'revolutionised sport in England by widening the catchment area for spectators and by enabling participants to compete nationally'. Later developments in automotive technology had similar effects, while the development of air travel widened sports tourism opportunities to a global scale.

Sports tourism in the nineteenth century, as now, involved both participants and spectators, with the former comprising those who travelled to compete and those travelling to use facilities or resources not available in their home area (Weed and Bull, 2004: 6). In the second half of the nineteenth century, the establishment of organisations such as the Football Association codified sport nationally and led to national travel to compete and spectate, something that is now taken for granted across a range of sports. In relation to travelling to use resources, skiing, hiking and climbing are each examples of activities that are unlikely to be available to participants in their home area. The Alps became an important ski destination, with 'a few adventurous visitors' travelling to the region by the 1890s (Withey, 1997: 217), and developing further in the early years of the twentieth century:

> In Switzerland, clusters of ski resorts to the east and west of the country, many with their own rail links, had emerged by the 1920s with Davos (nearly 6000 beds) and St Moritz (6000 beds) in the east and Villars (2000 beds) and Leysin (2800 beds) forming major resort centres.
>
> Towner, 1996: 250

The Alps were also important for climbing, with the Alpine Club in the UK and other similar clubs in other Western European countries existing to promote climbing as a sport. Less adventurous sports such as hiking and cycling did not necessarily need overseas travel, but were still dependent on people possessing the resources to travel to remoter rural areas and pay for accommodation. As such, much of sports tourism during this time, as indeed tourism generally, was still the preserve of those with means.

Key changes throughout the twentieth century were an increase in leisure time, both through a shorter working week and increasing holiday entitlement, and an increase in affluence, which together led to an increase in watching and participating in sport and in travel. Increasing affluence and time led to a change in attitudes that saw the 'democratisation' of both sport and travel, with involvement in sport, leisure and travel being not only enabled, but expected. Urry (2002: 5) noted that 'it is a crucial element of modern life that travel and holidays are necessary', and it was estimated that travel occupied 40% of people's free time by the latter part of the 1980s (Weed and Bull, 2004: 12). Furthermore, sport, while still pursued by some for the traditional motives of fitness, health, competition and achievement, is now increasingly participated in simply for fun and pleasure, or for reasons of body image and fashion. An increased emphasis on 'lifestyle choices' led to the combination of sport and tourism in the form of sports tourism, with perhaps two of the most popular activities being outdoor pursuits and international sports mega-events. While the former are linked to a range of motives and values relating to health fitness, image, excitement and, to a certain extent, fashion, the latter provide experience and spectacle.

The development of sports mega-events demonstrates the influence of globalisation and commercialisation on the twentieth-century growth of sports tourism. Horne,

Tomlinson and Whannel (1999: 277) describe international sport as 'a product of the jet, television and corporate capitalism' and, in fact, television in particular has influenced sports tourism. While this may seem strange, as television allows people to watch sport without ever leaving their home, Weed and Bull (2004: 13) point out that:

> . . . its great significance is that it has popularised a great many sports and highlighted their benefits and spectacle to a mass audience and this, in turn, has encouraged international exchange in sport and the expansion of international competitions (Tomlinson, 1996; Whannel, 1985). Not only has this led to many athletes travelling to participate in such competitions but also encouraged many people to travel to watch such events.

They also note that the drama and excitement of sports mega events, 'highlighted, if not exaggerated' by television coverage, have encouraged many people to want to experience the drama and spectacle in person. Consequently, sports events increasingly attract not only the traditional fan, but those searching for a 'spectacular tourist experience'. They are, perhaps, the most globally recognised type of sports tourism.

The sports tourism concept

While there have been a number of attempts at arriving at a definition of sports tourism, none have fully captured the essence of the activity. For example, Standeven and De Knop (1999) define sports tourism as:

> All forms of active and passive involvement in sporting activity, participated in casually or in an organised way for non-commercial or business/commercial reasons, that necessitate travel away from home and work locality.

On one level this all-embracing definition enables as wide an array of activity as possible to be covered by the term. However, in essence it involves no more than merely identifying tourist activity involving sport and is not particularly helpful in fostering a deeper understanding of the concept of sports tourism. In fact, it begs the question as to whether sports tourism is a serious subject for study or whether it is merely a convenient descriptive term with little explanatory value (Weed and Bull, 2004). Therefore, rather than attempting to provide a specific technical definition of sports tourism, perhaps a slightly different approach is required.

An important step in understanding sports tourism is to attempt to understand what factors identify it as a unique phenomenon that is more than simply the amalgamation of sport and tourism. Weed and Bull (2004: 37) suggest that the sports tourism phenomenon is constructed as much around experiences as activities, and so, although activities are an important part of sports tourism, other factors also contribute to its uniqueness. Of course, one such further factor is travel; however, in many cases, travel can be merely an instrumental factor in arriving at a unique place. The interaction of activity and place is clearly important, as a comparison of cycling to work through the pollution of a major city with cycling through beautiful countryside in one of the National Parks throughout the world shows. Yet this does not fully complete the picture, as for many participants an important part of the leisure experience is the people with whom participation takes place. In relation to sports tourism this may range from people with whom you interact every day, but with whom you have travelled to a distinctive place to take part in sports activities, to like-minded people you may or may not have met before, who are travelling from a range of places to the same destination for sports activities. Drawing these strands together, Weed and Bull (2004: 37) suggest the following conceptualisation of the sports tourism phenomenon:

> Sports tourism is a social, economic and cultural phenomenon arising from the unique interaction of activity, people and place.

While this conceptualisation is not a definition as such, it is perhaps of greater help in understanding the sports tourism phenomenon than any technical definition could be. However, this does not complete the discussion of the sports tourism concept, as there has also been some debate in the literature about the use of terminology.

In this chapter, the term 'sports tourism' is used to describe the phenomenon outlined above. However, other authors have argued that the term 'sport tourism' should be used, while Weed (1999, 2003), in addition to the term 'sports tourism' also uses the broader concept of 'the sport–tourism link'. The term 'sport-tourism link' refers to a broad concept that, in addition to tourism involving some element of sports-related activity, also embraces liaison between the sport and tourism areas on issues such as resources and funding, policy and planning, and information and research. As such it is a useful term to use in discussions of policy development and of partnerships between sport and tourism agencies. The use of the terms 'sports tourism' and 'sport tourism' are more problematic, and are the basis of some discussion among academics in the area. Gibson (2002: 115), along with many others in the field (e.g. Standeven and De Knop, 1999; Delpy, 1998) argues that the term 'sport tourism' should be used because 'sport' refers to the broader social institution of sport, while 'sports' refers to a collection of activities that have come to be defined as such. Consequently, the term 'sport tourism' encompasses 'a wider analysis of sport as a social institution rather than the micro view of individual sports' (Gibson, 2002: 115). However, the use of the term 'sport tourism' for these reasons implies a reliance on sport as a social institution to define and delimit the area of 'sport tourism'. Given that the conceptualisation outlined above describes sports tourism as a unique area of study derived from the interaction of activity, people and place, a dependence on the social institution of sport to characterise the area would be somewhat incongruous (Weed and Bull, 2004: xv). Furthermore, the concept of sport can in many cases be a misnomer that implies coherence where none exists and detracts from the heterogeneous nature of sporting activities. As one of the unique aspects of sports tourism is that the interaction of people and place with the activities in question expands rather than limits heterogeneity, the term 'sports tourism' is preferred, along with the focus on diverse and heterogeneous activities that the term implies.

Sports tourism provision

In one of the pioneering works in the field, Glyptis (1982) investigated the links between sport and tourism in five European countries and made some comparisons with Britain. She identified five 'demand types':

- general holidays with sports opportunities;
- activity holidays;
- sports training;
- spectator events;
- and 'up-market' sports holidays.

These, although proposed as relating to demand, essentially amount to a supply-side categorisation of sports holidays. Weed and Bull (2004) modified these categories to reflect the nature of contemporary sports tourism and used them to examine the range of sports tourism provision. In modifying the categories, Weed and Bull (2004: 123) noted that the 'activity holidays' category has come to imply outdoor adventure or countryside pursuits such as rock-climbing, pot-holing, hiking or trekking. Consequently this category was re-named 'sports participation holidays' to encompass the full range of sports activities that might take place as a prime purpose of a tourist trip. The 'spectator events' category allowed for the 'passive' aspect of sports tourism. However, Weed and Bull (2004: 37) noted that other categories, such as general holidays with sports opportunities, may also include passive sports tourism. In addition, there was a need to allow for active involvement in sports events, particularly mass participation events such as big city marathons. Consequently, they proposed that this category could be more usefully labelled 'sports events'. The final category, 'up-market sports holidays' has been identified (Weed, 2001a) as being characterised not by the nature of the sports opportunities offered, but by the luxurious nature of the accommodation and attendant facilities provided. As such, Weed and Bull (2004: 37) proposed that it would be useful to label this category 'luxury sports holidays' to reflect this more accurately. In addition to the updating of the individual categories, one final modification was required to allow for the inclusion of day-visits, which the vast majority of tourism definitions now include. This was achieved by simply replacing the word 'holidays' with 'tourism' where necessary in the categories. As a result, the updated sports tourism types proposed by Weed and Bull (2004) were:

- tourism with sports content;
- sports participation tourism;
- sports training;
- sports events;
- luxury sports tourism.

Tourism with sports content

This category is the broadest of the sports tourism types, including both the widest range of activities and the widest range of providers (Jackson and Weed, 2003). Tourism involving sport as an incidental activity rather than the prime purpose of the trip is sports tourism at its simplest and most unorganised. Consequently, types of provider can vary considerably, from large-scale multinational operators such as Thomsons to small leisure centres that would not consider themselves part of the tourism industry. However, the defining characteristic of this category is that sport is not the prime purpose of the tourism trip. Given such a defining characteristic, this category may overlap with sports events and luxury sports tourism, where it may also be possible that sport is not the prime trip purpose.

While this sports tourism type is defined by the fact that sport is not the prime motive, it is virtually impossible to characterise provision in this area. This is because the range of potential incidental sports activities is almost infinite. Many providers would not see themselves as part of the tourism industry, such as municipal sports facility providers or professional sports teams. These are, perhaps, 'incidental providers' and, along with the large-scale commercial tour operators, hotel chains, sports museums, and small-scale destination sports providers, make up the eclectic mix of provision in this category.

Sports participation tourism

While the previous category may be the broadest in terms of both activities and providers, the sports participation tourism category (where sport is the prime purpose of the trip) is perhaps the most obvious – essentially it refers to sports holidays (see Case 14.1). As with the previous category, there are some overlaps with other sports tourism types, particularly luxury sports tourism. Overlaps with other categories are best dealt with by exclusion. In this respect, active participation in sports events, except at the most basic level, is excluded from this category, as is any extended form of instruction or training. This category, therefore, encompasses the remainder of multisport or single-sport sports participation tourism and, with only a few exceptions, providers in this section tend to be drawn from the commercial sector.

Provision in this category is largely by commercial companies, the only exception being the 'not-for-profit' provision of accommodation and support by hostel organisations and cycle touring clubs. Within commercial provision for this category, it is only the multinational tour operators catering for the skiing market and the multi-sport provider Club Med that can be labelled as large-scale providers. Most other provision is by independent single-site operators, or small chains who often join together to produce, or subscribe to, guides or brochures both to market themselves and to help tourists to organise their own trip itinerary.

Case 14.1   Plas-Y-Brenin

Like the vast majority of sites providing for single- or multi-sport outdoor adventurous activity holidays, Plas-Y-Brenin in North Wales offers a wide range of water- and mountain-based sports and incorporates some basic 'dormitory' accommodation. It is the 'National Mountain Centre' for Wales and is run by the Mountain Training Trust, a registered charity set up by the British Mountaineering Council and the UK Mountain Leader Training Board.

Alongside provision for more experienced and advanced sports tourists, introductory two-day courses are offered in rock-climbing, mountaineering, kayaking and canoeing which include on-site accommodation, all necessary equipment, and supervision by qualified instructors. Specially tailored versions of these 'taster' courses are run to cater specifically for families and further 'intermediate' or 'technique development' courses are offered to encourage repeat visits. Provision is also made for clubs and associations, both to use the centre as a base for the surrounding natural facilities and to hold courses and seminars. The centre also offers personal development and corporate team-building activities.

Plas-Y-Brenin includes a range of training facilities, including an indoor canoe pool, a dry ski slope, indoor training and climbing walls, and equipment hire. It can provide for meals and functions, and has an on-site restaurant and bar. The full range of sports on offer are: rock-climbing, mountaineering, hillwalking, alpine climbing, ski touring, kayaking, canoeing, skiing, scrambling, sea kayaking, trekking, and orienteering. Its location in the lea of Mount Snowdon has made it a 'mecca' for many outdoor activity enthusiasts.

Further information: www.pyb.co.uk

■ Sports training

The sports training category is much narrower than the previous two sports tourism types. Quite simply it comprises sports tourism trips where the prime purpose is sports instruction or training. This might range from a weekend instruction course on dinghy sailing to an elite training camp at altitude for a national athletics squad (Weed, 2001a). Provision can be by both the commercial and public sector, with public sector provision often being that for elite athletes.

Providers of instruction for beginners, which Weed and Bull (2004: 130) identify as 'learn to' provision, are largely small-scale independent commercial operations, but courses often work towards achieving ability levels or certification linked to national sports governing body standards in both participation and coach education. Many commercial sector providers of advanced instruction and elite training (and the same sites will usually cater to both markets) are also often single-site operators (see Case 14.2). In some cases, elite training facilities may be subsidised by the public sector and, in these

Case 14.2   The amateur sports training market in Europe

The sports training market, while an identifiable sports tourism market niche, is too small to be economically viable for the large tourism operators. Consequently the market is mainly serviced by smaller, often family-owned, businesses (although there are some larger operators) which provide four types of product: sports resorts, structured training programmes, supported training sports tourism, and sports travel agency services.

Sports resorts sell accommodation with sports facilities to individuals or groups. Providers range from the well-known resort of Club La Santa in Lanzarote to small 'gites' in France. Club La Santa (**www.clubla-santa.com**) takes bookings from groups who wish to manage their own training, and also occasionally from other companies providing 'structured training programmes' within the Club La Santa facilities. 'Ferme La Garriguette' (**www.rasteau.co.uk/training.htm**) is one of the better promoted gites in France that provides for cyclists and triathletes. It is owned and run by the former manager of the GB Triathlon Team, who can offer advice on training.

Companies offering 'structured training programmes', such as Active People (**www.activepeople-uk.com**), Leisure Pursuits Group (**www.sportstoursinternational.co.uk**) and Robin Brew Sports (**www.robinbrew-sports.com**), use their in-house expertise along with contracted ex-athletes to coach customers through a week of intensive training. Leisure Pursuits Group is by far the largest of these companies, offering a wide range of products that would also place them in the sports travel agent category.

Supported training tourism provides accommodation, local knowledge of the area, and optional supported training (often running or cycling) with a guide. There is no structured programme and customers decide on their own level of activity. There are numerous touring and cycling centres providing such activities (e.g. Endless Ride – **www.endlessride.com**), while the service is also offered by many of the 'structured training programme' operators.

Leisure Pursuits Group also acts as a sports travel agent. Along with other companies, such as Sports Tours for Clubs (**www.sports-tours.co.uk**) and UK Premier Leisure (**www.ukpremiereleisure.co.uk**), Leisure Pursuits Group offers a full package of travel arrangements for large sports events for spectators or participants, and the booking of sports resorts.

Source: Derived from Belton (2003)

instances, it is unlikely that such sites would be available to any great extent to the advanced instruction market.

Sports events

Sports events refer to tourism where the prime purpose of the trip is to take part in sports events, either as a participant or a spectator. Provision may be by the commercial or public sector, or by a partnership of the two, and in many cases voluntary sports organisations are involved. Sports events can range in size from mega-events such as the Olympics and the football World Cup (see Case 14.3), to the smallest of local events such as a five kilometre fun run. Regardless of size or importance, all events will attract both participants and spectators (Jackson and Weed, 2003).

Provision for sports events in the overwhelming majority of cases will take place through a partnership of the public, commercial and voluntary sectors. The lead sector may vary, depending on the event, but it is unlikely to be the commercial sector unless it is an event for which that sector owns the trademarks and rights (such as World Series Baseball). Much that has previously been written on events has focused on their impacts, and such impacts are important to providers because in most cases they provide the motivation or impetus for provision.

Luxury sports tourism

Luxury sports tourism, unlike any of the previous categories, is not defined by reference to the nature of the sport involved in the trip, but by the quality of the facilities and the

Case 14.3   Global sports events

According to Law (1993: 97) the term mega-event, in an urban context, describes 'large events of world importance and high profile which have a major impact on the image of the host city'. They are 'usually viewed as a highly significant tourist asset . . . with the event directly attracting participants and the result-ing raised profile of the area also indirectly encouraging increased general visitation' (Bramwell, 1997: 168). Roche (2001) distinguishes between 'mega', 'special' and 'hallmark' events on the basis of the target attendance/market and the type of media interest involved (see Table 14.1).

Table 14.1   Types of event

Type of event	Example of event	Target market	Type of media interest
Mega-event	Olympic Games; football World Cup	Global	Global television
Special event	Grand Prix (F1); world regional sport (e.g. Pan American Games)	World regional/national	International/national television
Hallmark event	National sport event (e.g. Australia Games)	National	National television
Big city sport/ festivals	Regional sport event	Local	Local television

Source: Based on Roche (2001)

Special sporting events have emerged as major tourism policy instruments for governments keen to boost local business as a result of visitor spending (Mules, 1998). The economic benefits from mega-events are substantial. The total economic impact of the Montreal games in 1976 was reckoned to have generated between US$77 million and $135 million (or between US$124 million and $216 million if multiplier effects are included) while the estimated total impact of the Los Angeles games was US$417 million in value-added terms (Collins and Jackson, 1999). The 1996 Atlanta Olympics generated £645 million. Such figures may be exaggerated and, of course, do not reveal the extent of municipal debt and written off capi-tal involved (ibid). In fact, the hosting of the Atlanta games cost £557.9 million. However, there are other reasons why such events have become increasingly attractive to both local and national governments. They are seen as a means of changing the image of both the city and the state as a whole (Robertson and Guerrier, 1998). In fact, Weiler and Hall (1992: 1) argue that 'Hallmark events are the image builders of modern tourism' while Waitt (1999) suggests that the Olympic Games as spectacle is the ultimate tourist attraction. Such events can enhance the status of smaller states, as in the Seoul Summer Olympic Games, and also non-capital cities, as in the Barcelona and Los Angeles Olympics, the Adelaide Grand Prix, the Calgary Winter Olympic Games or the Victoria, British Columbia, Commonwealth Games (Collins and Jackson, 1999). The Barcelona Olympic Games also helped Spain demonstrate an alternative tourism product to the mass tourism of the 'costas' (Robertson and Guerrier, 1998) and the city has subsequently become one of the top European tourism destinations, being ranked fifth in terms of visitor numbers in the late 1990s after London, Paris, Rome and Dublin (Wöber, 1997). More recent work by Waitt (2003: 112), who examined the social impacts of the Sydney Olympic Games, has also suggested that such impacts are positive and can 'generate patriotism and a sense of community or belonging, particularly among the young and ethnic minorities'. He believes that such 'global sporting events provide the opportunity for government and city authorities to (re-)establish or increase the attachment and identification of people to place'. Whatever the overall benefits, there is intense competition among nations to host such prestigious events and governments are willing to help finance bids and fund the building of stadia and related infrastructure as well as send delegations on 'charm offensives' in order to help secure them. Sport England invested £3.4 million in the bid for the 2006 FIFA World Cup, a decision which the Government fully endorsed (DCMS, 2001).

Source: Weed and Bull (2004)

luxurious nature of the accommodation and attendant facilities and services (Weed, 2001a). Consequently it overlaps with all the other categories, as it simply caters for the luxury end of the market in each case. As such it may seem a strange category to include. However, the nature of the clientele attracted, the tourism experience provided, and the aims and objectives of the providers themselves, mean that it is a useful and legitimate category. Provision in this market is exclusively by the commercial sector and examples include country house golf hotels, the upper end of the skiing tourism market, and corporate hospitality at sports events.

The nature of luxury sports tourism provision is exclusivity, or at least the perception of exclusivity. Such perceptions can be created by both the standards of facilities and the reputation of the resort. The need for exclusivity means that provision tends to be by independent operators – if the provider were part of a chain this would detract from the perception of exclusivity. In addition, provision is entirely commercial, and potential profits in this sector can be quite large (Lilley and De Franco, 1999). Such large returns mean there is no need or desire for public sector investment or provision in this area.

Sports tourism impacts

While the impacts of sports tourism are wide-ranging and complex, it is perhaps in relation to sports events and sports participation tourism that they are most pronounced. As such, the discussions that follow will focus largely on the impacts and effects of these two sports tourism types, although the impacts described may also be attributable to other types, most notably tourism with sports content.

There is unquestionably a wide range of impacts resulting from sports tourism provision, of which the economic impact is perhaps the most obvious. Broadly, sports tourism is a dynamic and expanding sector of the tourism economy, and by definition this is attractive economically. Sports-related facilities and events can generate visitors from outside the local area, which generates economic benefit locally from sales of accommodation, food, beverages, gifts, admission fees, other spending at facilities, hire fees, use of transport, etc. Sport and its events may also generate sponsorship income, inward investment, media exposure, ongoing tourist appeal and secondary multiplier effects.

In 1996, Jackson and Reeves claimed that an estimate of 10%–15% of domestic holidays in Northern Europe having a sports orientation was not unreasonable. However, the authors called for a more specific and consistent focus on this information gap in future tourism statistic collection. Three years later, Collins and Jackson (1999) presented a 'conservative' estimate for the value of sports tourism in the UK which suggested an overall value of over £2.5 billion annually.

The impacts of sports events

It has tended to be in the area of sports events that most economic impact research has been conducted. The obvious direct benefits of major sporting events (new facilities and visitor spending) are supplemented in most cases by a post-event tourism boost. Resulting publicity and the positive influence on local tourism are clear advantages of staging such events.

Since the commercial success of the Los Angeles Games in 1984 (which realised a surplus of £215 million), there has been considerable competition to host the Olympic Games. Such hosting can be a catalyst for bringing forward general infrastructure investments that may have been on the drawing board for a number of years. As a result of the 1992 Games, Barcelona gained a ring-road, a new airport, and the redevelopment of an area of derelict waterfront for the Olympic Village, as well as the associated spending in the wider region of 422,000 visitors and other event-related income. The worldwide publicity and infrastructure investment that the Games brings should enable a host city to attract further general investment, future events and more tourists. Even a failed Olympic bid can attract investment to provide some facilities and infrastructure. Manchester gained a world-class Velodrome and several local infrastructure projects from its Olympic bid. The level of public investment is usually justified along these lines, with Whitson and Macintosh (1996) describing the importance that cities attach to establishing an identity as a 'world-class city' in the circuits of international business, culture and tourism. Invariably there is a cost to the host authority, but significant benefits to the wider economy (see Mules and Faulkner, 1996).

An important consideration is to include factors other than economic impacts in the cost/benefit assessment of sports events. For example, many such events, particularly those where regeneration is a major objective, often require the demolition of at least some existing provision or housing to make way for facilities, infrastructure or development. At worst, this can result in the traumatic break-up of entire communities. For example, in Edmonton for the Commonwealth Games of 1978 (Chivers, 1976) and in Calgary for the 1988 Olympics (Reasons, 1984) some working-class homes were relocated without consultation so that construction for the Games could take place. A similar displacement of indigenous communities took place in the development of Barcelona's waterfront for the 1992 Olympic Games and in Beijing's preparation for the 2008 Games. While many would see such redevelopment as a positive benefit that enhances the environment and image of the city, for those communities that are displaced the experience can be traumatic. In many cases, although these communities may have been living in comparative poverty and are usually relocated to improved housing elsewhere, such relocation is often to distant and unfamiliar suburbs far away from other families with whom friendships have existed for generations. The result is the destruction of working and social networks and, in some cases, entire communities.

Overall, however, sports event tourism is viewed as having primarily positive impacts in comparison to many commercial development forms. Sports tourism has played a significant part in a number of countries in the generation of community identity and pride and in the economic and social regeneration of decaying urban areas. In the immediate aftermath of apartheid in South Africa, Nelson Mandela spoke of the role of the 1995 Rugby World Cup, hosted and won by South Africa, in 'national building' after the years of internal turmoil and international isolation the country had suffered.

The impact of sports participation tourism

Sports participation tourism, particularly in rural areas, has been found to have made a number of significant impacts over recent years. Despite the evident sensitivity of rural environments and the fact that there will be some negative impacts of sports tourism development (see Standeven and De Knop, 1999), sports tourism has for the most part maintained a reputation as 'soft' tourism capable of contributing to the rural economy in a range of contexts across the world. Wright (2000), for example, describes how the use of the countryside by climbers and mountaineers can contribute to the economies of rural communities, specifically highlighting the generation of additional economic activity that assists in supporting local services such as shops, post offices and public houses. Climbing is a particularly good example of environmentally sustainable sports tourism, since the 'canons' and expected behaviours that are subscribed to by most climbers regard the defacing of mountain areas or rock faces as 'cheating'.

However, the growth of sports participation tourism in the countryside has led to increasing concern over the safety standards and environmental impacts of this sector. In the UK the Wales Tourist Board has established an Activity Holidays Advisory Committee to supplement the work of the British Activity Holidays Association, which maintains standards and operates a code of practice. Sport England has also noted its concern over the impact of activity-based holidays on the rural environment, where most such holidays take place.

The purely economic benefits of the development of rural sports participation tourism are arguably more unequivocally positive, particularly as traditional rural economic contributors are in decline in many areas. Countryside pursuits, such as hiking, climbing, orienteering, fell running and cycling, all increasingly contribute to the rural economy. In the UK, particularly as the National Cycle Network develops and rural districts and small local businesses invest in cycle tourism, it is emerging as a key element in rural economic development strategies. Jackson and Morpeth (1999) note that the National Cycle Network is seen as having the potential to generate £150 million in tourism receipts annually across the UK and over 3000 jobs nationally, particularly focused in rural areas. The 'C2C Cycle Route' from coast to coast across the rural north of England, for example, is estimated already to generate £1.5 million annually for the communities along its route.

However, a cautionary note should be sounded about an over-reliance on the leisure economy. For example, Keith *et al.* (1996) described how those counties in Utah, USA, that are dependent on tourism and recreation to maintain economic viability have a much greater annual employment variability than those counties which have a wider portfolio of economic activities. In fact, in the literature focusing on tourism's potential to generate employment, much similar concern has been expressed about the part-time, seasonal and casual nature of the jobs that are created (see, for example, Shaw and Williams, 2002). Such dependency on recreation and tourism can also result in a neglect of ecological and environmental concerns. For example, Weiss *et al.* (1998) studied reactions to ski tourism among ski tourists and ski resort residents in Austria and Belgium. They found that ski tourists and locals not financially dependent on tourism had a much higher ecological awareness than tourism-dependent locals. This was clearly a result of the latter group's vested economic interest in the industry and was further highlighted by the fact that differences between these groups on general environmental issues were minimal. Environmental concerns in relation to ski tourism were found to vary according to the extent of the personal sacrifice involved in addressing such issues.

Policy development for the sport–tourism link

There is a great deal of literature on the development of policy for the sport–tourism link that examines the problems affecting the extent to which sport and tourism agencies collaborate (e.g. Weed, 2001b, 2003). However, in this chapter the focus is on identifying those areas in which policy makers for sport and for tourism might reasonably be expected to work together. A useful tool in doing so is the 'policy area matrix for sport and tourism' developed by Weed and Bull (1997). The matrix identifies six broad areas for policy attention, these being:

- sports holidays (taken from Glyptis, 1982);
- facility issues;
- environmental countryside and water issues;
- resources and funding;
- policy and planning;
- information and promotion.

These areas are further sub-divided into 21 sub-groups, each of which are affected by a range of issues and considerations as illustrated in Figure 14.1.

Figure 14.1 Policy area matrix for sport and tourism

Sports holidays

Sports training	Activity holidays	'Up-market' sports holidays	General holidays with sports opportunity
Specialist facilities Major arenas Off-peak use Sports development	Nuisance activities Out-of-season tourism Water sports Cycling/walking Sports development Social goals	Conference market Nuisance activities	Water sports Leisure centres Conference market Sports development

Facility issues

Spectator events	Dual use of tourist facilities	Hotel leisure facilities	Use of tourism to sustain local facilities
Economic contribution Regional identity Specialist facilities Conference market Major arenas	Differential pricing Off-peak use Major arenas Specialist facilities Social goals	Out-of-season tourism Conference market Off-peak use	Major arenas Specialist facilities Differential pricing Leisure centres Social goals

Environmental, countryside and water issues

Farm diversification	Countryside access and integration	Marina Development
Nuisance activities EU funding	Water sports Cycling/walking Nuisance activities Social goals	Conference market Out-of-season tourism Major arenas Specialist facilities Water sports Nuisance activities Regional identity Leisure centres EU funding

Resources and funding

Supplementary funding	Joint bids for funding	Economic and social regeneration	Regional forums
Major arenas Specialist facilities Economic contribution Regional identity	Major arenas Specialist facilities Economic contribution Regional identity EU funding Social goals	Conference market Out-of-season tourism Major arenas Economic contribution Regional identity EU funding Social goals	Regional identity Social goals

Policy and planning

Marketing activity	Resolving conflicts	Codes of practice	Joint lobbying
Economic contribution Tourist information centres Leisure centres EU funding	Water sports Nuisance sports	Major arenas Specialist facilities Water sports Nuisance sports Social goals	Major arenas Specialist facilities Water sports Cycling/walking Nuisance activities Regional identity EU funding Social goals

Information and promotion

Information distribution channels	Research and advice
Regional identity Leisure centres Tourist information centres	Specialist facilities Major arenas Nuisance activities Conference market Economic contribution EU funding

Note: The categories used under Sports holidays pre-date the updating of Glyptis (1982) by Weed and Bull (2004)

Source: Adapted from Weed, M.E and Bull, C.J. (1997) Integrating Sport and Tourism: A Review of Regional Policies in England, *Progress in Tourism and Hospitality Research*, 3(2), 129–149. © John Wiley & Sons Limited, Reproduced with permission

The matrix aims to summarise those areas in which it might reasonably be assumed that agencies responsible for developing policy for sport and tourism might collaborate and such areas can be considered in relation to the interaction of activity, people and place discussed earlier. For example, in the Sports holidays area, a key consideration for major events relates to the post-event use of major arenas and specialist facilities. In the cases of the Atlanta Olympics (1996) and the Manchester Commonwealth Games (2002), the athletics stadia incorporated temporary stands which allowed for the adaptation of the facilities for the long-term use of the Atlanta Braves Baseball team and Manchester City Football Club respectively. In these examples the experience of place generated by and associated with athletics is different to that required for both baseball and football. Consequently, modifications to these stadia were made to ensure their long-term use, where a different group of people would expect a different place experience in watching a different type of activity. An example from the Facility issues area is provided by the City of Sheffield, which was keen to ensure that the facilities constructed for the World Student Games (1991) were suitable for dual use for both spectator events and general casual community sport. Here the requirement was for a place that would be capable of adaptation to produce different place experiences for different people participating in or watching a range of different activities. Consequently, the Ponds Forge swimming pool is one of the most flexible facilities in the world, and is continuously adaptable for use by Sheffield local residents, and as part of the city's ongoing sports events strategy.

The diversification of farms into tourism (see the Environmental, countryside and water issues area) can often comprise a significant element of sports tourism, with Busby and Rendle (2000) listing horse-riding, fishing, shooting and boating as part of this product. Farm tourism has become particularly important in some economically depressed areas of Europe, with the European Union offering funds to develop this type of recreational sports tourism product (see Davies and Gilbert (1992), for an overview of this sector in rural Wales). Here the experience of the place is changed, not by wholesale physical changes, but by its interaction with a new group of people participating in new activities.

Resources and funding is a key area where collaboration between sport and tourism interests could develop much further than is presently the case. While there are a number of US examples from the city marketing literature of the channelling of resources into projects that use high-profile sport to regenerate communities, there are also some less high-profile examples in relation to the use of resources for sports tourism as part of the marketing of rural areas. For example, the Adirondack North Country Region of New York State has developed a regional marketing plan based on cycle tourism with the aim of supporting the rural economy and sustaining local tourism services. In such cases the emphasis is on attracting new people to an area through the packaging and promotion of a range of new and existing activities. The aim is that new people and activities will serve to revitalise the place and consequently improve both the sports tourism experience and the lives of local residents. Related to such initiatives are areas of Policy and planning such as the development of codes of practice. In Wales, where activity tourism is an important market, the Wales Tourist Board established an Activity Holidays Advisory Committee to supplement the work of the British Activity Holidays Association, through which it liaises with the Sports Council for Wales to develop and maintain codes of practice to ensure the safety of activity holidays. In relation to Information and promotion, Gunn (1990) describes a collaborative initiative in South Africa relating to research and advice. The South African Tourism Agency and the Recreational Planning Agency collaborated on a joint research programme to identify tourism strengths in relation to sports and recreation facilities and resources. These final two examples highlight the ways in which the sports tourism experience might be enhanced by collaborative accreditation and research initiatives that ensure that people use the most appropriate places in the most effective and safest ways for the most appropriate activities.

Of course, the collaborations described above do not necessarily indicate the existence of sustained strategic sport-tourism policy development. In fact, although the research on which the matrix is based (Weed and Bull, 1997) revealed an increasing amount of sports tourism activity among policy agencies in England, such activity was not matched by any significant liaison between them. The vast majority of sports tourism activity that the agencies were involved in was promoted unilaterally, with no involvement of agencies in the other sector. Genuine examples of multilateral sport-tourism initiatives were few and far between, and more recent research indicates that this continues to be the case, not just in England, but worldwide.

Conclusion

The contemporary nature of sports tourism is such that it is no longer possible to view it as a tourism market niche. It is a multifaceted phenomenon that comprises a range of heterogeneous markets. Obvious differences within sports tourism are between those who watch and those who actively take part, between those who travel with sport as the prime purpose and those for whom sport is an incidental tourism activity, between those for whom sports tourism involves competition and those for whom involvement is recreational, and between those for whom different aspects of the activity, people and place interaction are important. There are, of course, many other dimensions on which sports tourists differ and this serves to illustrate the multidimensional nature of the sports tourism experience, to which providers must respond. For academics, interest in sports tourism has centred, *inter alia*, on impacts, participants, policy and provision, each of which have been examined in this chapter. Sports tourism, as both a phenomenon and an area of academic interest, has developed considerably in recent years, and the indications are that it will continue to grow still further.

Discussion questions

1   Outline the main types of sports tourism and provide examples of provision for each type.

2   Describe the impacts of sports tourism, both positive and negative, in both urban and rural areas.

3   Using a range of examples, discuss the areas in which it might reasonably be expected that policy makers for sport and tourism might work together.

Guided reading

A basic introduction to sports tourism, including good coverage of impacts, is provided by Standeven and De Knop (1999), while a more advanced discussion of the area, along with its theoretical bases, can be found in Weed and Bull (2004). Hinch and Higham (2004) discuss the developmental aspects of sports tourism, while the book edited by Hudson (2003) covers a range of sports tourism market niches.

Recommended websites

Readers are encouraged to visit the commercial websites mentioned in the text.

Key words

Luxury sports tourism; sports event tourism; sports participation tourism; sports tourism; sports training tourism; sport–tourism link; tourism with sports content.

Bibliography

Belton, S. (2003) The Supply and Demand of the Sports Training Tourism Industry. Unpublished MSc Thesis. Loughborough University, Leicestershire.

Bramwell, B. (1997) User satisfaction and product development in urban tourism, *Tourism Management*, Vol. 19, No. 1, 35–47.

Busby, G. and Rendle, S. (2000) The Transition from Tourism on Farms to Farm Tourism, *Tourism Management*, 21(6), 635–642.

Chivers, B. (1976) Friendly Games: Edmonton's Olympic Alternative, in J. Lorimer, and E. Ross, (eds) *The City Book: The Politics and Planning of Canada's Cities*. James Lorimer, Toronto.

Collins, M.F. and Jackson, G.A.M. (1999) The Economic Impact of Sport and Tourism, in J. Standeven, and P. De Knop, *Sport Tourism*. Human Kinetics, London.

Davies, E.T. and Gilbert, D.C. (1992) Planning and Marketing of Tourism: A Case Study of the Development of Farm Tourism in Wales, *Tourism Management*, 13(1), 56–63.

Delpy, L. (1998) An overview of sport tourism: Building towards a dimensional framework, *Journal of Vacation Marketing*, 4, 23–38.

Department of Culture, Media and Sport (2001) *Staging International Sporting Events*, Government Response to the Third Report from the Culture, Media and Sport Committee Session 2000–2001, presented to Parliament by the Secretary of Culture, Media and Sport by Command of Her Majesty, October 2001.

Gibson, H.J. (2002) Sport Tourism at a Crossroad? Considerations for the Future, in S. Gammon, and J. Kurtzman, (eds) *Sport Tourism: Principles and Practice*. LSA, Eastbourne.

Glyptis, S.A. (1982) Sport and Tourism in Western Europe. British Travel Education Trust, London.

Gunn, C.A. (1990) The New Recreation–Tourism Alliance, *Journal of Park and Recreation Administration*, 8(1), 1–8.

Hinch, T.D. and Higham, J.E.S. (2004) *Sport Tourism Development*. Channel View Publications, Clevedon.

Horne, J., Tomlinson, A. and Whannel, G. (1999) *Understanding Sport: An Introduction to the Sociological and Cultural Analysis of Sport*. E & FN Spon, London.

Hudson, S. (ed.) (2003) *Sport and Adventure Tourism*. Haworth Hospitality Press, New York.

Jackson, G.A.M. and Morpeth, N. (1999) Local Agenda 21 and community participation in tourism policy and planning: Future or fallacy, *Current Issues in Tourism*, 2(1), 1–38.

Jackson, G.A.M. and Reeves, M.R. (1996) Conceptualising the Sport-Tourism Interrelationship: A Case Study Approach. Paper to the LSA/VVA Conference, Wageningen, September.

Jackson, G.A.M. and Weed, M.E. (2003) The Sport-Tourism Interrelationship, in B. Houlihan, (ed.) *Sport and Society*. Sage, London.

Keith, J., Fawson, C. and Chang, T. (1996) Recreation as an Economic Development Strategy: Some Evidence from Utah, *Journal of Leisure Research*, 28(2), 96–107.

Law, C.M. (1993) *Urban Tourism, Attracting Visitors to Large Cities*. Mansell, London.

Lilley, W. and DeFranco, L.J. (1999) The Economic Impact of the European Grands Prix. Paper presented to the *FIA European Union and Sport Workshop*, Brussels, Belgium, February.

Mules, T. (1998) Events tourism and economic development in Australia, in D. Tyler, Y. Guerrier, and M. Robertson, (eds) (1998) *Managing Tourism in Cities: Policy, Process and Practice*. John Wiley & Sons, Chichester.

Mules, T. and Faulkner, B. (1996) An economic perspective on special events, *Tourism Economics*, 2(2), 107–117.

Reasons, C. (1984) Real Estate: the Land Grab, in C. Reasons, (ed.) *Stampede and City: Power and Politics in the West*. Between the Lines, Toronto.

Robertson, M. and Guerrier, Y. (1998) Events as entrepreneurial displays: Seville, Barcelona and Madrid, in D. Tyler, Y. Guerrier, and M. Robertson, (eds) (1998) *Managing Tourism in Cities: Policy, Process and Practice*. John Wiley & Sons, Chichester.

Roche, M. (2001) Mega-Events, Olympic Games and the World Student Games 1991 – Understanding the Impacts and Information Needs of major Sports Events, Paper Presented at the SPRIG Conference, UMIST Manchester, 1 May 2001.

Shaw, G. and Williams, A. (2002) *Critical Issues in Tourism: A Geographical Perspective*, 2nd edn. Blackwell, Oxford.

Standeven, J. and De Knop, P. (1999) *Sport Tourism*. Human Kinetics, Champaign.

Tomlinson, A. (1996) Olympic Spectacles: Opening Ceremonies, and Some Paradoxes of Globalisation, *Media, Culture & Society*, 18, 583–602.

Towner, J. (1996) *An Historical Geography of Recreation and Tourism in the Western World 1540–1940*. Wiley, Chichester.

Urry, J. (2002) *The Tourist Gaze*, 2nd edn. Sage, London.

Vamplew, W. (1988) Sport and Industrialisation: An Economic Interpretation of the Changes in Popular Sport in Nineteenth-Century England, in J.A. Mangan, (ed.) *Pleasure, Profit and Proselytism: British Culture and Sport at Home and Abroad, 1700–1914*. Frank Cass, London.

Waitt, G. (1999) Playing games with Sydney: marketing Sydney for the 2000 Olympics, *Urban Studies*, 36, 1055–1077.

Waitt, G. (2003) Social impacts of the Sydney Olympics, *Annals of Tourism Research*, 30(1), 194–215.

Weed, M.E. (1999) More Than Sports Tourism: An Introduction to the Sport-Tourism Link, in M. Scarrot, (ed.) Proceedings of the Sport and Recreation Information Group Seminar, *Exploring Sports Tourism*. SPRIG, Sheffield.

Weed, M.E. (2001a) Developing a Sports Tourism Product. Paper to the First International Conference of the Pan Hellenic Association of Sports Economists and Managers, *The Economic Impact of Sport*, February.

Weed, M.E. (2001b) Towards a Model of Cross-Sectoral Policy Development in Leisure: the Case of Sport and Tourism, *Leisure Studies*, 20(2), 125–141.

Weed, M.E. (2003) Why the Two Won't Tango: Explaining the Lack of Integrated Policies for Sport and Tourism in the UK, *Journal of Sports Management*, 17(3), 258–283.

Weed, M.E. and Bull, C.J. (1997) Integrating Sport and Tourism: A Review of Regional Policies in England, *Progress in Tourism and Hospitality Research*, 3(2), 129–148.

Weed, M.E. and Bull, C.J. (2004) *Sports Tourism: Participants, Policy and Providers*. Elsevier, Oxford.

Weiler, B. and Hall, C.M. (eds) (1992) *Special Interest Tourism*. Bellhaven, London.

Weiss, O., Norden, G., Hilschers, P. and Vanreusel, B. (1998) Ski Tourism and Environmental Problems, *International Review for the Sociology of Sport*, 33(4), 367–379.

Whannel, G. (1985) Television Spectacle and the Internationalisation of Sport, *Journal of Communication Enquiry*, 2, 54–74.

Whitson, D. and Macintosh, D. (1996) The Global Circus: International Sport, Tourism and the Marketing of Cities. *Journal of Sport and Social Issues*, 20(3), 278–295.

Withey, L. (1997) *Grand Tours and Cook's Tours: A History of Leisure Travel, 1750 to 1915*. Aurum Press Ltd, London.

Wöber, K. (1997) International city tourism flows, in J.A. Mazanec, (ed.) *International City Tourism*, 39–53. Pinter, London.

Wright, B. (2000) An Arm and a Leg: How Climbers' and Mountaineers' Money can Benefit Rural Communities, *Climber*, November, 88–89.

Chapter 15

The economic impact of tourism

John Tribe, University of Surrey

Learning outcomes

On completion of this chapter the reader should be able to:

- set the economic impact of tourism in a broader developmental context;
- explain the role of the state and the private sector in developing infrastructure and facilities for tourism;
- carry out simple cost–benefit analysis;
- explain the key economic impacts of tourism;
- explain the multiplier effect;
- outline the leakage effect and how it can be reduced.

Overview

Tourism can be a major contributor to national income and prosperity. Its main economic impacts include those on expenditure, incomes and employment as well as tax generation and foreign currency earnings (Archer, 1996; Wagner, 1997; Mules, 2001). In addition to this there is a range of favourable and unfavourable externality impacts (or indirect consequences) of tourism. In some countries economic impacts are particularly strong and tourism, for example, represents approximately 50% of the economic activity of the islands of Bermuda and the Bahamas (Conlin and Baum, 1995). Similarly, in terms of foreign currency earnings, tourism contributed over US$11 millions to the balance of payments account of France by the mid-1990s.

Tourism projects not only bring direct income and employment in the construction and running phases but can also have significant ripple (multiplier) effects on the local and national economy. The tourism industry is also increasingly seen as an appropriate vehicle to aid economic growth for developing countries. It is, however, sometimes difficult to determine the exact contribution of tourism to a country's economy because the boundaries between tourism and other activities can be blurred. For example, motoring, hotels and air travel can each have business or tourism elements. This has given rise to the development of tourism satellite accounts (see also Chapter 24).

Tourism development often requires substantial investment for infrastructure and various countries have different attitudes to the public/private sector mix in tourism development. Because of the complexity of favourable and unfavourable impacts associated with tourism development, cost–benefit analysis (CBA) is often used to offer a rational basis for decision-making when the state undertakes investment in tourism projects.

Tourism and economic development

The objective of this section is to examine how tourism can contribute to the long-term growth of economies and to the regeneration of areas affected by structural change.

Growth and development

Economic growth is defined as an increase in real output per capita of a country, generally measured by references to changes in gross national product (GNP) over a period of time. Growth is promoted by an increase in the quality or quantity of inputs into the economy or their more effective exploitation. Tourism is one of many industries that can be a source of economic growth. Like other industries its inputs can be examined under the headings of land, labour, capital and technology.

For tourism, climate, scenery, coasts and countryside are important resources classified under the input 'land' and it is by the exploitation of such resources that countries can use their comparative advantage against other possible tourist destinations. For example, the success of the French tourism industry is largely dependent on the country's natural endowments which attract tourism into cities, mountains, beaches and the countryside.

Turning to *labour*, it is the quality of the labour force that is important in increasing productivity and here improvements can stem from education and training programmes. On the other hand some destinations are able to capitalise on their cheap and abundant labour supplies to offer competitively priced tourism products.

Capital includes investment in new plant and machinery and its deployment enables labour productivity and economic growth to rise. Investment in infrastructure is important to develop the tourism sector and this includes airports, ports, roads and motorways. Jamieson (2001) outlines several key measures for creating a favourable atmosphere for investment in tourism infrastructure including:

- encouraging cooperation and integrated tourism development planning;
- creation of a positive investment climate;
- creation of special tourism investment zones;
- supporting human resource development;
- creating opportunities for strategic product development;
- adopting innovative means of delivering quality infrastructure development.

Technological developments have also led to improved performance of the tourism industry. These include continued improvements in air travel, reducing costs and increasing range as well as IT developments which have improved both information and marketing.

Case 15.1 illustrates the contribution of tourism to economic growth in Vietnam.

Regeneration

As well as being an important ingredient in national growth strategies, tourism may also be used in regeneration schemes. Regeneration is the term used to describe the process of economic redevelopment in an area that has suffered decline generally because of structural changes in the economy. In the UK structural changes have affected the countryside as agricultural incomes have declined and the general move towards deindustrialisation left areas such as Sheffield, Liverpool, South Wales, Birmingham and Manchester with declining local economies. There is no automatic process where a decline in one aspect

Case 15.1   Tourism and economic development in Vietnam

The year 1975 signalled the end of the US war with Vietnam and the country entered a period of international isolation and centrally planned economic development. It limited its trade and tourism exchanges to those with the USSR and its allies and tourism had a very limited economic impact on the country. However, a change in direction took place in 1986 when strict central planning was relaxed in favour of free enterprise. At the same time the period of international isolation was abandoned and restrictions on foreign investment and ownership were lifted.

Tourism was a key beneficiary of this change in policy direction. Vietnam has many of the basic tourism factors of production – unspoiled beaches, interesting landscapes, and cultural heritage. To this can be added a cheap and plentiful labour supply, but in the immediate post-war period the country lacked the capital to exploit its tourism resources.

This all changed after 1986 when foreign investors began to pump capital into Vietnam. For example, between 1988 and 1995, almost $2 billion was invested in over 100 hotel projects. These included multi-national hotel chains such as Hotel Metropole (France), the Hyatt and Marriot (USA) and Omni (Hong Kong). Tourism to Vietnam started a rapid period of growth. Arrivals rose from 300,000 in 1991 to over 1.3 million by 1995. By 1995, tourism earnings were estimated at over $400 million making a strong contribution to Vietnam's Gross National Product (GNP). By 2000, 130,000 jobs were provided directly by tourism as well as those in businesses related to the tourism industry. The industry's contribution to the country's GNP had reached 5.8%. By 2002 the country could boast 1940 hotels, nearly 670 guesthouses, bungalows and villas and 11 tourist villages. Tourist arrivals to the country continue to grow and international visitors to Vietnam reached 743,478 arrivals for the first quarter of 2004 – an increase of 4.3% compared with 2003.

There are two major problems facing Vietnam in its progress towards economic growth. First is the problem of foreign debt. The World Bank has classified Vietnam as a severely indebted low-income country and it owes over $26 billion in foreign debt. This hampers economic development. Investment is a key to economic development, but domestic capital is in short supply as Vietnam has to use a high proportion of its national income to repay interest and capital on its foreign debt. The second (related) problem is one of multinational enterprises. The lack of domestic capital has meant that much of Vietnamese investment in tourism has been supplied by multinational enterprises. The advantage of this is that tourism capacity is able to grow in the short run faster than otherwise might be the case. But the problem of investment by multinationals is that the multiplier effect of tourism and its benefits to the Vietnamese economy is reduced. This is because a high proportion of tourism expenditure is lost in leakages from the economy as profits are repatriated back to overseas shareholders of the multinationals. Both of these factors limit the ability of low-income countries such as Vietnam to reap the full benefits of the expansion of tourism. Additionally Vietnam suffers from poor basic infrastructure (road networks, airports and communications) and expansion of capacity here is again limited by lack of government funds to finance public investment.

of a local economy is compensated by a growth in another aspect. Because of this for many areas a point was reached where they became economically 'depressed' or 'deprived'. The economic indicators of localised economic depression include high levels of unemployment and below average per capita incomes and an ever-deteriorating spiral of economic decline.

Regeneration is generally about replacing the gap left by declining industries by implanting new centres of economic activity. Tourism projects can provide a popular focus for this. There is generally a threefold impact of regeneration. First, local jobs are provided at the construction stage of new projects. Next, local jobs are generated when the new projects are commissioned. Third, tourism projects often attract spending from outside the local area.

Smith (2003) examines the role of the cultural industries in attracting tourists and contributing to urban regeneration. Among the examples she cites are Sheffield in the UK, an area once renowned for its steel industry, which launched a cultural industries strategy in the 1990s and established a 'Cultural Industries Quarter' based around television, pop music and film. It also hosted the World Student Games in 1991. Schemes that have been successful in rural contexts include the Eden project in Cornwall and the Tate Gallery in St Ives.

State *versus* the private sector

Transport infrastructure is essential to many tourism activities. The provision of transport infrastructure, for example roads, railways and airports, requires considerable investment expenditure. However, it is very noticeable around the world that different governments have different approaches to investment. Taking the railways as an example, France has a very sophisticated system of national rail. At the heart of its system is the TGV (high-speed train). In order to run the TGV new, straight track had to be laid – a massive investment – and in France this was undertaken by the government. In the UK the story is quite different. The railway system was privatised in the 1990s and has since suffered from under-investment and a poor record of safety and reliability. So in tourism, as in other parts of the economy, proponents of growth-promotion policies tend to be split into those that support government intervention and those that prefer to rely on the free market.

Interventionists believe the government should play a key role in funding appropriate education and training, research and development and investing in projects and infrastructure. A compelling argument here is that without such intervention there would be insufficient investment in these areas. For example, to some extent private individuals will invest in education because it can be seen to offer a pay-back in terms of higher future wages. But an educated workforce brings wider economic benefits to a country. In this sense it is a merit good with public as well as private benefits and this is an argument for government subsidising it in order to capture its full benefits. There are two major arguments for government investment in infrastructure. First, the scale and risk is such that the private sector tends to be wary of such investment. Second, many of these involve 'public goods'. For example, it is difficult to charge for the use of, and yet exclude free riders from using, a local road network. This again means that such provision is unlikely to be profitable or attract private investment. Those who support public sector investment also readily look to the failings of the UK privatised rail system to make their point.

Against this, advocates of the free market blame government intervention for lower growth. They claim that government spending programmes 'crowd out' funds, leaving less available and at higher interest rates for the private sector. Similarly, it is claimed that the high taxes that are needed to fund public investment act as a disincentive for firms to invest. Supporters of the free market argue that profit is the best incentive for investment and that free trade and the actions of the price mechanism will ensure that investment and other resources are attracted to high-growth areas of the economy. Free marketers often favour 'supply-side' policies to promote private-sector investment. Supply-side policies include:

- reducing government expenditure to release resources for the private sector;
- reducing taxes to increase incentives;
- reducing trade union power to encourage flexible labour markets;
- reducing welfare payments to encourage individual enterprise;
- encouraging risk and entrepreneurship and privatisation;
- encouraging competition through deregulation;
- reducing red tape.

Opponents of public sector investment point to previous symbols of policy failure such as the development of Concorde (a supersonic aircraft) as representing the worst aspects of public sector investment – consuming ever-increasing sums of taxpayers' money and never achieving viable commercial sales. In contrast, Ryanair and easyJet are held up as virtuous examples of the success of private enterprise.

Cost–benefit analysis

Public sector investment can be complex. Whereas private-sector investment appraisal needs only consider profitability, public sector investment appraisal can include the consideration of wider public benefits as well as undesirable aspects. Cost–benefit analysis is a way of ensuring that all the costs and benefits of a project are identified and weighed up, including social as well as private ones. For a project or development to be socially acceptable the sum of the benefits to society (including external and private benefits) must exceed the sum of the cost to society (including external and private costs). This may be written as:

$$\Sigma B_S + \Sigma B_P > \Sigma C_S + \Sigma C_P$$

where Σ means 'the sum of', B_S = the benefits to society; B_P = the private benefits; C_S = the costs to society and C_P = the private costs.

Table 15.1 shows an example of possible private and social costs and benefits for a city-centre pedestrianisation scheme designed to attract tourists. Private-sector investment appraisal of such a scheme would calculate the private costs of the project and the private benefits, and since the private costs would almost certainly exceed the private benefits, the investment would not proceed. However, cost–benefit analysis would include the wider costs and benefits. For example, some extra costs such as noise and congestion associated with the construction phase might be identified. On the other hand social benefits of the scheme might include lives saved through improved road safety, greater public well-being caused by improved aesthetics from the project, and the effects on the local economy of new tourists and employment attracted to the area because of the project. In this case total public and private benefits would exceed costs. Thus there may well be an argument for public sector investment in the project. Case 15.2 illustrates the argument for public investment in tourist information centres in the USA.

Table 15.1	Cost–benefit analysis of pedestrianisation scheme
Costs	**Benefits**
Private costs	**Private benefits**
• Construction costs of project, e.g. – Labour – Materials – Architects' fees	• Rent of space to cafés
Social/public costs	**Social/public benefits**
• Longer journeys • Nuisance of construction period	• New jobs created • More tourist spending generated in the area • Fewer accidents • New amenity

---

Case 15.2   Costs and benefits of Welcome Centres

Pitegoff and Smith (2003) carried out an investigation into the provision of Welcome Centres by US State Destination Boards. These are traditionally operated at key vehicular entrance points to their states. They are often viewed as loss-making. However, they note that, if visitors change their trips in the state as a result of their Welcome Centre experience and this leads to an extra economic contribution to the state, then what was perceived as a loss in simple accountancy terms may actually contribute a profit for the state when these wider benefits are taken into account. In other words a wider public cost–benefit analysis rather than a strict accounting of the direct costs and revenues of the operation of these Welcome Centres can provide an economic argument for their continued existence.

Key economic impacts of tourism

Tourism is 'one of the largest industries in the UK (the fifth largest in England), worth £74 billion to the UK economy in 2001, about 4.5% of the GDP. It is a major employer in the UK: 2.1 million people have jobs in this sector, which is 7% of the UK workforce. Some 10% of all new jobs created are in the tourism industry, which demonstrates the importance of this growing industry to the UK economy' (Culture, Media and Sport Committee of the House of Commons, 2003). Case 15.3 illustrates the key impacts of tourism on the economy of Spain and the rest of this section analyses its impacts on expenditure and income, employment, taxation, the balance of payments and its external impacts.

Case 15.3   Tourism and development in Spain

Tourism has been an important driving element of Spanish economic growth in the period 1995–2002. Over this period it has contributed more than 10% of GDP per year with peaks in 2000 and 2001 in which it contributed more than 12% to the GDP. In 2002 foreign tourism brought more than 40,000 million euros to the Spanish balance of payments. Against this payments related to outbound tourism (tourism carried out by Spaniards outside of Spain) rose to 11,000 million euros. The difference between both shows a tourism credit balance of 29,000 million euros on the Spanish economy, equivalent to 4.3% of the GDP. Tourism has also played an important role in the generation of employment in Spain since activities in tourism industries tend to be labour intensive. Here, the typical tourism industries (hotels and other accommodations, restaurants, transport, travel agencies, etc.) generate more than one-and-a-half million jobs. This represents almost 10% of the total employment in Spain.

Two main problems have arisen from Spain's reliance on tourism. The first is its dependence on the economic prosperity of countries such as the UK, Germany and France. For example, Spain is particularly dependent on spending by German and UK tourists, who accounted for almost 50% of total visitors in 2003. However, the two countries displayed differing trends, with the number of German visitors falling and the number of UK tourists rising year-on-year over the 1999–2003 period. Earlier, recessions in those countries in the early 1980s and early 1990s caused tourism expenditure to fall in Spain. The second is that tourism employment tends to be low-skilled and seasonal.

Finally, the rapid pace of tourism growth in the 1960s and 1970s caused environmental degradation and this has threatened the prosperity of some of the earlier resort developments. However, by the late 1990s, tourism provision in Spain has become more environmentally aware and there have been successful programmes to rescue resorts such as Benidorm, Torremolinos and Magaluf from earlier planning mistakes.

The main sectors which benefit from tourism in Spain include:

- Accommodation, where receipts are predicted to amount to €10,592.2 million in 2003. This represents an increase of 17.7% on 1999.
- The car rental market, which is expected to reach a value of €995 million in 2003. This represents an increase of 3.6% on 2002.
- Tourist attractions, which are predicted to amount to €1373 million in 2003. This represents an increase of 46.8% on 1999.

Expenditure and income

It is not always easy to isolate spending on tourism from other expenditure in National Economic Accounts for it is not an industry in the traditional sense. Traditional industries are classified according to the goods and services that they produce (e.g. restaurant and café meals). However, classifying a good or service as a tourism good or service depends on the status of the customer (i.e. only includes those restaurant and café meals consumed by tourists). Most broad industry groups are involved to a greater or lesser extent in providing goods and services directly to tourists. However, while all the products that are produced and consumed in meeting tourism demand are counted in national economic accounts, the specific contribution of tourism is not readily apparent.

Because of this many countries now compile Tourism Satellite Accounts (TSAs). TSAs divide industries into tourism and non-tourism activities so that the direct contribution of tourism to the economy can be revealed and compared with more traditional industries such as manufacturing, agriculture and retail trade. TSAs are generally prepared using tourism surveys which can help estimate tourism values to the full range of economic activities. Typically TSAs are compiled using a combination of visitors' expenditure data from surveys conducted on tourists and industry data from national economic accounts. However, it should be noted that TSA estimates of tourism's value relates only to the direct impact of tourism. TSAs ignore tourism's indirect contribution to the economy (this is discussed later in this chapter under the heading of the multiplier). Using TSAs for Australia has shown that the tourism industry share of GDP was 4.7% in 2000–01.

Employment

The demand for labour is a derived demand. This means that labour is demanded in order to satisfy an end demand for a good or a service. Employment in the tourism sector is thus directly related to expenditure on goods and services by tourists. However, not all expenditure on tourism leads to the creation of domestic employment. For example, some expenditure will be made on overseas-provided services creating jobs overseas. By the same argument, domestic tourism goods and services will be supplied as a result of domestic tourists' expenditure as well as that of tourists from overseas.

The demand for labour will also depend upon the price of labour relative to other factors of production. For example, if the price of labour rises, producers will attempt to use more machinery (capital) where this is technically possible. It is generally the case that the tourism share of total employment is higher than its share of industry gross value added. This is because this sector tends to be more labour-intensive, on average, than other forms of economic activity.

Table 15.2 shows recent employment trends in tourism-related industries in Great Britain. It demonstrates a rise in employment in each of the component sectors and an overall contribution to national employment of 2.1 million (about 10% of the workforce). This represents an increase of about 27% in the period 1992–2002. However, in some areas of Great Britain tourism is of particular significance and is one of the main sources of economic activity. For example a 1993 survey by PA Cambridge Economic Consultants Ltd and the Southern Tourist Board found that approximately 20% of the workforce of the Isle of Wight was employed in the tourist industry and 24% of its GDP was generated by tourism.

In Australia, there were about 551,000 persons in tourism-generated employment in 2000–01, the number of tourism-employed persons grew by 7.4% between 1997–98 and 2000–01 and the tourism share of total employed persons in 2001 was 6.0%. Retail trade generated the most tourism employment, while the three areas of retail trade,

Table 15.2	Employment in tourism-related industries, Great Britain (thousands)				
Year	Hotels and other tourist accommodation	Restaurants, cafés etc.	Bars, public houses and nightclubs	Travel agents, tour operators	Libraries, museums and other cultural activities
1992	311.0	303.0	414.2	69.2	74.8
1996	399.1	487.9	506.4	104.0	73.9
2000	406.2	555.2	576.1	131.4	88.9
2002	418.0	545.4	535.9	133.6	81.4

Source: Adapted from Office of National Statistics, *Annual Abstract of Statistics*

accommodation, and cafés and restaurants accounted for more than half of the employment generated by tourism.

Table 15.3 shows the employment totals for the services and manufacturing sectors in Great Britain over the period 1980–2003. It shows a picture common in many post-industrial nations and illustrates the role of tourism in economic development. While employment in the services sector has grown in importance, manufacturing employment has shown a long-term decline. This is known as deindustrialisation. This is caused by three factors:

- First, technological progress enables productivity increases in manufacturing and thus the ratio of labour input to output declines.
- Second, manufacturing has been subject to intense competition from low labour-cost countries such as China and Vietnam, so many manufactured goods are now imported.
- Third, as incomes increase expenditure on services increases by a greater proportion (services demonstrate high income elasticity of demand).

Smeral (2003) discusses why, in general, tourism grows faster than the economy as a whole. He notes structural changes in demand and the differentials between productivity in tourism and manufacturing. He also notes that the demand factor explains why tourism's income elasticity is above 1 (i.e. demand rises proportionately faster than income).

Taxation

Recreation, leisure and tourism activities also offer an important stream of taxation revenue. A World Travel & Tourism Council (WTTC) research report forecast that travel and tourism's global direct, indirect and personal tax contribution would exceed $802.6 billion in 1998. This contribution is projected to grow to $1765.3 billion by 2010 and the industry's indirect tax contribution has been estimated at 10.6% of total tax rev-

Table 15.3	Employees by sector, Great Britain (millions)					
	1980	1985	1990	1995	2000	2003
Services	14.9	15.1	17.1	17.4	19.4	20.2
Manufacturing	6.4	5.0	4.7	4.0	3.9	3.4

Source: Adapted from Office of National Statistics, *Monthly Trends*

enues worldwide. Estimates for each of the 24 OECD (most developed) countries put the travel and tourism indirect contribution to tax revenues between 9% and 24%. As an example tourism tax revenues to the Province of Ontario, Canada, represent 3.7% of its total tax revenue. While most of tourism taxation revenues arise from income, sales and profits taxes there are some specific taxes on tourism such as air-travel taxes, departure taxes, overnight-stay taxes and environment taxes. Environmentalists argue that air travel is not taxed sufficiently. For example, in the UK there is neither VAT on air tickets nor tax on kerosene (jet engine fuel). They argue that taxes should be used to stem the rapid increases in demand for air travel, pointing to the environmental costs associated with this expansion.

The balance of payments

The balance of payments is an account which shows a country's financial transactions with the rest of the world. It records inflows and outflows of currency. For most countries the balance of payments has three main components – a current, a capital and a financial account. The main difference between these parts is that the current account measures the value of goods and services traded, while the capital account measures flows of capital, for example, investments. In addition there is a net errors and omissions item which arises because due to inaccurate data collection the figures don't always add up as they should.

Table 15.4 shows how tourism makes an important contribution to Australia's export earnings. For example, in 2000–01, international visitors consumed $17.1 billion worth of goods and services produced by the Australian economy. This represented 11.2% of total exports of goods and services. But although Australia's tourism exports have grown quite strongly since 1997–98, so have her exports of other goods and services. This has resulted in a slight decline in the tourism share of total exports since 1998–99. However, the data in Table 15.4 also shows that exports of tourism products compare favourably with other Australian 'traditional' export products. For example, exports of tourism products are higher than coal, and iron, steel and non-ferrous metals. This is true for many developed countries where earnings from invisibles can offset deficits on the visible account.

Table 15.4	Exports of tourism products and services, Australia			
	1997–98	**1998–99**	**1999–00**	**2000–01**
International visitor consumption (AUS$m)	12,792	13,446	14,611	17,100
Total exports (AUS$m)	113,744	112,025	125,972	153,140
Tourism share of exports (%)	11.2	12.0	11.6	11.2
Growth in international visitor consumption (%)	–	5.1	8.7	17.0
Growth in total exports (%)	–	–1.5	12.4	21.6

Source: Adapted from Australian National Accounts: Tourism Satellite Account 2000–01

Tourism is a net earner to the balance of payments of some countries and, for example, Blazević and Jelusić (2002) discuss the importance of tourism to the Croatian balance of payments. France and Spain boast large tourism surpluses, and tourism surpluses are rising rapidly for Turkey and China. On the other hand, Germany and Japan both have significant deficits in their tourism payments accounts, and the UK has a steadily deteriorating deficit. Table 15.5 shows how international tourism contributes positively to the balance of payments of the USA, although it is notable that expenditure on foreign tourism is rising faster than receipts from tourism.

Table 15.5	US international travel and tourism balance of trade, 1992–2002					
	1992	1994	1996	1998	2000	2002
Receipts/exports ($m)	$71,360	$75,414	$90,231	$91,423	$103,087	$83,593
Payments/imports ($m)	$49,155	$56,844	$63,887	$76,454	$88,979	$78,013
Balance ($m)	$22,205	$18,570	$26,344	$14,969	$14,108	$5,580
% change	17%	–17%	16%	–38%	–1%	–20%

Source: Adapted from Office of Travel and Tourism Industries, **http://tinet.ita.doc.gov**

Externalities

So far this chapter has examined the positive contribution of tourism to countries' national economies and, traditionally, economic analysis has measured impacts in terms of readily measurable variables such as employment, balance of payments and GNP. The objective of this section, however, is to draw attention to the issues raised by environmental economics.

Environmental economics involves a wider view of the impact of economic development and growth, taking into account well-being rather than just measuring how much richer people become in monetary terms. Initially, attention was turned to the so-called 'dirty industries' such as mining, oil and manufacture. However, tourism has not escaped from the critique of environmental economists. Here, issues such as global warming, acid rain and resource depletion have been highlighted as threats to economic growth and human welfare, and critiques and techniques developed by environmental economists can be readily used in the tourism sector.

For example, environmental accounting techniques seek to include a wide range of considerations when dealing with the costs and benefits of particular projects and industries. These include effects on the natural and built environment, as well as raw material and waste product issues. Air travel is a key issue here. Tourism accounts for more than 60% of air travel and is therefore an important source of air emissions. As incomes increase so long-haul travel becomes more popular. Air pollution from transportation for recreation and tourism has impacts at the local and global level. At the global level carbon dioxide (CO_2) emissions are significant, while at the local level pollution around London's Heathrow Airport, for example, often exceeds European Community maximum permitted levels due to a combination of traffic congestion and aircraft movements. This pollution includes carbon monoxide, sulphur dioxide as well as carbon particulates from diesel fuel and can cause asthma and other health problems.

However, when subjected to environmental scrutiny, the tourism sector can also display examples of previously unaccounted overall benefits as well as costs (e.g. habitat protection). Additionally, as well as being the perpetrator of negative environmental effects, the sector is sometimes the victim of environmental pollution caused elsewhere.

Multiplier effects

The analysis of data in the previous sections has looked at tourism contributions to national income and the economy at a single point in time. This is termed 'static' analysis. However, tourism expenditure, like any other form of expenditure, also has 'dynamic' or 'multiplier' (Archer, 1982) effects due to the circular flow of income and expenditure in the economy. The initial effects of expenditure will generate income but there will be further effects as that income generates expenditure and so on.

Calculating the value of the multiplier

For example, assume that there is an investment of £1m on a new hotel complex. Firms will hire factors of production to the value of £1m and therefore national income will rise by £1m. However, the effects of the investment do not stop there. The workers who earned money from building the complex will spend their money in shops and bars, etc. Thus the incomes of shop and bar owners will rise. They in turn will spend their incomes. In other words, an induced flow of income and expenditure will take place. The investment expenditure sets in motion a dynamic process, and the total extra income generated will exceed the initial £1m. This is known as the 'multiplier effect'.

The extent of the multiplier effect is determined by the level of leakages in an economy. The key leakages (or withdrawals) are savings, imports and taxes. Savings represents funds retained by households and firms. Imports result in expenditure flowing overseas, and taxes represent money taken out of the circular flow of income by the government in the form of income tax, VAT and corporation tax, for example. Where spending from the £1m investment finds its way into any of these leakages the multiplier effect will be diminished.

The existence of leakages means that money is flowing out of the economy hence reducing the ripple effect. So, in the example of the £1m investment in a hotel complex, perhaps £100,000 might be saved by workers, £50,000 spent on imported goods, and £100,000 taken in taxation (i.e. a total of £250,000 in initial leakages or 25% of income). In this example the initial effect of the hotel investment on national income is direct spending of £1m. Out of this, £250,000 is lost in leakages from the economy, leaving £750,000 to recirculate. This adds another £750,000 to national income in the next round but again when this income is spent 25% is lost in leakages. This process then continues, but with each round becoming smaller. It should be seen that the size of the multiplier effect will depend upon the amount of the original injection under examination and the leakages from the economy.

The Keynesian multiplier can now be formally analysed. This multiplier (k) shows the amount by which a change in expenditure (ΔEXP) in an economy leads to a change in national income (ΔY)

$$\Delta EXP \times k = \Delta Y$$

Thus if an increase in investment on a leisure complex of £1m led to a final increase in national income of £4m, then the multiplier would have a value of 4. There is also a formula for calculating the multiplier:

$$k = 1/MPL$$

where MPL = the marginal propensity to leak (the proportion of extra income that leaks out of the economy).

$$MPL = MPS + MPM + MPT$$

where MPS = marginal propensity to save (the proportion of extra income saved), MPM = marginal propensity to spend on imports (the proportion of extra income spent on imports) and MPT = marginal propensity to be taxed (the proportion of extra income taken in taxes).

In the above example, $MPS = 0.1Y$, $MPM = 0.05Y$ and $MPT = 0.1Y$, where Y = income. Therefore:

$$k = 1/(0.1 + 0.05 + 0.1)$$
$$k = 1/0.25$$
$$k = 4$$

Considerable research has been done into the impact of tourism expenditure using multiplier techniques, and multipliers are clearly an important issue for governments in assessing the contribution of tourism to economic activity. The main multipliers developed for impact analysis are:

- the output multiplier;
- the income multiplier;
- the employment multiplier;
- the government revenue multiplier.

Taking the case of the tourism income multiplier (TIM), values vary according to leakages, and empirical studies have found figures that include Canada (TIM = 2.5), UK (TIM = 1.8), Iceland (TIM = 0.6) and Edinburgh (TIM = 0.4).

Leakage reduction

It should be seen that analysis of the multiplier offers an insight into how the economic impacts of tourism development can be maximised to benefit the local economy. It can be seen that effort here needs to concentrate on the reduction of leakages. It is generally not feasible to influence the level of savings and taxation, which means that efforts need to be directed towards minimising imports. Here 'hire local' and 'buy local' schemes can help to retain as much tourism spending in the local area as possible.

It is for this reason that the multinational enterprises (MNEs) are often criticised for reducing the potential impact of tourism spending on their host economies. This can occur through a variety of routes and will be illustrated by considering the construction and operation of a hotel by a globally branded MNE. At the construction stage, building materials, fittings and senior construction workers may well be sourced overseas. At the operation stage such hotels will often employ expatriate managers and offer a range of high-value imported goods (e.g. wines, spirits and beers). They often have marketing tie-ups with other MNEs (e.g. car hire and air transportation) which magnify the leakage effects in imports. Finally, profits made on the enterprise are repatriated to the overseas shareholders.

A study conducted in Scotland found that there was a relationship between the size of tourism establishment and effects on local income and spending. It found that smaller organisations are more beneficial to local economies because of their tendency to shop locally and promote local produce. This is in contrast to larger establishments, whose central buying activities often take spending out of the local area.

Conclusion

Tourism is a significant and growing activity in many of the world's economies. Indeed the World Tourism Organization has claimed it to be the world's biggest industry. It can be an important strategy for economic development in less developed countries and a major driver of economic regeneration in mature economies. Approaches to the development of tourism range from strong government intervention to *laissez-faire* or free-market approaches. The main beneficial economic impacts resulting from the tourism industry are its contribution to expenditure and national income, provision of employment opportunities, tax revenues and as a source of foreign currency earnings. The impact of tourism expenditure on an economy is compounded by multiplier effects which arise as tourism expenditure ripples through supply chains in an economy. The benefits of the multiplier can be maximised by reducing the import content of tourist expenditure to ensure that the benefits of tourism spending remain in, and benefit, the local economy.

National Economic Accounts are not always well adapted to measure the full impacts of tourism. This is due, first, to the existence of 'externalities' which are not captured in market prices. These may include beneficial effects of tourism (such as improved labour productivity from the restorative effects of tourism) as well as negative effects. The latter include most notably the noise and pollution effects of air transport. Second, National Economic Accounts generally measure economic activity under old, established industrial classifications and therefore do not always record the full extent of tourism activities. Because of this tourism satellite accounts have been developed to capture the full economic impacts of tourism.

The economic impact of tourism is likely to increase as countries become richer for three reasons:

- Increased life expectancy and the rise in numbers of increasingly affluent pensioners will cause demand to rise.
- Increased wealth allows the benefits of growth to be taken in more leisure time This is particularly evident in continental Europe, where the working week has been reduced and holiday entitlement increased.
- Tourism has a high income elasticity of demand. This means that as incomes rise it attracts an increasing share of consumer spending.

Discussion questions

1 Explain the main impacts of tourism on the economy of a country.

2 What are the main arguments for investment in tourism to be left to the private sector as opposed to the public sector?

3 How does tourism exhibit multiplier effects and how can these be maximised in a developing country such as Vietnam?

4 In what ways do National Economic Accounts fail to fully account for the impacts of tourism?

Guided reading

The Economics of Recreation, Leisure and Tourism (Tribe, 2005) and *The Economics of Travel and Tourism* (Bull, 1995) each offer a full discussion of the wider economics of the tourism industry. Students needing a fuller explanation of some of the economic concepts should consult an economics textbook such as *Essentials of Economics* (Sloman, 2004). The *Compendium of Tourism Statistics* (WTO, 2002) offers economic statistics for a range of countries and the World Tourism Organization's website should be consulted for the wide range of publications containing economic data. The main academic journal publishing research articles in this area is *Tourism Economics*. Specific articles discussing the multiplier include Archer (1982) and Fletcher (1989).

Recommended websites

Statistics on UK Tourism: **www.staruk.org.uk/** .

The Tourism Education website: **www.tourismeducation.org** .

The World Tourism organization: **www.world-tourism.org/** .

Key words

Balance of payments; cost–benefit analysis; economic growth; externalities; gross national product (GNP); infrastructure; merit good; national income; tourism income multiplier (TIM).

Bibliography

Archer, B.H. (1982) The value of multipliers and their policy implications, *Tourism Management,* December, 236–241.

Archer, B. (1996) Economic impact analysis, *Annals of Tourism Research*, 23(3), 704–707.

Blazević, B. and Jelusić, A. (2002) Croatian balance of payment and tourism, *Tourism and Hospitality Management*, (8)1/2, 127–142.

Bull, A. (1995) *The Economics of Travel and Tourism.* Longman, Harlow.

Conlin, M. and Baum, T. (eds) (1995) *Island Tourism: Management Principles and Practice.* Wiley, London.

Fletcher, J.E. (1989), Input–output analysis and tourism impact studies, *Annals of Tourism Research*, 16, 514–529.

House of Commons Culture, Media and Sport Committee (2003) *The Structure and Strategy for Tourism*, Fourth Report of the Session 2002–2003, The Stationery Office, London.

Jamieson, W. (2001) *Promotion of Investment in Tourism Infrastructure.* UN ESCAP, New York.

Mules, T. (2001) Globalization and the economic impacts of tourism, in B. Faulkner, G. Moscardo and E. Laws (eds) *Tourism in the twenty-first century: reflections on experience.* Continuum, London.

Pitegoff, B. and Smith, G. (2003) Measuring the return on investment of destination welcome centres: the case of Florida, *Tourism Economics*, 9(3), 307–323.

Sloman, J. (2004) *Essentials of Economics.* FT Prentice Hall, Harlow.

Smeral, E. (2003) A structural view of tourism growth, *Tourism Economics*, 9(1), 77–93.

Smith, M.K. (2003) *Issues in Cultural Tourism Studies.* Routledge, London.

Tribe, J. (2005) *The Economics of Recreation, Leisure and Tourism.* Butterworth Heinemann, Oxford.

Wagner, J.E. (1997) Estimating the economic impacts of tourism, *Annals of Tourism Research*, 24(3): 592–608.

WTO (2002) *Compendium of Tourism Statistics.* World Tourism Organization, Madrid.

Chapter 16

Managing sociocultural impacts of tourism

Peter Mason, Luton Business School

Learning outcomes

On completion of this chapter the reader should be able to:

- recognise a range of sociocultural impacts of tourism and be aware of the context in which these occur;

- describe the nature of sociocultural impacts of tourism;

- identify relevant theories relating to the management of sociocultural impacts of tourism;

- identify the management implications of sociocultural impacts of tourism;

- demonstrate an understanding of different management approaches in relation to sociocultural impacts of tourism.

Overview

The chapter presents a discussion of important theories relating to the sociocultural impacts of tourism. It discusses the problems associated with trying to assess tourism's sociocultural impacts and attempts that have been made to overcome these. In terms of managing sociocultural impacts it is the demand side of tourism that is discussed in detail and there is discussion of the use of education, interpretation and regulation as management techniques. Several examples and case studies are presented from a variety of locations including Bali, Greece, Scotland, England and the Arctic region.

Introduction

As this chapter concerns the management of the sociocultural impacts of tourism, it is first necessary to understand the meaning of the terms society and culture. Sociology is the study of society and is concerned with the study of people in groups, their interaction, their attitudes and their behaviour (Ritchie and Zins, 1978). Culture is about how people interact as observed through social interaction, social relations and material artefacts. According to Burns and Holden (1995) culture consists of behavioural patterns, knowledge and values that have been acquired and transmitted through generations. It has been argued that 'culture is the complex whole which includes knowledge, belief, art, moral law, custom and any other capabilities and habits acquired by man as a member of society' (Burns and Holden, 1995: 113).

Culture is a major component of tourism, not only because it influences the way people, and in the tourism context this means particularly tourists and local residents, behave in relation to each other, but also because cultural manifestations can act as significant tourist attractions. In relation to tourism, there are many and varied cultural attractions. They include the following (Ritchie and Zins, 1978):

- language;
- handicrafts;
- art and music;
- traditions;
- gastronomy;
- types of work engaged in by residents;
- architecture;
- religion (including visible manifestations);
- dress;
- leisure activities.

The chapter begins with a discussion of the sociocultural impacts of tourism before moving on to a consideration of how these can be managed and the key players involved in this. Before proceeding with a discussion of sociocultural impacts it is important to be aware of the factors influencing these impacts. These are shown in Table 16.1.

Table 16.1	Major influences on the sociocultural impacts of tourism

- Who the tourists are (what is their origin? Are they domestic or international visitors? Are they from developed or developing countries?)
- In what type of activities are the tourists engaged? Are these passive/active? Are these consumptive of resources? Is there a high level/low level of interaction with the host population?
- What is the scale of tourism? How many tourists are involved?
- Where is tourism taking place? Is it in a rural/urban location, a coastal/inland location, a developed/developing country?
- What infrastructure (e.g. roads, sewerage systems, electricity supply) exists for tourism?
- What is the length of time that tourism has been established? (This is likely to influence the infrastructure.)
- The seasonality of tourism (time of year? importance of rainy/dry seasons)

Source: Based on Mason (2003)

Key factors, in relation to sociocultural factors, are who is involved in tourism and the nature of tourism activities engaged in. Of particular importance here is the nature of both visitors and host communities. The interaction of the two groups will be a major issue in affecting the types of impacts – when there is a large contrast between the culture of the receiving society and the origin culture, it is likely that impacts will be greatest.

Sociocultural impacts of tourism

Some of the more beneficial impacts of tourism on society include the following:

- the creation of employment;
- the revitalisation of poor or non-industrialised regions;

- the rebirth of local arts and crafts and traditional cultural activities;
- the revival of social and cultural life of the local population;
- the renewal of local architectural traditions;
- the promotion of the need to conserve areas of outstanding beauty which have aesthetic and cultural value (Mason, 1995).

In developing countries in particular, tourism can encourage greater social mobility through changes in employment from traditional agriculture to service industries and may result in higher wages and better job prospects.

However, tourism has the reputation for major detrimental effects on the society and culture of host areas. Tourism can cause overcrowding in resorts. This overcrowding can cause stress for both tourists and residents. Where tourism takes over as a major employer, traditional activities such as farming may decline. In extreme cases, regions can become over-dependent on tourism. Residents may find it difficult to co-exist with tourists who have different values and who are involved in leisure activities while the residents are involved in working. This problem is made worse where tourism is a seasonal activity and residents have to modify their way of life for part of the year. In countries with strong religious codes, altered social values caused by a tourist invasion may be viewed as nationally undesirable.

One of the more significant sociocultural impacts of tourism is referred to as the 'demonstration' effect. This depends on there being visible differences between tourists and hosts. Such a situation arises in many developing countries. In relation to the demonstration effect, it is argued that residents simply observing tourists will lead to behavioural changes in the resident population (Williams, 1998). Under these conditions, local people will note the superior material possessions of the visitors and aspire to these. This may have positive effects in that it can encourage residents to adopt more productive patterns of behaviour. But more frequently it is disruptive in that locals become resentful because they are unable to obtain the goods and lifestyle demonstrated by the visitors (Burns and Holden, 1995). Young people are particularly susceptible to the demonstration effect. Tourism may then be blamed for societal divisions between the young and older members of the local community. The demonstration effect may also encourage the more able younger members of a society to migrate from rural areas in search of the 'demonstrated' lifestyle to urban areas or even overseas.

The demonstration effect is most likely to occur where the contacts between residents and visitors are relatively superficial and short-lived (Williams, 1998). Another process, known as 'acculturation', may occur when the contact is for a longer period and is deeper. As Williams (1998: 153) noted:

> Acculturation theory states that when two cultures come into contact for any length of time, an exchange of ideas and products will take place that, through time, produces varying levels of convergence between the cultures; that is they become similar.

However, this process will not necessarily be balanced, as one culture is likely to be 'stronger' than the other. As with the demonstration effect, it is in developed-world/developing-world relationships where the process is most likely to occur. As the USA has one of the most powerful cultures, it is usually the American culture that predominates over the one from the developing country in any such meeting of cultures. This particular process of acculturation has been dubbed the 'McDonaldisation' or 'Coca-colaisation' of global cultures (McCannell, 1995; Mason, 1992). One of the perceived negative effects of this acculturation process is the reduction in the diversity of global cultures.

Although acculturation became an important process towards the end of the twentieth century, the desire of many tourists to experience a different culture is still a major motivation for tourist visits (Ryan, 1997). The motivation is to see and experience, at first hand, the actual culture and its manifestation, in terms of art, music, dance and handicrafts. This desire has contributed to a revival of traditional crafts as well as the development of new activities in a number of locations, including, for example, Bali (Mason, 1995; Cukier and Wall, 1994). In Bali, this in turn has promoted the growth of a souvenir trade that has made a significant contribution to the local economy.

However, on the negative side, the desire of visitors to experience the 'real' culture has brought into question the authenticity of the tourist experience. In some developing-world locations, for example Bali and the Solomon Islands, and developed-world locations with indigenous cultures, such as Canada, Arctic Norway and Finland, the provision of cultural artefacts and performances has become packaged for convenient consumption by visitors. Such commoditisation has contributed to challenges concerning the authenticity of the tourist experience. The commoditisation has led to pseudo-events that share the following characteristics: they are planned rather than spontaneous; they are designed to be performed to order, at times that are convenient for tourists; and they hold at best an ambiguous relationship to real elements on which they are based (Mason, 1995; Williams, 1998). Of particular concern, as Williams noted, is that these pseudo-events eventually *become* the authentic events and replace the original events or practice. For example, the keechak dance, part of a traditional religious ritual performed originally only on special occasions in Bali's Agama Hindu culture, has been shortened, taken out of its religious context and performed on a daily basis, to paying tourist groups (Mason, 1995). Tourists observing such an inauthentic pseudo-event may feel cheated, although this assumes that they have the knowledge in the first place to comprehend the local traditions and they may not even be aware that they are watching a pseudo-event. However, it can be argued that this type of performance may actually relieve pressure upon local communities and even help to protect the performance's real cultural basis from the tourist 'gaze' (see Urry, 1990). Nevertheless, there is danger that the local performers may, over time, forget the true meaning and significance of the practice or event now staged mainly for tourists. Likewise, traditional objects that are reproduced and marketed as tourist souvenirs may lose their meaning and value.

Immediately prior to the beginning of the age of mass tourism in the early 1960s, it was possible for a number of researchers and commentators to view the relationship between tourists from the developed world and residents of developing countries as a potentially positive one (see Tomljenovic and Faulkner, 2000). Such writers considered that tourism could act a positive global force for the promotion of international understanding. Approximately a quarter of a century later, views on tourism's potential to contribute to greater global understanding had changed somewhat. As Krippendorf (1987) argued, far from promoting more tolerance and respect, misunderstanding rather than understanding among different peoples was a more likely outcome of an encounter between visitors from the developed world and residents of the developing world. A major reason for this change in view was the advent of the age of mass tourism that, by definition, meant far greater numbers of tourists coming into contact with host populations.

Much of the preceding discussion has focused on the interaction between tourists and residents of tourist destinations, with an emphasis on the effects on the resident population. However, contact between tourists and residents also will clearly have an impact on the tourists themselves. This can contribute to the reinforcing of stereotypes, rather than the broadening of the mind that, according to the aphorism, travel experiences are meant to bring about. Nevertheless, there is increasing evidence to suggest that the impacts of experiences on tourists themselves can lead not only to changes in their attitudes, but may also result in behavioural changes. The Antarctic continent still remains relatively inaccessible and expensive to visit, but a growing number of tourists visited it in the last decade of the twentieth century. For many who travel there it is a 'once-in-a-life-time' journey. Those who visit often have a profound interest in nature and the wildlife of the continent and it would appear that they return from the Antarctic with not only increased knowledge, but also a far greater awareness of the need to conserve this unique wilderness environment (Mason and Legg, 1999). Therefore, it is possible to conclude that the experience of their visit has had such a marked effect that these tourists have become significant ambassadors for the continent.

A significant problem in assessing sociocultural impacts is that it is difficult to differentiate these from other impacts and hence particularly difficult to measure them. This partly explains why these impacts have been regarded in the past as less significant than economic impacts. Much of what has been written about sociocultural impacts of tourism has been based on research that has required those actually affected by these types of impact to assess the impact on themselves or on others. This form of research tends to be more qualitative and subjective in comparison with the more quantitative approaches used to assess and measure economic impacts of tourism, such as the multiplier. For some commentators, this qualitative approach is less acceptable than quantitative approaches as it is argued that it is less scientific. However, those who support the more qualitative approach would argue, among a number of points, that their techniques are more flexible and achieve a higher response rate and that their data is likely to be richer, more detailed and hence more meaningful (see Tribe, 2000).

A number of theories have been put forward regarding sociocultural impacts of tourism. One of the best known is Doxey's Irritation Index or (Irridex). Doxey (1975) claimed that the resident population, or hosts in a tourist area, would modify their attitudes to visitors over time and suggested there are a number of stages in the modification of resident attitudes. When tourists first visit, Doxey argued, they will be greeted with euphoria and then over time, as the tourist numbers grow, attitudes will move through stages of apathy, annoyance and finally to outright aggression towards the visitors.

Several pieces of research have been conducted to apply theoretical perspectives on sociocultural impacts of tourism. Getz (1978, 1994) attempted to apply Doxey's theory in the context of the Scottish Highlands. The study was significant as it was what Getz claimed to be a longitudinal study. Getz's study was in reality two snapshots taken at different dates and he investigated the Spey valley in the late 1970s and then again in the early 1990s. However, such return visits to the same investigation site are very unusual in tourism literature and hence the findings are particularly important. The sample size and content for Getz's studies of 1978 and 1992 were fairly similar to each other, but there were different individuals involved on each occasion. Each used a sample of 130 households. The main findings were as follows:

- In both surveys residents were mainly supportive of tourism.
- Despite mainly positive views, by 1992 there was much more of a negative feeling towards tourism. This was partly related to the fact that tourism was not found to be as successful as had been hoped in the 1970s.
- Those directly involved in, and hence dependent on, tourism were more likely to be positive about tourism.
- There was some support for Doxey's idea that, over time, locals had become more negative towards tourism. However, the attitudes appeared more linked to a general feeling of economic depression. Getz suggested that if an economic upturn occurred then views would probably improve towards tourism. Also, it would appear residents were particularly concerned that there were few viable alternatives to tourism in the area, so despite the lower satisfaction with tourism's impacts it was still felt that it was the best alternative. Hence the notion of 'trade-offs' was important here.
- The attitudes of locals had not greatly changed with the growth and change of the tourist industry and the number of tourists did not appear to have gone beyond a threshold in Speyside.

Hence, the research by Getz (1978, 1994) suggested that, unlike the theoretical statements of Doxey (1975), the attitudes of residents do not appear to change greatly over time. However, Getz noted some increase in negative attitudes to tourism in this time period, but not to the extent indicated by Doxey. Getz, in fact, discovered that attitudes to tourism by the host population were closely linked to economic fluctuations, both nationally and locally as well as to an awareness of the small range of other options to tourism in the local region.

Discussion question

1 Getz's findings from his research in the Spey Valley, Scotland were not consistent with Doxey's theory? What reasons would you give for this?

In the mid-1990s research was conducted into resident attitudes to tourism growth on the Greek island of Samos. The main results from this research are discussed in Case 16.1 as these findings provide a particularly good example of the variety of perceived different positive and negative sociocultural impacts of tourism from the perspective of local residents.

Case 16.1   Attitudes to tourism on the Greek island of Samos

The study was concerned with impacts of tourism on the host population in one town (Pythagorean) on the island, and their attitude to visitors and tourism in general. In the study, 20% of households in the town were given a questionnaire. As many as 71% of those questioned were involved in a tourism-related business and 59% had a member of the family involved in tourism. Most of those interviewed were relatively wealthy in comparison with the average Greek wage earner.

The main results were as follows:

- In general, residents favoured tourism (with as many as 80% strongly favouring tourism in their area).
- Some 84% indicated that the image of the town had improved since tourism developed.
- Residents were generally in favour of more tourism, indicating visitor numbers could increase.
- Specific questions were asked about the perceived social impacts. The top three factors seen to improve as a result of tourism were employment, personal income and standard of living.
- Sociocultural factors that were perceived to worsen as a result of tourism, in order of importance, were as follows: drug addiction, fighting/brawls, vandalism, sexual harassment, prostitution and crime in general.
- Those with direct involvement in tourism, perhaps not surprisingly, had more positive views on it. However, even those with no personal involvement indicated that tourism had positive effects, but were generally less keen and they also had more neutral and negative views in relation to other effects of tourism.
- Age was revealed as an important factor affecting views: the young were generally more in favour of tourism. Increasing sexual permissiveness was the only factor seen negatively by just about all groups, except the young.
- Length of time in the area was also important; the longer people had been resident, the less keen they were on tourism.
- Bigger family size also led to more positive views on tourism, and this was probably due to perceived job opportunities.
- More educated residents were more likely to have positive attitudes to tourism.

Source: Based on Haralambopoulos and Pizam (1996)

Discussion question

2 What would you suggest are the main reasons for the responses obtained in the survey conducted on the Greek island of Samos? How well do these findings relate to Doxey's theory?

The case study of the Greek island of Samos indicates that sociocultural effects tend to be unbalanced in relation to different groups in society with some being more affected than others. Hence, in the Samos example, those who were more actively involved in tourism were more likely to be supportive of it. This case study also indicates that it can be difficult to separate sociocultural effects from others. For example, on Samos respondents suggested that major sociocultural impacts of tourism could be considered under the headings of 'standard of living' and 'jobs'. These can also be considered as economic impacts and some researchers would include them in a discussion of economic impacts and not consider them as important sociocultural effects. The difficulty of separating out impacts under different headings also means that the management of impacts, including sociocultural impacts, is complex.

Managing sociocultural impacts

Discussion of the management of sociocultural impacts requires consideration of a number of factors that can be presented as questions:

- Who is managing?
- What is being managed?
- How is it being managed?
- Where is it happening?
- When is it happening?

Although presented as individual bullet points, the questions are linked and it may be difficult to separate, for example, the 'who' from the 'how' and the 'when' and the 'where'. However, the question relating to who is involved is a key factor, as the 'who' factor relates to decisions that will inevitably affect the 'what', 'how', 'where' and 'when'. This section of the chapter concentrates on the 'who' factor.

In relation to those involved in the management of sociocultural impacts, consideration needs to be given to individuals and organisations acting as managers, including government bodies, as well as members of the tourism industry. Tourism management clearly relates to the tourists themselves and will also need to consider the host or resident population. Hence, in summary, it is possible to suggest that the key players in the management of tourism's sociocultural impacts are as follows:

- tourists;
- the host population;
- the tourism industry;
- government agencies (at local, regional, national and international level).

Less obvious players, but nevertheless having very important roles, are the media and also voluntary/non-government organisations (including charities and pressure groups) (Swarbrooke, 1999).

Tourists are obviously of key importance in the management of the sociocultural impacts of tourism. Unfortunately, they are often viewed as the major cause of the problems of tourism. If they are perceived as one homogeneous group, then tourists are a relatively easy target for the so-called 'evils' of tourism. They are 'outsiders' and can be blamed by 'insiders' (the local people) for negative consequences of tourism. When the appearance of tourists and their behaviour is in marked contrast to those of the local population, it is also easy to point the finger of blame at them.

It should be noted that, unlike what is stated in much popular commentary on tourism, tourists are far from one homogeneous group. There are important demographic variables; for example, it is only necessary to consider 'seniors' travel in comparison with '18–30' activities to grasp this point. Tourism marketing media reveals that different types of holidays are targeted at male and female, heterosexual and homosexual tourists. Tourists engage in very different types of pursuits. Some forms of tourism are very active – sport tourism for example – while other types are relatively passive, such as sightseeing from a coach. Some activities consume resources and have marked sociocultural impacts, while others have minimal consequences. Tourists to one resort may vary according to seasonal factors; skiing in winter and walking in summer in a mountain environment for example. Additionally, an individual tourist may appear in one particular holiday location or a number of destinations in a variety of guises over a period of a week, a month, a year or a lifetime.

Managing the sociocultural impacts that result from tourists has involved two major approaches. One of these is to focus on the resource being visited, the supply-side approach, as it is usually termed, the other having been to concentrate on the visitor, or the demand side (Garrod, 2003). The following section of the chapter considers the demand side, the management of visitors, as this can be considered an appropriate and potentially successful approach when dealing with sociocultural impacts (Mason, 2002).

In relation to managing the behaviour of tourists, attempts have been made to regulate and/or to educate them (Hall and McArthur, 1996; Mason, 2002, 2003). Educating visitors who are at visitor attractions or destinations usually takes the form of what is known as 'interpretation'. Interpretation can be delivered via a number of different modes and in different formats, including books, maps and signs. It can involve the written word, but also the spoken word. In relation to the spoken word, tour guides can have a major role in the interpretation process (Weiler and Ham, 2001). Indeed, it is through the tour guides' direct involvement in interpretation that the inherent educational processes in interpretation can be demonstrated and the guide's role in managing sociocultural impacts is considered below.

A modern tour guide has five roles: leader, educator, public relations representative, host and conduit, which are in practice 'interwoven and synergistic' (Pond, 1993: 76). The guide's role as educator has been regarded by many as the most important (see Holloway, 1981; Pond, 1993). The main interaction involved in tour guiding is between the visitor and the guide. The tour guide also has an important role as a buffer between the visitor and the site visited (Ang, 1990). The role of the guide in this situation can be viewed as assisting in the interpretation of the site for the visitor.

If the tour guide is a member of the host community being visited, it is more likely that the guide will demonstrate cultural sensitivity towards this community. This should make it more possible for the visitor to gain a better understanding of the host community, which should enhance the likelihood of improved tourism management (ETB, 1991). Without this cultural sensitivity, it seems unlikely that a tour guide can accurately provide interpretation of the destination community (Christie and Spears, 1998; Yu, 2003). The effect that a culturally sensitive, as well as skilled and knowledgeable, guide can have on tourists is well expressed by Ridenour (1995). He relates the story of two friends visiting the Canyon de Chelly in the USA, an area once inhabited by significant numbers of Navajo Indians. One of the two friends makes an unguided walk and returns later with a broken piece of pottery. Her colleague, somewhat knowledgeable of Native American traditions, is annoyed and scolds her friend for picking up the shard. This provokes the response: 'What is wrong with me taking it, since I value it?'. The other friend counters with a question: 'Would you feel happy if somebody took a silver spoon that had belonged to your grandmother from your house, simply because they valued it?' Later in the day, with this situation still unresolved, the two friends take a walk led by a Navajo guide. During the walk the two learn about Native American spiritual beliefs and values. The one who took the shard is so taken by this new perspective that she admits what she has done and asks if she should return the shard. The guide responds: 'No, leave it with me. I will cleanse it and pray over it before returning it to the earth. You may pray that the spirits return to it' (Ridenour, 1995: xiii).

At present, it is not clear how successful interpretation as part of tourism management actually is, for only a limited amount of research has been conducted into its effectiveness. Stewart *et al.* (1998) indicated that, of the few evaluation studies that exist, effectiveness is usually determined by how much factual information visitors can recall. Such studies, however, provide little idea of how people use interpretation to help them *understand* places they are visiting, they argued. Orams (1994) concurred with Stewart *et al.* and argued that there is little evidence to suggest that interpretation programmes will necessarily lead to a change in the behaviour of visitors. Orams (1995) advocated the use of 'cognitive dissonance'. The theory of cognitive dissonance was developed by Festinger (1957) and the central concepts are dissonance, consonance and irrelevance. Festinger suggested that the existence of dissonance is psychologically uncomfortable and hence will motivate individuals to reduce it in an attempt to achieve consonance. The use of cognitive dissonance in interpretation, Orams (1995) suggested, would be an attempt to throw people off balance and put questions in their minds. This use of 'shock tactics' would be a way to get visitors to modify their behaviour. In addition, Orams (1994) suggested that the eliciting of emotional responses from visitors, as part of a strategy involving cognitive dissonance, may be the way to counter the problems inherent in educating tourists.

As has been stated earlier in the chapter, a host community can act as a major attraction for tourists. More often than not, it is the cultural manifestations of the community, including craft and art works, as well as less tangible factors such as music, dance and religious festivals that act as important attractions. In some cases, actually meeting members of a particular community and staying with them is a key motivation for certain types of tourist. Nevertheless, as with tourists, the host community is not homogeneous, but heterogeneous. Hence, it would be wrong to assume that there is such a thing as *a* host community – *any* host community is likely to be made up of long-term indigenous residents and recent domestic as well as international migrants. In addition to obvious variations in gender and age, a host community is likely to have individuals and groups with several different value positions, political persuasions and attitudes to sociocultural phenomena, including tourism. If it is acknowledged that communities are heterogeneous, then the importance of different interest groups and vested interests needs to be recognised. The acceptance of the notion of heterogeneous communities brings with it the realisation that the planning and management of tourism is a more complex and yet even more necessary task (see Mason and Cheyne, 2000). In accepting that communities are heterogeneous, Swarbrooke (1999: 125) suggests that they could be divided up in terms of:

- indigenous residents and immigrants;
- those involved in tourism and those not involved;
- property owners and property renters;
- employers, employees, the self-employed;
- elite groups and the rest of the population;
- those with private cars and those relying on public transport;
- affluent residents and less well-off residents;
- majority communities and minority communities.

The preceding discussion may have implied that host communities are passive recipients of tourists. This is not necessarily the case. There are several examples, particularly in developed countries and increasingly in the developing world, where local residents in a tourist destination are now actively involved in the provision for tourism and also its planning and management. This followed a groundswell of opinion in the early 1990s in favour of such participation (Middleton and Hawkins, 1998). However, this is not a particularly recent development and as long ago as the mid-1980s Murphy (1985) argued that, as tourism makes use of a community's resources, then the community should be a key player in the process of managing the sociocultural impacts of tourism. Swarbrooke (1999) suggested that the rationale for community involvement in tourism planning and management includes the following considerations:

- it is part of the democratic process;
- it provides a voice for those directly affected by tourism;
- it makes use of local knowledge to ensure decisions are well informed;
- it can reduce potential conflict between tourists and members of the host community.

One of the earliest communities to become actively involved in planning for tourism in their area was Erschmatt in the Valais region of Switzerland (Mason and Mowforth, 1995). In the early 1980s, the community created the Pro Erschmatt Society, which developed guidelines and a code of conduct to provide information on the perceived local needs for tourism and to indicate to potential tourism developers the views of the community. The code covered a number of economic and environmental as well as sociocultural aspects of tourism and was designed to manage tourism so that it brought maximum benefit to the local community (Krippendorf, 1987). The Pro Erschmatt Society code is shown in Table 16.2.

Table 16.2 The Pro Erschmatt Society code of conduct
The Pro Erschmatt Society supports a healthy tourism adapted to local needs that meet the following criteria:
• It must benefit the population as a whole and not individual speculators.
• It must not abuse the environment through speculation and thereby rob it of its recreational quality, but respect both the landscape and local architecture.
• It must take into account future generations and be based on medium- and long-term solutions, rather than short-term ones.
• It should allow the community to develop and should not impose a prohibitive infrastructural burden on it.
• It should not involve speculation leading to rocketing land prices, which makes property too expensive for the local population.
• It should not lead to a sell-out of our country.
• It must not generate dead holiday villages, inhabited for only a few weeks in the year.
• It must be based on autonomous local decision-making.
• It must create attractive jobs, take into account the local businesses and not waste land.

Discussion question

3 How effective are codes of conduct such as the Pro Erschmatt Society code likely to be in relation to the sociocultural impacts of tourism?

The Pro Erschmatt Society code makes a number of strong statements and is clearly an aspirational list, but could be criticised for being unrealistic in its aims (see Mason and Mowforth, 1995). Nevertheless, it does reveal a community concerned for the nature of tourism in its local area. However, the actual involvement of a community in attempting to manage sociocultural impacts will depend on a number of factors. These include the following:

- the nature of the political system at national and local level;
- the degree of 'political literacy' of the local population;
- the nature of the particular tourism issue;
- the awareness of the tourism issue in the community;
- how the tourism issue is perceived by members of the community; the history of involvement (or lack of it) in tourism-related issues;
- the attitudes and behaviour of sections of the media.

Murphy (1985) also suggested another important dimension about community involvement when he argued that it is relatively easy for a community to unite in opposition to a tourism development. However, it is far more difficult for a community to 'conceptualise, agree and then achieve its own long-run tourism future' (Middleton and Hawkins, 1998: 127). Jenkins (1993) indicated why this is a difficult process. He suggested that there are seven impediments to local participation in tourism planning. In summary, these are as follows:

- The public generally has difficulty in understanding complex and technical planning issues.
- The public does not necessarily understand how the planning process operates or how decisions are made.
- There is a problem of attaining and maintaining the representation of all views in the decision-making process.
- Apathy exists among some, if not a majority, of citizens.
- The cost in relation to staff time and money is increased.
- Decision-making takes much longer as a result of community participation.
- The overall efficiency (particularly in terms of time/money and the smooth running) of the decision-making process is adversely affected.

There is a multiplicity of government bodies that have a bearing on the management of sociocultural impacts. These bodies exist at different scales from national, through regional, down to local. Some European countries, such as France and Spain, have national bodies for tourism in the form of a Ministry or Department of Tourism. The UK has a Minister for Tourism but subsumes this relatively minor role and its public sector national tourism functions within the Department of Culture, Media and Sport. At the local and regional level, in the UK as well as in many other developed countries, there are not necessarily government agencies focusing specifically on tourism or government representatives with tourism knowledge and experience (Middleton and Hawkins, 1998). Such factors will have a significant impact on the ability of the public sector to influence the course of tourism development in a particular tourist destination. The main reasons for the involvement of the public sector in tourism management are as follows (Swarbrooke, 1999: 87):

- The public sector is mandated to represent the whole population and not just one set of stakeholders or interest groups.
- The public sector is intended to be impartial, with no particular vested or commercial interests.
- The public sector can take a longer-term view of tourism than, for example, the private sector.

The public sector in many developed countries has what may appear at face value to be contradictory roles. Governments may attempt to regulate tourism, but they also have a role in marketing tourism (Mason and Mowforth, 1995; Seaton and Bennett, 1996). Marketing is usually associated with promoting tourism, i.e. not controlling or regulating it. However, there are examples when marketing is used as a controlling measure. Such an example is that employed by the government agency, English Heritage, and the non-government organisation, the National Trust of England. These organisations work together in the marketing and management of two prehistoric sites in England. Stonehenge is the most visited prehistoric stone-circle site in the UK. Approximately 30 kilometres away is a similar prehistoric stone circle at Avebury, which like Stonehenge is a World Heritage Site. Stonehenge received approximately one million visitors per year in the last decade of the twentieth century, while Avebury received less than 200,000 visitors per year. The main reason for this great difference in visitor numbers is that Stonehenge is very strongly marketed to both domestic and international tourist groups. However, Avebury is deliberately not marketed to overseas visitors and there is also only a limited attempt to market it within the UK (Mason, 2003).

Although governments usually have a major regulatory role, in the UK, as Swarbrooke (1999) indicated, there is virtually no specific tourism legislation and this is particularly so in relation to sociocultural impacts of tourism. This has meant that public bodies and government organisations have tended to rely on the tourism industry regulating itself. However, there is no reason to believe that the tourism industry will be any more responsible for its actions in regard to sociocultural impacts than any other industry (Mason and Mowforth, 1996).

The public sector has also tended to rely on the education of tourists in an attempt to modify their behaviour in relation to potential and real impacts. Such voluntary efforts often involve codes of conduct targeted at visitors or sectors of the tourism industry in an attempt to regulate behaviour. As discussed earlier, educating tourists through interpretation at visitor sites is another commonly adopted approach. However, there is increasing evidence that these attempts at self-regulation are only achieving moderate success and there is likely to be a need for the introduction of externally imposed, government-backed legislation pertaining to certain sectors of tourism (Mason and Mowforth, 1996; Swarbrooke, 1999). Government legislation aimed at controlling tourist behaviour with the intention of minimising negative sociocultural impacts is also a possibility.

The preceding discussion has focused on the public sector playing a mainly reactive role in terms of attempting to regulate and control tourism. However, public bodies can be proactive and play a positive role in the management of sociocultural impacts. Governments may own or at least administer certain key attractions for tourism, including the cultural assets of built-environment attractions such as museums and historic buildings. These can be marketed and/or regulated in such a way that they provide models for private operators.

The tourism industry is often blamed for causing damage to destinations and showing little willingness to be involved in planning for long-term viability of tourism development (Mason and Mowforth, 1995). However, the complexity of the tourism industry makes it difficult to point the finger of blame directly at the cause of problems. Nevertheless, the tourism industry has been accused of (at least) (Swarbrooke, 1999: 104–5):

- being mainly concerned with short-term profit, rather than long-term sustainability of destinations;
- being relatively fickle and showing little commitment to particular destinations;
- exploiting the environment and local populations rather than conserving them;

■ not doing enough to raise tourists' awareness of issues such as sustainability;

■ being increasingly owned and controlled by large transnational corporations, who have little regard for individual destinations, their environments or communities.

The major way in which members of the tourism industry manage their operations is through what is known as the marketing mix (Middleton and Hawkins, 1998). The marketing mix can be summarised under four headings, the '4Ps' (see Chapter 6). These are as follows: product, price, promotion and place. Middleton and Hawkins (1998) add one other 'P' to this list, that of people. The marketing mix can be used by the tourist industry to manage the consumer, in this case the visitor or tourist. Hence, it is inevitable that the approach of the tourism industry will affect local communities that tourists come into contact with and, given that the approach is predominantly market-led, may be at odds or in conflict with attempts by government to manage tourism impacts.

Partly in an attempt to avoid or overcome conflict between the key players, tourism partnerships (or collaborations) have been put forward and operationalised recently. Collaboration and partnerships have been advocated in tourism because of the perceived benefits they can bring, of which the major one, it has been suggested, is that they can avoid the adversarial conflicts between different interest groups (Bramwell and Lane, 2000). In addition, the potential benefits of collaboration can be a greater democratisation of tourism decision-making, with the involvement of a range of players, the sharing of a range of views and the possibility of synergy and creative solutions to tourism problems. There are also a number of problems with collaboration. These include mistrust and misapprehension between the interest groups, embedded power relations which favour certain interests over others and perceived and real barriers that may entirely restrict access by some groups to partnerships. Also collaboration may be costly, time-consuming, not representative of some views and involve unbalanced power relationships.

Case 16.2 discusses the World Wide Fund for Nature (WWF) Arctic Tourism Project. This collaborative project involved a number of different players, including local government officials, tour operators, researchers/academics and environmental non-government organisations, in developing a framework and guidelines for linking tourism and conservation in the Arctic region. The case indicates a number of the potential benefits and problems of tourism partnerships.

Case 16.2   The World Wide Fund for Nature (WWF) Arctic Tourism Project

The WWF Arctic Tourism Project was established in 1995 with the aim 'to make Arctic tourism more environmentally friendly and . . . to generate support for conservation projects'. The major goals of the project were to:

● identify common interests of tourism and conservation and use these to reduce environmental problems and maximise the advantages for the Arctic environment and the local people;

● develop guidelines for Arctic tourism that not only educate tourists about conservation and appropriate behaviour, but that also generate political support from the tourism industry and tourists for WWF's conservation objectives.

The first meeting of the project took place in January 1996 in Longyearbyen, Svalbard, Norway, where the chief aim was the drafting of basic principles for Arctic tourism. The 43 participants, most of whom had been specifically invited by the WWF, covered almost all of the Arctic countries, and included tour operators, members of conservation organisations, representatives of indigenous peoples' groups, government representatives and scientists.

The meeting produced a Memorandum of Understanding (MOU) which made reference to minimising negative impacts of tourism, optimising benefits to local communities and promoting the conservation of nature. It suggested that cooperation between tour operators, as well as competition, could be in their interests. The memorandum recommended the creation of guidelines and codes of conduct for Arctic

▶

Case 16.2   Continued

tourism. It indicated the need for local involvement in tourism and advocated the use of a contract between local communities and tour operators. It also contained suggestions for operators to reduce the use of resources, to recycle and to minimise damage.

The next phase of the project was held in September 1996 in Cambridge, UK, and it transformed the MOU into 10 basic principles for Arctic tourism. Draft codes of conduct for both tour operators and tourists were produced as well as recommendations for communities involved in tourism. In March 1997, a second workshop was held on Svalbard. A number of those present at earlier meetings attended this meeting, representing a variety of communities of interest and coming from 12 different countries, including all the Arctic nations. The objective of the workshop was to refine, and develop a process to implement, the principles and codes of conduct. The workshop participants decided to create an Interim Steering Committee to guide the project. The Steering Committee members were elected by the meeting participants to represent indigenous peoples, destination tour operators, international operators, local tourism NGOs, conservation NGOs and the research community. It was decided that a number of pilot projects would be established to evaluate the usefulness of the various components of the guidelines project. Evaluation of the pilot projects was to take place one year later, at which point a new Steering Committee would be elected and the office of the permanent secretariat would be formalised.

In December 1997, the WWF Arctic Programme published *Ten Principles for Arctic Tourism, A Code of Conduct for Tour Operators* and *A Code of Conduct for Arctic Tourists*. These documents were the first to put this material into a widely available published form and 5000 copies were distributed to tour operators, tourist boards, environmental management organisations and government officials as well as to the general public. The intention was to promote awareness of the principles and codes.

In February 1998, a workshop was held in Iceland to bring together the Interim Steering Committee, interested tour operators, and tourism researchers. The purposes of the meeting were to:

- develop methods to measure compliance with codes;
- develop a structure for future implementation;
- examine funding sources;
- identify pilot projects to evaluate aspects of the principles, codes and implementation.

The project used the processes of negotiation and consensus building in an attempt to achieve its aims. A key problem was the lack of continuity, as not all participants at early meetings could make follow-on meetings. English was not the first language of most participants but was the main language of the project. Although many views were represented, not all voices were heard and some were more powerful than others. Meeting structures were relatively informal, but gave a good deal of ownership to participants, although may have contributed to a lack of direction at times. Despite these shortcomings, the project did build consensus and had notable achievements, not the least being the codes of conduct and the introduction of pilot projects to apply the codes and guidelines.

Source: Based on Mason, P., Johnston, M. and Twynam, D. (2000)

Discussion questions

4   Study the case and produce a table that is divided into two sections – one section should indicate the advantages of this form of collaboration and the other the disadvantages.

5   On balance do you believe tourism partnerships are likely to be successful or unsuccessful? Give reasons for your answer.

Case 16.2 presents a number of issues concerning collaboration and partnerships in relation to managing tourism impacts. One of the major issues was the nature of the arrangements for collaboration. In the WWF study, it is clear that not all of the parties who wanted to play a part were able to do so consistently. This problem of inclusion (or lack of it) is significant. Some stakeholders were unable to make it to all meetings, partly because of a lack of travel funds, others had problems communicating between meetings because of technical difficulties and some may not have participated because of the politics of WWF.

Although the WWF project had overall aims and reasonably clear objectives for each of the meetings, the arrangements were relatively loose and *ad hoc* and did not have a highly institutionalised structure such as a task force (see Hall, 2000). This appeared to suit most participants in that they were to some extent empowered and given a degree of ownership of the agenda and products. However, the project arrangements contributed to a problem of a lack of direction and leadership at times. Nevertheless, the WWF project appeared particularly good at building a consensus. Due to the nature of arrangements for the project, this process took the form of negotiated consensus building. Although not all participants agreed with everything that took place, their commitment to the idea that such a project was necessary took them beyond individual concerns to accept a majority view in order to keep the whole process moving.

The WWF project presented a major problem of coordination. As the focus was the Arctic region, it was by definition an international project. Participants came from many different countries as well as a variety of backgrounds and represented different views and stakeholders. On one level this led to potential communication problems, although attempts to resolve this involved the use of English as the key language. On another level the implementation stage was difficult to operationalise. Nevertheless, by the early part of the twenty-first century, codes of conduct had been created and a number of pilot projects had been put into action. It is still not clear what measurable success the WWF project has achieved, as these pilot projects and other initiatives still remain to be fully evaluated.

The issues presented in relation to the WWF project are not unusual. In fact, as Bramwell and Lane (2000) argued, such issues are to be expected. Hence, they need to be taken very carefully into consideration when evaluating collaboration as an approach to tourism management.

Conclusion

This chapter has indicated that there is a range of both positive and negative sociocultural impacts of tourism. Much has been written about the supposed negative impacts, including the demonstration effect, cultural damage, authenticity issues and specific factors such as increases in drug-taking, prostitution and crime in general. The negative consequences have been noted, particularly where there is a major cultural difference between the tourists and the local population.

Assessing sociocultural impacts is not easy and has tended to rely on obtaining attitudes of a range of respondents, particularly local residents, but also tourists themselves and other players in tourism. As local communities are not homogeneous, sociocultural impacts are perceived differently by different individuals. Some important research concerning sociocultural impacts has attempted to apply various theories, such as that of Doxey (1975) to specific contexts. Empirical research tends to suggest that local residents in many locations are willing to consider trade-offs in relation to tourism – they are willing to accept some negative consequences as long as tourism is perceived as bringing some benefits. This is particularly so where tourism is one of a small range of choices.

As tourism impacts do not fit neatly into categories, management of them can be complex. In terms of the management of sociocultural impacts, who is involved is particularly important. Hence tourists, host communities, the tourism industry and governments are key players. Education, largely through the use of interpretation, and self regulation, mainly in the form of codes of conduct, have been used as techniques to manage sociocultural impacts. However, it is not clear how effective these approaches have been as few evaluation studies have been conducted.

Partnerships (or collaboration) are an attempt to bring together different players in tourism. Partnerships are important in relation to the management of sociocultural impacts as they have the potential to lead to dialogue and consensus building, between frequently adversarial participants, around mutually acceptable proposals about how tourism should be developed. Information on the WWF Arctic Tourism Project has been presented and discussed and this has revealed some of the advantages of collaboration, as well as indicating the nature and effects of obstacles.

Discussion questions

6   In relation to a tourism development/activity in your area identify the main types of sociocultural impact. What characteristics do they exhibit? Arrange these impacts under the headings of positive and negative. Look again at the lists you have prepared and consider whether someone else asked to carry out this task would put the impacts under the same headings.

7   Consider an aspect of your culture that could be packaged and commoditised for tourist consumption. What would be the likely reaction of tourists? What would be the likely impacts of this commoditisation on the aspect of culture you have selected?

8   Why are sociocultural impacts of tourism difficult to assess?

9   How would you evaluate the effectiveness of interpretation as a technique in the management of the sociocultural impacts of tourism?

Guided reading

There are many sources on sociocultural impacts and the management of these impacts. Journals such as *Annals of Tourism Research*, *Tourism Management*, *Tourist Studies*, *Tourism, Culture and Communication*, *Tourism and Cultural Change* and *Tourism Analysis* should prove particularly useful. These journals also have articles, and occasionally special issues, on research methods used to investigate sociocultural dimensions of tourism. For example, *Tourism Management* had a special issue in February 1999 entitled 'Research Methods and Conceptualisations'.

Sociocultural impacts of tourism are also discussed in mainstream sociology and anthropology journals and on occasions in geography journals.

The UK based non-government organisation Tourism Concern was established initially because of perceived negative sociocultural impacts of tourism that were occurring as a result of tourism development. Tourism Concern produces a quarterly magazine, *Tourism in Focus*. This contains topical articles on sociocultural aspects of tourism, with particular reference to developing countries.

Recommended websites

Readers should search the websites of the journals mentioned in the Guided reading above for articles on sociocultural impact:

Annals of Tourism Research: **www.sciencedirect.com/science/journal/01607383** .
Tourism Analysis: **www.cognizantcommunication.com/filecabinet/Tourism_Analysis/ta.htm** .
Tourism and Cultural Change: **multilingual-matters.com/multi/journals/journals_jtcc.asp** .

Tourism Management: www.sciencedirect.com/science/journal/02615177 .

Tourism, Culture and Communication: www.cognizantcommunication.com/filecabinet/
Tourism_Culture/tcc.htm .

Tourist Studies: **tou.sagepub.com/** .

The Tourism Concern website – **www.tourismconcern.org.uk/** – is worth exploring. A number of useful resources are available from them; click on 'What we offer' and explore the menu headed 'Resources'.

Key words

Cultural, impacts, interpretation, regulation, social.

Bibliography

Ang, E. (1990) Upgrading the Professionalism of Tourist Guides, *Proceedings from the Travel Educators Forum*, 167–172, PATA Conference Singapore, 11–14 July, PATA, Singapore.

Bramwell, B. and Lane, B. (2000) Introduction, in B. Bramwell and B. Lane (eds) *Tourism Collaboration and Partnerships: Policy Practice and Sustainability*, 1–23. Channel View Publications, Clevedon.

Burns, P. and Holden, A. (1995) *Tourism: a New Perspective*. Prentice Hall, London.

Christie, M. and Spears, M. (1998) Training Tourist Guides: a comparative case study, in J. Klerk (ed.) *The Global Classroom: Conference Proceedings*, 20–23 August 1997, Drei Kant, Maastricht.

Cukier, J. and Wall, G. (1994) Tourism and Employment Perspectives from Bali, *Tourism Management*, 14(3), 195–201.

Doxey, G. (1975) A Causation Theory of Resident Visitor Irritants, in *The Sixth Annual Conference Proceedings of the Travel Research Association*, 195–198.

ETB (1991) *Tourism and the Environment: Maintaining the Balance*. English Tourism Board/Ministry of the Environment, London.

Festinger, L. (1957) *A Theory of Cognitive Dissonance*. Stanford University Press, Stanford, California.

Garrod, B. (2003) Managing Visitor Impacts, in A. Fyall, B. Garrod and A. Leask (eds) *Managing Visitor Attractions: New Directions*. Butterworth Heinemann, Oxford.

Getz, D. (1978) Tourism and population change: long-term impacts of tourism in the Badenoch and Strathspey District of the Scottish Highlands, *Scottish Geographical Magazine*, 102(2), 113–126.

Getz, D. (1994) Residents' Attitudes to Tourism, *Tourism Management*, 15(4), 247–258.

Hall, C.M. (2000) *Tourism Planning*. Prentice Hall, London.

Hall, C.M. and MacArthur, S. (1996) *Heritage Management in Australia and New Zealand*. Oxford University Press, Melbourne.

Haralambopoulos, N. and Pizam, A. (1998) Perceived Impacts of Tourism: The Case of Samos, *Annals of Tourism Research*, 23, 503–526.

Holloway, C. (1991) *The Business of Tourism*. Pitman, London.

Jenkins, J. (1993) Tourism Policy in Rural New South Wales – policy and research, *Geojournal*, 29(3), 281–290.

Krippendorf, J. (1987) *The Holiday Makers*. Heinemann, London.

MacCannell, D. (1995) *The Tourist Papers*. Routledge, London.

Mason, P. (1992) The Environmentally-Friendly Traveller, in M. Shales (ed.) *The Travellers Handbook*, 32–36. Wexas, London.

Mason, P. (1995) *Tourism: Environment and Development Perspectives*. World Wide Fund for Nature, Godalming, UK.

Mason, P. (2002) Why is the Visitor Always Guilty Until Proven Innocent? paper given at weekly seminar series organised by London Metropolitan University Centre for Leisure and Tourism, 6 April 2002.

Mason, P. (2003) *Tourism Impacts, Planning and Management*. Butterworth Heinemann, Oxford.

Mason, P. and Cheyne, J. (2000) Resident Attitudes to Tourism Development, *Annals of Tourism Research*, 27(2), 391–411.

Mason, P., Johnston, M. and Twynam, D. (2000) The World Wide Fund for Nature Arctic Tourism Project, *Journal of Sustainable Tourism*, 8(4), 305–324.

Mason, P. and Legg, S. (1999) Antarctic Tourism: Activities, Impacts, Management Issues and a proposed Research Agenda, *Pacific Tourism Review*, 3(1), 71–84.

Mason, P. and Mowforth, M. (1995) *Codes of Conduct in Tourism*, University of Plymouth, Research Paper No. 1, Department of Geographical Sciences.

Mason, P. and Mowforth, M. (1996) Codes of Conduct in Tourism, *Progress in Tourism and Hospitality Research*, 2(2), 151–167.

Middleton, V. and Hawkins, R. (1998) *Sustainable Tourism: A Marketing Perspective*. Butterworth Heinemann, Oxford.

Murphy, P. (1985) *Tourism: a Community Approach*. Methuen, London.

Orams, M. (1994) Creating Effective Interpretation for Managing Interaction between Tourists and Wildlife, *The Australian Journal of Environmental Education*, 10, 21–34.

Orams, M. (1995) Using Interpretation to Manage Nature-based Tourism, *Journal of Sustainable Tourism*, (4)2, 81–94.

Pond, K.L. (1993) *The Professional Guide*. Van Nostrand Reinhold, New York.

Ridenour, J. (1995) Foreword, in D.M. Knudson, T. Cable and L. Beck *Interpretation of Natural and Cultural Resources*, xiii–xiv. Venture Publishing, State College, Pennsylvania.

Ritchie, J. and Zins, M. (1978) Culture as a determinant of the attractiveness of a tourist region, *Annals of Tourism Research*, (5), 252–267.

Ryan, C. (1997) *The Tourist Experience*. Cassell, London.

Seaton, A. and Bennett, M. (1996) *Marketing Tourism Products*. International Thomson Business Press, London.

Stewart, E.J., Hayward, B.M., Devlin, P.J. and Kirby, V.G. (1998) The Place of Interpretation: a new approach to the evaluation of interpretation, *Tourism Management*, 19(3), 257–266.

Swarbrooke, J. (1999) *Sustainable Tourism Management*. CABI Publishing, Wallingford.

Tilden, F. (1957) *Interpreting Our Heritage*. University of North Carolina Press, Chapel Hill, North Carolina.

Tomljenovic, R. and Faulkner, B. (2000) Tourism and World Peace: a conundrum for the twenty first century, in B. Faulkner, G. Moscardo and E. Laws (eds) *Tourism in the Twenty First Century*. Continuum, London.

Tribe, J. (2000) The Philosophic Practitioner, *Annals of Tourism Research*, 27(3), 437–451.

Urry, J. (1990) *The Tourist Gaze*. Sage, London.

Valentine, P. (1992) Nature-based Tourism, in B. Weiler and C.M. Hall (eds) *Special Interest Tourism*, 105–128. Bellhaven, London.

Veal, A.J. (1994) *Leisure policy and planning*. Longman/ILAM, Harlow.

Weiler, B. and Ham, S. (2001) Tour Guides and Interpretation, in *The Encyclopedia of Ecotourism*, 549–563. CABI, Oxford.

Williams, S. (1998) *Tourism Geography*. Routledge, London.

Yu, X. (2003) *Conceptualising and Assessing Intercultural Competence of Tour Guides*, unpublished PhD thesis, Monash University, Melbourne.

Chapter 17

Managing the environmental impacts of tourism

Andrew Holden, Buckingham Chilterns University College

Learning outcomes

On completion of this chapter the reader should be able to:

■ understand that tourism can have both negative and positive environmental impacts;

■ comprehend how the behaviour of tourism stakeholders impacts upon the environment;

■ recognise the range of techniques available to manage the environmental impacts associated with tourism;

■ apply a selection of the techniques of environmental management.

Overview

The term 'environment' is a generic concept, encompassing different contexts including the cultural, social, political and economic. In this chapter, the term is used as being synonymous with a further context, and perhaps the most often assumed meaning of environment, that of nature. However, the reader should remember that how we use nature carries with it political, economic and social implications.

The impacts of human activities upon nature have implications for its biodiversity and the welfare of individual species. They also give rise to anthropogenic-centred concerns, i.e. concerns that we have of how these changes may affect the quality of our lives. For example, ozone depletion, global warming and pollution bring with them a range of health and lifestyle implications, such as increased occurrences of melanoma, flooding and respiratory complaints. The concerns of a significant number of people also extend beyond the anthropocentric, to include issues of the welfare of non-human fauna and flora. For example, concerns over animal experimentation and the loss of biodiversity, reflect how environmental ethics have become a feature of global society at the beginning of the twenty-first century (Holden, 2003).

In terms of the impacts that tourism can have for nature, it is important to realise that these may be both negative and positive. Although the focus of this chapter is upon the use of environmental management to mitigate the negative environmental impacts, it should be remembered that tourism can also encourage conservation, which is discussed later in the chapter. When considering the environmental impacts of tourism it is necessary to understand that often we are talking of incremental and cumulative effects. For example, one tourist who walks over a coral reef may kill the living organisms of the reef that are stepped on, but the overall damage to the reef will be minimal. However, if this behaviour is multiplied hundreds or thousands of times, the potential for greater and longer-lasting damage is increased. The more that tourists, businesses, and local people and governments use natural resources for tourism in an inappropriate way, the greater the potential for negative impacts.

Negative impacts

Although it may possibly seem strange to think that tourism could have negative impacts on nature, such effects were being observed by the 1960s. Milne (1988) comments that by the early 1960s there was already concern being expressed over the possible ecological imbalance that could result from tourism development in Tahiti in the Pacific. The observation of the effects of increasing numbers of tourists in the 1960s led Mishan (1967: 141) to write: 'Once serene and lovely towns such as Andorra and Biarritz are smothered with new hotels and the dust and roar of motorised traffic. The isles of Greece have become a sprinkling of lidos in the Aegean Sea. Delphi is ringed with shiny new hotels. In Italy the real estate man is responsible for the atrocities exemplified by the skyscraper approach to Rome seen across the Campagna, while the annual invasion of tourists has transformed once-famous resorts Rapallo, Capri, Alassio and scores of others, before the last war no less enchanting, into so many vulgar Coney Islands'.

Within Mishan's concerns, the 'visual' effects of tourism are evident. Tourism is, of course, heavily dependent upon the 'pleasing' visual qualities of the environment, but concerns over 'aesthetic pollution' are unlike scientifically measured changes in water quality. Thus the sense of sight is an important, if perhaps a somewhat subjective, means of determining tourism's negative impact. The replication of similar hotel construction on many coastlines of the world that fails to reflect the local culture, the construction of 'Playa del Anywhere', is a common criticism of tourism's environmental impact. For example, as Burac (1996: 71) comments on the development of tourism in the Guadeloupe and Martinique islands situated in the Lesser Antilles: 'The most worrying problem now prevalent in the islands relates to the anarchic urbanisation of the coasts . . . . Also, the built-up areas by the seaside are often not aesthetically attractive due to the diversity of architectural styles, the disappearance of traditional creole homes and the disorderly way in which public posters are displayed'. Besides the urbanisation of stretches of coastline, in mountain areas tourism has also created unsightly development. Besides hotel and apartment construction, the development of ski lifts and pistes has also been heavily criticised as a form of aesthetic pollution (Holden, 2000).

Returning to Mishan's (1967) quote, he refers to the dust from construction and the 'roar of motorised traffic'. Alongside the aesthetic, other types of pollution that may result from tourism include both air and noise pollution. The problems of air pollution associated with the transport of tourists must lead to a questioning of whether tourism can ever be truely environmentally sustainable. Particular concerns relate to the rapid increase in air travel in the second half of the twentieth century, a trend that is set to continue in this century. Per passenger, aviation produces more pollution than any other form of transport, accounting for 3% of the total amount of the world's carbon dioxide emissions or equivalent to the entire CO_2 output of British Industry (Malone, 1998). Besides contributing to global warming, air transport emits 2%–3% of the total global emissions of nitrogen oxides, which are believed to reduce ozone concentrations in the stratosphere (Friends of the Earth, 1997).

Air pollution is also associated with the development of airports for tourism. Health issues associated with airports include respiratory problems caused by emissions from aircraft and car traffic, and stress associated with noise pollution from air traffic. According to Whitelegg (1999) aircraft produce significant amounts of nitrogen oxides during take-off and landings. The potential effects of this pollution on health are dramatic, with aircraft engines being held responsible for $10\frac{1}{2}$% of the cancer cases in southwest Chicago caused by toxic air pollution (Whitelegg, 1999). Emissions of nitrogen oxides and hydrocarbons at lower levels also contribute to regional smog problems by forming low-level ozone on calm summer days, which is harmful to health.

A common misconception is to equate transport in tourism solely with airlines. However, the most common form of transport for domestic and international tourism is the car. For example, a very common pattern of summer holiday travel in Europe is for tourists from the countries of northern Europe such as Germany, Scandinavia, and the Benelux countries to drive down to the Mediterranean coast for their vacation. When domestic tourism is also taken into account, then the effect of the motor-car becomes even more prominent, as the majority of domestic trips are undertaken by car. For those people living in transport transit areas, the effects of tourism are predominantly ones of inconvenience associated with pollution and safety concerns. Although the social and health effects of transit traffic upon local communities is an under-researched area, Zimmermann (1995: 36) commenting on transit traffic through the European Alps remarks: 'The transit traffic is one of the most evident problems within the Alpine area. In several regions local populations' endurance levels have already been reached or exceeded'.

Within destination areas the air quality may deteriorate as a result of both extra traffic and construction. Just as Mishan (1967) commented on the problem of dust, Briguglio and Briguglio (1996) remark that the demolishing of existing buildings and the construction of new ones for tourism have generated vast amounts of dust on the Mediterranean island of Malta.

Noise pollution is another aspect associated with the extra transport traffic generated for tourism. According to Mieczkowski (1995) most complaints associated with tourism relating to noise are from air traffic. Noise pollution is particularly a problem for those residents who live around busy international and domestic airports, while noise from the construction of tourism facilities can also be a problem for residents and tourists. Briguglio and Briguglio (1996) observe that the building of hotels and other construction activity in destinations generate intense noise. Nightclubs open until the early morning, and increased car traffic from tourism movements, all add to the noise pollution experienced by both residents and tourists in tourism destinations.

The last common type of pollution is water pollution. Typically, this is a consequence of untreated sewage being pumped into the seas and oceans in tourism destinations. For instance, in the most visited tourist area of the world, the Mediterranean, only 30% of over 700 towns and cities on the coastline treat sewage before discharging it into the sea (Jenner and Smith, 1992). In the Caribbean Basin, where 100 million tourists annually join the 170 million inhabitants, only 10% of the sewage is treated before being discharged into the sea. The most worrying aspect is that, compared to other areas of the world, these figures are actually good. Other regular international tourist destinations such as east Asia and Africa and the islands of the South Pacific, with a few exceptions, have either no sewage treatment or treatment plants that are totally inadequate for the size of the population (Jenner and Smith, 1992). The problem of water contamination from human sewage is not caused exclusively by tourism but is reflective of an inadequate infrastructure to meet the needs of both local people and tourists.

Besides the consequences it can have for human health, causing diseases ranging from mild stomach upsets to typhoid through the intake of water contaminated by faeces, human sewage also causes eutrophication (nutrient enrichment) of the water. The pollution of the seas and oceans adversely affects tourism and subsequently the economic prosperity of those dependent upon it. Eutrophication may lead to a downturn in tourism demand as experienced on the Romagna coast of Italy in 1989. According to Becheri (1991), the total number of tourist bookings on the Romagna coast fell by 25% in 1989 compared to 1988, owing to the eutrophication of the Adriatic and the spread of algae on the surface of the water. The source of the pollution was from agricultural, urban and industrial wastes which were deposited in the River Po and subsequently flowed out into the Adriatic. Similarly, the fear of a typhoid outbreak in Salou in Spain in 1988 resulting from contaminated water led to a 70% decline in tourist bookings the next year (Kirkby, 1996). By the late 1980s, many Spanish beaches were considered dirty, with only three beaches on the Costa del Sol being considered clean enough for 'blue flag' status in 1989 (Mieczkowski, 1995). The decline in water and beach quality contributed significantly to a slump in tourism receipts in Spain in the late 1980s.

Besides the pollution resulting from the disposal of untreated human waste, water pollution is also caused by fertilisers and herbicides, which are widely used on golf courses and hotel gardens. The water containing the chemicals seeps through the earth to the groundwater lying 5 to 50 metres below the earth's surface and through aquifers it eventually reaches rivers, lakes and seas (Mieczkowski, 1995). Other sources of water pollution are caused by motorised leisure activities such as power boating, and even sun tan oil being washed off tourists when swimming can result in localised pollution. However, although tourism appears to be a culprit of much of the planet's water pollution it is important to realise it is only a contributory factor. The major sources of water pollution come from oil spills, industrial waste pumped into the sea, and chemicals used in agriculture.

Behaviour of tourism user-groups of natural resources

A key cause of the negative impacts that may occur from tourism is human behaviour towards the environment. Integral parts of the tourism system are:

- tourists;
- local people;
- governments;
- the tourism industry.

The behaviour of these groups will be highly influential in determining the extent to which the consequences of tourism upon the non-human world are either negative or positive. For instance, a major natural attraction for tourists is wildlife but certain aspects of human behaviour can adversely affect wildlife. While viewing of wildlife species in their natural habitats has become an attractive activity for an increasing number of tourists, this has meant the intrusion of humans into environments that had previously been the exclusive preserve of wildlife. Ironically, the desire of tourists to enhance their perceptions of nature by observing wildlife at close quarters can bring disruption to the natural behaviour of the wildlife they want to see.

According to Roe et al. (1997), the extent of the impact of tourism on wildlife can be related to the type of tourist activity and the level of tourism development. Mathieson and Wall (1982) add that the resilience of wildlife to the presence of humans will influence the degree to which tourism proves harmful to a particular species. For example, the type of safari tourism practised in the Serengeti Park on the Kenyan/Tanzanian border is representative of a highly developed level of tourism, involving local operators taking tourists into the park in minibuses and animals being surrounded by 30 or 40 vehicles with tourists taking photographs. The invasion of the territorial space of the animals and the associated increase in noise raises the stress level of animals, which is disruptive to their breeding and eating patterns. For example, cheetahs and lions are reported to decrease their hunting activity when surrounded by more than six vehicles (Shackley, 1996). The drivers of the minibuses are encouraged to ignore laws limiting the proximity of their vehicles to the animals by the extra tips they receive from tourists for getting close to them.

Sometimes the threat to wildlife from tourism can be more direct, especially in communities where the level of environmental education is low and locals do not have a high regard for the environment. For example, commenting on the backpacker operations that take tourists into the rain forest in Ecuador, Drumm (1995: 2) writes: 'Only 20% [sic] of local guides have completed secondary education, and very few are proficient in a language other than Spanish. Together with a social context which imbrues them with a settler frame of mind, antagonistic to the natural environment, the negative impacts of this operation are significant. Hunting wild species for food and bravado is commonplace during tours as well as the occasional dynamiting of rivers for fish. The capture and trade in wildlife species including especially monkeys and macaws is also very common'.

Besides wildlife, other natural resources may be placed under threat from the action of local people. For instance, coral is damaged by local people who break it off to sell as souvenirs, as in the Bahamas and Grenada, where rare black coral is made into earrings for sale to tourists. Local operators taking tourists out in boats to visit reefs sometimes drag their anchors through the coral causing localised damage, while tourists harm the coral by touching and standing on it. Additionally, shells are sometimes collected by local people to sell to tourists, as in areas of the Red Sea, the Caribbean and off the coast of Kenya. Key factors that are likely to influence the attitudes of local people to the surrounding environment include the level of economic development and the extent of the provision by government and the private sector of environmental education.

The positive effects

Although tourism can cause negative environmental impacts, it is important to balance this statement by giving consideration to the positive environmental effects of tourism. A key feature of tourism is that it gives an economic value to nature. Consequently, the partnership of tourism and conservation may offer an economic alternative to a more instrumental use of nature, such as, for example, agriculture, logging and mining. Even models of mass tourism, which may often be associated with over-development and the negative impacts of tourism, usually have as an integral part of their enjoyment reliance upon sea, sun and sand. Alternative types of tourism, such as nature tourism and eco-tourism, emphasise even more the centrality of nature to the tourist experience.

If it is evident that through the conservation of nature tourism results in economic benefits, then the incentives for conservation are enhanced. If through developing forms of tourism based upon the conservation of nature, governments can advance their economic priorities such as increasing foreign-exchange earnings and aiding the balance of payments situation, they are more likely to be encouraged to legislate to grant natural areas a protected status, such as a national park. Also, local communities who may because of economic necessity or material desire have used nature in an instrumental way with little emphasis upon conservation, may begin to prioritise conservation. A successful example of how tourism has been used to conserve a particular species is shown in Case 17.1.

Tourism can therefore act as an important catalyst to resource conservation. Certainly the need for careful environmental management and conservation will be prioritised where a strong link exists between the success of the tourism industry, the local

---

Case 17.1   Gorillas in Rwanda

An example of how tourism can be used to aid conservation is in the Parc National des Volcans in Rwanda, which is home to more than 300 of the world's remaining 650 mountain gorillas. Poaching has caused the decline in mountain gorilla numbers, an export trade of gorilla's hands for ashtrays to the Middle East being one lucrative outlet, as has the encroachment of agriculture leading to the removal of their habitat. Tourist visitation of the gorillas is controlled by the Office Rwandaise du Tourisme et de Parcs Nationaux, and part of the revenues generated from tourism go to conservation agencies, notably the Mountain Gorilla Project and the Dian Fossey Gorilla Fund. Visitors are taken out in small groups (maximum of eight) by well-informed local guides to see the gorillas in their natural habitat of dense bamboo forest. The total annual visitation to the park is between 5000 to 8000 tourists. The project has been proven to be a financial success, critically in its economic benefits to local people, who in turn have taken a more active interest in conservation. Economic benefits come from accommodating tourists and employment as guides and park wardens.

Sources: Mieczkowski, Z. (1995); Shackley, M. (1996); Lanjouw, A. (1999)

---

economy and the conservation of resources. As Mieczkowski (1995: 114) comments: 'The very existence of tourism is unthinkable without a healthy and pleasant environment, with well-preserved landscapes and harmony between people and nature'. The consequences for tourism destinations that do not maintain a high-quality environment were illustrated by the examples of Salou in Spain and the Romagna coast in Italy earlier in the chapter. This relationship between the economic success of tourism, the environment, and the tourist is shown in Figure 17.1.

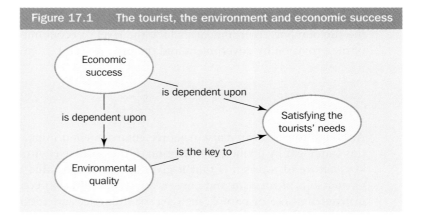

Figure 17.1   The tourist, the environment and economic success

This figure emphasises that a high-quality environment, including its physical resources, is a key element of satisfying the needs of the tourists and building long-term economic prosperity from tourism. It is therefore in the interest of the stakeholders to ensure that the landscape remains of a good quality. A key factor in achieving this is the careful environmental management of resources for tourism.

Environmental management

Having established that a high-quality natural environment is essential for tourism, a key question is how can it be maintained. Given that the negative impacts of tourism are partly related to the numbers of users of natural resources, an obvious starting point in the environmental management of tourism would be to control the numbers of users. One technique that attempts to do this is 'carrying-capacity analysis'. The World Tourism Organization (1992: 23) defines carrying capacity as being 'fundamental to environmental protection and sustainable development. It refers to maximum use of any site without causing negative effects on the resources, reducing visitor satisfaction, or exerting adverse impact upon the society, economy and culture of the area. Carrying-capacity limits can sometimes be difficult to quantify, but they are essential to planning for tourism and recreation'. Similarly, Mathieson and Wall (1982: 21) state: 'Carrying capacity is the maximum number of people who can use a site without an unacceptable alteration in the physical environment and without an unacceptable decline in the quality of the experience gained by the visitors'.

From these definitions it is evident that there are different elements to the concept of carrying capacity beyond purely physical considerations. According to Farrell (1992), there are at least four different types of carrying capacity, and O'Reilly (1986) identified economic, psychological, environmental, and social carrying capacities as being relevant to tourism. All have threshold levels beyond which the carrying capacity would be deemed to have been exceeded, leading to deterioration in the quality of the aspect under consideration. 'Economic carrying capacity' relates to the extent of the dependency of the economy upon tourism; 'psychological carrying capacity' is reflected in the expressed level of visitor satisfaction associated with the destination; 'environmental carrying capacity' is concerned with the extent and degree of impacts of tourism upon the physical environment; and 'social carrying capacity' is concerned with the reaction of the local community to tourism.

The four carrying capacities are not independent of each other, but it may be possible to exceed the threshold limit of one capacity for a limited amount of time without there necessarily being a detrimental effect upon another type of capacity. For example, it is possible that an increase in the number of walkers in a mountain area could lead to increased levels of destruction of flora from trampling, even threatening the ecological balance of the area, while the satisfaction of the visitors is not diminished. In this sense, carrying capacity has a perceptual element (Mason, 2003). However, if the number of walkers continued to increase and damage to the environment increased proportionally, eventually the level of environmental damage would lead to a threshold level being crossed where it detracted from the level of satisfaction with the wilderness being experienced by the walkers. Consequently, the whole notion of when damage occurs is debatable. As Wight (1998: 78) remarks: 'The term *damage* refers to a change (an objective impact) and a value judgement that the impact exceeds some standard. It is best to keep these two separate. In terms of human impact, a certain number of hikers may lead to a certain amount of soil compaction. This is a change in the environment, but whether it is damage depends on management objectives, expert judgement and broader public values'.

Early attempts in the field of tourism planning at identifying the carrying capacity of destination areas were pre-occupied with trying quantitatively to determine the number of tourists that could be accommodated in an area without causing 'unacceptable' environmental and social changes. Although the concept of carrying capacity had been evolving and developing in the field of recreation studies since the 1960s, it is only since the late 1980s that the concept has become of interest to tourism researchers and planners. One notable exception to this observation was a study carried out for the Irish Tourist Board by the United Nations in 1966, which attempted to define the numbers of visitors that different destinations in Donegal in Ireland could tolerate without harming the physical environment (Butler, 1997). However, owing to the highly complex nature of tourism, the notion of quantifying capacity limits is extremely problematical, not least because there are different types of tourist who will display various behaviours. This makes it difficult to legislate for the impacts they will have in a destination. A number of factors is likely to influence the carrying capacity of any particular destination as follows:

- Fragility of the landscape to development and change.
- Existing level of tourism development.

- Number of visitors.
- Behaviour of tourists.
- Environmental education of tourists and local people.
- Efficiency of environmental management.
- Levels of economic development.

Today the notion that there is a fixed ceiling, a threshold number of visitors which tourism development should not exceed, is largely discredited (World Tourism Organization, 1992; Williams and Gill, 1994). Coccossis and Parpairis (1996: 160) comment: 'However, until our understanding of the interactions between the environment and development – human actions – is much more profound, the concept of carrying capacity cannot be used in planning and practice as an absolute tool offering exact measurements but, instead, as one which is under continuous revision, development and research'.

Owing to the difficulty of quantification and fixed carrying-capacity limits, increased emphasis is being placed on indicator monitoring systems to identify potential problems. An extension of the carrying-capacity technique can be seen in the 'limits of acceptable change' (LAC) or alternatively called the 'limits of acceptable use'. According to McCool (1996: 1): 'The Limits of Acceptable Change (LAC) planning system was developed in response to a growing recognition in the US that attempts to define and implement recreational carrying capacities for national park and wilderness protected areas were both excessively reductionist and failing'.

As is indicated in the above definition, the LAC system, like carrying capacity, has its roots in wildlife management and recreational planning. It is only comparatively recently that the technique has begun to be talked about within the context of tourism planning and its application to the field is at present very limited. The main deficiency of carrying capacity analysis, as pointed out in the preceding section, is that many of the problems associated with tourism are not necessarily a function of numbers but of people's behaviour. The advantage of the LAC system is that it does not attempt to quantify the numbers of tourists that can be accommodated in the area. Instead the premise of the LAC system is the specification of the acceptable environmental conditions of the area, incorporating social and economic dimensions, and also its potential for tourism (Wight, 1998). The system is therefore reliant upon identifying the desired social and environmental conditions in an area, which subsequently necessitates the involvement of the community in determining the desired conditions.

The mechanics of the LAC system involve the adoption of a set of indicators which are reflective of an area's environmental conditions, and against which standards and rates of change can be assessed. Typically, the indicators would relate to the state of the destination's natural resources, economic criteria, and the experiences of local people and tourists. The indicators would therefore be a mix of the physical and the social. For example, the levels of water, air and noise pollution could be monitored; the percentage of the workforce employed in the tourism sector measured; crime rates and driving accidents associated with tourism recorded; and levels of tourist satisfaction evaluated. Such indicators would be symptomatic of the impact tourism is having within the destination, and the effect it is having on the quality of life of residents. The indicators should be regularly monitored and evaluated, and strategies identified by the managing authorities to rectify any problems, to progress towards the desired environmental and social conditions that the LAC system is intended to help achieve. It is important to point out that, owing to the nature of the indicators, measurement cannot be purely scientific, but is also dependent upon a citizen input besides a professional one. As the name suggests, LAC accepts that some change is inevitable, and provides a framework to monitor that change.

A further planning and management technique for tourism involves the use of 'zoning', which is a land management strategy that can be applied on different spatial scales, for instance within a protected area, or at a regional or even national level. According to Williams (1998: 111):

> Spatial zoning is an established land-management strategy that aims to integrate tourism into environments by defining areas of land that have differing suitabilities or capacities for tourism. Hence zoning of land may be used to exclude tourists from primary conservation areas; to focus environmentally abrasive activities into locations that have been specially prepared for such events; or to focus general visitors into a limited number of locations where their needs may be met and their impacts controlled and managed.

Zoning can provide a proper recognition of the resources that exist in the area and subsequently identify where tourism can and cannot take place. With specific reference to the use of zoning in protected areas the WTO (1992: 26) remarks 'a protected area can be divided into zone of strict protection (a 'sanctuary zone', where people are excluded), wilderness (where visitors are permitted only on foot), tourism (where visitors are encouraged in various compatible ways), and development (where facilities are concentrated).

An example of how zoning has been used in an attempt to balance the requirements of scientific research, conservation, tourism and other forms of commercial activity, is on the Great Barrier Reef Marine Park in Australia, as described in Case 17.2.

Case 17.2   Zoning on the Great Barrier Reef Marine Park, Australia

The Barrier Reef in Australia forms the world's longest coral reef stretching for almost 2000 kilometres along the north eastern coast of Queensland. The reef is home to approximately 350 species of coral, 1500 types of fish and 6 species of turtle. The development of international airports at the towns of Cairns and Townsville, which are conveniently situated for access to the reef, has meant that the number of tourists wanting to visit the reef has grown substantially since the late 1970s. The growth of tourism and other economic activities based upon the reef has meant that increased pressure is being placed upon it, and also that there is increased potential for conflicts between different user groups such as fishermen, tour operators (who can take groups of several hundred tourists on large catamarans and other boats to the reef), and recreationists such as scuba divers. The types of consequences that result from the use of the reef for tourism include:

- physical damage from anchors, moorings, snorkelling, diving, and people walking on it;
- collecting of marine fauna;
- the discharge of waste, litter and fuel.

The response to these problems was the establishment of the Great Barrier Reef Marine Park Authority (GBRMPA) to coordinate the management and development of the area. One of its functions was to zone the park to allow multi-use of the reef while preserving its ecology. They developed four different types of zones:

- *Preservation Zones* – areas in which use of the reef for virtually any use is prohibited;
- *Scientific Research Zones* – areas where scientific research is permitted under strict control;
- *Marine National Park Zones* – areas where scientific, educational and recreational uses are permitted;
- *General Use Zones* – areas where some commercial and recreational fishing is permitted.

Commercial tourism is permitted in the last two zones, and the zoning process also includes the designation of Special Management Areas, in which reefs that are being intensively used for tourism or other purposes can be protected or conserved. Another aspect of the GBRMPA's role is the environmental-impact management of the Barrier Reef. All proposed tourist operations are subjected to environmental assessment before they can be granted a permit to operate on the reef, and large scale developments or those that are assumed to produce unacceptable environmental impacts have to prepare environmental-impact statements.

Source: Simmons and Harris (1995)

The onus of the measures that have been stressed so far – carrying capacity analysis, limits of acceptable change and zoning – place emphasis upon the management of tourism through planning measures initiated by government. However, there has been since the 1990s an increased emphasis upon the corporate sector to demonstrate a responsibility to the surroundings they operate in. One type of environmental-management technique that is used by some tourism businesses is 'environmental auditing'. Goodall (1994: 656) comments:

> Environmental auditing provides the basis for such business practice[1] and is consistent with the view of management as a controlled cyclic process based on continuous monitoring of impacts and change, the development of knowledge and the feeding back of these into decision-making by formalised process.

The reasons why businesses may be encouraged to participate in environmental auditing fall into three main categories. First, the passing of environmental legislation and enforcement of punitive measures against tourism firms which are polluters of the environment may encourage companies to seek to improve their environmental quality. Second, if companies believe they can reduce their costs of operations and increase their profits through the utilisation of environmental auditing, they are likely to pursue it as a course of action. Last, some companies may be genuinely philanthropic and willing to adopt as many measures as they can reasonably afford to benefit the physical and social environments. They may also wish to appeal to a consumer market increasingly influenced by green issues.

According to Parviainen *et al.* (1995) an environmental or eco-audit would cover aspects of environmental management, including:

- the company's environmental and purchasing policies;
- the adequacy of its communication of environmental practices to its staff and their level of environmental training;
- impacts of the business upon the surrounding physical environment, including features such as air, water, soil, ground water, noise and aesthetics;
- energy usage;
- waste management and waste-water schemes.

They also point out that environmental audits form an integral part of a wider 'environmental management system' (EMS) for businesses.

Environmental management systems integrate strategic objectives for the environmental quality of a company's operation with the practical aspects of environmental auditing. The first stage of an EMS, is for a company to state clearly that it has an environmental commitment, which, if taken seriously, will subsequently influence the operations of the company. The next stage is to outline broad objectives of what it hopes to achieve; for example, one objective for a hotel may be to reduce the amount of untreated waste emitted into the sea. The company would then carry out an eco-audit of its operations, determine realistic targets of what can be achieved within a certain time frame, and develop mechanisms to achieve the targets. An essential part of the scheme is the ongoing monitoring of operations to determine whether the targets set for environmental improvements are being met. If they are not then strategies must be developed to rectify the situation. Developing an EMS is a long-term commitment and is likely to take several years to incorporate all the different stages from policy to review. The EMS system is not exclusive to any size of business but the resources available to any particu-

---

1 Author's note: improving the current environmental performance of tourism firms.

lar organisation will have an influence on the quality of the scheme. Importantly, it will require an investment of time and commitment from all employees of the organisation.

Within the EMS system, the eco-audit becomes a tool to evaluate the company's performance and to make subsequent alterations to environmental policy and plans of action. The use of EMSs in the tourism industry is limited, yet it offers an approach for businesses that is both environmentally beneficial and proactive. The benefits to the industry of using EMSs include:

- the reduced risk of financial liability for environmental damage;
- improving customer relations;
- reducing operating costs;
- improving access to lenders, insurers and investors;
- an EMS's voluntary nature is an efficient way of improving environmental resources without regulatory requirements and government interference (Todd and Williams, 1996).

One tourism company that took the initiative over the impacts of its operations upon the environment at the beginning of the 1990s is the large German-based tour group Touristik Union International (TUI). The use of environmental audits has now become a regular part of TUI's business operations as described in Case 17.3.

Case 17.3	Touristik Union International (TUI)

Measured by volume of sales, the German organisation TUI is the largest tourism operator in Europe, selling several million holidays per annum. TUI's interest in the environment represents a mix of concern about the impacts of mass tourism and a pragmatic business sense to respond to the demands of the German market, in which the environmental quality of destinations is known to have a critical influence on the level of customer satisfaction and subsequent demand. TUI has therefore realised that, by investing in the protection and conservation of the environment, it is helping to safeguard its own financial success for the future. In 1990, TUI was the first tourism company to appoint an environmental manager as a member of its management board, and it now has an established environmental unit in the company dealing specifically with environmental matters. Apart from carrying out environmental audits of TUI's operations, the unit also consults and liaises with: the governments of host countries; international and national public organisations holding responsibility for tourism and the environment; regional and local authorities; its business partners including hotels, airlines, car rental companies; and importantly its customers to make them aware of good environmental practices. The advantage of the TUI group in influencing policy over the environment is that owing to its size it has a huge political influence. The TUI approach is innovative in the tourism industry, because it incorporates environmental protection as a fundamental management function in the organisation of its companies.

Codes of conduct and environmental education

Given that the impacts of tourism are also related to user behaviour, codes of conduct and environmental education will also be important in the environmental management of tourism. The development of voluntary codes of conduct to mitigate the negative impacts of tourism and improve environmental quality has been encouraged by government, the private sector and non-governmental organisations (NGOs) in the last few years. The usefulness of codes of conduct in tourism *vis-à-vis* other approaches to improve tourism's interaction with the environment is described by the United Nations Environment Programme (UNEP) (1995: 3) thus:

A wide range of instruments can be used to put the tourism industry on the path to sustainability. Regulations, of course, are – and will remain – essential for defining the legal framework within which the private sector should operate and for establishing minimum standards and processes. Economic instruments are also being increasingly used by governments to address environmental issues. However, voluntary proactive approaches are certainly the best way of ensuring long-term commitments and improvements.

The primary aim of codes of conduct is to influence attitudes and modify behaviour (Mowforth and Munt, 1998). The objectives of codes of conduct for tourism are to (UNEP, 1995: 8):

■   serve as a catalyst for dialogue between government agencies, industry sectors, community interests, environmental and cultural NGOs and other stakeholders in tourism development;
■   create an awareness within the industry and governments of the importance of sound environmental policies and management, and encourage them to promote a quality environment and therefore a sustainable industry;
■   heighten awareness among international and domestic visitors of the importance of appropriate behaviour with respect to both the natural and cultural environment they experience;
■   sensitise host populations to the importance of environmental protection and the host-guest relationship; and
■   encourage cooperation among industry sectors, government agencies, host communities and NGOs to achieve the goals listed above.

These objectives cover a wide range of the stakeholders in tourism including:

■   the private sector;
■   government;
■   local communities;
■   tourists.

Consequently, the developers of codes of conduct come from a wide variety of organisations, including governments and national tourist boards, the tourism industry and trade associations, and non-governmental organisations such as Tourism Concern and the World Wide Fund for Nature. According to Goodall and Stabler (1997) the salient principles of the codes relating to the tourism industry include:

■   the sustainable use of resources;
■   reduction of environmental impacts, e.g. atmospheric emissions and the disposal of sewage;
■   reducing waste and over-consumption, e.g. increasing the amount of recycling; showing sensitivity for wildlife and local culture;
■   adopting internal environmental management strategies such as environmental auditing;
■   support and involvement of the local economy by using local suppliers where possible;
■   pursuing responsible marketing.

Codes of conduct may also be established for local communities who are affected by tourism. Such codes can be helpful in (UNEP, 1995):

■   advising on the role of the local population in tourism development;
■   safeguarding local cultures and traditions;

- educating the local population on the importance of maintaining a balance between conservation and economic development;
- providing quality tourist products and experiences.

An example of a local community code is one developed by the non-governmental organisation 'Tourism with Insight and Understanding', based in Germany. The code stresses the importance of community participation in tourism development, the need for respect of the local culture from tourists, and the need for tourism to play a balanced part in the economy of the region.

The final type of code is aimed specifically at the behaviour of tourists. Broad guidelines produced in such codes usually include:

- learning as much as possible about your destination;
- using suppliers (such as airlines, tour operators, travel agents and hotels) which demonstrate a commitment to environmental practices;
- respecting local cultures and traditions;
- aiding local conservation efforts;
- supporting the local economy by buying local goods and services;
- using resources in an efficient manner.

However, attempts to modify tourists' behaviour are not restricted to written codes. In an age of increasingly sophisticated media techniques and information technology, the use of visual imagery to raise tourists' levels of environmental awareness are important. An example of such a project which also demonstrates how partnerships between the different stakeholders in tourism can be environmentally beneficial is the initiative taken by the Association of British Travel Agents (ABTA) with two United Kingdom non-governmental organisations, Voluntary Service Overseas (VSO) and Tourism Concern, to produce an in-flight video highlighting the social and cultural concerns associated with mass tourism in The Gambia. The video aims to raise the level of awareness among tourists about the physical and cultural environments of The Gambia, importantly exploring the needs and wishes of the Gambians themselves. It is shown on flights to The Gambia operated by First Choice, a major UK mass tourism operator. Other videos are also expected to follow, about Thailand and Kenya, and also about general issues of tourism and the environment.

Although the development of codes of conduct offers a way forward in making all the stakeholders in tourism aware of their environmental responsibilities, there have been a number of criticisms made of them. According to Mowforth and Munt (1998) there exists a number of problems and issues arising with codes. These include:

- the monitoring of codes;
- the genuine philanthropy of codes *vis-à-vis* them being a cynical marketing ploy;
- the variability that exists between the codes.

The lack of evaluation of codes is also commented upon by Mason and Mowforth (1996: 163) who comment: 'There has been a clear lack of monitoring and evaluation of codes of conduct for the purpose of addressing their uptake and effectiveness'. In similar fashion, Goodall and Stabler (1997) talk of the limited practical usefulness of the codes because of their concentration upon principles, rather than informing tourist businesses on best environmental practice, and how this can be implemented in their own organisation. They also point out the spatial limitations of the majority of codes, which are destination-based, and consequently ignore the consequences of tourism in generating and transit areas.

Conclusion

The range of environmental management techniques referred to in the chapter reflects the complexity of the tourism system. Tourism as an activity is composite and complex. It involves a variety of different user groups, is spatially diffuse, and its impacts are sometimes difficult to differentiate from other causes. Hence, a range of proactive and reactive techniques is needed to manage environmental impacts. These approaches encompass land-use planning as well as economic, technological and psychological dimensions. Case 17.4 on Nepal asks students to consider how environmental impacts associated with tourism could be managed.

Case 17.4 The Annapurna Conservation Area, Nepal

Covering an area of approximately 7000 km² of central-north Nepal, the Annapurna Conservation Area (ACA) is often cited in the tourism literature as a successful example of community development through tourism (Gurung and DeCoursey, 1994; Simmons and Koirala, 2000). The management of this protected area by a non-governmental organisation (NGO), the King Mahendra Trust for Nature Conservation (KMTNC), through its Annapurna Conservation Area Project (ACAP), makes it unusual. It has received various international awards, including the 1991 British Airways 'Tourism for Tomorrow' Award, John Paul Getty Conservation Award 1992 and the World Wildlife Fund Conservation Merit Award for 2000.

It is the combination of the diversity of physical and cultural characteristics of Annapurna that have made it an attractive destination for trekking. The flora and fauna include 474 species of birds, 101 species of mammals and 1226 species of plants (ACAP, 2001). Examples of the rare fauna in the area include the snow leopard (*Panthera uncia*), the blue sheep (*Pseudois nayaur*) and the red panda (*Ailurus fulgens*) (Bajracharya, 1998). Notable geomorphologic features include the world's deepest river valley, the Kali Ghandaki, and two of the highest mountains in the world, Annapurna 1 and Dhaualgiri. The cultural diversity includes more than 10 ethnic groups who live in the ACA.

The diversity and beauty of this remote region, which is presently accessible only on foot has led to its popularity as an area for nature- and culture-based tourism, especially for tourists from Western countries, with numbers growing from approximately 37,000 in 1989 to nearly 80,000 in 2000. The long-term trend of arrivals is upwards despite recent political problems.

Trekkers tend to trek in organised groups or on an individual basis, often employing guides or porters. Although it is difficult to ascertain the exact number of support staff who visit the area, Bajracharya (1998) and ACAP (1999) estimate that one member of staff, the majority of whom come from outside the Annapurna area, supports each tourist. If this observation is accurate, then based upon the 78,000 trekkers who came to Annapurna in 2001, it is possible that up to 156,000 outsiders visited the area. The majority of these visits, about 60% of the total, is concentrated in the four months of March to April and October to November (Bajracharya, 1998).

Associated with the expansion of tourism in the Annapurna area was the depletion of forest resources, leading to the designation of the ACA in 1986 to prevent excessive environmental degradation (Parker, 1997) and especially deforestation (Gurung and De Coursey, 1994). For some commentators (Ives and Messerli, 1989; Gurung, 1992; Parker, 1997; Banskota and Sharma, 1998; MacLellan *et al.*, 2000) tourism and associated activities are the main culprits of deforestation. According to Gurung (1992), the increase in the numbers of trekkers after 1970 upset the ecological balance of Annapurna. Forests are typically used for timber to construct lodges to accommodate trekkers, to provide fuel for cooking and to heat waters for hot showers. However, a lack of ecological baseline studies, combined with the difficulty of disaggregating the impacts of tourism from other sources, makes the extent of tourism's effects difficult to determine scientifically. Consequently, the role of tourism as a major contributor to the alleged deforestation of the high mountains is contestable and Sofield (2000) suggests it is overstated.

Other environmental problems that have been associated with trekking in the ACA include littering and pollution. The issue of how to dispose of the thousands of plastic bottles bought for drinking water is a major problem. Either they must be burned or buried or alternatively taken to the town of Pokhara outside the ACA boundaries to be disposed of there. Other non-biodegradable rubbish includes plastics, glass bottles, tins, foils and batteries. A further issue relates to the pollution of water sources from setting toilets too close to the streams, the use of chemical soaps for bathing, and the washing of dishes and clothes in streams. However, in the same way as deforestation is a contested issue the extent to which trekkers are to blame for pollution problems is contestable. It is possible that increases in the levels of consumerism by locals and the behaviour of service staff coming into the area to support trekking have also led to increases in levels of littering and pollution.

Discussion questions

1 Referring to the case study, why is the environmental management of tourism necessary?
2 Accepting that negative environmental impacts are being caused by tourism, what would be the advantages of controlling the numbers of trekkers going into the ACA?
3 How could this be achieved?
4 How might environmental education be used to ease the pressures on natural resources that have been attributed to tourism? Your answer should consider all the user-groups of resources.
5 What kind of indicators could be developed to help monitor the limits of acceptable change resulting from tourism?

Guided reading

The following books are recommended:

Tourism and the Environment: A Sustainable Relationship? by C. Hunter and H. Green (1995)
Environment and Tourism by Andrew Holden (2000)
Tourism Impacts, Planning and Management by Peter Mason (2003)
Environmental Issues of Tourism and Recreation by Z. Mieczkowski (1995)

Recommended websites

United Nations Environment Programme main website: **www.unep.org** .
United Nations Environment Programme tourism website: **www.unepie.org/pc/tourism/home.htm** .
Green Globe 21: **www.greenglobe21.com** .

Key words

Carrying-capacity analysis; code of conduct; conservation; environmental auditing; impacts; limits of acceptable change; pollution; zoning.

Bibliography

ACAP (1999) *The Annapurna Ways*. King Mahendra Trust for Nature Conservation, Kathmandu.
ACAP (2001) *Annapurna Conservation Area Project: Two Years Retrospective Report 1998–2000*. King Mahendra Trust for Nature Conservation, Kathmandu.

Bajracharya, S.B. (1998) Tourism Development and Management in the Annapurna Area, in P. East, K. Luger and K. Inmann, (eds) *Sustainability in Mountain Tourism: Perspectives for the Himalayan Countries*, 243–253. Book Faith India, Delhi.

Banskota, K. and Sharma, B. (1998) Understanding Sustainability in Mountain Tourism: Case Study of Nepal, in P. East, K. Luger and K. Inmann, (eds) *Sustainability in Mountain Tourism: Perspectives for the Himalayan Countries*, 111–146. Book Faith India, Delhi.
Becheri, E. (1991) Rimini and Co – the end of a legend?: Dealing with the algae effect, *Tourism Management*, 12(3), 229–235.
Briguglio, L. and Briguglio, M. (1996) Sustainable Tourism in the Maltese Isles, in L., Briguglio,

R. Butler, D. Harrison, and W.L. Filho, (eds) *Sustainable Tourism in Islands and Small States*, 161–179. Pinter, London.

Burac, M. (1996) 'Tourism and Environment in Guadeloupe and Martinique, in L. Briguglio, R. Butler, D. Harrison, and W.L. Filho, (eds) *Sustainable Tourism in Islands & Small States: Case Studies*, 63–74. Pinter, London.

Butler, R. (1997) The Concept of Carrying Capacity for Tourism Destinations: Dead or Merely Buried?, in C. Cooper, and S. Wanhill, (eds) *Tourism Development: Environmental and Community Issues*, 11–22. John Wiley, Chichester.

Coccossis, H. and Parpairis, A. (1996) Tourism and Carrying Capacity in Coastal Areas: Mykonos, Greece, in G.K. Priestley, J.A. Edwards, and H. Coccossis, (eds) *Sustainable Tourism: European Experiences*, 153–175. CAB International, Wallingford.

Drumm, A. (1995) *Converting from Nature Tourism to Ecotourism in the Ecuadorian Amazon*, paper given at the World Conference on Sustainable Tourism, Lanzarote, April.

Farrell, B. (1992) Tourism as an element in sustainable development: Hana, Maui, in V.L. Smith, and W.R. Eadington (eds) *Tourism Alternatives: Potentials and Problems in the Development of Tourism*, 115–132. University of Pennsylvania Press, Philadelphia.

Friends of the Earth (1997) *Atmosphere and Transport Campaign*, **www.foe.co.uk** .

Goodall, B. (1994) Environmental auditing: current best practice, in A.V. Seaton, C.L. Jenkins, R.C. Wood, P.U.C. Deike, M.M. Bennett, L.R. MacLellan, and R. Smith, (eds) *Tourism: The State of the Art*, 655–664. John Wiley and Sons, Chichester.

Goodall, B. and Stabler, M.J. (1997) Policy perspectives on sustainable tourism, in M.J. Stabler, (ed.) *Tourism and Sustainability: principles to practice*, 279–304. CAB International, Wallingford.

Gurung, C.P. (1992) Annapurna Conservation Area Project, Nepal, in S. Eber, (ed.) *Beyond the Green Horizon: Principles for Sustainable Tourism*, 37–39. WWF, Godalming.

Gurung, C.P. and De Coursey, M. (1994) The Annapurna Conservation Area Project: a Pioneering Example of Sustainable Tourism, in E. Cater, and G. Lowman, (eds) *Ecotourism: A Sustainable Option*, 177–194. John Wiley and Sons, Chichester.

Holden, A. (2000) *Environment and Tourism*. Routledge, London.

Holden, A. (2003) In Need of New Environmental Ethics for Tourism?, *Annals of Tourism Research*, vol. 30, no. 1, 94–108.

Hunter, C. and Green, H. (1995) *Tourism and the Environment: A Sustainable Relationship?*, Issues in Tourism Series. Routledge, London.

Ives, J.D. and Messerli, B. (1989) *The Himalayan Dilemma: Reconciling Development and Conservation*. Routledge, London.

Jenner, P. and Smith, C. (1992) *The Tourism Industry and the Environment*. The Economist Intelligence Unit, London.

Kirkby, S.J. (1996) Recreation and the Quality of Spanish Coastal Waters, in M. Barke, J. Towner, and M.T. Newton, (eds) (1996) *Tourism in Spain: Critical Issues*. CAB International, Wallingford.

Lanjouw, A. (1999) *Mountain Gorilla Tourism in Central Africa*. Available from **www.mtnforum.org/ resources/library/mfb99a.htm** .

MacLellan, L.R., Dieke, P.U.C. and Thapa, B.M. (2000) Mountain Tourism and Public Policy in Nepal, in P.M. Godde, M.F. Price, and F.M. Zimmerman, (eds) *Tourism Development in Mountain Regions*, 173–197. CABI, Wallingford.

Malone, P. (1998) Pollution battle takes to the skies, 8 November, *The Observer*, London.

Mason, P. (2003) *Tourism Impacts, Planning and Management*. Butterworth-Heinemann, Oxford.

Mason, P. and Mowforth, M. (1996) Codes of Conduct in Tourism, *Progress in Tourism and Hospitality Research*, 2(2), 151–168.

Mathieson, A. and Wall, G. (1982) *Tourism: economic, physical and social impacts*. Longman, Harlow.

McCool, S.F. (1996) *Limits of acceptable change: A framework for managing national protected area: experiences from the United States*, paper presented at the Workshop in Impact Management in Marine Parks, Kuala Lumpur, Malaysia, August 13–14.

Mieczkowski, Z. (1995) *Environmental Issues of Tourism and Recreation*. University Press of America, Lanham.

Milne, S. (1988) Pacific Tourism: Environmental impacts and their management, Paper presented to the Pacific Environmental Conference, London, 3–5 October.

Mishan, E.J. (1967) *The Costs of Economic Growth*. Penguin, Harmonsworth.

Mowforth, M. and Munt, I. (1998) *Tourism and Sustainability*. Routledge, London.

O'Reilly, A.M. (1986) Tourism carrying capacity: concepts and issues, *Tourism Management*, 8(2), 254–258.

Parker, S. (1997) Annapurna Conservation Area Project: In Pursuit of Sustainable Development?, in R.M. Auty, and K. Brown, (eds) *Approaches to Sustainable Development,* 144–168. Pinter, London.

Parviainen, J., Pöysti, E. and Kehitys, S. (1995) *Towards Sustainable Tourism in Finland*. Finnish Tourist Board, Helsinki.

Roe, D., Leader-Williams N. and Dalal-Clayton, B. (1997) *Take only photographs: Leave only footprints*. International Institute for Environment and Development, London.

Shackley, M. (1996) *Wildlife Tourism*. International Thomson Business Press, London.

Simmons, D.G. and Koirala, S. (2000) Tourism in Nepal, Bhutan and Tibet: Contrasts in the Facilitation, Constraining and Control of Tourism in the Himalayas, in C.M. Hall, and S. Page, (eds) *Tourism in South and Southeast Asia*, 256–267. Butterworth-Heinnemann, Oxford.

Simmons, M. and Harris, R. (1995) The Great Barrier Reef Marine Park, in R. Harris, and N. Leiper, (eds) *Sustainable Tourism: An Australian Perspective*. Butterworth-Heinemann, Oxford.

Sofield, T.H.B. (2000) Forest Tourism and Recreation in Nepal, in X. Font, and J. Tribe, (eds) *Forest Tourism and Recreation Studies in Environmental Management*, 225–247. CABI, Wallingford.

Todd, S.E. and Williams, P.W. (1996) Environmental Management System Framework for Ski Areas, *Journal of Sustainable Tourism*, 4(3), 147–173.

United Nations Environment Programme (1995) *Environmental Codes of Conduct for Tourism: Technical Report, No. 29*. UNEP, Paris.

Whitelegg, J. (1999) *Air Transport and Global Warming*, **www.gn.apc.org/sgr/kyoto/jw.html** .

Wight, P. (1998) Tools for sustainability analysis in planning and managing tourism and recreation in a destination, in C. Hall, and A. Lew, (eds) *Sustainable Tourism: A Geographical Perspective*, 75–91. Addison Wesley Longman, Harlow.

Williams, P.W. and Gill, A. (1994) Tourism Carrying Capacity Management Issues, in W. Theobald, (ed.) *Global Tourism: The next decade*, 174–187. Butterworth-Heinemann, Oxford.

Williams, S. (1998) *Tourism Geography*. Routledge, London.

World Resources Institute (1994) *World Resources 1994–95*. Oxford University Press, Oxford.

World Tourism Organization (1992) *Tourism Carrying Capacity: Report on the Senior-Level Expert Group Meeting*, held in Paris, June 1990. World Tourism Organization, Madrid.

Zimmermann, F.M. (1995) The Alpine Region: Regional Restructuring Opportunities and Constraints in a Fragile Environment, in A. Montanari, and A.M. Williams, (eds) *European Tourism: Regions, Spaces and Restructuring*. John Wiley and Sons Ltd, Chichester.

Chapter 18

The accommodation subsector

Sherif Roubi and David Litteljohn, Glasgow Caledonian University

Learning outcomes

On completion of this chapter the reader should be able to:

- interpret different accommodation concepts;
- identify major markets for accommodation;
- develop an awareness of accommodation market dynamics, and related management concepts;
- appreciate the position of independent and corporate operators;
- understand the new forms of accommodation supply.

Overview

This chapter introduces the nature and role of commercial accommodation establishments in the tourism business. Hotels are often held as a benchmark against which other forms of accommodation are compared. This may be confusing at times because the term hotel does, in reality, cover several types of provision.

Different accommodation types are explained and important variables that drive accommodation operations are explored in order to help the reader understand the complexity of the sector.

Following study of this chapter the reader should also be knowledgeable in some of the technical terminology employed in accommodation operations. Because of the importance of hotels within the sector there is a natural focus on these units. However, the reader should be aware that many of the principles applied to the analysis of hotels could be applied to other forms of accommodation.

Case studies highlight particular features of the subsector: the first (Case 18.1) explains the nature of grading schemes and provides an example of the detail required in their operation; the second (Case 18.2) helps to highlight the diversity of accommodation provision by looking at the development of units where individuals invest in accommodation provision.

Introduction

Accommodation holds a central role in the tourism business. On the whole, destinations could not exist without accommodation. Economically its importance may be gauged by the fact that accommodation accounted for at least 27% of all domestic tourism spending in the UK in 2003 (United Kingdom Tourism Survey, 2004). On the other hand, tourists seldom decide to visit a location just because of its accommodation – though they may well decide that they will not visit if the accommodation is not of the standard and type they require, has a poor reputation or does not provide value for money.

Accommodation supply

As the chapter will show there are different types of commercial tourism accommodation. One of the most common is hotel accommodation. The size of this sector of the market is illustrated by the fact that for 2002 it was estimated that, globally, there were 15 million hotel rooms (Slattery, 2003).

The nature of accommodation supply may be judged by several dimensions. Naturally important factors relate to the physical characteristics of supply, aspects which will attract considerable attention during the course of this chapter. However, it is important to remember that accommodation provision also has important social dimensions. Hotels, as do other forms of accommodation, meet more than the physiological requirements of shelter for and body comforts of customers. The term 'hotel' originates from France, where the concept was developed, and spread across Europe and the USA from the mid- to late-eighteenth century as travel in these regions grew. The term was often used to distinguish this configuration of commercial hospitality from other cheaper forms of accommodation and privately provided hospitality. 'Hotel' is thus a culturally bound phenomenon. Much about hotels reflects customs of hospitality provision and operation rooted in the societies they sprang from, as well as from the times the concept became established. For example, locations are often chosen to appeal to certain types of user; establishments target particular customers through offering particular combinations of meals, drinks and other services.

Yet, both within the European/USA or western hospitality axis and internationally, there exist many variants to hotel provision. One view of contemporary hotel facilities nowadays is to recognise that they feature customised architectural features, large amounts of furniture, fixtures, and equipment, extensive artwork, and expansive public and back-of-house facilities (based on Cahill and Mitroka, 1992). This infers both a level of luxury from the consumer's perspective as well as high levels of capital and organisation necessary to maintain the operation. More generally hotels can be defined as:

> establishments that offer short-stay accommodation with an element of service which exceeds the functional elements of taking reservations, cleaning rooms and ensuring payments. Expected customer provision, over and above (overnight) accommodation, usually with a high degree of privacy, includes elements of meals and drink service which may vary from the basic to the sophisticated. To this can be added a range of different facilities and services. Hotels are considered commercial institutions, requiring financial reward from customers (or their agents), and are bound by relevant national legal and fiscal regulations.

Typically customers' purchases are based on daily (or nightly) rates. Hotels are normally run to make a profit; certainly they are not expected to make a loss.

Other common terms for commercial accommodation establishments include:

▨ lodging;
▨ inns;
▨ (youth) hostels (many of which may be operated on a not-for-profit basis by membership organisations);
▨ guesthouses;
▨ pensiones;
▨ boarding houses;
▨ bed and breakfast operations;
▨ taverns;
▨ hydropaths;
▨ sanatoria;
▨ apart-hotels, self-catering establishments, private lodges;
▨ holiday camps/villages;
▨ short-stay or limited-service lodging and timeshare developments.

Thus, there is a wealth of commercial accommodation options that serve a similar core function: the provision of accommodation. To match these differences there exist different management structures and methods. As indicated, this chapter will focus on the characteristics of commercial hotel provision but also includes further types of accommodation so that the full diversity of the sector is appreciated.

The capacity and siting of hotels and other types of accommodation is, at any one time, related to the nature of customer markets and past demand trends; for example, the extent of national and international tourism demand could affect the nature of supply at a particular location, as could the mix between leisure use and business-travel demand. Similarly, the future development potential for accommodation at any one location will reflect its current profitability and investors' views on how changes in underlying social, economic and travel trends will affect the extent of change required in accommodation provision.

To gain an accurate estimate of accommodation provision is not necessarily a clear-cut process. For example, the UK has no single accommodation registration scheme which all accommodation establishments must join. Each of the four major tourism organisations operates its own scheme; these have been amalgamated into Table 18.1 for the sake of simplicity. In addition, joining these schemes is discretionary – operators may opt not to participate. Thus the table, while useful in some respects, is incomplete as it

Table 18.1	UK serviced accommodation (establishments registered with regional tourism organisations, excluding Wales), 2002			
Establishment types	**England**	**North Ireland**	**Scotland**	**Wales**
Bed and breakfast and farmhouse	14,229	710	2,321	–
Guesthouse	7,016	147	948	717
Hotel (includes castles, lodges, motor hotels, motels, town house hotels)	9,201	129	1,255	–
Inns	2,635	–	145	–
Youth and group accommodation	740	56	187	–

Notes: The figures are for 'known stock' – those establishments which agree to abide by the National Tourist Boards' Code of Conduct, those which have ever agreed to abide by it and those which have otherwise become known to VisitBritain. Youth and group accommodation includes University accommodation.
Different countries operate different schemes, thus the above table simplifies data available.
Source: For complete details of the data available see UK Tourism Survey (2004)

does not include accommodation which has not registered with the tourist organisations. This situation is common in many countries.

The difficulty in obtaining comprehensive, comparative figures for accommodation stock, even in one country, to present in a table points to the difficulties in data collection for accommodation. These difficulties reflect not only the wide range of different accommodation types but also relate to a large number of small accommodation operations (they may offer only a few rooms for let), the ease with which operators may enter and exit the sector (for example, operating only at times of peak demand) and, in some cases, operators who operate on a limited basis, deciding to keep operations 'low profile', so income is not declared to taxation authorities.

Accommodation demand

To understand the nature of demand for hotel accommodation it is necessary to investigate a number of factors. The following analysis gives some general features of demand so that it can be better understood and explored in relation to a particular type of demand (e.g. conference) or demand at a particular location or type of location (e.g. rural Wales).

In the first place it is important to remember that the demand for accommodation is in great measure a *derived demand*: derived in the sense that the requirement to stay in accommodation (i) relies on the demand generated more generally for travel in society and (ii) often is made following the travel/location decision. In developed economies the reasons for travelling are many and varied, making it difficult to classify demand into particular segments. However, demand for accommodation can be examined in relation to four classifications, chosen for convenience in understanding why customers choose certain accommodation types and how operations may be organised – *purpose*, *locus*, *personal travel context* and *payment*. These categories, based on an individual traveller's perspective, should not be considered as exhaustive, though may provide a sound foundation for translating market characteristics into operational requirements.

Purpose

- Leisure travel: undertaken during an individual's leisure time and financed through personal finances.
- Business travel: undertaken as part of one's employment and financed through one's employer or through another form of sponsorship.

Locus

- Domestic: involves all travel which does not require crossing an international border.
- International: involves travel which crosses international borders.

Personal travel context

- Independent: where the traveller is travelling as an individual (e.g. by themselves or in a small group who make travel plans independently).
- Group: one where other travel specialists are involved (such as tour operators and conference organisers) which largely guides the nature of travel arrangements and the tourism experience.

Payment

- Customer pays: person who stays at the accommodation finances the stay through their own resources.
- Third-party payment: an organisation or an individual other than the customer who stays at the accommodation pays for the event.
- Payment is part of a longer-term customer investment, as will be the case when a purchaser commits to (a period of) occupancy for many years in the future.

An interesting point to note is that the person who stays at the accommodation (the visitor or customer) can be separate from the travel decision-taker. Decisions of where to stay and how much to pay are not always directly in the hands of individual visitors/customers. The choice of accommodation for independent leisure travellers may largely mirror their destination and accommodation preferences. However, if they buy a package offered by a travel intermediary the ability to choose a certain type or price level of accommodation is constrained by that intermediary. Similarly, business-travel demand will be shaped by the needs of employing organisations (who are financing the trip) – both in the destination chosen and the price band that they find acceptable. This distinction is important for hoteliers and other accommodation providers to consider when planning their marketing approach.

In many cases, even when the traveller is an independent decision-taker, it is likely that s/he chooses a destination before selecting an accommodation establishment; in these cases demand for an accommodation type will be a function of total demand for travel to that destination. This is not to imply that there will not be 'destination hotels' where the accommodation itself becomes the main reason for travel. However, this type of pull is apt to be limited to a few operations. Examples of types of 'landmark' or 'destination hotels' may be found in accommodation such as that marketed by Club Med, establishments with famous literary and/or heritage connections, or, in the case of individual trips, establishments which are being revisited for personal reasons (e.g. returning to a honeymoon hotel).

Once again diversity of supply poses problems in gaining reliable data on all the different types of accommodation markets. Understanding travellers' requirements greatly assists management to develop sound accommodation and service concepts and devise efficient and effective marketing strategies. For example, research by Wirth (1996) shows that on the one hand *corporate individual travellers* do not show a great deal of seasonality in their travel (i.e. it is spread relatively evenly throughout the year), stay during weekdays, rarely seek double occupancy, are not price sensitive, stay for two nights on average, require business facilities and amenities such as modems, fax, etc. and tend to demonstrate repeat patronage. They typically booked through travel agents, corporate travel departments and individual secretaries. On the other hand, *leisure group travellers* may show seasonality in demand depending on the destination, are indifferent with respect to weekdays and weekends timing, normally seek double occupancy for cheaper room rates, are price sensitive, stay between three and six nights, and require on-premises restaurants and large lobbies.

The UK exhibits a mature market for hotel accommodation. During the period 1998 to 2002 Key Note estimates that the balance between business (which it terms 'corporate') and leisure (termed 'consumer') markets in hotels only fluctuated between 65% business:35% leisure and 63%:37% (Key Note, 2003). No distinction is made in this estimate between national and international travellers and the market mix quoted applies to full-service hotels. A distinction may be made between the accommodation preferences of national and international markets by using data collected by the UK tourism agencies. Table 18.2 below contrasts types of accommodation used by UK residents (when in the UK) and overseas residents when visiting the UK. Thus hotel use accounts for only 29% of the accommodation used on trips by UK residents (though 41% of accommodation spending). This contrasts with 45% of trips (and 46% of spending) on international trips to the UK.

Table 18.2	Accommodation used on trips generated by UK and overseas visitors, 2003	
Establishment type	Use by UK residents for UK travel (% trips)	Use by overseas residents visiting the UK (% trips)
Commercial serviced accommodation		
Hotel/motel/guesthouse	29	45
Bed and breakfast (B&B); farmhouse	7	5
Hostel/university/school	1	4
Unserviced accommodation		
Rented house/chalet	6	3
Camping	3	1
Towed caravan	2	n.a.
Non-commercial accommodation		
Friends and relatives	42	n.a.
Mixed Commercial/non-commercial		
Second home/timeshare	2	2
Other	13	45

Source: United Kingdom Tourism Survey (2004). Due to different collection methods the data has been shown to provide a comparative analysis. However, some categories may not correlate precisely

At a glance it can be seen from Table 18.2 that, for many trips, there appears to be no call on commercial accommodation at all – for UK residents, 42% of trips are spent with friends and relatives (F&R). Also it is to be expected that significant numbers of the 'Other' category for overseas visits are accounted for by tourists staying with F&R.

This brief analysis emphasises the need for managers of accommodation properties to have an excellent understanding of their markets and the working of other organisations in the business of tourism that play a part in marketing of destinations and supply of particular customer services. The examples of accommodation preferences given in this section relate to the UK only and should not be taken as representative of other destinations. For example, resort destinations rely much more heavily on leisure markets.

One final point must be made in relation to accommodation demand. This is the need to separate market purpose from individual profile. As stated at the start of the chapter a major distinction between different areas of the market lies in the purpose of travel. This prioritises the trip rather than the traveller. Thus a traveller may, at one moment, want to stay in an up-market hotel (she is a business traveller); later in the month, when she and her family go on holiday, the decision may be made to stay in a self-catering *gite* in France for reasons of destination, personal preferences and economy.

Accommodation types

There is an array of different types of accommodation offerings – some of which have already been identified in Tables 18.1 and 18.2. When explaining this diversity in more detail, one is influenced by current, changing guidelines on provision as there are few strict definitions of accommodation types that are comprehensive enough to capture the diversity of supply. This short section attempts to give a general description of different accommodation types in order to better understand their different approaches to meeting the varied nature of demand.

A major reason for taking hotels as a benchmark is their commanding place in visitor preferences among commercial accommodation types. However, hotels themselves can be different. A common way of differentiating between them is to note which are licensed to sell alcoholic beverages in comparison to unlicensed establishments. This may be a useful distinction in some senses, and because it is a legal and licensing obligation in many countries it is also a statistic that can be given with a relatively high degree of confidence. But this distinction is inadequate to indicate the full range of establishments.

Accommodation types may be distinguished on between (a) the levels of service provided and (b) the breadth of provision in facilities and services. Normally the more personalised and sophisticated the degree of service provided the more up-market or upscale the nature of the operation. For example, a high level of meal service in a hotel would require restaurants to be open throughout the day and evening, with an extensive choice of menu items prepared and served by highly trained and competent staff. In a luxury unit there would be an expectation for a choice of type of meal services (i.e. different restaurants as well as individual room service).

Hotel operations span a wide spectrum of types, as indicated below. The categories are not precise.

- Luxury hotels: these provide highly personalised services in sophisticated facilities with generous space allowances for both individual customer areas (e.g. bedrooms and suites) and public areas (restaurants, bars). Design is highly specified in order to meet individual requirements and often to induce feelings of ornate/exclusive/elegant surroundings. Hotels in this category may include traditional luxury operations such as the Savoy Group in London (found at **www.the-savoy-group.com/**) as well as contemporary design/boutique hotels, e.g. Ian Shrager's Morgan Hotel Group (**www.morganshotelgroup.com/home.html**).
- Midscale hotels: these offer high standards of private accommodation and public facilities for food and beverage consumption. They will often provide a range of services and facilities for business and leisure travellers. Design combines functional aspects with elements of individuality. Private facilities of a high standard with attention made to specialist traveller requirements though less spacious and opulent than in luxury hotels.
- Budget hotels: these hotels may:
  - reflect a somewhat more constrained level of a midscale hotel with less generous space allowances in private areas and a lower level of investment in public areas – possibility limiting these to a breakfast area and/or a bar;
  - aim to provide a simple form of accommodation with private bedrooms sharing toilet and wash areas with little or no food and beverage facility.

■ Guesthouses and bed-and-breakfast establishments: both are often run by families, the latter using the family home, which may have undergone some extension and upgrade to cater for paying customers. In both instances customers may be offered a high degree of customisation in the service element, though levels of investment in facilities may be small and the range of services available limited.

More specialist hotel operations include:

■ Resort hotels: usually, but not necessarily or exclusively, aimed at leisure markets and focused on a single activity or a range of leisure facilities and services. Thus a spa hotel may offer hydropathic and associated treatments; golf hotels offer courses and tuition facilities. Many resort hotels offer a wide range of sporting and entertainment services so that tourists have little reason to leave the hotel environment if they have little interest in indigenous social and physical opportunities.
■ Conference hotels: these are hotels which possess conference facilities. They will require significant public areas devoted to auditoria/meeting spaces and food and beverage facilities with associated customer service and production areas (such as kitchens).

These definitions are neither exhaustive nor, indeed, are they comprehensive. For example, sometimes the last two categories may merge to become one as hotels strive to ensure that they have broad market appeal and can ensure high levels of usage.

Other operations tend to be more typified by lower service levels. In many cases the terms 'un-serviced' or 'self-catering' accommodation are used. The former is in most instances a misnomer as certain customer services are actually provided (e.g. concierge services, security and room cleaning) as well as advance reservation and payment systems. In no way should this lower level of service indicate either market levels lower than those of serviced accommodation or lower investment in facilities. Indeed, some of the options available under this general category may be luxurious and exclusive, though breaking away from conventional views of hospitality and accommodation provision. The listing below provides an indication of some of the major categories of self-catering accommodation.

■ Limited-service/short-stay units: these may include sleeping and working space and some cooking facilities, aimed to cater for stays of more than just a few nights in one location. They may often be considered as alternatives to hotels when provided in an urban location.
■ Holiday self-catering accommodation: this type is mostly located in rural/resort locations and may be let for more extended stays. Sleeping, catering and some recreational facilities usually available. The range includes purpose-built or converted properties (sometimes heritage properties) and, for some low-budget options, static caravans.
■ Holiday camps/centres, caravan and camping sites: this category encompasses sites which rent their own accommodation as well as those, like touring caravan sites, where visitors bring their own accommodation. They will cover a range of different service levels through provision of retail, entertainment and recreational services. They will range from the very large and relatively sophisticated centres such as Haven Holidays (**www.havenholidays.com/**) in the UK and Club Med internationally (**www.clubmed.com**) to those located at farms, etc. with limited facilities.
■ University-associated accommodation: during term/semester time this will cater for long-stay occupants (i.e. students). During the rest of the year this may be let out to groups or individuals for short stays. Support services are restricted; for example,

meals may often be limited to breakfast unless especially arranged, as may be the case with conference use.

■ Timeshare: this provides the opportunity to purchase ownership of accommodation in purposely operated and/or built properties. Typically there is multiple ownership of units with personal use restricted to a particular time period (e.g. a number of weeks) during the year.

The above list provides a brief introduction into different accommodation types. Case 18.1 provides an idea of how formal accommodation classifications systems work, after which a marketing model is presented to provide greater academic depth.

Case 18.1   Hotel classification and grading in the UK

The origins of formal accommodation grading systems appear to lie with motoring organisations in the UK, which developed them to advise their members of the standards of hotels and inns in the early 1900s. Their grading criteria, not unnaturally, reflected the priorities and prejudices of their turn-of-the-century upper and middle class members. A century later, many national tourist organisations sponsor their own classification and grading systems in addition to a range of private sector initiatives, which include the off-spring of the original motoring organisation schemes. Callan (1993, 1995) identified 13 major classification schemes in the UK.

Classification systems are a representation of the accommodation types (e.g. hotels, caravan sites) while hotel grading systems profess to be measures of the customer-orientated physical and service characteristics to provide a summary indication of the quality of a unit in relation to the rest of the sector. Grading is usually carried out annually through an organisation independent of the owners and operators. A fee paid by the hotel will cover inspection and administrative costs. To be able to judge an operation fairly, criteria used include quantitative and qualitative factors. Quantitative criteria provide objective measures of the range of facilities and amenities available. Qualitative criteria, as implied, are subjective measures. They relate to the perceptions of quality of the level of facilities and amenities available to customers; thus judgements can change from year to year even though the facilities do not alter (Callan 1993, 1995).

Not all schemes operate similarly; they may agree on the items to measure but will have different methods of measurement (e.g. quality of a bedroom), so it is necessary to understand the objectives and methods of each scheme. They use different symbols to denote quality – UK national tourist boards, with the exception of Northern Ireland, use crowns (N. Ireland uses an alphabetic system) while others use pavilions, suns, keys or a numeric code. Needless to say the systems also operate in different ways.

The English Tourism Council (ETC) 'Quality Standard for Hotels' categorises hotels into five classes ranging from one to five star. One-star properties represent an entry-level class and must meet the following minimum requirements:

● normally a minimum of six letting bedrooms;
● 75% of bedrooms with en-suite or private facilities;
● guest-controllable heating in bedrooms;
● restaurant or similar eating area;
● residential liquor license.

Progression to two star and above requires additional improvement in seven areas including:

● cleanliness;
● service – guest care;
● bedrooms – guest comfort;
● bathrooms, shower rooms, en-suite facilities etc.;
● food quality;
● public areas quality;
● and general.

Requirements in each area include quantitative and qualitative criteria. Table 18.3 illustrates the ETC's requirements for bed size, quality and access.

Case 18.1	Hotel classification and grading in the UK continued

Table 18.3	English Tourism Council's hotel classification scheme
One star ★	Minimum bed sizes (except clearly specified children's' beds in family rooms) as follows: Single: 190 × 90 cms/6' 3" × 3' Double: 190 × 137 cms/6' 3" × 4' 6" All beds (including supplementary beds, e.g. z-beds, sofa-beds, etc.) to be in good condition, with sound base and sprung interior, foam or similar quality, modern, comfortable mattress. All permanent beds to have secure headboard or equivalent. Access to both sides of all double beds.
Two star ★★	Easy access to both sides of all double beds.
Three star ★★★	Generous access to both sides of all double beds.
Four star ★★★★	A choice of larger bed sizes, e.g. queen and king. This could be achieved through the use of zip and link single beds. Very good quality beds (e.g. pocket-sprung mattress and base), in very good condition, with superior headboard or similar.
Five star ★★★★★	Single beds exceeding the 3ft (90 cm) minimum size. Excellent quality beds with superior headboard or similar.

Source: English Tourism Council (2004) *Quality Standard for Hotels*, Classification Scheme Manual, London

Analysis of accommodation may follow a more analytic market-oriented approach, as in the following marketing model. In this example the focus is on 'product' rather than the service element. However, here 'product' is taken as incorporating both physical facilities as well as service aspects of accommodation. Kotler, Bowen and Makens (2003) identified four product levels: core product, facilitating products, supporting products and augmented products. The core product of accommodation is therefore that of residential services for a temporary period. This represents rental (i.e. payment for temporary ownership and use of space) as the focus of business. For many hotel operations food and beverage provision is regarded as a facilitating product: it must be present for customers to be able to use the accommodation. Particularly in resort hotels the need to offer a varied meal experience becomes essential as tourists may stay for relatively long holiday periods with little choice of other restaurants. This situation is further pronounced in the case of cruise ships. Similarly, Hilton Hotels, catering for business travellers, provide a set of facilitating products for their guests including work desk and chair, task lighting, two-line phone and a surge protector at desk level (Olsen, West and Tse, 1998). Hyatt Hotels offer a fax, large desk, continental breakfast, coffeemaker, iron/ironing board and access to copier, printer and office supplies (Olsen, West and Tse, 1998). On the other hand, in budget hotels, which are essentially a 'no-frills' concept for the price-conscious travellers, food and beverage operations become supporting products, ancillary services offered to add value to the core product and possibly to help differentiate one operation from its competition. Augmented products are primarily intangibles such as location, atmosphere, service excellence and customer experience.

One final point to make is that accommodation operations are more disparate than described above. In the first place resorts may include several types of accommodation under one management. In the second place accommodation may be aimed at different markets; thus a large resort hotel may cater to both holiday and conference visitors at different times of the year or, indeed, at the same time. The important business concept to remember is that what is being 'sold' (rented) at one level is space: space for a particular purpose and with a particular configuration of facilities and services. The management of this exchange is considered in more detail in the next section.

Hotel unit operations and performance

Of all the different accommodation types a hotel is usually the most disparate in terms of operations and management. This is because a hotel usually involves the three core and facilitating operations of accommodation, meals and drinks – together with any other services that have been added such as entertainment, gambling, sports and leisure. Each of these areas will have a different investment and operational cost profile. For example, the provision of accommodation has a high investment (fixed) cost and a relatively low operational (variable) cost; variable costs will cover room cleaning, reservations and payment with little else. On the other hand a meals operation has high variable costs (cost of food and high wage costs); similarly operating a swimming pool will have a high variable cost in terms of staffing, security and maintenance as well as a high investment cost.

In relation to accommodation provision there are two important measures of business performance. One is the extent to which the rooms are used (capacity utilisation) and the other is the price at which the accommodation has been sold (revenue generation). In practice these measures can be calculated in a number of different ways.

Commercial operations have a profit requirement and the prices charged will have to ensure that the return from sales is sufficient to meet all the variable costs involved (gross profit) as well as the fixed costs (property, rates, insurance), taxation, shareholder requirements and so on. To this extent, prices will be set long term and be set at a level that is projected to meet these obligations and also provide a basis for upgrading/investment and the future health of the business. However, the cost profile of hotels (high fixed costs and low variable costs), together with the need for them (a) to meet day-to-day market conditions and (b) to face the position that a room not sold for a night is a sale lost forever, means that *in the short term* many managers have in practice a relatively high amount of discretion to vary their prices. This allows management to capitalise on the varied purposes, origins, timings, etc. of traveller markets. Thus a hotel aimed primarily at business travellers which experiences low occupancies during weekends may offer packages with substantial discounts. This will have the potential to provide accommodation occupancy when otherwise bedrooms would be empty.

As long as all the variable costs are more than covered a positive financial contribution is made to cover the fixed costs of the hotel. Therefore the transaction will benefit the operator at the margin. In addition, by attracting more residents to the hotel a greater demand for meal and bar services could follow, ensuring that these centres also gain more trade. Naturally it is essential that management looks into the potential financial benefits of pricing policies within an overall financial strategy for the unit. Offering low prices which only make a contribution to fixed costs is not a strategy that can be maintained for all customers. Discounting may also become a problem when there is an overall downturn in demand and many hotels at the same location engage in price competition; not unnaturally, if all that distinguishes one hotel from another is the price, customers are more than likely to opt for the one which provides the greatest value. Thus price competition becomes a vicious competitive spiral with hotels failing to gain sufficient profitability to ensure their long-term financial health.

When appraising the success of hotel operations, room occupancy is a main measure of capacity utilisation (other measures such as bed occupancy are not discussed here). It is shown as percentage and is usually calculated daily (or more accurately nightly) as well as on a weekly, monthly and annual basis. Thus, for a hotel which had, on a given night in June, 67 rooms occupied from a total of 100, its occupancy is 67%. The occupancy for June would be the average of the occupancy for each night. For the annual occupancy percentage the calculation could be shown as:

$$\frac{\text{Total rooms sold over the year}}{\text{Hotel rooms (100)} \times 365 \text{ nights}} \times 100$$

In practice not all 100 rooms may have been available over the entire year – for example, some rooms may have been redecorated while others may have been let out to travel writers for promotional purposes. In both cases these rooms will have been unavailable for letting to the public. To allow for these factors, a true measure of occupancy means that the denominator in the expression above will have to be reduced accordingly. Thus, if over the course of the year 25 rooms had been redecorated on a programme which lasted 10 days and seven travel journalists had been accommodated for two nights each, then the denominator would have to be reduced by 264 nights (i.e. $[25 \times 10] + [7 \times 2]$ nights).

Room revenue generation is measured by the room rate that the hotel obtains from the customer/paying organisation. This room rate in many cases is unlikely to the 'normal' rate quoted on the hotel website or brochure. In practice, many hotels will have a number of different rates; these could, for example, vary by the type of room, the inclusion of meals and other services, the time of week or year when the room is used (and when the reservation is made), the status of the buyer (e.g. discounts for preferred customers or tour operators who buy in bulk) and the necessary deduction of commission when a travel intermediary such as an online agent or travel agency has made the booking on the customer's behalf. Thus many businesses quote their 'Average Room Rate' (ARR) as a simple measure of the average room rate *achieved*; other hotels will report their 'RevPAR', which refers to revenue per available rooms over the period.

Naturally the higher the occupancy rates and the higher the rates at which room nights are sold, the more successfully a hotel generates income. However, these measures relate to only part of its income base. In fact, while over 50% of hotel revenue comes from accommodation, nearly 40% of hotel sales are generated from meals and drinks, the remainder coming from other sources such as telephone and rental (TRI Hospitality Consulting, 2002). Information on performance criteria can be updated by visiting the TRI Hospitality Consulting website (**www.trihospitality.com/** – look for 'hotelstats') and by accessing accommodation occupancy rates collected for national tourism organisations at Star UK (**www.staruk.org.uk** – find accommodation occupancy under 'Tourism facts by Topic').

This discussion can only be considered a brief introduction to performance measurement in hotels and accommodation. Other important factors to monitor relate especially to quality standards and staff/labour productivity. However, bearing in mind that attracting customers into the hotel is one of the main factors in its success, much attention is paid to both price and occupancy.

Prices for accommodation and elasticity of demand

At any one time both demand and supply factors affect the number of hotel and other room nights consumed. Generally these relationships may be examined in terms of elasticity of demand, a concept drawn from economics. Price elasticity of demand, discussed here, examines the relationship between changes in the price of a commodity and the amount demanded for that commodity – in this case the number of hotel rooms demanded (as measured by room occupancy) against the average room rates quoted. There are other types of elasticity that can be studied: for example, income elasticity of demand could examine the amount of travel in a society at different levels of income.

The concept of price elasticity simply examines the relationship between changes in the amount of good or service required (here a room night) as compared to the change in the price for that good or service. For comparability the change is shown in terms of a percentage (%) change. This is represented as an equation below:

$$\text{Price elasticity of demand} = -1 \times \frac{\text{the (\%) change in the quantity demanded}}{\text{the (\%) change in price}} \quad \textit{for a period (e.g. month, year)}$$

To ensure that a positive relationship is always shown positively a negative sign (–1) is included in the right-hand side of the equation. This is simply a matter of convenience and does not have a mathematical meaning. The definitions of different types of change relationships are shown in Table 18.4.

Table 18.4	Price elasticity of demand – relationships between changes in quantity demanded and prices	
Numerical value of elasticity	**Verbal description**	**Terminology**
Zero	Quantity demanded does not respond to price changes	Perfectly or completely inelastic
Greater than zero but less than one	Quantity demanded changes by a smaller percentage than price does	Inelastic
One	Quantity demanded changes by the same percentage as price	Unit elasticity
Greater than one but less than infinity	Quantity demanded changes by a larger percentage than price does	Elastic
Infinity	Purchasers are prepared to buy all they can obtain at some price and none at all at even a slightly higher price	Perfectly or infinitely elastic

Understanding price elasticity of demand can provide guidance on pricing policies for accommodation property managers. Given the amount of short-term discretion that managers may have in setting prices (as discussed previously), knowledge of relationships between price and quantity demanded is important. For example, offering a price discount will be effective (ineffective) in an elastic (inelastic) market because the percentage reduction (increase) in prices is met by a greater percentage increase (decrease) in occupancy rates and greater (lesser) revenue. The opposite can be true in a price inelastic market where discount policies may cause accommodation enterprises to realise losses. Percentage increase in prices in an elastic market causes lesser percentage decreases in occupancy rates and greater revenue.

Some work done in the USA is shown in Table 18.5 (Hanson, 2000). This examined changes in five different hotel segments by a comparison between quarterly occupancy room rates to average room rates for each market segment.

Table 18.5	Price elasticities for different hotel segments in the USA
Hotel segment	**Own/segment price elasticity of demand**
Luxury	+0.2
Upper upscale	+0.5
Upscale	+0.2
Midscale with F&B	+0.9
Midscale without F&B	+0.8
Economy	+0.3

Source: Adapted from Hanson (2000) and updates in conversation with Hanson 2005; changes include +/– changes to elasticity sign in order to conform to the approach taken in this chapter

The results from this exercise are unambiguous and show that, calculated in this manner, demand is price inelastic, i.e. demand will respond to decreases in price but the increase in occupancy engendered will be less than proportionate to the decrease in price. Table 18.5 shows various degrees of elasticity for the different hotel segments, with midscale hotels possessing the closest relationship to unit elasticity (i.e. quantity demanded changes by a larger percentage than does price). These results imply that hotel managements should be careful when considering an over-the-board decrease in average room rates at times of demand weakness; any expectations that revenue will increase to more than compensate for the price discount may not be met. This is not to say that different demand segments within hotel markets may not behave differently. For example it is generally held that leisure travellers are more price sensitive than business travellers.

From a supply perspective room prices are influenced by physical, economic and locational characteristics of properties. Bull's (1994) study on motels prices in Ballina in New South Wales, Australia, showed that significant variables of room prices included star-rating, age of the property, existence of a restaurant, distance in kilometres from town-centre crossroads and views on the river side of the highway. Other studies in the USA have confirmed this relationship between sophistication of the property and the prices charged (Carvell and Herrin, 1990). However, as indicated, it is important to note some important drawbacks in analysis of this type which concentrates on property types.

In relation to price elasticity, hotel property types/segments usually cater for different market segments (e.g. business and leisure), each possessing different price elasticities of demand. Further, demand conditions may alter by time periods examined: e.g. time of the week or time of the year. Thus management should be able to treat its demand markets differently and ensure it strikes an optimum balance in the rates offered (to different markets and by appropriate time periods).

While price levels may sometimes be taken as an indication of the quality of a unit, this relationship is mediated by strength of demand and level of competition in the same supply segment. An increase in the sophistication of hotel facilities and services may justify a price increase on cost terms; however, this does not take into account whether there is sufficient demand for this type of hotel or, indeed, if current levels of supply already cater adequately for markets able and willing to pay these rates.

Independent and chain hotels

To fully understand the complex nature of hotel businesses it is helpful to consider different types of hotel organisation. This section will focus on the characteristics and management issues which are faced by independent hotels and hotel chains.

A relatively simple organisational form is a small, independently owned and operated hotel. Here there is an owner-manager and only a small number of staff, several of whom may be family members. Independently operated hotels may, on the other hand, be large and require substantial input from non-family labour. In both of these cases the business will be focused around the opportunities that the hotel can meet, given its location, the local competition and the owners' aspirations, as well as the resource base that can be generated from this single operation.

A hotel chain is, as its name implies, a number of hotels which combine in some substantive manner. It has been defined as an organisation which comprises two or more hotel units which operate under a system of decision-making that permits coherent operation and, as desired, common strategies where functions at unit and corporate levels are linked to add value to each other by ownership or contractual relationships where these are seen to offer competitive advantage (based on Peng and Litteljohn, 1997). Thus a chain is a multi-site organisation with a management approach which decides what activities are best performed at unit or corporate level.

The organisational and management challenges of chains present significantly different challenges than those for single-site units. Because they are multi-site they will be geographically dispersed; this means that different units will be operating in different physical and competitive environments. Thus the physical features at locations may pose different operating challenges in terms of building and maintenance. The competitive environment will also present differences in terms of industry structure and competition, labour markets, different demand patterns and so on. Combined these factors present a requirement for a radically different type of management activity than that which faces the small, single-unit operator. For example, ensuring common standards of service quality across several units (if this is an objective of the chain) will present difficulties of a type that would not arise in an individual hotel.

Given these issues it may be helpful to consider why multi-chain units have become a prominent feature of the hotel business. The concepts of economies of scale and tourism applications were raised in the latter part of Chapter 2. For hotels, scale economies can be grouped under the following benefits:

- *Operations*: ability to negotiate with suppliers on trading requirements to provide bulk discounts/savings over the day-to-day costs of operating. These savings could include lower prices of food and beverage supplies, lower commission rates from credit-card companies, the ability to train staff more regularly and to a higher level, increased rewards and retention for craft and management staff due to greater variety of jobs within the organisation.
- *Capital costs and financial gain*: advantages of size in gaining large amounts of risk-associated capital because of the size and the wider risk base of the organisation.
- *Marketing*: advantages of referral from one unit to another and the ability to build a corporate (e.g. brand image) and provide associate back-up services such as central reservations. Large organisations may also develop strategic partnerships with other suppliers (e.g. airlines) which allow joint promotion and other revenue-enhancing activity.

Marriott, a large North American chain with units in many different parts of the world, was able to generate nearly eight million room nights during 2003 through its Worldwide Reservations Centers with an additional 13.3 million room nights coming through its special connections with airlines, travel agents and websites (**Marriott.com** and TravelWeb). For its franchised hotels in North America this translated into an average of 47,000 room nights during the year. Marriott was also able to offer a loyalty card to its customers. 'Marriott Rewards' has 19 million members worldwide (Marriott Hotels and Resorts, 2004).

Case 18.2   Condominium hotels

The nature of accommodation operations is becoming more complex. Conventional commercial accommodations see a clear separation between the operators, investors and customers. Often, though not necessarily, operations and ownership of property is under the same organisation. The customers or users have no tie to the operation and they pay for each individual stay.

However, there is now a growing number of accommodation operations which see different forms of investment and/or a different type of relationship between the investors and users. As usual, there are a number of different terms in use; many originate from the USA and most commonly are 'timeshare' and 'condominium hotels'.

Stephen Rushmore, president and founder of *HVS International*, has given three examples of what hoteliers and others would consider condominium hotels: Ritz-Carlton Boston, Ritz-Carlton Key Biscayne and Westin Grand Vancouver (Rushmore, 2001).

Ritz-Carlton Boston condo-units are located within the hotel. They are bought for personal residential use. Here there is no differentiation between users and owners: they are the same. Owners here are essentially homebuyers who preferred to purchase these units because of the state-of-the-art amenities and service (e.g. catering, spa and housekeeping) attached to them that would not be available in other residential properties.

At *Ritz-Carlton Key Biscayne*, condo-units are located in a building adjacent to the hotel. Here it appears that the owner/user is looking for a greater degree of customisation (cited in Lunt and Robins, 2004). Owners use their units during peak season for between one to four months. Again, units are integrated into the hotel so that owners can use its amenities and services. During the rest of the year owners authorise the hotel management company, which also assumes management of condo-units, to sublet their units to potential guests. Profit is split between them normally on a 50:50 basis. This seems to mirror timeshare arrangements. Timeshare developers build an integrated resort or accommodation complex and sell ownership interests typically in either one-week intervals or as packages of points that can be used in other locations to reserve resort accommodations which are either owned by, or have an affiliation with, the owners of the investors' 'home' investment. Members share in the occupancy rights of a development and therefore pay an annual maintenance fee after the initial purchase.

Westin Grand Vancouver, Canada, is a regular hotel, but units are owned by individual investors. Here owners and users are not the same. Individuals purchase these units for investments purposes through partial-ownership in an operating hotel. Units are pooled in a rental programme. Profit is shared between the Management Company and unit holders.

Figure 18.1 shows that condo hotels may be classified according to these functions. Ritz-Carlton Boston is residential on the one end of the spectrum and Westin Grand Vancouver is an investment on the other end, while in the middle Ritz-Carlton Key Biscayne serves residential purposes for some of the time and investment for the other.

Figure 18.1   Condo hotels classified by function

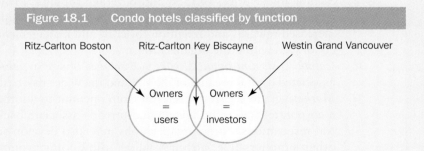

Stephen Rushmore suggests, however, that only Westin Grand Vancouver could be classified as a condominium hotel since the hotel itself has been 'condominiumised'. He suggests describing Ritz-Carlton Boston as a 'hotel with a primary residence condominium component', while Ritz-Carlton Key Biscayne would be described as a 'hotel with a secondary residence condominium component'.

Location

Accommodation must be provided at the point where customers want to use it. Unlike airplanes, for example, which can alter their routes to suit changing customer preferences, accommodation supply is rooted to its location. This is an accepted but under-theorised relationship. What follows in this section is an attempt to clarify discussion on accommodation/hotels and location. The material is structured to facilitate a traditional view that any hotel development should take into account demand characteristics at its location, while on the other hand also allowing for a more contemporary model of development where a hotel chain chooses a location to fit its hotel brand. Three levels of location are applied to hotel operations: (i) nature of place, (ii) local market access type and (iii) micro-site characteristics.

Nature of place. This is a general category that covers concentration of economic and tourism activity (including transport infrastructure) at the location. For example, places could be labelled as primary, secondary and tertiary. Primary destinations are national and international economic hubs. They are major commercial/leisure tourism centres with associated substantial long-haul public-transport infrastructure services. European examples include London and Paris. Secondary locations are those which possess considerable economic and social infrastructure with national and some international travel services. They often possess national prominence; UK examples include Edinburgh and Manchester. Tertiary places are peripheral to major sources of industry, commerce and related tourism where economic activity is dispersed rather than concentrated.

Local market access. This relates hotel location in relation to major transport/access characteristics and local tourism market resources. For example, there are factors which focus directly on transport: access to airports, motorways and railways. To this is twinned the access to the actual focus of the trip. Thus city-centre hotels normally provide easy access to cultural attractions and, for business travellers, commercial and government offices. Suburban hotels will usually share similar advantages to city-centre hotels, though they will be less convenient for major leisure attractions and professional, commercial and public sector organisations and will perhaps possess less convenient connections to transport infrastructure to and from the destination.

Resort hotels may be self-contained in accommodation, eating and drinking provision as well as associated entertainment, recreation and/or conference facilities. In this way they internalise their markets and provide an 'inclusive' location.

Micro-site characteristics. These refer to the micro-factors involved at a particular hotel site, for example:

- how close to convenient termini/stations/road-systems is the hotel for arriving and departing customers as well as those resident at the hotel?
- is it accessible by foot?
- is there a short or long journey by public transport?
- are these points of access safe and economical to provide (road access simple and on-site car parking available)?
- are levels of noise acceptable?
- is the environment a secure one?

If accommodation can provide benefits on these locational criteria management will be able to provide high values to visitors and charge a premium. Certainly location does have a significant effect on property values, which infers that location will have an effect on hotel revenues. For example, in the UK Roubi and Litteljohn (2004) found that economic factors such as population income and employment can add 20% to hotel property values while access to city centres, motorway systems and airports can add 4%.

Conclusion

This chapter has explored, at an introductory level, the nature of accommodation markets. The diversity of types and operations has been explained within a context of derived demand and destination location; while hotels are global in that they are present in many different parts of the world, like built heritage the sector is location-specific in that capacity and types of hotels will differ at each destination. However, while the 'hard' elements of accommodation infrastructure are location specific, the management of these units is not location bound – management approaches to ensure optimum use of capacity can be developed in, and transferred to, any part of the world. Adoption of effective management practices will help accommodation businesses, not always regarded as the most profitable of investment opportunities by financial institutions, to survive and prosper.

An introductory chapter risks ignoring important aspects or dealing with some issues superficially. In thinking about the future, the authors would recommend readers to pay attention to the following areas which, for lack of space, have been underplayed:

Operations: labour productivity and using labour to provide distinctiveness, as well as manipulating the built infrastructure (e.g. adding leisure facilities); the need to ensure that the total 'accommodation package' (i.e. services and facilities) provides customer satisfaction and value; the need to operate centralised reservation systems together with yield-management systems to ensure that space at accommodation units is used as effectively as possible. There is a need to ensure that all operations are professionally managed, as there is the need to ensure that operations meet sustainability goals in terms of their own operations and within the environments of the destinations that they serve.

Ownership and financial factors: the advantages of size in meeting operational challenges will become more acute than they have been in the past. The industry has traditionally been fragmented in terms of ownership while the need to raise finance in the light of growth predictions for tourism globally will only raise the need for this type of area to be examined. Also the relationship between investment and destination may become an issue, in relation to foreign-based entry of accommodation and tourism sectors.

Marketing and customer aspects: at a general level the power of other tourism intermediaries and accommodation operators is changing; for example, tour operators, e-bookers, budget airlines, conference organisers and so on all have shifting power in relation to accommodation. It is important that accommodation operators use these organisations and technologies to their advantage as much as possible, otherwise their finances may become less healthy. Branding, which has been one way that the industry has developed in the past 20 years, may help in this respect, but in Western markets, where customers are increasingly experienced travellers and, through the internet, can access levels of information not previously easily accessible, it may be that the hotel branding strategies of the late twentieth century do not meet customers' lifestyles or travel requirements.

Discussion questions

1 Compare the range of prices (mid-week and weekend) of a luxury (e.g. five-star) hotel and a branded budget hotel (e.g. Premier Travel Inn, Travelodge) in the same destination/location. Fully explain the differences you may find. (Hint: you may find it difficult to complete this topic just by accessing company/area tourism organisation websites.)

2 Discuss the significance of accommodation capacity, given national and international demand profiles, for hotels and similar establishments in 2001 for the management of the sectors shown in Table 18.6.

Table 18.6	Accommodation statistics for 2001		
Factor	Germany	Spain	UK
Number of establishments	38.5	16.4	50.5
Capacity (rooms)	884.5	685.7	555.0
Average size of establishment (rooms)	27.97	41.81	10.99
Nights spent, domestic residents	164,197	85,261	134,420
Nights spent, international visitors	32,876	143,421	49,781

Source: Derived from Office for Official Publications of the European Communities (2003); figures shown in thousands

3 Investigate accommodation occupancies using data from StarUK (**www.staruk.org.uk/**)
(Hint: try finding these through that section of the site dealing with 'Tourism Facts' then 'Tourism Facts by Topic', then open the latest available United Kingdom Occupancy Survey for Serviced Accommodation: Annual Report. Over the year chart the variations as follows:

- monthly differences between London and any one other region;
- differences between weekend and weekday occupancies.

Discuss the causes and consequences of these differences.

4 Examine the type of investment and commitment of holiday accommodation purchase in timeshare purchase. (Hint: you can do this by searching websites such as **www.macdonald-resorts.com/** or **www.rci.com/index** – look for 'timeshare', 'holiday ownership', 'vacation ownership' etc.) By relating these factors to more general changes facing the business of tourism, do you feel this type of option will grow in the future?

Guided reading

The following are recommended for further reading on hotel classification schemes:

Callan, R. (1993) An appraisal of UK hotel quality grading schemes, *International Journal of Contemporary Hospitality Management*, 5(5), 10–18.

Callan, R. (1995) Hotel classification and grading schemes, a paradigm of utilisation and user characteristics, *International Journal Hospitality Management* (14), 3/4.

The following are recommended for further reading on condominium hotels:

Lunt, M. and Robins, A. (2004) The Comforts of Home: Condominium-hotels are on the rise again, *ULI Magazine*, August, page 19.

Rushmore, S. (2004) Global Update: Hotel Investment Strategies, *Hotels Magazine*, November, page 28.

Recommended websites

For UK accommodation data, explore the Star UK website: **www.staruk.org.uk** .

For information on quality standards and award schemes in the UK: **www3.visitbritain. com/corporate/links/visitbritain/www_tourismtrade_org_uk.htm** .

To access the websites of major international and national hotel chains, visit John Beech's Travel and Tourism Information Gateway: **www.stile.coventry.ac.uk/cbs/staff/ beech/tourism/index** and click on 'Accommodation' .

Key words

Accommodation capacity; average room rate *achieved*; occupancy rate; price elasticity of demand.

Bibliography

Bull, A.O. (1994) Pricing a motel's location, *International Journal of Contemporary Hospitality Management*, 6(6), 10–15.

Cahill, M. and Mitroka, M.M. (1992) Estimating Hotel Replacement Cost, *The Appraisal Journal*, 60(3), 380–393.

Callan, R. (1993) An appraisal of UK hotel quality grading schemes, *International Journal of Contemporary Hospitality Management*, 5(5), 10–18.

Callan, R. (1995) Hotel classification and grading schemes, a paradigm of utilisation and user characteristics, *International Journal Hospitality Management*, (14), 3/4.

Carvell, S.A. and Herrin, W.E. (1990) Pricing in the hospitality industry: an implicit markets approach, *FIU Hospitality Review*, 8(2), 27–37.

Hanson, B. (2000) *Price Elasticity of Lodging Demand*. UCLA Investment Conference, 20 January 2000.

Key Note (2002) *Hotels* (Emily Pattullo, ed.), September, Key Note Publications, Hampton.

Kotler, P., Bowen, J. and Makens, J. (2003) *Marketing for Hospitality and Tourism*, 274–276. Prentice Hall, New Jersey.

Lunt, M. and Robins, A. (2004) The Comforts of Home: Condominium-hotels are on the rise again, *ULI Magazine*, Vol. 19, August 2004.

Marriott Hotels and Resorts (2004) **marriott.com/ corporateinfo/default.mi?WT_Ref=MIHome**, accessed 19 November 2004.

Office for Official Publications of the European Communities (2003) Table 19.8: Main indicators for hotels and similar establishments in European Communities. In *European Business, Part 5: Trade and Tourism*, Office for Official Publications of the European Communities, Luxemburg.

Olsen, M., West, J. and Tse, E. (1998) *Strategic Management in the Hospitality Industry*, 2nd edn. John Wiley & Sons, New York.

Peng, W. and Littlejohn, D. (1997) Managing complexity: strategic management of hotel chains,

Proceedings of Hospitality Business Development Conference. EuroCHRIE and International Association of Hotel Management Schools, Sheffield.

Roubi, S. and Litteljohn, D. (2004) What makes hotel values in the UK? A hedonic valuation model, *International Journal of Contemporary Hospitality Management*, 16(3), 175–181.

Rushmore, S. (2001) What Is A Condo-Hotel? Global update: hotel investment strategies, *Hotels Magazine*, November, 28.

Slattery, P. (2003) *Hotel Chain Growth and the Development Process, Otus and Co: Industry Writings*, **www.standr.co.uk/ind_writings.html**, accessed 14 November 2004.

TRI Hospitality Consulting (2002), *United Kingdom Hotel Industry 2002*. TRI Hospitality Consulting, London.

United Kingdom Tourism Survey (2004) *UK Tourism Facts 2003*, sourced from Star UK – statistics on tourism and research, **www.staruk.org.uk// default.asp?ID=708&parentid=469**, accessed December 2004.

Wirth, L.S. (1996) Market Segmentation and Analysis, in PKF Consulting (ed.) *Hotel Development*, 11–20. Urban Land Institute, Washington DC.

Chapter 19

Mass tourism businesses 1: tour operators

Tim Gale, University of the West of England, Bristol

Learning outcomes

On completion of this chapter the reader should be able to:

■ explain the central role of tour operators in the mass tourism industry;

■ identify what is included and excluded from different types of packages;

■ assess the significance of the market structure and the emergence of smaller specialist operators;

■ outline the competitive forces in the sector;

■ explain the need for, and implications of, vertical (and horizontal) integration;

■ identify various forms of consumer protection pertaining to tour operations.

Overview

This chapter aims to facilitate an understanding of the part played by tour operators in the supply of package holidays, or inclusive tours as they are otherwise known. In addressing the above learning outcomes, it focuses exclusively on outbound tour operators headquartered in the United Kingdom (albeit with extensive overseas interests), and is largely concerned with mass market operations, although several of the issues raised have some currency in the context of different types of operation (e.g. incoming, domestic) and, in particular, other major source countries (e.g. Germany).

Introduction: the history and importance of tour operations

It is difficult to overstate the significance of tour operations in bringing about the exponential growth in international tourist arrivals over the course of the late twentieth century (mirrored in the outbound statistics for many a developed country), and the associated economic, ecological and ethical consequences for host destinations. In occupying the position of *wholesaler* in the tourism chain of distribution, tour operators have effectively 'democratised' international tourism by passing on economies of scale associated with the bulk purchasing of air seats, hotel rooms and so on to the consumer in the form of lower prices, thereby removing the lead constraint on mass participation. They have also fostered an appetite for overseas travel by investing considerable sums of money in television and print advertising and, more importantly, brochures. These assume a key role in the social construction of tourism by promoting destinations in terms of certain generic attributes (e.g. guaranteed sunshine, palm-fringed beaches and well-appointed accommodation), which appeal to and reconfirm the expectations of the mass market (Shaw and Williams, 2002). This opens up the possibility of a critique, for such selective marketing frustrates ambitions to spread the benefits of tourism through-out local economies and fails to inform tourists of local ways of life that might be affronted by indulgent or ignorant behaviour (and which could constitute an attraction in their own right if sensibly promoted). Furthermore, the larger tour operators (i.e. multinationals such as TUI UK and MyTravel) have arguably done little to lessen the dependency of peripheral destinations, be they nations or regions, on the core of highly affluent source countries in which many such operations are headquartered by:

- using their undisputed bargaining power to pressure small- to medium-sized tourism enterprises with whom they do business (chiefly hoteliers and ground han-dlers) into accepting lower prices as a means of maintaining competitiveness;
- and focusing their operations in certain resorts thereby rendering them highly vul-nerable to external and uncontrollable variations in demand associated with exchange-rate fluctuations, oil crises, terrorism, and the like.

That said, this is not the place to pursue such a critique (see Chapter 22), neither should one forget what tour operators contribute to the 'tourism value chain', as summarised by Laws (1996: 172):

- selecting and packaging holiday elements;
- promoting and distributing them;
- providing information about destinations;
- ensuring affordable access to them;
- setting and monitoring quality standards in resorts;
- organising excursions and entertainments;
- managing relations with suppliers and distributors.

Tour operations as we would recognise them first originated in the 1850s with the pio-neering efforts of Thomas Cook, coinciding with the age of steam and the expansion of railway, cross-channel and deep-sea services. One hundred years later, a transport innova-tion of similar magnitude, the jet aircraft, paralleled the emergence of a second generation of tour operators led by Horizon Holidays and its founder Vladimir Raitz (who, along with Cook, is profiled in Case 19.1). Since the 1950s, the demand for international plea-sure travel has accelerated in those countries where such operations were instituted, notably the UK and Germany. In the former, inclusive tours account for a dominant, albeit recently declining, share of the market for overseas holidays (Table 19.1).

Table 19.1	UK outbound holidays, by independent and inclusive sectors (000s)					
	1998	1999	2000	2001	2002	% change 98/02
Independent	14,869	15,946	16,630	18,039	19,264	+30
Inclusive	17,437	19,077	20,055	20,631	20,638	+18
TOTAL	32,306	35,023	36,685	38,670	39,902	+24
% inclusive	54.0	54.5	54.7	53.4	51.7	

Source: Office for National Statistics (2003)

Case 19.1   Profiles: Thomas Cook and Vladimir Raitz

In 1841, Thomas Cook organised one of the first excursions by train, from Leicester to Loughborough, for a temperance meeting (a forum warning against the 'evils' of alcohol), which attracted a reported 570 customers at one shilling apiece. A printer by trade, he produced the 'first' tourist brochure for a trip to Liverpool some four years later, based on meticulous research of the city, its hotels and restaurants. Spurred on by these early successes, Cook extended his operation to Europe when, in 1855, he arranged the first of many tours to the Paris Exhibition (later issuing hotel coupons in conjunction with the trip). By 1863, he was promoting 'whistle-stop' touring holidays around Europe (largely for a middle-class clientele), and claimed his two millionth customer in 1868, prior to organising the first round-the-world excursion in 1872. By 1890, and after the addition of Egypt to his portfolio of destinations, Cook had pioneered a system whereby clients could exchange credit notes at contracted hotels in exchange for services rendered, which became the forerunner of the modern-day traveller's cheque. Today, the holding company that bears his name is registered in Germany, and owns the third largest tour operator in the UK.

In May 1950, eight months after founding Horizon Holidays, Vladimir Raitz arranged the first air-inclusive tour, a two week holiday for students and teachers to Calvi, Corsica (priced at £32-10-0). Capitalising on the gradual lifting of restrictions following the end of the Second World War, the widespread availability of aircraft for civilian use, rising affluence and the possibilities for advertising travel permitted by commercial television (which began transmission in September 1955), he soon expanded operations to include the destinations of Palma de Mallorca, Sardinia and the Costa Brava. With little direct competition, the company continued to grow throughout the 1950s and into the 1960s, acquiring its own travel agency outlet in Central London. However, its fall was to be even more rapid than its rise and in February 1974, a mere four years after recording a profit of £6 million at current prices, it was sold to Court Line in the wake of heavy losses attributable to unsustainable price-discounting on the part of competitors and the oil crisis of 1973/74 (which was precipitated by the Arab–Israeli war). Court Line collapsed later that year, stranding an estimated 40,000 customers abroad, and all that remained of Horizon Holidays was a Birmingham-based subsidiary which was sold, initially to Bass Breweries and then, in 1989, to Thomson Holidays (by which time it was the UK's third biggest operator). The brand was discontinued in 1995.

Source: Adapted from Laws (1996) and Bray and Raitz (2001)

Traditionally, the tour operator has co-existed with another intermediary or 'middleman' in the aforementioned tourism chain of distribution, the retail travel agent (whose various functions, in addition to the obvious role of providing a convenient high street location in which to compare and purchase tour operators' products, will be discussed in Chapter 20). That said, an increasing number of package holidays are booked direct with the tour operator, via the telephone or internet, and consumers may even bypass both intermediaries by purchasing transport and accommodation from the relevant principals (although this is thought, rightly or wrongly, to be a more expensive and difficult option in relation to overseas holidays). The situation is made more complex where tour operators own travel agents, in addition to certain components of production such as airlines and hotels; these 'vertically-integrated' tourism operations effectively constitute the supply chain in its entirety. On a related point, it might be argued that they are effectively 'producers of a new product rather than wholesalers of an existing product' (Holloway, 2002: 77), thus further confusing their role as intermediaries.

Table 19.2   Tourism chains of distribution

Role in (tourism) chain of distribution	Distribution channels			
	Forms of disintermediation			
	'Classic'	No retailer	No wholesaler	No intermediary
Producers (principals)	☺	☺	☺	☺
Wholesalers (tour operators)	☺	☺		
Retailers (travel agents)	☺		☺	
Consumers (tourists)	☺	☺	☺	☺

Table 19.2 illustrates the various means by which package holidays are distributed, as discussed above.

The package holiday or inclusive tour: definitions, diversity and development

At its most basic a package holiday may be understood as the pre-arranged combination of at least two of the following components, namely *transport, accommodation* and *other tourist services* (e.g. travel insurance, car hire and day/evening excursions). This is sold as a single product by a tour operator at an inclusive price, and necessitates a trip of at least 24 hours away from the purchaser's place of permanent residence. Such products typically involve international air travel by charter flight as opposed to scheduled carrier (known in the trade as 'ITC' and 'ITX', respectively) to a recognised 'short-haul' destination (i.e. within four hours' journey time of the origin airport, before allowing for transfers to/from the resort in question), for a period of 7, 10 or 14 nights in a single hotel or apartment, with 'pleasure' rather than 'business' in mind. That said, a great many package holidays encompass other modes of transport (e.g. by road, rail or sea), destinations closer to home and further afield (i.e. domestic, long-haul), short breaks and extended stays (i.e. from 1–3 nights to several months in the case of some retirees), a variety of serviced and self-catering establishments (including guesthouses, villas, caravans and cruise ships), 'circular' as well as 'linear' tours, and diverse motivations (e.g. educational trips). An extreme form of package holiday is the 'all-inclusive' holiday, where food and drink, activities, entertainments and even gratuities are paid for in advance and consumed on-site in privatised resort complexes or 'enclaves', such as those operated by Sandals and Superclubs in the Caribbean. At the opposite end of the continuum, one finds the 'no frills' holidays organised by the likes of Skytours and Just, the latter omitting to include transfers, in-flight meals and resort representatives (begging the question as to whether this constitutes a package at all, as posed by Holloway, 2002). Even overland expeditions to remote regions of natural and/or cultural significance, such as the Mayan Peninsula in Central America, constitute a type of package despite being perceived and promoted as 'independent travel' (Sharpley, 2002). Some tour operators have now diversified into selling seat-only aircraft flights, as do 'brokers' and 'consolidators', after European Union legislation enacted in January 1993 removed the legal as distinct from contractual requirement to build the trip into a package (Holloway, 2002).

A variety of tour operators ranging from large, multinational corporations to small, independent concerns are involved in the business of selling package holidays. Broadly speaking, they follow a similar programme of activities in planning, marketing and operating inclusive tours, implemented over a period spanning some two-and-a-half years including the holiday season. Figure 19.1 illustrates the typical package-holiday development cycle or tour operating calendar for a hypothetical 'summer sun' product, with indicative activities/dates corresponding to the prescriptions of Yale (1995), Laws (1996), Cooper *et al.* (1998), Holloway (2002) and Sharpley (2002). Here, it is presented as a seven-stage process:

1   **Company objectives/strategy**. The business objectives and strategic direction of the tour operator inform decisions made later in the cycle and, thus, constitute a necessary preliminary rather than a stage in itself. Such considerations are, of course, contingent on scale, but often come down to a trade-off between *profit* (e.g. by reducing costs and achieving higher margins on each package holiday sold) and *market share* (e.g. by increasing capacity and operating yield management systems to shift it).

Figure 19.1   The development cycle for a hypothetical 'summer sun' package holiday product

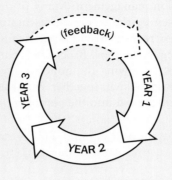

7. Destination management (May–Oct):

Transfer and reception of tourists

Customer care and following up of complaints

Supplier payments

6. Administration (Aug–Apr):

Set up reservations system

Accept and process bookings

Recruit and train resort representatives

5. Financial planning (Jul–Aug):

Estimate prices, based on current/forecasted exchange rates, inflation, price of fuel, etc.

Prices finalised and added (at the last available opportunity) to brochures

4. Sales and marketing (Apr–Oct):

Tenders for design, production and printing of brochures

Copy for text and illustrations commissioned

Brochure production, launch and distribution

Initial advertising, publicity and sales promotion

3. Capacity planning (Feb–May):

Establish target capacity figures

Set specifications of package

Negotiate with principals (airlines, hotels, transfer services, excursion operators)

2. Research (Aug–Dec):

Market trends/growth (tourist flows, competitors action, etc.)

Destination alternatives (encompassing ease of access, existing tourism infrastructure/services, local legal/political climate)

1. Company objectives/ strategy:

Profit *vs* market share, etc.

(feedback)

YEAR 1

YEAR 2

YEAR 3

2   **Research.** Forecasts of the overall size of the market and trends in demand assist the operator in selecting a set of potential destinations, each of which is then subjected to a feasibility study to determine ease of access, the existing infrastructure for tourism, and relevant political/legal factors, etc. This stage concludes with the derivation of a marketing strategy, equating the operator's objectives with the opportunities for product and/or market development revealed by this research.

3   **Capacity planning.** Target capacity figures are established, as are the specifications of the tour programme. The operator then undertakes contract negotiations with principals for beds, aircraft seats and any other services included in the package.

4   **Sales and marketing.** Tenders for the design, production and printing of brochures are put out early in the second year of the cycle. Text and illustrations for the brochure are then sourced and the layout agreed upon, before printing over the summer. Pricing panels are overprinted at the last possible moment to allow for any unforeseen financial risks (as identified in the next stage). Brochures are launched in the autumn (with large operators trying to beat their rivals to the launch), in parallel with media advertising and sales promotions (e.g. early-booker discounts).

5   **Financial planning.** Contracts with hotels and other local suppliers are usually made in the currency of the destination country, while those with airlines nearly always require payment in US dollars (USD). Airlines also reserve the right to adjust prices in line with the cost of aviation fuel. Hence, currency fluctuations and inflationary pressures can have a great bearing on the cost of a package holiday and care must be taken when finalising prices (towards the end of summer). That said, flexible pricing strategies are often employed post-launch (e.g. discounting on request, surcharges), and contracts may be renegotiated with principals prior to issuing subsequent editions of brochures.

6 **Administration.** Reservations systems are established in advance of distributing/launching the brochure, followed by the first bookings over the autumn and into the winter. With the exception of a core of employees holding permanent contracts, additional staff required to process bookings and represent the tour operator at the destination are recruited and trained on a 'just-in-time' basis, given the seasonal nature of the industry.

7 **Destination management.** Many of the activities that fall within this final stage are undertaken by the resort representative. These include transferring tourists to and from their resort, providing advice and dealing with problems as they arise, and overseeing excursions. Brochure accuracy reports are also compiled for rolling programmes. Following the holiday, payments are made to suppliers and complaints followed up (which, together with the data collated from customer feedback questionnaires, are fed into the planning process for the following year's programme).

Benefits to principals and consumers

Tour operators act as a 'bridge' between principals (i.e. airlines, hotels, ground handlers, etc.) and consumers, helping to match demand and supply. For the majority of principals, with neither sufficient resources available for marketing nor a reputation beyond the resort in which they operate, the tour operator is their only means of reaching overseas markets (although the internet is, to some extent, changing this). In addition, bulk purchasing should provide a guaranteed level of occupancy for principals, thus allowing them to circumvent to a large degree the problem of *perishability* (i.e. the irreversible loss of revenue associated with unused bedspaces, seats on aircraft or places on tours, which is especially unwelcome at times of low demand when fixed costs still have to be covered and temporary closure or cancellation is not an option). There are other benefits too, such as the availability of a holiday representative at the destination to mediate between principal and consumer in the event of a dispute, as well as simplified booking and payment arrangements.

With the obvious exception of those instances in which principals are owned by, or affiliated to, a given tour operator, package holidays are assembled via a system of sub-contracting, with the nature of the contract largely determining the benefits for the principal (not to mention the operator). Contracts with accommodation providers typically take two forms:

- An *allocation*, which favours the tour operator in that beds are contracted on a sale-or-return basis, with unsold stock being returned by an agreed release date (although the provider will often enter into such agreements with a number of operators by way of reducing the risk of non-occupancy, which carries with it the possibility of double-booking).
- A *commitment* or *guarantee*, an arrangement that benefits the principal who receives payment for beds regardless of whether or not they are sold (albeit at a lower rate compared to an allotment).

Aircraft seats may be contracted on scheduled ('ITX') or charter ('ITC') services, although the former tends to be reserved for specialist tours and bespoke packages given the expense involved. The latter may be booked in a number of ways, namely *a part charter* (essentially a block of seats), *a whole-plane charter* (an entire flight), or *a time charter* (an aircraft for the duration of the season). Flights may also be chartered with or without aircrew (known as *wet lease* and *dry lease,* respectively). There is something of a 'balancing act' to be struck by the tour operator in contracting seats on aircraft, as these constitute around 45% of the price of a package holiday (Holloway, 2002), hence unsold capacity can seriously impact on profitability. They are also relatively scarce in comparison to hotel beds and, therefore, tend to be monopolised by the larger operators on some popular routes.

The benefits of purchasing a package holiday for the consumer, as summarised by Sharpley (2002: 75), include:

- *price*, this being lower on account of the operator buying in bulk;
- the *convenience* of having a third party deal with arrangements which necessitate a level of expertise well in excess of that possessed by the individual (e.g. industry contacts, product knowledge, language skills, etc.);
- *reliability*, in that the tour operator lends an element of homogeneity to an otherwise heterogeneous product (e.g. in relation to their quality assurance procedures), in addition to providing a relatively safe and predictable environment for the tourist;
- *consumer protection*, in other words certain rights that are not afforded to the independent traveller (e.g. compensation where service standards fall short of those described in an operator's brochure, or where an operator ceases trading).

Market structure and (anti)competitive conditions: the polarisation of the tour operating sector into large 'mass' and small 'niche' operators

There are currently some 1400+ tour operators in the UK who hold an Air Travel Organiser's License (ATOL), this being a requirement of the Civil Aviation Authority (CAA) for any operation, except airlines, intending to sell seats on charter flights or block-booked scheduled services. Despite the large number of firms, which has remained relatively constant in the last few years, the market for air-inclusive package holidays is dominated by just four major operators: TUI UK (formerly Thomson Holidays), MyTravel (rebranded from Airtours), Thomas Cook (previously branded as JMC Holidays) and First Choice. Together, they accounted for 44% of the 27.5 million licensed passengers carried in 2000, rising to 55% if one takes into consideration other firms/brands within each operator's parent group of companies (Papatheodorou, 2003), such a high degree of concentration being typical of other Western European countries (and Germany in particular).

Accordingly, Sharpley (2002: 76) characterises the ever-changing structure of the UK tour operating sector as comprising:

- '[an] elite group of about 10 vertically integrated tour operators which collectively account for 70% of the air[-inclusive] holiday market . . .
- [a] central group of established, medium-sized operators which enjoy strong, niche market presence . . . [carrying] between 100,000 and 300,000 passengers a year . . . a number of . . . [these coming] under the ownership of the majors . . .
- [a] very large number of small, specialised operators, carrying up to 100,000 (but usually fewer) passengers, which focus on particular markets or destinations.'

One should note that the estimates cited above may be revised upwards, to reflect an overall increase in the number of passengers carried since 2000. In addition, the various trade associations that represent the interests of these outbound operators provide a clue as to the scale of the operation in question, in that many in the first and second tiers are members of the Association of British Travel Agents (ABTA), with some twenty of the largest constituting the informal but highly influential Federation of Tour Operators (FTO), while those in the third tier are more likely to pursue membership of the Association of Independent Tour Operators (AITO).

The market dominance of the top ten tour operating groups or companies is evident in Figure 19.2, which illustrates their share of the total number of passengers (30,545,690) licensed to all ATOL holders in the year to September 2004.

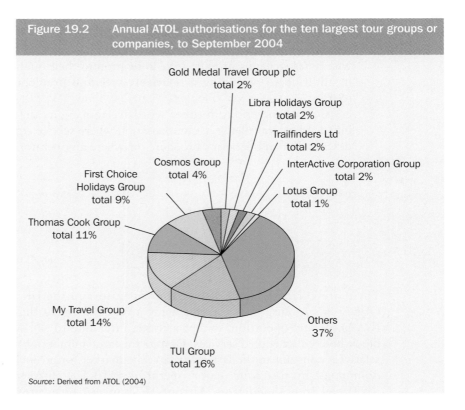

Figure 19.2   Annual ATOL authorisations for the ten largest tour groups or companies, to September 2004

Gold Medal Travel Group plc total 2%

Libra Holidays Group total 2%

Trailfinders Ltd total 2%

InterActive Corporation Group total 2%

Cosmos Group total 4%

First Choice Holidays Group total 9%

Lotus Group total 1%

Thomas Cook Group total 11%

My Travel Group total 14%

Others 37%

TUI Group total 16%

Source: Derived from ATOL (2004)

Agarwal *et al.* (2000: 244–5) suggest that concentration in the tourism industry *per se* takes the following forms:

▪ *strategic alliances* (most common among the airlines);
▪ *mergers, acquisitions and takeovers* (particularly in the tour operator, travel agency and accommodation subsectors);
▪ *franchising agreements* (these being behind the expansion of global brands in hospitality, such as Marriott);
▪ *marketing consortiums* (typically a means by which the smaller, marginalised retailers seek to compete with the majors by projecting a unified brand).

The second of these forms of concentration is most closely associated with integration, although the term could be extended to cover all four in that each offers the prospect of scale economies and/or the opportunity to exercise control over the manner in which principals' or operators' products are supplied, promoted and distributed. It occurs in one of two main ways, that is, *vertically* or *horizontally*. The former refers to a situation where firms occupying different positions in the supply chain merge to form one firm, or enter into a contractual arrangement whereby they operate *de facto* as a single organisation, with a further distinction between backwards and forwards integration (e.g.

Thomson Travel Group's purchase of Britannia Airways in 1965 and the retail travel agent chain Lunn Poly in 1972, respectively). The latter refers to occasions on which firms at the same level (e.g. two wholesalers or two retailers) come together as one; this is increasingly occurring on a pan-European basis (as with the recent acquisition of Thomson Holidays, the UK market leader, by Germany's foremost tour operator, TUI, itself the subject of a takeover by the German steel/utility company Preussag in 1998). Both types of integration should yield economies of scale, in addition to internalising an important source of revenue and enhancing reliability/quality (vertical), and increasing market share and opportunities to strengthen through expansion/diversification (horizontal). A third type of integration, *diagonal*, occurs between firms offering complementary rather than substitute products (e.g. package holidays and financial services), thus allowing for economies of *scope* as distinct from scale.

Integration is a logical response to, and also a reason for, the highly competitive environment in which both large and small tour operators function, the main features of which are (after Evans (1999) and Shaw and Williams (2002)):

- high-volume sales due to the large number of buyers and sellers;
- low-cost products, and slim gross margins, as a result of fierce price competition in the quest for market share;
- volatility of profits, coinciding with a downturn in the economic cycle;
- little differentiation between rival offerings in terms of their product features, with the attendant threat of substitutes;
- supplier power, where capacity is limited and tour operations are not significant to the supplier's overall business;
- potentially high fixed costs in relation to the contracting of travel, accommodation and other services;
- the risks associated with seasonality/perishability.

For those holding the 'upper hand' in merger, acquisition or takeover negotiations, integration offers the following benefits:

- it deters new entrants to the mass market (which, historically, have been attracted by the low capital outlays permitted by the subcontracting system and the ease of access to producers/retailers);
- it consolidates purchasing power over principals (especially in respect of accommodation, where 'large numbers of mostly small independent operators mean that supply conditions resemble those of perfect competition, whereas the concentration of ownership among tour companies mean that demand is delivered under oligopolistic conditions' (Shaw and Williams, 2002: 132);
- it provides a greater say in the sale of package holiday products;
- it allows for the possibility of 'instantly' diversifying into emerging and profitable niche markets, through horizontally integrating with a specialist operator (e.g. Trek America, which is now part of First Choice).

Correspondingly, Dale (2000, cited in Sharpley, 2002) considers the benefits of integration as a competitive strategy within the framework of Porter's (1980) 'five forces' model, whereby it is used to manage the threat of new entrants and substitute products/services, the bargaining power of buyers and sellers, and rivalry between competitors.

Naturally, there are 'winners and losers' implicated in such a strategy, and integration is regularly presented as being at odds with the interests of the small tour operator and the consumer in bringing about 'a position where the larger operators face little effective competition because the size of the next tier of competitors is so small' (Evans, 1999: 3). Horizontal integration has seriously challenged the *raison d'être* of the smaller operators (i.e. the sale of bespoke or alternative holiday products), as the majors move into market niches first carved out by independents frustrated at their inability to compete in mainstream markets on the basis of price. Meanwhile, it is contended that some vertically-integrated tourism operations have abused their dominant position by using their travel agencies' racking policies to covertly prioritise 'own-brand' holidays over competitors, while persuading agents to sell these products ahead of rival offerings via higher commissions and staff training (a practice known as *directional selling*, which does little to promote consumer choice). It should be added that the Monopoly and Mergers Commission found, in a 1997 report, no evidence of anti-competitive practices attributable to vertical integration, although it did oblige operators with a market share of 5% or above to declare their ownership links in brochures, retail outlets, etc.

On another note, integration has preceded some high-profile business failures (such as Court Line and its subsidiary Clarkson's Holidays in 1974, and Intasun together with its parent ILG in 1991), which Sharpley (2002: 77) attributes to one or more of the following factors:

- 'over-rapid growth based upon excessive borrowing to finance expansion;
- insufficient profit resulting from price-cutting to maintain market share;
- external factors, such as fuel price rises or political instability.'

In these earlier instances, integration either compounded the problems that led to the collapse of the above-named operators, or failed to insulate them against a downturn in the market which postdated the acquisition(s) in question. Together with MyTravel (see Case 19.2), itself under considerable financial pressure at the time of writing, they constitute a timely reminder that even the most integrated of operations are not invulnerable to risk. This would explain why several larger operators, MyTravel included, are now looking to cut capacity and sell off some of their assets (especially unprofitable overseas operations).

Case 19.2   Airtours/MyTravel

Airtours started life in 1980 as the tour operating division of a small travel agency, Pendle Travel, based in the north-west of England. Through a combination of vertical and horizontal integration (including the purchase of the Pickfords and Hogg Robinson retail travel chains in 1992 and 1993, which were merged to form Going Places, and Direct Holidays in 1998), it has since expanded to become the second largest UK tour operator in terms of market share (a position mirrored in several other countries in which it operates). As of 1999, the assets of its parent company included some 1600+ travel outlets, 40+ aircraft, 26 hotels, 10 cruise ships and two timeshare developments, with operations spanning four divisions: the UK Leisure Group, the Scandinavian Leisure Group, the European Leisure Group and the North American Leisure Group. The first of these incorporated the well-known Airtours, Aspro and Cresta branded holiday products, plus Going Places (with 728 branches), and reported a turnover for the year to September 1999 of £1838.3 million. That same year Airtours attempted to acquire First Choice, the fourth-largest UK operator in terms of market share, only for the European Commission to block its 'hostile' £850 million bid on account of concerns over the already high levels of concentration in the industry.

After turning in a poor set of financial results for 2001/02, compounded by the difficulties experienced by the industry as a whole in the wake of the terrorist attacks of 11 September 2001, the company (which rebranded itself as MyTravel in 2002) commissioned a review of operations resulting in the implementation of a three-pronged strategy of:

1 Lowering fixed costs (by reducing commitments to guaranteed accommodation, implementing job losses and retiring older, noisier, less fuel-efficient aircraft).
2 Improving asset utilisation (by cutting capacity, especially in relation to the travel portion and loss-making hotels).

3   Restructuring the UK charter and distribution business (by merging Going Places, MyTravel Airways, Airtours Holidays and six other UK-based businesses into one organisation headed by a single management team).

These measures came too late to prevent it posting a £358.3 million operating loss for 2002/03 (rising to £910.9 million after 'exceptional items and goodwill'), of which £325.4 million was accounted for by the UK business, with a further £36.1 million attributable to the now-disposed German operation (due, in part, to weak economic conditions in the 'Eurozone'), offset by a small profit of £7.3 million on joint ventures. The scale of these losses was put down to a combination of one-off costs associated with the sale of 'non-core' businesses, the war in Iraq, better than expected weather in Northern Europe and the UK, reported cases of the SARS virus in Canada, and poor pricing decisions on Summer 2003 products. Given the 'exceptional' nature of some of these problems, the capital derived from the ongoing implementation of the cost-cutting measures described above plus the proceeds of planned disposals (most recently in respect of the company's cruise ship operations), and a refinancing package agreed in June 2003, MyTravel (which has recently formed its own low-cost carrier, MyTravelLite) hopes to be back in profit by September 2005, although its optimism is yet to be shared by the trade press.

Source: Adapted from Page *et al.* (2001) and **www.mytravelgroup.com**

The rise and fall of some well established operators, over the recent past, is detailed in Holloway's (2002: 227–9) resumé of the changing structure of the UK tour operating sector, which highlights a number of significant acquisitions, failed bids for rival firms and collapses during the 1990s. The majority of those acquisitions relate to the 'big four', and have resulted in the ownership links summarised in Table 19.3 (note that this does not convey the totality of their operations in that it does not include overseas interests).

Table 19.3   The 'big four' UK tour operators' ownership links (as of 2004)

	Tour operations	Retail operations	Cruise operations	Airline operations
TUI UK	Austravel	Lunn Poly	Thomson Cruises	Britannia Airways
	Portland Direct	Manchester Flights		Thomsonfly.com
	Specialist Holidays Group:	Team Lincoln		
	(American Holidays, Crystal, Jersey Travel, Jetsave, Magic Travel Group, Thomson Breakaway, Simply Travel, Something Special, Spanish Harbour Holidays, Thomson Lakes and Mountains, Thomson Ski and Snowboarding, Tropical Places)	Travel House Group: (Callers Pegasus, Sibbald Travel, Travel House)		
	Thomson Holidays			
MyTravel	Airtours Holidays	Going Places		MyTravel Airways
	Aspro	Holidayline		MyTravelLite
	Bridge	Travelworld		
	Cresta			
	Direct Holidays			
	Escapades			
	Manos			
	Panorama			
	Tradewinds			

Table 19.3	Continued			
	Tour operations	**Retail operations**	**Cruise operations**	**Airline operations**
Thomas Cook	Club 18–30	Thomas Cook Retail		Thomas Cook Airlines
	Cultura			
	JMC			
	Neilson			
	Style Holidays			
	Thomas Cook Holidays			
	Thomas Cook Signature			
First Choice	2wentys	First Choice Holiday Hypermarkets	Royal Caribbean Cruises (strategic alliance)	First Choice Airways
	Citalia	First Choice Travel Shops		
	Eclipse			
	Exclusive Destinations			
	First Choice Holidays			
	Hayes and Jarvis			
	Meon Villas			
	Sovereign			
	Sunquest			
	Sunstart			
	Unijet			

Source: Company websites

Consumer protection: licensing/bonding and regulation

Package holidays, as products, are both *intangible* and *heterogeneous*. In other words they have no corporeal existence that would allow them to be 'road-tested' prior to purchase, neither is any one consumer experience the same as the next. Furthermore, given the array of services involved, including those provided at the destination by indigenous businesses, the potential for standards to fall short of those expected is considerable. Accordingly, Laws (1996) identifies a number of 'fail points' over the course of a typical inclusive tour, from purchase through to recollection. On a number of occasions (i.e. transfers, excursions, etc.) the tour operator is likely to be perceived as the direct source of any problem whereas, on others, the blame may be apportioned elsewhere (e.g. the travel agency, the airport/airline, the hotel or the ground-handling agent). However, regardless of who the tourist believes to be at fault, recent EU and UK legislation has placed liability for the quality of package holidays firmly with the tour operator, a position enshrined in the European Commission's Directive on Package Travel. This came into effect in 1993 and obliges operators to provide certain minimum standards of service, as advertised in their brochures, and appropriate redress where these are not met (even if the actions of a subcontractor, as opposed to the operator, are responsible for this). As a result, they tend to exercise a greater degree of caution than perhaps was the case in the past when subcontracting services to principals (with much of the informal sector, particularly in developing countries such as The Gambia, 'written off' as incapable of providing a quality product). To some extent, the cost of a package holiday has increased for consumers since the Directive was first implemented, as tour operators seek to protect themselves from the threat of litigation.

The origins of the other main form of consumer protection, namely that pertaining to operator failure, lay with the collapse of Fiesta Tours in 1964. This famously left around 5000 tourists stranded overseas with no means of returning home other than under their own initiative and at their own expense. The Association of British Travel Agents (ABTA) responded by setting up a 'common fund' into which 50% of members' subscriptions were diverted, with a view to providing the necessary capital to reimburse and, where necessary, repatriate tourists caught up in subsequent failures. It later established Operation Stabliser, in the absence of government legislation to regulate the industry, whereby ABTA tour operators had to sell their packages via ABTA travel agents and vice versa, with consumers purchasing holidays at their own risk if bought from an agency that was not a member. This lasted until 1993 and the implementation of the EU Package Travel Directive, which requires all 'travel organisers' to be *bonded* (see below). Meanwhile, the requirement for operators to hold an Air Travel Organiser's License, as explained earlier in this chapter, was introduced in 1972 by the Civil Aviation Authority. To this day, it remains the foremost statutory consumer-protection scheme in relation to air travel and, in order to obtain an ATOL, operators must undergo rigorous financial scrutiny and commit to arranging a bond with a preferred insurer that is sufficient to pay for the costs of reimbursing/repatriating tourists in the event of business failure, amounting to 25% of annual turnover, or 10% where the operator is a member of a recognised trade association such as ABTA or AITO (Sharpley, 2002). Where such protection is inadequate the CAA may draw on the (albeit depleted) Air Travel Trust Fund, financed by a 2% levy on the sale of package holidays and guaranteed by the government.

Thus, it can be seen that the emphasis in the tour operating sector has shifted from, as Sharpley (2002: 89) puts it, '*caveat emptor* (buyer beware) to producer liability', thanks to increasing regulation and consumerism.

Conclusion: whither the tour operator?

It is alleged that consumers of tourism products are becoming more sophisticated/experienced, as embodied in the concept of the 'new tourist' (after Poon, 1993). For these reconstituted pleasure seekers, a low price has ceased to be an imperative in itself. They are also less reliant upon the traditional sources of information as regards destinations, principally the travel agent and holiday brochure, with an increasing number of them enjoying access to the internet, digital television and a proliferation of paper-based and electronic guidebooks that 'tell it like it is'. Naturally, this brings into question the future for tour operations, and the larger, more integrated operators in particular (who, hitherto, have competed on the basis of price and the convenience of booking through one of their many 'high street' retail outlets).

Disintermediation, therefore, is a threat to the once seemingly secure position of the tour operator in the tourism chain of distribution. However, it may also be construed as an opportunity for operators to diversify into alternative supply channels by setting up or acquiring their own direct-sell subsidiary. Pertinently, we are now witnessing the emergence of the 'virtual' tour operator as a mass-market phenomenon, with the entry of the InterActive Corporation Group (owners of Expedia.com, TV Travel Shop, etc.) into the top ten tour operators by number of licensed (ATOL) passengers (Figure 19.2). In this respect, disintermediation appears to be more of a problem for travel agents than it is for tour operators (although, in many cases, they are effectively one and the same, thanks to vertical integration). Indeed, the expediency of purchasing tourism products direct from a principal or an operator, the potential for reducing the likelihood of an erroneous booking by cutting out an 'unnecessary' intermediary, and a growing recognition that agents are no longer the *definitive* source of advice on holiday options, all conspire to undermine the rationale for their existence. Already, this is starting to 'bite', as evidenced by

Airtour's announcement early in 2001 of its intention to close 120 branches of Going Places (Holloway, 2002). Such retrenchment reminds us that the future for tour operations in general (a volatile business at the best of times) is an uncertain one, the only certainty being that yet more operators will collapse before the decade is over.

Discussion questions

1   Using examples, state what is meant by 'integration' in the context of mass-market tour operations and suggest the implications of this for suppliers, consumers and (smaller) competitors.

2   Explain why a significant number of tour operators, both large and small, have collapsed and consider what might be done to reduce the risk of business failure on the part of those experiencing difficulties.

3   List the two main forms of consumer protection pertaining to package holidays and describe the characteristics of tour operating as a sector and as an activity that necessitate such measures.

4   Discuss the circumstances under which 'disintermediation' occurs in the tourism chain of distribution, and explain why this might be perceived as both an opportunity and a threat by the tour operator.

Guided reading

Although a little outdated, Laws (1996) provides a reasonably comprehensive and user-friendly treatment of tour operations, including chapters on the evolution of the inclusive-holiday industry, service quality management and agency distribution. More recent material of relevance may be found in introductory tourism textbooks such as Page *et al.* (2001), although these can be somewhat superficial in their coverage (with the notable exception of Holloway, 2002). Those looking for a practitioner's perspective are advised to consult Bray and Raitz (2001), a semi-autobiographical piece that skilfully weaves the erudite observations of the former with the anecdotal recollections of the latter. Meanwhile, academic journals such as *Tourism Economics*, *Tourism Geographies* and *Tourism Management* contain a number of relevant research articles at the other end of the theory/practice continuum. Finally, companies such as Mintel periodically publish reports with a focus on certain segments/activities (e.g. all-inclusive holidays).

Recommended websites

Association of British Travel Agents: **www.abtanet.com** . Provides a directory of members and information on featured destinations/specialist activities.

Association of Independent Tour Operators: **www.aito.co.uk** . Includes a specialist holiday search facility, a section on responsible tourism, and information on the Campaign for Real Travel Agents or CARTA (a reaction to the disputed sales practices of the high street agency chains).

Air Travel Organiser's Licensing website: **www.atol.org.uk** . Provides information for consumers and the travel trade, such as a list of failed companies, an explanation of the history of consumer protection and different types of bond, and the twice-yearly publication *ATOL Business* (with the most recent revenue and passenger figures).

Federation of Tour Operators: **www.fto.co.uk** . Contains a very useful fact file covering such issues as the tour operating calendar, seasonality, hotel contracting, reasons for differences in prices between the UK and the rest of Europe, and package holiday regulations.

Corporate websites of the four largest UK tour operators, with company histories and information on constituent brands:

First Choice: **www.firstchoiceholidaysplc.com** .

MyTravel: **www.mytravelgroup.com** .

Thomas Cook: **www.thomascook.info** .

Thomson: **www.thomsontravelgroup.com** .

Key words

ABTA; AITO; all-inclusive; ATOL; chain of distribution; disintermediation; integration; intermediaries; package holiday; principal; tour operator.

Bibliography

Agarwal, S., Ball, R., Shaw, G. and Williams, A.M. (2000) The geography of tourism production: uneven disciplinary development?, *Tourism Geographies*, 2(3), 241–263.

ATOL (2004) *ATOL business*, Issue 23 (January). CAA, London.

Bray, R. and Raitz, V. (2001) *Flight to the sun: the story of the holiday revolution*. Continuum, London.

Cooper, C., Fletcher, J., Gilbert, D. and Wanhill, S. (1998) *Tourism principles and practice*. Longman, Harlow.

Dale, C. (2000) The UK tour-operating industry: a competitive analysis, *Journal of Vacation Marketing*, 6(4), 357–367.

Evans, P. (1999) *Recent developments in trade and competition issues in the services sector: a review of practices in travel and tourism*. United Nations, New York.

Holloway, J.C. (2002) *The business of tourism*, 6th edn. Pearson Education, Harlow.

Laws, E. (1996) *Managing packaged tourism*. Thomson Learning, London.

Office for National Statistics (2003) *Travel trends 2002*. TSO, London.

Page, S.J., Brunt, P., Busby, G. and Connell, J. (2001) *Tourism: a modern synthesis*. Thomson Learning, London.

Papatheodorou, A. (2003) Corporate strategies of British tour operators in the Mediterranean region: an economic geography approach, *Tourism Geographies*, 5(3), 280–304.

Poon, A. (1993) *Tourism, technology and competitive strategies*. CAB International, Oxford.

Porter, M. (1980) *Competitive Strategy*. Free Press, New York.

Sharpley, J. (2002) Tour operations, in R. Sharpley (ed.) *The Tourism Business: an introduction*. Business Education Publishers, Sunderland.

Shaw, G. and Williams, A.M. (2002) *Critical issues in tourism: a geographical perspective*, 2nd edn. Blackwell, Oxford.

Yale, P. (1995) *The business of tour operations*. Longman, Harlow.

Chapter 20

Mass tourism businesses 2: travel agents

Claire Humphreys, University of Westminster

Learning outcomes

On completion of this chapter the reader should be able to:

■ explain the role of travel agents in the supply chain, and identify their strengths and weaknesses;

■ assess their use of information technology;

■ explain the importance of customer care and the strategies adopted to facilitate it;

■ outline their responses to the changing competitive environment;

■ identify the role of related stakeholders.

Overview

The purpose of this chapter is to introduce the reader to the business of travel agents. In the past decade the level of competition experienced by the travel agent has grown significantly. This is coupled with changes over the past few decades in the consolidation in ownership of travel businesses, with many travel agents now being owned by global travel companies that provide flights, accommodation and other elements of travel.

This chapter explores both the activities of the travel agent as well as examining the environment in which the mass travel agency business currently operates. The dynamic environment in which the travel industry operates does mean that the activities undertaken by agencies, both in terms of traditional 'high street' agents as well as online agencies, are having to be continually adapted and diversified to ensure a continuing income stream.

Introduction

The realm of the travel agent has significantly changed over recent years, most especially in the areas of the world where the travel industry is reaching maturity and where technology is providing the customer with other alternatives for purchasing travel products.

Mintel (2002) defined travel agencies as outlets at which holidays or other travel products can be purchased. These include the high street retailers as well as the many companies that now operate online. The Commission of the European Communities (1999) recognised that 'travel agents act as retailers. They generally act on behalf of a tour operator principal and are remunerated by a commission on the price of the holiday sold. Travel agencies supply other products such as air flights, either charter or scheduled, hotel and other accommodation bookings, car rental, insurance and other travel related services.

The travel agent, as retailer, can access products either from a wholesaler (the tour operator) or direct from the principal or manufacturer (such as a hotel or airline). This chain of distribution (Figure 20.1) can be perceived as similar to traditional industry, where the product flows from the manufacturer to the consumer.

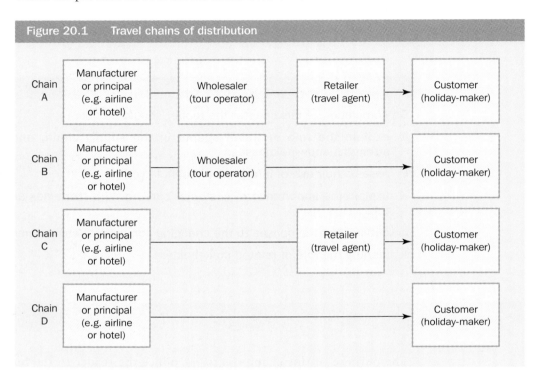

Figure 20.1   Travel chains of distribution

The role of travel agents

The main role of the travel agent is to seek suitable and available travel products on behalf of the customer. The travel agent acts as the retailing arm of the travel industry, linking both the tour operators and the principals, or direct providers of travel-related products to the traveller or holiday-maker.

The important difference between the travel agent and a traditional retailer is that the travel agent never purchases goods ahead of a request by a customer and therefore never holds stock. This is a benefit for travel agents, as they do not have capital tied up in stock holdings nor have stock which perishes or becomes out of date. Second, as the agent is not trying to make sales of products which are held in stock but can draw on any offered at that time, then the travel agent is usually under no obligation to overly favour specific products.

The implication is, however, that, where demand for a particular product is high and desired products are scarce, the travel agent can only make the sale if the tour operator provides enough availability; thus the travel agent has no opportunity to adjust supply for popular destinations. Theoretically, as every travel agent has an equal opportunity of accessing scarce travel products, the customer is not forced to one particular agent. However, as some tour operators own travel agencies to whom they provide details of offers on particular holidays, this means that in some cases parity among agents is not always achieved.

The travel agent is most commonly the provider of package travel (where several travel elements are provided for one price) but it is also common that individual products are provided, such as accommodation, rail tickets and flights.

The existence of travel agents

The number of travel agents around the world is difficult to estimate. Many travel agents are affiliated to association or member bodies, which operate to support the interests of their members. Table 20.1 identifies current membership by travel agents of leading associations around the world. In some regions the membership levels are a significant indicator (for example, the Travel Agent's Association in New Zealand estimates that members make up 90% of the total travel agents in the country), while in other regions the existence of several associations and membership bodies, or alternatively the lack of an effective organisation or limited expectation to be a member of a trade association, means that a far lower percentage of travel agents are registered.

Table 20.1 Membership of travel associations	
	Number of travel agent members (2004)
American Society of Travel Agents (ASTA)	3846
Australian Federation of Travel Agents (AFTA)	2300
Association of Austrian Travel Agents (ORV)	2300
Association of British Travel Agents (ABTA)	1548
Danish Association of Travel Agents and Tour Operators (DRF)	100
Association of German Travel Agents and Tour Operators (DRV)	3896
Irish Travel Agents Association (ITAA)	352
Japan Association of Travel Agents (JATA)	6312
Travel Agents Association in New Zealand (TAANZ)	520
Swiss Travel Association of Retailers	450

Source: Author's research

It is perhaps possible to predict more closely the total number of travel agents in a country when there is a legal or financial requirement to register the agency. For example, in Denmark travel agents are required to register for the Travel Guarantee Fund, which currently has 550 members (though that does include some airlines and travel organisers who are required to register). Lars Thykier, General Manager, of the Danish Association of Travel Agents and Tour Operators, suggests that approximately 200 of the 550 could be considered to be travel agents. In Australia, while licensing is undertaken on a state-by-state basis, membership of the Travel Compensation Fund (TCF) is a mandatory component of licensing and Lynne O'Neill at the Australian Federation of Travel Agents (AFTA) notes that anecdotal figures suggest that the TCF has approximately 4600 licensed travel agent members (of which approximately half are AFTA members). Malaysia also operates a licensing system, managed by the Ministry of Tourism, and they estimate that in the first quarter of 2004 there were 2100 travel agents operating, while in Hong Kong the Travel Agents registry had 1344 registered travel agents in 2004.

The use of travel agents varies from country to country. Dumazel and Humphreys (1999) noted that earlier research by Gilbert in 1990 suggested that at a time when 80% of travel purchases in the UK were made via travel agents, the level was nearer 25% in The Netherlands, Belgium, Switzerland and Luxembourg, whilst in France only 7% of bookings were made through travel agents. While there have been significant market changes since this research it is important to recognise that travel agency businesses vary across nations, in order to meet the expectations of their marketplace.

As demand for travel has grown, travel agency businesses have often tended to expand their operations. As a consequence many of the travel agency businesses today are operating several branches or outlets spread around their home country and in some cases overseas branches too. These 'multiples' have a number of advantages in operations over the single agency operation:

■ They can gain from a consolidation of marketing activity to reach extensive audiences.
■ Customers may place greater trust and confidence in the organisation as they are aware of the brand name.
■ The company can gain greater financial power through negotiating higher commission based on group sales.
■ Centralised purchasing of equipment such as computer systems can help reduce overheads for each outlet.
■ The cost of development of necessary technology systems can be borne across all outlets, thus allowing the group to seek greater competitive advantage.

Many of the multiples are linked through ownership to tour operators, and in Europe a significant number of travel agent brands are owned by just a few very large travel businesses, who operate at all stages of the distribution chain (Table 20.2).

Table 20.2	Travel agency ownership
Parent company	**Distribution network**
First Choice	UK and Ireland
	First Choice Holiday Hypermarkets, First Choice Travel Shops, Hays Travel
	Canada
	Sun Holidays, Dream Vacations, Travel Choice
MyTravel	UK and Ireland
	Going Places, Going Places TV, Holidayline, LateEscapes.com, MyTravel.com, Travelworld
	Europe
	Always, Gate Eleven, Globetrotter, Gullivers, MyTravel, MyTravel.com, MyTravel Reiswinkels, Spies, Saga, Skibby, Trivsel, Tjaereborg, Ving
	North America
	ABC Corporate Services, Diplomat Tours, DFW Tours, FlyCheap Vacations, Lifestyle Vacation Incentives, MyTravelco.com, MyTravel Retail, Resort Escapes, Travel 800
Thomas Cook	UK and Ireland
	Thomas Cook, Thomas Cook TV
	Europe
	Thomas Cook, Holiday Land, Alpha, Neckerman, Aquatour, Thomas Cook (formerly Havas Voyages), Broere Reizen
	Canada
	Marlin Travel, Thomas Cook
TUI AG	UK and Ireland
	Lunn Poly, Callers-Pegasus, Team Lincoln, Sibbald Travel
	Europe
	TUI, First Reiseburo, TUI TravelCenter, Nouvelles Frontières, Hapag-Lloyd Reiseburo, TV Travel shop, Lastminute.nl

Source: Author's research

While these large travel businesses dominate ownership of travel agents in Europe it should also be recognised that some companies operate multiple travel agency operations without being linked directly to major tour operators or principals such as airlines or hotel chains. In addition to this we find that some independent travel agency operations which have only one outlet (or in the case of 'miniples' a few branches) often link through trade associations to gain the benefits that would be experienced by multiple operations (for example, in the UK the National Association of Independent Travel Agents (NAITA) has over 1000 leisure and business travel members operating under their trading brand name of Advantage Travel Centres). The existence and growth in power of the multiples has led to a suggestion that in some countries the total number of travel agents may decline (Mintel, 2002).

Shelley (2004) has suggested, however, that 'the integrated model which Thomas Cook and their larger German rival, TUI operate – combining in-house airlines, tour operators and travel agents – has been undermined in recent years by the rise of independent travel, driven by the success of low-cost airlines'. Furthermore, in 2004, Travelocity, in a joint venture with Otto Freizeit und Touristik, acquired the online travelchannel.de. This followed its purchase of the French tour operator Boomerang Voyages, as part of their expansion into the European market (Yee, 2004a). Expedia, the US online travel agent expanded activities in the European market through the acquisition of Egencia, a French based corporate travel company, which also has operations in Belgium (Yee, 2004b). Such global ownership of both online and high street travel agencies creates powerful organisations, who are now starting to dominate this sector of the travel industry.

Case 20.1   Advantage travel centres

The members of the National Association of Independent Travel Agents (NAITA) have created an operating brand called the Advantage Travel Centre. Members of NAITA can use this brand name and promotional material when promoting their independent agency. The association suggests that the benefits for each agency are:

- *Marketing* – by using branded brochures, shop fascias and point-of-sale material, the customer will recognise the outlet and will gain enhanced trust through brand recognition.
- *Trade terms* – the collective buying power can ensure improved terms with suppliers.
- *Product range* – the collective entity can agree terms with a wider range of providers.
- *Training* – staff training and selling skills can be developed though specific programmes and educational visits for staff which are provided by the association.
- *Brand name advertising* and *direct mail campaigns* – these are designed to enhance customer awareness of the Advantage Travel Centre brand which can also benefit each individual outlet.
- *Business operations discounts* – this can include discounts on telephone and electricity bills, bonding and business insurance offers.
- *Web presence* – The **advantage4travel.com** website helps to bring customers in contact with the independent outlets.

Source: Edited from Advantage Travel centre promotional material

---

Discussion questions

1 Are there any concerns that need to be considered by the owners of an independent agency before linking their business with a trade association such as the Advantage Travel Centre group?

The activities of travel agents

The activities and skills of the travel agent are extensive. Vitally important is the ability to locate a product which meets the needs of the customer most suitably, thus requiring extensive product knowledge, although Holloway (1994) noted that as no individual could possible be aware of all products available to all destinations, agents must importantly have the knowledge and skill to locate information to help identify the products they seek on behalf of the customer. The travel agent also undertakes tasks such as ticketing, dealing with payments and administration of the bookings throughout the (often considerable) lead time prior to the date of travel. It is often the case that elements of the travel product purchased by the customer may be changed (for instance a flight time is altered) and therefore the travel agent provides significant after-sales service, ensuring that the customer is kept informed of these changes and dealing with any of the concerns of the customer due to alterations in travel product. Like any retailer the travel agent may also have to deal with customers who are unhappy with the product purchased and after travel return to complain. Therefore the travel agent has a responsibility to the customer existing long after the sale is made.

Interestingly, it is now expected that the travel agent also seeks to make additional sales of travel 'extras' such as airport parking, foreign currency, airport hotels, car hire, etc. These may not have otherwise been considered by the customer and can lead to greater levels of total sales (and thus greater commission for the travel agent). Commission on these services is often at much higher levels than for package holidays – perhaps as high as 20–30% of sales – and therefore provides a significant additional revenue stream for the agency.

The majority of travel agents will provide a full range of services to any client who wishes to use their service. However, some travel agents do choose to specialise; the business travel agent or global travel management organisations, such as Carlson Wagonlit, for instance, will arrange all the travel requirements for their corporate clients. Such an agency will offer a range of benefits to these clients, which may include either an on-site agency or a representative to handle enquiries, as well as additional travel services, such as arranging visas, foreign currency and providing travel information about the destination. The agency will also offer financial incentives to the corporate client by passing on bulk-purchase rewards and discounts. However, as Davidson and Cope (2003) remark, the business travel agent is likely to have to spend time amending bookings to meet the travel demands of the client, may need to provide a 24-hour service to meet client needs, may need to manage the travel arrangements in line with the travel policy set by the organisation and may have to deliver documents direct to the traveller or the airport as well as providing regular reports on travel expenditure to allow the corporate businesses to monitor and manage travel spend. These factors mean that, while the earnings on business travel bookings are often quite significant, the after-care and additional services that need to be provided have a significant impact on the operational costs of the travel agency.

| Case 20.2 | The activities of a travel agent manager |

As the manager of this busy travel agency I have a range of tasks to complete. Perhaps the most significant of my activities is to ensure that the customers are served efficiently and that they are sold products that suit their requirements. If a customer comes into the shop with a brochure and a specific holiday in mind then we will try to book that for them. If they have selected a holiday that isn't with our company we will see if any of the tour operators owned by our chain offer something similar, offering the same hotel at their selected destination, and provide a price comparison. But if the client chooses to use the original tour operator that is fine. I have heard that for managers of other travel agents they would have to write to their regional manager and explain why they didn't manage to 'cross-sell' the client onto one of their own products.

Our computer systems are vital for assisting us in making the majority of our sales. My staff will mainly sell packages offered by tour operators, principally brochure holidays, and this also includes accommodation-only packages. There are also systems that allow flight-only travel to be booked. When the customer wants something a bit more unusual then we may have to phone the tour operators and book this over the phone. It used to be very common to have to phone to check bookings but now the majority of bookings are completed using computer search-and-reservation facilities.

I also maintain the advertising material in the shop. The company wants all the shops to have a similar image so the main marketing material is universal but each day I will find travel offers that I think will suit my local market (as this differs from outlet to outlet) and I will display these in the window in order to tempt customers to come through the door. I also order the brochures, making sure that we have enough of those heavily demanded by my particular customers. My staff and I now have access to many brochures online so if for some reason we cannot give the customer a brochure then we can find the travel product online and print the required pages for the customer.

I have a lot of administrative tasks to complete. Each day I need to make sure that the payments we have taken from customers balance with our accounts total. This total is generated by the computer, which records all our bookings, forwards them to head office (they usually deal with ticketing) and sets reminders in my calendar to let me know when final payments are due and when tickets should be with me for the customer to collect.

I also have to ensure that the staff have up-to-date knowledge. This usually means that once a week all the staff meet for training updates; this could be about systems, products or promotions. Before coming to the outlet new staff would have had a week's training, to learn the systems and sales techniques. Once they are here, they put this into practice, with the rest of the team there to assist them if they have difficulties. Sometimes staff come to our outlet having completed a qualification, such as a National Vocational Qualification, that has taught them many of the necessary skills needed to be a travel agent.

All my staff receive a regular salary but they also receive commission on the sales that they make. When they sell 'extras' such as car hire, etc. they also receive additional commission. We have a centralised computer system which means that if the customer decides not to book straight away but comes back a few days later then the enquiry record can be retrieved and the consultant that dealt with the initial arrangements (rather than the one making the booking) gets the commission. This is the case even if the customer goes into another branch of our retail outlets to book – this makes it very convenient for the customer as they don't have to go back to the same shop and they don't have to go through all the details again in the new shop.

Another benefit we receive is the chance to travel on familiarisation trips. The regional manager (who looks after about 20 shops in this area) ensures that these trips are shared fairly. It means that perhaps once or twice a year I will be able to take a free trip (these could be short-haul for a couple of days or long-haul for a week). The trips are provided by tour operators and so the choice of destination is determined by the operator; they generally select destinations that they feel travel agents need more information about.

Customer care is vital in our business. I try to ensure that customers are greeted promptly and when the shop is busy I will ask the customer to complete a form telling us about their requirements and arrange for a member of staff to then call them back with details. In some of the larger outlets we now have a computer terminal to let customers search for their own holidays and they bring the printout to the agent to book. In those locations we often have tea and coffee facilities as well as lounge areas for the customer to relax while waiting to see a consultant. To ensure that staff are maintaining their customer care skills we are all secretly monitored through mystery shoppers. These may call into the outlet or may telephone – it is only afterwards that we find out that they were mystery shoppers and if we have received a good score then all the staff in the outlet receive a bonus. Some mystery shoppers are from our organisation and check such things as the appearance of the shop as well as the way in which the enquiry was managed. There are also mystery shoppers who are employed by major travel trade magazines.

Another important task of mine is to deal with customers who have complaints or difficulties after having travelled. We can help to ensure that their letter of complaint to tour operators is dealt with as well as helping to advise the client of their options when something has gone awry.

Over the years I have noticed that customers have changed; many are now much more knowledgeable about the products and destinations; they often come into the shop with a price found on the internet and ask us to beat it. Interestingly, however, many customers choose to book with us because of the customer care that they receive; they like to be able to easily ask questions about the travel product and seem to trust our knowledge. We now focus much of our attention on ensuring good customer care as this seems to make us an attractive option when customers decide to purchase their holidays.

Source: Interview with manager of First Choice travel outlet, 2004

The strengths and weaknesses of the travel agency business

The travel agent is a vital component of the travel industry. Its existence offers significant benefits both to the industry and to the customers who choose to use their services. There are, however, some drawbacks which must be considered (Tables 20.3 and 20.4).

Table 20.3	The strengths and weaknesses of travel agents for the travel industry
Strengths	**Weaknesses**
• The travel agent provides an interface between the customer and the travel providers, rather than these providers having to reach each customer separately.	• The level of turnover of staff in travel agencies is high, therefore leading to concerns regarding the range of product knowledge and level of training of the staff required to meet the demands of the customer.
• The travel agent ensures that the booking procedures are managed correctly, meets legal obligations and advises clients clearly of their rights as well as the implications of their reservations.	• The commission paid to travel agents is often a significant proportion of total costs and thus reduces potential profitability.
• The travel agent can encourage clients who might otherwise decide not to travel to purchase a travel product. The customer may be tentative due to concerns over the cost or safety and the agent can help to reassure the customer.	
• The travel agent can also seek to make additional sales of travel 'extras', thus increasing the total sales value.	

Table 20.4	The strengths and weaknesses of travel agents for the customer
Strengths	**Weaknesses**
• A wider range of products may be considered when purchasing travel as the travel agent can advise about many providers offering many destinations.	• The customer may not be informed of all the products available at the initial stage as the agent may focus on products which offer the agent greater levels of commission or where products are provided by the parent company of the travel agent.
• Special deals and offers may be used, which the customer may not be aware of, but which the travel agent can locate.	• The travel agent may not be in a position to reserve all travel products (for instance where principals only sell direct to customers).
• Confidence and peace of mind can be achieved when the responsibility for making reservations is placed in the hands of the agent.	• The customer may have to pay a fee for the service.
• A good agent should be able to save the client time as the customer will not have to spend time searching and reserving travel products.	

▓ Not all travel agents are mass tourism businesses – the changing role of the smaller travel agencies

In Europe it is the major travel companies, such as Thomas Cook and TUI AG, which dominate the travel agency industry. However, the independent travel agent has managed to continue to exist through the use of independent agency associations, thus offering increased bargaining power for their business.

The major selling point for independent travel agents is that they are independent! The agency can select from a wider range of travel providers and often can provide the customer with a unique level of service, focusing on providing greater levels of specialist knowledge, both of the products and of the customers themselves. This has in turn led to a growth in niche market agencies, which become exceptional by focusing on specific areas of the travel business rather than aiming to master the entire range.

Interestingly the small independent agency has begun to move away from operating in traditional premises and have moved to being businesses operated from home. In the USA nearly 10% of the members of the American Society of Travel Agents operate the business from their residence (Newman, 2004).

Travel agencies and their use of information technology

The development of both computer technology and communication technology has led to a significant change in the business practices of travel agents. Historically the travel agent would check on the availability of travel products by telephoning the tour operator or the principal to ask about products that were advertised in brochures. The affordability of personal computers along with the development of specialist travel reservation software, allowed tour operators the opportunity to create specialist systems, which instantaneously displayed current levels of availability to registered users, thus removing the need to make long telephone calls. This encouraged travel agents to invest in these systems, enhancing their response rates for customers and allowing the agent to search several tour operators for competitive prices. Now the tour operators are driving investment and such systems as Viewdata are being superseded by web-based technology, which can offer greater flexibility in both the range of information provided and the booking process.

The cost of accessing such technology has always been an issue for the small travel agency but for the mass travel agencies, the opportunity to bulk-purchase systems and to implement and manage them through standardised policies and procedures has meant that the use of such technology is now expected. The very large agencies are finding that customers are so comfortable with the web-based systems that it is possible to provide additional terminals in the outlets for customers to make their own searches (although they still need to speak to an agent to confirm the reservation). This has removed some of the time-consuming process away from the agent and into the hands of the customer, which has increased the efficiency for staff in outlets employing these additional terminals.

It can be recognised (TTI, 2001) that the use of technology has become a significant factor in the likelihood of success for all travel business. Effective use of technology will occur provided that:

- ▓ The systems and technology being employed is well-developed and that investment ensures that it continues to be developed and updated.
- ▓ All members of the distribution chain use the technology and that technology is available throughout the business process to ensure the effective sharing of information as well as efficiency of activities.

■ The integration of technology in the business practices must be rapid to ensure that the cost of operating dual systems is minimised.

Technology is not just being employed in booking travel products; there is an increasing use of technology to provide information, such as providing brochures on CD format and through internet sites. There is also the use of technology in the back-office systems, supporting the administration and accounting functions as well as using database technology to enhance client management and marketing.

The use of information technology in the reservations process

The use of computer technology in travel agencies has meant that the process of finding and reserving travel products has been significantly altered. This is not to say that the process is now quicker but that the agent can now locate a travel product using more complex criteria. In situations when the customer has decided upon a holiday, selected from a travel brochure, the travel agent can link directly into the reservation system of the provider and book the holiday. However, more commonly the agent is given only broad details by the customer, perhaps a destination and the time of year to travel; it is in this situation that a range of tour operators or principals systems may be selected, availability for the desired product will be examined and these options will be fed back to the customer for selection.

Once the product is located the travel agent can enter the customer details into the reservation system; this can then produce both the initial reservation documents but can also feed the client details and reservation information into both the client management system and the accounting system. Client management systems are designed to take the reservation details and store both client details and also the reminders required to progress the booking. These reminders ensure that letters are sent to the client when final payment for the holiday is due, ensure that tickets are received by the travel agent on time from the tour operator and ensure that these tickets are then forwarded to the customer prior to departure. In busy travel agencies it is exceptionally unlikely that just one agent staff will deal entirely with a booking, so client systems also ensure that reservation staff can make notes about the booking (held electronically) for any member of staff to access as necessary. This tries to ensure that effective communication between staff occurs for each booking.

The use of information technology to manage and maintain the client

Computerisation has permeated many areas of the travel agency business and now offers the management of customer information, in order to improve the relationship that the travel agent has with the customer – a significant change! The use of a database to manage the booking process has been acknowledged above but it is also important to recognise the need for the maintenance of customer information for the future. The recording of information about clients who may have contacted the agency, perhaps even been provided with quotes but may not have booked travel, are still of importance to the travel agency. It is some of these clients who the agency will seek to develop, in order to encourage them to become customers in the future. In most cases large travel multiples will not expect the individual outlets to use this information for marketing initiatives but will arrange this through the head office. The database is used by the individual outlet to identify customers who have made recent reservations and these people are then contacted to ask whether additional travel extras (such as airport parking, foreign currency, etc.) are required.

The use of non-face-to-face methods of communication to meet the changing demands of the customer is significant. Many travel agents now deal with reservations via telephone and email. It has been suggested (Beattie, 2004) that as a booking tool email takes 30% less staff time than telephone. There are, however, some considerations when employing this approach:

- The customer must feel that this method is most suited to them and not feel that they are losing some of the important contact with a travel agent which adds reassurance in their purchase of the travel product.
- The travel agent must be capable, both in terms of technology and staff skill, of dealing with such enquiries in a timely manner to ensure that the response is effectively provided.
- Legal issues such as terms and conditions can become difficult to convey when the client is not present.

Many airlines worldwide are now moving to e-ticketing, where the customer is provided only with a reference number rather than being issued with a coupon for travel. This has meant that for some travel agents the requirement to provide tickets for travel has been significantly reduced and as a consequence one of their many tasks has been removed.

Case 20.3 The response to customer email enquiries by travel agents

While accessibility to the internet is growing worldwide the ability to respond to emails sent by customers and potential customers has perhaps only been given limited business consideration. There is an obvious benefit for both the business and the customer in using internet technology to book travel. Customers can now search a range of information available through websites and can, at their convenience, email businesses to ask specific questions. These can then be responded to at the convenience of the business (especially useful when considering the problems faced with global travel that spans differing time zones). Poon (1993) suggests that technology can free up staff from administrative tasks to give more time to direct customer service, acting as a travel advisor to the clients rather than just processing bookings. Technology now allows the travel agent the opportunity to access both online and offline information and provide this conveniently to the customer. However, the ability to service the customer in this manner significantly influences the potential relationship with the customer.

The internet and email especially can help the organisation in developing a direct contact with the customer but the ability to do this in a professional and appropriate manner is perhaps an issue of concern. Strauss and Hill (2001) noted that responding promptly and appropriately to customer emails resulted in higher levels of customer satisfaction. Their research in Singapore explored the response levels of 200 travel agents and revealed that just over 28% replied directly to a request for a flight price. While 93% of those that responded did directly address the request, less than half opened the reply with a polite introduction thanking the customer for their enquiry. On a positive note more than three-quarters closed the mail politely and gave the name of the employee at the company who had composed the reply, which is important in enhancing customer satisfaction.

This research concluded that improvement should be made to email policies and training should be provided to agents in order to ensure that responses enhanced the relationship with the customer. While it is recognised that personalised responses are vital in ensuring that client questions are addressed effectively, it is useful for travel agent businesses to have a template which ensures that opening greetings as well as information about the agent and the agency is provided in the email. It was concluded that an ideal email response should be prompt, polite, personal, professional and promotional (for the agency). This should ultimately lead to an improved customer relationship and therefore an increase in business both in the short and long term.

Source: Adapted from Murphy and Tan (2003)

Discussion questions

4 Should travel agents give greater effort and time to email enquiries that are seeking higher-value travel products (such as business class flights or luxury holidays)? Is it easy to achieve such a focus when using email as a communication medium?

5 To what level should responses be standardised to ensure a consistent corporate message and corporate image?

■ Competing with online agencies and competition from direct-sell and other online providers

Vasudavan and Standing (1999) suggested that there has been a rapid growth in virtual travel agents (those that operate online). These online agencies use the same Computer Reservations Systems (CRSs) as high street agents but couple it with a range of additional information such as destination information, city maps, weather reports and currency rates. These online agents are normally available to the customer 24 hours a day. This has meant that the high street travel agencies are now facing stiff competition from those offering travel products and reservation facilities online. Perhaps the main advantage for the online companies is that the use of technology to allow customers to make the bookings directly via websites means that the overheads for the company are generally lower, as the need for fewer customer-facing staff brings immediate cost savings. Forrester Research estimates that in 2002 more than $22 billon was spent on online travel (not including the growing corporate management travel business), with the figure likely to grow to $50 billion by 2007 (Mintel, 2003).

The online provision can vary in its format (Buhalis and Licata, 2002). First, there are the online-only providers, such as **www.ebookers.com** and **www.travelocity.com** , who have created systems that allow real-time searches, driven by Global Distribution Systems (GDSs) such as Worldspan, Sabre, Amadeus and Galileo, offering a wide range of travel products and allow customers to confirm bookings instantly, making payment via credit or debit cards. Second, there are companies which are traditionally an offline provider (with many bricks-and-mortar outlets) who have chosen to create an online web facility to enhance their distribution opportunities (for example, **www.thomas-cook.com**). These mass travel agencies have often developed internet sites both in order to try to compete with the online agencies as well as encouraging their existing clients to consider this option which, providing the online technology is developed and managed efficiently, can bring cost savings.

Competing with these two types of online agencies are the internet portals (such as **www.yahoo.com**) and media companies (such as **www.telegraph.co.uk**) which offer travel information and travel products on their site, with the search and booking facilities being driven through an external travel provider (in the case of The Telegraph this is driven by a company called the Online Travel Company (OTC)). The design of these sites ensures that the customer sees the main company website (headers, logos, page links, etc.) but the content element central to the page is externally provided and inserted.

A further competitor has come from the principals who have joined forces to create multi-supplier travel portals (as seen with Opodo in Europe, Orbitz in the USA and Zuji in Asia), which allow customers to search across several providers simultaneously. Alamdari (2002) noted that many airlines are involved in such initiatives and suggests that the advantage for the airline is that, as well as benefiting from reduced fee-levels for the GDS system, they are also achieving sales online rather than through travel agents (thus avoiding having to pay commission). The use of online travel agencies has grown significantly in many key markets, such as North America and Western Europe, where correspondingly access and familiarity with the internet have ensured an extensive number of potential customers who are familiar and confident in using such technology. However, it has been recognised (Westbrooke, 2000; TTI, 1999) that while for package holidays and simple routes (return to one destination) the technology is very well developed for the customer, when the itinerary is more complex (such as round-the-world flights, multi-centre or tailor-made holidays) the booking is often referred to an agent directly, who can consider the range of special fares and deals to ensure that clients gets the most suitable product for their needs.

Interestingly, Mandelbaum (2004) has commented that despite dire predictions more than a decade ago that the internet would lead to the demise of the traditional travel agent, the reality has seen the demand for travel agents continue. He suggests that for customers a good travel agent can offer the following benefits:

- They now focus more on working for the customer's benefit, making sure that travel plans meet the client's requirements. When problems and difficulties occur the travel agent can assist in finding solutions.
- They can find low fares fast, and are often aware of latest deals and promotional offers. This can be much faster than internet searches.
- The knowledge and experience of the agent can usually ensure products that are suggested have a proven track record.

It appears that customers place great trust in travel agents. Dumazel and Humphreys (1999) reported that only 32% of customers would shop around after receiving advice from travel agents. This can mean that the travel agent has significant power in directing the customer towards or away from particular products or destinations.

Case 20.4   Booking business travel online   FT

Which is the better way to book business travel – through surfing the world wide web or calling a travel agent? For every story of a traveller who finds an online bargain, there is compelling evidence that travel agents are a much cheaper option.

One confirmed enthusiast for do-it-yourself reservations is Karen Bellis, programme manager for Shell LiveWire, an international scheme run by the oil company Shell to help young people start a business. She always checks the fares she is offered by her organisation's travel agency and in several cases has found better deals online. On one recent trip from London to Hong Kong via Brunei and Kuala Lumpur, Ms Bellis says she beat the agency price by £4000.

John Guarneri, Illinois-based travel manager for BP, is not convinced by this approach. BP uses Carlson Wagonlit Travel, the same agency as Shell, and he believes it makes much more sense to book through an agent. 'We have looked at studies and found that employees can beat the system between 3% and 6% of the time but the amount of time they spend on finding these deals is not worth it,' he says. 'Spending five hours beating the fares is not what they are paid to do.'

Mr Guarneri is sceptical about discounted web fares. 'A lot of web stuff is distressed inventory that cannot be used at the times the traveller wants to travel or involves awkward connections,' he says. 'Our negotiated corporate deals offer travellers a good price and flexibility.'

Mr Guarneri is also unhappy about employees not booking through a recognised travel agency. In the aftermath of the terrorist attacks on the US, travel managers had great difficulty tracking and helping travellers who had made independent arrangements.

Ms Bellis says she books a flight online only if the schedule is convenient and she never spends more than five minutes trying to beat the travel agency fare. She also uses the agency for journeys that are potentially difficult. This month, Ms Bellis visited Pakistan and went through the official channels to ensure that Shell LiveWire could trace her itinerary easily.

In spite of Ms Bellis's undoubted successes on the web, detailed quantitative research always concludes the agency option is cheaper. Topaz International, an air fare auditing company based in Portland, Oregon, took the fares quoted by travel agents and compared them with fares for the same flights on airline websites and

▶

from online retailers such as Expedia, Travelocity and Orbitz. The agent offered a better fare than any website in 93% of cases. On average, the fare was $170 (£116) cheaper. 'The web will come back with a great price, but for an 8pm flight involving several stops,' says Valerie Estep, president of Topaz. 'Overall it is better to stay with the fares offered by your agency.'

Travel agents make their bookings through the huge global distribution systems (GDSs) that still handle the overwhelming majority of scheduled flight bookings. The fares they can access are a mixture of published prices and specially negotiated fares loaded on to the GDS system by the airlines. These private fares are negotiated by the agency or by the corporate client, or by both.

For big companies pondering whether hotels should be booked online, there is the same argument as with air travel concerning the relative merits of spot and negotiated rates. 'There are a couple of nights a year when you will get a cheaper deal at the promotional rate but the corporate rate will win the other 350 days of the year,' says Damian Hinds, head of e-commerce for Six Continents. Brent Hoberman, chief executive of Lastminute.com, disagrees: 'The corporate discount may be 30% but we frequently offer reductions of 60–70%,' he says, although he admits most corporate travellers using Lastminute are from smaller businesses.

Source: Amon Cohen (2002a), Inside track: Toeing the line versus do-it-yourself, *Financial Times*, 28 May 2002

Discussion question

6 Is there a significant difference in the booking behaviour of business travellers to leisure travellers? Appreciating these differences, what could a travel agency do to capture a greater share of each of these markets?

Customer care

The skills required by the travel agent are diverse. It has already been acknowledged that extensive product knowledge (and the knowledge to find information about product offerings throughout the globe) is vital and that the agent must deal with a diverse range of administration duties, but the skills go much further. The agent is expected (and in many countries legally required) to provide information such as visa and passport requirements, health and travel safety advice and information about the terms and conditions of the booking.

The travel agent may also have to deal with distressed or irate travellers who may have had alterations to their travel plans made by the supplier prior to departure (changes to flight times are perhaps most common) or who may have experienced problems and disappointments during travel and wishes to complain. In such cases, it is the skilled travel agent who must both calm the customer as well as advise of their rights to seek a response from the supplier.

For many mass travel agent businesses there are standard procedures in place, which seek to ensure that all staff provide consistently high customer care. This can cover factors such as:

■ acknowledging a customer as they enter the outlet, even if all the agents are busy, so that the customer is confident that the agent will deal with their needs as soon as possible;

- ensuring that staff appear smiling and happy to deal with customers at all times;
- ensuring that the phone will be answered promptly and that when staff are unable to deal with the enquiry immediately then the client will be called back as soon as possible;
- ensuring that before the customers leave the outlet they are provided with the name of the consultant so that, should they wish to make further enquiries or to book the travel, they have a convenient point of contact.

Staff training

For many mass travel agency businesses the vast majority of the training received by an individual agent occurs while in the travel outlet. Once agents have received perhaps a couple of weeks of class-based skills training they are then allocated to a shop, where the manager and the existing staff help to guide the agent through the process of finding information and making bookings. Ongoing training may take the form of travel manuals, which agents read and then about which they complete questions and tests, to ensure that they have appreciated and understood everything. In some cases short courses, which update technology, customer care or sales skills, are operated and agency staff will attend these in turn to ensure that all agents in a store have full knowledge of procedures and systems.

In the UK modern apprenticeships now allow trainees to enter the profession through working in retail outlets whilst completing a portfolio which develops their knowledge and skills. Thomas Cook apprentices are given a week of training in product knowledge and sales skills as part of their company induction. They move then to the retail outlet, where they are allocated a member of staff as mentor as well as further support from a representative of the Travel Training Company, who support the modern apprenticeship NVQ qualification.

Staff motivation

Motivation can be a very personal thing and therefore it is not always possible to motivate two people using the same techniques. However, within a travel agency perhaps the most common motivation to make sales is that the individual agent receives commission, a percentage of the value of the sale, as a bonus.

However, as money is not the only motivator the reward of travel may also be used. Hitting a sales target or achieving the highest sales of a particular product may mean the chance to 'win' a holiday, i.e. to take a trip to a given destination.

The use of familiarisation trips

Many travel providers will offer travel agency staff travel products at reduced or no cost. These familiarisation trips (often called 'Fams' or 'Fam Trips' by the industry) are offered by tour operators and principals as part of the skills and knowledge development of sales staff. It is felt that by visiting a destination and experiencing all elements of the travel product, the agent should then be better placed to sell that product to the customer. However, it actually goes further than just product knowledge as the providers suspect that by providing such travel to the agent the perception of their company is enhanced, thus encouraging the agent to sell a particular company's product ahead of their competitors, thus gaining competitive advantage. In some cases the fam trips are offered as 'bonuses', where an increase in level of sales of a particular company's product will result in the travel being provided to the agent (or to the agency). This means that whilst the travel is a cost to the supplier this can be offset against the increase in sales. For example, *Travel Weekly* (2003) reported that travel agents could win a Cox and King's fam trip by signing up to receive a tour operator's training manual. For the tour operator this ensured that several agents would increase awareness of the operator's products while only a very small number would receive the benefit of a fam trip, thus ensuring wider product exposure among agents at minimal cost to Cox and King.

It is clear that there are advantages to the principals but there are also advantages to the travel agency. The agency can use the incentive of fam trips:

- to encourage staff to make greater levels of sales (and correspondingly greater levels of commission for the agency);
- as a motivator to encourage hard work from employees;
- as a means of useful staff development, enhancing the skills of the staff member, at very low cost to the agency.

For most mass travel agency businesses fam trips are regulated by the area manager, who ensures that all staff undertake trips that will benefit their skills development, that all staff receive a fair opportunity to participate in suitable trips, as well as ensuring that staffing levels in outlets can be maintained while agents are away.

Case 20.5 The abuse of familiarisation trips

There is a growing concern over the abuse of fam trips. In some cases the travel agents are using these not as educational experiences, designed to enhance their knowledge, but only as a 'free holiday', where the hospitality of the provider is not considered. While many hotels and travel providers will offer a reduced price or free travel to travel agents in order that these agents will then be better placed to sell their products to customers, it is often the case that the agent, having experienced the product, does not make any greater effort to offer that product (especially if it is not part of the parent company), or may not pass on the knowledge or experience to customers in a positive manner.

Travel press such as the American journals *Travel Agent* and *TravelAge West* each week publish details of fam trips being offered, in order that agents may select trips they desire to participate in. In most cases a companion rate is also offered, allowing agents to take a spouse or friend to accompany them on the visit. This is further suggesting that the agent views such travel more as a reduced rate holiday rather than personal development of product knowledge.

Discussion questions

7 Can a fam trip provider really expect a travel agent to be biased in their favour, purely by offering free or reduced priced travel? What are the implications if the operation of the fam trip goes poorly or it does not meet the desires of the travelling agent?

8 Does the benefit of offering reduced priced or free travel to agents actually ensure greater levels of sales in the long term for a particular company?

9 How might a tour operator reduce the risk of a fam trip just becoming a free holiday?

The use of mystery shoppers and the evaluation of service

The use of mystery shoppers to monitor the level of service provided by the staff has become common across many service-sector industries. Wilson (1998) suggested that mystery shopping, a form of participant observation, uses researchers to act as customers or potential customers to monitor the quality of processes and procedures used in the delivery of a service. The mystery shopper acts as a customer might, asking questions and making purchases. However the mystery shopper actually assesses the staff on their responses, measuring them against company procedures. The mystery shopper later reports findings to the management in order for them to evaluate whether service quality is being maintained. In most cases, mass travel agency businesses use mystery shoppers, either employed directly by the company or via specialist agencies. Research has suggested (Wilson, 1998) that the results of mystery shopping exercises are used to:

- diagnose weak points in an organisation's delivery process;
- encourage and motivate service personnel by linking assessment with appraisals, training and rewards;
- allow benchmarking of the organisation's service delivery processes in comparison with its competitors.

Interestingly, the mystery shopper process is also used by competitors or other organisations in order to evaluate the activities of travel agents. In the UK the trade journals *Travel Weekly* and *Travel Trade Gazette* undertake regular mystery shopper exercises in order to assess the activities of travel agents. The *Travel Trade Gazette* (TTG) allocates marks for:

- the appearance of agency staff;
- staff sales technique and personality;
- whether availability was checked;
- product and destination knowledge;
- whether the product offered was price-competitive and if any special offers were suggested;
- explanation and detail of the product offered;
- extras offered (such as car hire or currency);
- whether the product offered actually met the requirements of the mystery shopper.

The results of the mystery shopper exercise are published for each selected location, along with tips to help improve sales techniques. TTG regularly examines both mass travel agents and independent agencies and average scores are compared. While many agents try to offer superb customer service to achieve competitive advantage, when considering the rating across all agencies there appears to be very little to differentiate the mass travel agent operations (Table 20.5). Furthermore independent agents also achieve similar results.

Table 20.5 *Travel Trade Gazette* mystery shopper scores

Agents examined	Average score
Lunn Poly (Part of Tui)	57%
Thomas Cook	56%
First Choice	52%
All independent agencies	51%
Going Places (part of MyTravel)	41%

Source: Developed from Travel Trade Gazette, November 2003–April 2004

Case 20.6   Mystery shopping

In 1999 Thomas Cook decided to check on its staff and hired a company specifically to monitor the counter staff in travel agencies. The company sent mystery shoppers into the high street outlets to test out the behaviour of the staff. This was recorded, using hi-tech equipment such as video cameras hidden in clothing.

The training department of Thomas Cook suggested that the purpose of such an activity was not to gain information about the behaviour or skills of a specific individual but to allow the managers the opportunity to appreciate the activities of the staff and to discuss and explore ways in which customer care could be improved. However, it was not so well received by staff, who felt that such monitoring by Thomas Cook suggests that they do not trust their staff to deal with customers appropriately. With each shop being tested four times a year, it is a significant commitment by Thomas Cook to assess the activities of many staff.

Thomas Cook still undertake mystery shopping exercises. In 2004 they have chosen this technique to monitor their retail outlets (not their call centres) to ensure that the standards of service set for each shop are maintained and that the service by their staff adheres to company expectations. This is still outsourced to an external company, which completes this by assessing the retail outlet against key criteria such as brochure displays, the use of sales pads to fully identify the requirements and needs of customers and responses to the customer enquiries.

Thomas Cook are not alone in undertaking such studies of their front-line staff. Lunn Poly and First Choice travel agents are also tested by mystery shoppers, with the feedback going directly to the manager of the shop. The use of mystery shoppers to audit the behaviour and practices of staff has become commonplace. It has now extended to monitoring agents via telephone conversations to ensure that procedures and standards of service are maintained.

Source: Travel Weekly, 12 July 1999 and additional author's research

Discussion question

10   Is it fair to judge the service skills of staff based on such an interaction and are there some limitations to using the mystery shopper approach? How much can we learn about the behaviour of agents in a shop through one visit? Do you think that this approach is helpful for developing staff skills and motivations?

The changing competitive environment

The twenty-first century has certainly seen significant changes in the environment in which travel agencies operate. The global events of 2001 and their consequences for travel have meant that the level of competition for customers between all travel agencies, as well as different elements of the travel chain of distribution, is high and service quality has become ever more important in the need to both gain and retain the customer for repeat business.

Reactions to changes in consumer demand

There have been many reports that the growth of the internet for booking travel will lead to the death of the travel agent. However, this gloomy picture has yet to come to fruition. William Maloney, executive director of the American Society of Travel Agents, suggested that many travellers still prefer the personal service and added peace of mind that comes with making their travel reservation through a travel agent rather than making an online booking (Newman, 2004). There has also been a noticeable change in customers, who are often approaching the agent far better informed about the products that they are looking for and the range of options open to them. In some cases the customers may find the extensive range of information leads to 'overload' and as a consequence the travel agent is approached to act as an unbiased third party to help sift through it all (Gilden, 2004). As a consequence for these clients, the travel agent takes on a slightly different role, needing to swiftly evaluate the client's needs and then to provide an efficient booking service that instils confidence in the mind of the customer.

Consumers are becoming more knowledgeable about travel products and familiar with technology such as the internet, which can provide simple and convenient booking methods (encouraging more travellers to make their own arrangements independently). At the same time other media, such as CD brochures (which are produced by the mass tour operators and can hold perhaps a dozen different brochures at far lower cost than paper versions) and destination videos, have developed to provide greater access to product information. Therefore, it has become ever more important that the travel agent offers a significant advantage to the customer (to encourage the customer to use the agent rather than booking direct). As a consequence there has been a noticeable change in the ways in which travel agents operate. Many now offer late-night opening hours as well as offering booking slots (letting customers prearrange a time at their convenience to meet with the travel consultant). The redesign of the shops to meet the expectations of the clients is also underway, with the consultant moving around the desk to sit alongside the customer so that the customer can easily view the computer screens displaying the travel options.

Interestingly, in the UK it has also been noted that the main location of travel agent outlets, especially the larger operations, has been moving from high street shops to become large hypermarket operations in out-of-town sites. This has perhaps tied in with the growth in development of large retail parks that has been witnessed over the past decade in the UK. It may be the case that such locations for travel agents become common in other countries, where large-scale shopping malls are widespread and where the agent can provide for a large number of clients, who find the location convenient to reach and to park near where they can undertake many leisure activities as well as purchasing their holiday.

In the past, a culture of waiting to book until the last minute in order to get the best deals existed. The down-side for the customer was that they would have to be flexible on the holiday product. However in recent years there has been a shift in behaviour, driven by changes in approach of the large tour operators, who offered significant discounts on early bookings, free child places, and low deposit offers.

Reacting to changes in the business environment

Perhaps one of the most noteworthy changes for travel agents has been the significant reduction in commission earned from selling flights. Since 1995, major airlines, starting with those in the USA (American, Continental, Delta, Northwest, Trans World, United and US Air) jointly agreed to place a cap on commissions, to ensure that the high-volume low-price tickets cost the airlines little in commission, while commission on the high-price tickets were restricted by the cap, and thus limited the costs to the airline. In 1999 most US airlines also reduced the percentage of commission paid (from 8% to 5%), and European carriers followed suit, with commissions as low as 4%. In 2002 Scandinavian Airlines announced that it was to scrap commission payments to agents in Sweden, Norway and Denmark (though at that time not to agents in other countries) (Bray, 2002) while Finnair announced that it was to move to zero commission in September 2003 (Finnairgroup, 2003). Moving forward this approach has been taken by smaller airlines as well as the large carriers, and British Airways now pays a fixed commission rate per seat rather than offering a percentage of the ticket price (though business class seats earn a higher fee than economy seats). This has led to a serious reduction in income for travel agents and as a result many travel agents are now seeking to increase revenue both by focusing on areas where higher commission levels are offered (such as for accommodation and car hire) and by charging fees for the services they provide. In the USA Levere (2000) estimated that at least three-quarters of agencies charged service fees while Beattie (2004) comments that almost all New Zealand travel agencies charge fees (although interestingly most Australian leisure travel companies do not).

It is worth mentioning that in Asia the airlines have not acted so strongly in their attitudes to commission reduction. In a region where travel agents are far more predominantly used, with estimates that more than 80% of airline tickets are sold via travel agencies (Alamdari, 2002), and where access to the internet is low (perhaps with the exception of a few areas such as Japan, Hong Kong and Singapore), the airlines have generally kept commission to travel agents at levels between 7% and 9%. As a consequence the significance of the travel agent as a channel of distribution remains high in the region. However, Marketshare (an Asian-based travel research consultancy) forecast that the online travel market would be worth $12.5 billion for the Asia Pacific region in 2004 and predicted it to reach $16 billion by 2006 (AFX news, 2004). The growth is largely attributed to be due to the availability of sites in a wider variety of local languages and with consumers turning to online sources for access to regional low-cost airlines.

Furthermore, in the past travel agents were paid incentives by the owners of GDS systems to encourage the agents to use particular systems to make their bookings. However, the GDS owners have suggested that this can equate to an average 10% of their revenue and as a consequence it is likely that such payments to travel agents will be reduced (Cohen, 2002b).

Travel agents are also experiencing pressure on their accommodation sales. Where in the past hotels have provided preferential rates to travel agents, this is increasingly being undermined by the 'dumping' of cut-price accommodation on last minute internet sites. Hatton (2004: 104) recounts the case of 'a European hotel which sold a room via a dot.com site at €100 less than that the industry rate'. Not only does this mean that travel agents may lose such business but it can create ill feeling among the clients who do choose to use agents, if they feel their agent has not obtained the best deal for them.

Case 20.7   The competitive environment   **FT**

More and more airlines are reducing or eliminating the agent's commission, while the incentive payments agents receive for bookings from the global computer reservations systems are under threat. Add competition from the internet, plus a new tendency for customers to book direct with tour operators, and change looks likely even for agents who rely on package holidays for most of their income.

Travel retailers are being forced to change from their role as agents of suppliers to agents of their customers. Some, especially those managing travel for corporate clients, have already adjusted by charging their customers for services such as analysing staff travel patterns. But such is the pace of change that most agents, whether handling business or leisure travel, will have to charge customers for some bookings.

Lufthansa announced that commission for German agents would cease from September 2004, having already reduced it for agents in some other countries. In Germany the airline will market net fares to which it will add 30 euros to domestic and short-haul tickets and 45 euros to long-haul flights, representing the cost of handling bookings made direct with the airline.

Agents will be under pressure to retain the loyalty of corporate clients by ensuring they get the best negotiated or spot fares. Gerd Rieke, spokesman for Germany's Association of Business Travel Management, says some small independent travel agents will have a hard time. 'I would not be surprised if the big chains grew and many of those smaller agents were drawn under the umbrella of franchise organisations.'

First, the airlines lured customers from agents with cheaper fares available only via the airlines' websites. Now some have reached agreements with GDS operators so that agents can book the cheaper fares via their GDS screens but receive lower fees. British Airways has such a deal with Sabre and Galileo.

But the news for agents is not all bad. Ian Reynolds, Association of British Travel Agents' CEO, notes: 'There are still excellent opportunities for agents who can genuinely add value to customers' travel plans and provide a service that a customer can see is worth paying for.'

Source: Roger Bray, Agents suffer a squeeze from airlines, *Financial Times*, 21 January 2004

Discussion question

11   How might a successful travel agency replace earnings lost by the reduction in airline commissions?

The role of stakeholders and their effect on travel agency businesses

The actions and behaviour of travel agents are tempered by the public pressure exerted on the business by many stakeholders. These groups have a vested interest in ensuring that the business operates in a fair and appropriate manner for the good of the consumer, the industry and the environment in the long term.

For many travel agencies, stakeholders can include their trade associations, who seek to ensure that their members behave appropriately, are financially secure and operate their business within legal requirements. This is perceived as vital to ensuring that the customer has trust and confidence in the travel agent, thus enhancing competitive advantage.

Stakeholders can also include destination management organisations. It is noticeable that many destination promoters now work directly with travel agencies to promote their destination, offering travel agents fam trips and social events, as a means of educating the travel agent about that destination and its product offering (the attractions, culture, facilities, etc.).

Perhaps the main stakeholders, however, are the customers themselves and travel agents must now adapt their business operations to meet the changing demands of the travelling public.

Customers and their expectations

The expectations of the customer have changed significantly over the years. Customers have generally travelled more extensively, growing more confident about arranging travel independently. It has also become easier to reserve travel products directly and to access extensive information about travel destinations and product options, which has led to the customer now requiring the travel agent to provide value, beyond that which the customer can achieve alone. Therefore, for customers to use a travel agent they need to perceive that the travel agent will either achieve a better deal, can provide a more efficient service, can offer greater knowledge about the product (beyond that easily accessible in the mainstream media) or can access products not otherwise available to the customer directly. The suggestion is often made that it is the older generations that rely on travel agents as they are less comfortable with alternative means of accessing information. However, Hyde (2003) refutes this and suggests that it has more to do with the level of training and knowledge of the travel agent staff, travel agents only being as good as the advice they offer.

The links between travel agents, tour operators and principals

While many of the travel agencies throughout the world today are independent it is noticeable in some countries, including many in Europe, that the travel agency often has links through ownership with tour operators and also with the principals. This integration between different levels of the chain of distribution can bring both benefits and concerns.

The integration of travel agency and tour operator businesses

Many of the mass travel agency businesses are actually part of a much larger travel organisation. Integration (the joining together of several different elements of the business stream) can bring extensive financial benefits:

- Rather than having to pay commission to an outside agency the profit remains within the organisation.
- Economies of scale in operation (such as bulk purchasing) may be possible.
- Cross-selling of products (such as using the company-owned airline to take the client to the accommodation booked) can increase sales.

Integration can occur both horizontally and vertically. Horizontal integration is the joining of companies at the same point in the chain of distribution (such as two travel agencies) while vertical integration is the ownership of companies earlier or later in the chain of distribution.

The implications of integration for travel agents

For travel agents that are part of a mass travel enterprise there are some implications for their operations. ECTAA (2002) stated their concern that the rapidly changing business environment, with growing trends towards vertical integration and with the increase in technological developments leading to greater opportunities for direct-sell, meant that the travel agent's role was becoming more blurred. As tour operators and principals rely less and less on the travel agent to sell their product (and as commissions on sales to travel agents are reduced) the successful travel agency now needs to look to a variety of ways to ensure that income is earned. For mass travel agents who are part of a vertically integrated group some protection is provided by the favourable terms received on selling products of their parent company. However, pressure is often put on the travel agent to sell their parent company products ahead of other providers (known as directional selling or cross-selling).

Case 20.8	Horizontal and vertical integration – world of TUI

In 1972 Thomson purchased the travel agent Lunn Poly as a retail outlet for their burgeoning range of tour operators. However, the consolidation of travel companies has continued and in 2000 Preussag purchased Thomson holidays and has since rebranded under the TUI banner.

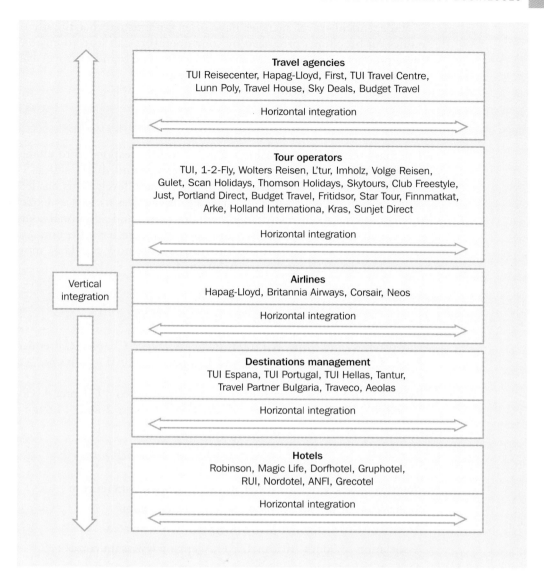

12 As more and more travel products are provided by a few mega-operators, should there be some government control of the industry? What are the implications of integration for the customer in the long term?
Will independent travel agents manage to survive in this market dominated by a few global players?

Whose holiday do you sell?

As many of the travel agents are affiliated through ownership to tour operators it is often
the case that the agent is expected to ensure that when a customer is purchasing a holiday
then they are at least given the chance to consider the owners' products. In many cases this
directional selling can be quite forceful. It can be further enhanced by the availability and
location of brochures. In some high street agencies it is only the owners' brochures that
are on display or that are located most prominently within the shop, further encouraging
customers to be more likely to select from these. Such practices were referred to the UK
Monopolies and Mergers Commission (MMC) for their anti-competitive practices and the
MMC (1998), while recognising that the lack of transparency of ownership did enhance
the opportunity for directional selling, concluded that such selling was not necessarily
leading to poor value for the customer and therefore did not seek to control such activity.

Independent travel agencies have often commented that the use of logos and brand names on brochures produced by tour operators can lead to customers believing that these products should be purchased from the same brand of travel agent, thus leading to further advantage for the integrated businesses.

Conclusion

The mass travel agency business has necessarily responded to changes in the environment driven by competition from the internet and direct sell as well as changes to earnings levels caused by reduction in commission levels. This has led to a range of differing responses, which include charging service fees as well as expanding the range of services offered to clients (drawing on alternative and additional sources of income). As a consequence, service quality and customer care have become a hugely significant factor in achieving success and the mass agents now regularly monitor their staff to ensure high levels of service are maintained.

Guided reading

Davidson, R. and Cope, B. (2003) *Business Travel*, Chapter 2. Prentice Hall, Harlow.
Page, S., Brunt, P., Busby, G. and Connell, J. (2001) *Tourism; a modern synthesis*, Chapter 6. Thomson, London.
Ryan, C. (ed.) (2002) *The Tourist Experience*, 2nd edn, Chapter 4. Continuum, London.
Youell, R. (1998) *Tourism: an introduction*, Chapters 2 and 4. Longman, Harlow.

Recommended websites

American Society of Travel Agents (ASTA): **www.astanet.com** .
Association of British Travel Agents: **www.abta.com/** .
Association of Canadian Travel Agencies: **www.acta.ca** .
Association of South African Travel Agents: **www.asata.co.za/** .
Australian Federation of Travel Agents: **www.afta.com.au/** .
European Travel Agents and Tour Operators Association: **www.ectaa.org** .
Guild of European Business Travel Agents: **www.gebta.org** .
Travel Agents Association of New Zealand: **www.taanz.org.nz/** .
United Federation of Travel Agents' Associations: **www.uftaa.org/** .

Key words

Chain of distribution; familiarisation trips; mystery shoppers; online agents; travel agent.

Bibliography

AFX News (2004) Asia Pacific e-commerce seen doubling to $16 billion by 2006, Agence France-Presse, 21 April 2004.

Alamdari, F. (2002) Regional development in airlines and travel agents relationship, *Journal of Air Transport Management*, Vol. 8, 339–348, Elsevier, UK.

Beattie, D. (2004) Aussies technology use lags, *National Business Review*, New Zealand, 30 April 2004.

Bray, R. (2002) SAS to cut fares and commissions, *Financial Times*, London, 18 June 2002.

Bray, R. (2004) Agents suffer a squeeze from airlines, *Financial Times*, London, 21 January 2004.

Buhalis, D. and Licata, M.C. (2002) The future of eTourism intermediaries, *Tourism Management*, UK, Volume 23, Issue 3, 207–220, June 2002.

Chen, J.S. and Gursoy, D. (2000) Cross cultural comparison of the information sources used by first-time and repeat travellers and its marketing implications, *Hospitality Management*, Vol. 19, 191–203.

Cohen, A. (2002a) Inside track: Toeing the line versus do-it-yourself, *Financial Times*, London, 28 May 2002.

Cohen, A. (2002b) BA's dogflight with the middlemen, FT.com, London, 2 July 2002.

Commission of the European Communities (1999) Merger Procedure Article decision, Case N. IV/M.1502. Office for Official Publications of the European Communities, Luxembourg.

Crocker, M. (2001) Consumer Travel Survey, *Travel Weekly*, USA, 24 September 2001.

Davidson, R. and Cope, B. (2003) *Business Travel*. Prentice Hall, Harlow.

Dumazel, R. and Humphreys, I. (1999) Travel agent monitoring and management, *Journal of Air Transport Management*, Vol. 5, 63–72.

ECTAA (2002) How does the European Union Impact the travel agents and tour operators, and how should it not, referring to the concrete subject of VAT, European Tourism Forum, Group of National Travel Agents and Tour Operators Associations with the EU, Bruxelles.

Finnairgroup (2003) Finnair to stop paying sales commissions to travel agencies, **www.finnairgroup. com/investor** , 28 February 2003.

Gilbert, D. (1999) European tourism product purchase, methods and system, *The Service Industry Journal*, 10(4), 665–679.

Gilden, J. (2004) As the traveler's world changes; the agent's role does too, *Los Angeles Times*, Los Angeles, 7 March 2004.

Hatton, M. (2004) Redefining the relationships – The future of travel agencies and the global agency contract in a changing distribution system, *Journal of Vacation Marketing*, Vol. 10(2), 101–108.

Holloway, J.C. (1994) *The business of tourism*. Pitman, London.

Hyde, J. (2003) If only they had an atlas, *The Observer*, London, 28 September 2003.

Levere, J. (2000) Changing Roles, *Airline Business*, USA, 48–76, October 2000.

Mandelbaum, R. (2004) Travel Agents – it still spays to hire one, even in the internet age, *Money*, Vol. 33, Issue 4, 68, April 2004.

Mintel (2002) *Travel Agents – UK*, June. Mintel, UK.

Mintel (2003) Online Intermediaries – revolutionizing travel distribution, *Travel and Tourism Analyst*, February 2003.

MMC (1998) *Foreign Package Holidays*, HMSO, London, in S. Hudson, T. Snaith, G.A. Miller, and P. Hudson, (2001) Distribution Channels in the Travel Industry: Using mystery shoppers to understand the influence of Travel agency recommendations, *Journal of Travel Research*, Vol. 40, 148–154.

Murphy, J. and Tan, I. (2003) Journey to nowhere? Email customer service by travel agents in Singapore, *Tourism Management*, 24, 543–550.

Newman, R. (2004) New Jersey travel agency continues to thrive despite online competition, *Tribune Business News*, USA, 22 February 2004.

Poon, A. (1993) *Tourism, technology and competitive strategies*. Wallingford, CAB International.

Shelley, T. (2004) Thomas Cook rules out disposals, *Financial Times*, London, 10 March 2004.

Strauss, J. and Hill, D.J. (2001) Consumer complaints by emails: an exploratory investigation of corporate responses and customer reactions, *Journal of Interactive Marketing*, 15(1), 63–73.

Travel Weekly (2003) Sign up for fam trip, *Travel*

Weekly, Issue 1698, Reed Publications, UK, 15 December 2003.

TTI (1999) The travel trade: Travel agents in Canada, *Travel and Tourism Intelligence*, No. 1, 71–86.

TTI (2001) Travel Distribution: The future of travel agents, *Travel and Tourism Intelligence*, No. 3, 57–80.

Vasudavan, T. and Standing, C. (1999) The impact of the internet on the role of travel consultants, *Participation and empowerment: an international journal*, MCB University Press, Vol. 7, No. 8, 213–226.

Westbrooke, J. (2000) Let the web do the walking, *Financial Times*, London, 13 May 2000.

Wilson, A. (1998) The role of mystery shopping in the measurement of service performance, *Managing Service Quality*, MCB University Press, Vol. 8, No. 6, 414–420.

Yee, A. (2004a) Travelocity makes German acquisition, *Financial Times*, London, 2 April 2004.

Yee, A. (2004b) Expedia extends European reach, *Financial Times*, London, 30 March 2004.

Chapter 21

Managing the transport subsector in tourism

George Goodall, Coventry Business School

Learning outcomes

On completion of this chapter the reader should be able to:

■ show an understanding of land, air and water transport systems and approaches to their integration;

■ understand the controls over the operation of scheduled and charter airlines;

■ explain the technological context of transport development;

■ understand the EU frameworks in which European transport operates;

■ identify the need and scope for policy intervention;

■ identify the key components of transport infrastructure.

Overview

This chapter focuses on the relationships between government, the tourist, and the operation of transport. It places transport by road, rail, air, and sea into an international, European and British regulatory context. This context will be used to explain who, how and why intervention is required to control transport providers and operators for the benefit of the business or leisure tourist. Transport is seen as a key component because without it international tourism in particular will not exist. What has to be recognised is that for a tourist to reach a destination often requires one or more different modes of transport to be used. These links may be made by tourists, by intermediaries, or by transport providers who seek to offer an integrated service.

Introduction

Transport is one of the key components underpinning human activity. Historically people walked to a destination, or used animals to carry goods to market. In its mechanical forms, transport enables people to travel long distances between, for example, home and workplace, while goods can be moved globally from point of manufacture to point of sale. The consequence of the introduction of mechanical transport has been to speed up journey times for people and goods when compared with non-mechanical forms. Speed may be an important determinant for both business and leisure tourists, along with cost and convenience. Statistical evidence indicates that visitor numbers are increasing substantially, as Table 21.1 illustrates. This growth in the number of tourists can put considerable pressure on transport systems to meet demand.

Table 21.1	Visitor numbers to European countries (millions)		
Country	1997	2001	% change
Greece	10.1	14.0	38.6
Cyprus	2.1	2.7	28.6
Spain	39.6	50.1	26.5
Portugal	10.2	12.2	19.6
Ireland	5.6	6.5	16.1
Germany	14.0	16.0	14.3
France	66.6	75.2	12.9
Italy	34.7	39.1	12.7
Malta	1.1	1.2	9.1
United Kingdom	25.5	22.8	−10.6

Source: World Tourism Organization (2003)

The provision of transport involves a number of different organisations acting individually or in combination. Three types of organisation can be identified.

- Government, at international, national and local levels, which develops the policy and rules for the operation of the different modes of transport. People form a government. They will bring to bear their experiences on the nature of the policy developed and the way in which it impacts on users and non-users alike.
- Infrastructure providers, who will implement government policy. These providers may be controlled by public- or private-sector bodies. In many cases the infrastructure will be constructed using predetermined techniques or practices that are based normally on government policy and rules. How a particular piece of infrastructure becomes operational may depend on how the project is managed.
- Transport providers, who use the infrastructure to carry business or leisure passengers. These providers will use mechanical devices that are controlled at both point of construction and in use by government-developed policies and rules.

In operating these three types of organisation, it has to be recognised that people are involved. It should be noted also that the people will, from time to time, move between the organisations, particularly when they become business or leisure travellers. The dividing lines between the types of organisation noted vary between country and country, due in large measure to the political make-up of the country.

Transport management in the United Kingdom

We have established that the start point for the effective and efficient management of transport is the development of policies by government. A transport policy can be developed from a political perspective or a technical perspective. Whichever political perspective is chosen, individuals and groups can lobby a government. In many cases government will be undecided and may seek independent advice, while in other cases government will want such advice to confirm its view. In the United Kingdom situation this often leads to the creation of a Committee of Inquiry (Rhodes, 1975).

A decision to make a new policy, or to amend an existing policy affecting all of the country, will be taken by central government. However, this decision may not be implemented without the approval of Parliament. Parliament will approve the policy ideas of central government in the form of an Act of Parliament. An Act of Parliament will allow subordinate legislation, in the form of Statutory Instruments, to be made by central government, but will require it to be approved by Parliament. All Acts of Parliament and Statutory Instruments will apply to individual citizens or corporate bodies. Central government can provide advice, often of a technical nature, to corporate bodies or individuals. This advice will not be approved by Parliament although it may be relevant when legal disputes occur.

One feature of government in the United Kingdom has been the creation of 'independent' government-funded organisations, or 'executive agencies', to oversee the implementation of policy. Transport has been a major area for these organisations, and two examples will illustrate this approach:

- The 1930 Road Traffic Act created Traffic Commissioners with the role of controlling the provision and safety of road bus transport. This role has changed over time, but the Traffic Commissioners still exist.
- The 1962 Transport Act created the British Waterways Board, with responsibility for maintaining canals. It remains extant, and is the only remaining nationalised transport undertaking in the United Kingdom.

Political decisions since 1980 have resulted in moving many of the costs of transport provision from the public sector to the private sector. While the public sector may continue to fund certain infrastructure provision, for example motorways, the construction of the work will be undertaken by the private sector. However, the money for motorway construction will be met from general taxation, so much so that non-motorway users will bear a proportion of the cost of construction and ongoing maintenance of the asset.

Once the infrastructure is in place, a tourist is likely to rely on the private sector to provide the vehicle to be used. The vehicle can be provided by either a company or an individual citizen, but it has to be manufactured. Its manufacture will have to comply with standards approved by Parliament. For example, if a coach is to be used to convey tourists, it will have to be fitted with a tachograph that monitors a driver's hours, and will have to meet noise emission levels specified by Statutory Instrument (Lowe, 2004).

Underpinning the efficient and effective management of transport is the combination of the activities of the public and private sectors for the ultimate benefit of the individual citizen. Whether travel is for business or leisure purposes, the facilities provided, in the form of infrastructure or vehicles, can be used for both purposes at the same time. It is possible for the provider of the vehicle to introduce differential charges, often based on the concept of 'level of service'. Travel by rail is a long-established mode that has charged different prices to individuals for the same trip.

Policy for transport is not normally unique to an individual country. Many organisations have been created that devise rules that are adopted subsequently by individual countries in their domestic legislation. The United Nations, through the International Civil Aviation Organization (ICAO), has developed standards for aircraft engine noise. These standards ultimately become adopted in the United Kingdom when a particular aircraft is issued with a Certificate of Airworthiness. The ICAO requirement will be adopted by many other countries, so that air travellers will know that a particular aircraft, irrespective of the company operating it, is safe. In Europe, the European Union (EU) has developed a range of policies that can be applied to transport. One example is the introduction of rules relating to the training of cabin crew on board aircraft that are certified as airworthy by member states. It should be noted that when new countries join the EU, existing regulations have to be applied by the new entrants, and often will require Parliaments' to introduce legislation for these purposes (C.E.C, 1969).

This section on transport management in the United Kingdom has shown that travel, whether for business or leisure purposes, is subject to many controls. While the controls have historically been aimed at safety, there is a growing body of evidence to show that environmental concerns, such as noise and air pollution, are entering into policy making. Their introduction is related to the concept of sustainable development, which for many transport providers is forming an important marketing element for attracting customers.

The following parts of this chapter will examine in more detail the ways in which the policy, infrastructure and providers engage in the management of travel. Examples will be drawn from the United Kingdom, Europe, and further afield. The information will be grouped under the four main modes of mechanical transport – road, rail, air and sea.

Managing transport by road

During the latter half of the twentieth century the provision of roads was based on the development of mathematical models and computer-generated forecasts. This work commenced in the USA in the 1940s and led to the concept of 'predict and provide': predict the traffic growth for, say, 30 years ahead and provide road space to meet demand. However, the American models omitted many types of movement (walking and cycling in particular), and did not consider environmental matters such as noise and air pollution (Banister, 2002: 134). These omissions were reflected in the approach adopted in many European countries with motorway construction continuing into the 1990s, as Table 21.2 indicates. Germany had special problems that resulted from re-unification, and the growth of the Green political party. The result was that many motorway schemes were abandoned in favour of upgrading existing roads and building by-passes around towns (Banister, 2002: 169–75). This approach has been adopted in the United Kingdom because of the growing concern of the social and environmental consequences of motorways (DETR, 1998).

In the European Union, a Common Transport Policy has been developed during the 1990s with a major theme of linking peripheral regions by means of Trans-European

Table 21.2	Motorway provision in European countries (kms)	
Country	**1990**	**2000**
Germany	10,809	11,712
Italy	6,193	9,766
France	6,824	9,766
Spain	4,693	9,049
United Kingdom	3,181	3,546
Netherlands	2,092	2,289
Belgium	1,666	1,702
Austria	1,470	1,633
Sweden	939	1,506
Portugal	316	1,482
Denmark	601	922
Greece	190	707
Finland	225	549
Luxembourg	78	115
Ireland	26	103

Source: Eurostat Yearbooks (2002, 2003)

Networks (CEC, 1992). This has involved improving road links in the United Kingdom to provide better access for vehicles from Ireland to travel to mainland Europe. Since 2000, however, it has become clear that the focus of European transport policy has moved towards the concept of sustainability. Policy has changed in the United Kingdom to reflect an increased emphasis on public transport (DETR, 1998). Similar changes have taken place in The Netherlands (Banister, 2002: 185–9) and France (Banister, 2002: 176–84). It remains clear that in the United Kingdom central government continues to dictate the scale and location of motorway provision, although new construction can be undertaken by the private sector, as the M6 Toll road demonstrates (DETR, 1998: 100).

If tourists are to travel by road, whether for business or leisure purposes, the provision of buses, coaches, cars and taxis will be required. Over the period 1950–1985 in the United Kingdom, central and local government owned many bus and coach vehicles, although private-sector vehicle ownership grew. The 1985 Transport Act led to the break-up and sale of the state-owned National Bus Company. The Stagecoach Group was one of the private-sector companies that grew by buying companies, and it had a 16% market share of passengers by 2002. The activities of the Stagecoach Group are considered in Case 21.1. Underlying the ownership changes since 1985 the Traffic Commissioners continue to regulate bus and coach operations. The regulation includes the need to hold a vehicle operator's license, to have drivers licensed, and to meet safety standards (White, 2002: 11–12; Hibbs, 2003: 106–10). In Ireland, however, the majority of bus and coach service operations continued to be provided by a state-owned company, Coras Iompair Eireann (CIE), although the private sector has been growing in importance through franchising of services (White, 2002: 5). Additional controls occur in the United Kingdom on vehicles themselves. These have been exercised through Statutory Instruments, which are being amended as a consequence of new European Directives. One example of these changes is that long-distance coaches are now permitted up to 15 metres in length (White, 2002: 41). A comprehensive discussion of these controls is provided by Lowe (2004).

Case 21.1   Stagecoach Group plc (1996–2003)

The Stagecoach Company, based in Perth, Scotland, provides public transport worldwide. In the United Kingdom it has benefited from a number of significant changes in central government policy since 1980. The period covered by this case study reflects the way in which a public transport company is able to change its transport focus when a financial opportunity occurs.

Bus operations in the United Kingdom formed the core business of the company in 1996. It had taken over companies formerly owned by central government and local authorities in the 1980s and early 1990s. In the same period it operated buses in Hong Kong, Kenya, Malawi and New Zealand. The company made purchases of bus operations in Sweden, Portugal and Australia in 1997. In subsequent years further bus operations were purchased in Hong Kong and the USA. However, the company sold its operations in Sweden, Portugal, Malawi, Kenya and Australia in the late 1990s. It took a policy decision to focus its bus activities in the United Kingdom, New Zealand and the USA. The company reported that a feature of its bus operations was the investment in new vehicles, many of which were obtained using hire-purchase agreements.

The central government decision to privatise the railways in the United Kingdom through the 1993 Railways Act resulted in Stagecoach deciding to re-enter the railway passenger market, having undertaken limited operations in 1992. In 1995 the company was awarded a passenger franchise for services from London to South West England, operating under the name South West Trains. Rolling stock was leased. Stagecoach extended its rail investment when, in 1996, it purchased the rolling-stock company Porterbrook, and with it an income flow from leasing rolling stock until 2012. Stagecoach, through Porterbrook, was able to obtain new orders for rolling stock from other train-operating companies, including National Express plc, that had moved into passenger-rail operations from a bus base. Rail operations were further expanded with the franchise for the Island Line (on the Isle of Wight), taking a 49% holding in the Virgin Rail Group, and operating the Sheffield Minitram system. The pattern of selling companies after a

▶

short period of ownership was continued. Porterbrook was sold to the Abbey National Bank in 2000. The company observed in 2002 that there should be 'vertical integration for the railways, which would be achieved by bringing the train and track under a single management structure (as this) would also align with the interests of passengers and shareholders alike'.

Stagecoach has over the period diversified into airport operations, shipping and highway infrastructure provision. It purchased Glasgow Prestwick Airport in 1998, but sold it in 2001. Shipping operations involved the purchase in 1998 of a New Zealand Company, Fullers Ferries. This activity continues and is managed as part of the New Zealand bus operations. Highway infrastructure provision commenced with an investment in a Hong Kong-based company that provides toll roads in China. This investment continued into 2003.

To accommodate these changes in areas of operation, Stagecoach has altered its management structure over the period since 1996. In that year the company had a number of subsidiary companies that were chaired by a main board director with a local managing director. Changes were introduced that resulted in the amalgamation of the UK bus area-management system into a single UK operation. Over the period 1996–2002 it introduced and abandoned management divisions dealing with Porterbrook and Aviation. In 2003 the company was divided into five management and financial-reporting divisions: UK Bus; Coach USA; Overseas Bus; Rail; and Investments.

Significant changes have taken place to the Stagecoach Board. In 1996 the board of directors comprised five executive directors, including the chairman, and three non-executive directors. In 2003 the board of directors comprised three executive directors and six non-executive directors, including the chairman.

While Stagecoach has developed its UK operations as a result of changes in national policies, particularly privatisation of bus and rail operations, the company noted in its 2003 Annual Report that its operations are 'best served by operators, government, local authorities and customers working together to improve our public-transport system'. Stagecoach has changed significantly over the period 1996–2003 from being a bus operator, to becoming a more integrated transport operator, with operations concentrated in bus, rail, and shipping passenger services. Its strategy is to continue 'as a leading international transport provider'.

Source: Stagecoach Group plc Annual Reports and Accounts, and author

Discussion Questions:

1 In what ways is the approach adopted by the Stagecoach Group, in buying and selling transport operations over short periods of time, appropriate to achieving integration of transport modes?

Coaches are used in a number of ways. Some airports use them to convey passengers from an aircraft to terminal buildings. At many destination airports in Europe coaches are used to convey leisure tourists to holiday accommodation where a packaged holiday is involved. The use of coaches for holidays is a limited market, although Leger Holidays, for example, offers coach tours from the United Kingdom to a number of destinations on mainland Europe (Leger Holidays, 2003).

Business tourists, and a growing number of leisure tourists, use hire cars and taxis for at least part of a journey. These vehicles are designed to specifications set by the United Kingdom government supplemented by growing EU regulation. Given that multinational companies such as Ford manufacture vehicles there is a growing model similarity, even if the vehicle names may differ. In many instances hire-vehicle services in particular are operated by international companies, with the use of franchise operations in some countries.

It is clear from the evidence that tourists will continue to use road transport as part of a trip. The roads will be designed to a specification determined by central governments, and provided in locations determined as part of central government policy. Vehicles operated on roads will be provided privately, but their design will be dictated by national governments. In some areas of vehicle design, such as noise, pollution control and safety, significant changes have been introduced by regulation.

Business travellers are more likely to use cars or taxis for part of their journey, particularly at destinations. The leisure traveller's choice of road transport will be determined by the type of holiday being taken. If the holiday includes flying, the coach will normally provide an important travel element at the destination, but if sea travel is involved, the travel is more likely to involve using the privately-owned car. What is also clear is that the traveller will be using a number of different transport types for travel outside the home country, but is likely to rely on using roads for part of the journey.

Managing transport by rail

Unlike transport by road, where a traveller can expect door-to-door transport, travel by rail is likely to be used for the 'line-haul' or main part of the journey, with other modes needed to link into the total journey. Rail transport differs between countries due in large measure to a combination of history and central government policy. This will now be explored.

In the United Kingdom, railways were provided originally by private companies whose operations were approved by Parliament. The private companies were nationalised in 1948 (under the provisions of the 1947 Transport Act), and operated by a state-owned body, the British Transport Commission (Bonavia, 1987). This ownership pattern is similar to that in a number of European countries where track and rolling stock are owned and operated by a single organisation (for example, SNCF in France and CIE in Ireland). In the United Kingdom today the railway system is no longer state-owned and operated, with all the assets being sold since 1994 (Banister 2002: 84–7)., Grouvish (2002) provides a comprehensive commentary on the changes to railways in Britain over the period 1974–1997. The privatisation and thus management of the rail network resulted in part from the contents of EC Directive 91/440/EEC, a directive on the development of the Community's railways (Grouvish, 2002: 262). The result was a threefold set of responsibilities – track and signalling, vehicle provision, and service operation – all undertaken by private-sector companies. The operation of passenger services involved the issue of contracts (franchises) to companies for a limited period of time (Grouvish, 2002: 517). Renewal of the franchises commenced in 2003. Examination of the companies that secured the passenger franchises reveals that in the majority of cases they were bus and coach operators (see Case 21.1).

To overcome the national funding complexity, the EU introduced directives that allowed payments by central governments for passenger services and connections to the network for freight movement (CEC, 1969). These provisions were introduced in the United Kingdom in the 1974 Railways Act. For passengers the 'public service obligation' funds are the most significant, and continue to be paid. Despite the availability of funding, the length of railway lines has been declining in Europe, as Table 21.3 shows, although some countries have added to their rail networks.

A growing trend is that some railway systems have been developed independently of the 'heavy rail' systems. Trams, or light rail systems, have been introduced in many urban areas of Europe over the period since 1980. Examples include Oslo, Stockholm, Hanover and Marseilles, and these replicate long-established urban systems in London, Paris and Berlin. Other railway developments have resulted in new links being provided between airports and city centres, including at London, Amsterdam, Newcastle-on-Tyne and Manchester. The provision of new track for high-speed travel has led to the TGV (*Trains de Grande Vitesse*) system in France, and the Channel Tunnel link between France and the United Kingdom. Some of the newer 'heavy rail' schemes are part of the Trans European Network system.

The use of railways for travel has declined substantially since 1950, due in large measure to competition from the private car. In the United Kingdom, use stabilised during the 1990s to some 6% of all travel (DETR, 1998). In France, however, the introduction of the TGV route between Lyon and Paris led to a substantial increase in travel by rail,

Table 21.3	Railway provision in European countries (kms)		
Country	1990	1999	% change
Luxembourg	271	274	1.1
Netherlands	2,780	2,808	1.0
Austria	5,624	5,643	0.3
United Kingdom	16,924	16,948	0.1
Italy	16,086	16,108	0.1
Sweden	10,801	10,799	0.0
Belgium	3,479	3,472	−0.2
Finland	5,867	5,836	−0.5
Denmark	2,344	2,324	−0.9
Ireland	1,944	1,919	−1.3
Spain	12,560	12,319	−1.9
Greece	2,484	2,299	−7.4
France	34,260	31,589	−7.8
Germany	40,981	37,536	−8.4
Portugal	3,126	2,813	−10.0
Total	**159,531**	**152,687**	**−4.3**

Source: Eurostat Yearbook (2002)

with business passenger diversion from air transport (Holliday *et al.*, 1991: 131, 162). The use of rail for leisure purposes is generally limited to day trips, or entertainment visits. There are a limited number of companies that offer rail holidays. Leger Holidays (2003) features 'escorted' rail holidays in Europe using TGV, but with coach and sea connections from the United Kingdom to Paris. In the United Kingdom motor-rail and sleeper services have been withdrawn, largely due to competition from air travel coupled with car hire from airports. Whether travel is for business or leisure purposes, the majority of passengers will be starting or finishing their journeys in large urban areas where more integrated transport systems exist, or are being provided.

Business travellers may use rail transport for both inter- and intra-urban journeys, although inter-urban travel may be limited to four hours in duration. The decision to use rail will be determined by intervening opportunities provided by other travel modes. For leisure travellers, time and cost may not be so critical, particularly if a journey is made at off-peak times. It is clear that there are very few packaged holidays using rail travel as the line-haul mode of transport.

Managing transport by air

Travellers undertake travel by air over longer distances in ever-increasing numbers. The provision of air transport has two different elements – airports and airlines – both of which are subject to central government policy control, including ownership. These two elements will now be considered.

In the United Kingdom airport provision has been the subject of a series of central government policy statements, the most recent being made in 2003 (DfT, 2003). The thrust of the 2003 policy has been to predict how many travellers there will be in 2030, and hence to determine how much runway capacity will be needed and where it should be located. This approach is based on the 'predict-and-provide' model used in highway planning and discussed under road provision. Central government leaves the provision of airports to owners who are local authorities or private companies, or a combination of the two (Graham, 2003: 28-31).

The development of private-sector involvement in airport provision and operation has grown substantially since 1980. In many instances public sector airport operators have involved international companies and banks. At Düsseldorf, Hamburg and Birmingham, the Irish company Aer Rianta has become part owner. In other cases, for example Vienna, central government has reduced its ownership to 50% (Graham, 2003: 13–17). Case 21.2 examines the ownership and management changes at Birmingham Airport, United Kingdom, since 1996.

Case 21.2   Birmingham Airport 1996–2003

Birmingham Airport is one of the largest airports in the United Kingdom. It had been operated by a succession of local authorities until 1986. The activities of the various local authorities were controlled by successive legislation, including the 1972 Local Government Act, the 1985 Local Government Act, and the 1986 Airports Act. The consequences of this legislation have been reflected in changes of ownership and how the airport has been managed.

From 1986, Birmingham Airport was owned by seven local authorities. To undertake its management, the local authorities formed a company, Birmingham International Airport plc. To simplify ownership relations, a 999-year lease over land and buildings was issued to one of the seven councils, Solihull Metropolitan Borough Council, which issued a 150-year lease to the company. In 1995 the company published a master plan outlining developments at the airport over the period to 2005, including terminal enhancements and an extension to the main runway.

One effect of the 1986 Airports Act was to allow the United Kingdom government to require local authority airport owners to sell part of their assets to private-sector investors. The effect would be to introduce private-sector capital and management expertise into airport development. The requirement to introduce the private sector into Birmingham Airport took effect in March 1997, and resulted in substantial organisational changes. These included:

- The formation of a new company, Birmingham Airport Holdings Ltd, which became the leaseholder and operator of the airport. The shareholding in the company became 49% owned by the seven local authorities, 48% owned by Aer Rianta International/NatWest Ventures (Nominees) Ltd and other companies, with the balance of the shares owned by an Employees Trust.
- Birmingham Airport Holdings Ltd purchased in 1997 Euro-hub (Birmingham) Ltd, a company that had constructed a second terminal building at the airport for use primarily by British Airways plc.
- Birmingham Airport Holdings Ltd acquired Birmingham International Airport Ltd (formerly the plc) in 1997.
- The holding company inherited the 150-year lease, and pays a rent of £200,000 per annum, together with dividends, to the seven local authorities. Dividends are also paid to the private-sector investors.

Passenger traffic at the airport has shown annual increases over the period 1996–2003. Table 21.4 shows the changes.

Table 21.4   Passenger traffic at Birmingham Airport 1996–2003

Activity	Year 1995–96	%	Year 2002–03	%
Passengers (scheduled)	3,226,087	59	5,239,621	63
Passengers (charter)	2,229,009	41	3,028,302	37
Total passengers	5,455,096	100	8,267,923	100
Air transport movements (ATM)	79,960		115,748	
Passengers/ATM	65		71	

Note: ATM's include both passenger and cargo flights.

Source. Birmingham Airport Holdings Ltd Annual Reports and Accounts

Case 21.2   Continued

The major change has been the increase in passenger numbers on scheduled services when compared to charter services. Table 21.4 also indicates a small increase in passengers per ATM, which confirms that spare capacity remains, but more significantly that the main runway cannot be used by fully-laden large passenger-carrying aircraft. At January 2004, the airport company had not commenced building the runway extension proposed in the 1995 Master Plan.

The holding company was investing in improving access to the airport site. New roads were provided from the adjacent motorway network, terminal facilities were improved, and additional car parking made available. Further improvements involved the development of an air/rail interchange facility linking the airport to Birmingham International railway station and bus services, and to the National Exhibition Centre. It is claimed by the holding company that the interchange 'dovetails completely with the "integration" that Government is seeking in its Transport Strategy'.

Income for airport operations comes from borrowings and from users of the site. Site users pay charges related to aeronautical activities, with occupiers of terminal buildings paying to rent space. The 2002–2003 figures show that aeronautical income grew by 1.9% over 2001–2002, but other commercial income grew by 7% over the same period. Together this amounted to over £100 million with a 64% (aeronautical) to 36% (commercial) split.

Birmingham Airport has seen some activity from 'no-frills' airlines. Ryanair has been operating scheduled services to Dublin for over 10 years using the 'no-frills' model. A long-term user of the airport, Jersey European Airways, rebranded first as British European Airways and more recently as flybe, became a 'no-frills' operator. The most recent 'no-frills' operator was MyTravelLite (a subsidiary of the packaged-holiday company, MyTravel Group plc), which established its first base at Birmingham Airport in 2003.

Over the period to 2003, a series of changes has been made to the company management at Birmingham Airport. This has seen the holding company create five subsidiary companies:

- Birmingham International Airport Ltd, responsible for airport terminal management and operation;
- Euro-hub (Birmingham) Ltd, responsible for terminal building operation;
- First Castle Development Ltd, a property-holding company;
- Birmingham Airport Developments Ltd, responsible for site development;
- Birmingham Airport (Finance) plc, responsible for financing.

The holding company board of directors is unusual in size and composition. In 2003 it consisted of 23 directors – 10 nominated by the seven local authorities, 10 nominated by the private investors, a chairman (all of whom are non-executive), and two executive directors. The private-sector non-executive directors represent Aer Rianta International, and Macquarie Airports (UK) No. 2 Ltd, which acquired the shareholding previously held by NatWest Ventures. None of the directors are appointed by the Employees' Trust.

During 2003 the importance of central government in policy making was reinforced when its White Paper *The Future of Air Transport* was published. Included was a proposal for a second parallel runway at Birmingham Airport. This will have to be provided by Birmingham Airport Holdings Ltd. Whether a second parallel runway is sustainable development, or economically viable, will not be known for a considerable number of years. However, if it is constructed in the period to 2030, it will help Birmingham Airport become 'the best regional airport in Europe'.

Source: Birmingham Airport Holdings Ltd Annual Reports and Accounts, and author

Discussion question

2 How could Birmingham Airport respond to the growth of 'no-frills' airlines, and what effects would any changes have on existing scheduled and charter service providers?

International policy has been of significance in the air transport system. The 1944 Chicago Convention established a range of internationally agreed technical standards for many areas of civil aviation, through the International Civil Aviation Organisation (ICAO), which became part of the United Nations in 1947. The ICAO continues to produce technical standards on a wide range of matters including aircraft engine noise. In a European context a number of policy initiatives have been developed by the EU. One ongoing area is in air traffic control where in 2003 'Single European Sky' directives were being developed (Cruickshank *et al.*, 2004). On the ground, competition has been introduced through a ground-handling directive (CEC, 1996), while member states can no longer control which airlines fly and which airports can be used for inter-state air travel.

The removal of direct state management from many airports in Europe during the 1990s has led to them developing their own mix of business and leisure traffic and operators. Growth of visitor numbers has been substantial, as Table 21.1 illustrates. Major developments in the 1990s have been the creation of 'no-frills' scheduled airlines, and charter airlines catering for the leisure traveller. In addition central governments are able to control ground development at airports through town and country planning legislation. Included in this control mechanism is the EU requirement for development to be accompanied by an environmental impact assessment that considers sustainable development (CEC, 1999).

Aircraft have changed substantially since the 1950s. These changes have included the development of larger aircraft using jet engines as the power source. These manufacturing changes have enabled more flights to be made. International action, particularly by the ICAO, has resulted in the development of more 'environmentally-friendly' aircraft. Propulsion units are now being introduced to meet ICAO 'Chapter 4' requirements (DfT, 2003: 33). The effects of these changes have been to reduce engine noise, but also to make aircraft more cost-efficient. Despite these changes to aircraft, airport operators remain able to control times when aircraft take off and land, particularly at night. Many airports have departure-time policies that favour the business traveller in preference to the leisure traveller. Leisure travellers on packaged holidays find that their departure times do not normally coincide with morning and evening peak times.

With the relaxation of legal controls brought about by deregulation in many parts of the world, three types of airline can be identified. These are:

- **Scheduled airlines,** which concentrate on carrying business travellers. They operate from a limited number of airports where there are good terminal capacity and long runways to accommodate international and intercontinental flights. London Heathrow, Paris Charles de Gaulle, Amsterdam, Madrid and Frankfurt are examples of airports used primarily by scheduled airlines. Scheduled airlines do use smaller airports where there are some intercontinental destinations. Birmingham Airport, for example, has scheduled intercontinental flights in summer 2004 to Dubai, Islamabad, New York and Tashkent.
- **Scheduled 'no-frills' airlines,** which have developed rapidly. Some international scheduled carriers developed their own 'no-frills' operations. The growth of this type of carrier has been due to a number of reasons. Deregulation and the expansion of the internet have been significant. The internet has allowed customers to book seats without having to involve travel agents and without a ticket being issued. In Europe the flights will be short-haul and may not use the same airports as the scheduled carriers. Cost minimisation is the key to their success, and it often involves using small airports. In the United Kingdom two operators dominate the market: Ryanair (an Irish company) operates from London Stansted, while easyJet has its main base at London Luton but operates from other airports, including Berlin. This domination has included taking over similar operations set up by scheduled carriers. What is clear is that these airlines are using the same type of aircraft operated by scheduled carriers, and are investing in new replacement aircraft. In Germany, Air Berlin has developed a similar low-cost operation to those of Ryanair and easyJet, but concentrating on destinations around the Mediterranean and encouraging the business traveller. It has developed a second operating base at Palma Mallorca, Spain.

■ **Charter airlines,** which have concentrated on passengers who have booked package holidays, although in recent years the operators have started to offer flight-only options. These airlines may be owned by tour operators: Britannia Airways (to be renamed Thomson) is owned by TUI AG, the multinational German tour operator. Because they operate for leisure travellers, their operations are often seasonal in nature. The majority of European charter airlines do not offer intercontinental flights, but for holidays to, say, the Caribbean the companies will often consolidate passengers onto a single charter airline. The aircraft are modern and similar to those used by scheduled operators.

Evidence demonstrates that deregulation can have both positive and negative benefits (Williams, 2002). For the customer the introduction of competition has led to lower fares. For airlines, however, it is apparent that many have been unable to continue in operation and have been taken over, or suffered financial collapse.

The discussion about the three types of airline has made reference to aircraft. All aircraft have to be airworthy, and have to use trained and competent crew. Each country has its own system of aircraft registration. In the United Kingdom, these functions are undertaken by the Civil Aviation Authority (CAA), an organisation that implements central government policy (similar to the Traffic Commissioners vehicle responsibilities). The CAA has other functions, particularly the regulation of packaged holidays through the Air Travel Organisers Licence system and the provision of advice to central government on aviation matters.

The air transport travel sector is growing continuously. In the United Kingdom the number of passengers is projected to rise from 180 million in 2000 to 500 million in 2030 (DfT, 2003: 149–54). These figures do not mean that aircraft numbers will double as the projections do not consider aircraft carrying capacity, since that is considered to be a matter for airline companies and aircraft manufacturers. Airbus Industrie, for example, is developing a new aircraft (A380) capable of carrying over 500 passengers. Another feature of the United Kingdom demand projections is the avoidance of suggesting which of the three types of airline a passenger will use.

This discussion of air transport has indicated that there have been, and will continue to be, substantial changes in airport provision and airline operations. The latter changes have resulted from major changes in aircraft technology, particularly propulsion that has reduced travel time. Business travellers have benefited from higher speeds offered by aircraft when compared with the alternative of travel by road, rail or sea. Anecdotal evidence indicates that there is a growth in the number of business travellers who are using 'no-frills' scheduled airlines, particularly where the total journey is of short duration, say one or two days. Leisure travel by air appears to have stabilised in recent years in the United Kingdom (Department for Transport, 2003: 152). How much this is due to market saturation, or to regulation, is not clear. What is evident is that the major packaged-holiday companies in the United Kingdom, while able to control prices through their ownership of airlines, are entering the 'no-frills' scheduled-service market. In 2004 TUI AG introduced no-frills scheduled services from Coventry to European destinations using its own airline, rebranded as Thomsonfly.

Managing transport by water

The use of shipping for passenger travel has changed dramatically since 1950 due to the growth of air travel. Gone are the scheduled passenger services between Europe and North America and Australasia. However, shipping remains an important travel mode in Europe, particularly when it combines passenger and goods movement.

Shipping policy has always had a major concern with safety. This has been augmented by a number of international agreements developed through the United Nations International Maritime Organisation in recent years (Pallis, 2002: 13–14). Accidents at sea inevitably result in design changes. For example, the 'Estonia', which sank in 1994 in the Baltic with the loss of more than 800 lives (Tesch, 1999: 27), led to changes in the design and operation of roll-on-roll-off (ro-ro) vessels' watertight doors being achieved through international agreement.

The European Union has been attempting to develop a common maritime policy since 1974. One of its initiatives was to attempt to create a European register of shipping, although this was abandoned in the mid-1990s (Pallis, 2002: 75). More recent EU policies have concentrated on safety, including ship inspections, training of crew, and the prevention of environmental pollution (Pallis, 2002: 139–40). The governments of member states undertake enforcement of these measures.

Shipping policy in the United Kingdom was reviewed in 2000 (DETR, 2000) with the encouragement to ship owners to register vessels in the United Kingdom. This has proved to be successful, especially as a range of fiscal measures was introduced at the same time. To implement the new policy the Maritime and Coastguard Agency was formed to promote ship safety and minimise marine pollution. In addition the policy included the recognition that dock facilities were required to meet the growth of cargo shipping and secure the improvement of passenger facilities. Similar policies for ports are being implemented around the Baltic (Tesch, 1999) and the eastern Mediterranean (Yercan, 1999a: 117).

Shipping services in Europe have been concentrated on 'short-seas' routes. These include services from the United Kingdom to Ireland, France, Belgium and The Netherlands (Heijveld and Gray, 1999), on the Baltic between Germany and Sweden, and in Greece between the islands. The vessels have been provided by private companies: the P&O Group spent £30 million in 2002 on converting two ro-ro ships to operate between Dover and Calais (Mintel, 2003). Brittany Ferries, a French-owned operator, has also invested in new ships over the past five years. Statistical evidence shows that shipping tonnages in EU countries have increased substantially. At 2003 Greece, Malta, and Cyprus had the largest tonnages (over 35 million each), while the United Kingdom fleet was over 15 million tonnes (DfT, 2003, Table 7.3(iv)). The major portion of these tonnages was cargo ships.

Port provision has been examined in central government policy documents. In the United Kingdom context, facilities are provided by port owners, or by shipping companies that own ports. These developments require planning permission, and in 2004 the United Kingdom government did not approve a cargo development at Southampton, with environmental concerns being a major reason for rejection. Facilities for passengers do not require the same land area as cargo facilities. This has enabled development to take place at Plymouth and Portsmouth in the United Kingdom, at Caen in France and on Corfu, Greece. Despite these investments the United Kingdom passenger numbers travelling by ship have declined from 37 million in 1994 to 29 million in 2002 (DfT, 2003). This decline has been due in large measure to competition from air transport and the Channel Tunnel.

One international growth sector for shipping has been the leisure cruising market. This market is dominated by companies operating from North America, including Carnival Corporation and Royal Caribbean. In 2002 some 500,000 passengers from the United Kingdom took cruising holidays (DfT, 2003: Table 3.1(a)). Package holiday companies entered the cruising market during the 1990s led by Airtours and Thomson. These packages were 'fly/cruise' holidays, often to the Mediterranean. In early 2004 Airtours (now MyTravel) withdrew from the market. New cruise ships are entering service, however, and the Cunard subsidiary of Carnival Corporation took delivery of

Queen Mary 2 in early 2004. It is anticipated that the majority of its voyages will start from American ports.

In terms of travel, it is clear that the majority of passengers will be using ships for leisure purposes, and will be relying on road transport for onward travel to a holiday destination, particularly where 'short-sea' crossings are being used. Despite the declining market and increased safety requirements, it is clear that shipping companies are prepared to invest in ships for leisure travel.

Discussion – business and leisure travel

The users of the four transport modes discussed have been referred to as business or leisure travellers. We will now discuss these two matters by asking the questions – what is business travel and what is leisure travel? Definitions of these two types of travel are not obvious from published sources. For the purpose of the discussion, the following definitions have been adopted:

■ Business travel involves a journey undertaken as part of a person's employment that is paid for by an employer. It can include attendance at meetings, conferences, exhibitions or trade fairs, all of which are part of an individual's paid employment.

■ Leisure travel involves a journey undertaken by a person for pleasure or leisure purposes where the traveller meets the cost of travel. It can include travel for holidays and visiting friends and relatives (VFR).

These two definitions do not include the broader consideration of where a person stays when away from home, or how long a period of time is involved in the activity of travel. However, they do relate to the purpose of travel and who pays for the travel.

There have been substantial increases in the number of people who travel over the decades since 1950. The World Tourism Organization (2003) provides comprehensive details of visitor numbers and their origins. Table 21.1 indicates that between 1997 and 2001 visitors to European countries, except the United Kingdom, grew. What the WTO statistics do not indicate is the scale of internal country trips, including visiting friends and relatives, and the type of travel purpose – business or leisure. Whatever the actual number of travellers, it is clear that transport facilities have to be provided, whether in the form of infrastructure or vehicles. The question that then arises is who will provide these two elements.

It is clear that for many years transport planning has used American-developed modelling techniques for highway provision as a basis for all infrastructure provision. This has resulted in the adoption of the 'predict-and-provide' approach that continues in the United Kingdom for air travel. What this approach omits is travel by non-mechanical transport forms, particularly walking. A further problem with this approach is that the trip is linked to land use at the destination point, which may not reflect the purpose of the trip. Thus many studies indicate that the 'journey to work' generates the vast majority of trips, but, in tourism terms, these are neither business nor leisure trips.

Policy makers in government have recognised that business and leisure travel is significant, but the statistics produced tend to use proxy words or phrases. This is most obvious in air travel, where statistics show whether a passenger travels by a scheduled airline (and by implication is a business traveller) or a charter airline (and is thus a leisure traveller). In the light of the development of 'no-frills' airlines, there is a lack of distinction between 'full service' and 'no-frills' scheduled carriers in the statistics (see Case 21.2).

Similar comments can be made for rail travel, where price and service are used as the mechanisms for distinguishing between business and leisure travel. This assumption may be correct in many cases, particularly as 'first-class' rail accommodation at weekends is often unoccupied, but available to leisure travellers at a small price supplement over standard-class fares.

The statistical evidence makes it clear that the making of travel policy that involves providing infrastructure by governments, whether at national or international levels, is neutral in terms of the purpose of travel. However, the providers of travel facilities – of the vehicles – are able to adjust the prices charged for their use. A range of other considerations affects choices of travel mode by people. These include the duration of travel, and the way in which different modes of travel are integrated with one another. There is increasing evidence that the integration of modes of travel is significant in making choices for investment (DETR, 1998; Case 21.2). This theme of integration has been developed in packaged holidays for leisure purposes more so than in business travel, particularly where travel is to destinations outside the home country of the traveller.

A significant international policy development that has occurred, and will continue to grow in the future, involves adapting the principles of sustainable development to travel. It is noted that the principle modes of travel involving the use of the internal combustion engine are being constrained by regulations. In Europe this is being achieved by environmental regulations affecting such matters as noise and atmospheric pollution. Vehicle manufacturers have been able to develop engines using different fuels, which are shown to provide financial benefits to users. These developments include the removal of lead additives from petrol engines. This type of technological change is being introduced into vehicle design irrespective of transport mode. The consequences of these changes is uncertain as the vehicle provider has to make a choice that includes the cost and expected life of the vehicle purchased, as well as the reactions of the users to the product. As vehicles are capable of being used for both business and leisure travel, it is not realistic to design for two separate markets. This is most obvious in the airline business, where companies operate the same aircraft irrespective of the type of traveller. It is clear that sustainability principles are becoming more significant in the making of transport policy, and can result in the provision of infrastructure and vehicles no longer being determined on a narrow cost basis.

Conclusion

The above review of business and leisure travel has indicated that there are a number of key changes that have occurred and are likely to continue for a number of years. Five key changes should be noted.

1 The growing importance of international agreements based on safety concerns.
2 The move on the part of governments to seek to integrate different transport modes to provide for the 'total journey'.
3 The move by transport providers to offer services by modes of travel that are different from their original core business.
4 The increasing significance of sustainable development as applied to technological changes in both infrastructure provision and vehicle design.
5 The increasing importance of long-distance travel for both business and leisure purposes.

There is a clear view that there will be uncertainties associated with travel. Two matters can be noted. First is the reliance on hydrocarbons, particularly oil, as the fuel of first choice. The volume of oil reserves is uncertain, but technological developments that involve the use of renewable sources could alter significantly all travel modes particularly where international travel is undertaken. Second is the development of electronic communications, particularly in business. The use of satellite audio-visual communications could lead to a decline of business travel, affecting significantly the travel providers operating in that market sector; meetings could take place without the need for travel.

It is suggested that neither of these uncertainties will affect business and leisure travel over the next 10 years. However, to ignore these types of change could well result in policy decisions relating to infrastructure provision for the next 20 or 30 years being taken using incorrect or misleading data. It will certainly confirm that the 'predict-and-provide' methodology was unreliable.

Discussion questions

3   Discuss, with examples, the alternative modes of travel between central London and central Berlin. Include time and cost as major considerations.

4   How will technological changes over the next 30 years alter the demand for leisure and business travel?

5   What are the benefits and disbenefits of using 'executive agencies' to implement government policy decisions?

6   Discuss the implications of sustainable development on the provision of transport for business and leisure travel over the next 10 years.

Guided reading

Transport management and planning issues may be investigated through a range of sources. White (2002) addresses the subject from a land-based perspective, with Hibbs (2003) examining the relationship between economic theory and transport policy, both from a United Kingdom perspective. Banister (2002) provides the context for transport planning and discusses the likely impact of sustainable development. The European dimensions of air travel are examined by Graham (2003) and Williams (2002). Sea-transport policy making is explored by Pallis (2002). No single book provides an overview of transport modes' use for business and leisure travel purposes.

Analytical information on a range of specialist business and leisure activities is available from companies such as Mintel and Key Note. Factual information can be obtained from Annual Reports and Accounts of transport and travel companies, such as the P&O Group plc, TUI AG and Carnival Corporation. Many of these reports are available online.

Transport relies heavily on decisions taken nationally and internationally. Publications by United Nations Agencies, the European Union, and the United Kingdom government all provide information on policy development, with much of the information being available online. Glaister *et al.* (1998) provides an overview of policy development in the United Kingdom to 1997.

Articles on business and leisure travel and on economic and policy matters can be found in the *Journal of Travel Research* and *Journal of Transport Economics and Policy*.

Comprehensive references are contained in all the titles listed in the bibliography.

For a detailed account of the early development of Stagecoach see Wolmar (1999).

Recommended websites

Birmingham International Airport: **www.bhx.co.uk/** . An untypically comprehensive airport website.

Eurostat: **www.europa.eu.int/comm/eurostat/** . The European Union's online statistical database.

John Beech's Travel and Transport Information Gateway: **www.stile.coventry.ac.uk/cbs/staff/beech/tourism/index.htm** . Explore the sub-pages on different modes of transport.

Stagecoach Group: **www.stagecoachplc.com/** . Has direct links to Stagecoach subsidiaries.

UK Department for Transport: **www.dft.gov.uk/** . An excellent source for UK data and policies.

World Tourism Organization: **www.world-tourism.org** .

Key words

Charter; business traveller; leisure traveller; no-frills.

Bibliography

Banister, D. (2002) *Transport Policy*, 2nd edn. Spon Press, London.

Bonavia, M.R. (1987) *The Nationalisation of British Transport: the early history of the British Transport Commission, 1949–1953*. Macmillan, Basingstoke.

Commission of the European Communities (1969) *Public Service Obligations in Transport*. Directive 1191/69/EEC. CEC, Brussels.

Commission of the European Communities (1992) *The Future Development of the Common Transport Policy*. COM (92) 494. CEC, Brussels.

Commission of the European Communities (1996) *Access to the ground handling market at Community Airports*. Directive 96/97/EEC. CEC, Brussels.

Commission of the European Communities (1999) *Air Transport and the Environment: Towards meeting the challenge of sustainable development*. COM (99) 640 final. CEC, Brussels.

Cruickshank, A., Flanagan, P. and Marchant, J. (2004) *Airport Statistics 2002/2003*. Centre for the Study of Regulated Industries, School of Management, University of Bath. University of Bath, Bath.

Department of the Environment, Transport and the Regions (1998) *A New Deal for Transport: Better for Everyone*. White Paper, Cm 3950. TSO, London.

Department of the Environment, Transport and the Regions (2000) *Modern Ports: A U.K. Policy*. DETR, London.

Department for Transport (2003) *The Future of Air Transport*. White Paper, Cm 6046. TSO, London.

Department for Transport (Annual) *Transport Statistics*. TSO, London.

Eurostat Yearbook (Annual). Office for Official Publications of the European Communities, Luxembourg.

Glaister, S., Burnham, J., Stevens, H. and Travers, T. (1998) *Transport Policy in Britain*. Macmillan, Basingstoke.

Graham, A. (2003) *Managing Airports*, 2nd edn. Butterworth Heinemann, Oxford.

Grouvish, T. (2002) *British Rail, 1974–1997: from integration to privatisation*. OUP, Oxford.

Heijveld, H. and Gray, R. (1999) The United Kingdom passenger car ferry industry, in F. Yercan, (1999b) (ed.) *op.cit*.

Hibbs, J. (2003) *Transport Economics and Policy*. Kogan Page, London.

Holliday, I., Marcou, G. and Vickerman, R. (1991) *The Channel Tunnel*. Belhaven Press, London.

Leger Holidays (2003) *European Summer Holidays. May 2003–June 2004*. Leger Holidays, Rotherham.

Lowe, D. (2004) *The Transport Managers and Operators Handbook, 2004*, 34th edn. Kogan Page, London.

Mintel (2003) Crossing the Channel. *Leisure Intelligence*, September 2003. Mintel International Group Ltd, London.

Pallis, A.A. (2002) *The Common EU Maritime Transport Policy*. Ashgate, Aldershot.

Rhodes, G. (1975) *Committees of Inquiry*. George Allen & Unwin, London.

Tesch, G. (1999) Ferry Transport in the Baltic Sea, in F. Yercan, (1999b) (ed.), *op. cit.*

White, P. (2002) *Public Transport: its planning, management and operation*, 4th edn. Spon Press, London.

Williams, G. (2002) *Airline Competition: Deregulation's Mixed Legacy*. Ashgate, Aldershot.

Wolmar, C. (1999) *Stagecoach*. Orion Business Books, London.

World Tourism Organization (2003) *Yearbook of Statistics (1997–2001)*. WTO, Madrid.

Yercan, F. (1999a) Analysis of recent developments in the passenger ferry services in the Eastern Mediterranean, in F. Yercan, (1999b) (ed.), *op. cit.*

Yercan, F. (ed.) (1999b) *Ferry Services in Europe*. Plymouth Studies in Contemporary Shipping. Ashgate, Aldershot.

Chapter 22

Developing mass tourism in developing nations

Marcella Daye, Coventry Business School

Learning outcomes

On completion of this chapter the reader should be able to:

■ identify the various definitions of developing nations including the use of non-economic measures;

■ explain the importance of political and economic contexts in which tourism operates in such nations;

■ identify the particular issues of tourism's economic, sociocultural and environmental impacts on developing nations;

■ explain the role of foreign developers and its implications;

■ explore the implications of developing all-inclusive mass tourism in developing nations.

Overview

This chapter reviews the importance of tourism as a tool of development for developing nations. It examines the main paradigms of development presented in modernisation, development and globalisation theories that have been proposed as approaches that may be adopted by developing nations in their quest to maximise the benefits of tourism development. However, the costs of tourism development are also highlighted in this chapter with respect to their economic, political, environmental and sociocultural impacts on the destination and peoples of developing countries. The case is also made that national governments in developing nations have a key role in the implementation and enforcement of policy and management measures to minimise the negative impacts of the industry. By providing the legislative and policy framework, and with judicious planning, national governments have the opportunity to enhance the benefits of tourism as well as to facilitate and to encourage sustainable tourism development. The question of the sustainability of mass tourism is also explored in this chapter with specific reference to the advantages and disadvantages of all inclusive hotel development as a developmental option. The chapter concludes by discussing the claims that alternative tourism is not a panacea for the ills of mass tourism and contends that in many cases mass tourism remains a viable form of tourism development for developing nations.

Tourism performance in developing nations

The World Tourism Organization's (WTO) statistics on the performance of international tourism show a pattern of remarkable growth and development of the industry especially over the past decade. Developing countries in particular appear to be the main beneficiaries of the rapid expansion and growth of international tourism. According to the WTO developing countries attained a higher level of income from tourism between 1990 and 2000 than developed countries. During this decade, developing nations achieved an overall income growth per international arrival of 65% combined, compared with 18% for Organization for Economic Co-operation and Development (OECD) countries and 7.8% for EU countries (WTO, 2002). This growth in tourism earnings has been accompanied by an expansion of developing nations' share of global international arrivals, doubling in volume from 20.8% in 1973 to 42% in 2000.

The sustained positive performance of tourism in generating income for developing nations makes a convincing case for the industry as a powerful tool for economic growth in developing nations. Even more significantly these performance statistics also suggest that tourism may be the singular industry where developing nations can attest to achieving higher percentage levels of growth than developed nations. Table 22.1 below shows that developing countries have achieved creditable increases in arrivals between 1990 and 2000. Relatively, total arrival levels for countries classified by the United Nations as 'least developed countries' (LDCs) is rather low, accounting for a total increase of 2185 between 1990 and 2000. However, for this period, this represents an increase growth of 74.8%, which is higher than the 39.3% increase in arrivals for OECD countries and 38.4% increase for EU countries. Table 22.2 shows that, in terms of absolute value, the rise in earnings has also been growing at a faster rate for developing countries than developed countries.

Table 22.1 International arrivals in thousands

Country groups	1990	2000	Increase	% increase
OECD	338,300	471,164	132,964	39.3
EU	204,961	283,604	78,643	38.4
Other countries	3,465	6,652	3,187	92.0
Developing countries	150,563	292,660	142,097	94.4
Least developed countries (LDCs)	2,921	5,106	2,185	74.8
Other developing countries	13,755	25,562	11,807	85.8

Source: WTO (2002) *Tourism and Poverty Alleviation*

Table 22.2 Absolute value (US$ million) of tourism expenditure by country group

Country groups	1990	2000	Increase	% increase
OECD	201,082	330,464	129,382	64.3
EU	119,998	179,041	59,043	49.2
Other countries	1,366	2,388	1,022	74.8
Developing countries	59,645	138,937	79,292	132.9
Least developed countries (LDCs)	1,021	2,594	1,573	154.1
Other developing countries	11,045	17,041	5,996	54.3

Source: WTO (2002) *Tourism and Poverty Alleviation*

However, it is also important to point out that in spite of these positive tourism indicators in developing countries, the international tourism industry is still dominated by the destinations of developed countries. As shown in Table 22.2, the considerable gap in tourism earnings and arrivals between the developed nations and developing ones remains staggering. Although tourism in developing nations is growing at a phenomenal rate and is achieving marginal levels of comparative advantage and enhanced competitiveness in the global market, yet their relative earnings from the industry remain substantially less than their competitors from the developed world.

Developing nations therefore account for a marginal share of the overall earnings from international tourism (Brohman, 1996: 52). According to Mowforth and Munt (1998: 15), global tourism is characterised by unequal and uneven development as first world countries command the giant share of income from international tourism and also receive and generate the largest volume of tourists. But this inequality can also be found among developing nations as well. In Africa, tourism activity is concentrated in three countries, Egypt, Morocco and Tunisia, which accounted for 52.6% of international arrivals in 1991, while in Southeast Asia, Malaysia, Singapore and Thailand accounted for 79.8% of all arrivals to the region (Mowforth and Munt, 1998).

Positive performance indicators pointing to the increase in tourism earnings in developing nations should therefore not eclipse the challenges that are contingent on maintaining and increasing income growth in tourism. Although many developing countries are endowed with natural assets such as beautiful landscapes, sun, sand and sea as well as authentic cultural heritage resources, yet they often do not have the requisite infrastructure such as airports, roads and human resources to deliver the quality tourism facilities demanded by mass tourists. So, although destinations in developing nations may therefore be showing rapid increases in international arrivals, this growth may belie their continued dependency on overseas capital investment, and expertise to sustain the industry.

More importantly, rapid growth in tourism does not mean that there is an overall improvement in the income and welfare of the general population. According to Burns (2004: 24–31), while tourism may succeed in increasing tourist arrivals and improving tourist infrastructure, it tends not to be as successful in delivering an equitable share of benefits for the more disadvantaged peoples of the destination. He argues that in order to assess the contribution of tourism to the development of a destination it is necessary to ask the question *cui bono* (who benefits?). This suggests that the extent to which tourism development improves the overall welfare of all the people of the destination should be considered when evaluating the contribution of the industry to 'sustainable human development' (Burns, 2004: 40).

Reid (2003: 4) also supports the view that tourism development, particularly in the destinations of developing nations, tends to be characterised by unequal incomes and erratic growth of their economies. He argues that, although local communities are often at the vanguard of the delivery of tourism services, they are usually the least to benefit from the returns of the industry. The people of local communities of many LDCs are often excluded from the planning and decision-making processes by many local developers, who tend to see them only as resources to be exploited.

Definitions of developing nations

Traditional measurements of development have focused mainly on economic indicators such as *per capita* income and gross national product (GNP) (Lea, 1988: 4). Generally, countries that are not ranked as 'high income economies' by the World Bank have tended to fall in the generic category of developing countries and have been tagged with the nomenclature of 'third world' countries, which is now less popularly used as a term to express the distinctions between the developed and developing world (Harrison, 1992: 1).

Developing countries are further categorised into 'least developed countries' (LDCs) and 'newly industrialising countries' (NICs). Some 49 countries in 2003 were designated as LDCs, of which 34 are in Africa, 9 in Asia, 5 in the Pacific and 1 in the Caribbean (WTO, 2003: 6). Those countries categorised as NICs are predominantly East Asian nations such as Singapore and Thailand (Brohman, 1996: 50). Some Eastern European countries have also been designated within the category of developing nations based on the World Bank *per capita* income classification, but they have not been traditionally termed as 'third world' countries (Harrison, 1992: 1).

Apart from low GNP *per capita*, developing nations are usually characterised by debilitating problems of poor health among most of the population, lack of access to water and sanitation, lack of educational opportunities, hunger and malnutrition, low levels of marketable skills as well as political insecurity and a high debt burden that perpetuates their economic vulnerability (WTO, 2003: 5). Other features of developing countries include low life expectancy, high maternal and infant mortality, poor civic amenities such as roads, electricity and telephone communications as well as high incidence of child labour. According to the WTO (2003) some 60% of the world's poor live in five countries: India, China, Nigeria, Ethiopia and Bangladesh.

Sharpley (2002: 27–31) also lists other non-economic development indicators of developing countries as their economic dependence on the agricultural sectors, the export of primary products and a limited industrial sector. He argues that developing nations are also characterised by 'socio-political structures that are ill equipped to address the challenges of underdevelopment' and this is evident in the high level of inequity in the distribution of economic and social benefits, which are generally dominated by the powerful elite groups in these countries.

The United Nations Development Programme (UNDP) advocates development as being more than growth in income levels to the consideration of indicators measuring the improvement in the standard and quality of life which also implies the widening and expansion of people's choices and improving their general well-being (WTO, 2003: 5). The 'human development index' (HDI) used by the UNDP in its measurement of development covers wider social indicators beyond GNP *per capita* and takes into account factors such as life expectancy, educational attainment and real income (WTO, 2003: 7). Based on these criteria, the HDI ranks countries as 'high human development' (HHD), 'medium human development' (MHD) and 'low human development' (LHD). In 1993, among the LDCs with the faster growing tourism arrivals that were ranked at medium human development were Cambodia, Bhutan, Peru and Cape Verde while the LDCs that were ranked at low human development included Chad, Zambia and Madagascar (WTO, 2002: 8).

Tourism and development

Tourism has been a major source of income earnings for developing nations and so can be exploited by them as a means of combating intransigent problems of poverty and economic dependency. However, there are varying views as to the development path that developing countries should take in order to improve their economic performance. Theories of modernisation, dependency and globalisation reviewed below represent the diverse perspectives or paradigms that have been generally suggested as appropriate approaches that may be used by developing nations in the quest for successful tourism development (Telfer, 2002).

Modernisation and dependency theories

Developing nations faced with the challenges of improving the income and welfare of their inhabitants are often attracted to tourism since it offers relatively rapid returns on investments and consistent inflows of foreign exchange earnings. Tourism has been presented by international agencies such as the World Bank and the International Monetary

Fund (IMF) as an opportunity for many countries marginalised on the periphery of world trade to link with advanced, capitalist economies that make up the core of the global economy (Scheyvens, 2002).

This approach to development has been mainly advocated by modernisation theories of development that contend that the closer developing nations are able to align their economies to developed ones, the better their prospects for economic growth and development. In other words, as proposed by modernisation theorists in the 1950s and 1960s such as W.W. Rostow, the path to development for developing nations is to become modernised, moving away from their agricultural-based economies and emulating the economies of the Western world by relying on their capital, technology and expertise to drive development (Clancy, 1998: 2; Scheyvens, 2002: 24). Modernisation theories therefore suggest that the economies of developing countries are essentially flawed and inherently weak, and therefore must be modernised, restructured, and reformed to achieve the economic growth and development that have characterised the economies of the developed world.

The emphasis of modernisation theory for development is on income generation and growth with the underlying assumption that the benefits of economic growth will eventually 'trickle down' to the local inhabitants. With specific reference to tourism, however, Lea (1988) notes that it is mainly elite groups in developing nations, who have joint interests with overseas investors and special trading arrangements with overseas counterparts, who usually are the main beneficiaries. Small local firms are often denied access to the lucrative tourist industry, based on their inability to provide the goods and services at the standard and volume required by the international, mass tourist market.

Critics of modernisation theories often point out that such approaches fail to deliver improvements to the general population, in particular to the most needy of these societies. Instead, they argue that the development of mass tourism in developing nations tends to reinforce their dependency on the developed world through arrangements with airlines for international transport links, with travel wholesalers to provide tourists and with transnational corporations (TNCs) such as brand named hotel chains. Political economists such as Britton (1982) have long argued that, while tourism has integrated many developing nations into the economies of the West, they have also become locked into an arrangement where their resources are exploited and kept subservient to the interests of overseas investors and the needs of foreign tourists.

With limited prospects for economic independence and limited ability to compete effectively in the international marketplace, developing nations remain perennially dependent on western capital to initiate and also to sustain tourism at their destinations. According to Brohman (1996), the negative impacts of foreign domination of 'third world' tourism involve loss of control by locals of their resources, which may detract from their overall well-being. Furthermore, locals are often subjected to top–down decisions made by elitist groups from outside the community and may also suffer economically as substantial leakage of earnings of most of the profits of the industry are repatriated to tourist generating regions.

Dependency theory therefore challenges the basis of modernisation theory, which maintains the economies of developing nations are backward and in need of modernisation and restructuring. Instead, dependency theory contends that capitalist economies, by their penetration of developing economies and the appropriation of their economic surplus as well as their monopoly of global trade, have instigated and perpetuated the underdevelopment of 'third world' countries (Khan, 1997). Consequently, mass tourism is usually rejected by dependency theorists as a preferred developmental option, mainly because it is associated with large-scale, foreign-owned investments, high levels of profit repatriation and leakage, limited participation in the industry and in decision-making by local peoples and excessive dependence on external markets. These characteristics are viewed by development theorists as evidence of a 'neo-colonial extension of economic forms of underdevelopment that reproduces historical patterns of structural inequalities between developed and developing nations' (Britton (1980) cited in Brohman (1996)).

Brohman (1996) cites two studies conducted in the Cook Islands and Thailand which found that small, locally-owned firms generated more income, employment and revenue in the economies of these destinations than large internationally-owned firms. This implies that tourism development that allows local communities to retain the lion's share of the earnings from the industry is essentially preferable for developing countries. Some have argued that tourism development that promotes the wider participation of local communities and contributes to the self-reliance of communities, and supports the overall development goal of the community is preferable to mass tourism development in optimising the benefits from the industry (Reid, 2003). Nevertheless, in the face of the realities of the global international market, the major proportion of tourism demand is for mass tourism products and packages. This poses questions therefore on the proposed viability of tourism development in developing countries in that it does not cater to the mass market (Khan, 1997).

Globalisation – its role in tourism development

The conception of the world as a global village is being continually affirmed with the increasing reduction of geographical, transport and communication barriers across both the developed and developing world (Scheyvens, 2002). According to Wahab and Cooper (2004: 319), globalisation may be defined as 'boundarylessness' inclusive of the various organisational and also national responses to this phenomenon. However, globalisation also goes beyond the shrinking of physical spaces and the removal of physical barriers to include the global assimilation of various cultures and lifestyle patterns. Critics of globalisation have highlighted the 'McDonaldisation' and 'CocaColaisation' across the world as a major threat to the cultural integrity of global cultures (Sharpley and Telfer, 2002). They also point to the fact that remote regions and countries are increasingly being drawn into global networks and alliances that at times appear to challenge the political exercise of the sovereignty of these nations.

While globalisation is not presented as a distinct model for development for developing countries, yet the currents of this new world order is such that nations are forced to respond to these exogenous forces in order to survive and to maintain control of their destinies. According to Wahab and Cooper (2004: 332), tourism is at the forefront of globalisation by the nature of its international operations and also as a driver of and a respondent to changes that are emerging with the growth of the industry. Within the tourism industry, global airline alliances, computer reservations systems and global distribution systems have been fostering the expansion of the industry into countries that were excluded from the global economy. Tourism has also benefited from the removal of barriers to trade and overseas investment as well as the free movement of labour contingent with legislative changes that are instituted due to globalisation (Madeley, 1999). The implications for developing nations are that globalisation offers both opportunities and threats that they cannot ignore. The opportunities for developing nations are greater access to capital investment in technology, training and new competencies for the local population as well as the building of new infrastructure. As part of their overall competitive strategy of internationalisation, travel and tourism transnational corporations in the airline, accommodation and travel distribution industries are attracted to developing countries in their quest to develop global brands, and to build alliances and partnerships that lessen their dependence on their domestic markets (Wahab and Cooper, 2004).

Undoubtedly developing nations reap the benefits of capital investment, employment, knowledge and skills transfer and the promotion of the industrialisation of the local economy that are consequent to the business operations of transnational corporations (TNCs). On the other hand, TNCs ultimately serve the interests of their major shareholders, and their operations in developing nations often result in the loss of locally created jobs as well as the viability of local small enterprises. Madeley (1999) notes that the main tourism TNCs are airlines, hotel and restaurant chains, tour operators and travel agencies, most of which are headquartered in developed countries. According to Madeley (1999), a study of international tourism estimated that some 13 TNCs dominate the tourism industry, of which 6 are from the US, 4 from France and 1 each from Australia, Britain and Canada.

Developing nations seem to have little influence in shaping international political trading arrangements that support the global operations of TNCs, with the trend towards liberalisation of trade regulations by the General Agreement of Trade in Services (GATS) (Madeley, 1999). Such arrangements have legitimated the operations of TNCs' incursions into developing countries, with local businesses unable to secure protective legislation that could shield them from the fierce competition the TNCs present based on their competitive advantages. Ultimately, the displacement of local enterprises as they become dwarfed by overseas competitors appears contrary to the long-term interests of developing countries, with some worrying prospects of rising inequality and the worsening of the life chances of the most disadvantaged of the developing world.

The overall commitment of TNCs to the welfare of their host country has been challenged by their readiness to use their power to influence government policy in their own favour even it may not be beneficial to the developing country. For example, Scheyvens (2002) cites the case of The Gambia that had imposed a ban on all-inclusive hotels in October 1999 based on perceived disadvantages of this type of hotel development on the economy and culture of the destination. However, the government decided to reverse this ban after a year when travel companies began to shift their clients to competitor destinations. The government of The Gambia has now implemented policies that encourage all-inclusive hotel development by offering tax incentives to developers.

Similarly, Marfurt (1997: 175) reports that in 1972, when Tunisia refused to grant a larger profit margin to a German tour operator, the response of the company was to reduce the country's tourist quota by one-fifth. This demonstrates the power of the TNCs to influence government policy in developing countries that rely on tourism as the main foreign exchange earner. However, the case of The Gambia is not indicative of all developing countries. For countries that are not as reliant on tourism, and where the national government embarks on an integrated plan of development that positions tourism on one of the various development options, there is the possibility of mediating the pervasive power of TNCs.

Madeley (1999: 8) argues that national governments of developing countries can play a role in trying to bargain with TNCs in order to secure more benefits for locals in terms of their operations. For example, governments could stipulate that international hotels utilise local suppliers for a proportion of their food and other services they may require.

Essentially, TNCs are reluctant to take on developmental projects in tourism especially when they seem to be high risk and offer no promise of early returns on investments. In such instances, national governments have had to take the lead in investment and then form subsequent partnerships with TNCs in order to build tourism clientele and to maintain the operations of the sector. In such instances, national governments are more likely to maintain control of the pace and scope of tourism development. For example, Clancy (1998) reports that in Mexico the government embarked on a planned statist approach to tourism development that had the long-term effect of balancing the extent of overseas domination of the local industry. According to Clancy (1998: 10), the Mexican government through the national tourist organisation, FONTUR, took the lead in 'planning, construction of infrastructure, offering funding for private investors and taking ownership of tourism enterprises'. In spite of intensive investment in the construction of their new resorts in Cancún, Ixtapa, Los Cabos, Loreto and Huatulco, there was a lack of interest in these areas among private international and foreign investors. International chains were then unwilling to build hotels in an area that seemed to 'have nothing'.

The response of the Mexican government was to build, own and operate their own hotels; at the same time they also offered preferential and subsidised loans to developers to encourage hotel construction. Although there was a general policy of limiting the extent of foreign ownership of businesses at the time, the government permitted foreign companies to form local conglomerates with private Mexican companies in order to share the investment risks. The success of this statist strategy was such that private investors were encouraged into taking over the lead in tourism development so that national Mexican chains now make up the largest and most dominant chains in Mexico. While benefiting from the 'name recognition, trust and ties with generating markets' of the major hotel brands of TNCs, Mexican developers were also able to share control of the local hotel market with overseas investors (Clancy, 1998).

By embarking on this statist model of tourism development, Mexico has been able to control the extent of overseas control of local tourism businesses while at the same time harnessing and benefiting from the inputs of TNCs in a more focused approach to tourism development. This Mexican approach seems to support Wahab and Cooper's (2004: 332) position that tourism should embrace globalisation, 'yet treat it with a localised focus if it is to succeed'. However, they also point out that globalisation of the tourist industry may be shifting the focus away from the divisions between developing and developed nations to global alliances that link special-interest groups in local destinations. The companies that benefit from global contacts are able to achieve competitive advantage over locals who operate only on the domestic level. Clancy (1998: 16) points out that this is the situation in the Mexican hotel industry, which is structured in a manner that 'ensures that only TNCs and large-scale Mexican capital reap most of the benefits associated the industry'.

The currents of globalisation seem set to continue to gain momentum and the ways in which developing nations can harness these forces for the benefit of their peoples are not clear. Still, developing nations involved in international, mass tourism are caught up into the maelstrom of these global changes and so have to engage in these global trends in their quest for improvement in the living standards and welfare of their people. The implementation of international trade agreements such as GATS may limit the extent to which national governments can protect their local operators. For example, the terms of GATS may stipulate that whatever subsidies, incentives and concessions are offered to local hotel companies should also be given to TNCs as well (Madeley, 1999). This is expected to pose real challenges for national governments in developing nations who desire to reap the benefits of TNC business but at the same time are also committed to the development of locally owned companies.

Case 22.1   Tourist liberalisation: local agents must adapt to survive

The Thai Travel Agents Association (TTAA) has warned of tough foreign competition as the tourism industry liberalises over the next two years. When this occurs under a World Trade Organization agreement, foreign travel agents will be allowed into the Thai market, bringing with them integrated services along with high investment budgets, know-how, technology and business networks.

'The advantage of foreign travel agents is "know-how". The Thai's strength is "know-who". If we can combine the advantage of foreign management with customer demand and behaviour we will survive, but if we don't agents can expect to be phased out in the long run', said Manus Pipathananunth, President of TTAA. He added that Thailand had 3000 inbound, outbound and domestic tour operators.

Of notable concern is the amount of money the foreign travel operators will be able to invest in Thailand. Their registered capital, for instance, is up to Bt15 million (US$275,000) compared with about Bt2 million (US$50,000) for Thai firms. The foreign companies also have networks that span the globe.

Manus said the country's tour operators would face serious competition in the next two years, with price-cutting expected to be fierce. 'The price war will reduce profit per unit in the tourism industry. Getting into the Thai tourism business is easy due to low investment and trade barriers', he said.

Source: new frontiers, Vol. 10, No.1 Jan–Feb 2004 available at **www.twnside.org.sg/tour.htm**

Discussion questions

1 What are the expected challenges to the domestic Thai travel agents of the impending liberalisation of the tourism industry?
2 What have been suggested as some of the ways that Thai travel agents can adjust to meet these challenges?
3 Do you think the Thai government has a role to play in assisting the local tourist industry to meet the challenges of globalisation?

Impacts of mass tourism on developing nations

It is a truism to say that once tourism takes place at a destination, impacts are inevitable for that country (Khan, 1997). These impacts are likely to be both positive and negative in terms of the economic, political and sociocultural outcomes for the destination (Archer and Cooper, 1994). For developing nations in particular, the negative impacts of tourism usually seem to be more acute because of the lack of resources and expertise to manage these impacts and to put in place planning measures to effectively minimise their costs to the country. Still, there has been considerable debate on the extent to which international mass tourism can be managed in such a way as to reduce the negative impacts and to make the industry more sustainable. The overall contention is that, while mass tourism continues to be the most dominant form of tourism activity and hence tourism development, efforts should be concentrated at managing the overall negative impacts of mass tourism rather than pursuing other types of tourism development that may not be as viable.

Economic impacts

The WTO and the World Travel and Tourism Council (WTTC) are the main international agencies championing the arguments in support of the positive impacts of tourism for both developed and developing nations. The case for the positive impacts of tourism on the economies of developing nations seems unassailable in light of the evidence of foreign exchange earnings and the contribution of the industry to the balance of payments. For example, the WTO maintains that apart from three countries that have petroleum export industries, tourism is the primary source of foreign exchange earnings for most of the 49 LDCs (World Tourism Organization, 2003). Tourism therefore presents a relatively low-cost prospect for developing nations to finance burdensome debt repayments, to pay for imports and to support the investment in requisite technology and skills for the development of their economies.

World Tourism Organization (2003) statistics show the importance of tourism as an invisible export for the balance of payments (BOP) earning of many developing countries. According to the WTO (2002), in the OECD and EU countries tourism accounted for some 28% of trade in services, compared to 43% for developing nations and 70% for LDCs. The importance of the contribution of tourism to the national earnings of developing countries indicates the positive economic impacts of the industry. However, this high level of dependence of developing countries and LDCs on tourism also exposes some of the structural weaknesses of their economies in terms of their lack of diversification and reliance only on one major source of foreign exchange earnings.

Nevertheless, the disadvantages associated with tourism development should be balanced with the reality that there may be few alternative options available for developing countries to embark on to provide export earnings. The World Tourism Organization (2002) therefore argues that tourism is able to play a vital role in poverty alleviation for developing countries and so should be chosen as a key developmental option. According to the WTO, some of the main beneficial economic impacts of tourism for developing nations include:

- improved links with consumers who travel to the destination thereby leading to opportunities for the sale of additional goods and services – micro-enterprises and small businesses can sell handicraft and souvenir products to potential consumers;
- access to international export markets that have been closed to traditional export products;
- opportunities for the cultural and wildlife heritage resources to provide earnings for poor, rural communities;
- increased employment opportunities for women so promoting gender equality.

Developing countries plagued by intractable unemployment are often attracted to large-scale hotel developments as they often provide jobs for large numbers of unskilled workers. Furthermore, skills training is usually provided on the job for local people who may not have had access before to formal training. The World Tourism Organization (2002) contends that tourism is more labour-intensive than manufacturing although less than agriculture. When compared with these sectors, however, tourism seems to be the most beneficial to developing nations in terms of relatively easy access to international investment capital, dynamic consumer markets and quick turnover in export earnings. Based on these positive benefits, tourism is usually well placed to be the lead sector and the main engine of growth for the national development strategies of developing countries. However, in order to optimise the economic benefits of tourism as a developmental tool for the country, national governments have to play a major role in maximising the benefits of tourism by providing the legislative framework, tax incentives and integrated tourism development planning.

Case 22.2 demonstrates the policy measures implemented by the government of Barbados in an effort to foster the growth of the local tourism industry through tax and fiscal incentives mainly directed in support of the accommodation sector. These measures were also directed at encouraging foreign investment as shown by the favourable fiscal concessions offered by the national government to investors in the industry. They were also geared to promote a diversified range of accommodation facilities ranging from the small hotel with a maximum of 75 rooms to larger properties of 250 rooms. However, these fiscal measures also include the restaurant and attraction sectors of the industry that demonstrate a comprehensive macroeconomic programme to develop tourism. The preservation of cultural and heritage sites is also encouraged by the government providing loans for activities to upgrade and maintain these attractions.

Case 22.2 Fiscal measures in support of tourism in Barbados

The government of Barbados has introduced a comprehensive set of fiscal measures to stimulate the development of new tourism products as well as expansion and revitalisation of existing accommodation and tourism entities. Outlined below are some examples of these policies that constitute the country's Sustainable Tourism Act.

1. Establishment of a fund to provide loans at concessionary interest rates for the refurbishment and upgrading of accommodation properties with fewer than 75 rooms.
2. Accelerated write-off of interest on loans up to $7.5 million where the loans proceeds are used to refurbish and upgrade accommodation facilities.
3. Accelerated write-off of interest on loans up to $30 million where the loan proceeds are used for the construction of new accommodation facilities of not fewer than 250 rooms where the property provides conference facilities.
4. Accelerated write-off of interest on loans up to $20 million where the loan proceeds are used for the construction of new accommodation facilities in non-coastal areas.

5 Accelerated write-off of interest on loans up to $15 million where the loans are used for the consolidation of properties in the small hotel subsector.

6 Accelerated write-off of interest on loans up to $3 million where the loan proceeds are used to refurbish and upgrade or construct facilities which emphasise our natural, historical and cultural heritage.

7 Provision of duty-free concessions to restaurants which meet specific criteria established by the Barbados Tourism Authority.

8 Accelerated write-off of 150% of any funds spent on marketing expenses incurred by accommodation facilities.

9 Accelerated write-off of 150% of expenditure incurred by hoteliers for training of staff by hotels and restaurants.

10 Provision of benefits for the first time in the form of duty-free concessions on construction materials for the establishment of timeshare properties.

Source: Poon (2004) *Successful Tourism Destinations – Lessons from the Leaders*

Discussion questions

4 What do you think are the main objectives of this policy framework?

5 To what extent should LDCs replicate these policy initiatives?

In their report *Tourism and Poverty Alleviation* the World Tourism Organization (2002) proposes that governments of developing nations can increase the economic benefits of tourism to the local economy and reduce poverty by pursuing specific strategies to increase tourist length of stay and the *per capita* expenditure of tourists and to attract higher yield market segments. The WTO further suggests that by developing complementary products, spreading the benefits of tourism geographically, reducing seasonality and providing incentives for small and medium enterprises, developing nations will be able to maximise the benefits of tourism and be better able to harness the industry as a tool for economic development.

As an economic activity, tourism yields income benefits for the countries that invest in this sector. Nonetheless, in real economic terms, tourism represents an opportunity cost to the economy of the country that has chosen to pursue it at the expense of other industries that may also provide income for the country. It has been suggested that tourism should be embarked on by developing countries only if it represents the best option for economic development for the country and if the use of the country's scare resources leads to no real costs to the society (Archer and Cooper, 1994).

However, the direct benefits of tourism in terms of positive balance of payments and export earnings is usually accompanied by secondary effects which occur when the direct inflow of foreign currency generates further income in the economy. The multiplier effect of tourism results when tourism earnings creates business turnover in an economy as it is 're-spent and create further rounds of economic activity' (Archer and Cooper, 1994). Developed countries tend to have higher tourism multipliers than developing countries since their highly diversified economies are able to utilise the tourism earnings generated from the primary effects of tourism.

By contrast, developing nations that have fewer linkages or business and productive enterprises that can be linked to the tourism industry also tend to experience higher levels of leakage of earnings from tourism. Leakage refers to loss of earning such as payments overseas for the delivery of the tourism product and services at the destination. These include payments to expatriate workers in the industry, food imports for hotels and payments for holiday packages in tourism-generating regions among others. Lea (1988) notes that linkages between the hotel sector and local businesses rely on the types of suppliers required and if the local business sector is able to meet those needs. He points out that as the number of hotels in the country increases, the supply of local product is often unable to meet this demand leading to 'growing dependence on imported food'. It may be concluded that stronger linkages within the economy mean fewer 'leakages' for the economy. The WTO (2002) maintains, however, that although 'tourism suffers from leakages, this impact is not greater than for other exports'.

Political impacts

According to Richter (1992: 37), developing nations tend to be less able to protect their tourist industry from their turbulent political environment than more developed nations. This is not only due to a lack of resources but also because many of these emerging nations are involved in the ferment of political currents that is viewed as inimical to the tourist industry. News stories of political conflicts and civil disturbances tend to be the focus of international media coverage and many developing nations do not ever hit the international screen except for instances of negative reportage. The tourism industry tends to respond negatively to incidents of political upheavals anywhere in the world, but developing nations are even more vulnerable since they lack the resources to launch sophisticated public relations and marketing campaigns as well as coordinated recovery strategies.

Richter (1992) points out that there were drastic downturns in arrivals to China following Tiananmen Square. The Caribbean island of Jamaica also suffered a decline in arrivals after reports of civil unrest in the country's urban centres even though they were far removed from the tourist resort areas of the country. After the 11 September 2001 terrorist attacks in the USA, tourist arrivals declined sharply, especially to the city of New York. Similarly, post September 11, the Caribbean region that depends on the US as a major source market for tourists also experienced a sharp decline of 13% in stopover arrivals and 4.1% for cruise passenger between 2001 and 2002 (Caribbean Tourism Organisation (2002) cited in Momsen (2004)). The tourism industry in the Caribbean did not recover arrival performance until 2003, two years after the terrorist attacks. According to Beirman (2003), the response of the USA travel industry to the crisis was to launch a sophisticated comprehensive recovery strategy that successfully wooed tourists back to the States within a year based on restoring confidence within their domestic market. However, as most Caribbean countries do not have a strong domestic market of tourists, the region tends to be more vulnerable to crises that increase perception of risk of overseas travel among tourists in the main generating regions.

Case 22.3 below shows that political tensions across neighbouring territories can also hinder tourism development.

Case 22.3   Tourism badly hurt by riots in Phnom Penh

The burning of the Thai Embassy and rage against other Thai premises in Phnom Penh have seriously hurt Cambodia's economic and tourism opportunities. The mob attack started on 29 January, only two days after the ASEAN Tourism Forum (ATF) was held in the city.

Tourism has become a key industry in Cambodia, with almost 800,000 foreigners visiting the country last year. During the ATF in January, the government launched 'Visit Cambodia Year 2003', but the Phnom Penh riot is expected to severely hamper the tourism campaign that aims to attract one million foreign visitors this year.

Another casualty is the Cambodian-Thai 'Two Kingdoms, One Destination' joint campaign that was introduced in 2001. Under the present ruling no official business is allowed and that has technically ended all bilateral cooperation in promotion and education between Cambodia's Ministry of Tourism and the Tourism Authority of Thailand.

As a result of the riots, flights were suspended and many tour groups cancelled their trips to Cambodia. Overland tourism vanished as border checkpoints were closed.

Source: new frontiers, Vol. 9, No. 1, Jan–Feb 2003 available at **www.twnside.org.sg/tour.htm**

As detailed in Case 22.3, rivalries between bordering nation states can disrupt both domestic and international tourism. Although tourism has been touted as a force for peace in bringing people of various cultures and ethnicity together, it is idealistic to expect the industry to transcend the realities of political polarities (Archer and Cooper, 1994). Tourism offers the opportunity for people of different cultural and national groups to experience social encounters and this may produce goodwill, but it is unlikely to resolve long-held antagonisms and recriminations between rival groups. While political stability is a distinct advantage for a successful tourism industry, most developing nations are pursuing tourism development in the face of social and civil unrest and turmoil.

Tourism in developing nations occurs across the spectrum of political governance ranging from democracies, communist states, repressive dictatorships, ruling monarchies and military regimes. These varied political systems may pose constraints to the development of international mass tourism in these destinations especially if there are political tensions between the ruling government and Western nations. In the case of Myanmar (formerly known as Burma), tourism has been a flashpoint for opposition groups, who launched a Burma tourism boycott in 1996 in response to an attack on the country's pro-democracy leader Aung San Suu Kyi. The opposition campaign has been agitating against overseas scheduled airlines and tour companies operating in the country to curtail their operations in a bid to weaken the income base of the military government (*new frontiers*, May–June 2003). In this respect, tourism has become the focus of political agitation and is being utilised by the opposition group as a combat zone for its political aspirations.

However, the political vulnerability and marginality of developing nations in the global arena is clearly demonstrated in terms of the travel advisories issued by major Western countries warning against travel to their destinations in the wake of national crises, terrorist attacks or natural disasters. According to Beirman (2003: 104) although they are not binding, travel advisories still tend to have a negative impact on travel insurance rates and on the decisions of tour operations for marketing and promoting the destination, as well as on prospective visitors to the destination. One of the greatest challenges for tourism officials in developing countries is coping with the impact of travel advisories, which often require substantial spending in public relations and media management to stem the effects of adverse publicity. The United States has only recently removed a long-standing travel advisory against travel to Kenya even though Kenyan political leaders have highlighted the devastating consequences of the ban on the tourism industry. Developing nations are much more vulnerable to these advisories as they have little negotiating leverage with Western nations in restricting their imposition in spite of the negative publicity they generate, with the corresponding impact of sharp decreases in arrivals and the spectre of price discounting. Nevertheless, trends indicate that the demand for travel is such that Western tourists in particular are accommodating higher levels of risk in travel, and there are some consumers who will respond to heavy discounts in the aftermath of crisis at a destination (Beirman, 2003). This seems to support the WTO's assertion that tourism is resilient and manages to survive and to restore itself even after major conflicts and political upheavals because of a generally strong consumer demand and appetite for travel.

Environmental impacts

The primacy of environmental and social impact assessments as essential tools of tourism planning has been advocated as an approach in minimising the negative impacts of tourism (Archer and Cooper, 1994). Mass tourism requires careful attention to the management of the level and pace of growth in order to deliver maximum benefits to the economy. If it does not receive this, mass tourism inevitably leads to environmental degradation, and tensions between hosts and guests that diminish the quality of the tourism experience and may jeopardise the long-term sustainability of the country's tourism sector. Therefore the growth of tourism in developing nations requires tourism planners to take into account issues of carrying capacity from the incipient stage of tourism development and to attempt to ascertain the 'threshold levels' of development that the destination can sustain (Sharpley and Telfer, 2002). There is the risk that developing nations that depend on tourism are likely to downplay these negative impacts of the industry and not include them in terms of the calculation of the overall costs of tourism development to the destination. Nevertheless, these are costs to the destination that cannot be ignored since, once these negative impacts start to take place, developing nations may find it more expensive to redress the problems. Often, developing nations are reluctant to impose strict planning regulations on the scope of tourism development in terms of spatial location and adherence to environmental standards, as they may not be able to attract developers who may prefer to invest in countries where such rules are not strictly enforced (Weaver, 2001b).

According to Brohman (1996), among the problems associated with mass tourism are 'spatial polarisation, environmental destruction, cultural alienation and the loss of social control by local peoples'. Tourism development in developing nations is mostly concentrated on the 'pleasure peripheries' such as beach coasts and in areas of high biodiversity. These fragile environments and ecosystems mainly constitute the 'pull factor', that is the appeal of the destination for tourists. Much of the indictment against mass tourism is that there is less concern for the environment when compared with alternative forms such as ecotourism which claims to promote travel that conserves the environment. According to Weaver (2001b), large-scale tourism has contributed to the loss of coral reefs and mangroves, the deterioration of water quality and the 'appropriation of high-quality farmland'. Intensive large-scale hotel development along beach coastlines, poor waste management and disposal of effluent from these facilities as well as lax planning regulations and their enforcement are examples of poor management practices that exacerbate problems leading to negative environmental impacts of tourism. However, it has been argued that negative environmental impacts of tourism can be controlled and minimised if there is careful adherence to judicious planning and management of the tourism industry.

Weaver (2001a: 111) contends, however, that best practices in the planning for mass tourism include the concentration of large numbers of visitors in a small area in order to facilitate efficient site-protection and reduce the level of space that visitors will use. He notes that the 700,000 visitors to South Africa's Kruger National Park each year access only 4% of the land.

But there are also environmental benefits from mass tourism based on the revenue that is generated which may indirectly contribute to the conservation of more fragile areas. For example, in Kenya tourist revenues from the wildlife reserves have been used to conserve these resources (Archer and Cooper, 1994: 75). Weaver (2001a: 111) also points out that ecotourism benefits when mass tourists engage in soft ecotourism activities, thereby increasing earnings for the preservation and conservation of delicate ecosystems and heritage resources.

Sociocultural impacts

The influx of large numbers of relatively affluent Western tourists to developing nations has been attributed to changes in the traditions, values, language and family structures of more traditional societies (Hashimoto, 2002). Arguably, tourism is not the only factor contributing to cultural change in developing countries; however, the emulation of the behaviour, lifestyle and language of tourists by locals at the destinations, termed the *demonstration effect*, is seen as a direct outcome of the encounter between tourists and their hosts. The loss of identity and respect for local traditions and culture that may occur through tourist–host interaction cannot be compensated by possible positive outcomes of motivations of locals to work harder to acquire Western lifestyles. Mass tourist destinations in the developing world display a common pattern of negative sociocultural impact such as the denigration of local cultural traditions to satisfy the desire of tourists for 'authentic cultural performances, the commodification of traditional art and craft for sale to tourists, and the stereotyping of native peoples' (Hashimoto, 2002).

Among the notable sociocultural impacts of tourism in developing nations is the increase in crime and prostitution particularly within resort communities. But as Hashimoto (2002: 224) points out, sex tourism is an invaluable source of foreign exchange for many developing countries, as in the case of the Philippines where it has been the third largest source of foreign exchange. However, sex tourism also exacerbates other social problems of sexually transmitted diseases and illegal drugs that are costly for destinations to manage.

The extent of the distribution of the benefits of tourism in the local community may also be a major factor in the attitudes and responses of local hosts to tourist development. Where there are large communities of unemployed locals, problems of tourist harassment occur where visitors are unduly pestered for money. In Jamaica, visitor harassment has been identified as the main source of dissatisfaction with the holiday experience on the island (Daye, 1997). Locals are likely to be alienated from the industry where they see little benefit or improvements in their living standards in spite of successful tourism development. Their alienation is also likely to increase if improvements to infrastructure and civic amenities are located only in resort areas and do not extend to their own communities (Daye, 1997). It is therefore an imperative for governments of developing nations to review their tourism development strategies to determine whether the inequalities in the flow of tourism benefits into local communities may be fostering negative attitudes to the industry among residents (Daye, 1997). Brohman (1996) and Reid (2003) advocate that increased participation and integration of community members in planning for tourism may be able to redress negative social impacts such as host alienation and inequitable distribution of benefits that results from mass tourism. Figure 22.1, a cartoon from a Jamaican newspaper, illustrates the tensions that may arise between host communities and tourists. Here the strict policing against tourist

Figure 22.1   *Jamaica Observer* cartoon

Source: *The Jamaica Observer*, 8 August 1996
Here a local Jamaican young man waves cordially to a tourist couple he meets in the main tourist resort area of the island and receives an equally warm reception from them. However, some policemen on patrol misread this greeting and with an extreme show of force chastise the young man stating that he has failed to heed police warnings to leave tourists alone, that is, not to harass tourists. The response of the local police to the young man leaves the on-looking tourist couple in shock and confusion as to the police response to their engagement with the young man.

harassment is shown to inhibit the cordial relations between hosts and visitors. The dilemma for tourist–host encounters in this situation is characterised by the confusion over the norms of behaviour for social interaction and the need for the destination to protect tourists from exploitation. The irony is that local hosts also appear to be exploited in the enforcement of tourist policing measures.

Sustainable mass tourism

Mass tourism featuring large-scale resort facilities, enclave development and a lack of participation of local hosts in the tourism development are features mainly associated with the negative impacts of tourism (Brohman, 1996). All-inclusive hotels in particular, that offer vacations with all food, beverage, airport transfers, baggage handling, the use of facilities and even gratuities all for one price, have been charged with contributing to high leakages, the marginalisation of locals and host alienation (Duval, 2004). However, Poon (2004) argues that for Jamaica, the all-inclusive concept has helped the destination in terms of insulating tourists from crime and harassment on the streets and beaches. According to Poon, all-inclusive hotels make up a quarter of Jamaica's hotel stock and have recorded significantly higher occupancy levels than traditional hotels all year round. As seen in Figure 22.2, all-inclusive hotels are top performers and, as noted by Poon, tend to be more profitable than non all-inclusive hotels. The relatively high success of all-inclusive chains particularly in the Caribbean suggests that they are likely to remain a dominant form of hotel development in the region (Issa and Jayawardena, 2003).

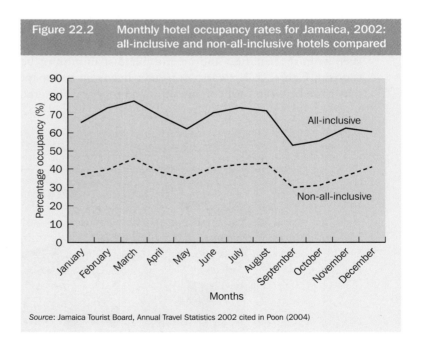

Figure 22.2   Monthly hotel occupancy rates for Jamaica, 2002: all-inclusive and non-all-inclusive hotels compared

Source: Jamaica Tourist Board, Annual Travel Statistics 2002 cited in Poon (2004)

Despite the positive performances of all-inclusive hotel development in destinations such as Jamaica, they are not viewed as 'sustainable' mainly because they are large scale. However, Weaver (2001b: 167) contends that mass tourism can be sustainable and goes even further to suggest that mega-resorts are in the best position to implement sustainable practices since their large-scale operations and income allow them to 'allocate significant resources specifically for environmental and social purposes'. Weaver (2001a) also points out that there are instances where so-called small-scale developments managed and run by local community members have been inappropriate and unsustainable. Case 22.4 is an example of small-scale tourism development that was not successful in producing an adequate level of benefits for the local operators or in satisfying the expectations of their guests.

Case 22.4   Culture clash as 'homestays' split villages

In January, a Thai ecotour operator, REST (Responsible Ecological Social Tours) received the 2002 World Legacy Awards by the US-based conservation group Conservation International and the National Geographic Travellers magazine. The project was honoured for its homestay programme in the Muslim community on the island of Koh Yao Noi near Phuket.

However, homestay programmes – as promoted by official tourism agencies, private operators and NGOs – have divided local communities. The homestay model, with strangers living under the same roof as homeowners, runs counter to local culture, argues scholar Srisak Vallibhotama. It has caused conflicts among local people, weakening communities. Conflicts arise because benefits from the programme were not evenly shared.

'It was unusual for the benefits to be enjoyed within a circle while others may receive nothing from homestay promotions,' he said. The Tourism Authority of Thailand (TAT) has promoted the programme without concern for the potential impact. 'Villages should build a guesthouse that which belongs to the community, rather than take individuals into their home. Villages would then take turns hosting visitors', he said.

To keep away tourists, angry villagers in Samut Songkhram cut down a lampu tree, a habitat for fireflies and a tourist highlight. People were forced to perform sacred ceremonies, sometimes more than once a day, in exchange for tourist money. Thai hosts tried too hard to please their guests, while guests, who were used to an urban lifestyle, could be too demanding.

Source: new frontiers, Vol. 9 , No. 1, Jan–Feb 2003 available at **www.twnside.org.sg/tour.htm**

It is therefore important to note that small-scale development is not always a criterion of success for tourism development. Gartner (2001) reports that in Ghana, even though there is a high level of local ownership of hotels, there are 'low levels of development and of ancillary economic development in the country'. Gartner also observes that the lack of international brand hotels and chains in Ghana has been a major factor in limiting the prospects of attracting to the country the numbers of international tourists and overseas investment capital required to make the local industry viable and even sustainable. This suggests that alternative forms of development may not necessarily be the most suitable development options for some tourist destinations. Weaver (2001a and 2001b) notes that there is a risk of alternative forms of tourism such as ecotourism mushrooming into mass tourism. This could lead to scenarios where ecotourism evolves into mass tourism, thereby making delicate ecosystems more vulnerable to denigration than would have probably been the case with mass tourism that is associated with highly developed and efficient waste-management systems and amenities geared to cater to high volume usage.

Sharpley (2002) argues that, although most mass tourism development leads to some environmental and sociocultural problems emanating from excessive or rapid tourism development, there are no clear development alternatives in achieving economic and social development for developing nations. He cites the case of the Dominican Republic, where the development of the budget all-inclusive market has resulted in the strengthening of backward linkages in both the agriculture and manufacturing sectors with tourism as the main source of foreign-exchange earnings for the country. Wheeller (1997) also questions the extent to which alternative forms of mass tourism are able to sustain viable levels of economic development for tourism and suggests that alternative forms of tourism development may not be the best option for those developing nations needing to maximise their investment in tourism.

Essentially, the decision to pursue mass tourism or alternative forms, or even both, depends on the unique features of the destination in terms of key variables such as tourism resources, competitive advantages and the role accorded tourism in national development. There are developing countries which have opted out of mass tourism and have been successful in their pursuit of alternative forms of tourism development. For example, Costa Rica has been identified as being a world-class ecotourism destination (Poon, 2004). Mauritius also has been highlighted by Poon as a destination that has successfully established a high-class tourist product based on a policy of 'selective tourism targeting quality rather than volume mass tourism'. However, the important point of emphasis is that alternative forms of tourism do not offer a panacea for developing nations to redress the negative impacts associated with mass tourism. As stated by Weaver (2001a), sustainable mass tourism is a possibility if judicious management, planning and enforcement are implemented by developing nations choosing this form of development as the engine of growth and economic well-being for their peoples. Packaged, large-scale mass tourism dominates the world demand for tourism in spite of trends towards independent, differentiated travel (Mowforth and Munt, 1998). As Sharpley (2002: 334) contends, mass tourism remains the most viable option for a successful tourism industry for many developing nations and offers the most likely means for these nations to improve the social and economic well-being of their people.

Conclusion

The level, scope and type of tourism development suitable for individual developing countries must be determined by their specific needs and goals and cannot be generally prescribed. The best option for tourism development therefore depends on the unique context of the destination. However, the extent to which tourism is integrated into the wider economy through backward and forward linkages is likely to determine the level of benefits that is gained by the wider community from the operations of the industry. Ultimately, the context of poverty and the need for economic growth and stability suggest that the success of tourism in developing nations will not only be measured by the number of tourism arrivals and *per capita* income derived from the industry. The industry's success in these countries will also be evaluated in terms of its contribution to the alleviation of poverty, the empowering of local communities and the equitable spread of benefits of tourism resulting in the improvement in the living standard and well-being of the people of developing countries that pursue tourism as the main engine of development.

Discussion questions

6   Critically review the advantages and disadvantages of the main development paradigms as approaches for the development of tourism in developing nations.

7   Why do developing nations seem to be less able to cope with the negative impacts of tourism than developed countries?

8   Discuss the view that mass tourism is one of the most viable forms of tourism development for destinations in the developing world.

Guided reading

Dahles, Heidi (1997) *Tourism, small entrepreneurs, and sustainable development: Cases from developing countries*. Department of Leisure Studies. Tilburg University–Atlas European Association for Tourism and Leisure Education, Tilbury.

Harrison, D. (1992) *Tourism and the Less Developed Countries*. Belhaven Press, London.

Sharpley, R. and Telfer, D.J. (2002) *Tourism and Development: Concepts and Issues*. Channel View Publications, Clevedon.

Recommended websites

Indigenous Tourism and Sustainable Development – The Case of Rio Blanco, Ecuador: **www.eduweb.com/schaller/Section3RB'sproject.html** .

New frontiers: **www.twnside.org.sg/tour.htm** .

ProPoor Tourism: **www.propoortourism.org.uk/Lesson_sharing.html** .

Third World Network: **www.twnside.org.sg/** .

World Social Forum: **www.wsf-tourism.org/home.asp** .

World Tourism Organization's *Tourism and Poverty Alleviation – Recommendations for Action*: **www.world-tourism.org/liberalization/poverty_alleviation.htm** .

Key words

All-inclusive hotels; alternative tourism; dependency theory; globalisation; impacts of tourism; mass tourism; modernisation theory.

Bibliography

Archer, B. and Cooper, C. (1994) The positive and negative impacts of tourism, in W.F. Theobald, (ed.) *Global Tourism*, 63–81. Butterworth Heinemann, Oxford.

Beirman, David (2003) *Restoring Tourism Destinations in Crisis: A Strategic Management Approach*. Allan & Unwin, Australia.

Britton, S. (1982) The political economy of tourism in the Third World. *Annals of Tourism Research*, 9(3), 331–358.

Brohman, J. (1996) New Directions in Tourism for Third World Development. *Annals of Tourism Research*, 23(1), 48–70.

Burns, P.M. (2004) Tourism Planning: A Third World? *Annals of Tourism Research*, 31(1), 24–43.

Clancy, M.J. (1998) Tourism and Development: Evidence from Mexico. *Annals of Tourism Research*, 26(1), 1–20.

Daye, M. (1997) Messages to Hosts: an evaluation of the effectiveness of tourism awareness programmes in promoting positive host attitudes towards tourism in Jamaica. University of Surrey. Unpublished MSc thesis.

Duval, D.T. (2004) *Tourism in the Caribbean: Trends, Development, Prospects*. Routledge, London and New York.

Gartner, W.C. (2001) Issues of sustainable development in a developing context, in S. Wahab and C. Cooper (eds) *Tourism in the Age of Globalisation*, 306–318. Routledge, London.

Harrison, D. (1992) *Tourism and the Less Developed Countries*. Belhaven Press, London.

Hashimoto, A. (2002) Tourism and Sociocultural Development Issues, in R. Sharpley and D.J. Telfer (eds) *Tourism and Development: Concepts and Issues*, 202–230. Channel View Publications, Clevedon.

Issa, J.J. and Jayawardena, C. (2003) The 'all-inclusive' concept in the Caribbean, *International Journal of Contemporary Hospitality Management*, 15(3), 167–171.

Khan, M. (1997) Tourism development and dependency theory: mass tourism vs. ecotourism. *Annals of Tourism Research*, 24(4), 988–991.

Lea, J. (1988) *Tourism and Development in the Third World*. Routledge, London and New York.

Madeley, J. (1999) *Foreign Exploits: Transnationals and Tourism*. CIR Reports & Briefings – Catholic Institute for International Relations, London.

Marfurt, E. (1997) Tourism and the Third World: Dream or Nightmare? in L. France (ed.) *The Earthscan Reader in Sustainable Tourism*, 172–175. Earthscan Publications Limited, UK.

Momsen, J.H. (2004) Post-colonial markets, in D.T. Duval (ed.) *Tourism in the Caribbean: Trends, Development, Prospects*, 273–286. Routledge, London and New York.

Mowforth, M. and Munt, I. (1998) *Tourism and Sustainability: Development and New Tourism in the Third World*. Routledge, London.

new frontiers, 'Burma Tourism Boycott to Escalate Following Crackdown'. *Third World Network* (online) Vol. 9, No. 3, May–June 2003. Available from **www.twnside.org.sg/tour.htm** (accessed 12 February 2004).

Poon, A. (2004) *Successful Tourism Destinations – Lessons from the Leaders*. Tourism Intelligence International, Bielefeld.

Reid, D.G. (2003) *Tourism, Globalization and Development*. Pluto Press, London.

Richter, L. (1992) Political instability and tourism in the Third World, in D. Harrison (ed.) *Tourism and the Less Developed Countries*, 35–46. John Wiley & Sons, Great Britain.

Scheyvens, R. (2002) *Tourism for Development: empowering communities*. Pearson Education Limited, Harlow.

Sharpley, R. (2002) Sustainability: a Barrier to Tourism Development, in R. Sharpley and D.J. Telfer (eds) *Tourism and Development: Concepts and Issues*, 319–337. Channel View Publications, Clevedon.

Sharpley, R. and Telfer, D.J. (2002) *Tourism and Development: Concepts and Issues*. Channel View Publications, Clevedon.

Telfer, D.J. (2002) The Evolution of Tourism and Development Theory, in R. Sharpley and D.J. Telfer (eds) *Tourism and Development: Concepts and Issues*, 35–78. Channel View Publications, Clevedon.

Wahab, S. and Cooper, C. (2004) *Tourism in the Age of Globalisation*. Routledge, London.

Weaver, D.B. (2001a) Ecotourism as Mass Tourism: Contradiction or Reality? *Cornell Hotel and Restaurant and Administration Quarterly*, 1 (April), 104–112.

Weaver, D.B. (2001b) Mass Tourism and Alternative Tourism in the Caribbean, in D. Harrison (ed.) *Tourism and the Less Developed World: Issues and Case Studies*, 161–174. CABI Publishing, New York.

Wheeller, B. (1997) Tourism's Troubled Times: Responsible Tourism is not the answer, in L. France (ed.) *The Earthscan Reader in Sustainable Tourism*, 61–67. Earthscan Publications Ltd, London.

World Tourism Organization (2002) *Tourism and Poverty Alleviation*. World Tourism Organization, Madrid.

World Tourism Organization (2003) *Tourism and Poverty Alleviation – Recommendations for Action*. World Tourism Organization, Madrid.

Chapter 23

The management of heritage and cultural tourism

George Goodall and John Beech, Coventry Business School

Learning outcomes

On completion of this chapter the reader should be able to:

- identify the subsectors of heritage and cultural tourism;

- evaluate heritage sites and their operation in the context of their effectiveness at presentation and interpretation;

- explain the management problems which arise from conflicting priorities such as contested space and preservation/access and how they can be addressed;

- explain the role of the voluntary sector and the management implications of volunteer staff;

- outline the increasing scope of 'heritage' and the emergence of vernacular, industrial and 'modern' heritage attractions.

Overview

This chapter focuses on heritage and culture as a sector of growing importance to tourism, particularly as modern development pressures have grown. Heritage and culture as tourism activities include visits to historic buildings and sites, museums and art galleries, viewing artefacts, attending performing arts, exploring natural history attractions and being exposed to other cultures. This presents a broad canvas of activities that are visited, and that have to be managed.

Heritage and culture are international in nature. This provides the starting point – the development of agreements at international and European levels to manage these assets. What is clear is that these agreements depend on national management, and the system operating in Britain will be considered. Heritage and culture, particularly when viewed by people who are not experts, have to be interpreted to them.

Developments over the past 50 years have shown that heritage and culture can be segmented. This has led to the growth of interest in the role played by technology, and views expressed as 'heritage that hurts'. What is clear is the need to accommodate the visitor at a particular location or activity. This can be achieved, but it requires appropriate funding, either through taxation or by gifts.

To enable a tourist to obtain the most from a visit, the importance of managing the asset is paramount. The scope of management is discussed in the context of the resource itself, finance, employees, and visitors. The significance of developing policy, goals and objectives, implementation, and monitoring are explored in the context of an integrated management activity.

The chapter includes a discussion of some of the dilemmas facing the heritage and culture sector of tourism, and concludes that heritage and culture, once lost, cannot be replaced by another original.

Introduction

Heritage and culture have been longstanding elements of tourism. It is evident from historical accounts that the rich members of European society engaged in travel for pleasure and culture. This travel included pilgrimages in the middle ages, and culminated in the Grand Tour during the seventeenth and eighteenth centuries when observations of galleries, museums, art, and music became important (Urry, 2002: 4). Mass tourism, including visiting the seaside, developed in the latter part of the nineteenth century and has continued to the present day. This type of tourism did not rely on the observation of heritage or culture as attractions, but on more natural phenomena including sun and water at coastal locations.

In discussing the role of heritage and culture in tourism, definitions are important. Heritage can be defined in terms of what is inherited by one generation from past generations. Culture can be defined in terms of shared norms, values, customs, artistic achievements held by a group of people at a certain time. What these two definitions indicate is that the combination of heritage and culture leads to considerations of human activity related to, and including, the built and natural environment, coupled with the way in which people have influenced and been influenced by their activities. These definitions have been expanded by Prentice (1993), Richards (1994), and Hughes (1996) to include visiting sites, attending performing arts and being exposed to other cultures.

Heritage and culture have been influenced by other disciplines. These include archaeology, anthropology and history. Archaeology involves the revelation of past human activity that has been lost for many years. The evidence of this activity has been buried for thousands of years, and can include human remains and artefacts which, when analysed, can help understand how civilisations operated. Civilisations depend on people, but humans have evolved over time. To trace the development of humans, the study of anthropology is important as it helps to indicate how humankind has changed in a physical sense. Did *homo sapiens* develop from apes? History relies in large measure on the written and spoken word. In many respects history converts spoken word into the written word to allow heritage and culture to become a study in their own right.

For many centuries individuals have collected artefacts. These often formed the purpose of undertaking the Grand Tour in Europe. Individuals often decided that, to keep their collections together, they would bequeath them to a public body or allow a public body to purchase them. The British Museum was started when Parliament approved the holding of a public lottery in 1753 to purchase the collections of Sir Hans Sloane and the Harleian manuscripts and provide for their housing. Other developments have taken place at a more local level where, in Dallas USA, for example, a public museum of art was created in 1903 (Scottish Museums Council, 1986). These two examples illustrate how heritage and culture have been maintained at public expense. Universities have maintained printed material for many years; for example The Book of Kells, dating from the ninth century, has been housed at Trinity College Dublin since the mid-seventeenth century (Meehan, 1994).

The development of heritage and culture in the twentieth century has seen a move from museum collections to the use of material *in situ*. This has been assisted by legislation that has sought to protect the best features of the built and natural environments and enable them to be available for future generations. Practice shows that three critical matters – management, finance and interpretation – have to be in place for a tourist to obtain an understanding of the significance of heritage and culture. The scope of these matters will be considered in this chapter.

International considerations

The development of international concern for heritage has been underpinned by voluntary organisations. The 1931 Athens Charter for the Restoration of Historic Monuments was typical of this approach, with the organisation becoming ICOMOS (the International Council on Monuments and Sites) in 1965. Similar developments took place with the formation in 1948 of IUCN (the International Union for Conservation of Nature and Natural Resources; in 1990 it shortened its full name to IUCN – The World Conservation Union). The role of the United Nations Educational, Scientific and Cultural Organization (UNESCO) in protecting heritage, culture and natural sites commenced in 1972 with the Convention Concerning the Protection of the World Cultural and Natural Heritage. This led to the designation of World Heritage Sites. The designation process is shown at Figure 23.1. At June 2004 there were 754 cultural and natural sites protected under the 1972 Convention. Protection does not mean that a World Heritage Site cannot be problematic, as Case 23.1 indicates.

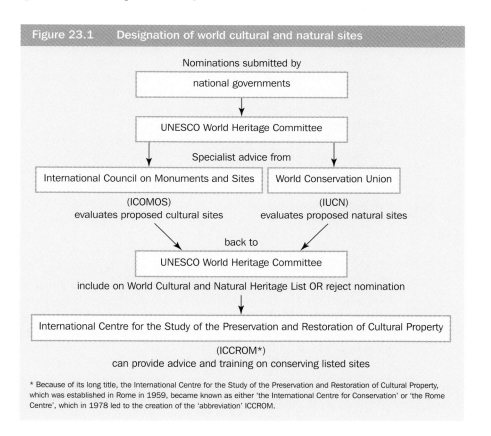

Figure 23.1 Designation of world cultural and natural sites

Nominations submitted by

national governments

UNESCO World Heritage Committee

Specialist advice from

International Council on Monuments and Sites | World Conservation Union

(ICOMOS)
evaluates proposed cultural sites

(IUCN)
evaluates proposed natural sites

back to

UNESCO World Heritage Committee

include on World Cultural and Natural Heritage List OR reject nomination

International Centre for the Study of the Preservation and Restoration of Cultural Property

(ICCROM*)
can provide advice and training on conserving listed sites

* Because of its long title, the International Centre for the Study of the Preservation and Restoration of Cultural Property, which was established in Rome in 1959, became known as either 'the International Centre for Conservation' or 'the Rome Centre', which in 1978 led to the creation of the 'abbreviation' ICCROM.

Discussion question

1 How does the World Heritage Committee assess the importance of culture when it decides to include a site on the World Cultural and Natural Heritage List?

Case 23.1   Machu Picchu, Peru

Machu Picchu is arguably Peru's most famous heritage site internationally. It received World Heritage status over twenty years ago, in 1983. It lies at the end of a major mountain ridge and was one of the Incas' largest cities. Following the collapse of the Inca empire, Andeans began to drift away from living on the tops of the mountains to living in the deep river valleys below. One result of this drift in population was that the exact site of Machu Picchu 'disappeared' from collective memory, and it was only 'rediscovered' by the US explorer Hiram in 1911. Since then, the vegetation which had completely reclaimed the site has been removed, and today the city can be seen in all its glory – a magnificent complex of walls, terraces and ramps made from large stone blocks which precisely interlock to an extent hardly imaginable from the perspective of today's sophisticated technology.

The position of Machu Picchu, as is so often the case with historic sites, does not lend itself well to today's transport infrastructure. With no road access from the outside world, a hardy few hike the Inca Trail from Cusco (at least a five-day hike), while most visitors travel by early morning train from Cusco along the river valley and then take buses to climb approximately 1000 feet to the site via a series of hair-pin bends on the purpose-built road, sending streams of dust across the valley. There is only a small hotel on site, so those unwilling to pay the premium prices charged or unable to find lodging at the hotel, which is normally fully-booked, have to take the last bus down at five o'clock to catch the last train back to Cusco, leaving the lucky few to savour sunset and sunrise in one of the world's most spectacular locations.

In late 1996 a scheme was announced to improve access to the site by building a cable car from Aguas Calientes, next to the station in the valley, to the main site. The visual impact this would have had on a site famous for both its staggering views and its sense of tranquillity, serenity and spirituality was enormous. A massive global campaign created so much protest that in 2001 the Peruvian government announced that the plans had been suspended indefinitely. It also announced that a master plan was to be developed for the coordination and supervision of all interventions at the site.

Discussion questions

2 If the cable-car project had gone ahead, what impact(s) do you think it would have had on visitation to Machu Picchu?

3 What do you see as a workable means of meeting the concerns of all stakeholders when proposing the introduction of radical change at a major heritage site such as this?

Sources: Various, including personal experience

There have been a number of other initiatives sponsored by the United Nations, including the 1992 Conference on Environment and Development (the 'Rio Summit') and the 2002 World Summit on Sustainable Development (the 'Johannesburg Summit'), which have raised the environmental and sustainability agendas. The effect of United Nations activity has led to a major impact on tourism, and in particular the development of short-break holidays to World Heritage Sites in Europe, for example, to Vienna, Prague, Rome and Florence.

European considerations

In the aftermath of war in Europe, the Council of Europe was founded in 1949 to 'achieve a greater unity between its members for the purpose of safeguarding and realising the ideals and principles which are their common heritage and facilitating their economic and social progress' (Council of Europe, 2001: 7). The Council of Europe is a governmental organisation that has developed a series of Conventions relating to cultural heritage, including:

- European Cultural Convention, 1954 (the Paris Convention);
- European Convention on the Protection of the Archaeological Heritage, 1969 (the London Convention);

- European Convention on Offences relating to Cultural Property, 1985 (the Delphi Convention);
- Convention for the Protection of the Architectural Heritage of Europe, 1985 (the Granada Convention);
- European Convention on the Protection of the Archaeological Heritage (revised), 1992 (the Malta Convention);
- European Landscape Convention, 2000 (the Florence Convention).

The Conventions are not legally binding until they are accepted by individual states. The Council has created a Cultural Heritage Committee to monitor the London, Granada and Malta Conventions through a Directorate of Culture and Cultural Heritage. Pickard (2001b: 1–11) discusses the role of the Council of Europe in the context of architectural and archaeological heritage and links to the work of ICOMOS, noting that some countries have reservations concerning these Conventions. What is evident is that there is a range of legal policy frameworks in member states, as the discussions by MacRory and Kirwan (2001) and Dambis (2001b) make clear. These legal and policy frameworks have led to the development of a range of management practices particularly where historic town centres are concerned. Negussie (2001) considers the case of Dublin, while Dambis (2001a) examines the historic centre of Riga. In both Dublin and Riga, culture and heritage are recognised as significant for the development of tourism within the local economy because of the money brought in by overseas visitors. Outside urban areas, the impact of the 1992 Rio Summit has led to the development of sustainable tourism policies that have been reviewed by Ellul (2000) for 21 countries in Europe. It is clear that a key policy component is the development of tourism master plans containing management schemes.

A second actor in Europe is the European Union. From its inception in 1957, it has not played a significant role in heritage and cultural matters except where there is a case for financing activities that create employment in tourism. The EU measures are part of the Environmental Action Programme, started in the 1970s and now in its Sixth Programme. One element of the programme has been the topic of nature and biodiversity. EU action has involved the production of the Directives on the Conservation of Wild Birds (79/409/EEC) and the Conservation of Natural Habitats and Wild Fauna and Flora (92/43/EEC). In management terms the EU directives make provision for the creation of Special Protection Areas that form part of the Natura 2000 Network.

The EU is also a source of funding for culture through its Structural Funds – the European Regional Development Fund (ERDF), the European Social Fund (ESF), the European Agricultural Guidance and Guarantee Fund (EAGGF) and the Financial Instrument for Fisheries Guidance (FIFG) – and various Programmes (Kaleidoscope, Ariane, and Raphael). This funding for 'culture is not only a means of maintaining or strengthening a distinctive identity, it is also a source of economic activity and new jobs' (EC, 1998). Some of the proposals are aimed at cultural tourism in Scotland, Sweden, Spain, and Portugal, particularly in rural areas, although financial contributions have been modest.

It is clear that the major player in heritage and cultural tourism at the European level is not the European Union but the Council of Europe, except for finance.

Discussion question

4 Discuss the problems of duplication of Council of Europe and European Union functions in heritage and culture.

National considerations

The review of international and European considerations has indicated that, for heritage and culture to be part of successful tourism, there must be legal, financial, and policy provisions in place in a nation state. This section will examine the heritage and culture elements with reference in particular to England and Wales.

Policy

The development of policy relating to heritage and culture can be divided into four main parts: ancient monuments, listed buildings, conservation areas and artefacts. As will be noted, the early concern was with the built environment; the consideration of the rural environment is a more recent phenomenon.

Ancient monuments

The policy of preserving very old structures developed in the nineteenth century. Writers such as John Ruskin and William Morris argued that to lose ancient buildings was not acceptable and that their retention was essential. The result was the creation of a voluntary organisation, the Society for the Protection of Ancient Buildings, and the production of its manifesto in 1877 setting out a conservation philosophy. The consequences of their activities led to the 1882 Ancient Monuments Protection Act, and the creation of a designated list of Scheduled Ancient Monuments (including Stonehenge). Since 1882 there have been a number of other Acts of Parliament that have strengthened public control over Scheduled Ancient Monuments, culminating in the legal recognition in 1979 that ancient monuments and archaeology can be inextricably linked (Act of Parliament, 1979).

The decision on which ancient monuments should be scheduled by a government minister has been dependent on appropriately qualified individuals who recommend particular monuments, buildings and areas that should be the subject of special protection (Mynors, 1999: 4). This approach has become formalised with the creation of such bodies as the Historic Buildings and Monuments Commission for England (English Heritage), Historic Scotland, the Ancient Monuments Board for Wales (Cadw[1]) and the Environment and Heritage Service in Northern Ireland. Case 23.2 reviews the way in which heritage and culture have been developed in Wales since 1999.

Case 23.2   Heritage and culture in Wales

The Ancient Monuments Board for Wales (Cadw) has provided advice to the Welsh Office (part of the UK Government) since 1984. Administrative control was transferred in 1999 to the National Assembly for Wales. The Cadw advice has dealt with conservation, presentation and promotion of the built heritage of Wales. It works in conjunction with the Royal Commission on the Ancient and Historical Monuments of Wales, the body responsible for recording the heritage of Wales.

In March 2003 the Minister for Environment in the National Assembly for Wales announced a review of the Historic Environment in Wales. However, during the review the administrative responsibility for Cadw and for the review itself were transferred to the Minister for Culture, Welsh Language and Sport. As part of these changes, a Cultural Forum, Cymru'n Creu, was formed. The outcome of the review was published in January 2004. It has resulted in minimal change to the operation of Cadw, although it would head up a sub-group of Cymru'n Creu to consider strategies and priorities for the historic environment. A longer-term development was the recognition that a 'Strategic Framework for the Historic Environment Records in Wales' would be produced to link the Royal Commission work closer to the Cultural Forum.

---

1 'Cadw' is a Welsh word which means 'to keep'; it is pronounced *KA-doo*.

However of equal significance was the recognition by the Minister that the safeguarding of the historic environment of Wales required the involvement of local government, the voluntary sector, and funding organisations (including the Heritage Lottery Fund). It is clear that the Cultural Forum is seen as the mechanism for linking the built environment with the language culture of Wales.

Source: Various

Listed buildings

Protection of buildings that were inhabited is a twentieth-century development in Britain, and stems from the introduction of town and country planning legislation. Since 1932 it has been possible to protect buildings of special architectural or historic interest from alteration or demolition without the consent of a local authority (Act of Parliament, 1932). The creation of lists of these buildings dates from 1947 (Act of Parliament, 1947) and required a Government Minister to produce these lists, based on advice from appropriately qualified people.

Currently there are three categories of listed building:

Grade I   buildings of exceptional interest, e.g. Buckingham Palace;

Grade II*   particularly important buildings of special interest, e.g. Birmingham Museum and Art Gallery;

Grade II   buildings of special interest, e.g. the BT Tower, which dominates the London skyline.

Control of alteration and demolition is exercised by local authorities through 1990 legislation (Act of Parliament, 1990). Local authorities and Government Ministers are advised by English Heritage (in England), or Cadw (in Wales) on all aspects of the processes.

Discussion question

5   National policy in Britain distinguishes between ancient monuments and listed buildings. In what ways could the system be simplified?

Conservation areas

The importance of the setting of an ancient monument or listed building is a recent development in England and Wales. This led to the introduction of 'conservation areas' in 1967. These are defined as 'areas of special architectural or historic interest, the character or appearance of which it is desirable to preserve or enhance' (Act of Parliament, 1990). Local authorities designate them without any control from central Government or the National Assembly. What is of significance is that these areas will often include areas of vegetation or parkland that are of equal importance to the appearance of the area. It is not a legal requirement that a conservation area contains listed buildings or ancient monuments, although many of them do include such buildings or monuments. One effect of conservation area designation has been the formation of 'amenity societies' (see Case 23.3).

Case 23.3   Village heritage – Hampton-in-Arden

Many villages in England and Wales have amenity societies with the object of maintaining the character of the village and its environs. Hampton-in-Arden, in the West Midlands, is such a village. Local residents formed an amenity society in 1968, at the same time that the village was designated as a conservation area. History has played an important part in Hampton-in-Arden. Mentioned in the Doomsday Book, the village has been owned by Kings of England. Pre-twentieth century history has been written up and

Case 23.3   Continued

published, but twentieth century changes had not been documented. The amenity society decided to collect and record village history since 1900 and to display its findings in the Hampton Heritage Centre that was created in 1992. The society has produced a range of publications including village walk leaflets, a book to commemorate the millennium (Bryant *et al.*, 2000) and a series of maps to illustrate the development of Hampton-in-Arden. Members of the amenity society, none of whom are professional heritage managers, produced all these. All these activities are undertaken on an annual subscription of £2 per member.

Source: Authors

Artefacts

The importance of moveable property to an understanding of heritage and culture should not be underestimated. The ability of wealthy citizens to have their portraits painted, or to collect a range of statues and manuscripts, was common throughout the world. During the nineteenth century, however, many of the owners of the artefacts decided that their collections should be made available for public benefit. This led to the creation of museums, art galleries and libraries. Some were owned by the state, others by local authorities, universities, and charities. An example is the Horniman Museum in London, developed from the collections of F.J. Horniman, a prominent tea trader – Horniman gifted the collections, the museum and the land it stood on to the people of London in 1901. Such generous gifts sometimes presented great difficulties for the recipients in terms of housing and presenting the gifted collections. For example, Sir William and Lady Burrell gifted over 9000 art works to the City of Glasgow in 1944, but it was not until 1983 that it was possible to open the display to the public in a specially designed building.

Over the past 50 years many museums and galleries have found it difficult to care for some 200 million individual artefacts and specimens (Carter *et al.*, 1999: 2). These are spread across over 2000 museums and art galleries in the United Kingdom, and absorbed £500 million of funding in 2000–01 (Re:source, 2001: 30). Many of the artefacts remain in country houses, and their owners produce guidebooks – a typical example being the National Trust Guide to Shugborough, Staffordshire (Robinson, 1989).

The UK National Lottery has given recent support to museums and galleries. This support is similar to that used to create the British Museum in 1753.

It is clear that for heritage and culture to be a component of tourism, the importance of a set of rules, backed by legal sanctions, should not be underestimated. Legal rules, however, depend on finance to enable heritage and culture to be discovered, collected and conserved. What is equally important is that experts are prepared to give time to supporting the legal activities of nations. The consequence is a vast collection of heritage and culture icons that need to be presented to tourists in such a way that their meaning and significance can be understood.

Interpretation

When tourists visit a site that has a heritage or culture attraction, they will ask questions. Answers, whether in verbal, written, or visual forms, will provide an interpretation of the site or activity. Much of the early work concerning interpretation at heritage and cultural sites derives from activities in United States National Parks. These activities have resulted in Freeman Tilden (1967: 8) developing a definition of interpretation, as

An educational activity which aims to reveal meanings and relationships through the use of original objects, by first-hand experience and by illustrative media, rather than simply to communicate factual information.

Tilden went on to outline six 'principles of interpretation' which can be summarised as four key messages regarding interpretation. Interpretation should:

- provoke a reaction from the visitor;
- relate to the personality or experience of the visitor;
- deal with all aspects of human knowledge;
- not be a dilution of interpretation to adults in the case of children.

Others have expanded Tilden's work. Lewis (1995: 26) has detailed interpretation from the perspective of the visitor. Goodey (1994) explored interpretative planning and provided specific advice. Roth (1998: 136) developed children's interpretation with a number of specific suggestions or 'tips', including establishing connection points with children's experiences through demonstrations, surprising information and anecdotes.

Underlying the whole question of interpretation is the need to develop an 'interpretation plan', based on a logical process. Binks *et al.* (1988: 6) suggested four key elements should form the basis of the plan:

- what to interpret, given labour costs and site constraints;
- choice of media, including leaflets, interpretation boards;
- visitor facilities, such as parking, toilets, shelter;
- management, dealing with staffing, finance and promotion.

They also noted that staff training, media updating and promotion should be included as part of the role of management. Management has the role of determining the type of interpretation, noted by Hall and McArthur (1998: 176) as verbal or non-verbal. Given the costs of using people as interpreters, many organisations fall back on non-verbal interpretation, such as signs and labels. Whether this approach can provide quality, and resulting consumer satisfaction, must be questionable, and certainly is unlikely to meet Tilden's definition of interpretation.

Discussion question

6 Discuss the relevance of Tilden's Principles of Interpretation in the twenty-first century.

What needs to be recognised is that there is no single model of interpretation that can be used in all situations. The basis of this statement will now be examined in relation to types of heritage and culture attractions, and organisations involved, particularly the National Trust.

Heritage and cultural attractions

There has been a substantial change in the nature of attractions from the nineteenth-century 'ancient monuments' approach, to a twenty-first-century approach that is moving into 'manufactured' heritage and culture. Whether this change of approach is best for heritage and culture has to be considered in the context that we are dealing with one of the growth areas of tourism (Poria *et al.*, 2003: 239).

In the United Kingdom, one of the largest organisations providing heritage and culture attractions is the National Trust. Attractions that it has preserved include buildings and monuments of historical importance, and coastlines. More recently it has diversified into acquiring important industrial sites and sites of social significance such as the Liverpool home of the McCartney family where The Beatles wrote many of their earlier songs.

The move by the National Trust into the acquisition of industrial properties has added a former Atomic Weapons Establishment site at Orford Ness, Suffolk, and the Quarry Bank Mill at Styal, Cheshire, to its collection. The significance of industrial attractions in their own right is typified in the Ironbridge Gorge, Shropshire, which includes a range of industrial processes such as china and tile manufacture (Blockley, 1999: 141–56).

There is little doubt that heritage in the form of buildings has changed over the past 100 years, in terms of what is now considered to be an attraction. Similarly culture has changed, as is often obvious from the contents of a particular building. It is suggested that heritage and culture attractions can be divided into three broad types: vernacular, industrial and modern heritage.

Vernacular heritage

The protection and preservation of buildings, designed over many centuries, comprises the earliest type. The habitable buildings were primarily residential, and were often designed by architects who are recognised today as being leaders in their time. This links to listed building criteria, where important factors include both architectural and historic interest. Many older buildings have been remodelled over time and are set in landscaped gardens (Robinson, 1989). Much of the architectural style has drawn on designs produced by the ancient Greeks and Romans. Many of the National Trust properties display a combination of these features, coupled with collections of artefacts. However not all buildings are of a grand scale. Many are small, and are representative of past ways of life, in particular in rural areas. These buildings, constructed of locally found materials, are more vernacular in nature than many of the 'grand houses', but do not attract many visitors.

Industrial heritage

This comprises three broad elements – the buildings used for the manufacture of products, the power sources used by the machinery in the factory and the means of transporting raw materials and finished products.

Textile mills powered by water typify early industrial heritage. An early example is the Arkwright Mill complex at Cromford, Derbyshire, that is being restored by a charity. This complex in the Derwent Valley was designated a World Heritage Site in 2001. The National Trust has acquired Quarry Bank Mill and is producing textiles for sale to visitors. Water power was replaced by coal to heat water to power beam-engines, with an example to be seen at Quarry Bank Mill.

Curiously, the move to protect and preserve industrial heritage in England is largely a recent phenomenon. Only during the 1990s has English Heritage established research and survey programmes to develop sound criteria for selection of industries and sites for conservation. Blockley (1999: 141–56) discusses the difficulties of preserving the Ironbridge Gorge and adapting it to become a tourist attraction.

Preserving transport heritage began in the 1950s, however, as the railways in particular were being drastically cut back. Adjacent to the Ironbridge site is the Severn Valley Railway. This particular railway was closed in 1963 and the first stretch was re-opened by enthusiasts in 1970. Although the driving force to re-open came from railway enthusiasts, the success of the reopened line has meant that the Severn Valley Railway has become a major tourist attraction, with railway enthusiasts now a minority of the visitors.

Modern heritage

It has to be remembered that many buildings and sites have been developed and redeveloped, often in the aftermath of war. Tilden observed that one element of interpretation was to provide a visitor with an emotional experience. Uzzell (1989: 33–47) discussed the interpretation of heritage and war and coined the phrase 'hot interpretation'. This phrase has been altered to become 'heritage that hurts' (Uzzell and Ballantyne, 1998: 152–71). What can also be recognised is that rewriting history in the light of new evidence can result in a villain becoming a hero. It is clear that with the passage of time, 'heritage that hurts' can become an important tourist attraction. Case 23.4 examines the importance to Guernsey of military fortifications as instruments of war, and their importance today as tourist attractions.

Case 23.4	Defending Guernsey

Guernsey has a long history of being defended against invasion from mainland Europe. The island had fortifications built between 1789 and 1815 to defend against attack from Napoleonic France. These fortifications were extended in Victorian times, and the larger ones continued in use until 1940. Invasion by German troops occurred in July 1940. Initially the Germans used the Napoleonic fortifications but added weapon locations and troop shelters, as occupation was part of the plan to invade Britain.

Guernsey formed an important part of Hitler's line of defence – The Atlantic Wall – and was to be an impregnable fortress in the form of an 'anchored battleship'. Building commenced with the German Army providing the main military manpower. Construction work was undertaken in part by the Organisation Todt, and was largely completed by autumn 1943. Guernsey was never retaken by the British and a German garrison remained until the surrender on 9 May 1945.

During 1945 and 1946 most of the fortifications and hardware were left in place, but made inoperable. However, the German fortifications contained vast quantities of metal. In 1948 the British Government implemented 'Operation Coast Line Clean-up' which resulted in the recovery of usable metal from the fortifications, the burial of shallow fortifications and their landscaping.

Attitudes have changed, and the States of Guernsey now has a policy of restoring and interpreting many of the fortifications on the island. Coupled with the physical restoration and interpretation is access to the contemporary records held in the Guernsey archives. Of equal importance has been the activity of volunteer members of the Channel Islands Occupation Society in undertaking research since 1973. The result of these activities means that military fortifications have become an important element of tourism on Guernsey.

Sources: Authors and Gavey (2001)

In 1996, Tunbridge and Ashworth had drawn attention to a previously neglected area of heritage deserving of research attention, which they called 'dissonant heritage'. They recognised that, since 'heritage' is a construct based on a contemporary interpretation of 'history', 'heritage' must be dissonant as it derives from a range of interpretations, many of which may be in conflict. An inevitable series of questions is:

- Whose heritage is being interpreted?
- By whom?
- For what purpose?
- Who is thereby disinherited? (Tunbridge and Ashworth, 1996).

Interest in 'dissonant heritage' as a tourism resource has resulted in what has been termed 'dark tourism' (Foley and Lennon, 1997) or 'thanatourism' (Dann and Seaton, 2001). Sites of large-scale tourist visitation now include, for example, concentration camps (Beech, 2000), where the nature of the dissonance is obvious, and slavery heritage displays (Beech, 2001), where the dissonance is less obvious to visitors – many do not identify with what is being presented, or do not wish to identify with what is being presented. In such situations a helpful concept is that of 'contested space' – various stakeholders have strongly-held and divergent views on whose heritage is being presented, and as a result of different interpretations of the history of a particular site they may seek different, and possibly incompatible, interpretations. An interesting example of 'contested space' can be found at prisons such as Freemantle, Western Australia, and Robben Island, South Africa, where visitors include former inmates and former guards as well as the merely curious.

Modern heritage also includes recently constructed buildings used for a variety of purposes. In Britain this is due to the recognition of the importance of architecture. The recently built cathedrals in Coventry and Liverpool are examples that, in a religious context, attract large numbers of tourists. An important twentieth-century development has been the opening of various museums (often based in old buildings) that illustrate technological developments associated with warfare. An example is Bletchley Park, where the Enigma code was broken during the Second World War, and which now houses the National Codes Centre. In a curious way technological developments are not associated normally with 'heritage that hurts', unless the interpretation makes the link for the visitor.

Considerations of culture raise a range of different questions. These include considerations of the scope of culture. We take the view that culture is related to people and what they do, rather than to the buildings or structures they operate from. The European Commission (1998: 6) posed the question:

> Are European cultural networks which develop around a theme or form of expression (television, music, cinema etc.) not the modern heirs of those great movements transcending linguistic and administrative barriers?

It went on to observe:

> . . . the continent is also a patchwork of enduring and highly varied local cultures. Many regions still have rich dialects, which are expressed mainly in spoken culture; many villages continue original festive traditions which channel the creativity and energy of a substantial part of the population.

To foster culture, the European Commission (1998) has supported financially a range of activities, including:

- A Celtic Film Festival, aimed at safeguarding the Celtic language and culture in Spain, France, Ireland and the United Kingdom;
- 'A home for cultural diversity' in Cosenza, Calabria, Italy, aimed at producing a melting pot of cultures, languages and religious faiths;
- 'First steps to becoming an Artist', to enable young artists develop their ideas, turn them into cultural products and gain a foothold in the professional art world.

These activities, however, do not appear to recognise the importance of recent migrants into Europe. In Britain the importance of people from the Indian subcontinent has been recognised, particularly in museums and galleries. This has to be seen in the context of the role of education in museums too (Hooper-Greenhill, 1997).

It is clear that heritage and cultural attractions form an important element in tourism. However, visits to a particular heritage or cultural site will be for a short duration, often as an optional day trip within a packaged holiday. This pattern of day trips is evident from the Re:source (2001: 78–81) examination of visitors to museums and galleries, the majority of whom live in close proximity to the site. Whether tourists to heritage or cultural locations spend a long or short time on a visit will depend on a range of interrelated factors. These include the interest of the visitor in the particular site or activity and the success of a marketing programme in drawing attention to what a site may have to offer. Some aspects may be controllable by a site, and it is these that will now be considered in the context of management.

Heritage and cultural management

Management in the context of heritage and culture includes a number of key components, such as the resource itself, visitor access to the resource and the reputation of the organisation responsible for the resource. It has to be recognised that heritage and culture operate within an ever-changing environment that is outside the control of individual bodies responsible for a particular site. Hall and McArthur (1998: 8–11) show that changes in the operating environment require changes to how management is developed. They suggest that management should be 'integrated', and incorporate concepts of 'quality', but should be capable of anticipating the future in a strategic manner.

Management can be seen to have concerns in four areas – the resource itself, finance, visitors and employees. However, these concerns have to be translated into a workable format – a management plan. This plan should be based on the Patrick Geddes 'traditional planning model' of survey, analysis and plan (Uzzell, 1998: 235). The plan element should have three components:

- the development of policy;
- the production of goals and objectives;
- the actions required for implementation.

all of which are time-related, and should include the requirement for monitoring and evaluation to enable continuous review to take place.

Cossons (1994) provides a basic outline of the format of what is described as a 'corporate plan'. He suggests that its preparation should be based upon a determination of the 'culture' of the organisation as expressed in a vision of its purpose. This can be achieved through a 'mission statement'. From this can be developed a series of objectives and priorities that will deal with 'programme areas', including marketing and visitor services. Underpinning the 'programme areas' is the 'financial plan'. What is fundamental throughout the process is the need to review past performance. Implicit in this model is the need to recognise the importance of quality, which Hall and McArthur (1998) consider to be fundamental to a successful management plan.

However, the management of an organisation needs to consider the wider context, which often requires an assessment of trends at international and national levels. These trends should include the legal, institutional and financial frameworks that affect a heritage or cultural organisation. In a British context Taylor (1994) provides a review of the countryside, while Hatton (1994), in discussing museums, recognises that change brings about uncertainty of a plan's outcome. While both of these reviews are dated, their messages should influence how a particular facility has to be managed. Botchway *et al.* (2002: 155–74) have recognised that any management model has to be able to respond to a turbulent operating environment, and that includes tourism.

The acceptance that an organisation requires an effective management structure led the National Trust, for example, to review its governance, and adopt a new structure in 2003, which recognises a reporting line and an advice line in the way it undertakes its operations. The changes proposed for the National Trust depended on legal amendments being approved.

It is clear that any heritage and cultural organisation has to be managed by introducing a 'management plan' or 'corporate plan', to use Cossons' (1994) phrase. This plan should include statements of policy, goals, objectives and implementation, and should reflect the needs of staff (both paid and volunteers), visitors and finance. Any management plan depends on human resources to produce it, manage its implementation and monitor it until such time as it needs to be reviewed. An example of site management advice can be found in ICOMOS (2002). The production of a satisfactory visit to a site is, in large measure, linked to how the staff interact with the customer. This aspect of heritage and culture sites will now be considered.

Discussion question

7　Evaluate the key elements of a 'visitor management plan'.

Staff and training

Heritage and culture locations will require staff to manage activity at the site, particularly if visitors are to be welcomed. The staff will be full-time, part-time or volunteers, or a combination of all three. Full-time and part-time staff will normally be paid, and will operate within the 'programme areas' noted by Cossons (1994). This group of staff will have to demonstrate a variety of skills that have to be related to a specific programme and site characteristics. It is suggested, for example, that different 'conservation' skills will be required in a national park, a historic house or an art gallery. Specialists, through prior training, will be essential at any site. But some staff requirements may not require site-specific skills, including accountants, marketers and managers. The importance of external events, such as changes in legislation, can mean that full-time or part-time staff may need training in other skills, such as in first aid.

The requirement to train or re-train staff will be an ongoing concern that needs to be reflected in the management plan. Training can be provided 'in-house' or it can be 'bought-in'. Whichever model is to be adopted will require consideration, and it can be undertaken as part of a risk-assessment strategy. Such a strategy will have serious consequences for sites where the public are admitted. All site owners and operators must exercise a duty of care to both staff and visitors. A further influence on training requirements can be stipulated as part of insurance requirements. For example, training will be required to minimise the theft of money or moveable property, especially when the latter includes valuable and/or irreplaceable artefacts.

It is common practice for many heritage and culture sites to use volunteers for certain activities. Yet a volunteer will require training which must be to the same standard as that provided for paid staff. Volunteers may be bringing to an organisation a range of skills, some of which can be used in managing the facility. The National Trust, for example, relies heavily on volunteers from among its members, to support the on-site activities of its paid staff. (See also Chapter 8.)

Irrespective of whether staff at a heritage or culture site are full-time, part-time or volunteers, it is clear that their skills and training have to be seen as long-term investments. How English Heritage approached one element of staff training is outlined by Griffin (1994: 256–7). Millar (1991, 1994: 270–9) indicates that a volunteer can be the future of effective management in the heritage and cultural industries. Case 23.3 illustrated the key role played by volunteers and a volunteer organisation in collecting, conserving and presenting heritage and culture. Case 23.5 gives an example of a small business in the heritage tourism sector, a sector that is typified by businesses with few employees.

Discussion question

8　What are the limitations to volunteers playing a greater role in site management?

Case 23.5 Habsburg Heritage

The Habsburg Empire ceased to exist in 1918. Until that point the dual monarchy, its western half ruled from Vienna and its eastern half ruled from Budapest, had covered much of central and eastern Europe, and its successor states include today's Austria, Bosnia Herzegovina, Croatia, the Czech Republic, Hungary, Slovakia and Slovenia plus parts of Italy, Poland, Romania and the Ukraine. The peoples of these modern states see little in their heritage that derives from what they see as their occupation until 1918 – it is hard to imagine an Italian from Trieste rushing to point out that it was an Austrian city from 1282 to 1918, for example – and only Austria sees any sense of direct continuity with its Habsburg past, so it might seem strange to set up as a tour operator and travel agent called 'Habsburg Heritage'.

Robert Avery did exactly that in 1989. For the previous eighteen years he had worked for the Anglo-Austrian Society and the Anglo-Austrian Music Society, two London-based cultural charities. Each charity is dedicated to promoting cultural links between Austria and the UK. Their membership includes both British people who enjoy Austrian culture and émigré Austrians seeking to reaffirm their cultural links with their cultural home. His work for the two charities focused on arranging visits for individuals and groups from the UK to Austria, and over the years he built up an extensive network of contacts in the travel trade in both countries.

Since setting up his own business, Robert has grown it considerably. In some respects his customers remain essentially the same segment – UK residents seeking to visit Austria for music and drama purposes. His range of destinations has grown considerably – as well as Austrian (by today's definition) destinations, such as Vienna and Salzburg, and former Habsburg cultural centres, such as Prague and Budapest, he also takes tours to places like Dresden and Weimar in Germany, never within the Habsburg Empire but with a considerable shared cultural heritage. Robert adds considerable value by personally guiding each tour, typically to a festival, and providing a series of informal talks to participants. Tours now depart from Manchester as well as London. Although he is almost perpetually on the move with his clients, Habsburg Heritage remains a small business – Robert's wife Jane, with occasional secretarial support, runs the administration of the Avery Empire from their small London office.

The mission statement of Habsburg Heritage is having 'the aim of bringing the culture of central Europe to the British public through a carefully selected programme of visits to the cities and countryside of the region and to smaller music festivals'.

Source: Personal contact and company website, **www.habsburg.co.uk**

Discussion questions

9   Could Habsburg Heritage maintain the quality of its service to its customers if it grew in scale and employed other staff?

10 Is 'Habsburg Heritage' a historically accurate name for Robert Avery's business? Does it matter?

11 In what ways might 'Habsburg' be developed as a brand?

Funding

Whatever the organisation, it is clear that a key consideration must be how funding is obtained and used to present heritage and culture to the tourist. This will be explored in this section.

In Britain, as in most countries, there are a variety of funding regimes in operation. The nature of the funding will depend on the perceived importance of the heritage or culture involved. Broadly there are four types of funding sources available: central government, local government, charities and other sources.

Central government

This type of funding will be for key locations, and may be direct to an organisation (for example the British Museum), or indirect through a secondary source (for example, to support University Museums as part of an educational grant). Money from the European Union can be included under this heading when provided through, for example, the European Regional Development Fund.

Local government

This type of funding will involve the use of money from central government, or that collected from the inhabitants of a local authority area, and used for museums or art galleries. National Parks are also funded in this manner.

Charities

Money will come from historic investments provided by an individual. Examples of charities include the Welcome Trust and the Gulbenkian Foundation, which have both supported heritage and cultural activities.

Other sources

Many individuals leave money to heritage and culture as legacies. The National Trust, for example, benefits from these individual gifts. Similarly trading companies in Britain make donations to charities, which may include heritage and cultural organisations.

The National Lottery, through the Heritage Lottery Fund, has supplemented these funding sources in Britain in recent years. Over the period since 1995 there has been a widening of the definition of 'heritage'. It can now include oral history and traditions based on language; small grants being made to collect recipes. For many smaller organisations, however, a key decision by the Heritage Lottery Fund was to reduce the 1:1 matched funding requirement when a grant was awarded to 10% on grants between £50,000 and £1 million, and 25% for amounts above that.

What has become apparent over the period since 1990 is the necessity to obtain funding from a combination of sources. Stonehenge, a scheduled ancient monument in the care of English Heritage, received a Heritage Lottery Fund grant of some £23 million to improve visitor conditions at the site. Birmingham City Council received £13.5 million to refurbish Birmingham Town Hall. The National Trust acquires property through grants and public subscription. All capital-funded projects will have an ongoing requirement for maintaining the asset, which may be funded in part by charging for admission.

It is clear that funding for heritage and culture depends upon complex arrangements. Volunteers play an important role by undertaking work or giving time without any direct financial contribution. A recent development to support heritage and culture has been the creation of an organisation, Heritage Link, that has the aim of coordinating the activities of the voluntary sector and of improving the effectiveness of that sector in lobbying central government.

Many issues associated with heritage and culture in Britain have benefited in recent years from television exposure. Channel 4 developed the 'Time Team' television series that has concentrated on archaeology, and has revealed many important finds that have led to increases in tourists. The BBC has produced the 'Restoration' series to make cases for bringing back poorly maintained buildings to their original states. What both of these television series have demonstrated is that, if we wish to maintain and preserve heritage and culture, ever larger sums of money will be required. This has been recognised in the Re:source report (2001: 10) as being a 'serious resources deficit'.

Discussion

Heritage and culture attract many visitors. How many visitors are attracted is unclear because of a lack of comparable statistics (Allin, 2000). While the European Union is seeking to resolve the problem, Hewison (2003) has noted that the quantitative data that has been collected has failed to provide any useful information on, for example, visitor numbers. The cause of this is due to differing definitions of heritage and culture. It is considered that this difficulty will grow in the United Kingdom with four sets of statistics now being produced (for England, Scotland, Wales and Northern Ireland) as a consequence of devolution.

If the statistical base for knowing how many tourists visit heritage and culture locations is a matter of uncertainty, an equally important cause could be the plethora of legal definitions. The World Heritage Site designation process is based on an assessment of built and natural environment provided by volunteer experts. If there are any cultural links underpinning the designation, it is considered that these will be accidental. Similar problems occur in Europe, where the Council of Europe has developed definitions of heritage in the 1985 Granada Convention (for architecture) and the 1992 Malta Convention (for archaeology, that replaced a 1969 Convention on the same topic). Pickard (2001b: 5) makes it clear that practice in individual countries continues to vary, due in large measure to the differing legal systems. The consequences of these legal differences make it difficult to implement wide-ranging protective conventions in Europe. Whether the heritage and culture definitions and legal differences make it harder to preserve buildings and artefacts should not be a major concern as the key point is that most countries have legal mechanisms in place that afford 'protection' to heritage and cultural assets. What is significant is the ability of the individual citizen to use the law to produce action by a state to preserve its heritage and culture.

Over the past century the legal protection afforded to heritage and culture has been based on a combination of administrative structures and individual professional expertise. In most European countries the administrative structure of government has provided the basis for recognising what is important. This is typified by the British system of scheduled ancient monuments and listed buildings. More recent developments have seen the growth of organisations that implement many aspects of government policy by concentrating professional expertise. These organisations are often divorced from the policy making exercised by government, as Case 23.2 demonstrates. The decision to divorce policy making from implementation of policy (including the financing of work to an asset) does result in longer decision taking. This can be seen in two ways. First, there is a need to negotiate with individual owners on the detail of what works may be required to enable public access to be maintained. Second, there is the process of securing approval through a town and country planning system for the work that is necessary. The combination of these two elements of the decision-making process leads to delay, and many different interpretations of what may be required. It is doubtful whether this type of complex decision-making process is beneficial to heritage and culture, particularly where activities depend on attracting tourists, as the tourist may not wish to visit a site that is not maintained to a high standard. However, a slow decision-making process can prevent unsuitable work being undertaken that will alter the original significance and purpose of heritage and culture.

The basis of heritage and culture requires the acceptance of a philosophy of conservation. What can also be of importance is the realisation that a conservation philosophy cannot remain the same over time. While William Morris, in the nineteenth century, developed a conservation philosophy for uninhabited ancient monuments, this has been diluted by the acceptance that new development may destroy the 'ancient'. The consequence has been the acceptance that recording culture and heritage may be the only way of making certain that some information is kept for future generations. Today this approach begs the question of who should decide what to keep and what to destroy. In Britain this decision is taken by non-specialists (councillors or Ministers) advised by specialists. With this system in operation, the views of the owners may be minimised in the interest of an ill-defined 'public good'. Conversely the benefits of conserving heritage and culture for the 'public good' can be ignored because of a greater perceived need to provide something new. This dilemma can be observed at Stonehenge, where the solution to a traffic problem could result in irreparable damage to the area surrounding the monument itself. (See **www.savestonehenge.org.uk/homepage.html** for details of the protest campaign.)

Many of the conflicts surrounding tourist accessibility can be resolved through the production of a management plan. The scale of a management plan is, in large measure, dictated by its purpose. The early British legislation (Act of Parliament, 1882) incorporated a scheme for the maintenance of ancient monuments and their management for the benefit of the nation. Similar schemes exist for the management of the National Trust and the properties that it owns (Act of Parliament, 1971). Both of these examples incorporate policy considerations. What has also become clear is that management plans incorporate many international ideas and changes in social patterns of demand by visitors.

One clear message is that the majority of management plans have to be site-specific. They will reflect what a particular location has to offer, changes in social practices and the needs of tourists. Tourism has generated the requirement for a management plan to ensure that a quality product exists (Hall and McArthur, 1998: 9–12). This broader site concern enables a tailored solution to be devised, including perhaps the inclusion of an assessment of visitor capacity. The National Trust (Act of Parliament, 1907) has been able to charge for admission to its sites, and has also introduced timed admission at a growing number of locations (for example, Chartwell, the home of Sir Winston Churchill, operates this system). Individual management plans will need to follow similar structural forms to those outlined by Cossons (1994: 12–20), but should recognise that tourists do cause damage to what they are visiting. All management plans should seek to ensure that the tourist is being offered a quality product (Hall and McArthur, 1998: 9–12). Such plans should be both comprehensive and integrated to reflect a wider spectrum of concerns and interests that will affect a particular location.

Damage is a continuing problem for heritage and culture locations, whether due to deliberate activities or natural causes. Repairs cost considerable sums of money, particularly if the aim of repairs is to replicate what has been lost. A major debate in Britain has been whether to charge tourists for admission to all sites. Charging for admission to certain nationally funded sites has been removed in recent years, with a large increase in visitor numbers (Martin, 2003). However, many sites are not funded by the state, including National Trust properties, yet they attract increasing numbers of tourists. Money is not only required for maintenance, but also for staff and marketing of a site. A visit to a tourist information centre will reveal significant quantities of marketing literature available to attract tourists. While it is possible to have such material sponsored, the site management will have to find a sponsor and persuade it to support the particular site or sites. Caution over likely visitor numbers, particularly where a charge for admission is made, is essential, as too many 'new' attractions fail because of over-optimistic visitor and revenue projections.

Discussion question

12   Discuss the case for charging tourists to visit a heritage or culture site.

Whether a tourist visits a heritage or culture attraction, the probability will be that there is little knowledge of what to expect on a site. It is for this reason that interpretation has become an essential element of heritage and culture tourism. Whatever the reasons for making a visit, there will be a need for some form of interpretation. Three main forms of interpretation can be isolated – passive, active, and inter-active – with the latter two relying on human presence at the site. The 'better' locations will realise that a 'quality' visit can be achieved only if interpretation has recognised the benefits of Tilden's 'principle of interpretation'. Many locations recognise that people are expensive and have moved into using modern technology. This brings problems particularly if the technology fails. Tourists passing on the negative message that major activities were not working because of 'equipment failure' are not ideal for ensuring a quality visit. Nevertheless, it is clear that allowing visitors to handle objects does have benefits in encouraging personal interpretation.

It has become clear that heritage and cultural tourism have developed significantly over the past 50 years and have seen a rise in visitor numbers. Nevertheless, it has been argued by Hewison (1987) that the heritage industry presents an obsession with the past rather than facing the future, and is replacing 'real' industry that is producing goods. This is certainly the case when an industrial unit which is not economically viable is re-opened as a 'living museum', a fate associated with many museums of mining. While there is some merit in Hewison's view, heritage and culture do rely on the development of management practices taken from industry. They also rely on education, in the form of life-long learning, to allow visitors to use what exists to enhance their knowledge and to capitalise on the use of non-work time.

> ### Discussion question
>
> 13 What is the case, if any, for removing state funding of heritage and culture?

Conclusion

Heritage and cultural tourism are recognised as one element of the business of tourism. This business, like any other, has to be managed so that the visitor can appreciate how a country, a specific location or an artefact fit into the broader search for human understanding. Humans are destructive by nature in the sense that they discard the old in favour of something new. Heritage and culture rely on conserving the old so that future generations can understand how the past has influenced the present. The achievement of conserving the past, yet encouraging tourists, has been based on the adaptation of a range of management principles to this sector. Management practices should be seen as encouraging integration of activities that acknowledge the importance of the tourist, but also the views of the population who are not tourists.

One of the major debates has revolved around whether the tourist should pay to visit heritage and cultural activities. This will depend on a range of considerations including ownership of the site, the financial support available and the importance of interpretation. The creation of a quality experience for tourists can be helped by a comprehensive management plan. What is becoming clearer is the educational role played by heritage and culture. Looking has to be supplemented by active interpretation as part of a visit. It is clear that the growth in the number of heritage and cultural tourists will have a major impact on the scale of this element of tourism.

Discussion question

14 What factors do you think contribute to the qualities of a tourist visit?

Guided reading

Heritage and culture are part of the extensive literature that deals with archaeology, architecture, anthropology and history. The management aspects are explored by Hall and McArthur (1998) in particular. Ashworth and Howard (1999) cover the European context, while reviews of management and legal matters can be found in Pickard (2001a, 2001b). Harrison (1994), while becoming dated, contains some valuable case studies on the scope of heritage management.

No consideration of interpretation should ignore Tilden (1967), nor the conference papers of Uzzell (1989). More recent work in the context of museums (Hooper-Greenhill, 1997) provides material to support Tilden's interpretation principles. Runyard (1994) deals with the attraction of visitors in the context of museum marketing.

There are many journals that deal with management and marketing that can be applied to heritage and culture. Specific international perspectives can be found in the *International Journal of Heritage Studies*, the *Journal of Heritage Tourism* and *Annals of Tourism Research*. *Cultural Trends* provides articles from a British perspective on a broad range of topics.

No reading list on this subject would be complete without reference to Hewison (1987) and his polemic on the heritage industry. While this is now dated, it does discuss a range of problems associated with heritage and culture.

Recommended websites

UNESCO World Heritage Centre: **whc.unesco.org/** .

International Council on Monuments and Sites: **www.icomos.org/ICOMOS_Main_Page.html** .

IUCN: **www.iucn.org/** .

ICCROM: **www.iccrom.org/** .

Council of Europe Heritage website: **www.coe.int/T/E/Cultural_Co-operation/Heritage/** .

Council of Europe Coventions website: **conventions.coe.int/** .

English Heritage: **www.english-heritage.org.uk/default.asp** .

Cadw: **www.cadw.wales.gov.uk/** .

Historic Scotland: **www.historic-scotland.gov.uk/** .

Environment and Heritage Service in Northern Ireland: **www.ehsni.gov.uk/** .

Dúchas (Republic of Ireland): **www.heritagedata.ie/en/index.html** .

John Beech's Travel and Tourism Information Gateway: **www.stile.coventry.ac.uk/cbs/staff/beech/tourism/index.htm** (click on Heritage).

BBC Restoration: **www.bbc.co.uk/history/programmes/restoration/** .

Channel 4 Time Team: **www.channel4.com/history/timeteam/** .

Cultural Trends: **www.tandf.co.uk/journals/titles/09548963.asp** .

International Journal of Heritage Studies: **www.tandf.co.uk/journals/titles/13527258.asp** .

Journal of Heritage Tourism: **www.irs.aber.ac.uk/bgg/jht.htm** .

Buchenwald Memorial Foundation: **www.buchenwald.de/index_en.html** .

Fremantle Prison: **www.fremantleprison.com.au/** .

Robben Island: **www.robben-island.org.za/** .

Key words

Artefact; culture; designation; heritage; history; interpretation.

Bibliography

Act of Parliament (1882) Ancient Monuments Protection Act. London.

Act of Parliament (1907) National Trust Act. London.

Act of Parliament (1932) Town and Country Planning Act. London.

Act of Parliament (1947) Town and Country Planning Act. London.

Act of Parliament (1971) National Trust Act. London.

Act of Parliament (1979) Ancient Monuments and Archaeological Areas Act. London.

Act of Parliament (1990) Planning (Listed Buildings and Conservation Areas) Act. London.

Allin, P. (2000) The Development of Comparable European Cultural Statistics, *Cultural Trends*, 37, 65–75. Policy Studies Institute, London.

Ashworth, G. and Howard, P. (1999) *European Heritage Planning and Management*. Intellect, Exeter.

Beech, J. (2000) The enigma of holocaust sites as tourist attractions – the case of Buchenwald, *Managing Leisure*, vol. 5, no. 1, 29–41.

Beech, J.G. (2001) The Marketing of Slavery Heritage in the United Kingdom, *International Journal of Hospitality and Tourism Administration*, vol. 2, no. 3/4, 85–106.

Binks, G., Dyke, J. and Dagnall, P. (1988) *Visitors Welcome: a manual on the presentation and interpretation of archaeological excavations*. HMSO, London.

Blockley, M. (1999) Preservation, Restoration and Presentation of the Industrial Heritage: A Case Study of the Ironbridge Gorge, in G. Chitty and D. Baker (eds), 141–156, *op. cit.*

Botchway, Q., Goodall, G.R., Noon, D.M. and Lemon, M. (2002) Emergence based Local Economic Development Model: a way forward in responding to turbulent operating conditions, *Entrepreneurship & Regional Development*, 14, 155–174.

Bryant, M., Parker, R. and Smith, H. (eds) (2000) *Hampton-in-Arden at the Millennium*. Brewin Books, Studley.

Carter, S., Hurst, B., Kerr, R.H., Taylor, E. and Winsor, P. (1999) Museum Focus, *Facts and Figures on Museums in the UK*, Issue 2. Museums and Galleries Commission, London.

Chitty, G. and Baker, D. (eds) (1999) *Managing Historic Sites and Buildings: Reconciling presentation and preservation*. Routledge, London.

Cossons, N. (1994) Designing and implementing corporate plans, in R. Harrison (ed.), 12–20, *op. cit.*

Council of Europe (2001) The Council of Europe and cultural heritage 1954–2000. Council of Europe Publishing, Strasbourg.

Dambis, J. (2001a) The Historic Centre of Riga, Latvia, in R. Pickard (2001a) (ed.), 187–201, *op. cit.*

Dambis, J. (2001b) Latvia, in R. Pickard (2001b) (ed.), 207–226, *op. cit.*

Dann, G.M.S. and Seaton, A.V. (eds) (2001) *Slavery, Contested Heritage and Thanatourism*. Haworth Hospitality Press, Binghamton NY.

Ellul, A. (2000) *Tourism and the Environment in European Countries. Nature and Environment Report 116*. Council of Europe Publishing, Strasbourg.

European Commission (1998) *Investing in Culture: an asset for all regions*. Office of the Official Publications of the European Communities, Luxembourg.

Foley, M. and Lennon, J.J. (1997) Dark Tourism – an ethical dilemma, in M. Foley, J.J. Lennon and G. Maxwell (eds) *Hospitality, Tourism and Leisure Management*, 153–164. Cassell, London.

Gavey, E. (2001) *A Guide to German Fortifications on Guernsey*. Guernsey Armouries, Castel, Guernsey.

Goodey, B. (1994) Interpretative Planning, in R. Harrison (ed.), 302–315, *op. cit.*

Griffin, J. (1994) Case Study 21.1: Changing a culture: the English Heritage custodian training programme, in R. Harrison (ed.), 256–257, *op. cit.*

Hall, C.M. and McArthur, S. (1998) *Integrated Heritage Management: Principles and Practice*. TSO, London.

Harrison, R. (ed.) (1994) *Manual of Heritage Management*. Butterworth-Heinemann, Oxford.

Hatton, A. (1994) The legislation and institutional context: museums, in R. Harrison (ed.), 157–170, *op. cit.*

Hewison, R. (1987) *The Heritage Industry: Britain in a Climate of Decline*. Methuen, London.

Hewison, R. (2003) Looking in the Wrong Place, *Cultural Trends*, 47, 85–89. Policy Studies Institute, London.

Hooper-Greenhill, E. (ed.) (1997) *Cultural diversity – developing museum audiences in Britain*. Leicester University Press, Leicester.

Hughes, H.L. (1996) Redefining Cultural Tourism, *Annals of Tourism Research*, 23, 707–709.

ICOMOS (2002) *Tourism at World Heritage Cultural Sites: The Site Manager's Handbook*. World Tourism Organization, Madrid.

Lewis, W.J. (1995) *Interpreting for Park Visitors*, 8th printing. Eastern Acorn Press, Philadelphia.

MacRory, R. and Kirwan, S. (2001) Ireland, in R. Pickard (2001a) (ed.), 158–183, *op. cit.*

Martin, A. (2003) The Impact of Free Entry to Museums, *Cultural Trends*, 47, 1–12. Policy Studies Institute, London.

Meehan, B. (1994) *The Book of Kells*. Thames and Hudson, London.

Millar, S. (1991) *Volunteers in Museums and Heritage Organisations: Policy Planning and Management*. HMSO, London.

Millar, S. (1994) Managing Volunteers: a partnership approach, in R. Harrison (ed.), 270–279, *op. cit.*

Mynors, C. (1999) *Listed Buildings, Conservation Areas and Monuments*, 3rd edn. Sweet & Maxwell, London.

Negussie, E. (2001) Dublin, Ireland, in R. Pickard (2001b) (ed.), 133–161, *op. cit.*

Pickard, R. (ed.) (2001a) *Management of Historic Centres*. Spon Press, London.

Pickard, R. (ed.) (2001b) *Policy and Law in Heritage Conservation*. Spon Press, London.

Poria, Y., Butler, R. and Airey, D. (2003) The Core of Heritage Tourism, *Annals of Tourism Research*, 30(1), 238–254.

Prentice, R. (ed.) (1993) *Tourism and Heritage Attractions*. Routledge, London.

Re:source (2001) *Renaissance in the Regions: a new vision for England's museums*. Re:source (The Council for Museums, Archives and Libraries), London.

Richards, G. (1994) Developments in European Cultural Tourism, in A. Seaton *et al.* (eds), 366–376, *op. cit.*

Robinson, J.M. (1989) *Shugborough*. National Trust, London.

Roth, S.F. (1998) *Past into Present: effective techniques for First Person Historical Interpretation*. University of North Carolina Press, Chapel Hill.

Runyard, S. (1994) *The Museum Marketing Handbook*. HMSO, London.

Scottish Museums Council (1986) *The American Museums Experience: in search of excellence*. HMSO, Edinburgh.

Seaton, A., Jenkins, C., Wood, R., Picke, P., Bennett, M., MacLellan, L. and Smith, R. (eds) (1994) *Tourism: The State of the Art*. Wiley, Chichester.

Taylor, G. (1994) The legislation and institutional context: the countryside, in R. Harrison (ed.), 127–147, *op. cit.*

Tilden, F. (1967) *Interpreting our Heritage*, Revised edn. University of North Carolina Press, Chapel Hill.

Tunbridge, J.E. and Ashworth, G.J. (1996) *Dissonant Heritage – The Management of the Past as a Resource in Conflict*. Wiley, Chichester.

Urry, J. (2002) *The Tourist Gaze*, 2nd edn. Sage, London.

Uzzell, D. (1998) Planning for interpretive experiences, in D. Uzzell and R. Ballantyne (eds), 232–252, *op. cit.*

Uzzell, D.L. (ed.) (1989) *Heritage Interpretation*, two volumes. Belhaven, London.

Uzzell, D. and Ballantyne, R. (eds) (1998) *Contemporary Issues in Heritage and Environmental Interpretation*. TSO, London.

Chapter 24

Conclusion – the future of the tourism industry

John Beech and Simon Chadwick
Coventry Business School; Birkbeck College, University of London

Learning outcomes

On completion of this chapter the reader should be able to:

- reflect upon the issues and challenges facing tourism businesses;
- identify techniques of forecasting and consider the problematic nature of tourism forecasting;
- identify emerging trends that managers of tourism businesses will need to address in the future;
- consider actions that managers of tourism businesses could take in the light of these emerging trends;
- consider future opportunities for the development of managerial practice and academic research as a result of the book.

Overview

In this concluding chapter the difficulties of facing the future in tourism are addressed. First the difficulties of gathering data on which to base forecasts are addressed and then forecasting techniques themselves are investigated. Next, some views on trends are reviewed and a model of future tourists is presented. Finally strategic techniques for planning for the future are discussed.

Introduction

All forecasting techniques are based on the principle of extrapolating past and present data into the future. In tourism this means gathering what can generically be called 'visitor numbers' and using them to predict, with varying degrees of certainty, how these data might project into the future.

If we are considering a small *visitor attraction* which is walled and has all entrances gated and provided with ticket offices, we can usually be confident that the data we gather from ticket sales is an accurate measure of the number of visitors. Even ticket sales are not always an accurate measure of visitor numbers – the number of visitors to a heritage steam railway, for example, will be greater than the number of ticket sales for travel on the railway as there will be visitors who simply wander around the station, visiting a museum and a gift shop, but not actually choosing to travel on the train.

Discussion question

1 With respect to a small visitor attraction you are familiar with, what techniques could you adopt to ensure that you were accurately recording the total number of visitors on a daily basis? How dependent would you be on the staff to ensure the accuracy of the data?

But what if we are trying to predict the future trend in visitor numbers of a *destination* such as Tenerife in the Canary Islands? Here we might assume that all visitors arrive either by aircraft at one of the two airports or by cruise ship at the one port. As with our small visitor attraction, numbers may be relatively easy to gather, but can we assume they accurately represent the number of tourists visiting Tenerife? In a word, no! The number will accurately represent the number of people moving onto and off the island, but we would be wrong to assume every one of them was a tourist – the number will include residents leaving and returning to the island.

Let us consider the case of what may appear to be a similar destination – Lloret del Mar on the Spanish Costa Brava. Here the situation is more complicated because the points of access and egress are less clearly defined – tourists do not neatly arrive through just two airports or one port; they can arrive through a number of airports, by train, by coach or by car and so it is effectively impossible to measure their number with any degree of accuracy by monitoring their arrival and departure. A different approach might be tried – we could monitor the number of nights they stay at a hotel. Here again though we cannot be sure that this is an accurate measurement. Even if the law requires that all people staying a night in a hotel must complete a process of registration at the hotel, there will be little chance that hotel staff will enforce the registration procedure 100% effectively – the authors have between them visited over 70 countries and can vouch for the fact that, even within the same city and indeed the same hotel, compliance depends on the person who happens to be on duty and the pressure they happen to be working under. We may also find problems with the way that data has actually been gathered. Often it will be aggregated into bed-nights per day or per week, and so it will no longer be possible to identify who stayed for how long – one person for seven nights will be recorded identically to seven people for one night for example.

If we were trying to measure the number of tourists visiting not just Lloret del Mar but the whole of the Costa Brava, we would face the same difficulties but on a much grander scale. At the extreme, imagine trying to measure the number of visitors to a country like Luxembourg, which you can drive through without stopping on the motor-way, or cross freely in and out of via country lanes thanks to the EU's 'open borders' Schengen Agreement. (Schengen, is in fact, a small town in Luxembourg where the agreement was signed in 1985. The countries that have signed this agreement are shown in Table 24.1.)

Table 24.1	Schengen countries		
Austria	Belgium	Denmark	Finland
France	Germany	Greece	Iceland *
Italy	Luxembourg	Netherlands	Norway *
Portugal	Spain	Sweden	

*Non-EU country
Source: Derived from EuroVisa, 2002

The map of Luxembourg shows that it has borders with France, Belgium and Germany and that it is crossed by motorways and railways. It also has an international airport. Trying to measure the number of people crossing the border into Luxembourg would be all but impossible.

To conclude this section, we have seen that the number of visitors can be difficult to measure with any level of accuracy. It depends a great deal on the circumstances of the place for which we are trying to measure this number. While it is practical and useful for a small visitor attraction with controlled entrances, it is not an effective measure for most purposes. What then could we measure as an effective alternative?

Tourism satellite accounts

Particularly if we are looking at tourism from a management perspective, it would be useful to know the economic impact tourism is having (see Chapter 15). This too is potentially fraught with difficulty. Remember the last time you were on holiday. Could you log the money you spent with accuracy? More to the point, could an observer have logged your spending?

Certainly to measure the economic impact of tourism with any level accuracy is a challenge. The challenge was taken up in the early 1990s by two international bodies, the World Tourism Organization (WTO) and the Organization for Economic Co-operation and Development (OECD). More recently the World Travel & Tourism Council (WTTC) has continued to develop this practice, as has Global Insight.

Tourism satellite accounts make an overall estimate of the economic contribution that tourism has made to a country or region. This they do from two elements, the more important being the extraction of existing data from a nation's or a region's accounts. To supplement this data surveys are conducted to estimate tourists' direct spend in the particular area. Finally, in most cases, a multiplier effect (see Chapter 15) is vectored in.

As the system of satellite accounting is based on the use of existing data, it works well at a national level where thorough data already exists, unlike data on visitor numbers. However, it has a weakness in that it is difficult to estimate accurately the second element – tourists' direct spend. Surveys are used to establish total spend in, for example, restaurants and then a 'tourists' share' is applied.

A further issue in establishing a tourism satellite account is the difficult decision of deciding how far to trace the effect of tourists' spend. Typically it is decided to restrict the measurement to tourists' direct spend.

Global Insight (2005) suggests that tourism satellite accounts offer a more comprehensive and accurate view of the tourism industry than more traditional methods. The particular advantages include the answers to these key issues:

- the extent of leakage from the local tourism economy;
- the ability to compare tourism subsidies with tax revenues generated;
- the adequacy or otherwise of capital investment;
- the rate of tourism growth compared to other sectors;
- the impact of the tourism sector on other sectors such as agriculture.

The WTO (2004), a major advocate of tourism satellite accounts, points out that the following information can be obtained from them:

- tourism's contribution to the economy of a given country and its ranking relative to other sectors and in comparison with other countries;

▨ industries that benefit from tourism, and to what extent, particularly industries that are not traditionally associated with tourism;

▨ the amount of tax generated as a result of tourism activity;

▨ data relative to visitor demand and the extent to which it is matched by domestic supply;

▨ improvement of knowledge concerning jobs.

Case 24.1   Preparing for a tourism satellite account in the UK

In 1998 the UK's Department for Culture, Media and Sport published a feasibility study showing its investigations into whether establishing a tourism satellite account was realistic.

The study noted that the following surveys were already collecting relevant data:

● United Kingdom Tourism Survey, jointly commissioned by the four national tourist boards in the UK;

● International Passenger Survey, conducted by the Office for National Statistics;

● United Kingdom Day Visits Survey, sponsored by a range of government departments and agencies with the Countryside Commission acting as commissioning agency;

● a number of non-governmental surveys conducted within specific subsectors.

An immediate difficulty was that there are discrepancies between the surveys and gaps in the information. Discrepancies included how deeply the breakdown of tourists' spend was investigated and inconsistencies with respect to the treatment of Northern Ireland. The gaps included tourists' spend on consumer durables and on particular forms of accommodation, and public-sector expenditure on infrastructure. The Department felt that the discrepancies could be resolved at reasonable cost but that filling the data gaps would involve considerable extra costs.

Existing data on the supply side was much less satisfactory, there being no database of tourism facilities. Accommodation registration was only compulsory in Northern Ireland. British Tourist Authority (BTA) data on visitation to tourist attractions did not distinguish between visits by tourists and by residents, a problem which would have to be resolved by establishing the ratio between the two through further surveys. Information on the supply of entertainment to tourists was very thin. Data on tourism infrastructure was also sketchy, especially with respect to supply by the private sector, and again tended not to distinguish between supply to tourists and to residents.

The existing National Accounts were focused on three areas:

● output – the supply of goods and services;

● income – remuneration for capital and current inputs;

● expenditure – the demand for, or use of, goods and services.

This raised a core problem in how they might fit with the economic activity of tourists. The crux of the problem 'of defining a tourism industry [was] the following question – "what is the correspondence between tourism activities and the output activities?". The answer is "very little" because tourism is demand-driven and not supply-driven – it is not like farming, forestry, fishing, quarrying, manufacturing, constructing, distributing, retailing, etc., for which the outcome is the production of a good or a service. The output corresponding to tourism activities is the provision of a range of services, none of which could have a "tourism trip" defined as its end use' (Department for Culture, Media and Sport, 1998: 23).

The specific proposal was to establish first a series of Tourism Economic Accounts (TEAs) and then derive Tourism Satellite Accounts (TSAs) from them. The latter would differ from the former in a number of ways, particularly by the inclusion of the value added generated in the domestic businesses supplying the businesses providing the services to the end users and by the application of 'tourism ratios' to distinguish between tourists' spend and residents' spend.

The report set out seven possible options, summarised in Table 24.2.

Table 24.2	Cost of TDA development options		
Option description		Duration/timing of option	Consultancy costs (£000s)
1 Do nothing			
Using existing data			
2 TEAs only		short term	15–25
3 TEAs and TSAs with expanded sector coverage		short term	65–75
4 TEAs and extra TSA topics		medium term	20–30
Adding to data development			
5 Further sectoral disaggregation on demand and supply side		medium term	optional
6 More survey work to increase robustness		medium term	optional
'Full' TSAs			
7 TEAs and TSAs using the output of options 5 and 6		long term	60–70

Note: Consultancy costs are recorded for each stage, but would be incurred cumulatively.
Source: Department for Culture, Media and Sport (1998: 44)

Source: Adapted from Department for Culture, Media and Sport (1998)

Discussion question

2 What are the issues that must be considered in deciding which option to pursue?

The basic principle which is being applied in the arguments of this chapter so far is that forecasts are established by projecting past and current data into the future. The limitation of this approach is that it takes no account of two factors which may have a significant impact on the way tourism develops:

◼ the sudden and dramatic influence of externalities such as the destruction of the World Trade Centre (11 September 2001), the Bali bombing (12 October 2002) and the Indian Ocean tsunami (26 December 2004);

◼ the element of uncertainty that derives from changing tastes and fashions – an uncertainty that increases the further we try to project into the future.

In the next section various visions and predictions of future trends based on experience and expertise as well as on econometric projection are considered.

Visions of the future – tourism

◼ The World Tourism Organization's *Tourism 2020 Vision*

The most comprehensive vision of the way tourism will develop in the twenty-first century has been set out by the World Tourism Organization. *Tourism 2020 Vision: Executive Summary* was published in 1997, with a revised version in 1998, and the main publication consists of six regional volumes covering Africa, the Americas, East Asia and Pacific, Europe, the Middle East and South Asia (a total of 452 pages, published in June 2001) and a concluding volume entitled *Global Forecast and Profiles of Market Segments* (139 pages, published in October 2001).

The research programme which generated *Tourism 2020 Vision* had begun as early as 1990 and had three general objectives:

- to identify the key trends in tourism supply and demand worldwide and by region;
- to identify their impact on the various sectors of the tourism trade;
- to identify the implications for policy making and relevant strategies (World Tourism Organization, 1998).

Key points of *Tourism 2020 Vision* are given in Table 24.3.

Table 24.3	Key points of WTO's *Tourism 2020 Vision*

- There will be 1.6 billion international tourist arrivals worldwide
- These tourists will spend over US$2 trillion
- China will become the top destination, and Russia will emerge as a top 10 destination; Thailand, Singapore and South Africa will have experienced major growth
- China will also have emerged as a major tourism generator, smaller only than Germany, Japan and the United States
- Europe will remain the top receiving region in spite of showing a drop in market share; East Asia and the Pacific will have become the second most popular region, taking this place from the Americas
- Europe will also remain the top generating region
- The Mediterranean coastlines will see a fall in market share from 30% in 1995 to 21% in 2020; the Indian Ocean countries will see a corresponding rise from 6.9% to 11.2%; the Mekong countries (Kampuchea, Laos) will see a rise from 5.1% to 11.4%
- Market segments which will achieve significant growth are ecotourism, cultural tourism, thematic tourism, cruising and adventure tourism
- Almost a quarter of international tourism will have become long-haul

Tourism 2020 Vision is nothing if not thorough in its methodology and its preparation, but it must always be borne in mind that it is a 25-year forecast and must therefore carry high levels of uncertainty as explained in the previous section. It must also be recognised that it focuses specifically on international tourism rather than domestic tourism.

The vision of the WTO is very much a projection of the past and present into the future – a forecast of what it believes is likely to happen. A different kind of vision is offered by the World Travel & Tourism Council (WTTC). The WTTC vision, called *Blueprint for New Tourism* (WTTC, 2003), is a *strategy* rather than a *forecast* – a view of what the WTTC *wants* to happen and will try and facilitate happening rather than a prediction of what *will* happen.

World Travel & Tourism Council

Blueprint for New Tourism has been considered in Chapter 9 as a strategy. The emphasis in this chapter is on what underlies the strategy and what its implications are. The vision is simply expressed in three strands:

Travel & Tourism [are seen] as a partnership, delivering consistent results that match the needs of economies, local and regional authorities and local communities with those of business, based on:

1 Governments recognizing Travel & Tourism as a top priority;
2 Business balancing economics with people, culture and environment;
3 A shared pursuit of long-term growth and prosperity.

(World Travel & Tourism Council, 2003: 3)

Governments recognising travel and tourism as a top priority

The core of the vision assumes a partnership, at least at an informal level, between key stakeholders – businesses, the state and residents – although there is no mention of other key stakeholders such as tourists and the environment. Notwithstanding this selectiveness, the WTTC 'invites *all* [author's emphasis] stakeholders to take up the *Blueprint*'s call to action and to commit to building New Tourism, helping to bring new benefits to the wider world' (World Travel & Tourism Council, 2003: 2). The emphasis in this first strand is firmly on high expectations of government. The strand therefore shows an undercurrent of lobbying on behalf of the private sector, the members of WTTC and, as such, it is not unexpected.

Business balancing economics with people, culture and environment

This strand is more revealing. It shows a will on the part of business to consider the impacts of tourism other than the economic one – specifically it states that business needs to consider sociocultural and environmental impacts.

The notion of balance is an important one. It implies that the potentially negative sociocultural impacts (see Chapter 16) and environmental impacts (see Chapter 17) must be considered in the light of the potentially positive economics (see Chapter 15). The profit motive cannot be the only motive for private-sector organisations, from which a duty of responsibility can be deduced – a theme returned to below.

A shared pursuit of long-term growth and prosperity

Again this is a more revealing strand. The reference to 'prosperity' simply recognises the importance of the profit motive for tourism businesses, but the reference to '*long-term growth*' has implications for the way in which the organisations conduct their business. In the latter half of the twentieth century businesses in the Western world had tended to plan strategically only for the short term, although Japanese businesses had tended to be much more long term in their planning.

The use of the word 'shared' reinforces the notion of collaboration between stakeholders.

Green Globe 21

Green Globe 21 has a benchmarking system designed to improve the sustainability of the tourism businesses which seek accreditation. An evolving system, it is designed to incorporate the Agenda 21 sustainability principles established by the Rio Summit of 1992 (see Chapter 23). Such a benchmarking system provides both a stimulus to drive the strategy of tourism businesses and a measure of the extent to which they have succeeded.

The Green Globe 21 key performance areas are shown in Table 24.4.

Benchmarking indicators have been developed in a range of travel and tourism sectors, set out in Table 24.5. The list includes sectors which can include global operators, such as 'accommodation' and 'tour operators', and sectors which are characterised by small business, such as 'farmstay' and 'aerial cableway'.

Several features of the benchmarking process need to be highlighted:

■ The emphasis is on reducing environmental impact. In one sense this is extremely good news in that it is encouraging the private sector to develop a much-needed awareness of tourism's impact on the environment. It makes clear that private-sector tourism businesses should not be solely preoccupied with positive economic benefits for themselves. However, it is disappointing that there is no parallel emphasis on minimising negative sociocultural impacts.

■ The examples of best practice that the WTTC promotes are largely drawn from small- to medium-sized businesses. Again, this is a move in the right direction, but

Table 24.4	Green Globe 21 key performance areas	
Key performance areas	**Benchmarking indicator**	**Benchmarking objective**
Greenhouse gas emissions	Greenhouse gas reduction	Reduction of emissions
Energy efficiency, conservation and management	Energy consumption	Minimise overall energy consumption
Management of freshwater resources	Drinking water consumption	Minimise drinking water consumption
Ecosystem conservation and management	Resource conservation	Reduce consumption of natural resources
Management of social and cultural issues	Biodiversity conservation	Conserve natural habitats and biodiversity
Land-use planning and management	Social commitment	Develop and maintain positive, productive and sustainable contributions to local communities
Air quality protection	Air quality	Improve air quality by reducing emissions from energy production
Noise control	Noise nuisance	Minimise noise disturbance from aircraft
Water waste management	Storm water management	High quality of storm water discharge off-site
Waste minimisation, reuse and recycling	Cleaning chemicals used	Reduced chemical discharge
	Solid waste production	Reduced generation of solid waste

Source: Adapted from **www.greenglobe21.com/Benchmarking_WhatIs.aspx**

Table 24.5	Green Globe 21 sectors for benchmarking		
Accommodation	Activity	Administration office	Aerial cableway
Airline	Airport	Attraction	Community
Convention centre	Cruise vessel	Ecotourism	Exhibition hall
Farmstay	Golf course	Marina	Railway
Restaurant	Resort	Tour company (wholesaler)	Tour operator
Trailer, holiday, caravan park	Vehicle	Vehicle hire	Vineyard
Visitor centre	Winery		

Source: Green Globe 21 (2004)

it does suggest that larger organisations, especially the global or multinational enterprises, have not leapt to benchmark with a similar alacrity.

While many of the benchmarks are couched in terms of achieving reductions to stated *absolute* levels to be achieved, some are couched in terms of *relative* reductions, typically as percentage improvements. A particular example is the benchmark for the (relative) reduction of greenhouse-gas emissions. For some idea of the scale of damage that jet aircraft engines cause to the environment use the FutureForests emissions calculator at **www.futureforests.com/calculators/flightcalculatorshop.asp** . This website also offers useful material on the dangers of excessive carbon dioxide emission. Some airlines (e.g. KLM and SAS) are, however, aware of the issues to the extent that they provide their own emissions calculators on the internet.

So far we have considered visions of the future from the perspective of an international governmental organisation – the WTO, and an international tourism businesses organisation – the WTTC. We now turn to visions of the future from two leading academics: Chris Cooper and C. Michael Hall.

Cooper's view

Chris Cooper, in *Tourism: Principles and Practices*, paints a dual picture of the future of tourism by drawing a distinction between those trends and issues which he identifies as 'beyond our control' (Cooper, 2005a) and those which are 'within our control' (Cooper, 2005b). It is tempting to equate 'control' with 'ability to manage' in this context, but this is not realistic as a closer look at the two categories reveals. His distinctions are set out in Table 24.6.

Table 24.6	Cooper's future trends and issues
Trends and issues beyond our control	**Trends and issues within our control**
Demographic and social trends	The new tourist
Political drivers: General Agreement on Trades and Tariffs (GATS); trade blocs; globalisation; redrawing of the political map	Need for effective segmentation
	Need for better planned and managed destinations
Safety, security and risk	Socioculturally and environmentally sustainable tourism
Climate change	
Human resources for tourism (education and training)	Organisations establishing guidelines for sustainability and acting collaboratively
	New and changing forms of tourism products

Source: Based on Cooper (2005a and 2005b)

The trends and issues which he identifies as *within* our control are certainly ones which we would expect to be able to manage. Managers in tourism organisations, whether large international companies such as tour operators and airlines or small businesses such as heritage visitor attractions, make decisions, albeit at a micro-level with respect to any overall trend, which reflect an attempt to control the development of the trend. The trends and issues in the left-hand column of Table 24.6, which Cooper sees as 'beyond our control', are certainly those which an individual manager's decisions will have relatively little effect on.

Taking an example from the right-hand column, a manager can have a direct influence on the development of a new tourism product, whereas he or she can have little direct influence on a demographic or social change, an example from the left-hand column. Certainly an individual manager can have no control over climate change, for example, but it does not follow that the items over which a manager has no control are items which he or she makes no managerial decisions about or responses to. Even where the item is 'beyond our control', we still respond to them with management techniques.

So, if we accept a distinction between the items in the two columns on the basis of whether we can control them, can we make sense of seeing them as having a distinction from a management perspective?

The distinction between the two columns makes sense from a managerial perspective when we recognise that it is the *nature* and the *scope of the effect* of the managerial responses that are different, rather than whether we make managerial responses or not. For issues and trends 'within our control' we proactively make micro-decisions the consequences of which are immediate within our own tourism organisations. For issues and trends 'beyond our control' our managerial responses are more reactive and there is less certainty of the outcome with respect to our own tourism organisations; however, our aggregated responses will influence the issue or trend in a general sense.

Cooper looks at each trend or issue in some detail. Key factors which emerge are the notions of 'challenge' – life in the future for a tourism manager is not going to be easy – and 'change' – our business environment will change, not necessarily in predictable ways, and we will have to respond with new tactics and even new strategies (see Chapter 9). Some examples of factors that can be found across a number of issues and trends are:

- sustainability;
- the new tourist;
- the need for precise segmentation.

Hall's view

C. Michael Hall reflects on the future of tourism in his scholarly *Tourism: Rethinking the Social Science of Mobility* (2004). He reflects not from a management perspective but rather from a multi-disciplinary perspective. His aim is to set Tourism Studies in a holistic social sciences context, so his perspectives include sociology, environmental studies, human geography and politics as well as management. Key points Hall (2004: 353) makes include:

- tourism has great *potential* for economic benefit;
- tourism managers will need to appreciate the *scale* of sociological and environmental impacts, and the conflicting interests of different stakeholders in these contexts;
- political instability and security issues will be very much on the agenda, as will health issues (biosecurity) and climate change;
- [with respect to tourism management students especially – authors' note] it is important to recognize that 'the scope of tourism studies is more than just an applied business discipline'.

Of particular relevance to tourism management students is Hall's (2004: 290) concern that, while there is now a greater than ever need for sustainability, growth in tourism may need to be constrained because of environmental considerations.

Visions of the future – tourists

Poon

Tourism 2020 recognises the significant role that technology will play in the development of tourism. This trend was recognised in 1993 by Auliana Poon, who wrote the influential *Tourism, Technology and Competitive Strategies*. In it she argued that

- major changes were taking place, to the extent that it could be considered that a metamorphosis was taking place;
- mass tourism had emerged as a result of key social, economic, political and technological changes following the Second World War;
- there were major constraints, mainly environmental but also sociocultural, to the continued growth of mass tourism;
- externally the tourism industry faced both limits to growth and the emergence of a new global best practice; internally the key forces were new consumers and new technologies.

These new consumers or 'new tourists' would be quite different from the old tourists of mass tourism. Their characteristics are shown in Table 24.7.

Table 24.7	Poon's new tourists
Old tourists	**New tourists**
Search for the sun	Experience something different
Follow the masses	Want to be in charge
Here today, gone tomorrow	See and enjoy but do not destroy
Just to show that you had been	Just for the fun of it
Having	Being
Superiority	Understanding
Like attractions	Like sports
Precautious	Adventurous
Eat in hotel dining room	Try out local fare
Homogenous	Hybrid

Source: Poon (1993: 10)

Beech and Chadwick

Unlike Poon's formative model of the 'new tourist', which offers an at least partially optimistic view of tourists as becoming more enlightened, the reality is likely to be that the twenty-first century's tourists will be MAVERICS, a mixture of 'good' and 'bad' and trying very much to 'do their own thing':

- **M**ulti-holidaying – taking several holidays a year;
- **A**utonomous – making up his/her own package, separately booking flights, accommodation, car hire, etc.;
- **V**ariegated – drawing their holiday experience from a range of niche tourism products. On different holidays, the tourist will play a range of the roles normally identified – sunlust tourist in the summer; culture-vulture for weekend breaks; skiing holiday enthusiast in the winter; visiting friends and relatives (VFR) throughout the year;
- **E**nergised – seeking activity and engagement; not only as a sport tourist or in the more obvious roles of adventure tourism, but also seeking activity and engagement when in the role of cultural tourist or even sunlust tourist;
- **R**estless – constantly craving something new; tending to tour rather than stay in one spot, mixing and matching the variegated niches in a single holiday, for example, part sunlust part ecotourist in a single package;
- **I**rresponsible – prone to voyeurism; insensitive to the role of 'guest'; largely unaware of the environmental impact caused by, for example, jet aircraft;
- **C**onstrained – constrained, that is, by what is presented and hence by what is directly available, for example, Brits don't get offered holidays in Senegal, although French tourists do. Brits will tend to go for more variegated holidays within established destinations in Africa such as Kenya and South Africa rather than start visiting Nigeria or the Cameroon;
- **S**egmented – easier to label as they consume tourism products, most significantly from the tourism product producers' perspective. Although MAVERICS are variegated and restless, and thus falling into a range of segments during even a specific holiday, tourist attractions will need to identify which segment its visitors occupy

on the day they come to visit – if they fail to do this, they will fail to meet the tourists' needs and the tourism businesses they run will become unsustainable economically.

But are MAVERICS actually mavericks? No, not in the sense that they are generally trying to subvert systems or operate outside the normal conventions. The use of the acronym MAVERICS does, however, highlight the individuality of the tourist and the lack of homogeneity – the quality of 'sameness' – in the tourist population.

Strategic implications of emergent themes and trends

Niche tourism

Both Poon's 'new tourists' and Beech and Chadwick's 'maverics' seek variety. The obvious way to develop a range of tourism products that offers the variety they seek is by developing niche tourism. Novelli (2005) has surveyed the growth and variety of niche tourism and the strands she identified are shown in Table 24.8.

Table 24.8	Niche tourism		
Special interest tourism	**Tradition and culture-based tourism**	**Activity-based tourism**	**The future of niche tourism**
Dark tourism	Cultural heritage tourism	Adventure tourism	Ethical tourism
Gastronomic tourism	Research tourism	Small ship cruising	Space tourism
Genealogy tourism	Tourism in peripheral regions	Sport tourism	Virtual tourism
Geotourism	Tribal tourism	Volunteer tourism	
Photographic tourism		Wildlife tourism	
Transport tourism			
Youth tourism			

Note: Some of these niches are discussed at length in other chapters, notably Chapter 14, Sports tourism, and Chapter 23, The management of heritage and cultural tourism.
Source: Based on Novelli (2005)

From a management perspective there are a number of specific implications in the growth of niche tourism:

- increase in the number of SMEs (see Chapter 8);
- increase in the reliance of volunteers to support niche-tourism products (see Chapter 14);
- a need for more specialist tour operators (see Chapter 19);
- increased demand for tourism products in countries so far bypassed by mass tourism (Chapter 22);
- greater emphasis on monitoring the business environment of niche-tourism businesses (see Chapter 9).

Case 24.2 is an example of how the potential of niche tourism is being explored.

Case 24.2   Space tourism

As far back as 1967 Hilton Hotels gave some serious thought to the development of a hotel in space, and in the 1980s market researchers began to turn their attention to the possible size of the space tourism market. A 1997 survey in the United States found that almost half those surveyed would be interested in cruising in space and would be prepared to pay an average $10,800 for the trip. A similar survey in 2003 suggested that both figures had risen considerably (Wainwright, 2005).

This, of course, seems very much in the realms of dreaming of very distant possibilities. But is it?

- In April 2001 Dennis Tito, a US millionaire, paid to travel on the Russian space shuttle for a visit to the Soyuz space station (he was followed in 2002 by a South African millionaire).
- In February 2002 the US space agency NASA announced criteria for the acceptance of space tourists.
- In October 2004 the privately-built SpaceShipOne flew to a height of over seventy miles and claimed the $10m Ansari X Prize, on offer to stimulate the development of private-sector space travel.

Space tourism is beginning to be addressed by speciality tour operators, Space Adventures being among the first. For the first time a major company has entered the space-tourism market – in December 2004 the Virgin Group established Virgin Galactic to develop space tourism using spaceships developed from SpaceShipOne. By mid-January 2005 Sir Richard Branson said he had 13,500 potential customers for the £100,000 flights. He predicted that such flights would take place within three years.

Sources: Various including **www.spacefuture.com**; **www.xprize.org**; **www.virgingalactic.com**

Case 24.3 shows how niches can be crossed to appeal to a very specific niche market.

Case 24.3   Steam railway holidays in China

As noted in Chapter 23, heritage steam railways developed in Britain in the second half of the twentieth century. At first the driving force was volunteer groups of steam enthusiasts and their clientele was other railway enthusiasts. As they grew in stature they became tourist attractions attracting a much wider market, comprising, particularly, families with children.

This shift in the composition of visitors left some of the hard-core steam enthusiasts disillusioned. To them, the steam railways had become commercialised, and in much the same way as many football fans became disillusioned with the way that 'the beautiful game' had fallen into the hands of 'big business' (see Beech, 2004). Preservation had resulted in a phoney form of presentation – once dreamy, deserted branch lines were now popular venues running Thomas the Tank Engine trains and Santa Specials, a far cry from the railway scene that was ostensibly being preserved.

These hard-core enthusiasts sought the authentic steam train rather than the preserved one. This led them to Eastern Europe and Turkey, and specialist tour operators, who typically, it transpired, were themselves steam enthusiasts, began to organise tours so that the 'genuine article' could be seen and filmed by British niche tourists. The collapse of the communist regimes in Eastern Europe led to the demise of even these steam railways and the hard-core enthusiast had to look even further afield – to China. The language barriers to arranging independent travel were even greater than they had been in countries like Poland and the Czech Republic, which provided distinct opportunities for the more entrepreneurial and adventuresome tour operator.

The Railway Touring Company is one such organisation. It has organised tours to Eritrea, Saudi Arabia, Peru and Namibia as well as China. Its China Tour combines the more predictable elements of any tour to China – the Great Wall, the Forbidden City and a Yangtze Gorges cruise – but also offers elements that would be of little appeal to the mainstream tourist; these include the Teifa (steam) railway, a trip on the last regular steam-hauled express train in the world, the Jitong (steam) railway and a visit to Daban Steam Locomotive Depot.

Sources: Various including **www.railwaytouring.co.uk**

Sustainability and responsibility

In the different views of the future explored above, two common themes which emerge are the need for tourism to be developed sustainably (the onus being on the producer) and responsibly (the onus being arguably more on the tourist).

These two themes are strongly interrelated. While there is a clear argument that for tourism businesses to produce unsustainable tourism products makes no sense in the longer term, short-term profits may draw them into doing so. Certainly the latter half of the twentieth century saw many examples of tourism development and the emergence of tourism products that were:

- either simply unsustainable (e.g. whale-watching and visiting coral reefs in some specific locations) because of the environmental damage they caused;
- or sustainable but only at the cost of permanent and irreversible change. Examples here include many Mediterranean sunlust destinations where the way of life for residents has fundamentally changed because of mass tourism.

Most businesses will argue that to be successful they must be customer-led – their business mission is to meet customer needs. If customers want tourism products that cause sociocultural or environmental impact, then the market is determining that that is what will be produced. The clear danger of such an approach is that it will break the virtuous spiral of sustainability (Figure 24.1).

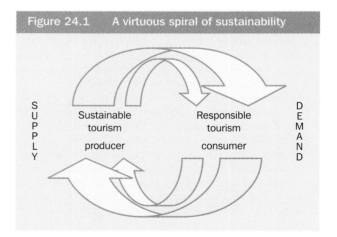

Figure 24.1   A virtuous spiral of sustainability

For the virtuous spiral to thrive, *both* key nodes – sustainable tourism production and responsible tourism consumption – must be maintained. If the tourism industry hides behind the argument that its only responsibility is to its customers and those customers are irresponsible in their tourism consumption, sustainability cannot be achieved.

The worrying alternative to this virtuous spiral of sustainability is a vicious spiral of unsustainability (Figure 24.2).

To break this vicious spiral of unsustainability it requires *either* one of the key nodes – the unsustainable tourism producer or the irresponsible tourism producer – to change.

The duality of the message is clear:

- producers need to design sustainable products;
- tourists need to be educated in the virtues of consuming tourist products responsibly.

A good example of a tourism product designed to be sustainable and yet with an appeal wide enough to attract not just responsible tourists is shown in Case 24.4.

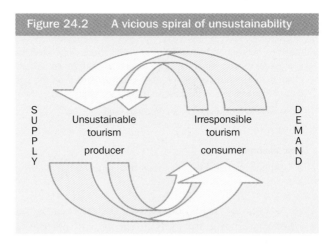

Figure 24.2   A vicious spiral of unsustainability

Case 24.4   Responsible sport tourism to Tanzania

The company responsibletravel.com was founded in 2001. Its aim was to help travellers find what it called 'real and authentic' holidays. The company describes responsible tourism in the following way:

> Responsible travel is a new way of travelling for those who've had enough of mass tourism. Responsible travel is very much about respecting and benefiting local people and the environment – but it's far, far more than that. If you travel for relaxation, fulfilment, discovery, adventure and to learn – rather than simply to tick off 'places and things' – then responsible travel is for you . . . Responsible travel is about bringing you closer to local cultures and environments by involving local people in tourism. It's about doing this in a fair way that helps ensure that they will give you an even warmer welcome! . . . The responsible traveller prefers smaller groups, and to meet some local people (as well as fellow travellers) rather than be surrounded by 1000s of people from back home. They don't like being herded about in a large crowd like nameless faces and understand that travelling in smaller groups makes local people and cultures more accessible.
>
> [Responsible travellers want] to get a little bit more out of their travels, and to give a little bit back to the special places and people that they encounter. They want deeper and more real travel experiences. The responsible traveller values authenticity – experiences integral to local people's traditions, cultures and rituals – rather than those created for tourism, or those whose existing meanings and uses have become lost as they have been packaged up for tourism. No more 'Greek nights' in resorts with the only Greek people there to serve food please!
>
> 'At the same time the responsible traveller understands that some cultural experiences are best kept private, and that their visit would be an intrusion. They believe that travelling with respect earns them respect. Responsible travel is also about helping people re-discover how to experience nature. . . . The responsible traveller understands local people's relationship with environments, and that income from tourism can be a powerful incentive for conservation.
>
> The responsible traveller values diversity – diversity of people, cultures and environments. They believe that they can grow as individuals through these experiences, and that their trip can make a positive contribution towards conserving global diversity.
>
> Above all else the responsible traveller wants to cut loose and experience their world. The experienced responsible traveller knows how difficult it can be to do the right thing – and is humble and learns from their mistakes. Whether they travel independently, or through a leading responsible travel operator, the responsible traveller makes and experiences a difference.

Among their more unusual offerings is a football tour in Africa. Like the steam railway tour in China described in Case 24.3, the holiday contains a conventional element. In this case the holiday includes visits to game reserves and a spell in Zanzibar for cultural tourism and a beach holiday, but the unusual element is one of participatory sport tourism. The traveller spends nine days in Lupiro, a small village in rural Tanzania 500 kms south west of Dar es Salaam. Two matches are played between travellers and locals, and training sessions are organised to allow travellers to get used to playing in the heat. At the conclusion of the tour a match is also arranged against local staff in Zanzibar.

The organisers argue 'that as the only truly global game, football has the positive power to change lives and communities – and transcend cultural barriers'. The notion of sport as a powerful force in uniting has been explored recently by Beech, Rigby, Talbot and Thandi (2005) in the context of international cricket

Conclusion

Tourism faces a period of growth but a period where it is operating in an uncertain business environment. Challenges which the tourism manager of the future must face include:

- changing choices of destination;
- changing shapes of holiday format;
- individual consumers who seek different tourism formats at different times and switch easily from marketing segment to marketing segment.

To rise to the dual challenge of sustainable tourism and responsible tourism, tourism organisations must not shirk from the need to shape tourism demand. Tourism organisations, including the commercial producers of tourism products, must follow the lead of, for example, *Tourism Concern*, and play a role in educating consumer tastes.

While tourism managers will inevitably pursue the goal of maximising positive economic benefit for their own organisations, they must be mindful of the economic impact they have, or fail to have, on receiving nations and their residents. At the same time, in order to achieve sustainability – and hence long-term profits – they must recognise the needs to:

- minimise negative sociocultural impacts on host communities;
- minimise negative environmental impacts.

To achieve these needs they will need to gain skills and knowledge beyond the confines of simply applied management theories.

Guided reading

Among the books mentioned in the text, the following are especially recommended:

- World Tourism Organization's *Tourism 2020 Vision*.
- Auliana Poon's *Tourism, Technology and Competitive Strategies*.
- Marina Novelli's (ed.) *Niche Tourism*.

For sustainable tourism, see John Beech's *Sustainable Tourism Management*. For responsible tourism, see *Tourism In Focus*, the magazine of Tourism Concern.

For a wide coverage of tourism statistics, see J. John Lennon's (ed.) *Tourism Statistics: International Perspectives and Current Issues*.

For an understanding of the need for understanding tourism from wider horizons than those of management, see C. Michael Hall's *Tourism: Rethinking the Social Science of Mobility*.

Recommended websites

Green Globe 21: **www.greenglobe21.com/** .

Tourism Concern: **www.tourismconcern.org.uk/** .

World Tourism Organization on Tourism Satellite Accounts: **www.world-tourism.org/ frameset/frame_statistics.html** .

World Travel & Tourism Council's *Blueprint for Tourism*: **www.wttc.org/blueprint.htm** .

John Beech's Travel and Tourism Information Gateway: **www.stile.coventry.ac.uk/cbs/ staff/beech/tourism/index.htm** .

To keep abreast of developments in the tourism industry, follow the Business of Tourism Management Blog: **businessoftourismmanagement.blogspot.com/** .

Key words

MAVERICS; niche tourism; responsible tourism; sustainable tourism; tourism satellite account.

Bibliography

Beech, J. (2004) Introduction – the Commercialisation of Sport, in J. Beech, and S. Chadwick, (eds) *The Business of Sport Management*. Pearson Education, Harlow.

Beech, J. (2006) *Sustainable Tourism Management*. Pearson Education, Harlow.

Beech, J., Rigby, A., Talbot, I. and Thandi, S. (2005) Sport Tourism as a means of Reconciliation: The case of India–Pakistan Cricket, *Tourism Recreation Research*, vol. 30, no. 1.

Cooper, C. (2005a) The Future of Tourism: Trends and issues beyond our control, in C. Cooper, *et al.*, (eds) *Tourism: Principles and Practice*. Pearson Education, Harlow.

Cooper, C. (2005b) The Future of Tourism: Trends and issues within our control, in C. Cooper, *et al.* (eds) *Tourism: Principles and Practice*. Pearson Education, Harlow.

Department for Culture, Media and Sport (1998) *Feasibility Study: Compiling a Tourism Satellite Account for the UK*. DfCMS, Available at **http://www.culture.gov.uk/NR/rdonlyres/ezdakgzim u5n2pgbvrdhpldrlqewwwjujnlitbiio6s5rzwrxivoahha ht7y6wnpwcbql3bppb7tvdopdtple5ehkyd/toursat. pdf** (accessed 20 December 2004).

EuroVisa (2002) *What are the Schengen countries?* **http://www.eurovisa.info/SchengenCountries.htm** (accessed 5 January 2005).

Global Insight (2005) *Tourism satellite account*, **http://www.globalinsight.com/Highlight/Highlight Detail1232.htm** (accessed 14 January 2005).

Green Globe 21 (2004) *Green Globe 21 Essentials*. Green Globe 21, Canberra.

Hall, C.M. (2004) *Tourism: Rethinking the Social Science of Mobility*. Pearson Education, Harlow.

Lennon, J.J. (2001) (ed.) *Tourism Statistics: International Perspectives and Current Issues*. Continuum, London.

Novelli, M. (2005) (ed.) *Niche Tourism: Contemporary issues, trends and cases*. Elsevier Butterworth-Heinemann, Oxford.

Poon, A. (1993) *Tourism, Technology and Competitive Strategies*. CABI, Wallingford.

Wainwright, P. (2005) *Space Future*. Space Future consulting Group, available: **http://www.spacefuture.com/home.shtml** (accessed 11 January 2005).

World Tourism Organization (1998) *Tourism 2020 Vision: Executive Summary* (revised edn). World Tourism Organization, Madrid.

World Tourism Organization (2004) *General Guidelines for National Tourism Administrations Relative to the Development of the Tourism Satellite Account*. WTO. Available at **http://www.world-tourism.org/statistics/tsa_project/TSA_guidelines_for_ NTAs_V1.pdf** (accessed 10 January 2005).

World Travel and Tourism Council (2003) *Blueprint for New Tourism*. WTTC, London.

End cases

These cases were originally published in the *Financial Times*, an internationally respected source of contemporary business commentary, and offer an entrée to a range of topics that lend themselves to further investigation by students or use by lecturers on a standalone basis in seminars.

The cases have been selected to provide a series of cases which:

- provide a contextualisation for the theoretical models and frameworks introduced in the main text;

- provide the lecturer with further material for use in seminars;

- provide the student with further opportunity to reflect on issues raised in the main text;

- stimulate students to conduct research beyond the limits of the cases.

An index follows that shows the content, title and page number of each case and a matrix is provided to show how the case studies may be linked to the 24 chapters of the book. The latter thus enables lecturers to identify easily which end case may be used with which chapter. Lecturers may find additional linkages, and the discussion questions provided may, of course, be added to.

To help students keep up-to-date on current tourism issues, a supporting tourism news service is available from *The BOTM Blog* at **www.businessoftourismmanagement.blogspot.com** . The Blog is regularly updated.

Index of end cases

Matrix of end cases

Chapter subject	A Iran	B TUI	C Nepal	D Olympics	E Smoking ban, England	F Dalmatia	G Liechtenstein	H Montenegro	I Havana	J The non-partisan middleman	K Travelocity	L Herzegovina	M The Costas	N Holiday package undone
1 Historical introduction									X				X	X
2 Industry structure		X												
3 The role of the state			X		X			X					X	
4 Organisational behaviour											X	X		
5 Human resource management					X									
6 Marketing	X		X			X	X				X			
7 Finance		X												
8 Small and non-profit organisations									X					
9 Business environment		X							X			X	X	
10 Quality and yield management				X										
11 Information technology											X			X
12 Law										X				
13 Visitor attractions	X													
14 Sports tourism				X										
15 Economic impacts				X		X						X	X	
16 Sociocultural impacts	X		X						X			X	X	
17 Environmental impacts				X				X						
18 Accommodation														X
19 Tour operators		X												X
20 Travel agents										X				
21 Transport								X						X
22 Developing countries	X								X					
23 Culture and heritage									X					
24 The future		X							X				X	X

Except for Arab pilgrims, few now visit Iran's Islamic splendours

The 17th century Naghsh-e Jahan square in Isfahan is one of the splendours of the world. Its fountains and gardens lure visitors to the stunning blue tilework of the Imam and Sheikh Lotfallah mosques, pre-eminent examples of Islamic architecture.

For a country with Iran's attractions – from Isfahan, 350km south of Tehran, to the 4,000-year-old remains at Persepolis, from the 1,500km Gulf coastline to northern mountains rising to 5,000m – tourist numbers are low.

Government figures for visitors mix tourists and others, giving a total of around 1m people for 2003 spending Dollars 900m (Euros 740m, Pounds 500m), but private operators say there are no more than 300,000 tourists a year.

A growing proportion of these are Arabs, who have replaced European visitors put off Iran by violence in the region in recent years.

Just five minutes' walk from the Naghsh-e Jahan square, the mid-range Sadaf hotel is packed with Bahrainis.

'Many more Arabs have been coming, since they don't feel welcome in Europe with all the suspicion of Arabs since September 11,' says Morteza Naderi, the general manager. 'Ninety-five per cent of guests in our hotel are now Arabs.'

These are not the rich Saudis and Kuwaitis who flock to Lebanon in the summer for the sea, glitzy shops, casino and dancing girls. Most Arab visitors to Iran are devout Shia Muslims who share their faith with the majority of Iranians.

'They go to Mashad for pilgrimage (to the shrine of Imam Reza, the eighth Shia imam) and they come to Isfahan for shopping,' says Mr Naderi.

Iranians have mixed feelings about the growth in Arab tourism, for while the business is welcome, there are long-standing tensions between the two peoples.

'There are many cultural differences,' says one hotelier.

While Iran adopted Islam from conquering Arab armies in the century after the prophet Mohammad's death in 632, Iranians waged a long and successful struggle to retain their culture and language. Some of Iran's greatest poets poked fun at the Arabs' desert ways.

Today, many Iranians pine for the European, American and Asian visitors who have been put off in recent years by the apparent dangers of the Middle East. Isfahan's up-market Abbasi hotel, once beloved by Europeans, has many empty rooms.

'Most countries have recovered from the downturn after September 11, but unfortunately for us, there was the war in Afghanistan and now Iraq,' says Ebrahim Pourfaraj, manager of the Tehran-based Pasargad Tours. 'People still confuse Iran with Iraq.'

Private-sector operators and government officials agree that Iran's image is a deterrent. 'The propaganda against us is very powerful,' says Ali Hashemi, deputy head of the state Tourism Organisation.

But recognising the industry's potential, the government has drawn up a plan for improvements. 'We need better facilities – hotels, transport – and more effective procedures for issuing visas,' says Mr Hashemi. 'We have already abolished the higher fees once charged to foreigners for entering sites.'

Iran's poor banking facilities are a practical problem. Without widespread use of credit cards and no ATM access to overseas accounts, tourists lack cashflow. Schemes for tourists to acquire temporary debit cards on arrival at the airport have had limited success, as retailers and hotels lack the means to process them.

This is a pity for the carpet-sellers, as today's European visitors to Iran tend to be older and richer than the backpackers who roamed the Silk Road in the days before Iran's 1979 revolution.

Such visitors are not deterred, says Mr Pourfaraj, by Iran's ban on alcohol nor by a dress code requiring women to cover their hair and body contours.

Source: Gareth Smyth, *Financial Times*, 11 September 2004

Discussion questions

1 What resources does Iran have that might be developed as significant tourism products?

2 What difficulties might a Western tourist face when visiting Iran? (Your answer should be evidence-based rather than a repetition of stereotyped views!)

3 What marketing strategies should Iran adopt if it wants to promote tourism?

4 How might Iran manage the potential problems of sociocultural impact that Western tourists would threaten?

CASE B   Germany's TUI reaches calmer waters

The travel group has had an eventful summer. This is the lull after the storm.

After a particularly trying past few months, Michael Frenzel, chief executive of TUI, Europe's biggest travel group by sales, might be excused for believing he has ridden out the storm. With TUI's cancellation of the partial listing of its Hapag-Lloyd container shipping business this week, the former WestLB banker has cleared up another uncertainty hanging over the German group.

Furthermore, TUI's shares, battered by heavy short-selling by hedge funds earlier this year, last week avoided expulsion from the Dax index of Germany's leading shares after rebounding on takeover talk.

Mr Frenzel played his part in underpinning TUI's share price, bringing forward the release of improved second-quarter results and feeding speculation of a hostile predator in the wings.

But even though the company has seen off the threat of Dax expulsion and a hostile bid has yet to materialise, other uncertainties continue to face the tour operator.

The first is the potential change to its shareholder structure.

WestLB owns a 31 per cent stake in the group, but has signalled it is ready to dispose of the holding.

It has indicated this for several months but held back on beginning a sales process because TUI shares were trading below book value.

The German bank was also keen to see TUI's future on the Dax and the tour operator's plans for the Hapag-Lloyd float resolved.

While it has clarity on the last two issues, analysts say a sale of the stake may be difficult.

In June TUI shares touched Euros 16.50 – the price per share paid by WestLB when it bought its stake. But since then the shares have dipped and closed last night at Euros 14.86, a significant discount to WestLB's book value.

TUI's decision to cancel the Hapag-Lloyd float may also be an impediment to a stake sale. 'It is difficult to see who the potential buyers are,' says Simon Champion, leisure analyst with Deutsche Bank.

'Our view is that there are no significant trade buyers. Any trade buyer would have to buy a mix of a tourism business and a container shipping business, which makes it less attractive than a pure play.'

TUI had been planning to float 30 per cent to 49 per cent of Hapag-Lloyd – which analysts have valued at about Euros 2.5bn (Dollars 3bn) – in what would have been Germany's second-biggest public offering of this year.

TUI had already said last month it did not need to float Hapag-Lloyd to meet its financial targets and that it was under no pressure to proceed.

However, there are other problems facing Mr Frenzel, not least the resignation yesterday of Chris Mottershead, the head of TUI UK, which runs brands such as Thomson and Lunn Poly.

Analysts said the resignation, which came unexpectedly when Mr Mottershead returned from a seven-week sabbatical, was not helpful to the tour operator.

Package tour operators have other problems to contend with.

First, like other travel companies whose core business is providing all-inclusive package holidays, TUI has been hit by fierce competition from online tour operators such as Lastminute.com and Ebookers, as well a change in travellers' booking habits towards more independent and adventurous holidays.

'TUI tends to just follow the others, rather than dominate with innovative new products,' says Klaus Linde, analyst at SES Research in Hamburg.

Second, although TUI has its own discount airline, Hapag-Lloyd Express, analysts say the group caught on too late to the dramatic rise of budget airlines such as Ireland's Ryanair and Easyjet of the UK.

Third, the brighter picture provided by TUI's improved performance and forecasts for a near-doubling of operating profits this year dims when one considers this compares with one of the weakest years in the travel sector's recent history.

The war in Iraq, ongoing concerns about terrorism and the outbreak of severe acute respiratory syndrome in Asia combined to decimate global travel in 2003.

Questions remain over what other routes the group might take.

Some analysts say that TUI, whose business model is based on quality mid-priced package tours, could attempt to go upmarket, or offer niche holidays, like its UK rival First Choice, to stave off the threat posed by online competition.

However, that strategy is risky as fixed costs are high in the luxury hotel business and the sector is highly susceptible to factors such as terrorism fears.

Whatever Mr Frenzel decides to do, he can ill afford to enjoy his late summer success for long.

Source: Sarah Althaus and Matthew Garrahan, *Financial Times*, 8 September 2004

Discussion questions

1 Conduct a PESTEL analysis for TUI and develop a TOWS matrix.

2 Using TUI's online financial accounts (www.tui.com/en/ir/reports/gb_2003/financial_statements_of_the_tui_group/profit_and_loss_statement/index.html), assess the company's financial position.

Nepal has been gripped by civil war for eight years and tourism has been hit hard, but optimists believe that a political solution is possible.

For a country beset by a triangular power struggle between its monarchy, political parties and communist insurgents, the Himalayan kingdom of Nepal appears remarkably resilient.

Its economy grew by 3.6 per cent last year and foreign tourist arrivals in the year to July increased by a third. Life in Nepal's capital, Kathmandu, was normal, the government said this week.

Yet this appearance of normality is deceptive. A Maoist-led blockade, which had paralysed travel into and out of Kathmandu for a week, was lifted on Tuesday after businesses, human rights groups and ordinary Nepalese complained of rising hardship.

The blockade, carried out through threats of violence, was the first time the Maoists, who rule vast tracts of remote countryside, had besieged the capital. It was the latest trial of strength in an eight-year civil war that has claimed over 10,000 lives.

The blockade has already cost the country's tourist industry, which offers livelihoods for some 1.25m people, up to Dollars 5m (Euros 4.1m, Pounds 2.8m) in cancelled bookings, reckons Basanta Raj Mishra, president of the Nepal Association of Tour Operators.

The Maoists have warned they will reimpose the blockade in a month unless the government frees jailed rebels and investigates alleged executions of leftwing activists, a claim that is part of its campaign to depose the monarchy in favour of a new, republican 'constitutional assembly'.

'The constitutional assembly option is the rational way out of the political crisis,' says Krishna Khanal, professor of political science at Nepal's Tribhuwan University. 'But our politics is not rational, so it is impossible to predict what could happen next.'

Nepal has not had a democratically elected government for more than two years. King Gyanendra, the constitutional monarch, has ruled through various pro-palace administrations and in June appointed a veteran politician, Sher Behadur Deuba, as prime minister.

Mr Deuba's government has promised peace but his shaky four-party coalition has not reached a consensus over how to deal with the Maoists' demands. At the same time, the main opposition Nepali Congress party yesterday renewed street protests in Kathmandu against what it sees as the king's increasingly autocratic rule.

Girija Prasad Koirala, Congress leader, accused the king of using the Maoist insurgency as an excuse to cement his power at the expense of democratic political parties.

Aid donors and governments such as India, the US and the UK have urged Nepal's political parties to form a united front to deal with the insurgency. But Mr Koirala's party has refused.

This bickering between the political parties is nothing new. Indeed, political analysts say it has only sharpened the Nepalese public's view that the country's 14-year-old experiment in creating a modern constitutional monarchy has failed.

The experiment has no doubt been complicated by the traditional authority of Nepal's monarch, who is worshipped in parts of Nepal as an incarnation of the Hindu god Vishnu, the preserver of social order.

But the palace's role in peacemaking is entirely secular. As the army's commander in chief, the king has the ability to call a fresh ceasefire with the rebels.

This is unlikely, however, while the army believes it has the Maoists on the run. The army says the 'failure' of the blockade was proof that the Maoists had lost support among the people.

'Only our military strength will make them surrender,' says Brigadier General Rajendra Thapa, army spokesman. 'There is no other way.'

Nevertheless, optimists believe a political resolution remains possible. The palace, the government and the Maoists say they want to resume peace talks, although observers worry that all sides have not shown about a lack of willingness on all sides to embrace compromise ahead of any talks. Negotiations.

In a sign of fresh momentum, the government this week announced the formation of a 'High Level Peace Committee' chaired by the prime minister.

CASE C   Continued   **FT**

Mohammad Moshin, the government's spokesman, said this committee would set up a peace secretariat 'in a matter of days', representing the start of the government's peace initiative.

The Maoists, however, have asked for mediation involving the United Nations. Kul Chandra Gautam, a Nepalese UN assistant secretary general, recently offered Kathmandu international assistance.

But the government has so far declined the UN's offer, falling in line with an approach espoused by neighbouring India, to avoid external mediation in separatist conflicts.

Source: Binod Bhattarai and Ray Marcelo, *Financial Times*, 28 August 2004

Discussion questions

1   How can the Nepalese government effectively develop tourism?
2   In what ways could the image of Nepal as a tourist destination be promoted?

CASE D   Raising the bar high in order to perform well   **FT**

It was always going to be difficult for Greece, a country of just 11m people, to stage a Summer Olympic Games.

But the humiliation of losing the 1996 centennial modern Olympics to Atlanta became a powerful incentive for Greece to overcome a reputation for inefficiency and prove itself as a modern European state.

Making a success of the 2004 Games has become the overriding priority for the centre-right government which came to office in March.

'We have set the bar high, but we are ready to stage an excellent Olympics,' Costas Karamanlis, the prime minister, who has personally overseen preparations for the Games, told a congress of his governing New Democracy party at the end of last month.

Costs are already projected to exceed the $4.6bn Games budget by at least $1.5bn, equivalent to 1.5 percentage points of Greece's gross domestic product.

The final bill, financed almost entirely out of public funds, is likely to be higher, according to the culture ministry which supervises Olympics projects.

Cost overruns for construction of Olympic venues may exceed 50 per cent. Road and transport projects were cut but may still exceed the budget by around 35 per cent, according to public works ministry officials.

Athens is not expected to reap immediate benefits from staging the Olympics. Ticket sales for sports events are lower than Sydney's, while a jump in hotel prices is blamed for lower tourist bookings.

'Americans are concerned about security, Europeans about high prices,' says George Antonopoulos, a travel agent. Tourist arrivals are projected to fall about 8 per cent this year in spite of the Olympics, according to Sete, an association of independent hoteliers and tour operators.

The security budget for Athens, the first city to stage an Olympics since the September 11 attacks has more than doubled to $1.5bn – over four times the amount spent at Sydney. Security measures, co-ordinated with a seven-country team, including from the US, Israel and the UK, may be intrusive.

More than 70,000 police, coastguards, emergency workers and soldiers will be on duty around Athens during the Games. Strict traffic restrictions for residents are in place to ease the movement of the 'Olympic family' – athletes, officials and VIPs – around the city.

Yet the popular mood is buoyant, thanks in large part to a boost to national pride provided by the Greek soccer team's unexpected victory last month in the Euro2004 tournament.

An opinion poll published last month showed 60 per cent of Athenians would stay in the city for the Games, although only 30 per cent have bought tickets for sports events.

'We are living in a new city,' says Yannis Papantoniou, a former economy minister who launched preparations for the Games in 1997. 'The Olympics have been a catalyst for completing infrastructure projects that would otherwise still be at the study stage.'

New transport systems – a suburban rail line, a tramway, extensions to the metro system and road upgrades – will reduce traffic jams and atmospheric pollution. Pedestrian walkways around the city's classical monuments have made them more accessible.

The main sports complex, with public spaces laid out by Santiago Calatrava, the Spanish architect who helped put Barcelona on the international map by redesigning the waterfront for the 1992 Olympics, would become an additional tourist attraction.

Services for business are set to improve. The public telecoms operator OTE has invested $300m to prepare for the Games, laying more than 1,200km of fibre optic cable, increasing the capacity of its cellular network and providing high-speed internet access.

Other benefits are less obvious. Hospitals have acquired new equipment because of the Games. The issue of construction safety has moved up the labour ministry's agenda. Public health standards have come under scrutiny for compliance with EU regulations.

Hoteliers have invested more than $500m in upgrading properties in Athens and the surrounding Attica area. The city's marinas and organised beaches have also had a facelift for the Games.

'For the first time in 30 years the capital offers a full range of high-quality accommodation, from luxury hotels to boutique properties. This will have a big impact on tourism over the next three years,' Antonopoulos says.

The framework is in place for Athens to enjoy lasting benefits from the Olympics by becoming a provider of high-quality services based on culture and tourism.

Source: Kerin Hope, *Financial Times*, 26 August 2004

Discussion questions

1 What particular problems arise with respect to ensuring quality (a) in the development of facilities and infrastructure before the Games and (b) during the competitions with events such as the Olympics?

2 What lasting impacts might the 2004 Olympics have on Athens? How might these be managed to ensure that they are maximised/minimised as appropriate?

| CASE E | Smoking ban 'could benefit economy by £2.3bn' | **FT** |

A ban on smoking in public places would benefit the economy by between £2.3bn and £2.7bn a year, Sir Liam Donaldson, the chief medical officer, claimed yesterday as he renewed pressure on the government for such a ban.

Most crucially, he said, the ban on smoking in pubs, restaurants and cafes would not reduce profits in the leisure, catering and hospitality industry.

Presenting his annual report, he provided headline figures to make the case from work he commissioned from the Department of Health's economics and operational research division. The actual study, however, and thus the assumptions behind the economic model, remain unpublished.

Sir Liam said he hoped the full study would be published as he presented figures arguing that reduced absenteeism, cleaning, fire service and healthcare costs, along with increased productivity, would more than offset a Pounds 1.1bn loss to the exchequer from a ban on smoking in public places.

Evidence from smoking bans in New York City, California and Miami showed taxable sales in the hospitality industry rising after smoke-free laws were passed, with no adverse impact on tourism.

'Concern about falling profits is unfounded,' he said. 'A major plank in the argument against smoke-free public places and workplaces is thus removed.'

Calling for legislation as 'a priority', Sir Liam acknowledged that he had differences with John Reid, the health secretary, on the issue. 'I do disagree with his reluctance to introduce legislation on smoking.'

Mr Reid had told him, however, that 'his mind remains open' and 'he does want to see more smoke-free public places and workplaces . . . his concern is how we get there'.

A ban would reduce smoking prevalence, discourage young people from taking up the habit and save lives, he said.

The only remaining issue was whether smokers had rights to defend. But the two-thirds of non-smokers in the population had the right to work and relax in an atmosphere 'that does not imperil their health' and 'both the national economy and the hospitality industry will get a boost'.

The time had come to act, he said, adding a call for National Health Service premises to become entirely smoke-free by the end of the year – something achieved in only 10 per cent of hospitals when a target to achieve that was first set in 1992. The only exception, he said, might be long-stay accommodation for the mentally ill.

He also warned that clinical research 'is threatened throughout our universities' as young doctors find it increasingly hard to combine academic medicine with service demands.

Even as medical schools were expanding rapidly, the number of lecturers was declining, with a 14 per cent drop in the number of clinical academics between 2000 and 2003. There was, he said, an urgent need to resolve the issue.

Source: Nicholas Timmins, *Financial Times*, 29 July 2004

Discussion questions

1 What are the implications of a smoking ban in restaurants and/or hotels for tourism?

2 From an HRM perspective, how might a compromise policy be possible – one where there was still a smoking option available for guests but adequate protection for tourism business workers?

CASE F   **Dalmatia woos the 'in-crowd'**   **FT**

The sector's growth has risen by 10 per cent in two years

Once the shooting stopped, it was really only a matter of time. With a stunning, largely unspoilt coastline stretching hundreds of kilometres along the Adriatic Sea, plenty of sunshine, historic sites and cheap prices, Croatia was waiting to be rediscovered as soon as western tourists saw it as a safe destination.

It has taken nearly 10 years since the war with the Serbs over the break-up of Yugoslavia, but, at long last, Croatia's tourism business seems to have turned the corner. Growth for the last two years has been close to 10 per cent. Hip guidebooks now tip Dalmatia – the southernmost stretch of Croatia's coast – as one of the finest summer destinations in Europe.

'We are aware Croatia is very "in" now,' says Maja Weber of Generalturist, the country's largest tour operator. She says revenues are up 30 per cent so far this year, and expects 10 to 20 per cent growth in its core business every year for the next decade.

That rise comes despite a slump in growth from Croatia's traditionally strongest markets for foreign tourists: Germany and Austria. Taking up the slack are visitors from the UK, France and the US, who tend to stay longer and spend more money. Helping the cause, the Croatian Tourist Board has run a highly successful advertising campaign across Europe, tagging Croatia 'the Mediterranean as it once was'.

The images of a scenic and sleepy holiday destination have proved a powerful draw for travellers turned off by the crowded and overdeveloped beaches of Spain and Italy. Unfortunately, the slogan might just as accurately describe the outdated facilities and levels of service tourists find in Croatia. The cheap prices are fading fast. Some hot spots, such as Dubrovnik, are as expensive as any destination in western Europe.

Tour operators and government officials agree Croatia needs more mid-range and high-end hotel rooms. The increased competition could, they say, keep prices down and improve the quality of services. Currently, half of all coastal accommodation is privately let apartments and houses. Campgrounds account for another 30 per cent.

Relief, however, is on the way. Zdenko Micic, state secretary for tourism in the Ministry of the Sea, Tourism, Transport and Development, says the country can add 100,000 new hotel rooms of three-star and higher quality by 2007.

In the first half of this year, he adds, more than Euros 250m was invested in renovating some of the 40,000 hotel rooms damaged during the war and currently out of use. All of these should be back in business by the end of next year. Additionally, the state is preparing a final push on hotel privatisation. About 30 companies, owning 150 hotels, will be sold by next year.

A handful of greenfield projects will be approved as well, especially four- and five-star resorts, but Mr Micic stresses the shoreline will not be overdeveloped. Indeed, the government has recently been destroying homes and other buildings built illegally on the coast.

If managed well, the tourism sector has the potential to be Croatia's main growth engine for several years. It already accounts for 40 per cent of export revenues. 'Tourism has been a big surprise for us,' says Zeljko Lovrinicevic of Zagreb's Economics Institute. 'Growth could remain at twice the rate of GDP growth. The sky is the limit.'

The industry, however, can be extremely vulnerable to energy prices, fears of terrorism and the fickle tastes of travellers. And for Croatia's pristine coast, another threat may be looming on the horizon.

Russia has recently been lining up support and applying pressure to link its Druzhba oil pipeline to Croatia's Adria pipe, which is currently used to transport imported oil arriving via the Adriatic. Under the scheme, the flow in the Adria pipe would be reversed and 15m tonnes of oil a year, mostly from Russia, would be exported to world markets from the Adriatic.

Tourism professionals are already concerned about two potential nightmare scenarios. Faced with a possible huge increase in tanker traffic through the Adriatic, many worry about oil spills and the dangers of dumped ballast water.

Though his government is considering the pipeline proposal with keen interest, Mr Micic is flatly opposed to it. 'I am very worried. If we create a future like that in the Black Sea, we will have no future in tourism. And we have more to make from tourism than from this pipeline,' he says.

Source: Christopher Condon, *Financial Times*, 13 July 2004

Discussion questions

1 How sustainable is tourism in Croatia?
2 What marketing strategies might Croatia adopt to recover the depleted German and Austrian markets?
3 Investigate the role of tourism within the overall economy of Croatia and the particular problems Croatia faced in moving to a post-Communist economy.

CASE G   **Liechtenstein buys a new look**   **FT**

Maligned and misunderstood, little Liechtenstein is trying to present a new face to the world. The country, squeezed between Switzerland and Austria, is attempting to rebrand itself.

Companies spend millions polishing their images and products. Governments also periodically have a stab often with dismal results. But none has gone so far as Liechtenstein, which has enlisted the services of Wolff Olins, an international branding consultancy.

In a sign of a developing trend, this company, whose clients include the Athens 2004 Olympic Committee, has since been hired to advise on the rebranding of New York City.

Gerlinde Manz-Christ, the Liechtenstein government's spokesperson and a driving force behind the branding initiative, says: 'We felt the need to explain some things and this seemed the right way of going about it.' For years, Liechtenstein appeared content with obscurity. The principality, ruled for centuries by a single family, had grown rich as a financial centre with a shady reputation.

Undemanding company laws, minimal taxation and banking secrecy had made Liechtenstein synonymous with letter box companies, opaque foundations and impenetrable trusts. Those same attributes created a money launderer's paradise. Recently, a constitutional crisis worsened matters. Change came with the election in 2001 of a new government. Legislation was passed to crack down on white-collar crime, and while financial services remain the key money spinner, ministers believed Liechtenstein could also attract more industry and tourism. 'The popular image had not caught up with the reality of Liechtenstein today,' says Mrs Manz-Christ.

But how does a country change its image? Further, can such efforts really be successful given that perceptions are built over years, if not decades?

'We received a lot of offers. But we didn't just want some PR campaign imposed on us. We wanted something sustainable,' says Mrs Manz-Christ, a diplomat who left her native Austria's foreign service three years ago to take on the Liechtenstein challenge. 'We needed to find another way.'

The first step was to set up the Image Liechtenstein Foundation group in March 2002, drawn from government, state agencies and leading trade associations and chaired by Otmar Hasler, the prime minister.

But while members agreed that action was needed, there was initially little unity on how to go about it. The foundation proceeded on two parallel tracks: assessing domestic and foreign attitudes to Liechtenstein to pinpoint weaknesses, and defining what messages should be pushed. By May 2003, recommendations were ready.

Some of these were obvious. The principality's internet site, previously a dull assemblage of administrative data, was relaunched as an attractive illustrated source on everything from finance to tourism, culture and history. Public relations efforts were also stepped up. Rather than waiting for people to call, 'we went out to meet opinion leaders and journalists ourselves,' says Mrs Manz-Christ.

Classic diplomacy also played a part. The principality's Lilliputian foreign service, restricted to embassies in Bern and Vienna, was expanded to eight foreign missions, including international administrative centres such as Brussels, Berlin, New York and Washington.

But the boldest step was recognition that such a tiny country needed more than traditional public relations or public diplomacy to get noticed, let alone improve its reputation. 'We realised we needed to start a branding process,' says Mrs Manz-Christ.

Last November, the foundation held a beauty contest to select a consultancy to translate its new positive messages into graphic form to create a 'brand' defining Liechtenstein, from which Wolff Olins was chosen. 'Liechtenstein is like a globally operating company, and people think in pictures. We wanted to put our message in a picture that, when people looked at it, they'd think: that's Liechtenstein,' says Mrs Manz-Christ.

'We'd done something vaguely similar for Copenhagen, Malmo and Lund linked to the opening of the Oresund bridge between Denmark and Sweden,' says Henning Rabe, a Wolff Olins consultant. 'But this was the first time I'd made a pitch to a hereditary ruler in his castle.'

Not only was its experience limited, Wolff Olins's involvement in one of the recent 'reputation management' exercises for Germany had left it no illusions about the task. 'It showed us how difficult it is to brand a country when you have got so many different interests and players,' says Mr Rabe.

'The real challenge was getting all the participants on board,' admits Mrs Manz-Christ. 'Other countries that have tried reputation management have failed because they haven't been able to get unity at home.'

The advantage of Liechtenstein was that it was small and under pressure. 'The country was ready and therefore open for something to happen,' says Mr Rabe. 'Everything had also been very well prepared through the foundation. And they were willing to take advice. In those circumstances, even a generally conservative client can be persuaded to take bold steps.'

Over six months, Wolff Olins worked with the foundation to turn its core messages into individual images and one over-arching logo. Last month, the symbols were unveiled. Each image is intended to portray one of the foundation's five key themes, be they finance, industry, dialogue, nature or home. The images have also been combined into a single unifying motif a so-called 'democratic crown'.

The crown will from now feature on everything from government handouts to private sector pamphlets, on a striking aubergine background. The colour was chosen for its distinctiveness but also because it combines red and blue, the colours of the royal house of Liechtenstein. Depending on space, the principality's full name or LI will stand under the crown. The letters themselves are composed of small white dots that are a rendition of the five sub-brands.

In time, Mr Rabe hopes the logo could appear on a range of products to project Liechtenstein's presence further.

'We have never been keen on merchandising. But with somewhere as small as Liechtenstein, they have got to go out and market themselves. It is not the sort of place people automatically go to, so merchandising could help'.

Mr Rabe is not specific about what might follow. But he speaks admiringly of how Switzerland, also a small country albeit much bigger than Liechtenstein, has developed an instantly recognisable identity thanks to its distinctive flag, reproduced on everything from penknives to pocketbooks.

'The aim is to have the logo on much more than paper,' says Mr Rabe. That does not mean coffee cups and cutlery, but upmarket goods, such as fashion accessories. 'We're already looking for companies that might be interested in manufacturing,' he says.

The Liechtensteiners acknowledge that the results will be slow. 'It will take time,' says Mrs Manz-Christ. 'More than five years; perhaps a generation.'

Source: Haig Simonian, *Financial Times*, 26 August 2004

Discussion questions

1 Evaluate the five key themes chosen from these perspectives:
   ■ other themes that might have been chosen;
   ■ their potential appeal to various market segments of tourists.

CASE H   Priority is preserving unspoilt coast   FT

The mountains rise a mile high, straight up from the sea, behind most of Montenegro's coastal resorts. The exception is the 13km long, wide sandy beaches of Ulcinj in the far south of the country. It is here that the bulk of the country's planned new hotel and resort building will take place over the next 20 years.

Today, the historic old town of Ulcinj is full of tourists from Kosovo, Bosnia and neighbouring Albania and the town beach is full of splashing children.

But the long, wide, sandy beach south of the town that extends to the Albania border is virgin territory, apart from a few raffia-topped sun shades and the odd cold drinks shack tucked away between the beach and the verdant marshland fed with water from the mountains in the distance.

Ulcinj is a rarity in Montenegro, a large stretch of flat land. The first view of the sea from the peak of the winding highway through the mountains from the capital Podgorica is more typical.

On the right, as the road tops the ridge is the ancient walled town of Budva with its red tiled roofs, palm trees and an extensive yacht basin far below. To the left, the island hotel of Sveti Stefan, joined by a narrow isthmus to the mainland. Stretching to the horizon is a deep blue sea.

That the Montenegrin coast remains so unspoilt is partly due to the mountains, partly its location at the far end of former Yugoslavia and partly to the isolation imposed by a decade of war and mutual hostility in the neighbouring Yugoslav republics, but spared Montenegro itself. The result is that, for now at least, the coast in many parts reminds older visitors of the tourist resorts of 1970s Italy.

Preventing this exquisite coastline from sharing the excesses of Spain, Turkey and other mass tourism venues is one of the main aims of the 20-year tourism development plan drawn up with the help of German and US advisers and finally approved by the Montenegrin parliament with only one dissenting vote last month.

That such a risk exists can be seen in the rash of new hotels, cafes and seaside homes thrown up over the last 12 months in small towns and villages along the coast as cash-rich businessmen and locals poured money into property in a country where other investment opportunities remain limited.

The government estimates that up to 200,000 beds are available for tourist use at the height of the season in July and August, but that only 3,200 are of 'western' quality.

Given that the majority of tourists remain low income visitors from neighbouring Serbia, Albania, Kosovo and Bosnia or old habitués from the Czech Republic, Slovakia and latterly Ukraine and Russia, this has not been a big problem.

But the basic thrust of the plan is to make Montenegro more attractive to an up-market clientele, partly by building more modern hotels for traditional sun and sea holidays, and partly by encouraging ecologically sound and aesthetically pleasing facilities for winter-skiing, hiking and boating in the four national parks, of which Durmitor with its glaciers, high mountain lakes and forests is the most spectacular.

Other attractions include white water rafting in the Tara river and other steep river gorges and boating and fishing on Lake Shkoder. The Norwegian fjord type inlets at Kotor Bay and Tivat are also ripe for further development of sailing schools, sailing and windsurfing.

In order to prevent over-building in the historic, mainly Venetian-built small towns along the coast, the development plan calls for the concentration of traditional sun-sea-sand type holidays in new hotels to be built behind the long sandy Ulcinj beach. Ulcinj lies 20kms beyond the port city of Bar with its rail link to Belgrade and direct ferries to Ancona and Bari in Italy.

Apart from the attractions of a safe sandy beach, a rarity on this side of the Adriatic with its mainly rocky, indented coastline, the Ulcinj area also enjoys easy access to Lake Shkoder, one of the largest and least spoiled fresh water lakes of Europe, teeming with carp and other lake fish. Only six metres above sea level, the lake is nevertheless ringed with spectacular high mountains and is accessible by boat up the Bojana river which spills into the sea at the end of the Ulcinj beach.

It is difficult to over-estimate the importance to Montenegro of a well thought out and executed plan. Predrag Nenezic, the young and energetic minister of tourism, says: 'We plan to go step by step but hope that within five or six years we will be recognised as a quality destination. The aim is to achieve revenues of about €500m by 2015 rising to €1.1bn by 2020'.

This compares to current Central Bank estimates of about €100m in 2001 when 525,000 tourists visited. This was sharply up on the previous year but contrasts poorly with the 1.1m tourists who arrived in 1989, the year before the Yugoslav crisis erupted. This year, the omens are good with expectations of 650,000 visitors, 22 per cent of them from Europe, Japan and the US.

One of the minister's main concerns is to ensure that the necessary infrastructure development, including the provision of fresh water, which flows in abundance from the nearby mountains, and the development of a pollution-free waste water collection and solid waste treatment facilities, does not disturb the ecological balance. Road connections also have to be carefully planned.

Big tourism-related construction projects include a new road tunnel through the mountains to connect Podgorica with Bar, which is due for completion later this year, and a road bridge across the mouth of the Bay of Kotor. This remains at the project stage, and is fiercely contested by many people in the area who fear it will destroy its tranquillity. They argue that it would be cheaper to augment the current ferries which carry trucks and cars.

There is less controversy over the road tunnel. This will bring traffic from the capital to the coast in less than 45 minutes and help ensure that some tourist facilities could be used all the year round. It would boost local business out of season while allowing easier access from Podgorica airport to the coast for the growing number of charter and regular flights bringing foreign visitors. Tivat airport on the coast is also being developed and expects to receive 2,500 charter flights this season.

Source: Anthony Robinson, *Financial Times*, 11 July 2004

Discussion questions

1 To what extent do you think the Montenegrin government will be able to reorientate tourism towards a Western market?

2 How might tourism be developed without destroying the 'tranquillity' which is a major part of the current attraction?

3 By further investigation, assess the needs for development of transport infrastructure to support tourism growth.

Peering into the concave bowl of Havana's camera obscura, Ariel was becoming more and more irritated. It was a hot and humid afternoon. And the bored official guide was not only sending his small audience to the edge of sleep as he mechanically pointed out the Cuban capital's churches, forts and museums, he was also, Ariel insisted, getting his facts wrong about the city's architectural heritage.

Later, as we revived ourselves with sweet espresso coffee and mineral water at the Cafe del Oriente, Ariel, a single man in his 50s, extolled the polychrome ceramics and geometric ornamentation of the Bacardi building (the rum company's pre-revolutionary headquarters on Calle Monserrate) but he claimed that the guide had forgotten many other fine examples of art deco, a style that, like much else in Cuba, seems to have arrived later and in a more eclectic form than elsewhere.

What, Ariel asked, about the Americas apartment block on Avenida Galiano or the art deco ornamentation on Calle O' Reilly?

We had met only a few days earlier. Ariel seemed like a good person to show me around the city. He was a university lecturer in literature, he was enthusiastic about the city's architectural gems and its ambitious restoration plan and – what's more – had lots of time on his hands.

For the past few years, Ariel said, he had been unable to find work in Havana and now, like many Cubans, is *inventando*, making a living in the burgeoning informal economy. Twice a week he cleans houses rented by foreigners in the brighter western suburbs, earning about $12 a week.

That is enough to allow him to survive in a tiny high-rise flat on a sprawling housing estate to the east of the city. And it is more than most of his neighbours get – even professionals earn no more than 650 pesos or about $26 a month – but life is tough. Ariel travels to work crushed along with 300 or so other suffering passengers inside the camello (camel), one of the giant articulated trucks that the hard-pressed Cuban government has converted into buses.

When I visited, his cramped flat vibrated with the boom-boom of Cuban hip-hop from across the block, as Ariel showed me his art deco knick-knacks and statuettes, period furniture and precious English and German porcelain inherited from his grandmother.

Books, international travel, even the bars and restaurants of old Havana – such as Bodeguita del Medio and Floridita – are out of reach for Cubans. Nor, even if he could afford it, could Ariel aspire to spend much time in the Old Havana hotel Ambos Mundos, made famous by Ernest Hemingway, or La Sevilla, where Al Capone once rented a whole floor and Italian opera singer Enrique Caruso stayed in the 1920s.

Under legislation designed to curb prostitution, Cubans are not allowed to stay overnight in hotels.

Many poorer Cubans still live in the tenements of Old Havana and are said to be benefiting from the city's improvement. But when we visited, it sometimes seemed as if the restored sections were an enclave or a theme park reserved for the Italians, French, Canadian and other foreign tourists.

Near the San Francisco church, I made a phone call and Ariel drifted off on his own to visit a curious small garden dedicated to the memory of Princess Diana. But he was quickly warded off by a security guard. I could understand why so many Cubans quietly and despairingly grumble about 'tourist apartheid'.

We headed a few blocks eastwards toward the commercial centre, to an area that Ariel remembers visiting as a boy but which is now generally off the track beaten by the 800,000 or so tourists who visit the city each year. Once the throbbing heart of bourgeois Havana, Galiano Avenue has – as yet – seen little improvement.

The square opposite the El Encanto department store, which burned down in 1961 after a fire caused by CIA saboteurs, is still desolate.

The elite stores where Ariel recalls his grandmother buying her porcelain and fine cloth have been left to rot. The Fondo & Cia once sold jewellery, silver, watches and *objetos de arte* but it is now an empty shell, its yellow-and-blue tiled facade crumbling.

Opposite, at what was once a top department store, shop assistants with glum defeated faces sell tiny paper packets of detergent, boiled sweets and cheap toys for Cuban pesos. In one of the shop's original display cases there are three hairdresser's plastic capes, half a dozen children's colouring books and a blue wire skipping rope. Above another there is a sign in its original lettering which reads 'cakes and biscuits'. Inside are 12 carefully arranged packets of spaghetti.

In the Bizarre Ingles shop, cheap second-hand clothes are hung alongside bunches of plastic flowers. At the exit a case contains bags of green and black buttons, a length of black wire and a stack of long-forgotten greeting cards, printed to celebrate the 20th anniversary of the revolution in 1979 and each costing 20 centavos.

Next door, the Casa Quintana luxury goods store is now a gloomy photography repair shop. In the window are blown-up prints of a man and a woman in traditional Cuban costume in old Havana, the technicolour long faded and the yellow backing papers wilting with age. Several ancient cameras are propped on display stands, quietly gathering dust.

Source: Richard Lapper, *Financial Times*, 16 August 2003

Discussion questions

1 What strategies could be adopted to avoid 'tourism apartheid'?

2 Outline opportunities for the development of small and not-for-profit tourism organisations in Havana.

3 How can Havana (a) relaunch tourism products which were available in its pre-Castro era and (b) design new tourism products?

As the days grow shorter and the winds wilder, brochures advertising next summer's holidays begin to drop on to the mat. Most of the brochures are gloriously produced – none more so than the lavish book of sun-dappled, semi-timbered, blossom-fringed properties offered by English Country Cottages.

I have a high regard for English Country Cottages, having stayed in seven of its properties. They are not cheap, but the company guarantees a certain level of comfort. A tendency towards riotously floral interior decoration apart, English Country Cottages has never let me down.

The cottages are not owned by the company. They belong to individuals who market them through English Country Cottages, which does the bookings and collects the payments. The owners pay about 25 per cent of the holidaymaker's fee for the service.

To escape such charges, some cottage owners have got together to publish collective brochures of their own, encouraging customers to book with them directly rather than through intermediaries.

Browsing through one such brochure, from Premier Cottages, I was interested to note that three of the properties I previously booked through English Country Cottages have defected to Premier. A fourth, multi-cottage complex has hedged its bets by marketing some of its cottages through English Country Cottages and some through Premier.

Would I risk one of the independently-marketed cottages? I might, if a telephone conversation with the owner persuaded me that it was clean and well-run. Some of the independents' prices are lower than those of English Country Cottages; others are not. But English Country Cottages performs a valuable service. It inspects holiday accommodation – something I do not have time to do myself.

I do not pay for this service directly; the cottage owner does. I asked Nick Rudge, English Country Cottages' marketing director, whether his company offered cottage owners greater exposure in return for higher commission. 'Absolutely not,' was his reply, and I have no reason to disbelieve him. As I said, his company has never let me down.

The clients of Marsh, the world's biggest insurance broker, will be thinking no such sweet thoughts. The law suit against Marsh from Eliot Spitzer, New York's attorney-general, illustrates what can happen when the relationship between middleman, provider and customer breaks down. (If proved, Mr Spitzer's allegations will also show how much sections of US business have learnt from Enron, WorldCom and Martha Stewart: nothing.)

Marsh was taking money from both sides: from companies paying fees for advice on where to buy insurance, and from insurance companies who paid Marsh 'contingent commissions' to push business their way. Marsh told the insurance-buying companies that it was their advocate, rather than the insurance companies'.

By Mr Spitzer's account, this was nonsense. His suit alleges that as well as failing to ensure it obtained the best rates for its clients, Marsh set up bogus bidding competitions between insurance companies.

Probably the worst instance in the Spitzer suit concerned the school district of Greenville, South Carolina, which hired a project manager to run an $800m expansion and renovation of its schools. The project manager asked Marsh to advise it on insurance, for which the broker was to receive $1.5m.

In an attempt to make the bidding look more intense than it was, Marsh attempted to persuade an insurance company to enter a bid which would be reasonably competitive but not as low as the front-runner's. When the insurance company refused, Mr Spitzer's suit alleges, Marsh submitted a fictitious bid on its behalf.

The alleged practices, if proved, were disgraceful. However, whenever a middleman takes money from the supplier, there is the possibility that the end user's best interests will be compromised. This is true even where there is no hint of fraud.

Take the December 2003 judgment of the European Court of First Instance against British Airways. The judgment upheld a fine of £6.8m ($8.7m) imposed on BA by the European Commission in 1999 for operating anti-competitive loyalty schemes with travel agents. Under the scheme, BA increased commissions to travel agents who sold higher volumes of its tickets. Virgin Atlantic successfully argued that this encouraged travel agents to steer customers towards BA. (BA changed its arrangements in 1999 and is appealing against the court's decision.)

Do cases like these mean we should avoid middlemen? We should certainly have a hard look at whether we need them. Individual travellers should only hand over money to a travel agent who can offer a lower air fare than any obtainable over the internet or from the airline directly.

The only other reason to use travel agents is if they know destinations and hotels inside out and can offer better advice than you find on the web.

As for insurance brokers, it is difficult to see why individuals or companies use them. Price comparisons are easily made from our screens. Large companies, who are experienced insurance buyers, would be better off investing in some in-house expertise. This goes against the fashion for outsourcing, but the Spitzer suit suggests there is still a case for doing some non-core things yourself.

If there are insurance buyers, such as the South Carolina education authorities, who feel they need someone to guide them through the thicket, they should pay a fee and make sure the broker is not getting anything from the other side. Brokers who will not give such an undertaking are best avoided.

Finally, if, like me and my holiday cottages, you do rely on other people's expertise, use them only for as long as they honour your trust. Marsh has forfeited its trust, and it will take more than the resignation of Jeffrey Greenberg, its parent company's chief executive, to win it back.

Source: Michael Skapinker, *Financial Times*, 27 October 2004

Discussion questions

1 How does putting together your own holiday package increase your risk of becoming drawn into legal action?

2 Investigate what happened with respect to BA's appeal against the European Court of First Instance (use websites such as **www.travelmole.com** and **www.travelweekly.co.uk**) and the battle between BA and the travel agents.

CASE K   **Leader on the route to success**

Not many chief executives welcome failure, but for Michelle Peluso, chief executive of Travelocity, it is part of the equation that leads to success.

Ms Peluso, who became head of the second largest US online travel company last year, says that innovation requires risk and that risk sometimes leads to failure. But the next step, which she describes as 'learning from and embracing failures', is crucial to success.

'If an idea fails, there's a lot of finger-pointing and a lot to lose,' says Ms Peluso, speaking at her desk in Travelocity's offices in New York. 'You have to break that cycle if you want to figure out how to innovate.'

Many chief executives are reluctant to talk about failure. But Ms Peluso, a youthful Oxford-educated 32-year-old, is ready to confront it. 'As a leader, I'm willing to own up to things that weren't the best strategies.'

Ms Peluso no doubt finds the topic of failure easier to broach because Travelocity is currently enjoying some renewed business success.

Last quarter, it reached profitability after two years of losses and growing competition from its rivals: Expedia, which stole the company's former number one position by expanding its lucrative holiday package and merchant hotel businesses; and Orbitz, the third largest online agency, which went public last December.

Now, a combination of revenue momentum from new businesses, aggressive cost control and market share gains means that the company is expected to report $10m to $15m in adjusted operating profit this year, compared with a $28m loss in 2003, according to CIBC World Markets, an investment bank. This improved outlook was boosted last month when Travelocity paid $32.8m to acquire the remaining 50 per cent of the Travelocity Europe joint venture it did not already own – excluding German operations – from Otto Group, a Munich-based catalogue retailer.

In recovering the ground lost to her rivals, Ms Peluso has sought to steer an independent course. When, two years ago, she began to build Travelocity's merchant hotel business, she resisted following Expedia's lead, even though it enjoyed margins of 20 per cent to 30 per cent on hotel rooms. 'We were clearly behind,' she says. 'But being second to market also gave us a chance to say: "What's working? What can you improve?" '

For example, after talking to hundreds of hoteliers, she found them frustrated that online agencies were manually faxing customer reservations to hotels – an inefficient process that meant reservations would sometimes get lost. Ms Peluso decided to invest in technology and training that allowed direct connection to hotel reservation systems. New technology also meant that hotels could be paid immediately instead of up to 60 days later, which was the norm with the old system.

Taking the time and money to invest in what she calls 'seamless connectivity' was risky and prompted questions from investors. 'They wanted to act quicker,' says Ms Peluso.

'They asked: "Are we sure this is the right approach?" Especially because it was clear that there was a [rival] model that was working.'

But Ms Peluso insisted on the strategy. 'Business models have to be more than just about the bottom line,' she says. 'They have to be about suppliers and the customer.'

Two years on, her strategy seems to be paying off. Last month, InterContinental Hotels (IHG), whose brands include Holiday Inn, certified Travelocity as an official third-party distributor because of its hotelier-friendly policies. On the same day, IHG announced that it would sever ties with Expedia and hotels.com, both owned by InterActiveCorporation. But, despite IHG's crackdown, some analysts do not think Expedia is at risk of losing its number one position. At the end of 2003, Expedia's market share was 39 per cent, Travelocity's 20 per cent and Orbitz's 18 per cent, according to PhoCusWright, a travel research company.

Ms Peluso is hopeful, however. And, at any rate, she explains that Travelocity's 'supplier-friendly' business model is in line with the company's philosophy of doing things differently and having a long-term view.

In the hurried online world, this is no easy task. But it was her appetite for new thinking that catapulted her to the top of the company. Five years ago, she helped launch site59, a last-minute travel website and a pioneer in vacation packages.

Travelocity, which was trying to beef up its holiday packages, bought site59 in 2002 for $43m.

Leading Travelocity's 2,500 employees in about a dozen sites across the US is a different task to heading site59, which had 80 staff in its New York office. But Ms Peluso still strives to give Travelocity a feeling of intimacy.

She holds regular informal lunches with employees to encourage feedback and discussion, she sends a regular e-mail to staff and she awards a weekly prize in which employees at all levels are nominated by colleagues for outstanding and innovative work. In a bid to erode old-fashioned hierarchies, she even bakes brownies for employees.

Ms Peluso says that she learned this style of management from her father, an entrepreneur who started an environmental engineering firm in New York. The company had hundreds of employees, but she says that 'he knew all their names' and made a point of getting to know them.

But her big professional mentor was Sandy Moose, the first female consultant at the Boston Consulting Group, where Ms Peluso worked for three years after completing her degree at the Wharton School at the University of Pennsylvania.

Recognising the value of mentoring, Ms Peluso now mentors 25 'exceptional' Travelocity employees. 'You have to devote time to make them passionate about their work,' she says.

'Being a leader is about giving different people what they need psychologically from you,' she adds. 'Your style has to evolve.'

Ms Peluso's idiosyncratic approach to leadership was also shaped by her varied education. She studied philosophy, science and economics at Oxford, where she completed a master's degree, and she did a stint as a White House fellow, working for Alexis Herman, secretary of labour during Bill Clinton's presidency.

This political experience was useful for learning the art of the possible. 'In government, knowing the right answer won't always get things done,' she says. 'You have to understand how to use spheres of influence.'

It was also useful for developing interests beyond the narrow world of e-commerce. Unusually for a senior business chief, she still manages to read one or two books of fiction, non-fiction and poetry each week. 'I always read before I go to bed,' she smiles. 'Otherwise I would stay up thinking about Expedia.'

Source: Amy Lee, *Financial Times*, 1 September 2004

Discussion questions

1 Using internet resources, investigate how Travelocity and its rivals have fared since the article was written.

2 Discuss how leadership style influences business development.

3 How can Travelocity advertise its services and hence attract customers?

| CASE L | Vision of booming spiritual village | **FT** |

Bosnia-Herzegovina boasts a number of enviable tourist destinations: from its Olympic mountains outside Sarajevo to the cosmopolitan capital itself and cherished beauty spots, such as the ancient Ottoman bridge in Mostar, now completed renovated. But for all the country's visible gems, it is an inner, invisible beauty that draws the most visitors.

Situated high in the mountains of Herzegovina, the village of Medjugorje, whose name literally means 'between the hills', is as unlikely a tourist haven as can be found. In a region sadly known for conflict, Medjugorje has become a haven of spiritual peace for millions of visitors – a holy site of growing importance to many Catholics.

The village's special importance – indeed its entire industry – rests entirely on the testimony of six parishioners, who claim to have been confronted by an apparition of the Virgin Mary in the summer of 1981. She introduced herself as the Queen of Peace, according to their story, and all six claim she continues to appear to them privately.

However, they make these claims without the blessing of the church. Early on, a bishop in nearby Mostar condemned the apparitions. His judgment has never been reversed and the Vatican remains silent on the matter, preferring not to designate Medjugorje an official place of pilgrimage.

During recent visits to Bosnia-Herzegovina, Pope John Paul II gave the village a wide berth. But official scepticism is no deterrent to the faithful. 'Can't you just sense the presence of our Lord more closely here than in other places?' a retired Canadian bishop asked a capacity crowd of more than 1,000 North American pilgrims packed into Medjugorje's parish church last month.

The tabular content relating to this article is not available to view. Apologies in advance for the inconvenience caused. With similar exhortations on their lips, thousands of clergymen now visit the village every year to concelebrate mass, their parishioners in tow. Whatever the legitimacy of the visionaries' claims, the village's resulting commercial success is indisputable. It is, by far, the country's top tourist destination, ahead of Sarajevo and Mostar.

An estimated 20m visitors have streamed into Medjugorje since 1981, turning what, two decades ago, was a poor farming community into a boom town. Bosnian tourism officials have failed to keep a good count, but figures in the parish register show enthusiasm is strong and rising. More than 1m people took communion in Medjugorje last year.

Most come by the coach-load, crossing over the border after visiting Dubrovnik, Croatia. They settle in dozens of new hotels crammed around the parish church.

Mario Vasilj, executive director of JWT Medjugorje, a local joint venture with the Irish tour operator, Joe Walsh Tours, says the Medjugorje phenomenon is now gaining ground in new markets after two decades of heavy European interest. '2004 is the first year that Americans came in great numbers,' says Mr Vasilj.

This may cause headaches in the Vatican City but it should be great news for Bosnia's tourism industry. Efforts to advertise Bosnia-Herzegovina as an exotic place for 'adventure holidays' have not yet yielded a significant rise in visits, though the country has much to offer.

Lord Ashdown insists tourism development is a priority. Annual tourist overnights have never exceeded 1m since the war and progress is slow. Overnights last year rose less than 0.2 per cent, to 902,000.

Blame the war, industry experts say. A country once frequently visited on European ski vacations and bus tours through the former Yugoslavia is now infamous as the staging ground for Europe's bloodiest war since 1945. Pilgrims, assured by local church leaders that a visit will be peaceful, may be the only visitors undeterred by an exaggerated perception of security risks.

'What we really need to do is to change the image of this country. People have an outdated, black and white picture of Bosnia in their minds,' says Semsudin Dzeko, head of the Sarajevo-based Tourist Association of the Federation of Bosnia and Herzegovina. He suggests a humble rebound in the tourism industry is more likely than a sharp rise in visits. Bosnia will never be seen as a mass attraction on the scale of nearby Dalmatia, on the Croatian coast, he says.

From a business perspective, this is precisely what Medjugorje achieves, not more. The average visitor stays for one or two nights, then heads back to Dubrovnik. Only wholehearted enthusiasts – many of whom refer to the village simply as 'Medj' – stay on for longer prayer retreats.

Little of their money stays in the country. Most group tours are booked by foreign agencies. Local hotels and restaurants profit, but rates are extremely cheap. The trinket-dealers lining Medjugorje's streets do brisk business but they import most of their merchandise: porcelain Virgin Mary statuettes from Italy, plastic angels made in China.

Only a few local businesses involve themselves in production. One assembles rosaries using imported Italian beads; another publishes postcards, and a third casts Mary statuettes.

Everywhere are the signs of a place bent on getting rich quickly – tempting half-hearted pilgrims to doubt. But above the village, barefoot and deep in prayer, those who climb the sharp, stony path up Apparition Hill never seem to notice.

Source: Eric Jansson, *Financial Times*, 23 November 2004

Discussion questions

1   How could economic leakage from Medjugorje be reduced?

2   Identify ways in which culture clashes might inhibit the development of tourism.

3   What actions could be taken to reduce the risk of sociocultural impacts on Medjugorje from tourists?

| CASE M | Image starts to wear a bit thin | |

The Costas have become relatively expensive.

It is official: Spain's image as Europe's premier cheap and cheerful holiday destination for sun-starved northern Europeans is starting to wear thin. The cheer may still be there: Madrid alone has more bars and restaurants than some Scandinavian countries.

However, an eight-year credit and property investment boom, along with the introduction of the euro, has made Spain's Mediterranean Costas expensive compared with beach resorts in emerging destinations such as Turkey, Croatia and north Africa. While the country received a record 52.5m tourists last year, growth in internet bookings and budget flights, along with changing leisure habits, mean visitors are spending less time in the country.

Revenue growth in the sector, which accounts for about 12 per cent of gross domestic product and 11 per cent of employment, was just 0.4 per cent for the first half of this year, well below inflation. Last year, revenues grew 3.7 per cent year-on-year, a far cry from the 9 per cent average experienced between 1995 and 2002. The latest statistics, which also point to a flattening-out of the number of tourists entering the country each year, prompted Pedro Mejia, the secretary of state for commerce and tourism, to ring the alarm bells last month. 'The sun and beach hotel operators will have to modify their products in order to be attractive,' he said. More research in feeder markets such as the UK and Germany was needed, along with improved service and conditions.

For many in the private sector, the government's wake-up call simply comes as official recognition of strategy decisions in the late 1990s. From being an essentially

Spanish chain in 1999, NH Hoteles, for example, is now just as well known in Latin America and central Europe, where it invested about Euros 1bn building its franchise in less than four years. It now derives more than half its revenues outside Spain and is looking towards eastern Europe for future growth.

'After looking at what had happened in the Spanish market in the 1990s, and taking into account what was still being planned, we saw a certain imbalance between supply and demand in the main cities,' says Ignacio Aranguren, head of strategy at NH Hoteles. 'It was then that we embarked on international expansion.'

Most of the group's competitors tell the same story. Sol Melia, Barcelo and the Riu group have grown aggressively outside the home market, with mixed results. 'If you look at the globalisation of the large hotel chains in recent years, you can see that they've been pretty clear about which direction they had to take,' says Josep-Francesc Valls, head of tourism studies at the Esade business school in Barcelona. 'On the other hand, property developers still find that residential and hotel development on the Mediterranean coasts offers the best returns.'

According to the Bank of Spain, foreigners bought almost 100,000 holiday homes in Spain last year, spending a record Euros 7.2bn.

Foreign demand for a second or retirement home on the Spanish coast is still there, but there are signs that growth is starting to slow. New housing starts this year are forecast at 585,000, down 15 per cent year-on-year. Some property developers are starting to follow the bigger operators abroad. Confronted with increasingly squeezed margins at home and diminishing tracts of beachfront land, they have crossed the border into Portugal.

Necso Inmobiliaria, which specialises in coastal villa developments, recently spent Euros 14m on a tourist complex on the Portuguese Algarve. The project, near Albufeira, includes 58 holiday flats, a golf course, two five-star hotels, two aparthotels, a congress centre, medical clinic and seven kilometres of beach.

Prasa, another property developer, this year announced the purchase of Portuguese developer Lusotur Inmobiliaria in Vilamoura for Euros 360m. In the future, says Mr Valls, developers will also have to abide by tougher environmental regulations as regional and local authorities follow the lead of Lanzarote, one of the Canary Islands, where a 10-year moratorium on tourism-related construction has been in force since 2000.

A recently-completed study concluded that Lanzarote's economic sustainability would only be assured through refurbishing and improving existing tourist infrastructure, preserving and promoting the island's unique ecosystem and recovering traditional industries such as agriculture and fishing.

Even on the Mediterranean coast, some companies look set to benefit from a flight to quality. MedGroup, a property investment vehicle for the Soros group in Spain, is spending nearly Euros 700m developing seven resorts and communities, encompassing nearly 6,000 residential units, 1,700 tourist units, five hotels and five golf courses.

According to Ferran Blanch, marketing director, there is latent demand on the coasts for more 'people-friendly' managed communities. 'Our business is based on identifying the needs of a local authority area and complementing existing tourist and residential developments,' he says.

Spanish cities, meanwhile, are adapting to the world's growing love affair with cultural or special-purpose tourism. Construction of the Guggenheim museum, and the subsequent arrival of cheap flights, has transformed Bilbao from a grungy industrial city into a cultural drawcard for foreign and Spanish travellers.

Thanks largely to its rebirth ahead of the 1992 Olympic Games, Barcelona is now one of the most-visited cities in the world. With its mix of museums, interesting architecture, lively streetscape and trendy beach resorts, Barcelona has become the model for other coastal cities in Spain looking to become more than an airport for the tacky beach resorts beyond. Valencia is a case in point. Awarded the task of hosting the 2007 America's Cup, the Mediterranean port is undergoing a multi-billion dollar face-lift to ready it for the expected deluge of spectators, journalists and participants.

Madrid has promised it a high-speed train, which would put it just over an hour from the Spanish capital, and about Dollars 2bn in public money will be spent on improving port facilities and urban infrastructure. A speculative property bonanza is already well under way, and entrepreneurs are busy remodelling or opening new restaurants, bars and shops.

The Real Club Nautico is also investing heavily. Not to be outdone, Madrid, too, has pitched itself as the venue for another global event: the 2012 Olympic Games. While most Spaniards are, arguably, enthused by the fun and cachet both events would bring to the country, pragmatists still abound.

'When a one-off event is held in a country such as ours, it can have negative as well as positive consequences,' says Mr Aranguren. 'The number of hotel beds required is often overplayed: after two weeks, one month or three months of success, businesses can wind up in crisis. The fact that Madrid may or may not host the 2012 Olympic Games will not change our business criteria.'

Source: Mark Mulligan, *Financial Times*, 26 October 2004

Discussion questions

1 How can the changes in the last half century be explained by evolutionary theories of tourism?
2 Argue the cases for and against the two strategies proposed: redeveloping to aim for the same market with the same product; and developing new tourism products. Which do you think is the better choice for the future?
3. Has Spain become too dependent on tourism? How could tourism development be linked to development of other sectors of the economy?
4 Investigate the change in the residents' lifestyle on the Costa over the last fifty years.

CASE N   **The holiday package undone**

Murderous attacks in Morocco. British Kenya-bound aircraft grounded for fear they will be shot down. War in Iraq. Sars. Tourists opting to stay home.

The travel industry has had its troubles before – notably during the last Gulf war – but it has never seen anything like this. These difficulties will eventually pass, but Goldman Sachs has declared that the industry as we know it will never recover.

In particular, the investment bank says, the giant European package tour operators have had their day. The companies that created a new industry, offering millions of northern Europeans holidays in the sun, are being undone by the internet.

In the past, tour operators used their buying power to purchase rooms, aircraft seats and car hire at knock-down rates. They then packaged these and sold them at prices far lower than holidaymakers could have achieved on their own. Now, says Goldman Sachs, holidaymakers can get better deals alone. Its London-based leisure analysts examined the tour operators' offerings, then attempted to book similar holidays themselves, largely relying on the internet.

In 70 per cent of cases, they were able to put together cheaper deals, with an average discount to tour operators' prices of 26 per cent. The traditional package holiday, they concluded, 'is in terminal decline'.

If true, it will be a significant event in internet history. In its 1990s heyday, the internet's champions claimed it would change everything. They said it would lead to 'disintermediation', a horrible word that meant consumers would be able to dispense with intermediaries such as bookshops, banks or supermarkets. They would go directly to the internet to get what they wanted. New online companies would be the beneficiaries.

It has not worked out that way. With the exception of Amazon.com, most companies that have succeeded on the internet have been established organisations, such as Tesco or the large banks. Like much else associated with the internet, disintermediation appeared to have been hyped.

So has it now finally arrived, and is it about to inflict significant damage on the package holiday companies? On the face of it, the idea makes no sense. Tour operators are not hugely profitable. They may bully hoteliers into cutting their rates, but the brutally competitive nature of the business means they have to pass much of the benefit on to consumers. Goldman Sachs estimates the margin on a mass market package holiday before interest and tax is little more than 3 per cent.

It is not as if tour operators are charging rip-off prices. How can individual travellers buy holidays 26 per cent cheaper? Why would a hotelier offer lower prices to a lone buyer than to a large operator offering to book his rooms for an entire season?

There are two explanations, one transient and one longer-lasting. The transient explanation is that, with so few tourists around, there are plenty of vacant rooms and empty aircraft seats. In normal times, hoteliers and airlines would charge the highest possible price for any rooms and flights that the tour operators had not snapped up, particularly at peak season. But these are not normal times. Rather than leave their facilities empty, the providers of tourist amenities prefer to offload them for whatever price they can get. Here, the internet does have an effect. Not only can individual travellers use it to compare prices; so can the hoteliers, driving prices down even further as they attempt to attract what little custom is available.

But longer-term trends are damaging tour operators – and these are only partly the result of the internet. The rise of Europe's low-cost airlines, led by Ryanair and EasyJet, has provided tour operators with stiff competition. The two airlines did not start out relying on the internet. Ryanair sold tickets through travel agents. EasyJet had its own telephone centre.

But they have now adopted the internet with enthusiasm, driving down costs for themselves and their customers. What is more, travellers who have booked their EasyJet air tickets can click on a neighbouring hotel site run by another company. Like the tour operators, these companies buy hotel accommodation in bulk. Travellers can take advantage of their lower prices, while assembling their own package holidays.

The potential problem for the traveller – and the cost advantage for the low-cost airlines – is that holidays bought in this way offer nothing like the consumer protection that Europe's tour operators have to provide by law. Paying for the bonds that protect package travellers adds to the tour operators' costs and makes their holidays that much more expensive.

What can the package tour operators do? They can offer reliability. Holidays are precious; time is short and paying for them takes a substantial slice out of most people's disposable income. But even prize-winning tour operators cut corners, not telling travellers that the sea view is obscured by an electricity pylon or forgetting to mention the motorway 200 metres from the villa. Brands matter more than ever when people buy online. Few holiday companies understand that.

The upmarket specialist companies can offer something different, such as new destinations and activities. For mass market operators, the future looks grim. They should do better when travellers return, but they will not win back all the business they have lost. When times are bad, excess accommodation and flights will be dumped on the market, and the transparency of the internet will ensure they sell at ever-lower prices. Europe's tour operators have never been a great investment prospect. They look worse than ever.

Source: Michael Skapinker, *Financial Times*, 21 May 2003

Discussion questions

1 How seriously should the tour operators be concerned by the arguments made here?

2 If they do accept the changes that are suggested will actually happen, how could they reorientate their businesses and the products they offer?

3 What opportunities are there for tour operators to take advantage of advances in information technology?

4 Can no-frills airlines ever serve the less popular destinations or will they always be focussed on just the mass tourism destinations?

5 What are the implications for hoteliers if tour operators go into decline?

Glossary

ABTA Association of British Travel Agents. Represents the interests of the larger UK tour operators and travel agents (with around 670 members as of 2000), and operates a bonding scheme whereby customers booking with ABTA members have their holidays protected should the operator/agent in question collapse.

Accommodation capacity The measure of accommodation stock at a defined destination. May be given by various different measures: e.g. number of establishments; number of main units within an establishment (e.g. rooms, caravan stances); capacity in terms of residents (e.g. bedspaces).

Accounting period Normally one year, the period for which accounts are drawn up.

AITO Association of Independent Tour Operators. Performs a similar function to ABTA, although its membership (and therefore its agenda) differs in comprising some 160 of the smaller UK tour operators.

All-inclusive hotels Resort facilities that offer all meals, activities and entertainments on site. All holiday expenses at these hotels are covered by one pre-paid price. Caribbean destinations are noted for their high-profile brands of all-inclusive hotels which offer unlimited alcoholic drinks, snacks between meals and motorised sports all included in one price.

All-inclusive A form of package holiday where the majority of services offered at the destination are included in the price paid prior to departure (e.g. refreshments, excursions, amenities, gratuities, etc.).

Allocentric Of a minority of tourists – adventurous, outgoing, self-confident, independent, needing little tourist infrastructure. Enjoys high contact with locals.

Alternative tourism In essence, tourism activities or development that are viewed as non-traditional. It is often defined in opposition to large-scale mass tourism to represent small-scale sustainable tourism developments. AT is also presented as an 'ideal type', that is, an improved model of tourism development that redresses the ills of traditional, mass tourism.

Artefact An object; an item of material culture.

Assets Something of value that will provide future benefit or utility, can be used to generate revenue. Usually owned, so simply described as 'things we own'.

ATOL Air Travel Organiser's License. A requirement of the Civil Aviation Authority for all UK tour operators wishing to sell air seats on chartered or scheduled services. Necessitates a financial 'health check' and the putting up of a bond to cover the expense of reimbursing/repatriating tourists in the event of operator failure.

Average room rate achieved The average of the room rates resulting in room sales which a hotel has experienced for a given time period.

Balance of payments Record of one country's financial transactions with the rest of the world.

Benchmarking Measuring your performance against that of best-in-class companies, determining how the best-in-class achieve those performance levels and using this information as a basis for your own company's targets, strategies and implementation (Pryor, 1998).

Benchmarks Points of reference or comparison, which may include standards, critical success factors, indicators, metrics.

Bureaucracy An organisation typified by formal processes, standardisation, hierarchic procedures, and written communication.

Business travel Travel for a purpose and to a destination determined by a business, and where all costs are met by that business.

Capacity management A process that seeks to ensure that their organisations operate at optimum capacity while maintaining customer satisfaction levels.

Capital expenditure The cost of long-term assets such as computer equipment, vehicles and premises. Importantly these are bought to use over several years and not to resell.

Carrying-capacity analysis Originally a term applied in ecology referring to the maximum number of animals of a given species that a particular habitat could support. In the context of tourism, it refers to the maximum number of tourists a destination can support.

Case A case describes a dispute taken to court, and specific cases set legal precedents – a legal principle, created by a court decision, which provides an example or authority for judges deciding similar issues later.

Chain of distribution The means by which products (package holidays in this instance) are distributed from producers (principals) to consumers (tourists), often via wholesalers and retailers (tour operators and travel agents).

Chaos theory Views organisations/businesses as complex, dynamic, non-linear, co-creative and far-from-equilibrium systems the future performance of which cannot be decided alone by past and present events and actions. In a state of chaos, organisations behave in ways which are simultaneously both unpredictable (chaotic) and patterned (orderly).

Charter A legal contract between an owner and an organisation for the hire of a means of transport for a particular purpose. An individual traveller will use an intermediary to arrange to be carried on the transport. Often applied to a flight which is the result of a charter.

Class action A lawsuit filed by a number of people in a similar situation, e.g. participants in a particular package holiday might file a class action against the tour operator rather than take action individually.

Code of conduct Guidelines advising a tourism stakeholder, including tourists, on how to behave in an environmentally responsible manner.

Collaboration The process of working together in pursuit of common objectives.

Competitive strategies Offensive or defensive strategies that aim at providing strategic competitive advantage and at increasing the competitiveness of an organisation.

Computer reservation systems (CRS) Computerised Reservation Systems used for inventory management by airlines, hotels and other facilities. CRSs can allow direct access through terminals for intermediaries to check availability, make reservations and print tickets.

Conservation Can be broadly interpreted as action taken to protect and preserve the natural world from harmful features of tourism, including pollution and overexploitation of resources.

Contract A legal agreement entered into by two or more parties.

Control Monitoring and, if necessary, adjusting the performance of the organisation and its members.

Cost–benefit analysis Full analysis of public and private costs and benefits of project.

Cost-plus pricing A method of pricing where an amount, to cover profit, is added to costs to establish the selling price; this is an internally orientated pricing method.

Critical incident point (CIP) A critical incident point or 'moment of truth' is any event which occurs when the customer has (or even perceives that he has) contact with a service organisation.

Cultural See 'culture'.

Culture A set of shared norms and values which establish a sense of identity for those who share them. Typically applied at the level of nation and/or race.

Customer 'An organization or a person that receives a product' (ISO, 2000: 10).

Decision-making unit (DMU) The combination of inputs to a purchasing decision.

Delegation The assignment to others of the authority for particular functions, tasks, and decisions.

Dependency theory This theory maintains that developing countries are kept in a position of dependency and underdevelopment due to existing economic and institutional power structures sustained by leading Western nations. Dependency theorists argue that the policies and activities of multinational corporations, national, bilateral and multinational aid agencies such as the World Bank and the International Monetary Fund (IMF) tend to widen the gap between rich and poor countries and perpetuate the dependency of developing nations.

Designation The act of conferring a legal status on a building which requires compliance with specific legislation on conservation and preservation.

Discretionary income Money received from employment or other sources which can be freely spent on leisure pursuits (such as travel and tourism) after general living costs, taxation, etc. are taken into consideration.

Discrimination Unequal treatment of persons on grounds which are not justifiable in law, e.g. in the UK, discrimination on the grounds of sex or race.

Disintermediation A process by which the consumer 'bypasses' the services of an intermediary or intermediaries in the chain of distribution, in order to purchase products direct from those who supply them. In the travel industry, examples of disintermediation include airlines selling tickets direct to the public over the internet, thus cutting out the travel agent in the selling process.

Distribution The process employed to provide customers access to the product. For travel products distribution focuses largely on the ways in which the customer can reserve or purchase the product.

Diversification The process of developing new products for new markets, in order to achieve business growth.

Due diligence Taking what is considered in law to be reasonable care.

e-commerce Internet facilitated commerce, using electronic means for promoting, selling, distributing, and servicing products.

Economic growth An increase in real output *per capita*.

e-mediaries Electronic booking systems (usually web-based) which combine commerce and the traditional intermediary role of travel agents. Products and services are usually sourced from a range of other product providers allowing customers to book a range of different tourism and travel services from one website, and may enable price/product comparisons between competing suppliers.

Employee relations Covers communications, employee participation in management decisions, conflict and grievance resolution, trade unions and collective bargaining.

Environmental auditing Inspection of a tourism organisation to assess the environmental impact of its activities.

Environmental management systems Systems established by tourism organisations with the aim of mitigating negative environmental impacts.

Environmental scanning The process of collecting information to carry out a systematic analysis of the forces affecting the organisation and identifying potential threats and opportunities with a view to generating future strategies.

Evolutionary theories Theories of tourism which see destinations evolving, in the sense that the types of tourists change, or evolve, over time.

Exclusion clause This is a term in a contract that tries to exclude or limit the liability of one of the parties if there is a breach. Such clauses often take the form of 'small print' in the standard terms and conditions of the dominant partner in the contract, e.g. tour operators.

Externalities Those costs or benefits arising from production or consumption of goods and services which are not reflected in market prices.

Familiarisation trips (fam trips) Visits to tourism destinations made in order to experience and learn more about the destination. Such trips are usually organised either by tour operators or by destination managers to improve knowledge of the destination. When travel agents are taken on such trips it is expected that their increased knowledge will lead to greater level of sales of holidays to that destination.

Force majeure This is an unforeseeable or uncontrollable situation or train of events that would excuse a breach of contract.

Global distribution system (GDS) The reservation network which links bookers such as travel agencies to travel suppliers' booking systems.

Globalisation Generally defined as the network of connections of organisations and peoples across national, geographic and cultural borders and boundaries. These global networks are creating a shrinking world where local differences and national boundaries are being subsumed into global identities. Within the field of tourism, globalisation is also viewed in terms of the revolutions in telecommunications, finance and transport that are key factors currently influencing the nature and pace of growth of tourism in developing nations.

Group norms Informal standards of behaviour and performance that develop from the interaction of the group.

Heritage Today's perception of a pattern of events in the past.

History A pattern of events in the past.

Human Resource Management (HRM), concerned with the strategic management of human resources to achieve a competitive advantage.

Impacts Effects, which may be either positive or negative, felt as a result of tourism-associated activity. Tourists have at least three kinds of impacts on a destination: economic, sociocultural and environmental. Tourism also has effects on tourists, in terms of possible attitude and behaviour changes.

Industry structure An explanation of the functions, form and interrelationships of individual elements, organisations and activities within a defined industrial sector (such as tourism).

Info-mediaries Organisations which provide websites/electronic guides as an information resource, sharing other resources such as web links to organisations that sell tourism/travel. The infomediary may be an organisation or company in its own right, or may form part of an individual company's or organisation's customer service.

Information systems Systems that use information technology to capture, transmit, store, retrieve, manipulate, or display information.

Infrastructure Construction needed to support economic development.

Inseparability The characteristic of service consumption being inseparable from its production, meaning that any errors made in production are seen by the consumer.

Institutions Institutions are 'an established law, custom, usage, practice, organization, or other element in the political or social life of a people; a regulative principle or convention subservient to the needs of an organized community or the general needs of civilization' (Scrutton, 1982: 225, in Hall and Jenkins, 1995).

Intangibility The characteristic of not being touchable – a good is tangible whereas a service is intangible.

Integration The linking (through changes of ownership such as mergers, acquisitions and takeovers) of different stages of the chain of distribution to form larger, more powerful organisations. Integration can be vertical (where links are developed with suppliers and distributors) or horizontal (where links are at the same stage of the distribution chain).

Intermediary An organisation within the chain of distribution whose function is to facilitate the supply of a given product from producers to consumers. In the travel industry examples are travel agencies and tourism information offices.

Interpretation An educational process that is intended to stimulate and facilitate people's understanding of place, so that empathy towards, conservation, heritage, culture and landscape is developed.

Invisible trade Trade in services.

Labour market The pool of employees from which an employer can fill vacancies.

Leadership Influencing and directing the performance of group members towards the achievement of organisational goals.

Leisure travel Travel undertaken for pleasure and unrelated to paid work time.

Liabilities An obligation to pay money or provide service in the future. Simply described as 'things we owe'.

Lifecycle The particular pattern through which a destination evolves.

Limits of acceptable change Environmental indicators that can monitor changes over time as a consequence of tourism.

Litigation Legal action to resolve an issue before a court.

Luxury sports tourism Active or passive sports tourism serviced by high-quality facilities and luxuriant accommodation and attendant services.

Marginal or contribution pricing A method of cost-plus pricing which focuses on the variable or marginal cost only and thus establishes the lowest possible selling price.

Market-orientated pricing A method of pricing that benchmarks prices against competitors when deciding on price.

Market segmentation Market segmentation is a marketing approach that encompasses the identification of different groups of customers with different needs or responses to marketing activity. The market segmentation process also considers which of these segments to target.

Mass tourism Traditional, large-scale tourism commonly, but loosely used to refer to popular forms of leisure tourism pioneered in southern Europe, the Caribbean, and North America in the 1960s and 1970s.

Mature market A market in which a wide range of substitutable products or services are available to consumers who exhibit a sophisticated approach to consumer decision-making.

MAVERICS Characterisation of tourists of the future as multi-holidaying, autonomous, variegated, energised, restless, irresponsible, constrained and segmented.

Mediation An attempt to settle a dispute using a neutral third party.

Merit good One with public as well as private benefits.

Midcentric Of the majority of tourists – displaying a mix of allocentric and psychocentric characteristics. Prefers to be cushioned from contact with locals.

Mode of travel The type of transport used to make a journey between an origin and a destination, and can include walking and cycling as well as all forms of mechanical transport.

Modernisation theory The socioeconomic development and process that evolves from a traditional society to modern economies such as the United States and Western Europe. Harrison (1992) argues that modernisation is a process of Westernisation where developing countries emulate Western development patterns.

Motivation Internal and external forces and influences that drive an individual to achieving certain goals.

Mystery shoppers These researchers investigate companies through using their services, while pretending to be customers (or potential customers). They usually monitor such areas as the level of customer service and product knowledge.

National income A measure of the total level of economic activity which takes place in an economy over a year.

Negligence Failing to exercise what is legally considered to be reasonable care.

Net worth/Total net assets The net value of all operational assets and liabilities; shows the amount of money invested in operational capacity of the business. Calculated by deducting current and long-term liabilities from the value of fixed assets and current assets.

Niche tourism Small specialised sector of tourism which appeals to a correspondingly tightly-defined market segment.

No-frills A low-cost scheduled travel package based on minimising operator service and costs, which are passed on to the consumer as a low price.

Non-profit Non-profit organisations are those which are driven by non-financial organisational objectives, i.e. other than for profit or shareholder return.

Occupancy rate The measure of capacity utilised within an accommodation unit for a given time period (e.g. day, week, month or year).

Online agency Travel agencies who operate using the World Wide Web to provide information to potential customers as well as allowing the customer to book travel and related products without the necessity of speaking to a salesperson.

Operations management 'The ongoing activities of designing, reviewing and using the operating system, to achieve service outputs as determined by the organization for customers' (Wright, 1999).

Opodo A web-based booking site linking the reservation systems of cooperating airlines, allowing bookers to compare times and prices for particular journeys.

Organisation A deliberate arrangement of people to achieve a particular purpose.

Other recruitment difficulties Includes poor recruitment/retention practices, poor image, low remuneration, poor employment conditions which arise despite sufficient skilled individuals.

Owners' equity Combines the original investment and any retained profit to show the total value of the owners' interest in the business.

Package holiday Also known as an inclusive tour. Defined in law as 'the pre-arranged combination of at least two of the following components when sold or offered for sale at an inclusive price and when the service covers a period of more than 24 hours or includes overnight accommodation: (a) transport; (b) accommodation; and (c) other tourist services not ancillary to transport or accommodation', as set out in Section 2(1) of the European Union's Package Travel Regulations, 1992 (cited in Sharpley, 2002: 72–3).

Perishability The characteristic of being perishable. In tourism the term is used to describe, for example, a particular hotel room on a specific night or a particular seat on a specific flight – they cannot be 'stored' and sold later, so they are perishable.

Personal disposable income (PDI) The amount an individual has left over for personal expenditure on goods and services, after payment of personal direct taxes, national insurance and pension contributions.

Personnel Concerned with the practical management and administration of people at work.

PESTEL analysis Examines the political, economic, sociocultural, technological, (physical) environmental and legal forces within which businesses operate and which act on them.

Physical evidence The tangible evidence of a service, including everything which can be seen, touched, smelt and heard.

Politics Politics has been defined in many ways. According to Heywood, politics is 'The activity through which people make, preserve and amend the general rules under which they live' (Heywood, 1997: 410). According to Davis *et al.* (1988: 61) 'Politics is the process by which the structure, process and institutions are brought to a decision [including non-decisions] or outcome. It is an endless activity; while politics operates, all decisions [and non-decisions and actions] are provisional'. So politics means no decision or action is final. All decisions and actions of a government or institution of the state are open to question and are up for debate and argument and are, ultimately, subject to change.

Pollution Harmful effects on the environment as a by-product of tourism activity. Types include: air; noise; water; and aesthetic.

Porter's forces A model which suggests that the profit potential for companies is influenced by the interaction of five competitive forces: rivalry in the marketplace; the threat of substitutes; buyer power; supplier power; and barriers to entry into the market for new players.

Positioning The process of ensuring potential customers have a desired perception of a product or service, relative to the competition.

Price elasticity of demand A measure of the variability that can be expected in sales when prices are changed. Unity elasticity would see equal increase in sales in reaction to a decrease in price. Inelastic demand would not change when prices went down or up.

Principal A term that encompasses accommodation providers, carriers, ground handlers and any other provider of services to tourists, except for those whose primary function is to package and distribute tourism products (i.e. tour operators and travel agents).

Process 'A set of interrelated or interacting activities which transforms inputs into outputs' (ISO, 2000: 7).

Process control A systematic use of tools to identify significant variations in operational performance and output quality, determine root causes, make corrections and verify results (Evans and Lindsay, 1999: 345).

Process design Involves specifying all practices needed, flowcharting, rationalisation and error prevention (Rao *et al.*, 1996: 540–1).

Process improvement A proactive task of management aimed at continual monitoring of a process and its outcome and developing ways to enhance its future performance (James, 1996: 359).

Process management Planning and administering the activities necessary to achieve a high level of performance in a process and identifying opportunities for improving quality, operational performance and ultimately customer satisfaction. It involves design, control and improvement of key business processes (Evans and Lindsay, 1999: 340).

Product 'The result of a process' (i.e. output), which may be either a service, or a good (hardware or processed materials) or software (e.g. information) or their combination (ISO, 2000a: 7).

Profit The excess of revenue over expenses; if expenses exceed revenues in a given period the organisation will make a loss.

Psychocentric Of a minority of tourists – preferring 'away' to be like 'home'; requiring appropriate tourism infrastructure.

Public policy Is whatever governments choose to do or not to do (Thomas Dye, 1992: 2). Such a definition covers government action, inaction, decisions and non-decisions as it implies a very deliberate choice between alternatives (see Hall and Jenkins, 1995).

Quality The degree to which a set of *inherent* characteristics of a product fulfils customer requirements (ISO, 2000).

Regulation Control through formalised processes.

Relationship marketing Relationship marketing is a business philosophy which aims to develop strong relationships with a range of stakeholders, such as suppliers, media, intermediaries and public organisations, as well as with customers.

Requirements Stated, generally implied (as a custom or common practice for the organisation, its customers and other interested parties) or obligatory needs (ISO, 2000).

Responsible tourism Type of tourism which is practised by tourists who make responsible choices when choosing their holidays. These choices reflect reponsible attitudes to the limiting of the extent of the sociological and environmental impacts their holiday may cause.

Retained profit The profit left in the business at the end of the accounting period after all deductions and appropriations have been made.

Revenue expenditure The cost of resources consumed or used up in the process of generating revenue, generally referred to as expenses.

Revenue management Revenue management is a management approach to optimising revenue, often based on managing revenues around capacity and timing (yield management), for different market segments or from different sources of funding.

Sales Revenue from ordinary activities – not necessarily cash.

Seasonality A phenomenon created by either tourism supply or demand (or both) changing according to the time of the year.

Service encounter The moments of interface between customer and supplier.

Services marketing mix The addition of People, Physical Evidence and Process to the four areas of activity more usually associated with marketing products – Price, Place, Promotion and Product.

Servicescape The location in which the service encounter takes place.

Skills gaps Employers perceive existing employees have lower skill levels than needed to achieve business objectives, or where new, apparently trained and qualified for specific occupations, entrants still lack requisite skills.

Skills shortages Lack of adequately skilled individuals in the labour market due to low unemployment, sufficiently skilled people in the labour market but not easily geographically accessible or insufficient appropriately-skilled individuals.

Small business A small business is one which has a small number of employees, profit and/or revenue. Often these are owner-managed, with few specialist managers. Some definitions of small businesses distinguish between businesses with under 10 employees, which are micro-businesses, and those with 10–49 employees, which are classified as small businesses.

Social Relating to human society and interaction between its members.

Sports event tourism Tourism where the prime purpose of the trip is to take part in sports events as either a participant or spectator.

Sports participation tourism Active participation in sports that is the prime purpose of the tourism trip.

Sports tourism A social, cultural and economic phenomenon arising from the unique interaction of activity, people and place.

Sports training tourism Sports tourism trips where the prime purpose is sports instruction or training.

Sport–tourism link Not just sports holidays, but all areas in which a link between sport and tourism might be of mutual benefit (e.g. joint facility development, marketing and information provision).

Stakeholder Any person, group or organisation with an interest in, or who may be affected by, the activities of another organisation.

'The state' 'The state is a set of officials with their own preferences and capacities to effect public policy, or in more structural terms a relatively permanent set of political institutions operating in relation to civil society' (Nordlinger, 1981, in Hall and Jenkins, 1995). The state includes elected politicians, interest or pressure groups, law enforcement agencies, the bureaucracy, and a plethora of rules, regulations, laws, conventions and policies.

Statute The law as made by parliament, e.g. in the UK, the Disability Discrimination Act (1995). A statute is made up of many parts called 'sections' or 'provisions'.

Statutory instrument The vast majority of delegated legislation in the UK is in the form of statutory instruments governed by the Statutory Instruments Act 1946.

Strategic information systems Systems designed to support the strategic management decision processes and implementation.

Strategy pyramid A visual way of representing the different levels of the strategy conceptualisation and implementation process. The most general assumptions are shown at the apex and the practical, implementation actions are at the base.

Suppliers Individuals, companies or other organisations which provide goods or services to a recognisable customer or consumer.

Sustainable tourism Tourism that is economically, socioculturally and environmentally sustainable. With sustainable tourism, sociocultural and environmental impacts are neither permanent nor irreversible.

SWOT (Strengths-Weaknesses-Opportunities-Threats) analysis Brings together the internal and external environmental scanning to identify the business's internal strengths and weaknesses and external opportunities and threats.

Tort A civil wrong.

Tour operator An individual or organisation in the business of (bulk) buying, and subsequently bundling, the various components that make up a package holiday (see above), for sale via a travel agent or direct to the consumer.

Tourism flows The major movements of tourists from specific home areas to destinations.

Tourism income multiplier (TIM) Exaggerated effect of a change in tourism expenditure on an area's income.

Tourism satellite account System of accounting at national or regional level which reveals the total direct impact of tourism on the economy.

Tourism system A framework that identifies tourism as being made up of a number of components, often taken to include the tourist, the tourist-generating region, the transit-route region, the tourist destination and the tourism industry (Leiper, 1990).

Tourism with sports content Tourism products that include participation in sport that is not the prime purpose of the trip.

Tourist attractions Tourist attractions are defined as being destinations for visitors' excursions which are routinely accessible to visitors during opening hours.

Visitors can include local residents, daytrippers or people who are travelling for business or leisure purposes. Formal definitions exclude shops, sports stadia, theatres and cinemas, as these meet a wider purpose, although in practice tourists may consider the excluded categories to be tourist attractions.

TOWS (threats-opportunities-weaknesses-strengths) matrix Uses a SWOT analysis to develop strategies by matching strengths with opportunities, using opportunities to reduce weaknesses, using strengths to overcome threats, and reducing weaknesses and avoiding threats.

Travel agent The retailer of travel and related products. While this refers to the sales person employed to sell travel products, the term is often applied in reference to the business that is established to sell travel products (the travel agency).

Variability Because the production and the consumption of a tourism experience are inseparable and because differing circumstances and people will affect each experience, those experiences are prone to variance and create a challenge for tourism managers to achieve consistency of standards.

Virtual organisation Organisation in which major processes are outsourced to partners.

Working capital Operational assets and liabilities needed for everyday operation, e.g. cash or bank overdraft, stock and trade creditors, known as net current assets/liabilities.

Yield management 'A revenue maximization technique which aims to increase net yield through the predicted allocation of available . . . capacity to predetermined market segments at optimal price' (Donaghy *et al.*, 1997a).

Zoning Different ecosystems may be zoned in terms of their robustness to pressures from tourism in an attempt to mitigate environmental damage.

Bibliography

Davis, G., Wanna, J., Warhurst, J. and Weller, P. (1988) *Public Policy in Australia*. Allen and Unwin, North Sydney.

Donaghy, K., McMahon-Beattie, U. and McDowell, D. (1997) Yield Management Practices, in I. Yeoman, and A. Inglold, (eds) *Yield Management: Strategies for Service Industries*. Cassell, London.

Dye, T. (1992) *Understanding Public Policy*, 7th edn. Prentice Hall, Englewood Cliffs, NJ.

Evans, J.R. and Lindsay, W.M. (1999) **REFERENCE DETAILS WANTED** [Chapter 10 but 2002 in text]

Hall, C.M. and Jenkins, J.M. (1995) *Tourism and Public Policy*. Routledge, London.

Harrison, D. (1992) *Tourism and the Less Developed Countries*. Belhaven Press, London.

Heywood, A. (1997) *Politics*. Palgrave, New York.

ISO (2000) *Quality Management Systems – Fundamentals and Vocabulary*. ISO, Geneva.

James, P. (1996) *Total Quality Management: An Introductory Text*. Prentice Hall, Hemel Hempstead.

Leiper, N. (1990) Tourist attraction systems, *Annals of Tourism Research*, 17, 367–384.

Nordlinger, E. (1981) *On the Autonomy of the Democratic State*. Harvard University Press, Cambridge, MA.

Pryor, L.S. (1998) Benchmarking: a self-improvement strategy, *Journal of Business Strategy*, Nov/Dec, 28–32.

Rao, A., Carr, L.P., Dambolena, I., Kopp, R.J., Martin, J., Rafii, F. and Schlesinger, P.F. (1996) *Total Quality Management: A Cross Functional Perspective*. John Wiley & Sons, New York.

Scrutton, R. (1982) *A Dictionary of Political Thought*. Pan Books, London.

Sharpley, J. (2002) Tour operations, in R. Sharpley, (ed.) *The Tourism Business: an introduction*. Business Education Publishers, Sunderland.

Wright, J.N. (1999) *The Management of Service Operations*. Continuum, London.

Index